MINNESOTA IN A CENTURY OF CHANGE

MINNESOTA IN A CENTURY OF CHANGE

The State and Its People Since 1900

EDITED BY CLIFFORD E. CLARK, JR.

MINNESOTA HISTORICAL SOCIETY PRESS · ST. PAUL · 1989

The publication of this book was made possible by a generous grant from The St. Paul Companies, Inc.

MINNESOTA HISTORICAL SOCIETY PRESS
St. Paul 55101

Manufactured in the United States of America
10 9 8 7 6 5 4 3 2 1

International Standard Book Number
0-87351-234-0 Cloth
0-87351-238-3 Paper

This publication is printed on a coated paper manufactured on an acid-free base to ensure its long life.

Library of Congress Cataloging-in-Publication Data

Minnesota in a century of change : the state and its people since 1900 / edited by Clifford E. Clark, Jr.
p. cm.
Includes index.
ISBN 0-87351-234-0 : $35.95. – ISBN 0-87351-238-3 (pbk.) : $19.95
1. Minnesota – History – 1858- I. Clark, Clifford Edward, 1941- .
F606.5.M56 1989 89-30925
977.6'05 – dc19 CIP

Contents

Preface

This book had its genesis in a major monetary gift presented to the Minnesota Historical Society by The St. Paul Companies to mark the 125th anniversary of its origin in 1853 as the St. Paul Fire and Marine Insurance Company. This generous gift, given by the holder of the oldest business charter in Minnesota to the state's oldest cultural institution, was intended to assist the Society in producing a new, one-volume history of Minnesota.

Initially, the Society planned a volume to be written by three historians under the editorship of June Drenning Holmquist, then assistant director for publications and research. Before the project was well under way, however, the untimely death of June Holmquist in February 1982 combined with later events to cause a rethinking of the original plan. Consequently, a planning group was named, and after consulting with numerous scholars and reviewing the published works on the state's past, it formulated a new plan for a volume of topical essays focusing on the history of Minnesota in the twentieth century. The planning group included Russell W. Fridley, then director of the Society, Jean A. Brookins, assistant director for publications and research, Lucile M. Kane, then a senior research fellow, William E. Lass, professor of history at Mankato State University, Deborah L. Miller, research supervisor, and John McGuigan, then managing editor of the Minnesota Historical Society Press.

The decision to focus on the twentieth century recognized that most standard reference works on Minnesota's past cover the nineteenth century well but fall short in interpreting developments after the 1930s. The choice to have individual authors write essays on specific topics, while a departure from the more usual chronological historical treatment, allowed the volume to present a rich variety of voices and interpretations.

Implementing the plan became the responsibility of Brookins, Miller, and McGuigan. Our first goal was to name a volume editor who would assist in selecting authors and who would work with them in developing and completing the essays. We met that goal when Clifford E. Clark, Jr., professor of history and American studies at Carleton College, Northfield, agreed to join the project.

The charge to create a list of topics important to Minnesota's development since 1900 and to match that list with scholars having relevant interest and expertise was laden with both opportunities and frustrations. The opportunities lay in selecting subject areas that are vital to a survey of the past nine decades and that will bring new historical information and understanding to readers. More opportunities opened as we reviewed a select list of scholars in several disciplines whose work related closely to the envisioned volume. But we also encountered frustration when the growing list of topics had to be trimmed repeatedly to keep the volume at a reasonable size. Disappointment fueled frustration whenever a chosen scholar was unavailable to write an essay on a topic that we considered important. We have, however, been gratified by the cooperative spirit with which authors, editors, and Society staff members have worked together.

The seventeen essays on the pages that follow provide a multifaceted view of the transitions and sometimes dramatic changes that have affected the people of Minnesota since 1900. Many of their subjects are common to histories of the state, such as politics, government, and education; others are less so, such as religion, rural life, and the labor movement. Although we endeavored to give broad coverage of the twentieth century, we realize that readers will miss some topics that have not been included. For each one found lacking, we hope that readers will discover another that is newly illuminated for them by the essayists in this volume. Many additional subjects that appear throughout the work can be traced in the comprehensive index. The broad range of source materials used by the authors is fully documented in notes appearing at the end of each essay; therefore, a comprehensive bibliography has been omitted.

Without The St. Paul Companies' strong interest in, and dedication to, Minnesota's heritage, exhibited by its grant to the Society, this project would not have been possible. We are grateful for the company's generosity and for the leadership role it has long played in ensuring the preservation of the past. We also express thanks to Russell Fridley, Lucile Kane, and Bill Lass – the originally designated trio of authors – for their help in recasting the project and for their continuing interest in it, and to Nina M. Archabal, the Society's present director and former deputy director for programming, for her strong support. Professor Clifford Clark has earned our admiration for skillfully coordinating the essays into an interrelated whole – an effort that depended on the cooperation and good will of the authors, who are identified on pages xi–xiii.

Critical manuscript reviews by W. Roger Buffalohead, Carl H. Chrislock, Hazel Dicken Garcia, Rhoda R. Gilman, Lucile Kane, Anne R. Kaplan, Bill Lass, John McGuigan, Deborah Miller, Ann Regan, Carl Ross, and Nicholas Westbrook helped in shaping the essays for this volume. Deborah Miller guided much of the research assistance provided to authors by Richard M. Chapman, Mark Haidet, Valerie Hauch, James A. Roe, and Alan R. Woolworth. A strong proponent of photographs as historical documents, Miller also worked closely with the authors to select the evocative and informative images that illustrate the essays.

To our colleagues on the Society's staff, particularly those in the reference and special libraries and the manuscripts and archives reading room, we extend thanks for assistance cheerfully given to authors, researchers, and editors. A vote of appreciation is due the MHS Press's dedicated staff supervised by managing editors John McGuigan and his successor Ann Regan. Project editor Elaine H. Carte, especially, deserves compliments for her own judicious editing and for overseeing the assignments given to others. Editors included staff members Anne Kaplan, Ann Regan, Sarah P. Rubinstein, and Deborah Swanson plus free-lancers Carolyn Gilman and Ellen B. Green. Providing editorial and research assistance were Dawn Haug and James Roe. The index was compiled by Sarah Rubinstein, assisted by Ann Regan and Gloria Haider, who also produced corrected computer disks of the manuscripts. Christine Watkins handled numerous production details, and production supervisor Alan Ominsky oversaw design by Lois Stanfield and map production by Gregory Chu and Yeong-Ki Beck of the University of Minnesota Cartography Laboratory, as well as typesetting, printing, and binding.

To everyone who gave us advice, encouragement, and assistance along the way, we offer our sincere thanks.

Jean A. Brookins
Assistant Director for
Publications and Research

Contributors

ARNOLD R. ALANEN, a geographer by training, is professor in the Department of Landscape Architecture and School of Natural Resources, University of Wisconsin, Madison. He is co-author of *Main Street Ready-Made: The New Deal Community of Greendale, Wisconsin* (1987). A native of northeastern Minnesota, he is writing a history of Iron Range communities and immigrant groups.

THOMAS J. BAERWALD, director of the Geography Department at the Science Museum of Minnesota, St. Paul, has worked as a researcher and exhibit planner in topics relating to urban geography and land use. He has also been active in efforts to promote the teaching of geography in Minnesota and the nation.

DAVID BEAULIEU is manager of the Indian Education Section, Minnesota Department of Education, and former chair of the Department of American Indian Studies, University of Minnesota. He spent a year as a fellow at the Newberry Library in Chicago and has served as vice-president of Sinte Gleska College in Rosebud, South Dakota.

MARJORIE BINGHAM is a teacher in the St. Louis Park Public Schools. For nine years she served as director of Women in World Area Studies, St. Louis Park, where she developed curricular materials for secondary world studies classes. She is co-author of a series of books exploring the historical role and status of women in countries throughout the world.

JOHN R. BORCHERT is Regents Professor of Geography at the University of Minnesota, Minneapolis, where he has taught since 1949. His teaching and research have dealt especially with the geography of natural resources, land development, and settlement in the Upper Midwest. He is a founder and former director of the university's Center for Urban and Regional Affairs. His most recent book is *America's Northern Heartland* (1987).

CLARKE A. CHAMBERS, a third-generation Minnesotan, has taught American social history at the University of Minnesota, Minneapolis, since 1951, where he is also director of the Social Welfare History Archives. He has written *Seedtime of Reform: American Social Service and Social Action, 1918–1933* (1963) and other works on social welfare history.

RICHARD M. CHAPMAN is a doctoral candidate in history at the University of Minnesota, Minneapolis. His research has focused on such topics as social welfare, religion and reform, and Latin American history. He is writing a dissertation on the work of women in religious-based welfare organizations between 1920 and 1940.

CLIFFORD E. CLARK, JR., is professor and chair of the History Department at Carleton College, Northfield. His publications include *Henry Ward Beecher: Spokesman for a Middle-Class America* (1978) and *The American Family Home* (1986). He has participated in numerous public programs in Minnesota on topics of intellectual history and popular culture.

DANIEL J. ELAZAR is professor of political science and director of the Center for the Study of Federalism at Temple University, Philadelphia. He also teaches political science at Bar Ilan University, Israel. He is the author of *Cities of the Prairie: The Metropolitan Frontier and American Politics* (1970) and co-author of *Cities of the Prairie Revisited: The Closing of the Metropolitan Frontier* (1986).

GEORGE S. HAGE is director of the Minnesota Journalism Center and professor emeritus, School of Journalism and Mass Communication, University of Minnesota, Minneapolis. He is the author of *Newspapers on the Minnesota Frontier, 1849–1860* (1967) and co-author of *New Strategies for Public Affairs Reporting* (1976).

THOMAS HARVEY is a city planner for the City of St. Paul and a doctoral candidate in geography at the University of Minnesota. He has worked extensively as a researcher and consultant on topics of historical geography, including a study of town founding, development, and urban form for the Minnesota Historical Society.

JOHN E. HAYNES is specialist in twentieth-century political history in the Manuscript Division, Library of Congress, Washington, D.C. Although trained as a historian, he has spent most of his career in political posts, including staff positions in Minnesota state government and the U.S. Congress. He is the author of *Dubious Alliance: The Making of Minnesota's DFL Party* (1984).

KIRK JEFFREY is professor of history at Carleton College, Northfield. In addition to the rise of modern corporations, his research interests include American environmental thought and the history of family and women. He is co-author of the book *Understanding Quantitative History* (forthcoming).

KARAL ANN MARLING is professor of American Studies and art history at the University of Minnesota, Minneapolis, where she has taught since 1977. Her publications include *The Colossus of Roads: Myth and Symbol along the American Highway* (1984) and *George Washington Slept Here: Colonial Revivals and American Culture, 1876–1986* (1988). She is completing a history of the Minnesota State Fair for the Minnesota Historical Society Press.

DAVID L. NASS is professor of history at Southwest State University, Marshall. He has done extensive writing and consulting on such aspects of rural life as outmigration, rural electrification, and farmer activist movements. Among his publications is *Public Policy and Public Works: Niagara Falls Redevelopment as a Case Study* (1979).

PETER J. RACHLEFF is associate professor of history at Macalester College, St. Paul. His 1984 book on black labor in the South will be issued in paperback under the title *Black Labor in Richmond* (1989). He is completing a book on the Hormel strike of 1985–86 to be entitled *P-9 Proud,* and his other works in progress include the early history of the Independent Union of All Workers in Austin.

D. JEROME TWETON is professor of history at the University of North Dakota, Grand Forks. He has published extensively on the history of agriculture in the region, including *Depression: Minnesota in the 1930s* (1981) and *The New Deal at the Grass Roots: Programs for the People in Otter Tail County, Minnesota* (1988).

Minnesota's counties and county seats. The youngest of the state's eighty-seven counties – Lake of the Woods – was added in 1922.

MINNESOTA IN A CENTURY OF CHANGE

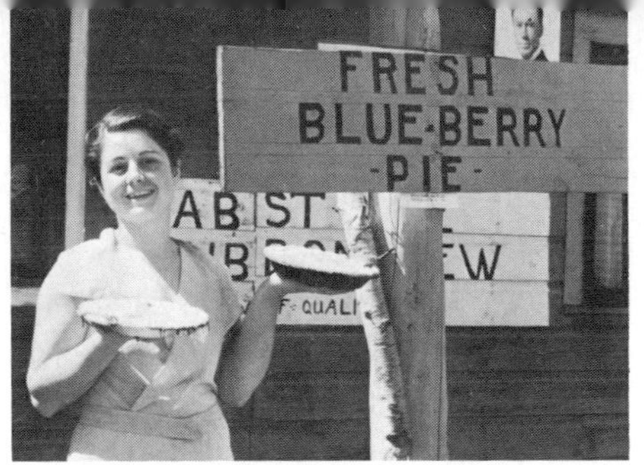

CLIFFORD E. CLARK, JR.

Minnesota: Image and Identity

Trying to understand Minnesota's history in the twentieth century is much like putting together a jigsaw puzzle. The edge pieces are easy to identify: they make up the popular image of the state, the one that is presented in tourist and promotional literature or dramatized in national magazines. According to that image, Minnesota is a wholesome natural environment, a land of ten thousand lakes and cold winters, a state populated by hard-working people – descendants of hardy Scandinavian settlers – who have used innovative technology to develop the latest manufacturing processes. As *Time* magazine put it in 1973, "By a combination of political and cultural tradition, geography and sheer luck, Minnesota nurtures an extraordinarily successful society."[1]

But it is harder to fill in the center pieces of the puzzle. One wonders, for example, whether the promotional image of the state is accurate. Outsiders from the East and West coasts may perceive the state, in the words of *National Geographic Magazine* in 1949, as a land of "vision and versatility," but how accurate is that perception?[2] Does the state live up to its reputation as innovative and forward looking? Has it always been viewed as a recreational paradise, a land of ten thousand lakes? Is there a common bond between those who live in the Twin Cities and those from the iron ranges or the Red River valley? Does it even make sense to speak of a state as having a distinct identity?

Because the relationship between the image and the actual development of the state provides an important insight into Minnesota's sense of identity, it is fitting that this new history of Minnesota in the twentieth century begin with questions about the popular image of the state. As historian Michael Walzer has suggested, since state boundaries are always somewhat arbitrary and political units have no palpable shape or substance, a state "must be personified before it can be seen, symbolized before it can be loved, imagined before it can be conceived." Hence the popular image of Minnesota is the key to its own sense of identity. Although this image is derived to some extent from actual experience, it is also constructed out of Minnesotans' hopes for the future. Like the fish story about the one that got away, the image of the state has expanded beyond simple descriptions of reality to encompass the hopes and dreams of its people. Indeed, the mythology of what the state is and should be has even shaped the ways in which the state has developed. In short, the popular image of the state, as it has evolved since 1900, provides clues to what Minnesotans value, what they want, and – to some extent – what they have become.[3]

The state's twentieth-century image has been synthesized from multiple sources, beginning with nineteenth-century immigrant guidebooks and railroad brochures, continuing with publications by state tourism promoters, elaborated in governors' messages, reinforced by the work of the Minnesota Historical Society, expanded with essays by popular authors in the periodical press, given shape by the people themselves in cities and small towns around the state, and extended through the century in coverage in national magazines and on radio and television. Surprisingly, the events that have drawn the most national attention to the state – the publication of Sinclair Lewis's *Main Street*, or the daring solo flight across the Atlantic Ocean in 1927 by Charles A. Lindbergh, Jr. – have contributed little to Minnesota's image in the world. Instead, most of the information about Minnesota has been internally generated – the product of Minnesotans' efforts to attract immigrants, tourists, and industry to the state.[4]

Perhaps the central theme of the popular image of the state begins with the physical environment itself. To the white settlers of the nineteenth century, Minnesota was a frontier paradise, a Garden of Eden whose lush farmlands and dramatic forests promised unrivaled opportunity and abundance. A writer reflected this point of view in an 1883 article in *The Northwest*, a magazine published by the Northern Pacific Railroad, with the question: "Why is it that people will emigrate to Dakota [Territory] – that they will pass through this 'Garden of the World' – the Park Region of Minnesota, where we find all that nature does for the good of man in the handiwork already prepared for homes of mankind?" Here was the classic early vision of the state as a land of fertile soils, breathtakingly beautiful lakes and forests, and wholesome recreation.[5]

Within this Garden of Eden, Minnesotans pointed to the richness of the agricultural resources in the southern and western parts of the state as the basic source of the state's power. At the turn of the century, Gov. John Lind summed up that feeling when he said in 1899 that "while we can point with pride to our manufacturing, lumbering, and mining industries, it is after all the condition of the Minnesota farm that marks our progress. It is the barometer of our prosperity, and it commands for us the proud position which we occupy among our sister states." As late as 1911, for example, of the state's forty-five million acres of agricultural lands, fewer than half were under cultivation. Thus Gov. Adolph O. Eberhart could proudly assert that "Minnesota possesses the greatest agricultural resources of any state in the Union."[6]

One governor after another stressed the potential of this vast agricultural domain for increased production. Farming was pictured not only as the source of the simple, good life, the traditional yeoman-farmer vision

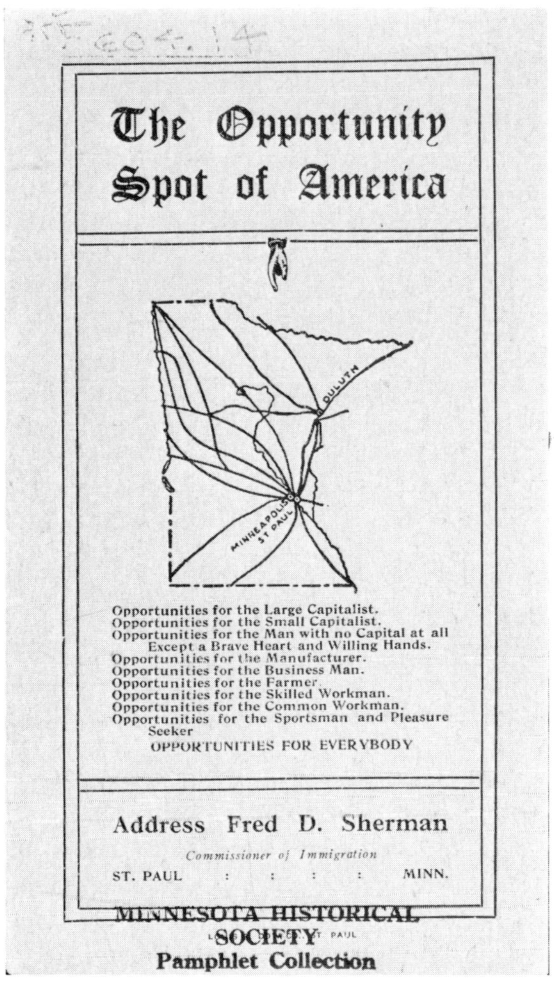

Cover of pamphlet issued by the state commissioner of immigration, about 1913

that could be traced back to the writings of Thomas Jefferson; it was also tied by state promoters to investment opportunities and scientific innovation. In a pamphlet issued about 1913 and entitled *The Opportunity Spot of America,* H. J. Maxfield, commissioner of immigration, boasted about the profits to be made on a Minnesota farm. "There are many farmers who have come to Minnesota, from the older states," he asserted, "who have discovered that with the same cash and labor expenditure they can secure a larger MONEY RETURN per acre than they could from their old farms that they disposed of for twice or three times the cost of their Minnesota farms." Promoters of the state insisted that the scientific methods of cultivation and skillful seed selection developed by the agriculture department of the university would give Minnesota farmers a technological advantage over competitors in other states. To support this assertion, they pointed out that the state ranked third in total production of all wheat varieties in 1912 and that Minneapolis was widely recognized as the flour-milling capital of the country. Hogs, cows, and sheep could all be raised more efficiently and cheaply in Minnesota than elsewhere, the promoters maintained. By 1911, the dairy industry could boast of 814 creameries and a state inspection system that guaranteed the quality of Minnesota dairy products.[7]

Even during the 1920s and 1930s, when a depression in farm prices brought foreclosures on farm mortgages and put the industry in a precarious position, promoters continued to tout the benefits of farming in Minnesota. But now they argued that agriculture needed state support in order to improve. Governors recommended increased state expenditures on agricultural research and moved to help farmers by promoting cooperative marketing, maintaining a system of rural credits, encouraging lower transportation rates, and supervising the grading and weighing of farm products. As late as 1941, Gov. Harold E. Stassen continued to assert that the state's broad agricultural base was its greatest source of new wealth. Even in the 1950s, when manufacturing at last surpassed agriculture as the state's dominant industry, government officials continued to praise the farm economy as a source of Minnesota's strength and progressiveness. Farmers were trustworthy and hard working. Living in close contact with the soil for several generations, they represented the tradition of the sturdy yeoman – a tradition that had roots deep in the American past.[8]

In addition to praising the extraordinary potential of the state's farmlands, nineteenth-century Minnesotans boasted about the seemingly boundless mineral and timber resources. Nevertheless, government officials were forced by 1900 to recognize that the forests had largely been cut over, and they urged that efforts be made to replant them. Concern for depleted forest resources and growing tax delinquency in parts of northern Minnesota prompted several governors by the late 1920s to stress the need to buy these lands back and turn them into vast state parks. The drive coincided with a growing interest in the use of the state's lands for recreation. Aware of the lure of Minnesota's fishing and hunting potential, organizers in 1917 founded the Ten Thousand Lakes of Minnesota Association to promote tourism. Pooling financial contributions from fifty communities around the state, the association placed advertisements in state and national newspapers and in magazines like *Outing*, funded a movie about canoeing down the Mississippi River that was shown around the nation, and published circulars, leaflets, postcards, and booklets praising the state's splendid outdoor recreational opportunities.[9]

So successful was this effort to promote Minnesota's recreational resources that the state took over the functions of the association in the early 1930s by setting up a tourist bureau within the Department of Conservation. "From a scenic standpoint, Minnesota bows to none," said the bureau; it was careful, however, as earlier Minnesotans had been, to play down the region's less desirable features – particularly its cold winters and mosquito-plagued summers. Although critics of this Garden-of-Eden vision might have suggested that the state's dreadful winters made it more like America's Siberia, defenders had long boasted that activities like the Winter Carnival in St. Paul changed the cold northern winter into a "season of movement and merriment, of out-door sports, and in-door sociability." Minnesotans in 1888 had bragged that "Nature had given to Min-

Come to Minnesota

Drive north to the land where Ten Thousand Lakes are linked by motor highways organized and maintained for your pleasure and convenience. Come to the piney woods for your motor journey.

A new delight at each turn of the road. Climate, Scenery, Sport, Good Roads, and those well equipped, comfortable hotels that bring a day's journey to its fullest possibility of enjoyment. All roads lead to Minnesota. Take the nearest one and come.

Write today for complete information and our personal service.

Ten Thousand Lakes of Minnesota Association
Fourth and Cedar Streets, St. Paul, Minn.

Illustration of advertisement which appeared in national magazines and trade publications to attract the motorist to Minnesota.

Advertisement placed in state and national publications by the Ten Thousand Lakes of Minnesota Association, 1918

nesota an invigorating climate, fit to produce a race of men as hardy and active as any the world has seen," praise that was continued over the years as boosters promoted the state as a center for winter recreation. The tourist bureau proclaimed in its 1932 report that "Minnesota's facilities for cold weather activities are fully as complete as those of St. Moritz, Switzerland, and Lake Placid, New York, much of whose income is derived from winter sports enthusiasts."[10]

The bureau's report to the state legislature was also blunt in setting forth its objectives: "One of the prime efforts of the Bureau at its inception will be to sell every Minnesotan on the fact that he lives in America's greatest year-around playground, an area which at the same time maintains one of the highest ratings as regards agricultural productivity and industrial achievement." Thus, the physical wonders of the state were to be consciously promoted to Minnesotans themselves. State leaders clearly saw the positive gains to be achieved from convincing Minnesotans that they had the best of all possible worlds – substantial economic opportunities within an unlimited recreational paradise.[11]

This emphasis on outdoor recreation coincided with a new, nationwide stress on health and physical fitness that began at the turn of the century and has endured throughout the decades. The trend, partly a reaction against a society whose emphasis on consumption was seen as enervating and dissolute, was strengthened by medical and nutritional research on the importance of exercise and physical fitness. It was reflected in the founding of the Boy Scouts in 1910 and the Girl Scouts two years later, as well as in the efforts of the progressive movement to expand the national park system dramatically. Minnesotans were quick to capitalize on the potential of their unusually diverse physical environment. As urban congestion grew in the East and the Midwest, few people could resist the attraction of the state's great physical beauty. As one *National Geographic* writer put it in 1935, "The Ten Thousand lakes offer an irresistible lure; the sandy lakes perfect for wall-eyed pike and bathing at Detroit Lakes or Alexandria, the rocky, pine-girt lakes of the Arrowhead, fashionable White Bear Lake and Lake Minnetonka, broad Mille Lacs Lake, or Lake Superior itself, marvelous in its pale-blue atmospheric effects and its rugged shore down which cascade after cascade comes splashing."[12]

In the 1920s and 1930s, state leaders took advantage of the national interest in outdoor sports and recreation by creating more state parks and making them accessible to tourists and Minnesotans alike. The earliest parks had been established to commemorate important historical events. Camp Release, near Montevideo, was created in 1889 to mark the site where 269 captives were released by Dakota Indians in 1862. Early parks at Birch Coulee (1889) near Morton and Fort Ridgely (1896) near Fairfax also commemorated events of the Dakota conflict, reminding the public of that chapter in the state's frontier heritage. Itasca State Park and Forest, with its thirty-one thousand acres of lakes and woods, was established in 1891 to preserve the beauty of a site that had held the dreams of generations of explorers – the headwaters of the Mississippi River. Other sites, such as Alexander Ramsey State Park (1911) near Redwood Falls and Jay Cooke State Park (1915) south of Duluth, were named in recognition of important individuals. The state tourist bureau proudly announced in 1939 that "Minnesota is rich in historic lore. . . . Today, throughout the state, there are 105 historic sites indicated by marker plates or monuments. Many of them are scattered throughout the 46 state parks, recreational areas and wayside parks. . . . Sites of old forts, missions and Indian battles are found in all parts of the state, and, as you drive along Minnesota's 11,500 miles of paved highways, you will pass many scenes where Minnesota history was made."[13]

When state parks assumed a new function as sites for healthy outdoor life around 1920, state leaders began to build parks whose main purpose was to enhance recreational opportunities. Interstate Park, which had been established in 1895 along the St. Croix River near Taylors Falls, preserved one of Minnesota's most scenic areas. As their names suggested, many of the newer parks – Whitewater (1919) near Winona, Scenic (1921) in northern Itasca County, and Inspiration Peak (1931) near Brandon – were also designed to attract tourists. A 1932 brochure reassured its readers that many of the parks now had new road systems, redesigned campgrounds, and special picnic areas. "Camping facilities are of the best and one could spend many delightful days in outdoor activities in and around Scenic Park."[14]

State interest in expanding the park system mushroomed in the 1950s

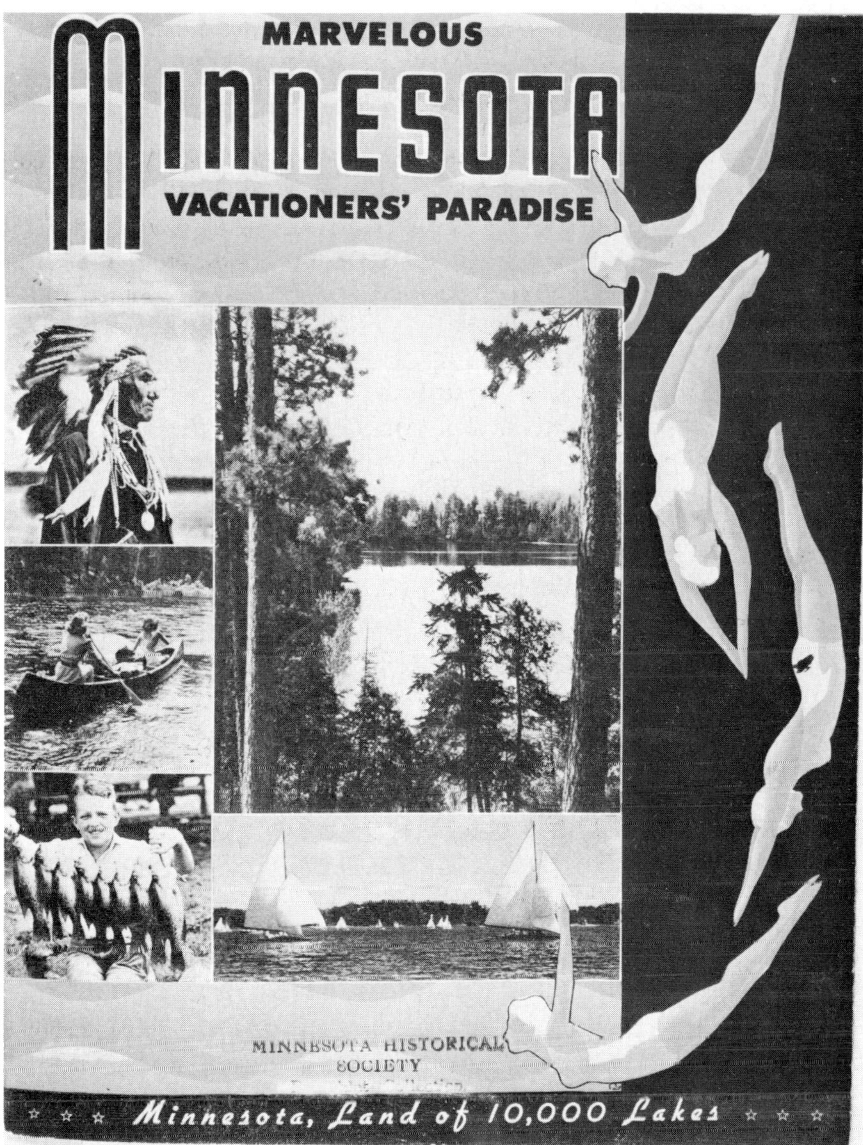

Cover of brochure published by the Minnesota Tourist Bureau, 1943

and 1960s when interstate highways and the outdoor-life movement made it possible for thousands of urban people to "get away" to a lake or forest retreat "up north." Fourteen new parks were added in those years. In addition to providing camping and fishing facilities, the state sought to preserve some of the landscape in its original condition. "A STATE PARK is a typical portion of the State's original domain of adequate size whereby a small portion may be provided for concentrated use," suggested a 1955 brochure, "and the remainder preserved in a primeval condition, accessible only by a system of foot trails and waterways, by which the present and future generations may study the flora, fauna and geologic structure of a beneficent Nature, 'unspoilt, unimproved, and unbeautified' by Man's attempt to improve on the work of the Master Engineer."[15]

As the references to "primeval condition" and the "work of the Master Engineer" suggested, the state had tacitly adopted the position – first put forward in the late nineteenth century by naturalist John Muir and painters Frederick E. Church and Albert Bierstadt and later popularized by the counterculture movement of the 1960s – that the natural wilderness was part of God's great book, a realm that had moral lessons to teach to a society obsessed with its material possessions.[16] Parks were seen as an antidote to the commercialism of everyday life, a place of escape from the frenzied pace of the urban workweek. Minnesotans, because of their easy access to the unspoiled landscape, could have their cake and eat it too: they could enjoy the material benefits of the modern commercial world while balancing them with the restorative sustenance of nature. In the 1960s, when middle-class Americans embraced the glorification of the simple, outdoor life, Minnesotans could picture themselves as living in the ideal environment.

In promoting these virtues of Minnesota's natural environment, the state was reinvigorating the myth of the frontier that historian Frederick Jackson Turner had articulated in the 1890s. According to Turner, the contact with the wilderness had operated as a selective factor in American history, nourishing self-reliance and pragmatism, individualism and democracy. By confronting nature and by building farms and towns on the frontier, the immigrant settler had developed into the new American. Contact with nature had thus assured a process of renewal and rebirth. In its 1973 cover story, captioned "The Good Life in Minnesota," *Time* picked up the same idea. The state still retained a frontier quality because of its 15,291 lakes and twenty-five thousand miles of rivers. The splendid natural resources of the state, together with the relatively small population and "Ice Age" winters, had created a more resourceful and reliant citizen. After all, *Time* explained, "Nature is close (20 minutes from a downtown Minneapolis office building to a country lake) and is generally well protected." It was the message that the state's Department of Business Research and Development had been preaching since its establishment in 1947, but it also built on Minnesotans' love of the outdoor life.[17]

The state rejoiced in its newfound media preeminence as a society with a frontier ethos in the modern world, congratulating itself on a park system that had indeed been created in part to preserve that image. But the interpretation of the state that was expressed in the *Time* article had always had its critics. Writing fifteen years earlier in *Harper's*, conservationist Leona Train Rienow declared that the Minnesota landscape had been pillaged, the virgin forests reduced to bleeding stumps, the lakes denuded of fish, and the iron ranges reduced to vast treeless pits that gaped like open sores on the body of nature. In the 1920s, Minnesotans in the Izaak Walton League and other organizations had protested deteriorating water quality in the upper Mississippi River because of sewage dumped into that waterway by the cities of Minneapolis and St. Paul. The construction of the lock and dam system on the river after 1917 had compounded the problem by creating, in effect, gigantic sewage pools that festered and smelled. Responding to the crisis in water quality, the state legislature funded a study and then created a Twin Cities sanitary district; finally, with the help of the Public Works Administration, the district opened a $15.7 million sewage-treatment plant in 1938.[18]

Public concern about deterioration of the natural environment developed in those years as a response to a specific problem – water pollution – that had become a serious threat to public health. But the 1960s witnessed the culmination of a battle to protect the northern wilderness that was provoked not by fear of pollution but by concern over the loss of the primeval forests of spruce, fir, hardwoods, and pine. As early as 1909, under the leadership of Pres. Theodore Roosevelt, the federal government had created Superior National Forest in northeastern Minnesota. Ontario followed suit and established its own Quetico Provincial Forest Reserve across the border. In 1926, after much debate, the U.S. Forest Service agreed not to build roads in the Superior, Little Indian Sioux, and Caribou areas of the Superior National Forest; they were to remain accessible only by water. Loggers were allowed to operate so long as they provided "natural screens along lakeshores, campgrounds, and similar areas."[19]

Conservationists, lumber and power companies, and recreational land supporters continued to debate the ways in which the forested land of northern Minnesota should be used. Congress passed the Shipstead-Nolan Act in 1930, creating a massive protected area that included Superior National Forest and encompassed more than four thousand square miles, almost the size of the state of Connecticut. During the Great Depression, the state of Minnesota responded to bankruptcies and lumber-company tax defaults on cutover lands by establishing twelve state forests in its northernmost counties, containing 1.4 million acres adjacent to or inside the park area. Recreational proponents, including naturalist Sigurd F. Olson and landscape architect Ernest C. Oberholtzer, worked for a wilderness canoe country in part of the international park, arguing that the recreational value of the area surpassed its potential as a source of timber. Successive battles followed, first to limit the roads and then to forbid the use of airplanes to fly visitors to remote campsites. Eventually – after the roadless areas had been renamed the Boundary Waters Canoe Area in 1958 – regulations were put in place to prevent the thousands of campers who visited the area from spoiling it with their trash and the lumber companies from destroying the landscape through logging.[20]

The war culminated in the passage of the Wilderness Act of 1964, which redefined the area as one where "man himself is a visitor who does not remain." The question of limiting logging and the use of motorboats, snowmobiles, and houseboats on federal lands and waters continued to be hotly debated, but all of these activities were now subject to restrictions. The act reserved certain areas for canoe use, barred the enlargement of cut zones, and set up stiffer rules for loggers. Minnesota, under the persistent and visionary leadership of Oberholtzer and Olson, had succeeded in controlling the use of wilderness lands, but the beauty of these remote areas brought with it the problems of attracting too many visitors.[21]

The vision of preserving a natural wilderness where recreation and the development of natural resources could exist side by side was thus difficult to implement in practice. Recreation, which brought an average of 171,000 visitors to the area yearly by 1976, threatened to change the character of the environment. Recreation and preservation were at odds with each other, in a tension that would continue as the twentieth century neared its end. Minnesotans had succeeded in preserving a natural landscape that could keep the state's frontier mystique alive, but the success came at the cost of compromising the ideal of preserving the northern part of the state as a pristine natural wilderness.

While the conservationists were working at midcentury to preserve the state's natural environment, the Minnesota Historical Society began to assume a new role as preserver of historic real estate. In 1910, when preservationists had sought to buy and restore the Henry H. Sibley house in Mendota – the oldest surviving private residence in the state – they had enlisted the services of the Minnesota Chapter of the Daughters of the American Revolution. Similarly, in 1931 it was the state that acquired the Lindbergh house near Little Falls and turned the land around it into a park.[22]

Not until 1958 did the historical society become actively involved in rescuing historic sites. The immediate occasion for this new responsibility was a crisis that developed when the state highway department announced plans to create a highway interchange by bulldozing Fort Snelling, the military post built in the 1820s at the confluence of the Minnesota and Mississippi rivers. The public's response was swift. Concerned citizens strongly protested the proposed destruction. The state then made a commitment to protect and develop the site, and archaeological excavations conducted by the historical society during the next few years uncovered the foundations of more of the original buildings. The historical society became custodian of the site and began to reconstruct the fort and develop it into a center for interpreting the state's early history.[23]

In 1961 the historic fort and the area around it were designated as Fort Snelling State Park. As in the northern park systems, the goal was not simply to prevent the destruction of valuable resources, but also to increase the public's pride in and awareness of the accomplishments of the state. A Fort Snelling promotional brochure published as work was under way at the fort stressed that "the Park is much more than the old Fort"; it promised trails for the nature lover, areas for picnickers, swimming beaches, and athletic and game areas. "For the amateur historian and archeologist," the brochure continued, "viewing the restoration as it goes forward may, in some ways, be as rewarding as a tour of fully restored old Fort Snelling could ever be."[24]

Besides restoring the fort to its 1825 condition (a project that was completed in 1978), the historical society developed a major interpretive program, complete with costumed soldiers and workers who re-created the texture of life on the frontier. The site promised to present a new kind of public history, featuring vivid reconstructions of the past that were directed to ordinary men and women and their children. Billed in the brochures as "a gateway to the past," the old fort became a new symbol for the revitalization of the mystique of the state as a frontier society. The description of the rough-and-tumble life at the fort, with its low pay, fatiguing routines, shiftless soldiers, and primitive living conditions, could serve as a constant reminder to Minnesotans of the state's humble beginnings and many achievements.[25]

Minnesota was part of a national, grass-roots movement to protect the record of the past. Responding to what it later called the "widespread hunger for history in our land," the historical society embarked on an ambitious program of historic preservation and interpretation. In the Omnibus Natural Resources and Recreation Act passed in 1963, the state legislature recognized historic sites as one of the "natural resources of the state." It created the Outdoor Recreation Resources Commission to work with the historical society in establishing a historic sites program. The legislation was explicit about the purpose of this arrangement: historic sites not only provided "a rare educational experience for young and old alike" and a "practical laboratory for students," but they also had a "sound, economic, dollars-and-cents" purpose. "[The sites] can strengthen the state's appeal to tourists," stated the commission. "The automobile traveling public has found that such sites add purpose to vacations."[26]

Given this legislative support, which was supplemented by the state Historic Sites Act of 1965 and the National Historic Preservation Act of 1966, the historical society launched a major program of historic renovation and restoration. Its role in increasing public awareness of state history, especially through its work at historic sites, made the society one of the primary shapers of the state's historical consciousness after World War II. Not surprisingly, the tremendous popularity of this celebration of Minnesota's history contributed to the rebirth of the frontier mystique in the twentieth century.

In the 1950s, state publicists added a new dimension to the now-familiar litany about Minnesota as a frontier state – an emphasis on the creative, entrepreneurial potential that was available to what would come to be called "high-tech" industries. The emphasis on support and encouragement of new business and industry had, of course, been written into the frontier thesis from its start. As Turner had suggested, the frontier had given rise to the most striking characteristics of the American intelligence, including "that coarseness and strength combined with acuteness and inquisitiveness; that practical, inventive turn of mind, quick to find expedients; that masterful grasp of material things, lacking in the artistic but powerful to effect great ends." Writer Frederick G. Vosburgh, following up this theme in a *National Geographic* article entitled "Minnesota Makes Ideas Pay," suggested that the state's wonderful outdoor life produced not only a healthy population but also a new creativity with state businesses. Citing the production of high-altitude balloons by General Mills, the development of Scotchlite reflective material by Minnesota Mining and Manufacturing, and the research into industrial heating controls by the Minneapolis-Honeywell Heat Regulator Company, Vosburgh exclaimed that "scientific tinkering gets results."[27]

In their speeches, Minnesota's governors regularly connected the state's wonderful recreational environment with the generation of new ideas and business. Gov. Orville L. Freeman suggested in 1956 that the attractiveness of the natural environment was the single most important factor in getting new business to locate within the state. The Sperry-Rand plant built in St. Paul that year and the expansion of IBM into Rochester were but the most recent signs of the vitality generated by life in Minnesota. As the Department of Business Development asserted in 1957, in the true frontier tradition, "Today the people of Minnesota are largely native born, but they still display the rugged individualism, the high productivity, and the stability of their forebearers [*sic*]." This same sentiment was echoed by *Time* sixteen years later when it noted that Minnesota had become one of the nation's leading "brain-industry" centers. By 1973 the state had more than 170 businesses in electronics and related technical fields, employing more than seventy thousand people.[28]

If the lingering frontier spirit supported new high-technology industries, it also appeared to create an ethic of cooperation and community-mindedness. From this civic spirit came a new interest in the arts: the Guthrie Theater was founded in 1963, and the following decade saw the expansion of the Minneapolis Institute of Arts and the Walker Art Center and a new home for the Minnesota Symphony Orchestra. Searching for an explanation for the dramatic growth of the arts within the state in the 1960s and early 1970s, the *Time* writer said that "Minnesotans tend to be participants in their communities, perhaps because for so long they were comparatively isolated and developed traditions of mutual reliance."

Large corporate interests in the state have also given generously to support civic institutions. Minnesota has gained a "national reputation for philanthropy," according to a local journalist, because of the generous grants made by corporate and private foundations to educational institutions, the arts, and social services. Since the 1940s, Dayton Hudson Corporation has given away 5 percent of its pretax earnings; by the 1980s, about seventy Minnesota firms had adopted this practice, with another forty contributing between 2 and 5 percent. In 1984, William Ouchi, author of the best-selling management guide *Theory Z*, was pointing to Minnesota's brand of public-private teamwork as a model for recapturing America's competitive edge.[29]

Despite the tendency of commentators to attribute Minnesota's achievements to its residual frontier mystique, this image has exerted a negative as well as a positive influence. It has, for instance, tended to stress the value of white, northern European culture over that of Indians, blacks, or immigrants from other places. Certainly, the public press has loved to celebrate the white ethnic makeup of the state. As the *Time* writer put it, that heritage had created a melting pot that shaped the state's character. "They [the Scandinavians], together with its large Anglo-Saxon and German strain, account for a deep grain of sobriety and hard work, a near-worship for education and a high civic tradition in Minnesota life. Such qualities helped to produce the intelligent calm – and the stolidity – that characterize the efficient Minnesota atmosphere."[30]

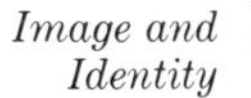

ATTITUDE

. . . a factor that can affect your company's efficiency and profit.

Business success is strongly influenced by people—employees, community and government. Minnesota people have an outstanding resumé.

The attitude of our 1,200,000 workers is reflected in their reliability. They lose only 4.65 workdays per year compared with the national average of 8.2. Minnesota has grown in Value Added by Manufacturing faster than the national rate. New industries, notably electronics and food processing have thrived here.

Some of the reasons for Minnesota's superior performance are found in the recent "Quality of Life" study by Dr. John O. Wilson, formerly of the Midwest Research Institute, Kansas City. It ranks all 50 states on nine socio-economic and political factors. Minnesota's overall rank is Number 2—and still improving.

We think the comparative ranking of the 50 states on each of these points will be helpful to you. Please write on your letterhead for a complimentary copy of "The Quality of Life in Minnesota."

minnesota!
10,000 LAKES

Send request to:
J. Kimball Whitney, Commissioner, Department of Economic Development
57 West 7th Street, St. Paul, Minnesota 55102

Promotion included in a special advertising section placed in Fortune, *October 1968, by the Minnesota Department of Economic Development*

This emphasis on the northern European origins of Minnesota's population has often relegated groups whose numbers were never large, such as Russian Jews, to virtual invisibility. Historian Marilyn J. Chiat, who has examined the history of the more than eight thousand Jews who lived in small towns outside the Twin Cities in the 1930s, commented in 1988 that "when I started this, the historian in me was sick and tired about the characterization of 'white bread Minnesota.' I found that it wasn't. It's more like pumpernickel bread [with communities made up of a variety of ethnic and religious groups]." Similarly, spokespeople for the Indian, Hispanic, and other minority communities have often argued that comparisons of their groups in the popular press with Minnesotans of northern European stock have often created false stereotypes and minimized their contributions to the state. Because of the power of the popular image of the state as a place where people of northern European background are dominant, other ethnic and religious groups have been aware of constant pressure to change. One Mexican American who lived in St. Paul in the 1930s remembered thinking of himself as being "different." He said, "I was darker, and I felt that in order to be American, you had to be white, you had to speak English well, and you had to eat American food."[31]

Notwithstanding its destructive and coercive impact on groups outside of the dominant culture, the frontier mystique has remained alive in the state, both rationalizing Minnesota's achievements and diverting attention from its faults. Winters have become recreational opportunities and builders of character rather than oppressive reminders of a bone-chilling climate. Farming, despite its uneven financial rewards, has continued to be praised as a source of the state's self-reliance. Even the isolation created by the scattering of Minnesota's relatively small population has been turned to an advantage.

From the essays that follow, readers can judge the extent to which the public self-image of the state in the twentieth century has corresponded to reality. Minnesotans have long prided themselves on the quality of life in their state. The question remains about the degree to which the state has fulfilled its ideals and whether those same ideals have acted as a positive force.

Our analysis of the state's history in the twentieth century begins appropriately with Thomas J. Baerwald's study of the state's physical landscape, the basic environment that various groups have reshaped over time and that has both stimulated and hindered economic development. Pointing out how the patterns of exploitation of land and water resources have shifted during the century, Baerwald examines the questions that people – farmers, miners, citizens in both city and country – have asked about the proper use of Minnesota's environment.

The next two essays, by John R. Borchert and Thomas Harvey, focus on the growth of regional urban centers and their impact on towns in the surrounding countryside. The expansion of railroad and highway systems, the shifting economic base of communities, the growth of new communications systems, and suburban residential sprawl have transformed the built environment in the state. As these writers make dramatically evident, sweeping economic and social changes have taken place in the state since 1900. Nowhere have these changes been more evident than in the lives of farmers and miners. David L. Nass charts the ups and downs of the farm economy and its impact on the state's rural population. In a similar fashion, Arnold R. Alanen documents the shifting fortunes of people on the iron ranges as the iron-mining industry has expanded and then collapsed.

The economic life of the state has been a complex story during the twentieth century, including intense labor struggles, as well as industrial and business successes and failures. Peter Rachleff shows how the state's vigorous and at times radical labor movement has fought over the years to gain power in the workplace, often within the context of national economic trends that have had great impact on state labor issues. Examining the growth of industry, Kirk Jeffrey demonstrates how key inventions, a knack for marketing, and investment in basic research have enabled a number of Minnesota firms to compete in world markets. In his look at the precarious world of agribusiness, D. Jerome Tweton charts the cycles of that business and the shifting nature of crop and animal production. George S. Hage analyzes growth and change in the media, including newspaper publishing and broadcasting. His account shows how a small number of aggressive entrepreneurs have come to dominate the popular media in the state.

Daniel J. Elazar and John E. Haynes next examine Minnesota's unique political culture. Elazar charts the evolving structure of state and local government while Haynes explores the distinctive features and changing agendas of the political parties. Both writers show how Minnesota's open political process has encouraged active and often innovative debates about social issues and methods for resolving social problems.

In his essay on Indian life during the twentieth century, David Beaulieu details the efforts of Indian leaders to improve the economic and social circumstances of their people, and he traces some of the complex issues that have characterized the period. He describes ways in which Indians have adapted their culture to the urban environment.

Marjorie Bingham provides a perspective on the century in relation to changes in the lives and work of women. She surveys the growth of women's networks throughout the state as it has opened up new opportunities for women and has increased their political and economic involvement in community life. Looking at the dramatic expansion of educational institutions within the century, Clarke A. Chambers chronicles the growing importance of the state's schools, colleges, and universities. Searching for the ways in which religion has affected people's lives, Richard M. Chapman demonstrates the influence of the church on communal life, ethnic identity, and social reform. Each of these essays illustrates the diverse and pluralistic nature of life in the state at the end of the century.

Karal Ann Marling's concluding essay on culture and leisure brings us back to the questions about identity and self-image with which we began. If the popular image of the state was in part created by Jessica Lange, Garrison Keillor, Prince, and other media stars, Minnesotans' ongoing search for identity has itself become one of the distinctive features of life in the state. Whether they escape to a northern lake, participate in a town festival, or go to the Guthrie Theater, Minnesotans pride themselves on the opportunities for leisure and recreation that are available to them. Most Minnesotans would agree with *Time* magazine's comment that theirs "is a state where a residual American secret still seems to operate. Some of the nation's more agreeable qualities are evident there: courtesy and fair-

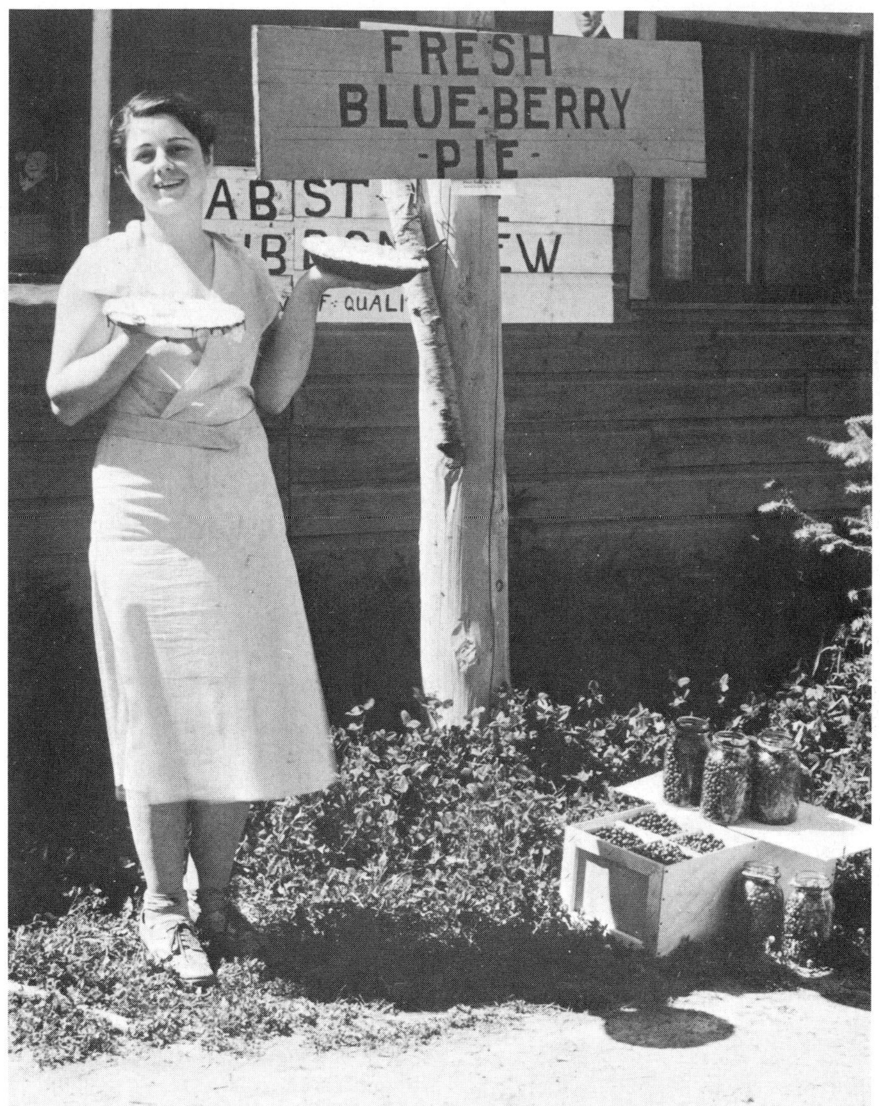

Photograph of a "high-school miss at Ash Lake" that illustrated a National Geographic Magazine *article about Minnesota, March 1935*

ness, honesty, a capacity for innovation, hard work, intellectual adventure and responsibility." The mythic world of Lake Wobegon that many Minnesotans picture themselves as living within is not without its flaws, but it does contain enough reality to sustain the hopes of the majority of its population. Journalist Carol Byrne summed it up in another way: "East, West, urban, rural, young, old, black, white and even androgynous. Minnesota is all of these things, and so is America. Maybe it's just as well that we are a couple of years behind the rest of the country. It gives us a chance to put it all together. We are the middle, where the pendulum stops."[32]

NOTES

The author is grateful to Sarah Crippen Madison for helping to track down much of the material used in this essay.

1. "Minnesota: A State That Works," *Time*, Aug. 13, 1973, p. 24.
2. Frederick G. Vosburgh, "Minnesota Makes Ideas Pay," *National Geographic Magazine*, September 1949, p. 291.
3. Michael Walzer, "On the Role of Symbolism in Political Thought," *Political Science Quarterly* 82 (June 1967): 194. The power that myths possess not only to crystallize peoples' ideas but also to shape the future was explored by Richard Slotkin in *Regeneration through Violence: The Mythology of the American Frontier, 1600-1860* (Middletown, Conn.: Wesleyan University Press, 1973), 3-24, and *The Fatal Environment: The Myth of the Frontier in the Age of Industrialization, 1800-1890* (New York: Atheneum, 1985), chap. 2.
4. June Drenning Holmquist, ed., Introduction to *They Chose Minnesota: A Survey of the State's Ethnic Groups* (St. Paul: Minnesota Historical Society Press, 1981), 4; "Home Town Eager for News as Lindbergh Speeds over Sea," *New York Times*, May 21, 1927, p. 3.
5. "The Park Region of Minnesota," *The Northwest*, April 1883, p. 11.
6. Lind, *Inaugural Message of Governor John Lind to the Legislature of Minnesota, 1899* (St. Paul: N.p., 1899), xxvii; Eberhart, *Inaugural Message of A. O. Eberhart* (Minneapolis: Syndicate Printing Co., 1911), 25.
7. Maxfield, *The Opportunity Spot of America* (St. Paul: N.p., [1913]), 3-4 (quotation), 10-12; Lind, *Inaugural Message*, xxviii-xxix.
8. Theodore Christianson, *Third Inaugural Message of Theodore Christianson* (St. Paul: Riverside Press, 1929), 35; Harold E. Stassen, *Inaugural Message* (Minneapolis: Allied Printing, 1941), 6; Orville L. Freeman, "Minnesota Builds toward New Frontiers" (Speech presented to security analysts, Chicago, Ill., June 12, 1956), 5-6, typescript available at Minnesota Historical Society (MHS).
9. Samuel Van Sant, *Inaugural Message* (St. Paul: Pioneer Press Co., 1901), 13; Theodore Christianson, *Third Inaugural Message*, 26-27; Ten Thousand Lakes of Minnesota Association, *Report of Activities . . . for the Year Nineteen Hundred Eighteen* (The Association, n.d.), 3-7.
10. Minnesota Commission of Conservation, *First Biennial Report . . . for the Years of 1931 and 1932* (St. Paul: The Commission, 1933), 56, 57; *Northwest Magazine*, Winter Carnival Edition, 1887, p. 26; "Our Winter Festival," *Northwest Magazine*, February 1888, p. 1.
11. Commission of Conservation, *First Biennial Report*, 55.
12. See Samuel P. Hays, *Conservation and the Gospel of Efficiency* (Cambridge, Mass.: Harvard University Press, 1959); Glanville Smith, "Minnesota, Mother of Lakes and Rivers," *National Geographic Magazine*, March 1935, p. 316.
13. Works Progress Administration, *The WPA Guide to Minnesota* (New York: Viking Press, 1938; St. Paul: Minnesota Historical Society Press, 1985), 291, 309, 313, 316, 395, 405, 412; Steve Hall, *Itasca: Source of America's Greatest River* (St. Paul: Minnesota Historical Society, 1982), 6-13; Minnesota State Tourist Bureau, *Welcome to Minnesota: Land of 10,000 Lakes* (St. Paul: The Bureau, 1939).
14. Russell W. Fridley, "Preserving History in Minnesota's State Parks," *Minnesota Naturalist* 8 (Spring 1957): 26-28; Harold W. Lathrop, "Minnesota State Parks," excerpted from *Minnesota Conservationist*, nos. 33-37, February-June 1936, available at MHS; Minnesota Department of Conservation, *Minnesota State Parks and Monuments* (St. Paul: The Department, 1932), description of Scenic State Park.
15. Minnesota Department of Natural Resources, *Resource 2000, 1975 DNR Bonding Proposal, 1975-77 Biennium* (St. Paul: The Department, 1975); Minnesota Department of Conservation, *Minnesota State Parks: Memorials, Recreational Reserves, Waysides and Monuments* (St. Paul: The Department, 1955), 2.
16. Barbara Novak, *Nature and Culture* (New York: Oxford University Press, 1980), 3-17.
17. Frederick Jackson Turner, "The Significance of the Frontier in American History," in *The Turner Thesis: Concerning the Role of the Frontier in American History*, ed. George Rogers Taylor (Boston: D. C. Heath and Co., 1972), 3-28; "A State That Works," 24, 31, 33. See also Henry Bradshaw, "Happy Land of Sky-Blue Waters," *American Magazine*, April 1952, p. 38-39, 93-98; Minnesota Department of Business Research and Development, *First Biennial Report: 1947-1949* (St. Paul: The Department, 1949).
18. "Lament for Minnesota: One Hundred Years of Pillage," *Harper's Magazine*, May 1958, p. 57-59; Philip V. Scarpino, *Great River: An Environmental History of the Upper Mississippi, 1890-1950* (Columbia: University of Missouri Press, 1985), 160-81.
19. R. Newell Searle, *Saving Quetico-Superior: A Land Set Apart* (St. Paul: Minnesota Historical Society Press, 1977), 15, 31-32; the quotation from the federal policy is on p. 32.

20. Here and below, Searle, *Saving Quetico-Superior,* 87, 105, 112, 125, 165, 218, 221, 223–26.

21. The quotation from the Wilderness Act is found in Searle, *Saving Quetico-Superior,* 221.

22. Here and below, MHS, *Historic Resources in Minnesota: A Report on Their Extent, Location, and Need for Preservation* (St. Paul: The Society, 1979), 54–55; Department of Conservation, *Minnesota State Parks and Monuments,* description of Charles Lindbergh State Park.

23. June D. Holmquist and Jean A. Brookins, *Minnesota's Major Historic Sites: A Guide,* 2d ed. (St. Paul: Minnesota Historical Society, 1972), 6–8.

24. Fort Snelling State Park Association, *Welcome to Fort Snelling State Park* (Minneapolis: Fort Snelling State Park Association, n.d.).

25. MHS, *Historic Fort Snelling* (St. Paul: The Society, n.d.).

26. MHS, *A Historic Interpretation Program for the State of Minnesota* (St. Paul: The Society, 1977), 1; here and below, Holmquist and Brookins, *Minnesota's Major Historic Sites,* viii, 83; Minnesota Outdoor Recreation Resources Commission, *An Historic Sites Program for Minnesota* (St. Paul: The Commission, 1964), 2.

27. Turner, "Frontier in American History," 27; Vosburgh, "Minnesota Makes Ideas Pay," 291, 311, 315 (quotation), 316. For an example of state promotion on this theme, see Minnesota Department of Business Development, *Minnesota Welcomes New Industry* (St. Paul: The Department, 1957), esp. 2–5, 16–17.

28. Freeman, "Minnesota Builds toward New Frontiers," 8; Department of Business Development, *Minnesota Welcomes New Industry,* 2; here and below, "A State That Works," 31, 33 (quotation), 34.

29. *Star Tribune* (Minneapolis), Mar. 21, 1988, p. 1A, 4A (quotation); "Minnesota's Magic Touch: A Public-Private Alliance Creates Jobs and High-Tech Companies," *Time,* June 11, 1984, p. 54.

30. "A State That Works," p. 34.

31. *Star Tribune,* Dec. 5, 1988, p. 1A, 5A (quotation); Susan M. Diebold, "The Mexicans," in *They Chose Minnesota,* ed. Holmquist, 95. For an account of the views of some Indian professionals about stereotypes of Indian problems, see *Minneapolis Star and Tribune,* June 5, 1985, p. 3B, 4B.

32. "A State That Works," p. 24; "As Minnesota's Symbols Have Changed, So Has America," *Minneapolis Star and Tribune,* Sunday Magazine, Nov. 2, 1986, p. 9. In her essay "Minnesota: Left of Center and Out of Place," Annette Atkins described the conflict in Minnesotans' image of their state – a sense of its superior natural resources and high quality of life, yet a nagging fear of having the state perceived as " 'flyover land' – the space between the coasts where nothing happens." (In *Heartland: Comparative Histories of the Midwestern States,* ed. James H. Madison [Bloomington: Indiana University Press, 1988], 9 [quotation], 28–30.)

THOMAS J. BAERWALD

Forces at Work on the Landscape

Minnesota's landscape is a quilt of swatches woven over the centuries by natural and human forces. By the late twentieth century, row crops blanketed the rolling plains of the state's southern counties like corduroy draped on a poorly made bed. Within the undulating terrain of the northeast – largely covered by the white trunks and silvery green leaves of aspen and birch trees – long, reddish gray gashes marked the sites where miners had torn iron ore from the earth. Buildings were scattered throughout Minnesota, but they clustered most densely in cities where roads and rails linked factories, office towers, and shops with quiet neighborhoods of houses sheltered by deciduous trees. Lakes dotted the state unevenly, and streams and rivers wended their way toward its borders. Along the shorelines were structures ranging from shacks to mansions, but most waterfronts were still bordered by pasture or forest.

The landscape thus mirrored the activities of its people, just as it had always reflected the lives, work, and play of Minnesotans. At times the pace of landscape change had been cataclysmic, and at other times it had been slow. The appearance of the region changed little during the centuries of occupancy by Indians because these early residents were few in number and highly concentrated in the river valleys.[1] More dramatic transformation of the land began when settlers arrived from Europe and Africa via eastern North America in the first half of the nineteenth century. By 1900, loggers had cleared most of the vast pine forest of the northeast, farmers had plowed the virgin prairie in southern and western Minnesota into fields and pastures, and urban settlers had established more than a thousand cities, towns, and villages.[2]

The farmers, builders, and industrialists of the nineteenth century had used relatively simple plows, saws, shovels, and rails. Although their counterparts in the twentieth century had larger and more powerful equipment, they reshaped the state in more subtle ways, and changes in Minnesota's landscape were thus less dramatic. These changes remained a register, however, on which the state's people rewrote the answers to their most fundamental questions. Just as the furnishings of a home tell about the family that lives there, Minnesota's landscape changes showed how the state's residents and visitors altered their ways of life in the twentieth century.

Patterns of Change in Life and Work

The number, location, capabilities, and aspirations of Minnesotans changed markedly after 1900. More than 4.2 million people lived in Minnesota in the mid-1980s, about 2.5 million more than in 1900.[3] At the start of the century, Minnesotans were scattered evenly across the southern and western parts of the state, with about a third of the people living in larger cities, especially Minneapolis and St. Paul. As the century progressed, however, Minnesotans showed a growing preference for urban living in all parts of the state.[4]

The most dramatic example of this urbanization was the growth of the Twin Cities. In the ten Minnesota counties included by the U.S. Census Bureau in its tabulations of the Twin Cities metropolitan area, population increased fourfold from 1900 to 1980; by 1970, more than half of the state's residents lived there. In other parts of Minnesota, counties with larger cities grew by a factor of almost 2.3 over the first eighty years of the century; the figure for counties containing smaller cities was 1.8 for the same period, and for counties with little urbanization it was only 1.15. The increase implied in the last category is misleading, however, because the combined population of these forty-one counties actually peaked in 1940 and declined 10 percent by 1980.

Besides becoming more numerous and moving into urban areas during the twentieth century, Minnesotans also changed their ways of life. Most of them, as in the nation as a whole, became more mobile. Before World War I people generally traveled by foot, atop or behind horses, or on streetcars and railroads. Automobiles and trucks greatly increased the convenience and range of travel, however, and Minnesotans bought these vehicles in rapidly growing numbers. Automobile registrations in the state rose from 2,500 in 1905 to 747,000 in 1940 and more than 2.4 million in 1983. Truck registrations rose more slowly at first, but the number increased to almost 200,000 in 1950 and exceeded 850,000 in 1983. Greater use of motor vehicles put pressure on governments at all levels to provide better roads, leading to an increase in paved roads in Minnesota from 67 miles in 1906 to more than 33,000 by 1981.[5]

To accommodate their automobiles and trucks, Minnesotans built garages next to their houses, added service and repair stations in commercial areas, and dedicated large tracts of land to parking lots and to freeways, interchanges, and frontage roads. University Avenue, the most important Twin Cities thoroughfare in 1900, was only a third as wide as the fourteen lanes of interstate highways 94 and 35W that passed just south of downtown Minneapolis starting in 1967, and the interchange that opened at highways 35E and 494 in 1984 in northern Dakota County con-

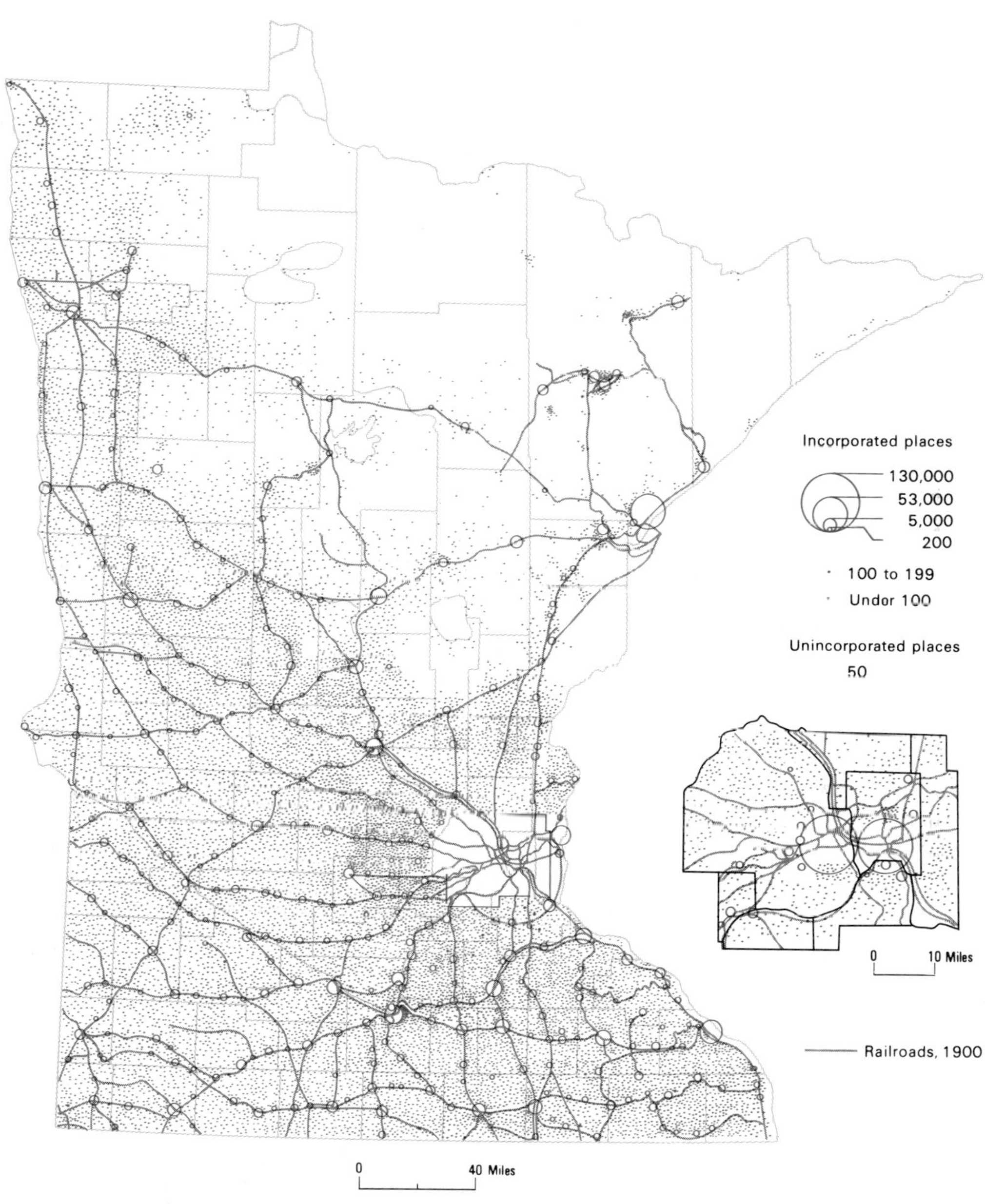

Distribution of the population in 1900, when less than a third of the state's people lived in the Twin Cities metropolitan area. Source: *Borchert and Gustafson,* 1980 Minnesota Atlas, *209.*

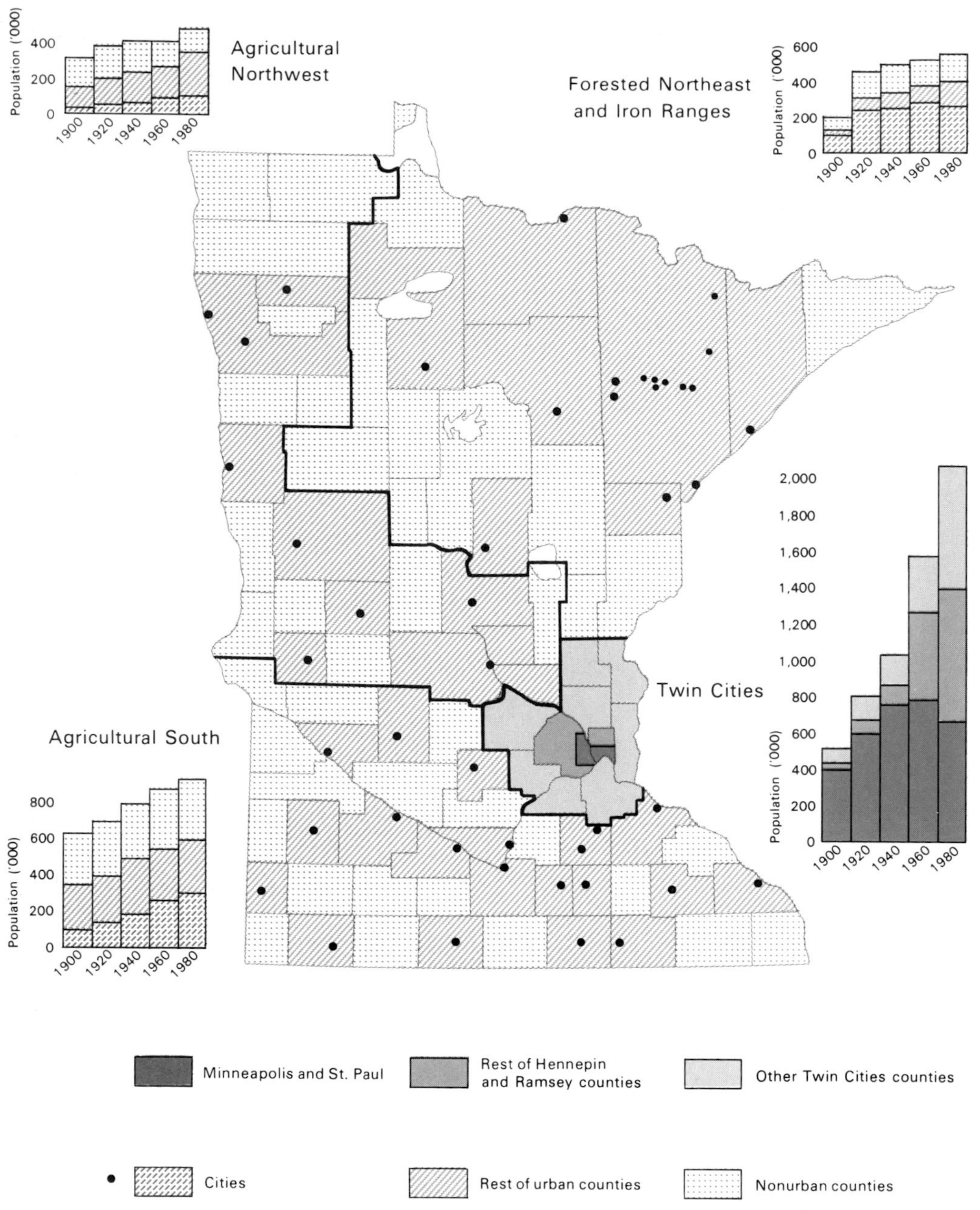

Population change in major land-use regions, 1900–80. Source: *Data are taken from census reports as described in n. 3.*

sumed almost 150 acres, an area roughly comparable to the average size of a Minnesota farm in 1900.[6]

Automobiles, trucks, telephones, airplanes, and other high-speed modes of transportation and communication dramatically changed the ways in which Minnesotans viewed and used different places. In the early years of the twentieth century, people rarely traveled more than a few miles from home because of the expense and time involved. Cities were

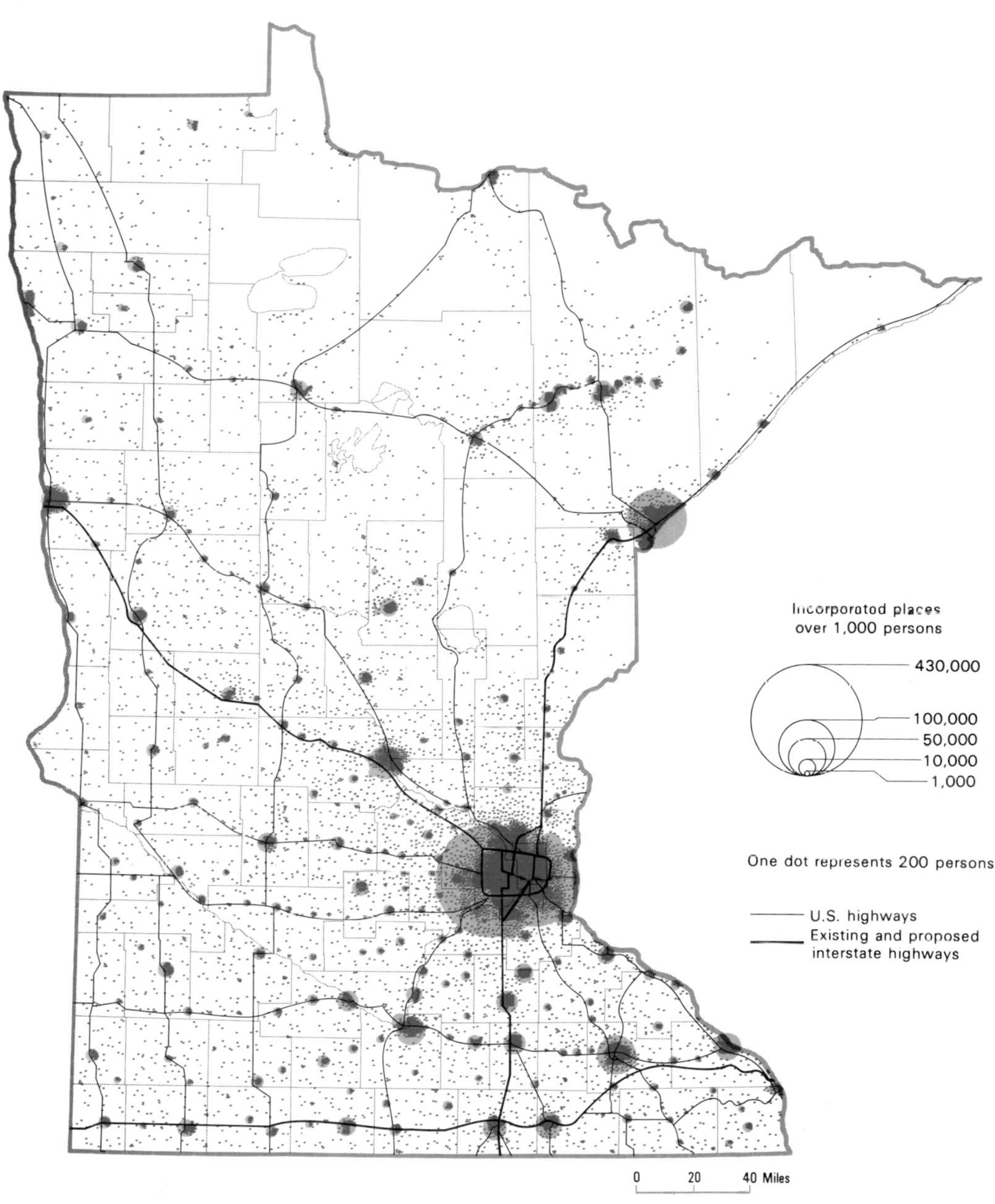

Distribution of the population in 1970, when the Twin Cities had grown to include more than half of the state's people. Source: *Borchert and Gustafson,* 1980 Minnesota Atlas, *211.*

densely packed near core employment concentrations or along relatively short streetcar lines, and urban settlements in rural areas were strung out along railroad lines at distances geared to travel by foot or wagon over crude roadways.

As transportation improved, however, Minnesotans traveled farther and faster. Some people sought out lower-priced sites for housing on the outer margins of urban centers, and others purchased property on remote lakes for second homes. Merchants responded to the greater personal mobility and shifting population patterns by redefining the types and locations of stores and service establishments. By the 1980s, rural residents – whose grandparents had perhaps spent a full day journeying round trip to the county seat – drove to cities to shop at enclosed malls that served people in a half-dozen counties. The potential of trucks as a means of moving freight allowed manufacturers and wholesalers to relocate from the limited number of sites along waterfronts and rail lines to cheaper sites along suburban freeways and in smaller urban centers throughout the state.

Other facets of individual and corporate life underwent equally profound changes during the twentieth century. Machines played larger roles in economic production and leisure activities. Larger machines that did more work completely altered the way in which farmers raised crops and livestock, loggers harvested trees, miners removed ores, factory workers made products, and service people performed their jobs. The stoves, refrigerators, freezers, dishwashers, and other appliances that Minnesotans bought were increasingly sophisticated. People spent their leisure time using devices – radios, television sets, outboard motors, snowmobiles, and countless other contraptions – that were unknown to their parents and grandparents. The concept of leisure itself changed as the century unfolded. Employees worked fewer hours each week and took longer vacations, and the number and range of activities in which they could spend their nonworking hours multiplied. Recreation became a major economic activity in its own right, with many parts of the state increasingly reliant on tourist dollars to fuel local economies.[7]

Landscapes of the Regions

The ways in which Minnesotans changed the landscape in response to the demographic, economic, and social forces of the twentieth century varied substantially from one region to another. People grappled with critical questions that reflected the natural features and human activity of their particular region, and their answers left different imprints on the landscape. Throughout the century, Minnesotans used the state's land in four major ways. Three of these dominant land uses – farms, forests, and mines – were concentrated in specific regions, whereas the other – urban settlement – was more dispersed. Comparable changes in use and appear-

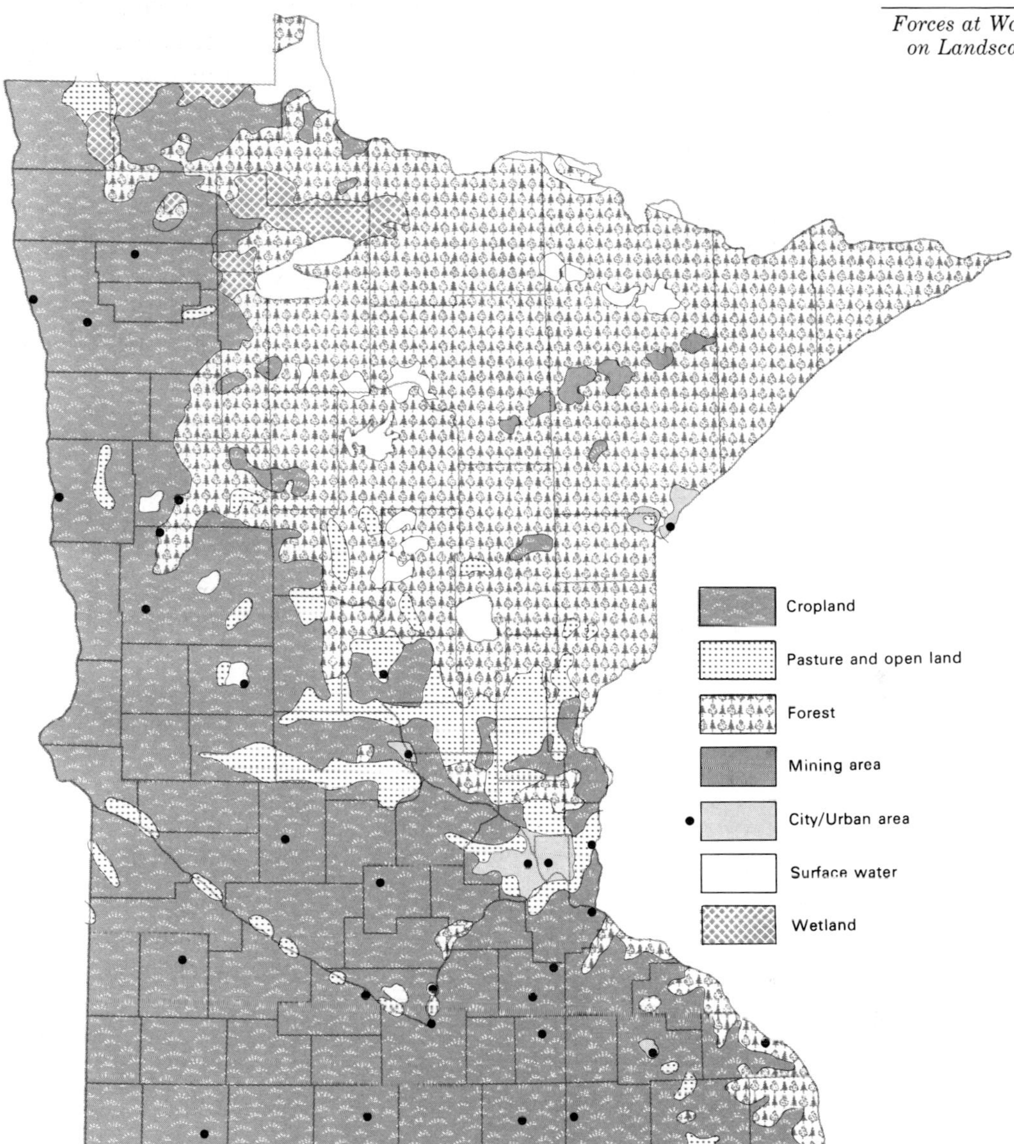

Generalized land uses in Minnesota, 1969. Source: *Adapted from MLMIS,* Minnesota Land Use.

ances were also evident on surface waters and wetlands, which, like the cities, were unevenly scattered across the state.[8]

The Agricultural South and West

Farming remained the most important land use in southern and western Minnesota during the twentieth century. Since the early 1900s, about half of all land in the state had been used for agricultural production, and another 5 percent was semiproductive or fallow. In more than thirty counties southwest of a line connecting Hallock, Detroit Lakes, Little Falls, and the Twin Cities, more than three-fourths of the land was farmed, help-

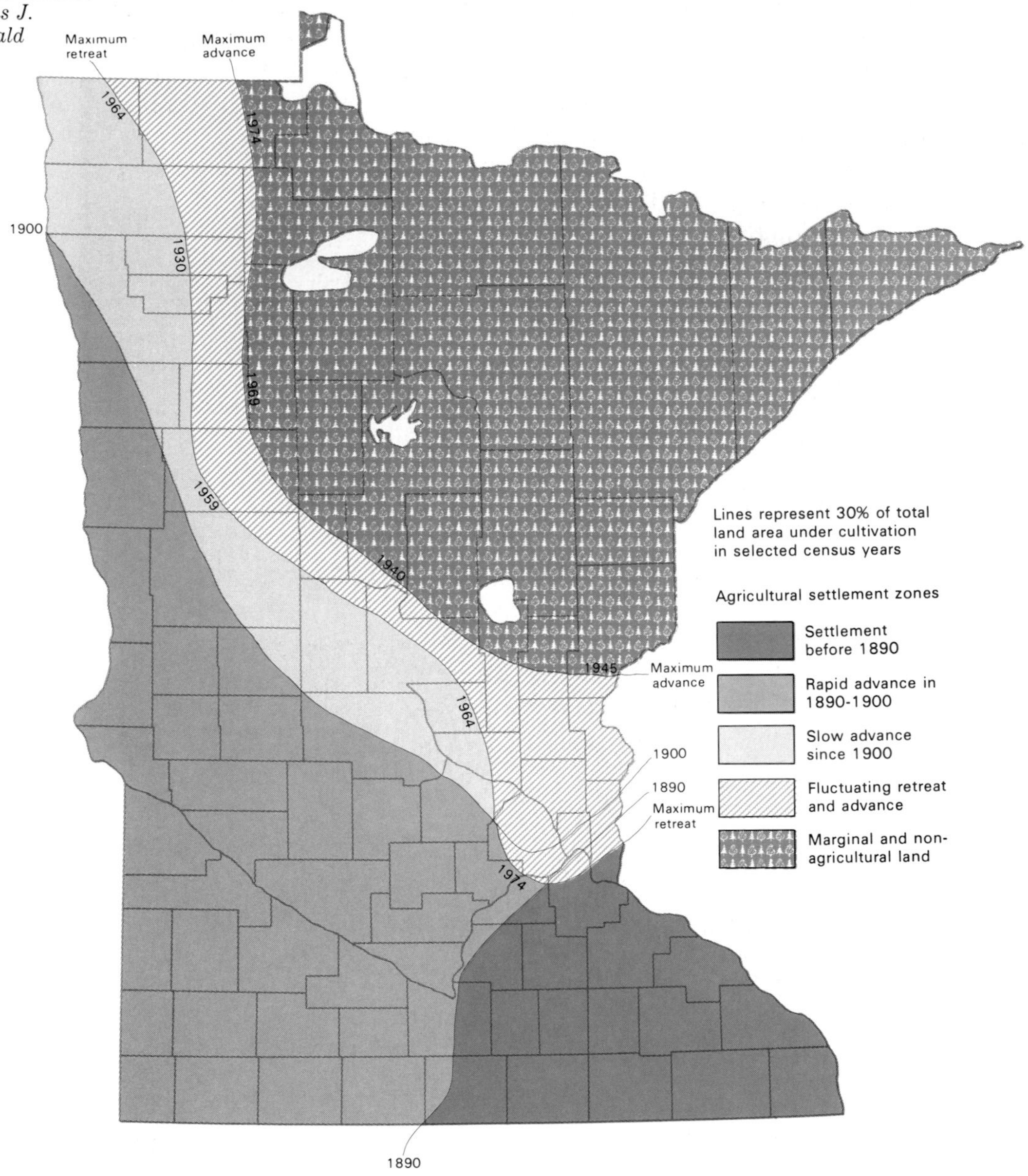

Changing frontier of cultivation since 1890. Source: *Borchert and Gustafson,* 1980 Minnesota Atlas, *63.*

ing boost the state's total annual production of agricultural goods to $7 billion by 1985.[9]

"What should we raise?" and "How should we operate our farms?" were two questions that Minnesota farmers repeatedly had to answer. On the northeastern margins of the state's agricultural heartland, where soils were less fertile and climates cooler, the answers to these questions were crucial, with economic survival hinging on variable outcomes. In the 1910s, farmers continued to push the state's agricultural frontier into the rolling terrain another fifty miles or so to the northeast of a line from East Grand Forks to Fergus Falls and the Twin Cities, and some farmers tried to establish farms in the recently cleared forest lands of St. Louis and nearby counties. Farming along these margins was more difficult than in the rest of the state, however, and less favorable weather and lower market prices forced many farmers to give up in the 1920s. Some hopeful newcomers obtained abandoned farms after conditions improved, expanding the state's agricultural frontier in the 1930s and, later, in the 1970s, but it retreated during the rougher times of the 1920s, 1950s, and 1980s. The last retreat caused the fuzzy boundary of farm activity in Minnesota to be just slightly farther east in the mid-1980s than it had been at the start of the century.[10]

Every year, each Minnesota farmer tried to anticipate which combination of crops and livestock would be most successful. Even when yields were high, the question had to be posed anew the following year. Farmers in the same area tended to respond in similar ways, but regional patterns of crop and livestock production changed considerably over the decades in response to fluctuations in climate, market prices, diseases, pests, availability of hybrids and livestock breeds, and a host of other factors beyond the farmer's control.

In 1900, southern Minnesota farmers raised corn, small grains, and hay in small fields and kept a variety of animals in barns and barnyards. Wheat was the mainstay of northwestern Minnesota farm production, covering more than one-third of the cultivated land in counties of the Red River valley.[11] As the pioneer crop that farmers raised in a newly settled area to generate cash, wheat had moved steadily west through the state with the wave of new agricultural settlement during the nineteenth century. Farmers who worked the same property for a number of years gradually diversified into a broader mix of crops and livestock, but the rise of the giant flour mills in Minneapolis and the spread of railroads to the northwest supported wheat production in the Red River valley through the early decades of the new century.[12]

Corn, the favored feed for cattle and hogs, became the most important crop in southern Minnesota counties after 1900, and the development of hybrids that matured rapidly and thrived in cooler weather permitted farmers north of the Minnesota River to raise corn successfully by the 1950s. Through the first half of the century, farmers frequently grew corn in a three-year rotation with hay and a small grain like oats or barley.[13] Although well suited to the Minnesota climate, oats lost much of their market when tractors replaced horses and mules as the primary means of power for field machinery throughout the nation. As late as 1949, however, oats were still Minnesota's second crop in terms of acreage and production value, and in 1964 in some northwestern counties they were grown on more than 40 percent of the cropland.[14]

Starting in the 1950s, crop-rotation schemes slowly changed. Rows of tall cornstalks were still most common in southern Minnesota, but the acreage on which oats were grown declined by two-thirds between 1949 and 1986, and barley acreage dropped nearly in half between 1949 and

1974. To complement corn, farmers turned to soybeans, which were grown on six times as many acres in 1986 as they had been in 1949. The rapid adoption of this bushy legume resulted from the breeding of hybrids that could survive in Minnesota's shorter growing season and the development of oil-based products that boosted demand and made soybean prices higher than for any of the small grains.[15]

Some crops remained popular with farmers over time, although the areas in which they were produced often shifted. Sugar beets were a mainstay in the Minnesota River valley until the 1920s, but two decades later other crops had become more profitable in southern Minnesota. Farmers of the Red River valley, however, where the climate was unfavorable for corn and soybeans, continued to grow sugar beets. Another major crop in northwestern Minnesota by the 1950s was potatoes, which also remained locally important on the sandy plains north of the Twin Cities.[16] Contracts issued by large canneries in many towns since the first decade of the century encouraged some south-central Minnesota farmers to grow peas, sweet corn, and other vegetables. Cultivation of forage crops shifted in response to the changing location of dairy farming, and purple-flowered alfalfa had become the preferred hay crop by the 1930s in the central and southeastern parts of the state where dairying was common.

Some crops were favored by Minnesota farmers for a shorter period of time. Wartime shortages encouraged Red River valley farmers to produce flax in the 1940s. This oil crop was grown on more than 1.6 million acres in western and northwestern Minnesota in 1949, but lower prices in subsequent decades caused most farmers to plant other crops; by 1986, statewide flax acreage dropped to a mere 35,000 acres. Many northwestern Minnesota farmers were briefly infatuated with sunflowers beginning in the 1970s, as new hybrids and expanding markets boosted statewide acreage from 68,000 in 1968 to 1.4 million in 1979 before problems with disease and lower prices caused farmers to cut production to only 155,000 acres in 1985.[17]

The ascendancy of corn and soybeans as the predominant crops of southern Minnesota and the evolution of northwestern Minnesota agriculture to include production of wheat, potatoes, sugar beets, and small grains were ways in which Minnesota farmers reevaluated the operation of their farms. In the early decades of the century, Minnesota farmers usually raised both crops and livestock. Most crops were directly consumed on the farm as feed; roughly three-fourths of Minnesota's total farm output in 1930 consisted of livestock products. Farmers began to specialize in the 1940s, however, and by the 1980s many were concentrating solely on production of a limited number of crops or livestock breeds or were ending all livestock operations. Almost three-fourths of all Minnesota farms had dairy cattle in 1925, but the share declined to only one-fourth by 1982.[18]

Livestock farmers also changed the ways in which they kept animals. Early in the century, cows were milked for a few years and then slaughtered. By raising breeds that were selected to convert feed efficiently into either milk or meat, however, farmers increased the overall production of

Cattle, hogs, and chickens sharing a Swift County barnyard, 1935

both products significantly. The total number of dairy cattle in Minnesota dropped by almost one-third from 1929 to 1986, but the later cows produced substantially more milk. In contrast, the number of cattle raised solely for beef increased more than ten times between 1929 and 1974. Hog production remained relatively constant throughout the century, averaging about three million head, but numbers sometimes fluctuated dramatically: in the late 1970s, favorable prices led farmers to boost production to more than five million head. But increased specialization in livestock production caused the prototypical Minnesota farm of the 1910s and 1920s – in which cattle, hogs, chickens, and other livestock rooted together in the same barnyard – to vanish. By the late 1980s, most livestock farmers raised only one kind of animal, and the few who kept more than one kind usually segregated them in the interests of efficiency.[19]

Asking questions about crops and livestock was only one way in which Minnesota farmers grappled with changes in farm operation. Many farmers adopted the successful strategy of increasing the size of their operations. From 1920 to 1940, Minnesota's roughly 200,000 farms averaged about 165 acres in size. After World War II, as the economic advantages of larger farms became apparent, many farmers bought property from neighbors who were less successful or who were retiring. By 1986, only 93,000 farms operated in Minnesota, but these units averaged more than 320 acres. Fewer than half as many farmers were working almost as much land as their predecessors had earlier in the century.[20]

Larger farms permitted more efficient use of field machinery, which became larger and more complex as the century progressed. After the 1910s, tractors gradually replaced horses as the motive power for pulling plows, tillers, and harvesters, and sophisticated equipment enabled farmers to plant larger fields and process higher volumes. Corn farmers harvested an average of 36 bushels per acre in 1920, but that figure increased to 122 bushels by 1986. Improvements in machinery also helped farmers in the work of milking cows and of feeding and cleaning up after livestock. As a result, the herd on the average dairy farm grew from fewer than ten cows in 1929 to forty-five in 1986.[21]

As farm size doubled and the number of farms fell by half, many farmsteads were abandoned. Because the farmer who acquired the vacant buildings had little incentive to remove them, thousands of decrepit buildings simply withered as time passed, unsteady monuments to the families that had once worked smaller farms in different ways. These buildings were one way in which the changing scale and character of agriculture were mirrored in the evolving landscape of southern and western Minnesota. The land itself was not dramatically altered, except by massive drainage projects in south-central and northwestern Minnesota that were started in the 1800s and continued through the first half of the twentieth century. By 1960, drainage improvements had been made on about a third of the state's agricultural land, and artificial drainage served more than half of the land in the south-central part of the state, along the middle Minnesota River valley, and in northwestern Minnesota. In Renville and Yellow Medicine counties more than thirty dollars per acre had been spent installing and maintaining drainage improvements by 1960.[22]

The numerous ditches and straightened natural channels of the drainage projects moved water off the land more effectively. Farmers used to harvest the grasses of the "wet prairies" for hay, but by the turn of the century the lure of using the land for more profitable row crops en-

P. G. Jacobson's ditch and tile machine at work on a farm near rural Madison, Lac qui Parle County, about 1910

couraged many to drain every possible acre. By the 1950s, however, other factors – increased flooding, pressure from environmentalists worried about water quality and from hunters seeking to maintain wetlands as wildlife habitat – significantly reduced the number of new drainage projects and encouraged reestablishment of wetlands on some tracts.[23]

In other parts of Minnesota, farmers concerned about rapid soil erosion turned to such soil-conservation practices as contour plowing, strip-cropping, and terracing. These techniques were first used extensively in the 1930s in southeastern Minnesota, and they were later adopted on parcels near the Minnesota River and in the hills of central Minnesota. In flatter areas of the state, concern over erosion focused instead on winds. A few long shelterbelts were planted to protect croplands in the Red River valley in the 1930s, but most trees maintained on Minnesota farms were the L-shaped windbreaks north and west of farmsteads that were planted to protect the buildings when the farms were first established.[24]

Less visible were the changes arising from increased use of chemical fertilizers, pesticides, and herbicides. Early in the century, farmers spread manure, mulched plants, and rotated crops to maintain soil fertility, but the development of synthetic fertilizers allowed them to save time and increase production. By 1974, commercial fertilizer use averaged more than thirty tons per square mile in some south-central and northwestern Minnesota counties, and the state average was sixteen tons. The runoff of fertilizers into surface waters encouraged harmful levels of plant growth in many lakes and ponds.[25]

As Minnesota agriculture changed, so did the appearance and function of buildings and other structures on farms. Outbuildings that once sheltered animals became important for the storage of machinery. On cash-grain farmsteads of southern and western Minnesota, large barns in which dozens of animals had been kept were converted to machine storage by the 1980s. Older buildings were gradually replaced by simpler structures, especially the metal-sided pole barn, an oversized garage that was inexpensive to build, easy to maintain, and efficient to use. Utilitarian structures on grain farms included round, metal grain bins that saved farmers the rental costs of elevator storage by allowing them to store thousands of bushels on the farm until market prices were favorable or the grain could be consumed by livestock. Because the bins permitted dry storage of soybeans, shelled corn, and other grains, they replaced the wire-mesh corncribs and ventilated wooden and tile structures in which whole ears of corn were stored and the gable-roofed wooden granaries designed to hold other crops.[26]

Livestock farms were similarly transformed. Barns remained the focal point of dairy farms throughout the twentieth century, but the increased number of cattle meant the relocation of grain storage and calf rearing to other structures. Stricter health requirements mandated construction of separate milk rooms for the cooling and storage of milk and the cleaning of equipment, adding another fixture to the dairy farmstead. Forage crops were stored in wooden silos in the 1800s, but concrete and masonry silos became common in the early decades of the twentieth century; starting in

Although a silo remained from a previous livestock operation, this Dodge County farm raised only commercial crops in 1987, storing most of its output in large metal storage bins.

the late 1940s, these were in turn joined by colorful, glass-lined steel silos. Because they were airtight, the tall blue and green cylinders were more efficient than the earlier silos, but their high price added to the financial stress experienced by many farmers in the 1980s.

The appearance of other livestock farms also changed. Beef producers began using feedlots in the 1960s, keeping cattle in barns or nearby lots most of the time. Until midcentury, most hog farmers used small A-frame houses scattered throughout fields to isolate farrowing sows, and they sheltered larger pigs in small hog houses. Starting in the 1960s, however, larger, well-ventilated hog houses with concrete floors, conveyor belts for efficient feeding, and separate stalls for each sow became more common. Poultry buildings changed most drastically. The small chicken coops that were a familiar fixture on tens of thousands of farmsteads in the state were removed as poultry production became concentrated at a few farms, where chickens were raised as broilers or egg-layers in long, narrow sheds that accommodated thousands of birds. Turkeys were housed in comparable numbers in sheds during the winter and around long, semisheltered feeding troughs during warmer months.

With livestock confined to feedlots and specialized houses, and with fewer crop-farmers raising any livestock, fences had become rare features on Minnesota farms by the 1980s. Farmers had been able to remove the fences that kept animals from roaming through pastures and stubbled fields earlier in the century, thus allowing the greatest possible area on which to plant crops and operate large machines. Single strands of electrified wire were easily erected where some fencing was needed, and just as easily removed afterward. Large machinery also became evident along rural roads as farmers drove to fields arranged in a complex, noncontiguous pattern, many of the fields rented by the farmers who worked them.[27]

The house where the farm family lived also reflected the changing ways of rural life. Most 1900 farmhouses were variations of simple, two-story wooden boxes, but many older houses were modified in their appearance over time. After World War II, split-level houses, one-story ramblers, mobile homes, and other suburban styles became common. Many were occupied by farmers, but a larger share housed the nonfarm families that purchased large lots in rural settings. The complex linkage between urban and rural life was also evident in transmission lines, which made electrical service available everywhere by the 1950s, and in satellite dishes, which became the preferred means of television reception in the 1970s.[28]

The Forested Northeast

As nineteenth-century farmers were establishing the state's agricultural system in southern and western Minnesota, loggers in the northeast were cutting most of the white, red, and jack pines that grew on well-drained soils, as well as many of the spruce and fir trees that flourished in swamps and bogs. The clearing of the massive conifer forests continued into the first decades of the twentieth century, with production peaking in 1905. The lumber sawn in the state that year would have filled about 240,000 freight cars. New technology, both in the forests and at sawmills, had hastened the clearing, as had the expansion of railroads to transport timber that was remote from waterways. Sawmills in Minneapolis started to close the following decade, however, and by 1929 the closing of a Virginia mill that once kept three thousand loggers busy in nearby forests symbolized the end of the logging boom in northeastern Minnesota.[29]

"How should we use the state's forests? How should we manage the forests?" These questions confronted northeastern Minnesotans after the clearance of virgin conifers from millions of acres. Farmers faced similar questions, but the range of feasible alternatives was far more limited in the forests than in the state's agricultural areas. The cutover lands of the northeast had poorer soils, more rugged land, a cooler climate, and lower population densities. And the time horizons within which decisions had to be made varied enormously: farmers reconsidered production and management decisions at least every year, but trees required decades to mature. The people who made the decisions were also different: farmers had more control over their destinies than did the people who relied on the forest economy of northeastern Minnesota, where choices about land use and management were usually made by corporations or government agencies.

After the loggers left, vast tracts of northeastern Minnesota were fields of stumps beneath a patchwork blanket of dead branches and small trees. This dry tinder was often blackened by fires that swept rapidly across the litter, often scorching nearby towns. Between 1908 and 1918, Chisholm, Baudette, Cloquet, and Moose Lake were all destroyed by forest fires.[30] Some fires spurred natural regeneration of conifers, especially jack pine, but aspen and birch trees rapidly took root and shaded out the slower-growing pines on most of these tracts, as well as on uncharred cutover acres. Conservationists and some forest-industry officials who had not moved to the Pacific Northwest when the Minnesota pineries were depleted started replanting pines in the 1910s, and the Civilian Conservation Corps planted seedlings on tens of thousands of acres in the 1930s. The replanted tracts reached maturity as groves of stately evergreens forty to fifty feet high after 1970. But most cutover tracts were never reseeded, and a 1977 inventory found that 45 percent of the state's forested land was dominated by naturally regenerating aspen and birch trees.[31]

The changes in Minnesota forests during the twentieth century were matched by changing forms of human habitation and economic activity. As the boom ended, loggers gradually abandoned the camps they had built in the woods, as well as the makeshift towns and rail spurs. In larger towns, business leaders adapted structures in the wake of the shift from lumber to activities exploiting the new mix of dominant trees. Aspen and birch made poor lumber, but they pulped well, and paper mills were established along the Mississippi, St. Louis, and Rainy rivers starting in the first decades of the twentieth century.[32] The general growth of office paperwork throughout the nation provided steady markets for these mills, which were regularly expanded and renovated. In later decades, the forest-products industry established processing plants for a variety of fabricated boards and finished products ranging from windows and doors to hockey sticks and chopsticks.[33]

The way in which loggers harvested the forests of northeastern Minnesota also changed dramatically over the century. Many operations were still done by hand or with simple tools in 1900. Specialized lumberjacks felled trees and removed branches on site with axes and crosscut saws. Transportation tended to be labor intensive, with workers stacking the logs high on horse-drawn sleds in winter or on crude skids that horses pulled to rivers in warmer months. Mechanization slowly began to change Minnesota logging in the first decades of the century, however. Small tractors gradually replaced horses as a means of pulling logs to railheads, where timber was shipped out over newly constructed rail lines.[34] Another wave of technological improvements came in the 1940s and 1950s, as chainsaws became the common tool for felling trees and tractorlike skidders were used to drag whole trees to roadside lots where they were loaded on trucks for hauling to mills.[35]

By the early 1970s, the conversion to mechanized harvesting was complete. Loggers used giant tractor-mounted feller bunchers to grab one or more tree trunks at ground level, snip off the trees (leaving no stumps above the ground), and fling them into a nearby pile. Skidders then dragged the trees to loading sites, where portable mills ground them into wafers that were blown into semitrailers, or where portable saws removed the branches and cut logs for loading onto flatbed trailers. Finally, trucks hauled the wafers and logs from harvesting sites to the mills. Mechanization thus substantially increased the productivity of the workers in the state's forests. Koochiching County logger Oscar Bergstrom invested less

Minnesota lumberjacks using axes and saws to fell and trim trees, around 1900

than $400 to $500 per worker in 1947, when he expected each employee in a thirty-man crew to cut one cord of wood each day. By 1983, average productivity had risen to forty cords per person per day, but the equipment required for the four- or five-man crew had a replacement value of nearly $1 million.[36]

As operations became more capital intensive, fewer loggers were needed; 50,000 workers were employed in the harvest of Minnesota forests in the years before 1950, but this number fell to about 3,700 in 1981. The life-styles of loggers also changed: few lived in cabins within walking distance of their work sites, as did many loggers in earlier decades; most commuted to work in pickup trucks from homes in town.

The management of forests underwent a parallel transformation. Spurred by concern about depletion of forest stocks and increasing danger from fire, the U.S. and Minnesota governments started acquiring land for national and state forests in the early decades of the century. The largest of these in Minnesota, Superior National Forest, was established in 1909. The state and county governments also received considerable acreage in tax-delinquent property after lumber companies had exhausted the timber potential of many sites. By the 1960s, more than half of Minnesota's commercial forest land was publicly owned. Improved fire control was one of the first benefits: the fire towers built in the 1920s and 1930s helped forest workers to spot fires quickly, and the clearing of large swaths of land for firebreaks helped control them.[37]

The Gunflint Trail passing through the second-growth aspen-birch forests of Cook County, 1936

Private companies were periodically allowed to cut timber on these public lands, but forest managers encouraged other uses as well. Starting in the 1930s, recreational facilities were built for the public. Weekend visitors and vacationers were able to travel on new roads to the lakes and streams within the forests for fishing and boating, to explore the forests on special trails built for hikers, skiers, and snowmobilers, or to hunt in habitats that were being steadily improved. Only when trees reached maturity were loggers permitted to remove them, and even then their activity was limited to small, backwoods areas – usually forty acres or less – that were unnoticed by most visitors.[38]

The multiple-use policy was not embraced by all Minnesotans, however. As early as 1902, the state's Federation of Women's Clubs was lobbying for creation of a national park in northern Minnesota to protect large stands of virgin pine from the onslaught of loggers. That debate eventually resulted in adoption of a "primitive plan" for Superior National Forest in 1925, with nearly twelve hundred square miles in the northern part of the forest being set aside for preservation in a pristine state. Proponents of economic development of forest and mineral resources, however, continued to clash with groups that wanted to expand the wilderness area. Congress finally sided with the preservationists in the 1960s when it set aside part of Superior National Forest as the Boundary Waters Canoe Area, where motorized boats and vehicles were prohibited. Controversy over the use of this area raged for another decade, and renewed challenges to the wilderness area were expected in the 1980s as mining companies considered potential new forms of mineral exploitation.[39]

The Iron Ranges

The forests of northeastern Minnesota were substantially leveled by the start of the twentieth century, but exploitation of the state's iron-ore deposits had just begun. More than two billion years of complex geologic history had produced three linear formations near the surface that were

MINNESOTA: "WHICH DO I GET?"

Debate over use of northeastern Minnesota forests as depicted by a St. Paul Daily Pioneer Press *editorial cartoon, January 6, 1902*

rich in iron, but these high-grade ores were not identified until the 1860s and 1870s.[40] Mining on the Vermilion Range of northern St. Louis County began in earnest in 1884, and the first shipments left the Mesabi Range of Itasca and St. Louis counties in 1892. Marketable iron ore was not identified in the Cuyuna Range of Crow Wing County until 1904, and commercial extraction began there in 1911.[41]

Until midcentury, high-grade natural ores containing at least 50 percent iron were mined from all three ranges.[42] Production levels rose and fell in response to changing market conditions; production peaked during and immediately after the two world wars, but it plunged in the early 1930s and to a lesser extent in the 1960s as high-grade ores that were economical to extract became scarce. New technology, however, permitted the processing of taconite, a lower-grade rock found in abundance along the Mesabi Range. As demand for iron ore increased in the late 1960s and early 1970s, production levels rose again; but by the 1980s a depressed national economy and competition from lower-priced foreign iron and steel sent Minnesota iron-ore production to the lowest levels in a half-century.

Minnesota's iron ranges, like all landscapes dominated by mining, came to exhibit both the physical characteristics of mineral extraction and the personal adjustments that the people made in response to the wild fluctuations in economic activity. Mining employment rose and fell with production levels throughout the century, ranging from more than twenty thousand workers when the mines were most active to about four thousand during recessions. Population levels in the region were more stable. Twenty-five thousand people lived on the three ranges and in related Lake Superior communities in 1900, a figure that quadrupled to roughly 100,000 in 1920. After that date, population remained about the same, although the early years of taconite production temporarily boosted the total to 115,000 people in 1960.[43]

"What should we mine? How should we relate mining to other economic activities?" Even more than in the forests of northeastern Minnesota, the key questions asked by people on the iron ranges were ultimately answered by large corporations and government, and most of the decision makers were based entirely outside the region. Local decisions were usually responses to conditions determined elsewhere – "How can we take the greatest advantage of favorable conditions? How can we weather rough times?" Seen from a distance, the landscape of the iron ranges was a record of national and global forces, but on close examination it reflected the repeated adjustments of people who persevered in the face of unstable conditions.

Because most mines on the Vermilion and Cuyuna ranges were underground, they had little effect on the landscape. Standing on the surface were skeletal headframes at the tops of mine shafts, conveyors to haul ore to rail sidings, small houses for workers, and extensive piles of the timbers used to support shafts below the ground. In contrast, the open-pit mines that dominated the Mesabi Range were overwhelming. The term *massive* described almost every aspect of Mesabi mining. Individual mines covered hundreds of acres and went as deep as four hundred feet. Huge shovels,

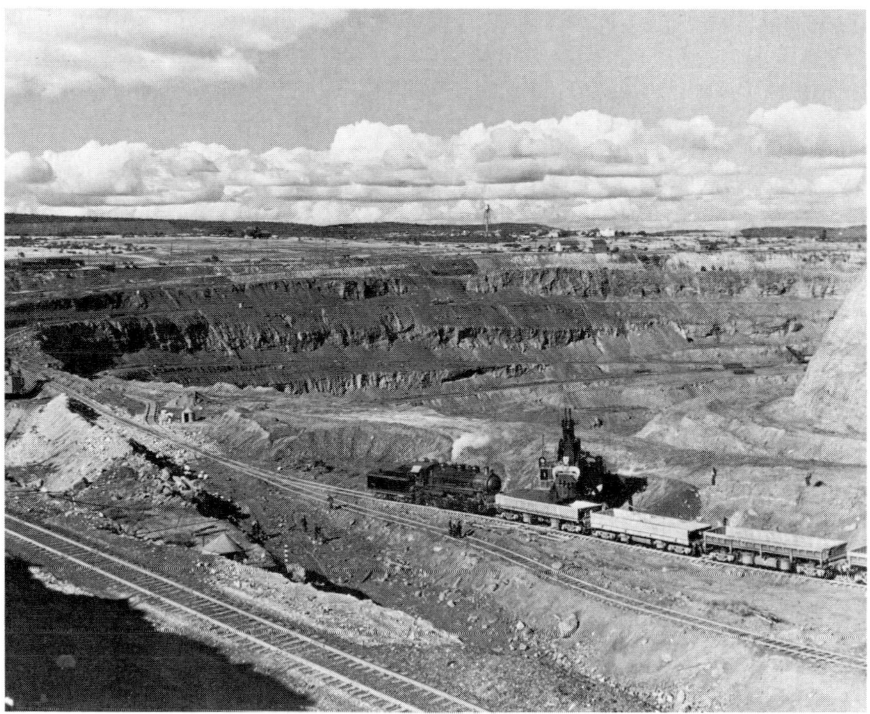

The Hull-Rust-Mahoning mine north of Hibbing in 1940, with railroad tracks totaling more than fifty miles

originally powered by steam but increasingly electrified after the 1920s, removed dozens of tons of rock with each scoop and loaded the rubble into railroad cars. Workers repeatedly relaid tracks along the terraced sides and bottom of the pits to get the ore out most efficiently. Overburden removed during early stages of mine operation was heaped into mesas that perched eerily on horizons throughout the range. Railroad lines slashed through forests to connect the mines with Lake Superior, where mammoth ore docks permitted rapid loading of ore into ships.[44]

As the high-grade ores were depleted after World War II, University of Minnesota experimenters worked to develop ways to tap the lower-grade taconite. By 1955, mining companies were using the new methods to crush this hard rock, separate out the iron, and bind it with clay into pellets that were easily shipped and smelted. Eight taconite-processing plants were in operation or under construction in northeastern Minnesota by 1979, and taconite pellets made up more than 70 percent of the iron shipped from the state. Mines on the Vermilion and Cuyuna ranges had closed by the late 1970s, and almost all of Minnesota's iron in the 1980s came from taconite.[45]

The shift to taconite processing altered the geography of the iron ranges because the best deposits were in the eastern half of the Mesabi Range. From a distance, the outsized open pits and slag heaps of the taconite mines were similar to their natural-ore predecessors, but giant shovels now loaded rock into dump trucks so large that they required separate motors for each wheel. The trucks carried the rock out of the pits to nearby crushing and pelletizing plants from which trains of compact hopper cars carried pellets to traditional ore docks on Lake Superior. In most plants, large basins near the plants were filled with the nonferrous tailings left from the processing.[46]

The roller coaster of iron-ore production on Minnesota's iron ranges repeatedly spurred local political and business leaders to attempt to diversify the region's economy. Pressures were especially great during recessions. For the corporation, the decision to close mines and plants at a distant locale was a purely economic one, but the unemployed workers had strong psychological and social ties to the area and were reluctant to leave to find jobs elsewhere. Recreation, forestry, and light industry were especially favored activities among homegrown entrepreneurs. Mesabi Range developments included industrial plants, a historical theme park – the Iron Range Interpretative Center (Ironworld USA), which opened in the Hibbing area in 1977 – and a skiing complex built near Biwabik in 1984. On the Vermilion Range, Ely became best known as a gateway for canoers, and the underground mine at Tower Soudan reopened as a state park. Cuyuna Range communities catered to tourists seeking relaxation and excitement on Crow Wing County lakes. The search for other minerals also intensified in northeastern Minnesota after 1970, as new scientific discoveries raised hopes that the region's geologic formations had economically extractable deposits of copper, nickel, and uranium. The resilience of iron range residents and their ability to wait for new discoveries were sorely tested by the depressed economy of the U.S. steel industry in the mid-1980s, however, and many people were forced to move from the region in search of jobs elsewhere.[47]

The Urban Settlements

Minnesota's urban settlements covered slightly more than 2 percent of the state's land in 1980, a minor share compared with the land consumed by farms and forests. Urban acreage had more than doubled since the start of the twentieth century, however, and as the end of the century approached, these settlements housed and provided workplaces for about three-fourths of the state's people.[48] Answers to the questions that urban Minnesotans asked about different facets of their daily lives – "Where should we live? How and where should we work? How should we spend our leisure time?" – repeatedly changed the landscapes of the state's cities, towns, and villages.

In 1900, Minnesota's cities and towns were trade and raw-material processing centers.[49] Warehouses and transfer terminals abutted rail lines and sidings in all but the smallest settlements. Wood-frame sawmills fronted rivers in the northeastern forests, whereas limestone-block flour mills stood beside streams in the southeast. Throughout southern and western Minnesota, clapboard- or tin-sided grain elevators that resembled shoe boxes sprouted beside railroad stations. Banks, stores, government buildings, and other establishments serving local residents stood near the industrial cores, and these central functions were surrounded by dwellings. In larger cities, four- to six-story apartment buildings were common near downtown; two-story frame houses for one or two families were farther away, especially along streetcar lines. In smaller communities, frame houses predominated in a compact ring around downtown.[50]

As early as 1910, the economic bases of Minnesota's cities started to change. The rapidly diminishing flow of logs down the Mississippi and other rivers forced sawmills to shut down from that time into the 1930s. Starting in the 1920s, many of the flour mills around the Falls of St. Anthony in Minneapolis and in smaller centers of southeastern Minnesota closed as companies constructed new mills in locations like Buffalo, New York, and Kansas City, Missouri, that were favored by changing freight rates and new areas of wheat production.[51] Some factories processed local resources, such as United States Steel's mill in western Duluth and the Armour meat-packing plant in South St. Paul, both constructed in the 1910s; but most new industrial operations made products that were assembled in Minnesota because of the inventive, entrepreneurial, and production skills of company leaders and workers. By the 1940s, factories in larger cities manufactured goods ranging from paper bags to thermostats in two- to three-story brick buildings beside rail lines radiating from the downtowns.[52]

The expansion of industrial and warehouse activities along railroad lines in the early decades of the century was paralleled by the building of houses along a rapidly expanding network of streetcar lines in Minnesota's larger cities. The residential areas served by streetcars by the 1920s were more than four times the areas that were accessible in the pedestrian-oriented cores before fixed rail transit began in the 1890s. As a result, urban Minnesotans built more single-family, detached houses on larger lots through the first three decades of the century. As residents moved away from the downtowns, storeowners followed, establishing themselves at critical points along the streetcar networks. A clearly defined commercial hierarchy evolved, with the number, size, and range of establishments at a specific place directly related to the number of passengers getting on and off streetcars there.[53] Major junctions had multistory brick buildings on all corners, with busy stores below and professional offices above. Blocks along lines with moderate traffic had smaller businesses at the corners separated by three-story, walk-up apartment buildings, and more distant points on lesser-traveled lines had only small convenience stores at alternate corners amid a sea of single-family houses. In settlements that lacked public transit, the accretion of new houses was more gradual, and downtown remained the location of most commercial enterprises.

The urban pattern that evolved along the iron ranges was unique in Minnesota. The string of mines that stretched for sixty miles along the Mesabi Range, twenty miles along the Vermilion, and fifteen miles along the Cuyuna was replicated with a string of cities, towns, and smaller enclaves known as locations.[54] These settlements sat beside the mines and were sometimes moved when ore deposits were discovered beneath their foundations, as happened at Hibbing in 1919. Iron range communities had traditional rectilinear street grids, but the peculiar mix of stores and services and the distinctive architecture of the many churches catering to immigrants, many from southern and eastern Europe, gave range communities a different look. These towns used revenue from mine taxes to build impressive schools, auditoriums, and municipal centers that became landmarks on the ranges.[55]

After World War II, the economic character, geographic structure, and general appearance of Minnesota cities and towns changed substantially. Finance, administration, and services became the fastest-growing economic sectors. In the Twin Cities, for example, only half of all workers in 1940 had managerial, professional, or clerical jobs, but the proportion in 1980 was about 60 percent.[56] The dominance of office-based economic activities was manifest in the proliferation of office towers in both downtowns, the expansion of the state capitol complex in St. Paul, and the overflow of the University of Minnesota's main campus to the west bank of the Mississippi River in Minneapolis.

As Minnesota's larger cities reshaped their economic structure, they expanded outward. People drove automobiles on a growing network of streets and highways, enabling the Twin Cities metropolitan area to grow from roughly 150 square miles at the start of the century to more than 800 by 1980. Builders early in the postwar period constructed small, single-family houses in easily developed areas, such as the plains south of Minneapolis and in its northern and northwest suburbs. Starting in the 1960s, however, small walk-up apartment buildings along major suburban highways became common, and the mix of new single-family houses included a greater share of larger, higher-priced units on hillier sites.[57]

The expansion of housing was matched by dispersion of economic activities into outlying districts of the state's urban centers. Stores were strung out along major streets during the early postwar period, in a manner reminiscent of the streetcar pattern, but clusters of stores behind small parking lots were common by the mid-1950s. The opening of the Southdale shopping mall in Edina in 1956 signaled a new era that saw the building of many enclosed, regional shopping malls in the state. In the Twin Cities, almost a dozen multilevel malls competed for the $11 billion that Twin Citians spent in retail stores in 1986, with each mall offering scores of shops on multiple levels among three or more large department stores. In Duluth, Rochester, St. Cloud, and Mankato, a single suburban mall became the preeminent shopping locale, whereas for other Minnesotans "a trip to the mall" meant a drive to a shopping center outside the state in Fargo or Grand Forks, North Dakota; Sioux Falls, South Dakota; or La Crosse, Wisconsin.[58]

After 1960, factories, warehouses, and offices also spread into the metropolitan suburbs. Large, windowless, one-story buildings with room nearby for trucks and employee parking housed processing and storage operations on spacious tracts along suburban highways. In the Twin Cities, glass-walled office and hotel towers were built amid the low-rise office parks along other freeway stretches and near major shopping centers. By the late 1970s, the larger suburban concentrations held a range of functions comparable to that of the traditional downtown. More than 40 per-

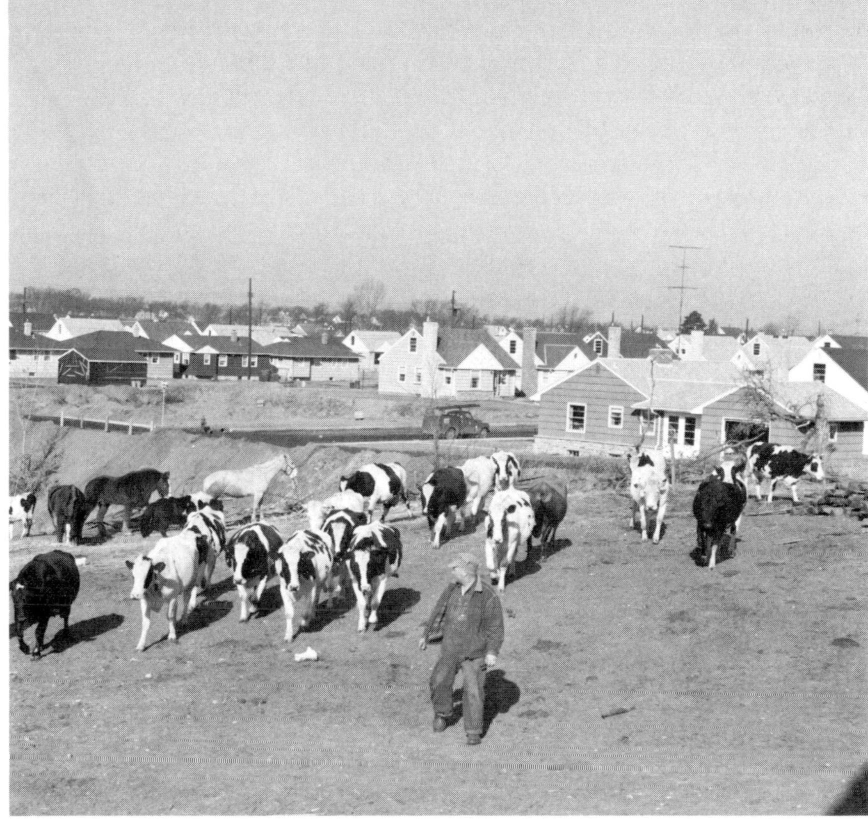

Suburban housing encroaches on a farm pasture at Penn Avenue South and 62d Street in Richfield, early 1950s.

cent of all Twin Cities jobs were located in the suburbs by 1970, and commuters were likely to drive from home to job entirely within the suburbs. This extensive development of Twin Cities suburbs in the postwar era made the metropolis one of the least dense in the nation, but the integrity of the Twin Cities as a single, coherent urban center was affirmed by the complex interrelationships among the area's nearly three hundred local government units.[59]

The rapid growth of suburban housing, commerce, and industry caused abandonment of large tracts in the state's major central cities. Downtown redevelopment in Minnesota began in earnest in the mid-1950s when merchants taxed themselves to create Nicollet Mall in Minneapolis. The following decade, private landowners in Minneapolis and the city government in St. Paul began to build a network of skyways, glass-walled bridges that connected downtown buildings at their second stories and that reoriented shopping patterns from ground-level stores facing the streets to upper-level interior spaces. By the 1970s, Minneapolis and St. Paul were actively assisting in land acquisition and clearance and in the financing of multipurpose projects. Most prominent of these were Town Square in St. Paul and City Center in Minneapolis, essentially suburban malls topped by towers containing offices and hotel rooms.[60] Abandoned structures were also cleared and new factories and houses built in parts of the Near North neighborhood of Minneapolis, the West Side of St. Paul, and along rail frontage in the Midway district of both cities. Young professionals seeking central locations began renovation of the large Victorian houses just west of downtown St. Paul.[61]

Redevelopment took place on a smaller scale in other cities. St. Cloud tried to rejuvenate downtown retailing with a pedestrian mall, Mankato built an enclosed shopping center, and Duluth fashioned a skyway system to link offices, stores, and a new convention center. Rochester's downtown remained that city's primary employment center as skyways and underground arcades connected the towers that housed the Mayo Clinic and related hospitals and hotels.[62]

Improved personal mobility affected the string of cities along Minnesota's iron ranges as well. In the early years, most miners and their families lived near the sites where they worked, but bus transportation starting in 1914 and greater use of automobiles after World War II allowed iron range residents more flexibility. They took frequent trips to other range communities, and by the 1950s they regularly traveled away from home for work, shopping, and recreation.[63] This "dispersed city" was functionally integrated like the urban centers in other parts of Minnesota, but its linear shape gave it a distinctive appearance. Urban settlement patterns along the Mesabi Range changed after taconite processing began in the mid-1950s. Because more taconite was mined in the eastern part of the range, plants there spurred renewal of larger cities like Hibbing and Virginia and establishment of new towns at Hoyt Lakes, Babbitt, and Silver Bay. These three communities, which were developed by mining companies, combined homogeneous single-family houses with nondescript commercial structures, all dwarfed by massive taconite-processing plants.[64]

In some smaller Minnesota cities – those having between five thousand and fifteen thousand people – shopping centers and college campuses were added to the landscape after World War II, but the fates of these communities more often were tied to the success of their industries. Traditional industries closed in some cities, as in Red Wing, where the potteries could not remain competitive; dozens of cities also lost their creameries by the 1960s, as a few dairies in the central and southeastern farming regions grew to handle most of the state's milk.[65] Older industries in other communities maintained or expanded their operations, as did meat-packers in Austin and Albert Lea, canneries in south-central Minnesota communities like Le Sueur, Owatonna, and Blue Earth, poultry-processing facilities in Willmar and Worthington, and sugar-beet refineries in several Red River valley locales. Another dimension of the changing industrial scene in smaller Minnesota cities was the success of homegrown companies and of branch plants that were attracted by low labor costs.

Although towns and villages with fewer than five thousand residents sometimes succeeded in attracting small factories to their peripheral industrial parks, their stores often did not fare as well. The new business typically occupied a site along the highway bypass or major street entering the town, but vacant storefronts were scattered along the few blocks that constituted downtown. The unstable prospects for merchants in these towns in the 1980s were still better than for those in the smallest villages and hamlets, however, where the grain elevator often remained as the only operating economic unit as local residents drove over continually upgraded highways to shop at larger urban centers. Many older residents of rural counties in southern and western Minnesota moved to senior-citizen housing complexes or towers in county seats and other medium-sized towns, the only major structures built in those communities for several decades.[66]

The State's Waters

While Minnesotans slowly transformed the appearance of the land throughout the twentieth century, they also modified the 6 percent of the state's area covered by rivers, lakes, and other surface waters and the 3 percent covered by wetlands on which vegetation was partially submerged by shallow water.[67] They evaluated the state's waters in relation to two major questions – "How should we use the waters? How can we maintain or enhance their quality?" As with land resources, the answers to these questions changed over time.

In 1900, surface waters were viewed in utilitarian ways. Rivers and streams were transportation routes, sources of water for drinking and in-

A steam-powered stern-wheeler on the Mississippi River pushing coal barges past the Robert Street Bridge in downtown St. Paul, 1917

dustry, conduits for waste disposal, generators of power where they fell from one level to another, and sites for fishing. Lakes were bodies from which to draw water, cut ice, or catch fish. Wetlands were perceived to have little value, and in farming areas they were often drained to free land for crop production.[68]

As the century progressed, Minnesotans made changes in these water resources with the goal of improving their usefulness or eliminating their undesirable characteristics. Dams had been built before 1900 along the upper Mississippi River and lesser streams to ensure consistent flows and to control flooding, and the damming of rivers continued in the first half of the new century. Eleven locks and dams were renovated or built on the Mississippi River from just above the Falls of St. Anthony to the Iowa border between 1940 and 1960, turning that section of the river into a stairstep series of pools through which a channel nine feet deep was maintained. The dams permanently flooded large tracts of valley bottom, generally improving wildlife habitat in the Upper Mississippi River National Wildlife and Fish Refuge, which had been established in 1924.[69] Paddle steamers continued to move up and down the Mississippi, and smaller excursion boats plied that river and smaller streams into the 1930s; after World War II, however, freight shipments on Minnesota's surface waters consisted mostly of strings of barges pushed by tugboats on the Mississippi and Minnesota rivers and larger freighters that docked at the state's ports on Lake Superior. When the St. Lawrence Seaway was opened in 1959, Duluth got a temporary boost of activity, but tonnage never approached the levels forecast when the seaway was planned.[70]

After the 1920s, Minnesotans viewed their lakes less as places to cut ice during winter (a need that mechanical refrigeration equipment began to meet) and more as places for recreation during warmer months. The state's first resorts were established in the 1920s in the central lakes district between Brainerd and Bemidji. By the late 1960s, more than 3,500 resorts operated in the state, most within an area bounded by a line connecting Little Falls, Glenwood, Detroit Lakes, Grand Rapids, and Onamia. The earlier resorts typically included boat docks and ramps for lake access and a half-dozen or more buildings ranging from rustic log cabins to pastel-colored, clapboard-sided structures. The size and range of activities in many resorts increased after midcentury, as resort owners sought to attract more customers by providing swimming pools, beaches, and campgrounds. A shift from dependence on fishing characterized the large resorts built since 1970. These resorts, which operated throughout the year, included such features as bars, restaurants, nightclubs, dinner theaters, tennis courts, golf courses, and riding stables. They accommodated guests in lodges that differed from metropolitan motels only in their location among trees on a lakeshore.[71]

The rise of resorts was paralleled by growth in the number of lakeside vacation homes. As automobiles allowed more Minnesotans to spend time at the lake after World War II, property that had been used for only a few weeks each summer saw intensive use on weekends throughout the year.

Crude log cabins were improved or replaced, and many Minnesotans who retired in the 1970s and 1980s made the "lake place up north" their permanent home. Retirees and people catering to the tourist trade were the groups most responsible for population increases in Beltrami, Cass, and Hubbard counties, which had lost population throughout the middle decades of the century.[72] Closer to the Twin Cities, Lake Minnetonka and White Bear Lake were surrounded in the first decades of the century by cottages owned by city residents who used railroads and streetcars to reach their weekend retreats; as automobile use increased and road networks improved after World War II, however, these lakefront tracts held elaborate year-round residences for people who commuted to Twin Cities jobs. The juxtaposition of many different styles and sizes of dwellings along the suburban lakefronts was a striking zone of contrast visible in the Minnesota landscape of the mid-1980s.[73]

Water pollution emerged as a major concern during the twentieth century, and Minnesotans undertook measures to improve the quality of the state's surface waters. Communities dumped raw sewage directly into rivers in the early decades of the century, but city governments built large, increasingly effective treatment facilities along rivers and lakes starting in the 1930s. By the late 1970s, factory managers were boasting about the expensive improvements their companies had made to ensure that discharges met federal and state standards. The overall impact of these measures was a general improvement in the water quality of many Minnesota water bodies, although the long-term accumulation of heavy metals and pesticides still restricted use of the Mississippi River in the mid-1980s.[74]

Farmers generally stopped draining small marshes in southern and

Capt. Billy Fawcett's Breezy Point Lodge on Big Pelican Lake in the central lakes area of Crow Wing County, 1926

western Minnesota by the 1960s, and in later years the state government and hunting and environmental groups restored some of these wetlands.[75] The massive peat bogs of north-central and northeastern Minnesota were exploited twice on a large scale during the twentieth century. Attempts in the 1930s to drain some of the bogs to create new farmland were unsuccessful, although remnants of ditches could be seen more than fifty years later. The energy crises of the 1970s spurred renewed interest in these areas as sources of fuel, but market conditions retarded such development in the 1980s, when the limited amounts of peat removed were used mostly for horticulture.[76]

Perceptions and Limitations

Minnesota's landscape has been modified in the twentieth century through continuous, cumulative action by millions of people. By building and maintaining homes, working at jobs, shopping in stores, traveling from one place to another, and spending leisure time in countless ways at countless places, Minnesotans have altered the landscape created by natural forces and shaped by their predecessors. The process of landscape change is ongoing, and forces that affect the perception and use of the land will continue to influence Minnesota in future years.

Some forces counteracted one another, creating tensions that had different impacts under different circumstances. Human activities repeatedly reached natural limits, as when rivers dammed to control floods silted their channels, forcing periodic dredging to maintain acceptable depths for navigation and to prevent floods even more disastrous than those before the "improvements" were made. Just as farmers altered their row-cropping practices in the 1930s to reduce soil erosion, many of them reexamined the heavy application of chemicals in the 1980s in light of questions about its long-term impact on soil composition and fertility. Similarly, the impact of continuous metropolitan expansion on the ability of the Mississippi River to absorb storm-water runoff forced separation of sewer systems in the Twin Cities area, a project scheduled for completion in the late 1980s.

Other tensions arose from the different perspectives, attitudes, and expectations that people had about what had been and ought to be done with Minnesota's land and water.[77] A forester's opinion about the use of large machines to clear trees from a stand was not the same as that of a metropolitan family driving through the woods on a summer weekend. Similarly, iron miners did not describe open-pit mines as "ugly scars," as did some visitors to the iron ranges, and farmers found large metal sheds attractive because of their practical simplicity, although others viewed them as eyesores compared with the traditional barns they had replaced. Low-density suburban houses and shopping centers were criticized as homogeneous and sterile by those who preferred the diverse settings and populations of central cities, but many Minnesotans were attracted to houses on large lots and to shopping centers with convenient, free parking.

Certain conflicts hinged on fundamental differences in values. Some people took a totally functional view of the world, whereas others placed a higher value on aesthetic qualities. Skyways were hailed by many Minnesotans as ways to revitalize the state's largest downtowns, but some architects criticized the skyways for marring the facades of the buildings they connected. Similarly, projects that were meant to spur economic development were challenged by people who believed that the damage to the environment would be too great, even when weighed against the jobs that the projects would create.

Nonetheless, the landscape of Minnesota was subject to overriding realities, many of them totally beyond the control of the state's people. Physical characteristics – weather, soils, and terrain – fostered the success of certain activities and caused others to fail. Economic forces influenced decisions about the implementation and maintenance of projects over the long run, and the influx of people, resources, and ideas from other places strongly affected the ways in which Minnesotans acted within their own state. Just as the landscape of Minnesota changed in subtle yet substantial ways through much of the twentieth century, the perceptions of the people who brought about those changes and the forces to which they were subject were slowly evolving. Minnesota would look different in the twenty-first century, and the nature of those differences would reveal much about the processes that continued to shape the state.

NOTES

1. Elden Johnson, *The Prehistoric Peoples of Minnesota*, 3d ed. (St. Paul: Minnesota Historical Society Press, 1988), 15-27; Ronald J. Mason, *Great Lakes Archaeology* (New York: Academic Press, 1981), 295-324, 350-72; H. E. Wright, Jr., "The Environment of Early Man in the Great Lakes Region," in *Aspects of Upper Great Lakes Anthropology*, ed. Elden Johnson (St. Paul: Minnesota Historical Society, 1974), 13-14.

2. Theodore C. Blegen, *Minnesota: A History of the State*, 2d ed. (Minneapolis: University of Minnesota Press, 1975), 13-14, 315-407, esp. 316-18, 340; William W. Folwell, *A History of Minnesota*, rev. ed., vol. 3 (St. Paul: Minnesota Historical Society, 1969), 251-55.

3. Population data here and below are drawn from United States, *Census*, 1900, vol. 1, part 1, p. 215-30; 1940, vol. 1, p. 537, 539-50; 1980, chap. A, part 25, p. 10-24.

4. John R. Borchert, *America's Northern Heartland* (Minneapolis: University of Minnesota Press, 1987), 44-49; John R. Borchert and Donald P. Yaeger, *Atlas of Minnesota Resources and Settlement* (Minneapolis: Department of Geography, University of Minnesota, 1968), 27-31; John R. Borchert and Neil C. Gustafson, *Atlas of Minnesota Resources and Settlement* (Minneapolis: Center for Urban and Regional Affairs, University of Minnesota, 1980), 205-10.

5. U.S. Department of Transportation, Federal Highway Administration, *Highway Statistics: Summary to 1975* (Washington, D.C., 1975), 52, *Highway Statistics* (Washington, D.C., 1981), 163-66, and *Highway Statistics* (Washington, D.C., 1983), 17; Minnesota Department of Highways, *Fiftieth Anniversary, 1921-1971* (St. Paul, 1971), 25.

6. Lucile M. Kane and Alan Ominsky, *Twin Cities: A Pictorial History of Saint Paul and Minneapolis* (St. Paul: Minnesota Historical Society Press, 1983), 47; U.S., *Census*, 1900, vol. 5, part 1, p. 2.

7. Minnesota Department of Energy, Planning, and Development, *Minnesota in the Eighties . . . Its People and Its Land* (St. Paul, 1983), 34-37.

8. John R. Borchert, *Perspective on Minnesota Land Use – 1974* (Minneapolis: Center for Urban and Regional Affairs, University of Minnesota, 1974), 9-27; Minnesota Land Manage-

ment Information System (MLMIS), *State of Minnesota Land Use, 1969* (Map no. 1, Minneapolis, 1969).

9. Borchert, *Perspective on Land Use*, 9-27; MLMIS, *Minnesota Land Use;* Vic Spadaccini and Karen Whiting, eds., *Minnesota Pocket Data Book – 1983-1984* (Minneapolis: Blue Sky Marketing, 1983), 241-329; Minnesota Agricultural Statistics Service, *Minnesota Agriculture Statistics – 1987* (St. Paul: U.S. Department of Agriculture and Minnesota Department of Agriculture, 1987), 7.

10. Borchert and Gustafson, *1980 Minnesota Atlas*, 61, 63.

11. U.S., *Census*, 1900, vol. 6, part 2, p. 169-70.

12. Ralph H. Brown, *Historical Geography of the United States* (New York: Harcourt, Brace and Co., 1948), 336-38; Merrill E. Jarchow, "King Wheat," *Minnesota History* 29 (1948): 25-28. See also Hildegard Binder Johnson, "King Wheat in Southeastern Minnesota: A Case Study of Pioneer Agriculture," *Annals of the Association of American Geographers* 47 (1957): 350-62; Henrietta M. Larson, "The Wheat Market and the Farmer in Minnesota," *Columbia University Studies in History, Economics, and Public Law* 122, no. 2 (1926): 55-256; Fred Lukermann, "The Changing Pattern of Flour Mill Location," part 2, *Northwestern Miller* 261 (Jan. 27, 1959): 12-14.

13. Borchert and Yaeger, *1968 Minnesota Atlas*, 43-46, 53; John Fraser Hart, *The Look of the Land* (Englewood Cliffs, N.J.: Prentice-Hall, 1975), 104-8, and "Two Corn Belt Farms," *Journal of Cultural Geography* 5 (1984): 7-17. See also John C. Weaver, "Changing Patterns of Cropland Use in the Middle West," *Economic Geography* 30 (1954): 1-47, "Crop-Combination Regions in the Middle West," *Geographical Review* 44 (1954): 175-200, and "Crop-Combination Regions for 1919 and 1929 in the Middle West," *Geographical Review* 44 (1954): 560-72.

14. Borchert and Yaeger, *1968 Minnesota Atlas*, 43-45, 54; here and below, U.S., *Census of Agriculture*, 1950, vol. 1, part 8, p. 77, 81, 88.

15. Agricultural data here and in the following three paragraphs are taken from Borchert and Yaeger, *1968 Minnesota Atlas*, 43-63; Borchert and Gustafson, *1980 Minnesota Atlas*, 64-77; Minnesota Agricultural Statistics Service, *Agricultural Statistics – 1987*, 4, 19-51. See also Hart, *Look of the Land*, 144-47.

16. Blegen, *History of Minnesota*, 566.

17. Minnesota Crop and Livestock Reporting Service, *Minnesota Agricultural Statistics – 1976* (St. Paul: U.S. Department of Agriculture and Minnesota Department of Agriculture, 1976), 15; Minnesota Agricultural Statistics Service, *Minnesota Agricultural Statistics – 1981* (St. Paul: U.S. Department of Agriculture and Minnesota Department of Agriculture, 1981), 41.

18. Blegen, *History of Minnesota*, 390-96; Borchert and Yaeger, *1968 Minnesota Atlas*, 76-77; Borchert and Gustafson, *1980 Minnesota Atlas*, 64; U.S., *Census of Agriculture*, 1925, part 1, p. 788; 1982, vol. 1, part 23, p. 1, 15.

19. Hart, *Look of the Land*, 116-18, 140-50; Borchert and Yaeger, *1968 Minnesota Atlas*, 46-48; Borchert and Gustafson, *1980 Minnesota Atlas*, 77-84; Minnesota Agricultural Statistics Service, *Minnesota Agricultural Statistics – 1982* (St. Paul: U.S. Department of Agriculture and Minnesota Department of Agriculture, 1982), 55, and *Agricultural Statistics – 1987*, 65; Willard W. Cochrane, *The Development of American Agriculture* (Minneapolis: University of Minnesota Press, 1979), 129-38, 198-200.

20. Borchert and Yaeger, *1968 Minnesota Atlas*, 46-47, 68; Borchert and Gustafson, *1980 Minnesota Atlas*, 61-104; Minnesota Agricultural Statistics Service, *Agricultural Statistics- – 1987*, 6.

21. Borchert and Yaeger, *1968 Minnesota Atlas*, 45-47, 59, 66, 73; Borchert and Gustafson, *1980 Minnesota Atlas*, 88-93; Cochrane, *American Agriculture*, 108-9, 126-38, 197-200; Hart, *Look of the Land*, 84-85; U.S., *Census*, 1920, vol. 6, part 1, p. 494; Minnesota Agricultural Statistics Service, *Agricultural Statistics – 1987*, 55, 61.

22. Minnesota Historical Society (MHS), *Minnesota Farmscape: Looking at Change* (St. Paul, 1980), 15; Borchert and Yaeger, *1968 Minnesota Atlas*, 47, 74-75; Borchert and Gustafson, *1980 Minnesota Atlas*, 93, 95; Hart, *Look of the Land*, 117-18, 146-47; Ralph W. Tiner, Jr., *Wetlands of the United States: Current Status and Recent Trends* (Washington, D.C.: Fish and Wildlife Service, U.S. Department of the Interior, 1984), 42-45. See also Bert Henningson, "Farm Surpluses – A Policy and Its Consequences," *Roots* 16 (Fall 1987): 3-13.

23. Robert T. Moline, "Cultural Modification of Wet Prairie Landscapes," in *AAG'86 Twin Cities Field Trip Guide*, ed. Thomas J. Baerwald and Karen L. Harrington (Washington, D.C.: Association of American Geographers, 1986), 194-96; Tiner, *Wetlands of the United States*, 43.

24. Blegen, *History of Minnesota*, 565; Works Progress Administration (WPA), *The WPA Guide to Minnesota* (New York: Viking Press, 1938; St. Paul: Minnesota Historical Society Press, 1985), 71-72, 305, 408-10, 423; Hart, *Look of the Land*, 115.

25. Borchert and Gustafson, *1980 Minnesota Atlas*, 93–94; Cochrane, *American Agriculture*, 308–10.

26. Here and following four paragraphs, Hart, *Look of the Land*, 85–88, 116–23, 169–70; MHS, *Minnesota Farmscape*, 2–16.

27. Everett G. Smith, Jr., "Road Functions in a Changing Rural Environment" (Ph.D. diss., University of Minnesota, 1962), 53–87.

28. Cochrane, *American Agriculture*, 227-28; MHS, *Minnesota Farmscape*, 6; David Nass, "Bringing Electricity to Minnesota's Farms," *Roots* 16 (Fall 1987): 29–33.

29. "Lumbering in Minnesota," *Roots* 4 (Fall 1975): 22, 26; Ellen B. Green, "Timber!" *Roots* 11 (Fall 1982): 4–7.

30. Blegen, *History of Minnesota*, 592; Bertha L. Heilbron, *The Thirty-Second State: A Pictorial History of Minnesota* (St. Paul: Minnesota Historical Society, 1966), 177–79; "Forests," *Roots* 1 (Winter 1973): 19.

31. Borchert and Gustafson, *1980 Minnesota Atlas*, 104–8; WPA, *Guide to Minnesota*, 359, 465–68; Pamela J. Jakes, *The Fourth Minnesota Forest Inventory: Area* (St. Paul: North Central Forest Experiment Station, U.S. Department of Agriculture, Resource Bulletin NC-54, 1980), 11.

32. Harold T. Hagg, "Buena Vista: Vanished Boom Town," *Gopher Historian* 17 (Winter 1962–63): 6–13; Peter Smith et al., "Minnesota's North Country," in *AAG'86 Guide*, ed. Baerwald and Harrington, 227–28; Blegen, *History of Minnesota*, 324, 329; WPA, *Guide to Minnesota*, 343, 357, 434.

33. Borchert and Gustafson, *1980 Minnesota Atlas*, 122, 127–28, 130; *Minnesota Directory of Manufacturers, 1985–86* (Burnsville: Nelson Marketing Services, 1985), sec. 3.

34. Blegen, *History of Minnesota*, 329–32; E. G. Cheyney, "The Development of the Lumber Industry in Minnesota," *Journal of Geography* 14 (1916): 194; Agnes M. Larson, *History of the White Pine Industry in Minnesota* (Minneapolis: University of Minnesota Press, 1949), 176–81; Heilbron, *Thirty-Second State*, 175–77; William E. Lass, *Minnesota: A History* (New York: W. W. Norton and Co., 1977), 148–51; Smith et al., "Minnesota's North Country," 234–35.

35. Here and below, Patrick J. Weicherding, James R. Schramek, and William R. Miles, *Forest Management* (St. Paul: Agricultural Experiment Station, University of Minnesota, 1974), 27–32.

36. Here and below, "Mechanization Puts State Logging Industry on the Endangered List," *Minneapolis Tribune*, Mar. 27, 1983, p. 1D, 3D.

37. Blegen, *History of Minnesota*, 405–7; Borchert and Gustafson, *1980 Minnesota Atlas*, 286–97; WPA, *Guide to Minnesota*, 24, 359, 465–68; Minnesota Department of Energy, *Minnesota in the Eighties*, 25–29.

38. Borchert and Gustafson, *1980 Minnesota Atlas*, 292; Weicherding, Schramek, and Miles, *Forest Management*, 3, 40–44; WPA, *Guide to Minnesota*, 467.

39. Newell Searle, "Minnesota State Forestry Association: Seedbed of Forest Conservation," *Minnesota History* 44 (Spring 1974): 28; WPA, *Guide to Minnesota*, 467; Russell W. Fridley, "A State That Works," in Blegen, *History of Minnesota*, 709.

40. Richard W. Ojakangas and Charles L. Matsch, *Minnesota's Geology* (Minneapolis: University of Minnesota Press, 1982), 37–40, 125–32.

41. "Men, Money and Ore," *Roots* 2 (Spring 1974): 4–13; Blegen, *History of Minnesota*, 364–67, 372–73; David A. Walker, *Iron Frontier: The Discovery and Early Development of Minnesota's Three Ranges* (St. Paul: Minnesota Historical Society Press, 1979), 49–58, 99–106, 248–56. See also Arnold R. Alanen, "Years of Change on the Iron Range," *this volume*, 155–60.

42. Data regarding the iron content of ores were published annually in a directory issued by the Mines Experiment Station of the University of Minnesota. See, for example, John J. Craig, *Mining Directory of Minnesota – 1933* (Minneapolis: University of Minnesota, 1933), 197.

43. Borchert and Gustafson, *1980 Minnesota Atlas*, 54–58; N. Yaworski et al., *Technology, Employment, and Output per Man in Iron Mining* (Philadelphia: Work Projects Administration, National Research Project, Rep. E-13, 1940), 208; Minnesota Department of Economic Security, *Nonagricultural Wage and Salary Employment Hours and Earnings: January, 1950–December, 1984* ([St. Paul], 1985), 15; Minnesota Department of Jobs and Training, *Nonagricultural Wage and Salary Employment Hours and Earnings: January 1980–December 1987* ([St. Paul], 1988), 7; John W. Webb, "An Urban Geography of the Minnesota Iron Ranges" (Ph.D. diss., University of Minnesota, 1958), 43–52.

44. WPA, *Guide to Minnesota*, 95–96, 318, 367; Walker, *Iron Frontier*, 43–46; Richard Olsenius, *Minnesota Travel Companion* (Wayzata: Bluestem Productions, 1982), 51, 59; Gordon Levine, "The Iron Range, North Shore, and Duluth – Timber, Taconite, and Tourism," in *AAG'86 Guide*, ed. Baerwald and Harrington, 247.

45. E. W. Davis, *Pioneering with Taconite* (St. Paul: Minnesota Historical Society, 1964),

3-4, 178-79; Borchert and Gustafson, *1980 Minnesota Atlas*, 51-53; Walker, *Iron Frontier*, 258-59.

46. Davis, *Pioneering with Taconite*, 1, 202; Borchert and Gustafson, *1980 Minnesota Atlas*, 61.

47. Levine, "Iron Range, North Shore, and Duluth," 241-62; Minnesota Department of Energy, *Minnesota in the Eighties*, 30-33.

48. Spadaccini and Whiting, eds., *Pocket Data Book*, 150; MLMIS, *Minnesota Land Use;* Minnesota Department of Energy, *Minnesota in the Eighties*, 1-4, 39. See also John R. Borchert, "The Network of Urban Centers," *this volume*, 57, 70-91.

49. Thomas J. Baerwald, "Minnesota Cities and Towns," *Architecture Minnesota* 2 (July-August 1976), 19-23; Borchert, *America's Northern Heartland*, 44-49; Borchert and Gustafson, *1980 Minnesota Atlas*, 205-20.

50. Heilbron, *Thirty-Second State*, 216-27; Judith A. Martin and David A. Lanegran, *Where We Live: The Residential Districts of Minneapolis and Saint Paul* (Minneapolis: University of Minnesota Press, 1983), 3-10.

51. Ronald Abler, John S. Adams, and John R. Borchert, *The Twin Cities of St. Paul and Minneapolis* (Cambridge, Mass.: Ballinger Publishing Co., 1976), 17-20; Heilbron, *Thirty-Second State*, 221; Kane and Ominsky, *Pictorial History of Twin Cities*, 207, 231; Lukermann, "Flour Mill Location," 12-14; Victor G. Pickett and Roland S. Vaile, *The Decline of Northwestern Flour Milling* (Minneapolis: University of Minnesota Press, 1933), 5-23.

52. Blegen, *History of Minnesota*, 392-93; Borchert, *America's Northern Heartland*, 67, 75; Don W. Larson, *Land of the Giants* (Minneapolis: Dorn Books, 1979), 121-33.

53. Abler, Adams, and Borchert, *Twin Cities*, 21-22, 29-33; Borchert, *America's Northern Heartland*, 61; Kane and Ominsky, *Pictorial History of Twin Cities*, 89; Martin and Lanegran, *Where We Live*, 4-5, 15-18, 83-99; Thomas J. Baerwald, "Overview of St. Paul and Minneapolis," in *AAG'86 Guide*, ed. Baerwald and Harrington, 5-6, 11; Alan R. Lind, *Twin City Rapid Transit Pictorial* (Park Forest, Ill.: Transport History Press, 1984), 31-57.

54. Borchert and Yaeger, *1968 Minnesota Atlas*, 87-97; Webb, "Urban Geography of Iron Ranges," 312-30; Arnold R. Alanen, "The 'Locations': Company Communities on Minnesota's Iron Ranges," *Minnesota History* 48 (Fall 1982): 95.

55. WPA, *Guide to Minnesota*, 97, 321-24; Olsenius, *Minnesota Travel Companion*, 54-55; Levine, "Iron Range, North Shore, and Duluth," 244-52.

56. Borchert, *America's Northern Heartland*, 203-14; U.S., *Census*, 1940, vol. 2, part 4, p. 195.

57. Borchert, *America's Northern Heartland*, 152-54; Borchert and Yaeger, *1968 Minnesota Atlas*, 187-90; Abler, Adams, and Borchert, *Twin Cities*, 54-58.

58. Abler, Adams, and Borchert, *Twin Cities*, 34, 55-57; Thomas J. Baerwald, "Southwest Suburban Traverse," in *AAG'86 Guide*, ed. Baerwald and Harrington, 108-9, and "Land Use Change in Suburban Clusters and Corridors," *Transportation Research Record*, no. 861 (1982), 7-12; Kane and Ominsky, *Pictorial History of Twin Cities*, 233, 251; U.S. Census Bureau, *Statistical Abstract Supplement: State and Metropolitan Area Data Book, 1986*, 178.

59. Thomas J. Baerwald, "The Emergence of a New 'Downtown,'" *Geographical Review* 68 (1978): 308-18, "Land Use Change," 7-12, and "Southwest Suburban Traverse," 107-40; U.S., *Census of Population and Housing, Census Tracts, Minneapolis-St. Paul, Minn.*, 37; Abler, Adams, and Borchert, *Twin Cities*, 57-65; Kane and Ominsky, *Pictorial History of Twin Cities*, 237-38.

60. Abler, Adams, and Borchert, *Twin Cities*, 43-47; David Gebhard and Tom Martinson, *A Guide to the Architecture of Minnesota* (Minneapolis: University of Minnesota Press, 1977), 28-31, 81-86; David A. Lanegran, "Public-Private Cooperation in Major Twin Cities Redevelopment Projects," in *AAG'86 Guide*, ed. Baerwald and Harrington, 95-106.

61. Martin and Lanegran, *Where We Live*, 47-59, 63-81, 126.

62. Levine, "Iron Range, North Shore, and Duluth," 256-58; WPA, *Guide to Minnesota*, 272-73; Borchert, *America's Northern Heartland*, 118; Cotton Mather and Ruth Hale, *Prairie Border Country* (Prescott, Wis.: Trimbelle Press, 1980), 47-50.

63. Borchert and Yaeger, *1968 Minnesota Atlas*, 86; Borchert and Gustafson, *1980 Minnesota Atlas*, 61; Webb, "Urban Geography of Iron Ranges," 176-88.

64. Olsenius, *Minnesota Travel Companion*, 31; Davis, *Pioneering with Taconite*, 143, 156-57, 170-75.

65. Borchert and Gustafson, *1980 Minnesota Atlas*, 78-80, 205-12; MHS, *Minnesota Farmscape*, 21.

66. Hart, *Look of the Land*, 163-69; Heilbron, *Thirty-Second State*, 216-31; Borchert, *America's Northern Heartland*, 197-99.

67. Borchert, *Perspective on Land Use*, 17; Spadaccini and Whiting, eds., *Pocket Data Book*, 150; MLMIS, *Minnesota Land Use*.

68. Blegen, *History of Minnesota*, 5-7; Borchert and Gustafson, *1980 Minnesota Atlas*, 26-39, 292, 297; Moline, "Wet Prairie Landscapes," 194-96. See also Thomas F. Waters, *The*

Streams and Rivers of Minnesota (Minneapolis: University of Minnesota Press, 1977); "Minnesota's Rivers" and "Rivers Are News," *Roots* 6 (Spring 1978): 4-23.

69. Blegen, *History of Minnesota*, 349, 483-84; WPA, *Guide to Minnesota*, 360, 426; Waters, *Streams and Rivers*, 220-21, 237-40; "Minnesota's Rivers," 16; Olsenius, *Minnesota Travel Companion*, 236-40.

70. Blegen, *History of Minnesota*, 466, 561; Borchert, *America's Northern Heartland*, 178; Heilbron, *Thirty-Second State*, 188.

71. Olsenius, *Minnesota Travel Companion*, 85-87; Smith et al., "Minnesota's North Country," 224-27.

72. Borchert, *America's Northern Heartland*, 111-19; Borchert and Gustafson, *1980 Minnesota Atlas*, 255, 259-61; U.S., *Census*, 1980, chap. A, part 25, p. 8.

73. Abler, Adams, and Borchert, *Twin Cities*, 53; Baerwald, "Southwest Suburban Traverse," 117-18.

74. Carol Gersmehl, Janet Drake, and Dwight Brown, *Minnesota Water: A Geographical Perspective* (Minneapolis: Water Resources Research Center, University of Minnesota, 1986), 18-25; Waters, *Streams and Rivers*, 242; Minnesota Department of Health, *Minnesota Fish Consumption Advisory – May, 1987* (Minneapolis, 1987).

75. Moline, "Wet Prairie Landscapes," 196.

76. WPA, *Guide to Minnesota*, 424; Borchert and Gustafson, *1980 Minnesota Atlas*, 12-16; Minnesota Department of Natural Resources, *Minnesota Peatlands* (Map with accompanying text; St. Paul, 1978); Sara Webb, "Research in the Peatlands," *Imprint* (James Ford Bell Museum of Natural History) 1 (Summer 1984): 6-7; H. E. Wright, Jr., "Red Lake Peatland: Its Past and Patterns," *Imprint* 1 (Summer 1984): 1-3.

77. Joan Iverson Nassauer, *Caring for the Countryside* (St. Paul: Agricultural Experiment Station, University of Minnesota, 1986).

A critical point in the urban network—the bridges spanning the Red River between Fargo, North Dakota, and Moorhead, about 1950

JOHN R. BORCHERT

The Network of Urban Centers

The first two decades of the twentieth century saw the culmination of an era in Minnesota's urbanization. The railroad builders had completed a dense network of main and branch lines across the state, and the advance of the agricultural frontier had ended. The land of Minnesota was settled. Except for metropolitan suburbs founded later in the century, virtually no new place names would be added to the map of the state after 1920.[1]

The Pattern on the State Map

The rail system extended market accessibility to every corner of the state's suitable land, thus multiplying the commercial value and productivity of farms. Exponential increases in the flow of commodities from farm to market, of goods from factory to countryside, and therefore of money, spurred the development of an urban system based on agriculture. But more than commercial agriculture underlay the growth of the cities: the rail net augmented the river routes in reaching the timber wealth of the northern pine forests, as it augmented the Great Lakes waterway in providing access to the mineral wealth of the Lake Superior district.[2]

As urban and farm markets grew in volume and diversity, entrepreneurs opened shops and offices in the cities and manufacturing and service enterprises multiplied atop the growing base of transportation and trade. A few types of small businesses were repeated at many places: grocery stores and saloons, for example, stood beside the country churches and town halls at the smallest crossroads settlements, at the center of each of the state's nearly two thousand organized townships. Other businesses were found in bigger units at fewer places: dry goods stores, bakeries, specialty shops, hotels, newspapers, and law offices were more likely to be concentrated at the seats of the state's eighty-seven counties. And some activities came in still larger packages at still fewer places – for example, big department stores, wholesale traders and warehouses, major hospitals and medical specialists, major mills and factories.[3]

From the vast seedbed of country crossroads and town centers, only eighty-seven could be chosen to be county seats, and from these and a handful of specially endowed mining or waterpower locations, fewer than thirty emerged as the state's diversified, multicounty retail-trade centers. From that group, just seven grew to become principal centers of wholesale trade, services, and industry as Minnesota moved into the twentieth century. The Twin Cities of Minneapolis and St. Paul stood at the top of the pyramid, and Duluth, with its twin port of Superior, Wisconsin, was second. These centers were major crossroads not only in Minnesota but in the entire Upper Midwest. The other five centers were smaller cities in the state's farming region: Winona, Mankato, St. Cloud, and the interstate cities astride the North Dakota boundary at Fargo-Moorhead and Grand Forks-East Grand Forks (see table).[4]

At the opening of the century, all seven of these urban areas stood at critically important locations in the network of railroads and waterways. When the midwestern rail net was completed, three overlapping, fan-shaped sets of lines spread across the map of Minnesota. Two of the three sets radiated from the great terminal ports at the western end of the Great Lakes. One was focused on the preeminent transportation hub at Chicago, where the Lake Michigan waterway terminated in the rich midwestern prairies, and the other fanned out from Duluth-Superior, where the Lake Superior route terminated in the northern forest and mining country. The third set reached into the hinterland from the historic head of Mississippi riverboat navigation at the port of St. Paul and the adjacent industrial waterpower site at Minneapolis.

The Twin Cities system dominated most of the state. It reached out in every direction – to the northern forests and iron ranges, to the northern Great Plains, Canadian prairies, and Pacific Northwest; to the Iowa prairies and the distant midcontinent centers of Omaha, Kansas City, and St. Louis; to Chicago-Milwaukee and the lesser lake ports of Ashland, Sault Ste. Marie, and Green Bay. Through that system, Twin Cities firms had become major organizers of the economy of both the state and of a larger "empire." For most purposes the Northwest Empire reached from northwestern Wisconsin to Montana, for some purposes from Michigan's Upper Peninsula to Puget Sound and the Canadian prairies.[5]

The Duluth system had its independent connections with the East by way of the iron ore, coal, and grain that were shipped on the Great Lakes waterway. Rail lines fanned out from the Twin Ports to the Red River valley, the eastern Dakotas, and the Missouri River waterway at Yankton and Sioux City. The Chicago-Milwaukee system sent a major corridor to the Twin Cities, but lesser radials bypassed Minneapolis-St. Paul on both the east and south. The North Woods lines headed from Chicago and Milwaukee directly to the Lake Superior timber and ore ports, and the Prairie lines ran west across southern Minnesota and northern Iowa directly to South Dakota's James River valley and the historic Black Hills gold camps.

Population Change in Minnesota's Urban Centers, 1900-84
(Given in Thousands)

Urban Center	1900	1910	1920	1930	1940	1950	1960	1970	1980	1984
Twin Cities	570	731	842	992	1,098	1,268	1,614	1,988	2,155	2,247
Minneapolis	203	301	381	464	492	522	483	434	371	358
St. Paul	163	215	235	272	288	311	313	310	270	266
Suburban area[a]	204	215	226	256	318	435	818	1,244	1,514	1,623
Twin Ports	86	123	145	146	145	153	157	152	145	136
Duluth	53	78	99	101	101	105	107	101	93	86
Superior	31	40	40	36	35	35	34	32	30	29
Suburban area[b]	2	5	6	9	9	13	16	19	22	21
Fargo-Moorhead	47	54	63	72	78	89	106	121	137	144
Fargo[c]	10	14	23	30	34	41	50	58	71	78
Moorhead[d]	5	6	7	9	10	16	25	32	33	32
Remainder of counties[e]	32	34	33	33	34	32	31	31	33	34
Grand Forks-East Grand Forks	26	31	32	35	39	44	56	69	75	77
Grand Forks	8	12	14	17	20	27	34	39	44	44
East Grand Forks	2	3	3	3	4	5	7	8	9	8
Remainder of Grand Forks County	16	16	15	15	15	12	15	22	22	25
St. Cloud	56	63	73	81	87	92	102	123	141	147
St. Cloud[f]	9	13	18	24	27	32	37	45	49	48
Remainder of counties[g]	47	50	55	57	60	60	65	78	92	99
Mankato	47	43	46	51	54	59	67	77	79	79
Mankato-North Mankato	12	11	15	17	20	24	30	38	38	37
Remainder of counties[h]	35	32	31	34	34	35	37	39	41	42
Winona	36	33	34	35	38	40	41	44	46	47
Winona	20	19	19	21	22	25	25	26	25	25
Remainder of Winona County	16	14	15	14	16	15	16	18	21	22
Rochester	23	22	28	35	43	48	65	84	92	96
Rochester	7	8	14	21	26	30	41	54	58	58
Remainder of Olmsted County	16	14	14	14	17	18	24	30	34	38

Sources: Data are taken from census reports as described in n. 4.

a. Includes Anoka, Carver, Chisago, Dakota, Hennepin and Ramsey (except central cities), Scott, Washington, Wright, and Sherburne (except Haven, Palmer, and Clear Lake townships and Clear Lake city) counties in Minnesota; St. Croix County in Wisconsin. **b.** Includes Proctor, the townships adjoining Duluth, and Douglas County, Wisconsin (except Superior). **c.** Includes West Fargo. **d.** Includes Dilworth. **e.** Cass, North Dakota, and Clay, Minnesota. **f.** Includes Sauk Rapids. **g.** Stearns and Benton counties; Haven, Palmer, and Clear Lake townships and Clear Lake city in Sherburne County. **h.** Blue Earth and Nicollet counties; remainder of Nicollet County includes city of St. Peter.

Lines from the Twin Cities and Duluth crossed at some of the trade centers at county seats in western and southwestern Minnesota, giving those places direct access to the two competing regional distribution and collection centers. Lines from the Twin Cities also crossed prairie lines from Chicago and Milwaukee at other trade centers across southern Minnesota, giving them a special advantage. Location at the intersection of lines in two railroad grids was essential if a county seat was to emerge as

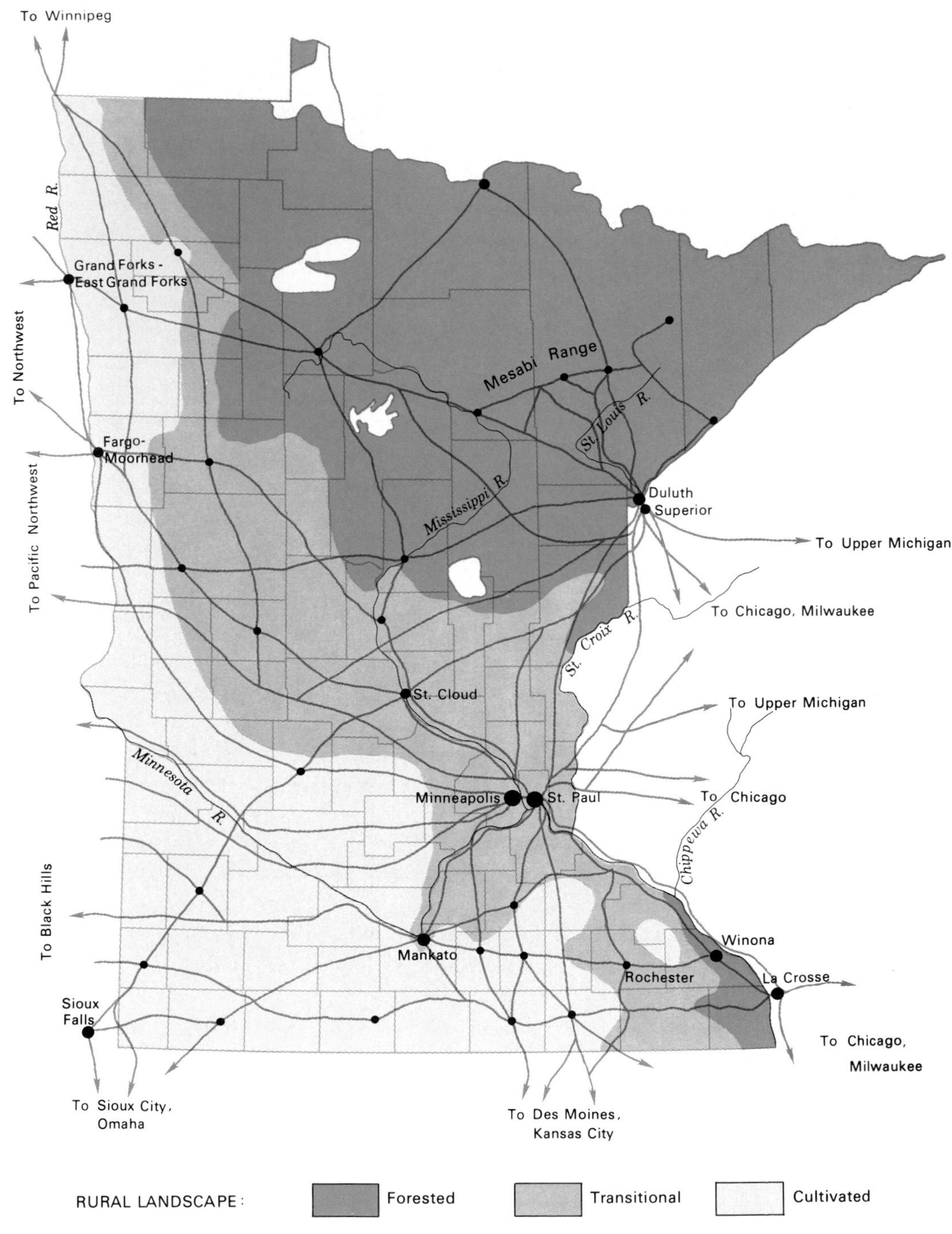

Minnesota's seven principal urban centers in the network of railroads and waterways at the opening of the twentieth century

Rafts of logs floating on the Mississippi River past Winona, about 1905

a larger, multicounty trade center in the agricultural region of Minnesota in the late 1800s and early 1900s.

The principal cities that emerged early in the twentieth century in western and southern Minnesota were exceptionally well located in the rail system. The first northern transcontinental, the Northern Pacific, had built its Red River bridge at Fargo-Moorhead in the early 1870s, and James J. Hill's Great Northern had followed with Red River crossings at Fargo and Grand Forks. These cities were gateways between the Twin Cities, the Twin Ports, and the northern Great Plains; Fargo, in particular, served as a distribution point for almost all of North Dakota.[6]

Winona's initial advantage came from a combination of river and rail routes. From the pineries of its upper watershed in northern Wisconsin, the Chippewa River poured a massive stream of commercial logs into the Mississippi just above the port of Winona. The pioneer Winona and St. Peter Railroad – and the wagon road it replaced in the 1860s – moved the sawn timber westward to lumber markets on the treeless prairies. An especially important gateway to those prairies was Mankato, which served briefly before the Civil War as the terminal port of the Minnesota River on the southern Minnesota prairie frontier, before the railroad made that function obsolete. The Chicago-based Chicago and Northwestern Railroad bought the Winona and St. Peter in 1867 and extended the line to the Missouri River and Black Hills in the next two decades, placing Winona and Mankato at intersections of important lines in both the Twin Cities and Chicago webs. The railroad system strengthened Winona's position in the lumber trade – for as long as the trees lasted – and assured Mankato's place as the largest wholesale center in the farm trade of the southern Minnesota prairies.[7]

In St. Cloud's trade area, fast growth of the country's largest rural German-Catholic population had played a major role in moving that city into the family of future Minnesota metropolitan areas. St. Cloud enjoyed

Postcard view of South Front Street in Mankato, about 1900

an initial advantage as the railhead and stagecoach center on the Twin Cities–Red River route in the 1860s and as the site of the Midwest's most valuable commercial granite deposits. In the 1880s, the major railroad activity that developed at the intersection of the Duluth–Missouri River and Twin Cities–Pacific Northwest lines strongly reinforced St. Cloud's position.[8]

Of all the urban areas wholly or partly on the map of Minnesota when the twentieth century opened, these seven boasted the largest populations, the most buildings, the most solid facades on Main Street, and perhaps the most convincing of all measures of development at that time: an electric streetcar network converging on downtown from the neighborhoods. The Twin Cities constituted the metropolis of an empire, a new place to be noticed on the national map. Duluth and Superior, which together formed a booming port for the world's greatest iron-mining region, had joined the cities at the Ruhr-Rhine confluence in Germany as one of the two largest freshwater ports in the world. From small towns in 1870, they had grown by 1920 to have a combined population almost one-fourth that of the Twin Cities. The other five were farm trade centers for smaller but extensive regions that covered large parts of Minnesota and adjoining states. Of the cities that the U.S. census would identify in the 1980s as Minnesota's metropolitan centers, only Rochester was not on this early list.[9]

The Legacy of the Early Twentieth Century

Although the railroad settlement pattern was completed and stabilized between 1900 and 1920, this period was also a time of impending revolution. Electric streetcars, from the famous Snelling Shops in St. Paul and from more distant factories in Chicago and St. Louis, were rumbling along the streets beside a slowly shrinking stream of horse-drawn wagons and buggies and a swelling stream of horseless carriages from factories in Michigan, Ohio, Indiana, and Wisconsin. Even in the shadow of the Snelling Shops, people were talking about building automobiles with names like Minneapolis and Luverne, and a sprawling new plant at St. Cloud was trying to turn out the Pan automobile for the booming national market. By 1920, the mileage of gravel roads in southeastern and central Minnesota finally exceeded the mileage of railroads. Following the slogan of the Good Roads movement, farmers were cooperating with the effort to "pull Minnesota out of the mud." Just as important, the cities were ceasing to be big islands in the mud. The shallow leading edge of the wave of cars, trucks, and paving had arrived and would soon flood across the American scene.[10]

At the same time, the people living in the cities sensed the growing complexity of their environment. From less than one-sixth of the state's population in 1870, the urban share had risen to a third at the turn of the century and to more than 40 percent by 1920. In 1916, the League of Minnesota Municipalities – one of the pioneer leagues of cities in the nation – began to publish the journal *Minnesota Municipalities*. The first few issues carried articles on topics that, in retrospect, seem prophetic: central station heating, parks and playgrounds, sewerage, city planning, the "bill board nuisance," saloon licenses, and the legal power of cities to annex land, extend public improvements, and accommodate growth.[11]

As Minnesota's cities stood at the eve of the transformations of the auto era, the landscapes of the major centers reflected the remarkable improvements that had been made in the short period since pioneer settlement. The cities were similar to the degree that they had been built at about the same time, with the same technology and by people with common ideas and goals; yet they were different because of their contrasting locations in the rail network, natural resource patterns, and distance from the nation's eastern economic core. And there was no better way to see those landscapes than to ride the streetcars.[12]

Cities in the Farming Region

Everything was up-to-date in downtown Fargo-Moorhead, Grand Forks-East Grand Forks, St. Cloud, Mankato, and Winona in 1920. Facades rose three to six stories high, and the urban landscapes included busy railway stations, brick pavement, traffic lights, electric streetlights, motorized fire departments, and automatic railway-crossing gates, as well as streetcars. A remarkable number of garages and car dealerships had appeared, including only the second Ford automobile agency in the world, opened by the Tenvoorde brothers in downtown St. Cloud.[13]

At the same time, effects of differences in age and changing fortunes were becoming apparent. The downtowns of the cities along the Red River were new architectural products of the settlement boom in that wide, fertile valley between 1880 and 1910 – cities built entirely within the memories of people less than fifty years old. In contrast, the Victorian architecture of downtown Winona reflected its lumber and railroad boom a generation earlier and the twenty years of slow growth that had accompanied the decline of the lumber industry after 1900.[14] In all the cities, aging areas between the railway stations and the pioneer river landings were deteriorating. As reminders of the maintenance and replacement needs that relentlessly follow new growth, those areas foreshadowed the renewal projects that would emerge in the 1950s and 1960s.

The industrial and wholesale districts that followed the railroad tracks from the downtowns to the edges of the cities showed similar contrasts. In Fargo-Moorhead, the corridor stretched through the two downtowns for most of ten miles from the stockyards and packing plants at West Fargo to the sprawling railyards and shops at Dilworth, Minnesota. The spread of agriculture across North Dakota had given Fargo-Moorhead one of the largest volumes of wholesale trade per capita among all the cities of the United States, and the substantial brick warehouses and spacious sheds in that corridor left little doubt about the importance of those cities in the regional economy.[15]

In Winona, however, two miles of lumber mills and yards that had dominated the riverfront in the 1890s had disappeared almost completely by 1920. Acres of buildings had housed sawmills, planing mills, sash and door factories, and livery barns. The mills had taken white pine logs rafted from the upper Chippewa and some from the upper St. Croix, and trains had hauled away millions of board feet of lumber and millwork to build the new generation of houses, barns, sheds, and stores on the southwestern Minnesota and South Dakota prairies. But by 1920 the northern pine forest was cut over and the prairie towns and farms were built. At the site of the original levee, where the city began, the old waterfront freight house stood amid open land that even the 1894 insurance maps simply labeled "ruins." The structure had been obsolete since railroads put a virtual end to river packet traffic in the 1870s and 1880s. As Minnesota's cities moved into the automobile era, Winona already carried the economic problems of both a lumber town and a river town.[16]

Yet the place was far from dead. The railway belt that paralleled the river told a more complicated, and more typical, story of industrial change since 1890. A pioneer carriage factory still operated; pioneer flour milling and brewing had expanded. New plants had opened to make insulating material, agricultural specialties, and boxes. The J. R. Watkins Medical Company had expanded its famous door-to-door medicine and extract business to the national market. The company's new limestone office and plant now towered over the old east end of the city. In the west end, the sprawling division headquarters and shops of the Chicago and Northwestern Railway were a busy legacy from the early Winona and St. Peter Railroad – a major link in the rail expansion westward across South Dakota. Although lumber had gone, commerce survived and other industries changed ownership, grew, and diversified.

Railway and industry corridors in the other cities had similar symbols of change and adaptation, each in its distinctive physical setting. In St. Cloud's suburban Waite Park, about a thousand workers were employed

Abandoned Pan Motor Company building near St. Cloud, 1936

in the acres of shops, foundry, rolling mill, and lumber and timber storage of the Great Northern maintenance base. Nearby, the extensive but ill-fated Pan automobile works awaited gradual reoccupation by other industries. More than a dozen granite plants on the edges of the city exploited the area's unique building-stone deposits, exposed local labor to some of the most sophisticated industrial skills of the time, and linked local sales forces to national markets. And there were flour mills of Yankee origin and the brickyards, pickling and sauerkraut plants, and bobsled works (rural Minnesota's winter substitute for wagon works) that accompanied German culture.[17]

A new identity was still emerging for East Grand Forks. When the streetcar line reached the city in 1911, the Minnesota side of that urban area virtually monopolized the beer-distributing business. Ten beer depots – representing all the major brewers of Duluth, the Twin Cities, and Milwaukee – were lined up along the railroad sidings. But Prohibition changed that, and rapid exhaustion of the pineries in the Red Lake River basin closed the big sawmill that had been the east side's primary employer.[18]

Mankato's new rail-industry corridor had been built by removing tracks from city streets and consolidating them along the riverfront behind the new retaining wall. The corridor bustled with wholesale activity that reflected its location in the heart of the state's richest farm market. Oil and gasoline storage facilities were thriving as the number of farm trucks, tractors, and cars in the trade area started to climb. The expanded, modernized Hubbard Milling Company had established its base for years to come, and the Carney family had taken over the Connecticut-owned cement plant and added to the product line. Both these firms reflected the trend of locally owned industries to expand to ensure their survival. At the same time, however, Chicago acquisitions in meat packing, creamery packaging, and bulk oil distribution reflected the trend toward rising chain and absentee ownership, as well as the historical Chicago influence across southern Minnesota.[19]

As they bumped and rumbled through the residential neighborhoods of these cities in the 1920s, the streetcars passed single-family homes and duplexes, lawns and gardens, churches, schools, and corner stores along the grid of streets lined with elm and maple trees. Extensive middle-class neighborhoods reflected the growing importance of trade and services in the economic base, and other neighborhoods housed affluent business and professional families. Fine houses built early in the 1900s, with garages for newly acquired automobiles, stood on the south side of Fargo, and Winona featured blocks of nineteenth-century mansions south of downtown. Many of the Winona mansions were monuments to fortunes from the city's early commerce and lumber trade. In 1927, the Watkins family built the largest and finest piece in that architectural collection – a monument not only to a new local fortune but to a new era in ways of building a fortune.[20]

Streetcar lines also served the tightly packed districts of immigrant worker cottages, especially in cities having an important railroad and industrial base; examples included the heavily Polish western section of St. Cloud and eastern sections of Winona. Dozens of churches lay along the lines, witnessing to the diversity of ethnic populations. The size and age of Winona as a river city led to many examples: the splendid Methodist church memorialized the Yankee legacy in the business community, and Roman Catholic parishes spoke for the French, Irish, and Polish traditions in the city's history – especially massive, ornate St. Stanislaus, rising above its modest east-end surroundings. The line west from central St. Cloud passed near three different German denominational churches – reflecting in perhaps a perverse way the hope of frontier priest Francis X. Pierz that "the choicest pieces of land in this delightful territory would become the property of thrifty Catholics who would make an earthly paradise . . . and who would bear out the opinion that Germans prove to be the best farmers and the best Christians in America."[21]

And the streetcar lines reached out to college campuses, parks, and fairgrounds, often where the sharp edges of the cities met the surrounding sea of farmland or bordering rivers. The College of St. Teresa and St. Mary's College in Winona and Concordia College in Moorhead were measures of the importance of pioneer religious communities; similarly, the normal schools at Mankato, St. Cloud, and Winona, the agricultural college at Fargo, and the university at Grand Forks showed the early importance of those cities in their state's economies. More broadly, however, these institutions reflected the powerful cultural and economic features of the region – concern for human development, agricultural and technological improvement, and religious ethnicity.

Although Rochester was not among Minnesota's seven largest urban centers in 1920, its growth during the first two decades of the century had been more than three times the net increase at neighboring Winona and Mankato. The boom was linked to the growth of the Mayo Clinic, and seeds of the city's future claim to metropolitan status had been evident on insurance maps drawn in 1899. Several blocks from the original mill site on the Zumbro River, a two-story brick building was labeled "Dr's Off." Even at that time, two of the city's three largest nonindustrial structures were St. Marys Hospital and the supporting Franciscan Sisters' Academy of Our Lady of Lourdes at the western outskirts. The beginnings of the Mayo medical center were on the scene when the century opened.[22]

In 1920, Fargo-Moorhead illustrated how cities grow. Winona showed how they adapt and survive. Rochester was proving how dynamic the whole system can be. Yet all of these cities, despite their comparatively short histories, reflected the importance of location, individuals, beliefs, ideas, and community of interest in the continuous building and rebuilding of a city.

The Twin Ports

In the early 1900s, Duluth-Superior emerged as the second-ranking urban center in the entire Northwest. The "Zenith City of the Unsalted Seas," as journalist Thomas Foster had named Duluth in 1868, had become a vital U.S. shipping center. The broad estuary of the St. Louis River formed the harbor, sheltered from the open water of Lake Superior by the low, narrow, five-mile-long sandspit called Minnesota Point. Inside the harbor, a wider, industrially developed spit called Rice's Point reached from the Minnesota mainland to within a mile of the Wisconsin shore and provided the bridge connection across the lower bay. The country rose gently toward the south on the Wisconsin side, with an abundance of land suitable for development. But behind Duluth, a rocky, brushy escarpment towered more than five hundred feet above the city. Southwest of Rice's Point, where the escarpment retreated from the bay, a wide terrace accommodated the city's railroad yards and heavy industry. In contrast, northeast of Minnesota Point the high, rocky country rose immediately from the lakefront to form the most picturesque section of the new metropolis. The top of the escarpment commanded spectacular panoramas of the cities and of the harbor edge of downtown.[23]

From Duluth's spacious harbor extended rail routes to the Twin Cities and the iron ranges, as well as direct connections to the Twin Cities–Chicago corridor and the northern transcontinentals. Central Duluth's impressive office, hotel, retail, and warehouse facade crowded around the historic railhead just inside Minnesota Point. The smaller downtown of Superior stretched along the main street leading inland from the waterfront opposite the end of Rice's Point.

More than ten thousand ships – including some of the Great Lakes fleet of graceful passenger cruisers – entered or left the harbor in the peak year of 1929, most via the Duluth ship channel through Minnesota Point at the doorstep of downtown. Half the cargo was iron ore; outbound northern plains grain and incoming Appalachian coal accounted for most of the other half. Along about twenty miles of the forty-nine-mile harbor frontage, facilities of national manufacturers and distributors sprawled among the rocks, scrub woodlands, and marshes.[24]

Houses along 24th Avenue East in Duluth, about 1915

Each separate industrial node provided an employment focus for a neighboring cluster of houses. Those neighborhoods were a crazy quilt of ethnic groups from Finland, eastern and southern Europe, and French Canada. Some of the immigrants had come to northeastern Minnesota to work in the booming port; others had come to the mines and the lumber camps and then to the lakehead. In 1930, foreign-born people still accounted for a quarter of the population of Duluth, and among these immigrants men outnumbered women more than four to three.[25] The main upper-income spoke of residential development projected northeastward from central Duluth along the escarpment on the Lake Superior north shore. The downtown technical, professional, and business corps lived on the slope of the escarpment, and many of the city's sizable group of wealthy families occupied the line of mansions – including the famous Congdon estate – near the cliff at the edge of the lake.

The whole collection of settlements was linked by a highly efficient, nearly linear streetcar system.[26] The age of the buildings, the smoky landscape of factories and railroad yards, and the presence of an immigrant European labor force gave the place a flavor of lower Great Lakes and eastern industrial cities that seemed strange in this remote northern setting. The landscape expressed the large-scale absentee investments, quick fortunes, surge of immigration, and hopes that had driven the area's remarkable growth. Few signs revealed that the boom had ended and that Duluth-Superior would see virtually no increase in population during the rest of the century.

The Twin Cities

The mature rail network that had developed by the turn of the twentieth century nourished the regional metropolis at Minneapolis-St. Paul. Between 1890 and 1920, population of the Twin Cities more than doubled. The metropolis had accounted for nearly one-third of the nonfarm growth of the territory from Upper Michigan to western Montana, and nearly one-eighth of the population of the region lived in the metropolitan area. One of the nation's ten leading rail centers, the Twin Cities were the northwestern anchor of the nation's principal rail corridor between the Middle Atlantic seaboard and the Midwest. St. Paul's Hill family had a controlling influence in the major railroads in the northern transcontinental corridor. Minneapolis had become the world's leading flour-milling center and still clung to the title in 1920. Throughout the territory, financial, mercantile, and professional interests that were based on these railroad and grain industries dominated their competitors from other major metropolitan centers.[27]

The very name of the Twin Cities implied unity and duality. St. Paul's developers exploited the practical head of navigation on the upper Mississippi River, together with the nearest easy access to the upland below the Falls of St. Anthony. Developers at Minneapolis (and its earlier neighbor, St. Anthony) exploited the greatest natural industrial waterpower site in the central United States. The two cities, which were ten miles apart, had separate commercial centers, municipal governments, and newspapers. By creating separate terminals in each city, the railroads reinforced the duality, but beyond that they created an empire in need of a metropolis. And what was the metropolis? Viewed from the outside, it appeared to be "the Twin Cities." From the inside, however, the view of the metropolis fragmented into one of institutionalized special interests, each group looking from its respective city past its neighbor to the world beyond.[28]

While the transcontinental railroads were being built, the Twin Cities trade and service territory expanded almost entirely to the west. Because the two cities were barriers to each other in the time-consuming process of switching rail shipments to the hinterland, Minneapolis held a growing advantage in regional trade during the steel-rail era from the 1870s to 1920. In response to those regional forces, the population of Minneapolis passed that of St. Paul between 1870 and 1880, the period when rivalry between the cities was least subtle and most intense. During the remainder of the rail era, the population on the Minneapolis side grew to exceed that of St. Paul by about three to two, a ratio that persisted into the 1980s. Although Minneapolis interests could afford to be more conciliatory and cosmopolitan, the feeling of contest continued. After 1920, highways, suburbanization, and air travel would change the entire context of the rivalry, but its driving special interests would not relax quickly. Historian Lucile M. Kane's description of the relationship in the mid-nineteenth century lost its pertinence only slowly and selectively in later years: "And yet for all the ties that bound them, the cities were rivals. . . . The rivalry was bitter and pervasive, and local newspapers piled fuel onto the blaze as they espoused the causes of their cities." Nevertheless, the special interests of commercial centers, newspapers, and city officials were superimposed on a massive, intricate metropolitan system that was evolving to an increasing degree without reference to them. Metropolitan, regional, national, and world business had to be done.[29]

Much of that business took place in an impressive corridor of rail yards, warehousing, and manufacturing that extended nearly twenty miles from the north edge of Minneapolis, through the two downtowns, to South St. Paul, with stubs running to the South Side of Minneapolis and to St. Paul's East Side and West End. In western St. Paul, a north-south short line, the Minnesota Transfer Railway Company, linked the main lines within the corridor. The Transfer served as a belt railway on the common edge of both cities and a locus for extensive industrial and commercial development beginning around the turn of the century that came to be labeled the Midway district. The downtowns and the University of Minnesota were the largest concentrations of activity in the corridor. Although each downtown earned part of its living serving a local market that roughly matched its city, the downtowns were also home to thousands of businesses and government offices serving the whole Twin Cities regional trade and service territory.[30]

The industrial-railway belt included the flour mills, terminal elevators, stockyards, and packing plants for which the Twin Cities were well known, but it was also an entrepreneurial seedbed. Hundreds of small firms served the regional market for farm supplies, the country stores, and the giant grain-milling industry. They also supplied consumer goods to the fast-growing metropolitan market, competing wherever they could with more costly or less well-adapted imports. They made household heating and plumbing equipment, some of the earliest commercial refrigerators and light bulbs, generators and motors; paint, pumps, steam tractors and threshers, garments and shoes; printing presses, books, magazines, office forms, calendars, playing cards, pioneer brands of mouthwash and shaving cream. The list of names easily goes far beyond the major national brands of flour or the regional beers – Burma Shave, Lavoris, Mazda Lamps, Minneapolis Moline, Minneapolis Heat Regulator Company, Minnesota Mining and Manufacturing, Northern Pump, Kluge, Seeger Refrigerator, Brown and Bigelow, Munsingwear. Many of these firms grew to manufacture for the nation and the world. They spawned a constant stream of ideas, new products, successes, expansions, moves, and failures – and a large, growing base of employment. Even the companies that were largest by the 1980s were only moderate in size at the end of the railroad era, and hundreds were smaller and less well known.[31]

Perhaps 55 percent of all the income earned in the Minneapolis–St. Paul metropolis in 1920 depended on business within the Northwest region that reached from northern Michigan to Montana and from the Canadian border to northern Iowa. The other 45 percent depended on business with the rest of the United States and with the world. The Twin Cities had clearly emerged as both the regional metropolis and the region's principal gateway to its national and international markets.

The Loop in Stillwater, twenty miles from downtown St. Paul—the easternmost point on the 390 miles of track operated by the Twin City Rapid Transit Company in 1912

One of the nation's model streetcar systems radiated from the two downtowns. By 1920, the lines served about eighty square miles of neighborhoods that housed most of the metropolitan population; they also reached beyond the main urban frontier to the summer suburbs on Lake Minnetonka and White Bear Lake and to the industrial satellites at Stillwater and South St. Paul.[32]

The streetcar lines came to identify different sectors of the cities. Clusters of lines from different neighborhoods converged on a few major bridges and viaducts on their downtown approaches, and people who lived in these clusters and their accompanying spokes of growth gave the different corridors regional names—Northeast, Southeast, South, Southwest, and North in Minneapolis; East Side, North End, Como, and West End in St. Paul. The lines also set the location of tens of thousands of jobs that were in the neighborhoods rather than in the downtowns or rail-industry corridor. Thousands of neighborhood shops and offices concentrated in the strips that fronted the trolley lines. About seventy-five miles of neighborhood commercial strips had developed on radial and crosstown lines by

1920 – grocers, druggists, hardware merchants, doctors, dentists, morticians, and hundreds of other small businesses.[33]

Only southwest and south Minneapolis and the western and southwestern parts of St. Paul had direct access to downtown without significant rail or river barriers. As a result, the growing population of white-collar commuters who worked in the downtowns tended to live in those directions, creating by the turn of the century a higher-income region of the metropolis southwest of the main rail-industry corridor that was separated from a lower-income region on the northeast. Newly arrived immigrants congregated within or northeast of the rail-industry corridor, and these were the neighborhoods that came to have the national parishes and synagogues of the streetcar city.

Terrain brought still more variety to the real estate market within each corridor. Flat land was abundant, but the higher, rolling land was preferred, as were sites on lakeshores and river bluffs. People who could pay the most for housing settled in the southwestern lakes district of Minneapolis, on the river bluffs in St. Paul, and in the block-wide strip of elite homes built along Summit Avenue, which ran from the "summit" above downtown St. Paul to the river bluffs opposite south Minneapolis. Across the tracks from the downtowns, neighborhood professionals and business proprietors were more likely to be on the heights in northeast Minneapolis, on the rolling uplands of the unique campus suburb of St. Anthony Park, or overlooking Como or Phalen lakes in St. Paul; lower-income, less-skilled residents lived in smaller houses on land that was lower, flatter, farther from water, or closer to the noise and soot of the railroad yards.[34]

Among Minnesota's streetcar and railroad era cities, the regional metropolis was already by far the biggest and most complex. But the gap was destined to widen in the auto era that was breaking on Minnesota and the nation.

Transformation during the Auto Era

During the 1920s, a swelling fleet of cars and trucks rapidly took the place of horses, wagons, and buggies on city streets. Ridership on the streetcar lines declined precipitously: except within the Twin Cities, where service continued on the Twin City Lines until 1954, all the state's systems were abandoned during the Great Depression.[35] Abandonment of the streetcar lines was little more than a symbol of the wrenching changes that the auto era brought to the cities. Vast areas were rendered obsolescent because they lacked space for parking, loading docks, peak-hour traffic, or garages.

At first, the changes of the new era brought pure excitement. In the heart of the city, new paving, traffic signals, parking meters, billboards, and the din of motors and horns replaced smokestacks and streetcars as symbols of urban centrality. Although the railroad corridors and downtown facades were still the dominant locations of business and industry, the underlying obsolescence became evident as auto-era building gradually accounted for more and more of the stock of urban structures. A sluggish rate of new construction during the depression, and the virtual hiatus during World War II, delayed the impact. But the full reality of the revolution emerged quickly in the postwar building boom that began about 1946.[36]

Perhaps the most profound impacts of the internal combustion engine on the cities were indirect. One, the replacement of horsepower by tractors on the farms, led average farm size to increase two to three times over the half-century from 1920 to 1970, and the change continued somewhat chaotically into the 1980s. With only one-half to one-third as many farms, one-half to two-thirds of the farm labor force shifted to nonfarm jobs. Beyond that, the growth of productivity and income increased the market for many kinds of capital goods and supplies. Construction and maintenance of roads, electric power and telephone lines, greater sales and distribution of fertilizer, feed, and equipment – all created jobs in town.[37]

Bigger and fewer farms, combined with automobiles and improved rural roads, also triggered drastic changes in the need for towns and cities in the locations where they had developed in the era of the railroad, wagon, and buggy. Thanks to cars, trucks, and good roads, farmers could travel twenty-five miles to town with no more expenditure of time or income than they had once used to travel three miles. Trade and services that had been dispersed at hundreds of small towns and hamlets became concentrated at a few dozen county seats or multicounty trade centers, and the enlargement of trade territories and purchasing power led to still further growth at those favored locations. Increased trade meant the creation of a market for totally new kinds of professional and business services and specialty retailing, as well as an enlarged urban middle class.[38]

The same forces that shifted population growth toward the larger urban centers also spread the resulting urban growth over larger areas at lower density than had ever been possible before the days of cars, trucks, and highways. Metropolitan industries decentralized, adding still another growth factor to the urban centers in the farming region. The new urban population dispersed widely into sprawling, low-density subdivisions and into the surrounding countryside.[39]

Good roads made an enormous amount of new land accessible for urban development. In the time it once took a person to ride from downtown St. Cloud to the streetcar stop nearest a house on the outskirts and walk home, a car could travel twenty or thirty miles. In 1920, about two hundred square miles of land lay within an hour's travel time, by streetcar and foot, from the center of the nearer of the two downtowns of the Twin Cities. In 1970, the comparable area was nearly five thousand square miles! During the same period, the metropolitan population had grown from 840,000 to almost 2 million. The supply of land thus grew more than twenty times while the population tripled, a greatly increasing land supply that held prices down and further encouraged the dispersal of growth.[40]

Places in the farming region that were largest early in the century tended to be those most affected by the forces of concentration and dispersal in the auto era (see table on page 57). The notable exception was Winona. Trapped between the nearby larger center at La Crosse and the booming medical service center at Rochester, its population only held steady through most of the period. Meanwhile, Fargo-Moorhead, Grand Forks-East Grand Forks, St. Cloud, and Rochester advanced in the 1960s and 1970s to the census status of standard metropolitan statistical areas – an event that automatically put them on the strategic maps of a host of national business chains and marketing organizations. Only the Twin Cities felt the ultimate impact of the complex forces set in motion in the auto era and the later air age. Those forces included the national decentralization of industry, off-farm migration, spectacular growth of the Midwest farm economy, and low-density dispersal of urban growth. At the same time, the virtual halt in expansion at metropolitan Duluth-Superior reflected their isolation from the direct effects of the growth in farm trade and off-farm migration that were felt at the other cities. It also reflected events in the mining hinterland, where an enormous increase in machine productivity was accompanied by a decline in the labor force and extreme instability in the demand for iron ore. While the Twin Cities population increased by a factor of 2.5 between 1920 and 1980, the population of the Twin Ports remained virtually the same.[41]

Urban Centers in the Farming Region

Striking new patterns emerged on the land in the urban growth centers of the state's farming region after 1920. Maintenance problems had begun to accumulate in the downtown districts during the long austerity of the 1930s and World War II. After the war, downtown property owners began to make cosmetic improvements, a few putting up one- or two-story buildings to accommodate chain retail stores serving the booming population of young families. At the same time, however, the postwar building boom seriously reduced the advantage of downtown locations. The great mass of new housing, which was separated from downtown stores by the narrow or congested streets of the older city, faced outward toward developing commercial strips on the new highway approaches and bypasses.

The problem of deteriorating downtowns festered slowly through the 1950s and worsened dramatically in the 1960s. At first, paint began to peel here and there and fittings became worn. One by one the department stores closed. The chains moved to the malls on the highway outskirts, and even the names of proud, home-owned stores disappeared from the main streets – closed or shifted to the malls. Specialty shops, professional offices, and movie theaters – their numbers reduced by competition from television – followed the department stores out of town. Then the old hotels – except those in Rochester's booming medical complex – closed down. Most were victims of age, style, and parking problems. Moreover, as the railroad stations declined in importance and stores and offices moved out, the hotels lost the ambience and centrality of their downtown surroundings. Vacant fronts and downgraded retailing became the signs of a shrunken, lower-income trade area.[42]

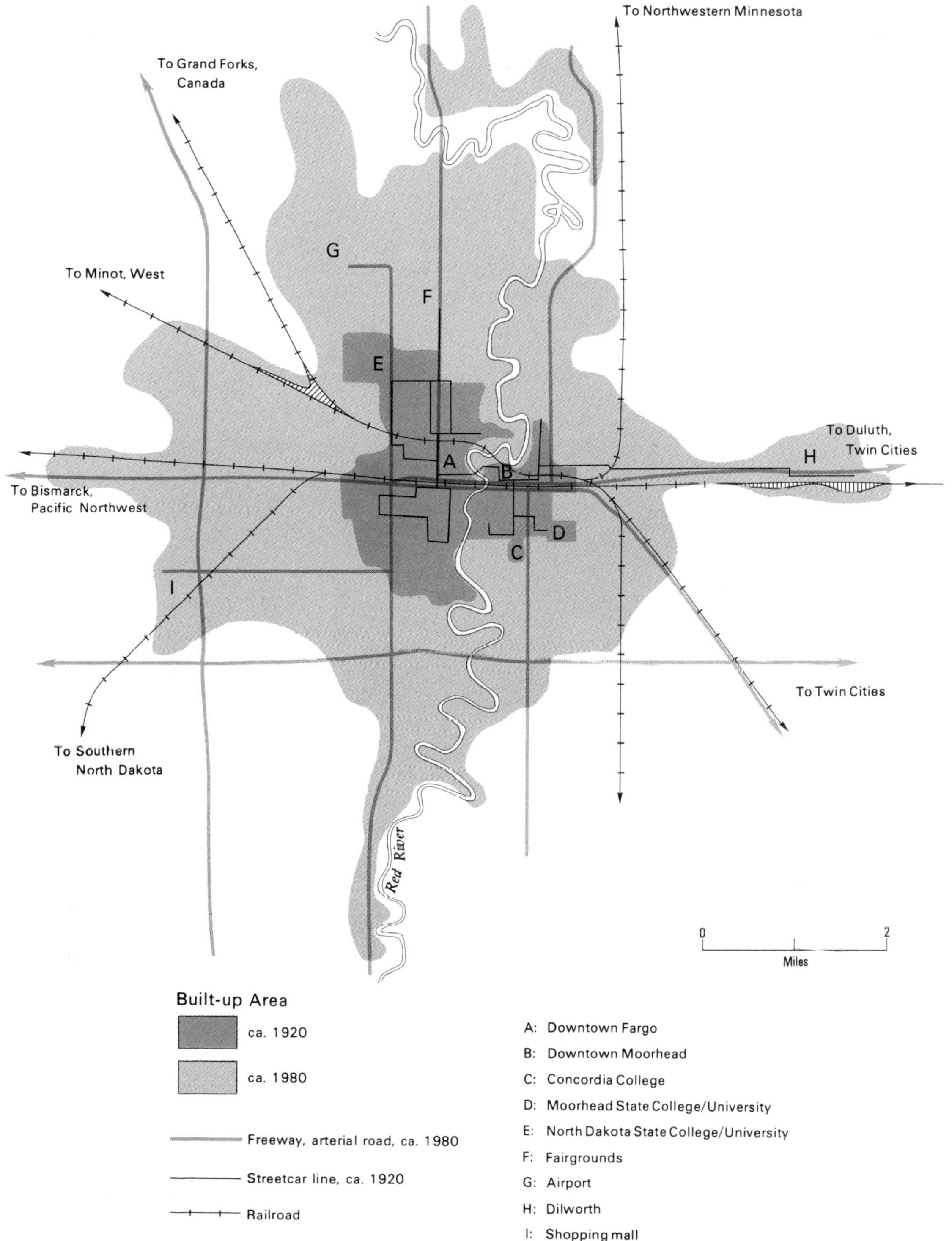

Compact urban area of Fargo-Moorhead near the end of the streetcar era (about 1920) and the varying extent of low-density expansion during the auto era (into the 1980s). The following five maps show a similar growth process in other Minnesota urban centers. Sources: *See n. 41.*

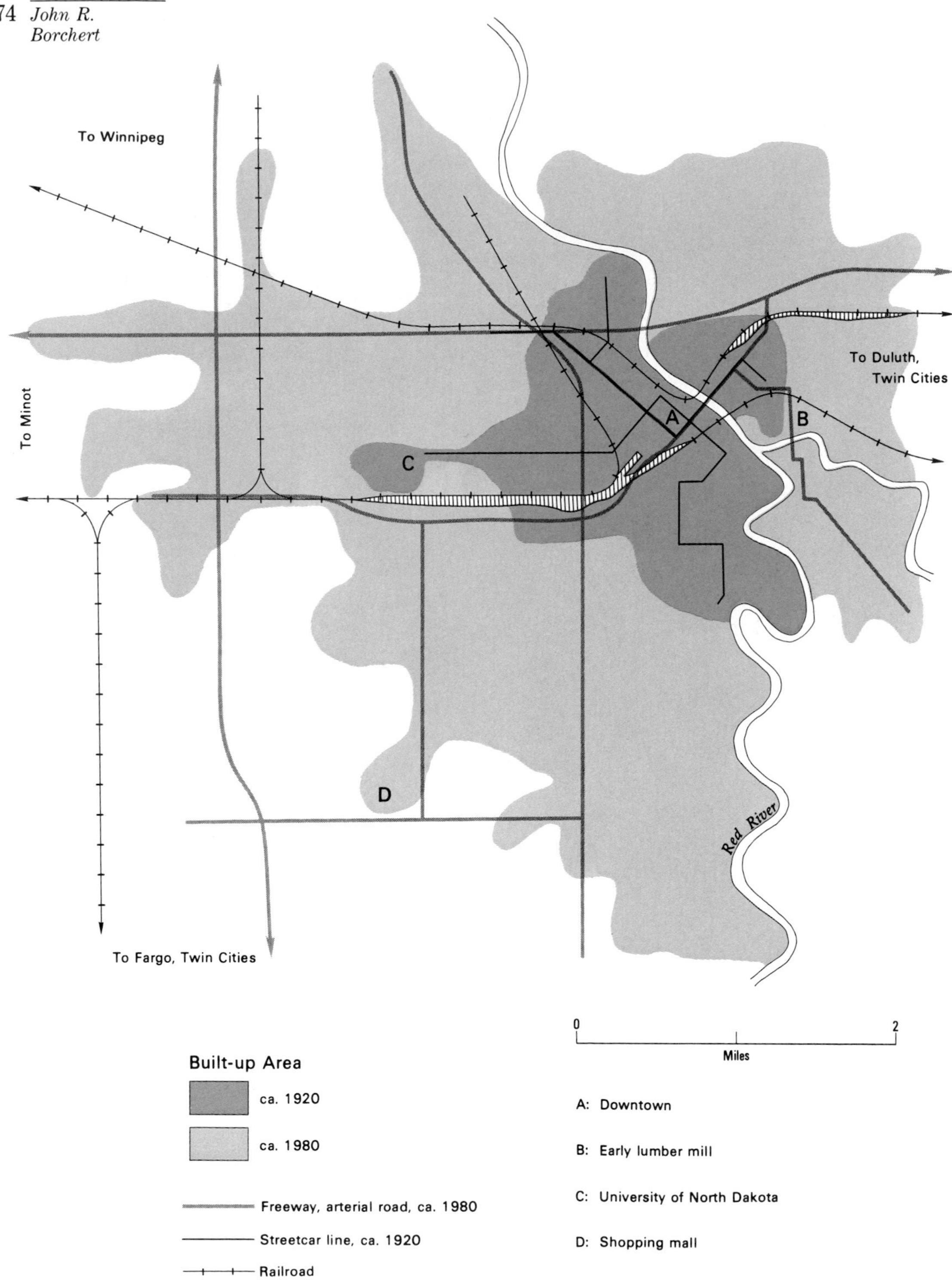

Compact urban area of Grand Forks-East Grand Forks about 1920 and later auto-era expansion

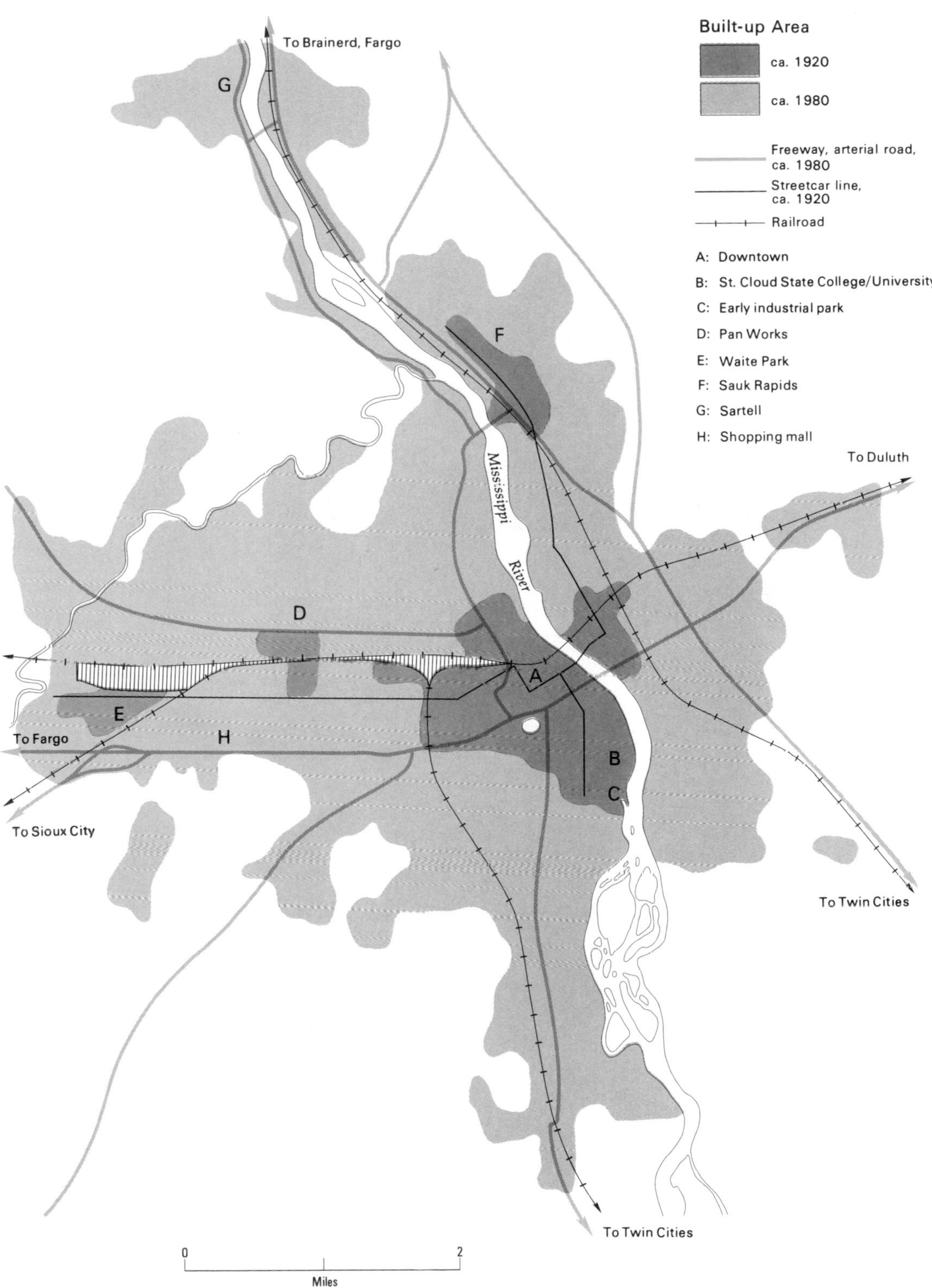

Compact urban area of St. Cloud about 1920 and later auto-era expansion

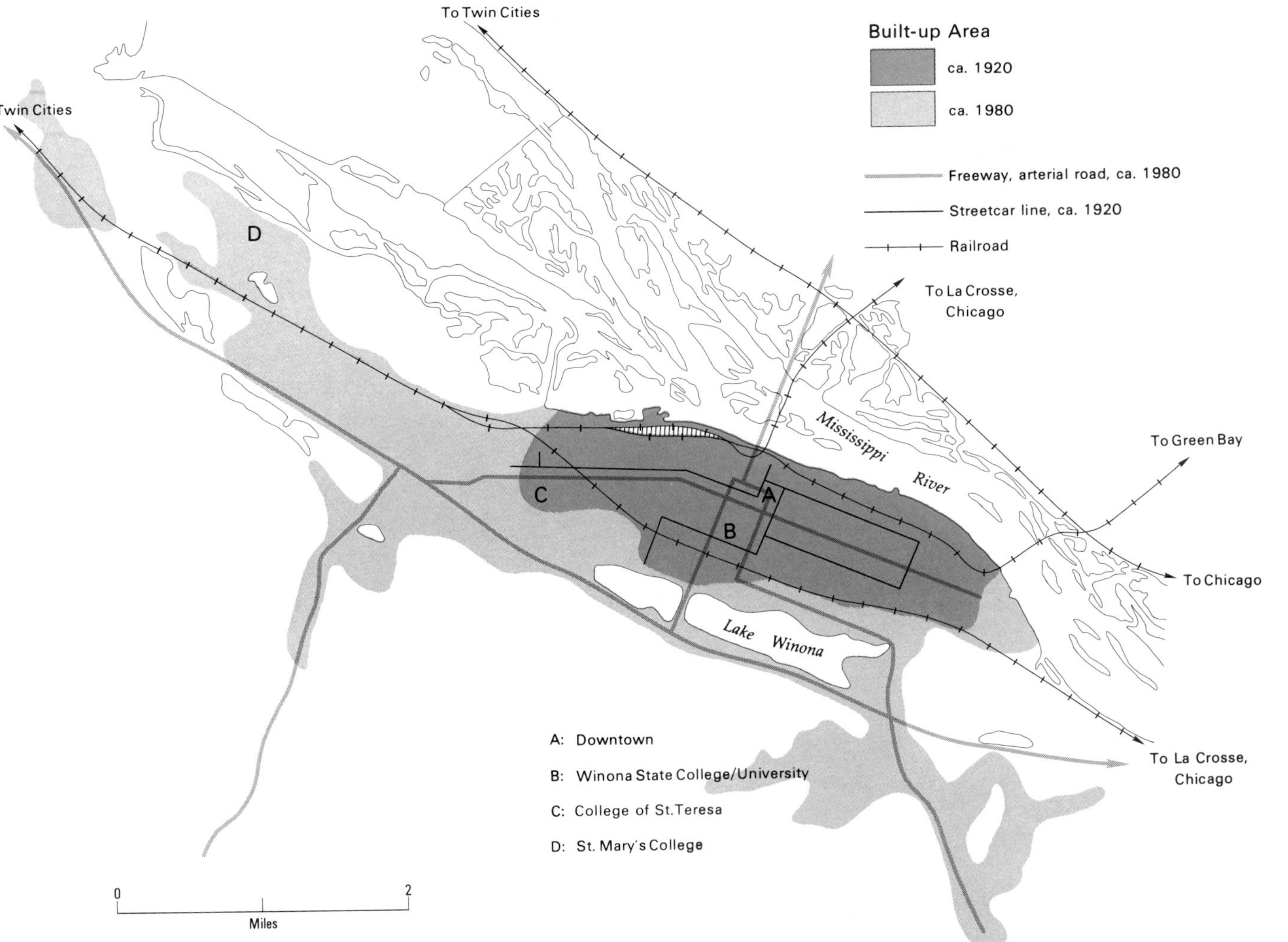

Compact urban area of Winona about 1920 and later auto-era expansion

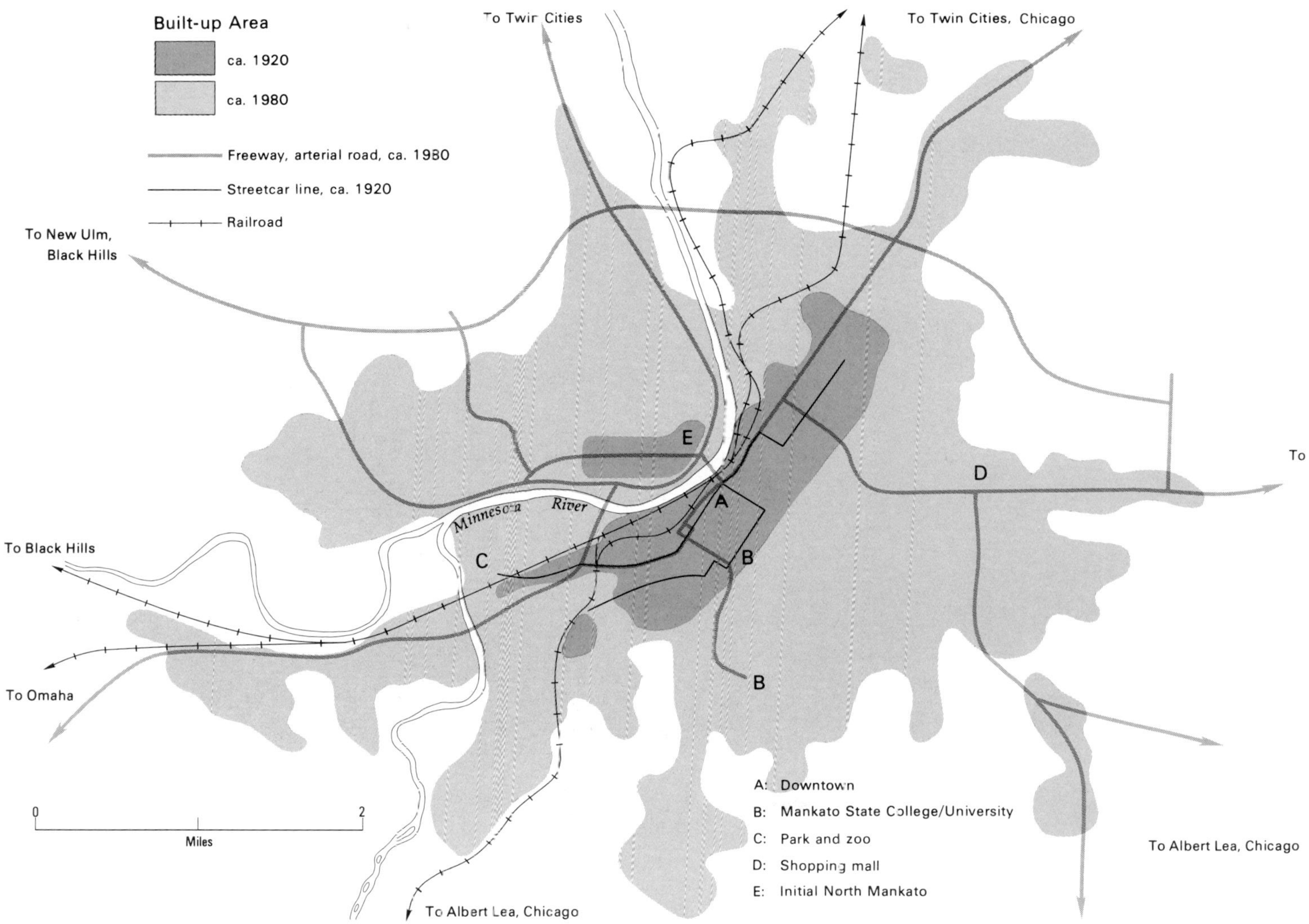

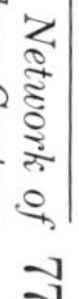

Built-up Area

ca. 1920

ca. 1980

Freeway, arterial road, ca. 1980

Streetcar line, ca. 1920

Railroad

To New Ulm, Black Hills

To Twin Cities

To Twin Cities, Chicago

To Rochester, Chicago

To Black Hills

To Omaha

To Albert Lea, Chicago

To Albert Lea, Chicago

Minnesota River

E A D C B B

0 Miles 2

A: Downtown
B: Mankato State College/University
C: Park and zoo
D: Shopping mall
E: Initial North Mankato

Compact urban area of Mankato about 1920 and later auto-era expansion

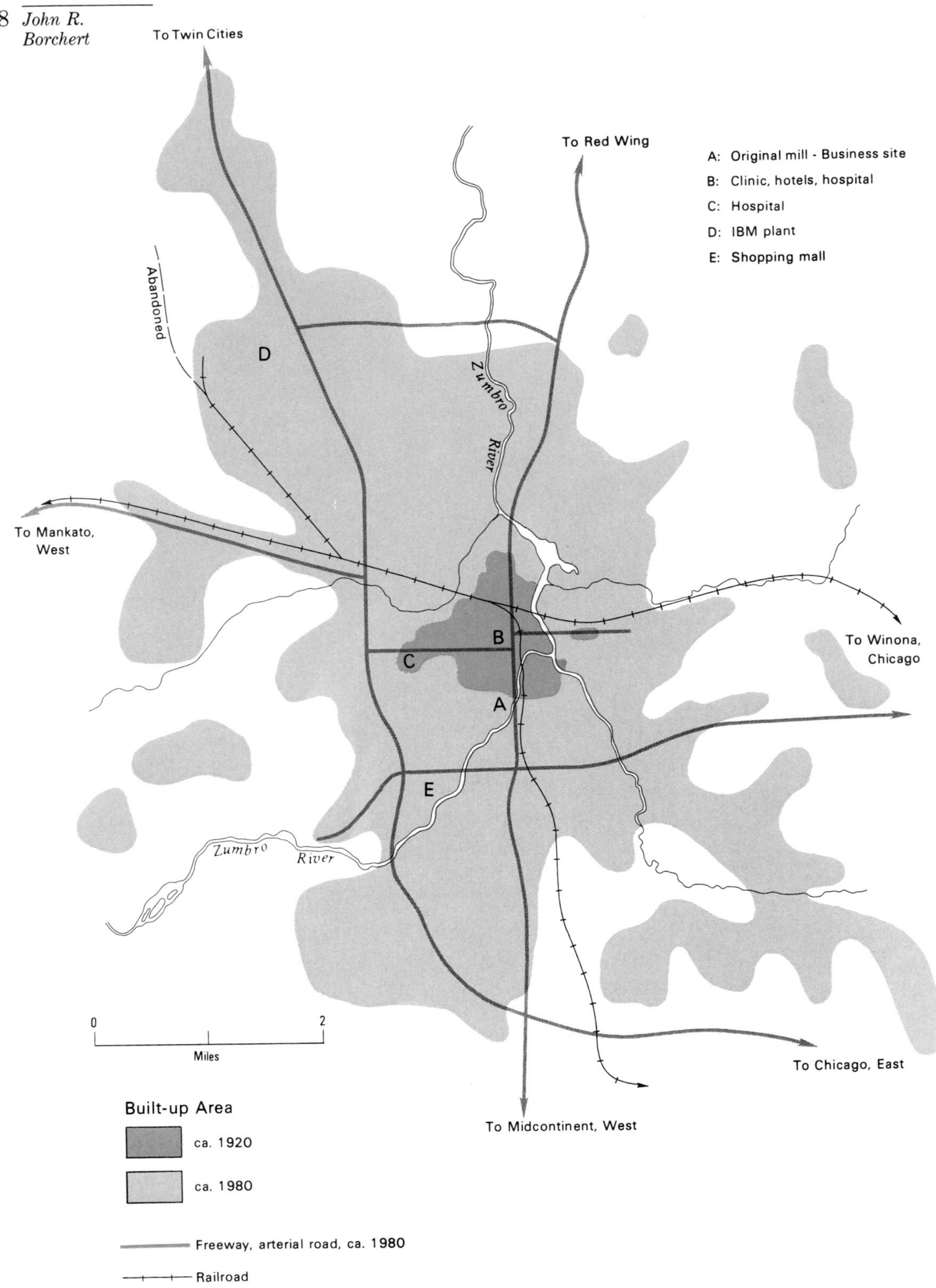

Compact urban area of Rochester about 1920 and later auto-era expansion

By 1960, the need for action had become clear, especially to those who had the most at stake. Local banks and utility companies had no desire to watch the value of property dissolve before their eyes in the communities to which they were anchored. City officials were anxious about the loss of commercial tax base. And part of the reaction to blight and decay reflected the genuine spirit of loyalty of that small group of people in any city who provide the thread of continuity amid the turbulence of mobility and social change. Congress helped to produce action in the 1950s by appropriating federal housing funds for renewal and redevelopment projects in the central areas of small and medium-sized cities.

Many actors had to join hands in the effort to renew the downtown districts. The city had to issue bonds to raise funds for the improvements. For the city to be able to justify the investment, private developers had to make commitments to buy the land and build on it. A long-range land use plan was essential to guide the public investment, reassure developers, and meet the requirements of the federal housing agency. Neighborhood activists in the deteriorated fringes of the downtown had to be satisfied that a significant amount of housing would be included in the project, and real estate agents had to be reassured that the project would not destroy the private housing market. Ideological differences emerged between those who believed in public action in the development field and those who did not. Public officials, business leaders, churches, and voluntary organizations gradually formed coalitions to launch actual projects, but the process was slow.

Through the late 1950s and the 1960s, downtown renewal programs of this sort spread rapidly across the country. Beginning with Fargo, leaders in Upper Midwest cities were among the first in the country to recognize that the old central areas could not be adapted to the new locational circumstances of the auto era without organizational and financial initiative on the part of the municipality. With the loss of their railroad-streetcar centrality, the downtowns no longer had the same natural attraction for new investment. Yet much that was there still had importance and utility. Some of the durable old buildings were usable and vital symbols of the history and continuity of the city. Local business and professional leadership – and, most of all, the municipality itself – refused to abandon the districts to grime and decay. In the last analysis, the local government was the one special-interest institution that simply could not walk away. And it would gradually become clear that the downtown was only the earliest and most densely developed area of the city in which the fundamental, long-term need for systematic maintenance and replacement would appear.

Although the Twin Cities tapped the greater part of the federal funds in the region, smaller cities in Minnesota and along the state's borders were quick to discover and match the growing array of financial grants. Through the 1960s, *Minnesota Municipalities* kept local officials posted on new federal grant legislation. Economic development, housing, and planning authorities worked together to monitor the growth and aging of their cities and to formulate strategies for maintenance and development. By

1965, all Minnesota cities having more than ten thousand in population and 70 percent of those having more than twenty-five hundred had established city planning departments. Many went on to organize development agencies and corporations.[43]

In each case, the strategy evolved to include landscaping and cosmetic improvements to the city's historic retail core, new hotels, offices, partly subsidized new housing for the elderly, new civic buildings, subsidized parking ramps, and conversion of old warehouses to shops, restaurants, and housing. National chains attracted the capital for the new hotels. Local and regional business and financial institutions built the principal office buildings and financed many of the conversions of warehouses and other large, old structures. Maturing of the postwar baby-boom age cohort provided a continuing supply of entrepreneurs to fill the office space and open the new shops. But old, poorly maintained areas of mixed commercial-industrial-residential buildings from the railroad era persisted in the 1980s at the edge of the renewed downtown, and retailing was slow to revive in the face of ever-growing competition from suburban malls.[44]

In the aging neighborhoods of the streetcar era that surrounded each old commercial core, the original housing stock by 1980 was approaching an average age of eighty years – which was also near the average life expectancy of dwelling units in the United States.[45] In many of these neighborhoods, the housing had been filtered down to the lowest-income inhabitants of the city – people on welfare, minimal pensions, or minimum-wage jobs. Public low-cost housing or new apartments had replaced some of the late-nineteenth and early-twentieth-century homes. As in the downtown, city government faced the need to invest in new or rehabilitated public improvements in order to attract the new investment that would maintain or replace the old housing.

While one group worked to revitalize the old inner city, others were building the new, postwar outer city. Populations of most of these places tripled or quadrupled in the auto era, and the use of land grew at least twice as fast as the population.[46] The larger lots, parking space, and sprawling one-story buildings that came with automobiles and trucking contributed to the surge in land use, but there were other factors as well. The building boom of the late 1940s and 1950s compensated for fifteen years of deferred construction because of depression and war. In the 1950s and 1960s, school and playground areas expanded to accommodate the children of the baby boom. When the postwar boom matured in the 1960s and 1970s, shopping centers, high schools, and other civic construction expanded faster than the population. And when the baby-boom generation married in the late 1960s and 1970s, the number of households multiplied in a similar fashion. Through it all, the growth in material wealth created the need for more space to store, use, and dump the swelling volume of goods that everyone in the community purchased, used, and discarded.

Powerful forces attracted or impelled the new development in particular directions. The middle-class residential market had always expanded in directions away from the railroad-industry corridor, and that tendency was more pronounced than before as the auto era increased the proportion of the population in the middle class. And people were attracted more than ever by amenities: those who could pay the most shifted from the tree-arched main streets near downtown to the country club area, and people in the upper-middle-income sector settled in developments that exploited riverfront parklands in Fargo, bluffs and rolling uplands in Rochester, Mankato, and North Mankato, and riverside areas on the edge of St. Cloud.

Commercial and industrial developments shifted and expanded to open tracts along the highway bypasses at the edge of the city. Industrial and warehouse expansions tended to stay close to both highway and rail – and, in Winona, to the river port as well. The big shopping malls looked for open tracts near the outer edge of major residential growth – preferably the upper-middle-income sector – and near the major highway bypass. Not only did this location provide an advantage over the older downtown retail location in the city market, but it also made the new malls accessible to small towns as far as fifty or sixty miles away. Thus the malls captured most of the retail market of the growing city and an enlarged share of trade from the surrounding smaller towns as well.

The Upper Midwest's World Port

In the auto era, Duluth-Superior presented a striking picture of maintenance and growth amid obsolescence and abandonment. The spacious harbor was still the centerpiece of the urban area in the 1980s, but some of the great railroad-era docks and storage yards were overgrown by brush and aspen, edged by rotting pilings around quietly silting slips. Hundreds of acres of railway yards were used at only a fraction of their capacity, and the United States Steel mill was cold and rusting. Five thousand transportation jobs and perhaps half as many industrial jobs had disappeared from the port area between 1929 and 1980. Residential growth had been minuscule around the bay since World War II, and much of that growth had been in the vicinity of the planned community of Morgan Park, built by the steel company in 1913 and still considered desirable because of its amenities.[47]

Still, the Twin Ports were the scene of much activity. Tens of millions of bushels of grain moved through the banks of terminal elevators on Rice's Point and the Superior waterfront. The steel economy was depressed, but millions of tons of taconite pellets moved each year through the ore docks in southwestern Duluth and on the southeastern outskirts of Superior. A new terminal transshipped Montana coal bound for electric utility plants in the lower Great Lakes region. Although the St. Lawrence Seaway had fallen short of expected use, general cargo freighters tied up at Duluth's postwar terminal at the westernmost end of the seaway. An ultramodern paper mill was in operation on the Duluth side of the harbor. But beneath the activity lay uncertainty about the future of the taconite shipments, grain trade, and general cargo upon which the ports depended: all were extremely unstable streams in an environment of changing technology and world markets.

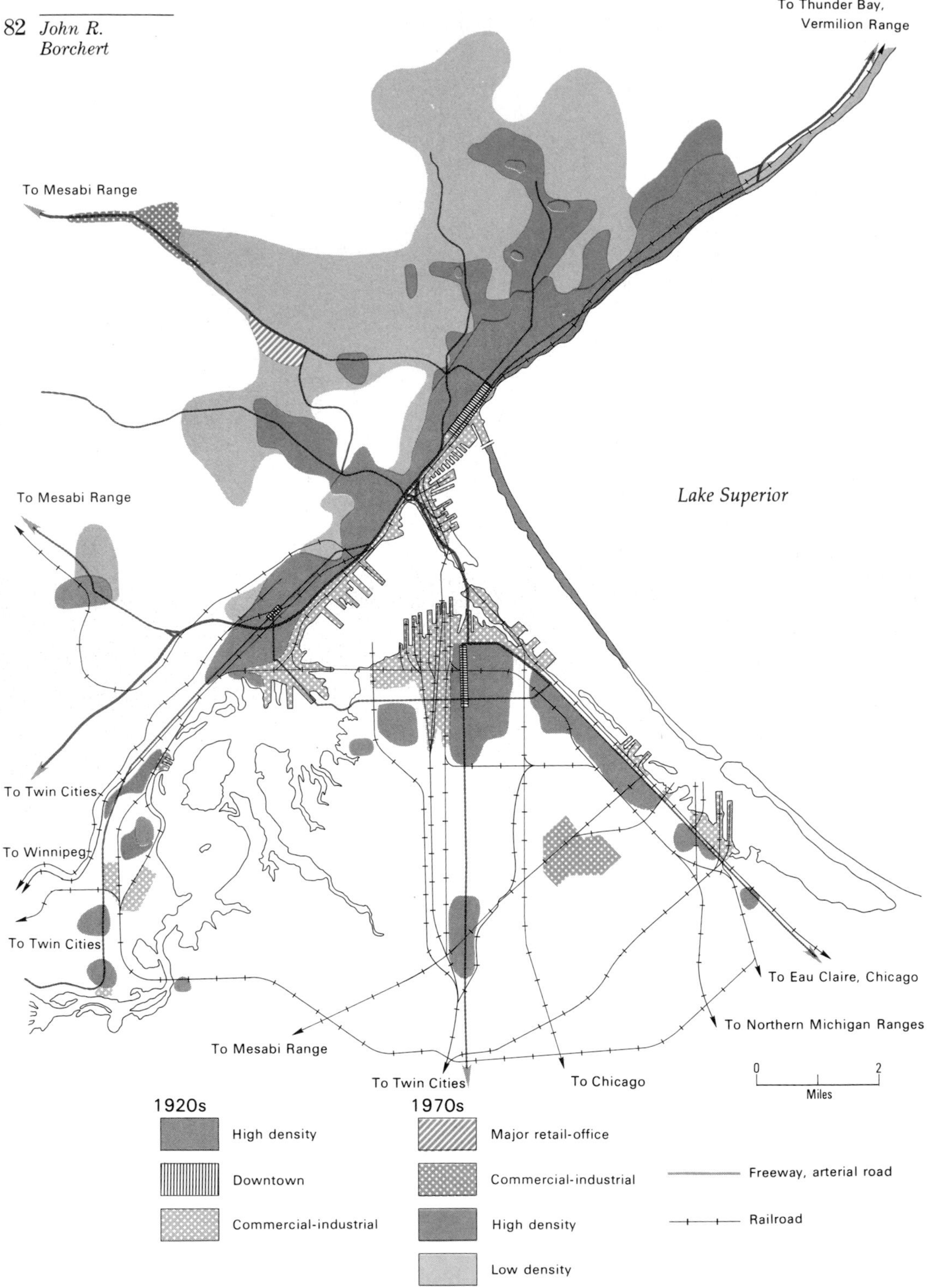

Built-up areas of the Twin Ports–Duluth and Superior, Wisconsin–in the streetcar era and selective expansion during the auto era, mainly on the heights of the Minnesota side. Sources: *See n. 41.*

Duluth and its harbor, with the site of the future Duluth Arena-Auditorium in the foreground, 1963

In contrast, outside the port and the rail-industry districts, Duluth-Superior had undergone maintenance and even expansion since the 1920s. Net population growth of the metropolitan area had been near zero for more than half a century, but new housing in the eastern uplands had replaced older, deteriorated housing in the core and industrial sections. To compensate for the loss of jobs in transportation, warehousing, and manufacturing, employment had grown on the campuses on the east side – especially at the University of Minnesota – in the services downtown, and at the military air base in the 1950s and 1960s.[48]

Many signs gave evidence of the continuing rehabilitation. Historic preservation and redevelopment projects were gradually lifting the face of the downtown of the railroad and streetcar eras and creating a new civic facade at the place where massive rail yards once bordered the harbor around the first northern transcontinental rail terminal. A network of modern highways and spectacular bridges was gradually stitching together the patchwork of settlements that made up this unusual and picturesque metropolis. A long-enduring planning program kept nudging the pieces into place, and energy for the continuing maintenance and redevelopment effort came from a remarkable reservoir of local leadership and generous state and federal grants.

In the 1980s, Duluth-Superior presented an unusual and dramatic view of the powerful effects of service growth, industrial transformation, federal and state expenditures, and international interdependence in the auto era. Unlike many other cities, the Twin Ports were not buried in layers of recent growth. Therefore, they offered an exceptionally clear exposure of the maintenance and obsolescence problems that beset most cities. The problems were not unique to the Duluth-Superior area, only more prominent there because of the slow counteracting growth. Many other cases of prolonged nongrowth of cities have appeared in the historical geography of the northeastern United States and other areas around the North Atlantic. If the Twin Ports followed those precedents, they might feel an occasional resurgence. But their nongrowth experience was likely to be shared by many other cities in coming decades. The communities at the head of Lake Superior were indeed coping with obsolescence, but they were also running an urban laboratory experimenting with the future.[49]

Regional Metropolis

Minnesota's most dramatic transformation during the auto era came in the Twin Cities, which grew not only with the Upper Midwest agricultural and industrial economy but also as a node in the worldwide system of exchange among metropolitan markets. Between 1920 and 1980, the population of the urbanized area grew from 840,000 to more than 2 million. The regional metropolis absorbed half the net out-migration from the rest of the Upper Midwest and accounted for more than half the population and employment growth in the entire region. A new 800-square-mile outer city surrounded the pre-1920, 50-square-mile inner city.[50]

Although the 1920s building boom was the first in U.S. history to be affected by automobiles, most development followed the direction of earlier streetcar expansion by simply filling in excess subdivisions from earlier boom years. Other development, however, foreshadowed things to come. With the skyscrapers of the 1920s, the downtowns were building upward more than outward, but the building boom on the outskirts allowed older units to be abandoned faster. That abandonment showed up first in the oldest, most obsolete areas of the central city, producing a widening "gray zone" around the downtowns. Then the first large department stores outside the downtowns opened in connection with the Sears Roebuck and Montgomery Ward mail-order houses in south Minneapolis and St. Paul's Midway district – precursors of the suburban malls.[51] Auto-era forces of change had begun to appear, but they were slowed by the 1929 crash and the fifteen years of austerity that followed.

When a new boom erupted in 1946, almost every household owned an automobile. In the frenetic effort to build houses, grade streets, run the electric power and gas lines, and do the basic landscaping, local public agencies had money left only to build elementary schools as the baby-boom

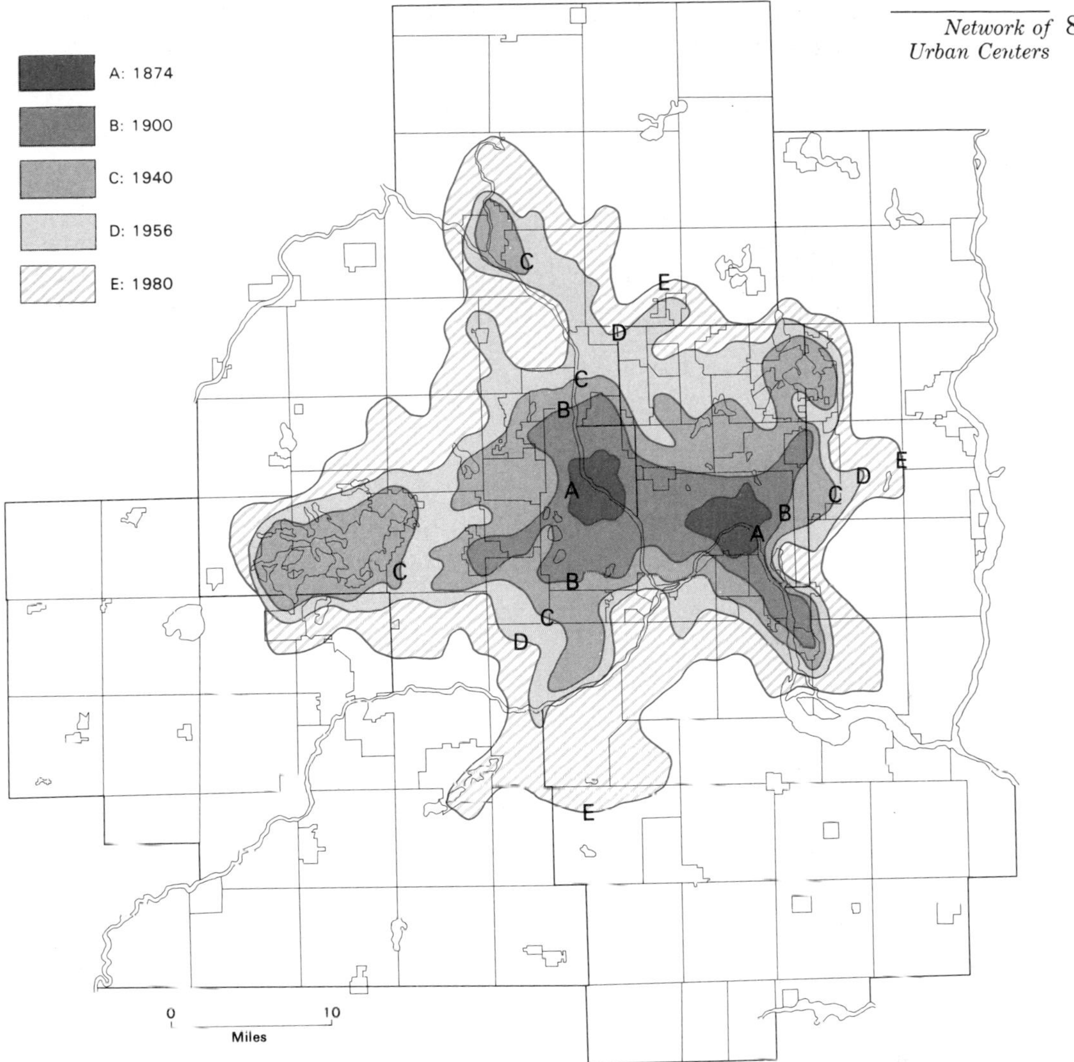

Successive positions of the frontier of urban development in the Twin Cities beginning in 1874 as superimposed on the familiar boundaries of the municipalities that comprise the metropolitan area in 1980. Sources: *See n. 41.*

youngsters approached age six. Most suburban business was transacted in places that were little more than enlarged crossroads centers inherited from the recent agricultural past. Growth ran far ahead of sewer and water extensions, and the few paved arterials were congested. By the time the baby boom ended about 1958, a sea of new single-family houses had pushed several miles beyond the edges of the 1920 streetcar city. Most of the people living in the fast-growing suburbs traveled on inadequate roads and city streets to the central cities for jobs, medical care, shopping, and entertainment. Highway needs, secondary-school construction, sewer problems, and downtown crowding begged for attention.[52]

But new forces emerged dominant in the 1960s. Although growth of the suburban ring continued, maturation was replacing boom. By 1960 the

Road construction in a housing development in Richfield in the 1950s

Twin Cities suburbs were home to nearly 500,000 Minnesotans who had emerged as a major market, labor force, and tax base with large and urgent demands. In the late 1950s, freeway construction was under way and plans for the full network were nearing completion. Extensive improvement of connecting highways and arterials accompanied the building of the freeways. As sections of the network were finished in the 1960s and 1970s, more and bigger office and medical centers, shopping malls, and industrial parks developed near the major interchanges. A girdle of freeways around the metropolitan area connected the new mass of job locations, homes, and shopping areas. The belt freeways also linked the new outer city with major radial highways that led inward to the downtowns and outward to the rest of the state and region. The two downtown centers had become a part of a constellation having multiple foci for the metropolitan area and the regional economy.[53]

Highway and business improvements were soon accompanied by long-awaited suburban community improvements. Municipalities began to build new sewer and water systems. School districts consolidated and built large, new high schools for the now-adolescent baby boom. Church congregations left their temporary quarters in quonset huts, schools, and taverns and moved into new buildings. Wold-Chamberlain Field became the Minneapolis–St. Paul International Airport as the Metropolitan Airports Commission made its first round of large-scale additions. Sagging, frame, nineteenth-century town halls were replaced by municipal civic centers, libraries, and fire stations. And city, county, and regional parks, an outer ring of golf courses, state junior colleges, and a state zoological garden filled remaining gaps in the development matrix.

Management problems became increasingly apparent during the time of frenetic expansion and also of major public construction. These public improvements were the responsibility of scores of different municipalities, state agencies, and special districts that constituted the metropolitan area. The different levels of government were using local, state, and federal revenue in what was supposed to be an effort to build a coherent skeleton for the outer city. As a result of the need for coordination, the legislature created the Metropolitan Planning Commission in 1957 and converted it to the stronger Metropolitan Council in 1967.[54]

The housing market also matured. In the fifteen years that began in 1955, single-family units dropped from nearly 100 percent of new housing construction to about 66 percent. Apartments and, later in the 1970s, condominiums made up the other 34 percent. Compared with the earlier boom years, a larger number of new housing units were in excess of the number needed to accommodate new growth, and this surplus could be used to replace old units. Dwellings at the bottom of the housing chain were abandoned at a record rate as people all the way down the chain moved into new quarters. Most of the new housing was built in the outer city, and housing in the inner city was rapidly abandoned. Contemporaries viewed this abandonment as a problem, but it was probably a symptom of an unprecedented, if inadvertent, effort to improve the physical condition of the cities.[55]

St. Louis Park's Miracle Mile Shopping Center, 1953

Residential expansion of the suburbs finally slowed in the 1970s. But it revived considerably in the 1980s when part of the baby-boom generation appeared on the scene yet again, this time as affluent, early-middle-age families moving up from starter houses in the older districts to new homes on the outer suburban frontier – space-age "Victorian" and "farmhouse" styles with a contrived, standardized eclecticism that seemed certain to become as distinctive of this episode as the rambler was of the 1950s. In contrast to the postwar boom of the 1950s, the new subdivisions were almost all built with sewers and paved streets; they tended to fill in the open areas between older bits and pieces of sprawl and to increase the overall density of the metropolis.[56]

By the mid-1980s there was indeed a new outer metropolis. Built to accommodate more than 1.7 million people and their automobiles, it included all of the suburbs plus the post-1920 outer edges of the central cities. It spread across rolling land, around hundreds of lakes and ponds, through tens of thousands of acres of woodlands. It had abundant parks and playgrounds. On its inner margin were the major parks that had been developed nearly a century earlier on the urban periphery at the end of the pioneer boom period of Minneapolis and St. Paul. On the outer margin, the new city graded into new regional parks and preserves and into farmland that was the target of a metropolitan preservation program. The outer city, which was held together by several hundred miles of metropolitan freeways and a highly developed grid of arterials, focused on perhaps ten major regional shopping and office centers and a vastly upgraded metropolitan airport. Fifty-two percent of metropolitan sales were in garish suburban commercial strips that had been farmland in 1920, and shopping malls had captured 12 percent of retail sales. The outer city contained more than half of the office space built since 1967 and well over half of the more than 1.2 million jobs in the metropolitan area. Although the older downtowns were headquarters for most of the largest business firms, the belt freeway ring was the home to the greatest number and to the youngest, fastest-growing ones.[57]

In the center of this auto-era ring, entirely within the limits of Minneapolis and St. Paul, lay the inner city – a legacy from the rail and streetcar era. The two downtowns were twin cores of the inner city, and they had been the scene of fitful and partial replacement of old buildings almost from the beginning. Yet, by 1955 all redevelopments accounted for less than one-tenth of the inner city area. In the other nine-tenths, obsolescence and abandonment led to a spreading blight of low income and low investment; and these areas housed most of the cities' large share of Minnesota's racial minorities.

Because of the great accumulation and declining value of their structures, the inner cities suffered from higher taxes, lower accessibility, and higher land preparation costs for new development than locations in the suburbs. Yet for those who believed that the Twin Cities metropolis was here to stay, it was clear that this relatively small area in the middle of it merited recycling.

Strong counterforces began to converge on inner-city problems in the late 1950s. The combined effects of these forces – whose origins were impressive – were partly related, partly coincidental. With 90 percent federal financing, the interstate freeways finally penetrated the inner city in the 1970s. Coupled with other federal aid opportunities, the freeways triggered comprehensive plans for redevelopment. Leading the effort were city government, large corporations with local control and inner-city headquarters, medical centers, and neighborhood associations. Major developers and financial backing were attracted from other centers of investment capital in the United States and abroad. The cities borrowed heavily to buy land, clear it, prepare it for new development, and make the accompanying public improvements. Private organizations, in turn, committed themselves heavily to new construction. And the neighborhoods worked in the political arena to keep a share of the subsidies directed toward family housing and improvements in older residential areas.[58]

When people in the baby-boom generation first entered the housing market in the 1970s, unprecedented inflation had produced high building costs and high interest rates. Because many of them could not do as their parents had done – go to the outer fringe and build a new house – they turned inward. With private financing and limited public subsidies, and encouraged by widespread city improvements, they bought into the vast stock of older housing in the transition zone between the inner and outer cities and set out to improve it. Although most were average young families renovating average old houses, some higher-income young families renovated fine old mansions and "gentrified" once-prestigious neighborhoods – notably St. Paul's Summit Hill and Minneapolis's Kenwood and southwest lake district.[59]

A historic preservation movement also converged on the inner city in the decade of the 1970s. In the 1880s and 1890s, the monumental buildings erected in the Twin Cities reflected the rise of the Northwest Empire after completion of the northern transcontinental railroads. Eight to ten decades later, the cities faced for the first time the prospect of abandoning and destroying architectural landmarks that commemorated important people and institutions in Upper Midwest history. Since the oldest, most durable, and best located of these buildings were in or near the downtowns, the major targets of that first round of historic preservation were in the inner city.[60]

Thanks to these converging forces of downtown redevelopment, residential rehabilitation, and historic preservation, the inner city in the early 1980s was probably in the best physical condition in its history. Much of the outer city was still being built, and even the older parts of it had not yet begun to show serious or widespread deterioration.

Yet the future seemed uncertain. To anyone who looked around and reflected, it was obvious that the aging that perplexed the inner city of the rail and streetcar era would inevitably spread to the outer city of the auto era. The impressive cost of building the outer city would be transformed into the even more impressive cost of maintaining and replacing it. But the stream of federal subsidies had greatly diminished, and its future seemed in doubt. Competition for public revenues at all levels was as severe as ever, as was reluctance to raise taxes. The traditional middle-income class upon which the entire character of the auto-era city so heavily depended seemed to be narrowing as America became more like the rest of the world, in a more global economy.[61]

Although local municipalities were likely to continue to take the initiative in the recycling effort, as they had in the older central cities, it was not clear where the money would come from. Roland F. Hatfield, the state's politically conservative tax commissioner, had observed in 1965 that a combination of public demand for more services, increased urbanization, inflation, and higher costs of maintenance and replacement would require more public revenue. Predicting that income from automatic tax increases would lag behind increased demands, he forecast the need for further tax increases and improvements in the tax structure.[62] Twenty years later, his words seemed more relevant than ever.

Even the future of the traditional rivalry between St. Paul and Minneapolis had become cloudy. The special interests that underpinned the rivalry in the early years – downtown merchants, newspapers, and city officials – were operating in a drastically changed environment. In the auto-era transformation of the metropolis, the two downtowns no longer dominated in their share of either office or retailing functions, although downtown Minneapolis was still the largest concentration of office towers and the paramount skyline symbol of the metropolis, and St. Paul was still the state capital. The major newspapers played a narrower and somewhat uncertain role within the burgeoning mass of print and electronic communications. Many of their advertisers were business firms that transcended the metropolitan area and in many cases were present only in Minneapolis or in neither of the two historic downtowns. The newspapers were competing in a market that rarely divided along Minneapolis–St. Paul lines, a reality that was confirmed when the Minneapolis paper dropped that city from its name in 1987 in favor of an identification with the entire Twin Cities.[63] Thus two of the three traditional special interests had lost much of their relevance as participants in the rivalry.

Only the two central-city governments persisted with seemingly as much parochial power as ever. Yet that ecology had changed, too: Bloomington, with the historical accidents of its large expanse and encompassing of the major corridor of belt freeway development, had emerged as Minnesota's third-largest city. Its boosters sometimes threatened to turn the historic twins' rivalry into a three-city affair. But that effort, too, was hopelessly complicated by the diversity of interest among other large suburban municipalities – such as Eagan, Edina, Plymouth, or Eden Prairie – positioned elsewhere on the belt freeways. As the old dual rivalry began to look at times more like a struggle against anarchy, new players emerged in the form of entities whose territories covered multiple municipalities. They included the state agencies for transportation, education, and conservation; special districts for waste control, airports, and parks; the county governments – especially large and populous Hennepin; and the Metropolitan Council. Nevertheless, a vast lore and the weight of

Construction site for the new Minneapolis Convention Center, 1988

current practice assured the persistence of "Minneapolis-St. Paul" as the common name for the urban mass that many people in the rest of Minnesota and western Wisconsin had long accurately, often affectionately, simply called "the Cities."

Urbanization of the Countryside

If organizing the cities was difficult, that problem stemmed partly from their being so hard to define. By the 1970s, the populations of the state's major cities were, in many ways, not at all confined to their contiguous, built-up areas or even to their metropolitan areas as defined by the U.S. census. A sprawling urban network covered much of the state in a triangular pattern with corners at Lake Superior northeast of Duluth, at Fargo-Moorhead, and at La Crosse, Wisconsin.

The sprawl was partly the result of dispersal and new development of industries and business services. Outside the Minneapolis–St. Paul metropolis, in the cities and towns along the region's highway network, hundreds of firms took advantage of an exceptional combination of location features. The sites had relatively easy access to the Twin Cities not only for markets and supplies but also for shopping, arts and entertainment, administrative offices, and the airport. They were within easy reach of the attractive residential environments of the lake districts. And they adjoined the state's main farming region, with its markets for agricultural supplies and equipment and its sources of agricultural raw materials.[64]

Some of the firms, and the homes of many of the people who worked in them, were located in the surrounding countryside rather than in developed urban areas. Employees commuted to new houses, old farmhouses, and mobile homes that were scattered along lakeshores, among woodlots and forests, on hilltops and the edges of cornfields. The commuter sheds of neighboring cities and towns overlapped one another on the map. Commutation from the belt freeway ring of the Twin Cities reached out forty to sixty miles, and from the smaller metropolitan areas it extended as far as twenty-five to thirty-five miles.[65]

Beyond the commuting range, the houses of urbanites had traditionally been second homes for summer vacationing at the lake. But after World War II, skiing and snowmobiling changed those places to year-round recreational colonies. As years passed, a swelling stream of vacation homeowners moved there permanently when they retired. Other people with footloose occupations such as sales, consulting, writing, or the arts also shifted their residences from the city to the country.[66] A schoolbook salesman, puttering in his boathouse north of Brainerd, once commented to me: "I can cover my territory in western Minnesota and North Dakota from here just as well as from Edina – and I'm where I want to be." (He did not mention the sewage disposal problem, which would eventually require a large outlay on his part and a subsidy from the rest of the country, as well.)

The growing number of business services and industries, along with the growing population of the lake districts, generated need for trade and services at the county seats and crossroads. Still more people settled in the countryside to provide services to the swelling stream of truck and auto traffic in the main highway corridors in the network – especially those extending from the Twin Cities to Fargo and to Duluth and the Mesabi Range.

By the 1970s, the outcome was a map of nonfarm population growth virtually heedless of municipal boundaries. Focused on the Twin Cities, the sprawling urban system not only covered most of the northeastern half of Minnesota but spread across much of neighboring western Wisconsin and two counties of eastern North Dakota. Outside the Twin Cities seven-county metropolitan area, the region's total population growth in the 1970s was 233,000. Sixty-two percent of the increase occurred outside any incorporated municipality, in rural townships or unorganized county territory. In the Minnesota counties alone, those rural township governments accommodated nearly nine-tenths as much nonfarm (that is, urban) population growth as the seven-county Twin Cities area did between 1970 and 1980, and more than the combined growth in all of the incorporated cities of the state outside the Twin Cities area.[67] With the completion of the interstate freeway system and slower population growth in the 1980s, the dispersal was slower. But by that time the new pattern was firmly established.

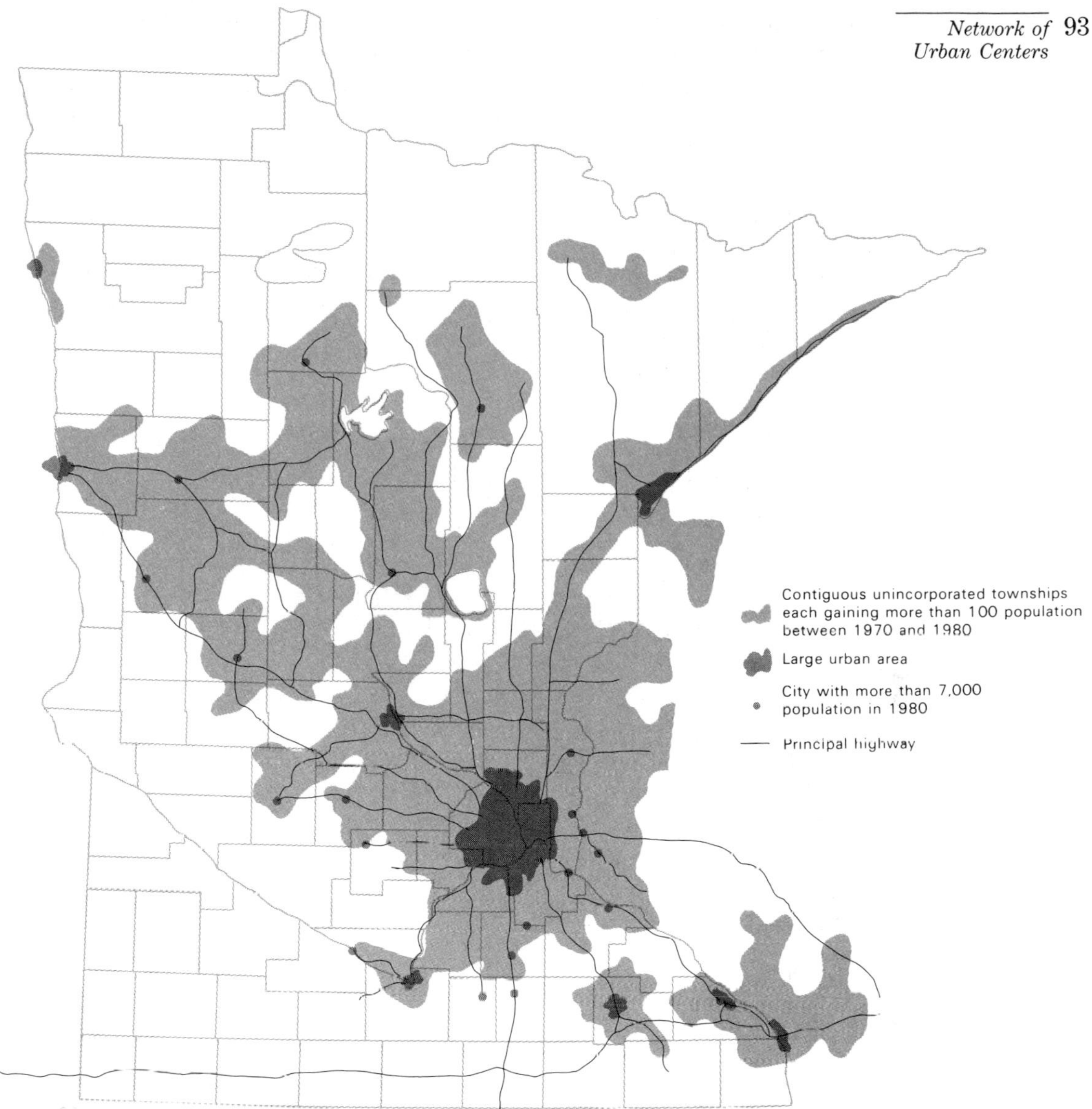

Regions in which the population of each rural township gained at least one hundred people between 1970 and 1980. Source: *Data are taken from census reports as described in n. 67.*

The "spread city" was tributary to a system of major highways. One part of the system was a set of branching radial routes reaching out from Minneapolis-St. Paul to Willmar, St. Cloud, and Fargo-Moorhead; to the lake districts; to Duluth-Superior and the North Shore; to Mankato, Rochester, Winona, and La Crosse; and to the coulee country of western Wisconsin. Besides the radials, there were "crosstowns": for example, La Crosse and Winona to Rochester; Little Falls through St. Cloud to Willmar; Walker to Detroit Lakes and Fargo-Moorhead.

The terms *radial* and *crosstown* surely recall the patterns of city streetcar lines in the bygone days of the early 1900s. Yet they also describe the circulation pattern of the large-scale regional urban system that evolved in less than a century from those much smaller, more identifiable, and more isolated cities. But leaders in the sprawling urban system of the 1980s continued to face questions about management and development that their predecessors discussed in the forums of the League of Municipalities twenty-five and even seventy years ago – public improvements, maintenance, rebuilding, finance. The principles have been remarkably persistent, while the scale and complexity have changed almost beyond recognition.

NOTES

1. Richard S. Prosser, *Rails to the North Star* (Minneapolis: Dillon Press, 1966), 55-56; John R. Borchert and Donald P. Yaeger, *Atlas of Minnesota Resources and Settlement* (St. Paul: Department of Geography, University of Minnesota, 1968), 35.

2. John R. Borchert and Neil C. Gustafson, *Atlas of Minnesota Resources and Settlement* (Minneapolis: Center for Urban and Regional Affairs, University of Minnesota, 1980), 172.

3. John R. Borchert and Russell B. Adams, *Trade Centers and Trade Areas of the Upper Midwest* (Minneapolis: Upper Midwest Economic Study, 1963).

4. Refer to the table for a summary of population changes in the state's urban centers since 1900. United States, *Census*, 1920, *State Compendium: Minnesota*, 11-12, 15, 24; 1920, *Population*, vol. 1, p. 548-50; 1930, *Population*, vol. 3, part 2, p. 437, 440; 1950, *Population*, vol. 1, p. 49-9; 1950, *Population*, vol. 2, part 23, p. 11, 14-15, 21, 25; 1960, *Population*, vol. 1, part 36, p. 11, 14-15; 1970, *Population*, PC(1)-B36, p. 35; 1980, *Population*, vol. 1, chap. A, part 25, p. 8, 11, 40; 1980, *Population*, vol. 1, chap. B, part 36, p. 7-8; 1984, *Current Population Reports*, Series P-26, West North Central, p. 43-74, 109, 112, East North Central, p. 114. The table shows the population of central cities and associated counties for urban centers regarded by the U.S. Census Bureau as standard metropolitan statistical areas, or the equivalent areas for Mankato and Winona; areas included do not coincide with the Census Bureau's definition in all cases. In 1900, population outside the central cities lived mainly on farms or in rural farm trade centers. The beginning of suburban growth around a central city is indicated by a distinct upturn in population in the outlying county areas. Around the Twin Cities, suburbanization was already under way in the first decade of the century, and the suburbs passed the central cities in population during the 1950s. Suburbanization began dramatically in the Rochester area in the 1950s and around St. Cloud in the 1960s. The same process began outside Duluth-Superior in the early 1900s, Mankato in the 1950s, and Winona in the 1960s, but it proceeded slowly in all three places. Suburban spillover has never been significant in the Red River valley, except for the surge that accompanied the growth of the Grand Forks Air Base in the 1960s.

5. Borchert and Adams, *Trade Centers*, 23-26; Mildred L. Hartsough, *The Twin Cities as a Metropolitan Market* (Minneapolis: University of Minnesota Studies in the Social Sciences), 83-88, 112, 174; here and below, John R. Borchert, *America's Northern Heartland* (Minneapolis: University of Minnesota Press, 1987), 42-44, 61-67. Some of the passages on Duluth-Superior and the Twin Cities in this essay are drawn from the text of *America's Northern Heartland*, chaps. 3, 6, 7.

6. Here and below, Prosser, *Rails to the North Star*, 12, 17-18, 27-28.

7. James Hellie, *Mankato at the Bend of the River* (Master's thesis, University of Minnesota, 1945), 50-53.

8. Gertrude Gove, "Micropolis in Transition: An Episodic Sketch, 1853-1940," in *Micropolis in Transition*, ed. Edward L. Henry (Collegeville: St. John's University Center for the Study of Local Government, 1971), 156-65; John J. Dominik, Jr., *Three Towns into One City: St. Cloud, Minnesota* (St. Cloud Area Bicentennial Commission, n.d.), 28-31.

9. Russell L. Olson, *The Electric Railways of Minnesota* (Hopkins: Minnesota Transportation Museum, 1976); United States, *Census*, 1870, *Compendium*, 234, 366; 1900, *Population*, vol. 1, part 1, p. 215-30; 1920, *Abstract*, 58-59; 1980, vol. 1, chap. B, part 25, p. 7. For information on the state's smaller communities, see Thomas Harvey, "Small-Town Minnesota," *this volume*, esp. 103-9.

10. Alan Ominsky, "A Catalog of Minnesota-Made Cars and Trucks," *Minnesota History* 43 (Fall 1972): 101–4; Arthur J. Larsen, *The Development of the Minnesota Road System* (St. Paul: Minnesota Historical Society, 1966), 462.

11. U.S., *Census*, 1870, *Compendium*, 60, 229–35; 1920, *State Compendium: Minnesota*, 8; *Minnesota Municipalities* 1, no. 1 (February 1916), and no. 3 (June 1916).

12. Olson, *Electric Railways of Minnesota*, 7–8.

13. Gove, "Micropolis in Transition," 167, and *A History of St. Cloud, Minnesota: 1853–1970* (N.p., 1970), 30, available at Minnesota Historical Society (MHS).

14. *Insurance Maps of Fargo, North Dakota* (New York: Sanborn Map Co., 1922); *Insurance Maps of Moorhead, Minnesota* (New York: Sanborn-Perris Map Co., 1899, and Sanborn Map Co., 1922); Hiram M. Drache, *The Day of the Bonanza* (Fargo: North Dakota Institute for Regional Studies, 1964), 24, 25–30; *Insurance Maps of Winona, Minnesota* (New York: Sanborn-Perris Map Co., 1894, and Sanborn Map Co., 1917).

15. *Insurance Maps of Fargo, North Dakota* (New York: Sanborn Map Co., 1922); U.S., *Census*, 1930, *Distribution*, vol. 2, esp. p. 792, 1117.

16. Here and below, *Insurance Maps of Winona, Minnesota* (New York: Sanborn-Perris Map Co., 1894, and Sanborn Map Co., 1917); Work Projects Administration, *Wisconsin: A Guide to the Badger State* (New York: Duell, Sloan and Pearce, 1941), 67, 73.

17. *Insurance Maps of St. Cloud, Minnesota* (New York: Sanborn-Perris Map Co., 1898, and Sanborn Map Co., 1904, 1919).

18. *Insurance Maps of East Grand Forks, Minnesota* (New York: Sanborn Map Co., 1904, 1909, 1926); Borchert and Yaeger, *1968 Minnesota Atlas*, 7, 11.

19. *Insurance Maps of Mankato, Minnesota* (New York: Sanborn-Perris Map Co., 1900, and Sanborn Map Co., 1907, 1924).

20. Beulah Buswell, *Watkins United Methodist Home* (Winona: The Home, n.d.), 3–6.

21. Patrick H. Ahern, *Catholic Heritage in Minnesota – North Dakota – South Dakota* (St. Paul: Archdiocese of St. Paul, 1964), 43, 78–99.

22. U.S., *Census*, 1920, *State Compendium: Minnesota*, 31–33; *Insurance Maps of Rochester, Minnesota* (New York: Sanborn-Perris Map Co., 1899, and Sanborn Map Co., 1921).

23. Dora Mary Macdonald, *This Is Duluth* (Duluth: N.p., 1950), 65; Works Progress Administration (WPA), *The WPA Guide to Minnesota* (New York: Viking Press, 1938; St. Paul: Minnesota Historical Society Press, 1985), 236; *Insurance Maps of Duluth, Minnesota* (New York: Sanborn Map Co., 1908).

24. John R. Borchert, *A Look at Minnesota Industry* (St. Paul: Minnesota Education Association, [1954]), 2–24, pamphlet available at MHS; WPA, *Guide to Minnesota*, 241–42.

25. U.S., *Census*, 1930, *Population*, vol. 3, part 1, p. 1203.

26. Olson, *Electric Railways of Minnesota*, 319.

27. U.S., *Census*, 1920, *State Compendium: Minnesota*, 8; Hartsough, *Twin Cities as Metropolitan Market;* Borchert, *America's Northern Heartland*, 51–53, 61.

28. Richard Hartshorne, "The Twin City District: A Unique Form of Urban Landscape," *Geographical Review* 22 (1932): 431–42, esp. 440; Calvin F. Schmid, *Social Saga of Two Cities* (Minneapolis: Minneapolis Council of Social Agencies, 1937), 12–16.

29. U.S., *Census*, 1920, *State Compendium: Minnesota*, 8; 1980, vol. 1, chap. B, part 25, p. 10–11; John R. Borchert, "The Twin Cities Urbanized Area: Past, Present, Future," *Geographical Review* 51 (1961): 47–70, esp. 62–64; Lucile M. Kane and Alan Ominsky, *Twin Cities: A Pictorial History of Saint Paul and Minneapolis* (St. Paul: Minnesota Historical Society Press, 1983), 10.

30. Hartshorne, "The Twin City District," 432–33; Kane and Ominsky, *Twin Cities*, 81.

31. Here and below, Borchert, *America's Northern Heartland*, 61, 66.

32. Olson, *Electric Railways of Minnesota*, 19–22.

33. Here and below, Ronald Abler, John S. Adams, and John R. Borchert, *The Twin Cities of St. Paul and Minneapolis* (Cambridge, Mass.: Ballinger Publishing Co., 1976), 21–28, 33.

34. Borchert and Yaeger, *1968 Minnesota Atlas*, 202-6.

35. Olson, *Electric Railways of Minnesota*, 135; Prosser, *Rails to the North Star*, 104.

36. John S. Adams, "Residential Structure of Midwestern Cities," *Annals of the Association of American Geographers* 60 (1970): 37–62, esp. 50–51.

37. Chauncy D. Harris, "Agricultural Production in the United States: The Last Fifty Years and the Next," *Geographical Review* 47 (1957): 175–93; here and below, Borchert, *America's Northern Heartland*, 103–9, 175–79.

38. Borchert and Adams, *Trade Centers*, 21–22; Joan Finch, *Upper Midwest Retail Trade Centers* (Minneapolis: Upper Midwest Council, 1982), 26, and *Shopping Centers and Medium Sized Cities: The Upper Midwest Experience* (Minneapolis: Upper Midwest Council, 1982); Neil C. Gustafson et al., *Recent Trends/Future Prospects: A Look at Upper Midwest Population Changes* (Minneapolis: Upper Midwest Council, 1973), 4, 8–9, 26–44.

39. John R. Borchert and Frank E. Horton, "Geography and Urban Public Policy," in *Geographical Perspectives and Urban Problems*, ed. Frank E. Horton (Washington, D.C.: Na-

tional Academy of Sciences, 1973), 1-24, esp. fig. 11; Borchert and Gustafson, *1980 Minnesota Atlas*, 148.

40. John R. Borchert et al., *Perspective on Minnesota Land Use – 1974* (Minneapolis: Center for Urban and Regional Affairs, University of Minnesota, and Minnesota State Planning Agency, 1974), 40-43; U.S., *Census*, 1920, *State Compendium: Minnesota*, 8; 1970, *Number of Inhabitants: Minnesota*, 44.

41. John R. Borchert, *The Urbanization of the Upper Midwest: 1930-1960* (Minneapolis: Upper Midwest Economic Study, 1963), 19; Borchert, *America's Northern Heartland*, 150-52; U.S., *Census*, 1980, vol. 1, chap. B, part 25, p. 7. The maps of the Fargo-Moorhead and Duluth-Superior urban centers are based on those appearing in Borchert's *America's Northern Heartland*, 142, 150.

42. Here and below, John R. Borchert, Earl E. Stewart, and Sherman S. Hasbrouck, *Urban Renewal: Needs and Opportunities in the Upper Midwest* (Minneapolis: Upper Midwest Study, 1963), 1-4, 10-25.

43. "Survey: Municipal Planning Agencies in Minnesota," *Minnesota Municipalities* 50 (May 1965): 138.

44. Finch, *Shopping Centers*, 16-34.

45. Michael E. Gleeson, "Estimating Housing Mortality," *Journal of the American Planning Association* 47 (1981): 190-91.

46. John R. Borchert, Thomas L. Anding, Donald V. Klein, Ellis Waldron, and C. Lee Gilbert, *The Why and How of Community Planning: Comparative Studies of Problems and Actions in Fourteen Upper Midwest Cities* (Minneapolis: Upper Midwest Economic Study, 1963), 12.

47. Here and below, Borchert, *America's Northern Heartland*, 151-52.

48. Virginia Hyvarinen and Jeanette Smith, "Education, Hospitals and the Duluth Public Library," in *Duluth: Sketches of the Past*, ed. Ryck Lydecker and Lawrence J. Sommer (Duluth: American Revolution Bicentennial Commission, 1976), 267.

49. Borchert, *America's Northern Heartland*, 152.

50. U.S., *Census*, vol. 1, chap. B, part 25, p. 7; Borchert, *America's Northern Heartland*, 161-63

51. Kane and Ominsky, *Twin Cities*, 180, 188, 214-15.

52. Abler, Adams, and Borchert, *Twin Cities of St. Paul and Minneapolis*, 51-57; Borchert, "Twin Cities Urbanized Area," 68-69; Twin Cities Metropolitan Planning Commission, *Metropolitan Land Study* (St. Paul: The Commission, 1960).

53. U.S., *Census*, 1960, vol. 1, part 25, p. 32; Twin Cities Metropolitan Council, *Industrial Expansion and Migration in the Twin Cities Metropolitan Area: 1960-1970* (St. Paul: The Council, 1973), 19; Marlin Gilhousen, *Industrial Parks in the Twin Cities Metropolitan Area, 1960-1983* (St. Paul: Twin Cities Metropolitan Council, 1984), and *Shopping Centers and Retail Centers in the Twin Cities Metropolitan Area* (St. Paul: Twin Cities Metropolitan Council, 1985); Twin Cities Metropolitan Council, *Regional Land Use Trends: 1970-1980* (St. Paul: The Council, 1982), 1-3.

54. Arthur Naftalin, *Making One Community out of Many* (St. Paul: Twin Cities Metropolitan Council, 1986); Ed Knudson, *Regional Politics in the Twin Cities: A Report on the Politics and Planning of Urban Growth Policy* (St. Paul: Twin Cities Metropolitan Council, 1976), 1-3.

55. John R. Borchert, David Gebhard, David Lanegran, and Judith A. Martin, *Legacy of Minneapolis: Preservation amid Change* (Minneapolis: Voyageur Press, 1983), 165-81.

56. Twin Cities Metropolitan Council, *Information Bulletins* (Residential Building Permits Issued, 1984, 1985, January-June 1986; St. Paul: The Council, 1985, 1986).

57. Twin Cities Metropolitan Council, *1983-1985 Employment Estimates* (St. Paul: The Council, 1986); "The 1985 Twin Cities Office Space Census," *Corporate Report Minnesota*, April 1985, p. 81-160; analysis of headquarters locations and assets of corporations listed in *Corporate Report Fact Book 1983 Edition* (Minneapolis: Dorn Communications, 1982).

58. Abler, Adams, and Borchert, *Twin Cities of St. Paul and Minneapolis*, 43-49.

59. Judith A. Martin and David A. Lanegran, *Where We Live: The Residential Districts of Minneapolis and St. Paul* (Minneapolis: University of Minnesota Press, 1983), esp. 5-6.

60. Borchert et al., *Legacy of Minneapolis*, 181-82; Lucile M. Kane, *The Falls of St. Anthony: The Waterfall That Built Minneapolis* (St. Paul: Minnesota Historical Society Press, 1966, 1987), 181-95.

61. Twin Cities Metropolitan Council, *Regional Fiscal Profile* (St. Paul: The Council, 1979), and *Regional Service and Finance Study* (St. Paul: The Council, 1984).

62. Roland F. Hatfield, "The Fiscal Climate in Minnesota," *Minnesota Municipalities* 50 (February 1965): 40-42, 60.

63. *Minneapolis Star Tribune*, Aug. 31, 1987, p. 1A.

64. Borchert and Gustafson, *1980 Minnesota Atlas*, 109-55.

65. Gustafson et al., *Recent Trends/Future Prospects*, 45-47; Neil C. Gustafson and Mark E. Cohan, *Population Mobility in the Upper Midwest: Trends, Prospects and Policies* (Minneapolis: Upper Midwest Council, 1974), 21–25; John R. Borchert, Thomas L. Anding, and Morris Gildemeister, *Urban Dispersal in the Upper Midwest* (Minneapolis: Upper Midwest Economic Study, 1964), 1–3; John Fraser Hart, "Population Change in the Upper Lake States," *Annals of the Association of American Geographers* 74 (1984): 228–42.

66. John R. Borchert, George W. Orning, Joseph Stinchfield, and Les Maki, *Minnesota's Lakeshore: Resources, Development, Policy Needs* (Minneapolis: Center for Urban and Regional Affairs, University of Minnesota, 1970), 20, 33–38; Philippe Cohen and Joseph Stinchfield, *Shoreland Development Trends* (St. Paul: Minnesota Department of Natural Resources, 1984).

67. U.S., *Census*, 1984, *Current Population Reports*, Series P-26, West North Central; 1980, vol. 1, chap. A, part 25.

Plate commemorating the centennial of the town of Perham, Otter Tail County, 1971

THOMAS HARVEY

Small-Town Minnesota

KSTP-TV may think Madelia is dying, BUT WE DON'T!!" The quarter-page advertisement in the *Madelia Times-Messenger* of April 30, 1986, expressed optimism about a small town closely identified with the agricultural crisis of the 1980s. Townspeople were understandably upset. Madelia, in Watonwan County in southern Minnesota, had experienced more than its share of bad press following a Region Nine Development Commission report on the town undertaken for U.S. Sen. David F. Durenberger. The senator's staff had asked three of Minnesota's regional development commissions to gather information on typical towns for hearings on the farm crisis. The *Minneapolis Star and Tribune* reported the study under the headline "Depressed Madelia Consents to Undergo In-depth Examination." KSTP portrayed the town in an April 21 documentary called "Foreclosing on a Dream."[1]

Madelia responded with a local editorial that called the survey a "carnival," accused the television producers of maligning the "little city," and went on to list the many positive aspects of the town. Several months later, the Minneapolis newspaper published a commentary entitled "Amid the Gloom a Small Town Finds a Reason to Hope," written by a Madelia native living in the Twin Cities. A town resident had told him that "as rational people think about a more perfect society in the future, they will ultimately 'reinvent what we already have in our small communities' " – places that have "willing people, innovative public-private cooperation, a solid work ethic and rich life style."[2]

Outsiders may not have shared the rosy view of some residents about the town's present and future, but it was hard not to share the town's sense of disappointment following the television documentary. The people had trusted the station to present a balanced view. Instead it had depicted a town in rapid decline, the fate, it implied, of many of Minnesota's agriculturally based towns. In fact, Madelia's main street was more prosperous in the mid-1980s than the business districts of many towns in the state. Although population had declined from 2,316 in 1970 to 2,096 in 1985, changes in numbers had not been significantly different over the century from those in towns of similar size. On the other hand, despite some increases in industrial employment in the community, farm-related businesses had declined precipitously and retail sales were down. Of the seven implement dealers in Madelia in the late 1960s, none was in business in 1985, and both of the town's hardware dealers reported that they could not sell out if they wanted to.[3]

Madelia in 1986 presented themes common in small-town history. The impact of the agricultural crisis of the 1980s was serious, but no more so than other crises that towns had faced. The presumed demise of small towns had been a recurring theme since before the turn of the century, yet hundreds of Minnesota towns showed every sign of continued survival. Nostalgia for small towns was another recurring theme. Every decade or so writers produced a spate of books and articles praising the "good life" in small communities, counterbalancing the view, also widely held, that these places were culturally deprived and socially regressive. The myths and images of small-town life fluctuated, but a basic interest in that life seldom waned.[4]

Images and Expectations

Minnesota towns have played a substantial part in establishing and maintaining America's image of the small town. Edward Eggleston's 1873 novel *The Mystery of Metropolisville,* set in the townsite speculation era of the 1850s, was based on life in Cannon City. One of the books in the *Little House on the Prairie* series by Laura Ingalls Wilder was set in the area around Walnut Grove in the 1870s. It was in 1920, however, that Minnesota towns achieved national prominence – even notoriety – with the publication of Sinclair Lewis's *Main Street.* The novel's Gopher Prairie became the epitome of small-town life. Lewis attacked almost everything about small prairie towns, but his real focus was the social conformity and lack of culture. He had grown up in Sauk Centre, in western Stearns County, and he wrote the novel after a visit to the town in 1916 when he was thirty-one years old. His depiction of Gopher Prairie/Sauk Centre was decidedly narrow, yet it grew to be highly influential in shaping American thinking about small towns.[5]

The novel brought immediate acclaim, was voted a Pulitzer Prize in 1921 (though the jury was overruled by the trustees of Columbia University on the grounds that the novel failed to present a positive view of American life), was read by two million readers in just two years, and was made into a movie in 1923. Its message no doubt rang true to many people. The book also provoked strong reactions. Following its success, Charles P. Hall wrote "Sane Street," a maudlin pamphlet extolling the virtues of small-town Red Wing. *Main Street* also inspired reflective essays over the years as journalists traveled to Sauk Centre to take the pulse of the small-town Midwest.[6]

Main Street in Sauk Centre as it appeared in 1957, thirty-seven years after publication of Sinclair Lewis's book of the same name

About the time Lewis was writing his novel, sociologists conducted extensive social surveys of towns much like Sauk Centre. In the early 1920s, the Institute of Social and Religious Research in New York undertook a study of 140 American villages with populations between 250 and 2,500, including the Minnesota towns of Blackduck, Elk River, Wells, and Windom. Another institute publication, *Village Communities*, included Litchfield (disguised as "Lincoln") as one of eight national case studies. Within the state, University of Minnesota economists studied Ada, in the Red River valley, and Braham, in northeastern Minnesota.[7]

Not until the 1980s, however, did Minnesota again provide the focus of the nation's small-town mythology with Garrison Keillor's Lake Wobegon. It was perhaps appropriate that stories of Lake Wobegon, located in a township supposedly lost from the government's land survey, would be brought to life by a native of a town-qua-suburb (Anoka) of the Twin Cities. (According to Minnesota writer Paul Gruchow, "Urban people have tended to make up myths in which small towns are wonderful and in which people are charming and basically good and decent at heart; and small town writers have tended to be in the Sinclair Lewis vein." Keillor, Gruchow noted, was "basically an urban writer with an urban view of small towns.")[8]

Sociologist Edmund deS. Brunner commented in 1927 that "Main Street has an importance beyond its size. To the city, it is the representative of rural America; to the farmer, it is the interpreter of the city. Both need it; neither fully understands it."[9] The relative importance of Minnesota towns has declined since that time, and massive improvements in transportation and communications have greatly diminished the cultural gaps between town and city. But the significance of small towns has remained strong because they promise to provide a sense of community – balanced between the isolation of the farm or hamlet and the frenzy of the big city – that many people want. In a society that values growth and competition above all else, small towns succeed as model communities by failing to become cities.

Formal town founding was a vital part of the state's early history, the urban side of the story of frontier expansion. Few towns "just happened"; rather, they were deliberate attempts to market real estate. An entrepreneur's action in establishing a town reflected the desire to attract settlers and businesses and to capture local rural trade. The sentimental view of small towns in the twentieth century has obscured the fact that dozens of places were originally envisioned as "New Chicagos." With rare exceptions, the founders of towns intended to plant the seeds of cities in rural areas. This intention was reflected in such town names as Minnesota City (founded in Winona County in 1852; 1980 population of 265) as well as Minneapolis; in the expansive original plats of towns (Kasota, in Le Sueur County, had more than sixty blocks and enough lots for several thousand people, rather than the 739 living there in 1980); and in the promotional literature of town promoters.[10]

No one believed, of course, that every town would become a city. A long history of American urban settlement had proven otherwise.[11] But individuals acted on the belief that their choice would be the right one. As small towns stabilized – and thus remained small towns – some residents moved on to try their opportunities elsewhere. John W. North, founder of Northfield in 1855, left the town in 1861 for Nevada, where he developed Washoe City; in 1870 he moved to California and founded the city of Riverside.[12] Merchants often moved to seek their fortunes in different towns and different trades.

Those who founded towns after 1900 had more limited expectations about the future. By the turn of the century, the competitive fortunes of most places – except for the boom towns of the iron ranges – were settled. Continued growth and rampant promotion were no longer major issues; keeping the towns vital was. Most small towns struggled to attract and retain commerce, industry, and some features of urban life. Creating new jobs and other opportunities for residents who wanted to stay was not easy. The average Minnesota town grew at less than the rate of natural increase, and most towns declined both relatively and absolutely in jobs and services during the twentieth century.

Stagnation and decline, however, did little to diminish the desire of people to identify with their hometown. Regardless of size, towns were centers of settlement and imageable places, and Minnesotans fought to preserve the identity of places that seemed barely viable. The loss of a school, passenger depot, or post office was exaggerated by the loss of the identity that those facilities had provided to the town. In the least successful places, these losses accumulated over time until little was left but the identity itself. In 1979, the moribund hamlet of Willow Creek in Blue Earth County found itself taken off the official state highway map. The unincorporated "town" consisted entirely of a belly-up store, with a single family living on the site. But another 300 people who lived in the surrounding countryside identified with Willow Creek and petitioned successfully to have it returned to the map. "The determination of the Willow Creek residents to preserve the identity of their community is resounding," said the state commissioner of transportation. "If by putting Willow Creek back on the official state transportation map we can contribute to this endeavor, we will be happy to do so."[13] Even townspeople who left for other opportunities carried this sense of identity with them. Former residents of the Beltrami County town of Kelliher (1986 estimated population of 332) began holding annual picnics in the Twin Cities in 1931. The fiftieth anniversary event in 1981 drew more than 200 people – as many as the town itself might have attracted with a local event.[14]

At the heart of this question of town identity is the related one of definition. What features or population size qualifies a place to be described as a small town? The historical basis of the ideal American small town, according to two researchers in community development, is the agricultural marketing center that "typically began with the opening of public land to settlers and grew through the accumulation of people seeking their fortunes as farmers, merchants, skilled craftsmen, and similar small-scale capitalists and entrepreneurs."[15] Geographer John Brinkerhoff Jackson wrote: "A contemporary definition of the town is hard to come by, and we almost always refer not to the town but to the *small* town as a social and cultural entity, a definite type of community with special social and cultural and economic characteristics."[16]

"Small town," "country town," and "Main Street town" suggest certain functions and familiar images. Hundreds of Minnesota towns fit the picture, more or less. But many other towns are either too large or too small, too independent of agriculture or tied to large urban centers to match the image. And few people agree about how small or large a "small" town is. The U.S. Census Bureau has considered incorporated places with populations of more than 2,500 to be urban – including communities that most people would refer to as "towns" – and has labeled smaller incorporated places as rural. For the purposes of this essay, small towns are defined as those incorporated places that had a 1980 population of less than 25,000 and that were outside of urbanized areas – that is, beyond the contiguous built-up areas of major cities.[17]

Although the figure is arbitrary, it works well in Minnesota. Only two cities – Winona and Mankato – had more than 25,000 inhabitants in 1980 without being classified by the Census Bureau as metropolitan. At the lower end of the scale, some unincorporated places exceeded the populations of incorporated towns, but reliable population figures for unincorporated communities are not available. Incorporated places included some towns that at one time had more than 100 residents (the minimum needed to incorporate during the twentieth century) but that had dropped below that threshold. Failed and failing towns are as much a part of history as successful ones.[18]

In 1980, Minnesota had 747 small towns with a total population of 1,005,735 – 25 percent of the population of the state; urbanized areas held 52 percent of the state's population, and the remaining 23 percent lived in unincorporated rural areas. Taken together, small towns gained in absolute population during every decade between 1900 and 1980, even though the growth rates differed considerably over the decades from those for the state as a whole. Small towns also showed a remarkable stability in the proportion of the state's population they held, ranging from 21 to 26 percent. This proportional stability masks some significant demographic trends, however. Urbanized areas grew at a faster rate than small towns, while rural areas declined in population: small towns were thus holding their own – as a proportion of the state's population – but at the expense of a shrinking farm population. Also, as the number of incorporated places increased, the change in the average size of towns between decades varied from a 7 percent decline to a 13 percent increase. Finally, the averages obscure population change from town to town. In general, larger towns grew faster than smaller ones, but even towns of similar sizes showed quite different population trends. Instability is normal for small towns. Drastic swings in size from decade to decade have made planning for population change difficult from statewide and regional perspectives, and almost impossible for individual towns.[19]

The Course of Town Development

The forces that shaped the towns in the nineteenth century had little power in the late twentieth century, but patterns persisted in the location, size, and look of towns. It is easy to trace the beginnings of towns and cities in Minnesota. Starting in 1851, territorial and state laws required that town founders file a plat map with county officials before lots could be sold. The plat certified that the townsite had been surveyed, established its location, and designated the form of streets, blocks, and lots. Individuals, railroads, and townsite companies filed more than one thousand plats between 1849 and 1900. Paper towns – with a plat but no settlers – were common before 1870, but after that date most places saw some measure of development. Few townsites were entirely unsuccessful, though many did eventually fail.[20]

A turn-of-the-century map of town origins and functions would show distinct regional patterns corresponding to four major rural and small-town settlement areas.[21] In the southeastern region of the state – the area east of Mankato and south of Minneapolis – water sites provided the initial impetus for town development. A handful of Mississippi and Minnesota river towns served as river-oriented trade centers, including the lumber center of Winona and the agricultural center of Red Wing. More towns were located at waterpower sites on smaller, unnavigable streams. Grain

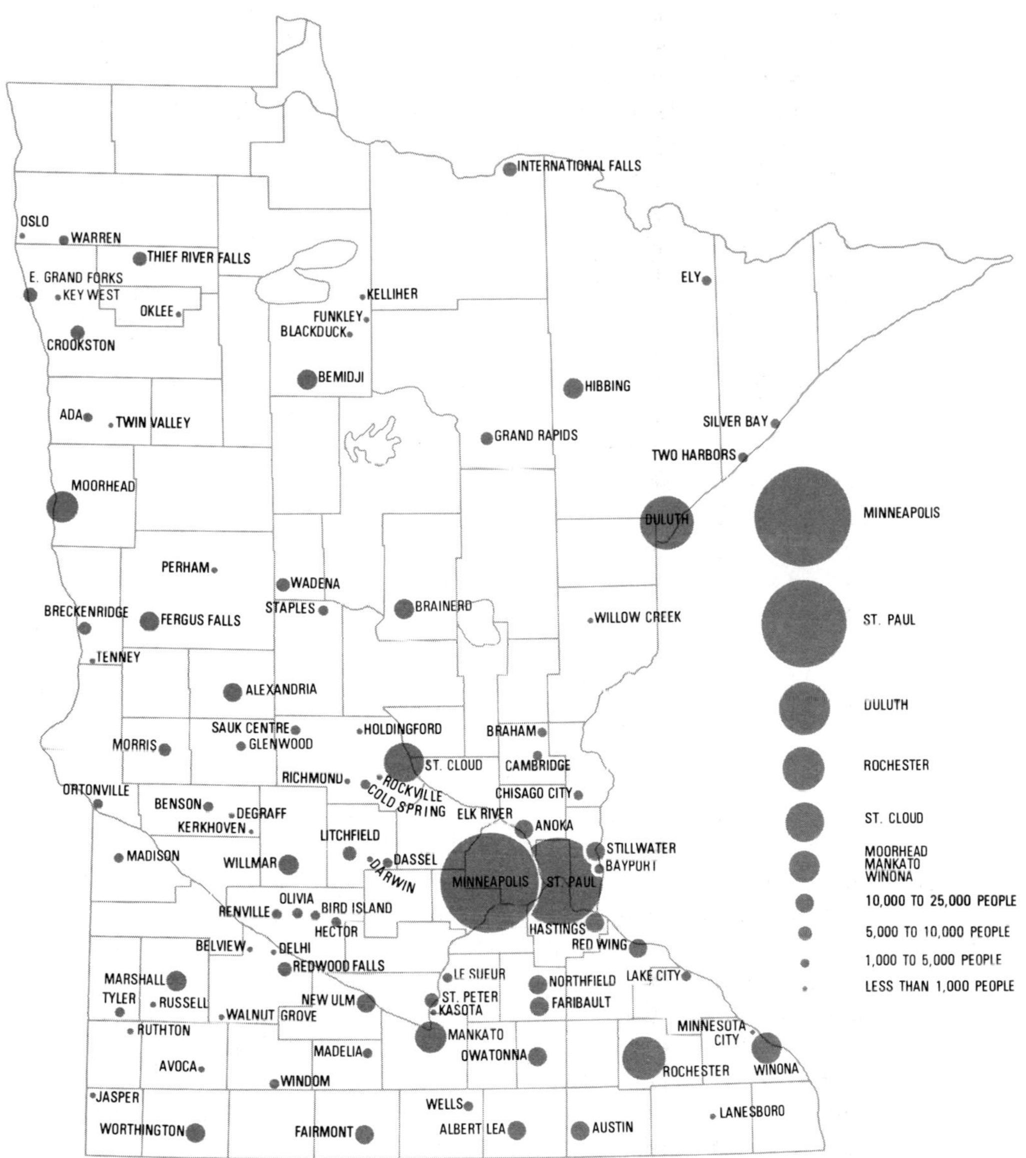

Location of some of Minnesota's 747 small towns, where one-fourth of the population lived in 1980, shown in relation to its eight urban centers

A Main Street postcard from Oklee, Red Lake County, 1910

milling was an important local activity, and a dense network of small farms led to the establishment of many local service hamlets. Large-scale processing and manufacturing of agricultural products characterized such centers as Austin and Owatonna. Effective settlement preceded the rail building of the 1870s.

The prairie counties in the western half of the state were settled after 1870, hand-in-hand with the expansion of the railroads. The tracks created a new transportation network, and rails – not waterways – were the key to a town's fortune. In southeastern Minnesota, towns subsidized the rail companies with land and cash donations. In the western prairies, on the other hand, the rail companies usually created the towns. Few "inland" towns – off the tracks – ever existed, and as many as half the towns in the region were controlled directly by the railroads or their subsidiary townsite agents. In Lyon County, every town was founded by a railroad. Rail dominance and cash-crop agriculture on a large scale led to scores of small elevator towns and farm trade centers, a few major processing centers, and several transportation-dominated rail-division points.

Central Minnesota reflected the transition from the settlement pattern of the southeastern region to that of the western counties. Wright and Carver counties, for example, were areas of intense speculative townsite platting in the 1850s, and some successful towns were established at waterpower sites. Major industrial centers did not develop, however, and rail expansion in the latter part of the century laid a new network of towns over the old. The region retained some of the inland towns of the era before the railroads, but it also had rail-created towns dating from the late 1880s. Towns like Sauk Centre embodied a mix of elements. Settled in 1856 at a mill site on the Sauk River, the town was later tied into the rail network.

In the region north and east of the agricultural prairie counties, specialized resources strongly influenced small-town development. Lumber and iron ore gave rise to dozens of ephemeral towns and to a few successful ones. Of all the regions of the state, the northeast had the most volatile small-town history, including paper-town speculation, thriving lumber camps that disappeared entirely, and iron-mining towns whose fortunes fluctuated decade by decade. Places served a variety of functions over time. Brainerd was both a major rail-division point and a lumber town; Ely's beginnings centered on iron ore, whereas in the 1980s recreation dominated; and Grand Rapids combined wood processing and recreation.

Towns that were successful by 1900 continued to be the major settlements in the state in later years. Initial advantage was the paramount factor in town growth. Outside of the state's urbanized areas, only 10 towns had turn-of-the-century populations of more than five thousand. They ranked among the top 31 cities and towns in 1980. Of the state's 747 small towns in 1980, 400 were incorporated by 1900. In 1980, 320 still had fewer than 2,500 residents. Forty-three towns disincorporated between 1900 and 1980, but this decrease was offset by 390 new incorporations during that period. In addition to the incorporated towns, the state had another 973 small trade centers in 1905. Although some of these were towns that would later incorporate, most were hamlets that would not survive as more than a name on the map.[22]

Pre-1900 settlement rules continued to operate during the first two decades of the twentieth century. Between 1900 and 1920, about 320 new towns were platted. New municipalities were established around Minneapolis and St. Paul, and company towns were developed along with the mines in northeastern Minnesota.[23] In the western counties, and especially in the northwest, branch-line railroads that were built into lightly

The town of Madison, seat of Lac qui Parle County, 1899

settled territory led to the creation of dozens of towns. Excluding the wildly speculative 1850s, the decade from 1900 to 1910 proved to be one of the most productive – as far as town creation was concerned – in the state's history. The number of incorporated small towns increased from 400 to 624 between 1900 and 1920. Few places platted after 1900 were outright failures, and a high percentage eventually incorporated, but they did not grow to a large size. Built to serve limited trade functions in rural areas and competing with established centers, the newer towns had little hope of rapid growth. Small initial plats show that the proprietors had modest expectations.

At the beginning of the twentieth century, Minnesota's towns reflected the characteristics of their different geographic settings, use of regional resources, local transportation facilities, and age. Yet the distinguishing histories and special aspects of particular towns should not be overstated. Even in the nineteenth century, towns showed remarkable homogeneity in their business patterns, architecture, and land use. Growth and development tended to minimize differences: transportation shifted from water to rail to roads, "river towns" and "lumber towns" became general-service trade centers, and local residents became part of national networks. Changes during the twentieth century brought towns even closer together.

Railroads were vital connections for towns in the nineteenth century, and that importance carried over into the next century. The trains provided the critical link between towns and major urban markets, and they brought life to farm villages. Harmful effects of the siting of railroads, however, are illustrated in this 1915 appraisal by economist Louis D. H. Weld of the stunted growth of one town: "Ada has failed to gain appreciably as a business center [because] the section immediately adjacent to the village has not furnished sufficient business to make up for the gradual cutting down of tributary territory. At first it had a very extensive tributary area, extending fifteen or twenty miles into Dakota and a like, or even greater, distance to the east. Furthermore, Crookston (thirty miles away) was the nearest point of any importance on the north, and Moorhead (also thirty miles) on the south." But Great Northern branch lines built between 1883 and 1886 at points fourteen miles west and fourteen miles east of Ada effectively reduced the town's trade territory.[24]

If Ada businesses benefited from a thirty-mile-radius trade zone, the farmers at the edge of the territory did not. Groups of farmers petitioned railroads to build new lines and new towns, depots, and grain stations. Competing rail lines complied – so long as the captured trade was from a rival line. Where competition was lacking, railroads saw little reason to invest in trackage or even to send cars to collect grain. In 1902, the Great Northern Railway Company prepared a map showing the competitive situation in the Red River valley. According to the text on the map, "Competition is especially strong with the C.M.&St.P.Ry. at stations between Wahpeton and Moorhead. All stations from Downer to Angus & Grand Forks to Neche are competitive with opposite points on the N.P.Ry. A good supply of cars is needed early in the season at Euclid, Ives, Angus,

Workers paving a street in Kerkhoven, Swift County, during the 1920s

Warren & Schurmeier. The following competitive points may be deprived of cars to give supply to adjacent G.N.Ry. stations: Wahpeton, Fargo, Moorhead, Glyndon, Crookston, Grand Forks & Grafton. – For example, rather than draw grain to Grafton, where it will be divided with N.P., good supply of cars should be furnished at Audubon, Nash & Herriott to prevent grain being hauled to Grafton."[25]

Growing numbers of automobiles and trucks, especially after 1920, heightened the competition between towns. Rural roads were poor until the Good Roads movement gained momentum early in the century, and it was a push by town business people more than farmers that led to state legislation around 1913 authorizing township taxation and professional road improvements. An associated change was the increased number of tractors on farms and the expansion of average farm size. Fewer farmsteads meant a shrinking of the trade potential of a small town's rural hinterland. Farmers were also able to travel farther to shop, leading to the growth of larger trade centers as they absorbed services from smaller ones. The importance of railroads began to decline at about the same time. In 1929, trackage in Minnesota peaked at nearly 9,400 miles. Railroads were still essential in the towns they served, but abandonment became commonplace and many towns lost their rail connection. Improved highways helped to compensate for rail loss, although the forced switch to trucking usually put town businesses at a competitive disadvantage. As late as 1984, threatened track abandonment spawned an organization in Alexandria and Fergus Falls that worked to convince Burlington Northern to reconsider abandonment in that area of western Minnesota.[26]

Town Landscapes

The ideal of the small town is often expressed in physical images – Main Street, the courthouse square, a baseball diamond, grain elevators, and the town water tower. Function, as well as the record of successes and failures, are all reflected in the landscapes of Minnesota's towns. Although minor differences between towns are visible, one quickly senses the "peas-in-a-pod situation" that geographer Wilbur Zelinsky noted of towns in the Midwest, "where the form and substance of the next town [are] soporifically forecast by the last." These small towns are highly legible places, with predictable street layout, land use, and architecture.[27]

The image is based on the moderately successful town having a population of between one thousand and five thousand people. A highway runs along the edge of town, and railroad tracks divide the good and bad sides of the community. Farmland extends right up to the edge of the built-up area. Businesses line the several blocks of Main Street, which forms a T with the railroad. Sinclair Lewis captured the landscape of Sauk Centre and similar towns in *Main Street.* The book describes all parts of the town in detail, but the novelist focused on the commercial district because it represented the materialism and strident boosterism of the midwestern town.[28] The identification is narrow, as are all stereotypes, but it has merit. It acknowledges the relentlessly economic view of community well-being that looks for evidence of success in the retail activity at the center of town.

This emphasis on Main Street, however, overlooks the importance of other parts of the town, as well as the places that are too small or too large to fit the stereotype. Wide railroad rights-of-way, for example, that were owned and controlled by rail companies are common to virtually all small towns. At one time, the swath of trackside land was filled with line elevators and coal and lumber yards, all controlled or licensed by railroad subsidiaries. Later in the century, only cooperative grain elevators remain along the tracks, and little evidence of the dominance that railroads exerted over towns survives. Depots have been sold and moved, becoming as common in reconstructed pioneer villages, on farmsteads, or on town lots as along the tracks. Station services are concentrated in the larger depots in county seats or regional centers, and the wide swaths of railroad land, with the tracks abandoned and removed, pass through built-up blocks. Communities once took pride in maintaining trackside parks, but with no passengers disembarking at the station, the parks and bandstands have disappeared with the depots. Warren, the seat of Marshall County in northwestern Minnesota, has kept its park, complete with a gazebo built as a garden club bicentennial project, alongside the depot. In most towns, however, parks are located on the outskirts of town near the baseball field, on a few lots at a major street corner (typically war memorial parks), or out on the highway to welcome automobile travelers.

Residential areas flank the commercial street of the twentieth-century small town. Churches and schools are located away from businesses, either at the far end of Main Street or in the residential areas. Houses, predominantly frame structures, are modest in appearance. Small cottages and bungalows are common, and larger houses are typically two-story, unadorned cubes. Because blocks were not developed all at once, the architectural styles are mixed. New ranch-style houses stand next to turn-of-the-century ones, unlike the pattern in suburban developments where houses are clustered by income. Many properties remain undevel-

Postcard mailed from the Norman County town of Twin Valley, 1917

oped, giving small towns an open appearance despite lot sizes that are typical of large cities. Even in very small towns, an Elm Street or its equivalent is lined with substantial homes, and larger towns may even have a "Quality Hill" district.[29]

The solid blocks of two-story brick buildings that are so much a part of Main Street imagery are rare and thus worthy of preservation where they are found. Years of neglect, alterations, and fires have left few commercial streets intact. Many towns simply never saw a substantial investment in the buildings on Main Street. Banks, which generally exceeded local architectural standards, were often built in the most modern architectural style of their period and continued over the years to provide the highlight of commercial architecture in many towns. As historian William T. Morgan noted, they served "as symbols of security, strength, and character." Louis Sullivan's Owatonna bank is the state's most famous example. Even the modest brick and stone building erected by the Citizens State Bank of Oslo about 1905 was a striking contribution to the business district of this Red River valley town.[30]

Courthouses were the most impressive small-town landmarks. Counties showed a remarkable investment in their courthouses, and the county-seat towns benefited from the countywide investment in the structure and drawing power of government functions. It is little wonder that the late nineteenth century was marked by county-seat wars. The rise of state and federal government functions in the twentieth century added even more to local employment and drawing power in the county seats. Post offices were the only government facilities available in other towns, and even very small towns put up fierce opposition to their closing.

Opera houses, movie theaters, and libraries have been the formal cultural outlets in small towns. Early in the century the opera house hosted such popular entertainment as band concerts, dances, and traveling vari-

New Ulm's Art Deco movie theater, 1935

ety shows, and when movies became available they were shown there until specialized theaters were built. By the 1980s many of the movie theaters were themselves closed, though in Madelia, at least, the progression continued when the former theater became a video rental store. Libraries have represented some of the finest local efforts to improve the cultural life of the community. Beginning in 1899, the Carnegie Corporation provided funds to many small Minnesota communities to establish libraries, encouraging them to construct sophisticated, architect-designed buildings.[31]

Size has been the main variant in town form. The very small towns – those having fewer than 250 residents – did not develop the full range of functions found in the typical town. Main Street was not completely built up, even for a two-block stretch. Formal cultural facilities never existed. These towns always depended on larger places, and they were reduced in the late twentieth century to providing minimal local services – a grain elevator, a gas station, and a bar. Bigger places had more of everything. At a certain population size, say 7,500, the main commercial street was outgrown. A central business district developed, though it was one without high-rise buildings. In Brainerd, with just over 11,000 residents, the water tower and church steeples have remained the prominent landscape features. A single main street no longer existed in these bigger towns by the 1980s, but it was easy to find the principal intersection in town. Although commercial and industrial establishments were more clearly separated than in smaller places, the centers of each were not far from one another.

Strip developments along the highway leading into town have become the focus of activity in many of Minnesota's small towns, with shopping malls, gas stations, restaurants, and motels as the most visible elements.[32] But all along the highway strips are signs of the agricultural economy. Space-extensive businesses like farm equipment lots and bulk fertilizer plants require too much room to locate on Main Street or along the railroad tracks. Other farm-oriented services, including banks and lending agencies, have located near these businesses. Strip developments first appeared in the 1950s in towns that were large enough to have a built-up Main Street, and their growth directly competed with the businesses in that traditional center of the town. In the following decades, strips grew and added functions while Main Streets declined. The strip has reflected the investment and agglomeration of functions in county seats, and as a result the larger towns have absorbed many functions that were once provided in smaller places. In effect, the small village strip came to be located miles away in another town. Like Main Street, the strip is linear, utilitarian, and multifunctional. The architecture is newer and simpler, but no less homogeneous in style, than the commercial blocks in town. The only architectural highlights are the signs. Although the landscape of the strip does not capture one's attention, by the 1980s it had become critically important in assessing the viability of small towns.

Less visible than the stores and businesses, but vital in establishing a town's image, have been the public utilities. Running water, gas lines, and sewers vastly improved the quality of life for those who could afford them, but electricity was the symbol of urban success in the early decades of the century. Litchfield's power plant supplied local electric power, pumped the town water supply, and furnished heat to public buildings and most businesses. Most important, according to Brunner, was "the current for the thirty-two five-globe white-way lights through the business district" that was provided free of charge. When electric lighting was uncommon, the "White Ways" in the heart of a town were one way of claiming urban status. They were introduced in California in 1906, and the idea spread quickly across the country. Thief River Falls, a Red River valley town, built one of the earliest municipally owned hydropower plants in the state. In 1913 merchants pushed for a White Way, and Thief River Falls promoted itself as "Power City."[33]

In 1914 Minnesota led the nation in municipally owned utilities, and 912 Minnesota communities had electric power by 1928. This total included the larger cities, but also some unincorporated places with as few as sixteen residents. Most towns were served not by municipal power plants but by the vast network of public-utility power lines that crisscrossed the state. After 1945, the pace of technological change and its nearly ubiquitous geographic spread greatly diminished the differences and distances that had isolated communities from each other. Telephones, improved highways, and cable television allowed towns to "plug in" to national cultural and economic networks.[34]

Making a Living

Small towns have often been identified by the particular functions they serve – lumber town, mill town, mining town, or railroad town – and the identity has meaning on a local scale for residents and on a statewide scale in terms of regional images. The pictorial maps that are common on postcards draw upon this functional identity, but they are acceptable only insofar as they reflect common perceptions. Minnesotans have come to share images of particular towns, yet it is difficult to classify the towns by function because roles change over time. Image and reality are often at odds. Historical and cultural events, the natural environment, transportation networks, and local entrepreneurship combine to produce particular functions in each town, and as those factors change, so do town functions. Past images linger, however, and local identity is not always an accurate reflection of a town's present dominant role.

By the 1980s, all towns offered a mix of services, and extreme specialization was rare. They served as collecting and sometimes processing points for the materials produced in their immediate vicinity, basic activities that required a transportation network, warehouses and factories, and financial institutions. Retail stores, service enterprises, theaters and recreational facilities, churches, welfare organizations, and schools were found, to a certain extent, in most towns.[35]

The prototypical small town earlier in the twentieth century was the agricultural trade center where townspeople's livelihoods were dependent, directly or indirectly, on supporting farm trade territories and selling goods to farmers. Of the three Minnesota towns best described in the 1910s and 1920s, Braham, in northeastern Minnesota, was the smallest, with a population in 1910 of 406 and in 1920 of 511. Ada, in the Red River valley, had 1,432 residents in 1910 and 1,411 in 1920, and it had the advantage of being a county seat. Litchfield, in central Minnesota, was the largest of these towns, with a 1920 population of 2,790.[36] Each was a farmers' town. Three-quarters of the economic life of Litchfield was based on agriculture. Four grain elevators, a woolen mill, three produce companies, and a livestock shipping operation marketed farm products, primarily to the Twin Cities. Dairying was important around Braham, but potatoes were the most important cash crop. Braham and nearby towns had both potato warehouses and processing plants, but few other agricultural industries. Wheat and other grain cash crops accounted for more than two-thirds of Ada's agricultural trade, followed by livestock marketing.[37]

As the century progressed, business services (including repair, banking, insurance, and real estate) and wholesale and retail trade became ubiquitous in towns having more than 2,500 residents. Few towns specialized in these functions. Wholesale and retail trade tended to be more important urban functions in the south and west of the state, where agriculture was important, than in the north and east. The northeastern region saw high levels of service employment in resort and tourist towns, including Wadena and Grand Rapids. Manufacturing was significant in southeastern Minnesota, especially the processing of agricultural products—meat-packing at Austin, vegetable freezing and canning at Le Sueur, and diversified farm-products processing at Fairmont, Owatonna, and Red Wing. Diversification allowed some towns to retain jobs and residents despite individual firm failure. As economist Robert J. Holloway noted in his 1954 study of Minnesota towns, "Industry is not a new phenomenon in Red Wing, for Red Wing has probably forgotten more industry than some cities ever knew." These enterprises included two mattress firms, a fur-processing company, a sorghum plant, and a cigar factory. The firms were thriving when Red Wing was a busy sawmill and river transportation center.[38] Despite high levels of farm production, western Minnesota did not develop agricultural manufacturing towns; turkey processing grew in importance at Willmar and Worthington, however, and small processing plants became more common in the western counties after the 1950s.

Larger towns characteristically offered a wide range of professional services. Certain types of service employment led to specialized towns and cities. Rochester became famous for its medical services, but smaller towns with state hospitals (such as Cambridge) also showed a degree of medical specialization. Education was another professional service, and several towns were specialized as college towns. Northfield, with St. Olaf and Carleton colleges, was the premier example. Education, along with other institutions, was important in St. Peter and Faribault; and as the state's higher-education system grew rapidly after 1950, that specialization gained significance in Bemidji, Crookston, Marshall, Morris, and other towns.

Dramatic changes occurred in town economies, usually because of major shifts in technology and the larger economy. The timber industry declined throughout the state, leaving former lumber-mill centers like Stillwater with little lumber processing. Manufacturing of lumber products remained significant in International Falls, Grand Rapids, and Bayport. Some Minnesota towns were linked to the exploitation of economic minerals. On the iron ranges of northeastern Minnesota, the mining industry was the reason for existence for many communities. Although mining towns like Ely were able to diversify into tourism when the mining industry declined, economic hardship remained a problem in the 1980s for many towns on the ranges. Processing of iron ore increased with the rise of the taconite industry in the 1950s, and towns like Silver Bay saw their fortunes rise and fall as demand for taconite fluctuated. Other Minnesota towns had important quarrying industries, including granite at Ortonville and Rockville and quartzite at Jasper, but the quarrying did not dominate the towns as mining did in the northeast.

The transportation specialization that arose during the railroad era declined statewide with reductions in train service, routes, and employment. Still, some towns retained importance as division points where crews changed and repair shops were located. Brainerd, Staples, Breckenridge, and Glenwood served these functions on transcontinental rail lines. Transportation at Two Harbors was associated with the movement of iron ore from mines to Great Lakes ore boats.[39]

Classification by function, however, glosses over important differences in the kinds of jobs that people had – differences that have been crucial to urban viability and identity. A lumber town is far more vulnerable to long-term industrial decline and short-term product demand than a food-processing center, even though the lumber town may provide a more engaging image. The Forest History Center at Grand Rapids, for example, had no twentieth-century equivalent in the meat-packing industry.

Communications improvements and public utilities allowed footloose industries in the 1980s to locate almost anywhere they chose. With dependable, cheap labor forces, towns found themselves able to compete with cities for new industry. Business relocation and expansion had been a part of the history of small-town vitality, with even successful firms relocating to larger towns and cities. Brandt Brothers Manufacturing, run by three brothers in Chisago City in the early years of the century, made and marketed a highly successful potato-bud hand sprayer. In 1909 the firm moved to Hastings (which promised that taxes would never exceed ten dollars a year), and for a time after the move the firm (renamed Hudson Manufacturing) was one of the Northwest's largest distributors of agricultural equipment. Richard Sears started a small mail-order firm in Redwood Falls that eventually became Sears, Roebuck and Company after his move to Chicago in 1893. But dozens of towns could claim remarkable success because of people who stayed. The decisions of individuals often had great impact and visibility in small towns. In Perham, businessman Darrell Nelson almost single-handedly kept the town's economy alive. He founded Tuffy's Dog Food, the largest employer in town, and sold the firm to Star-Kist in 1971. He then developed Barrel O' Fun potato chips, and later sold it. He constantly reinvested in the community by buying businesses that were about to close and then selling them to young people on favorable terms.[40]

Townspeople and Their Institutions

Minnesota towns are more than physical landscapes or trade centers. They are also places where people live. Regardless of the size, function, or fortune of a town, social and cultural life has taken on similar proportions in the state's smaller communities. Thus Sinclair Lewis could write that Gopher Prairie's Main Street was "the continuation of Main Streets everywhere."[41] Schools, religious institutions, clubs, and celebrations have long been the centers of a community's life and the expression of its spirit. And it is community, in both its positive and negative aspects, that has inspired the critiques of both social scientists and novelists.

Almost invariably, sociologists and economists have seen communities or neighborhoods as extending beyond a town's municipal limits to include its immediate farm-trade hinterland. The writers have taken it as a given that townspeople and farmers should get along. Of Litchfield, Brunner wrote: "The absence of definite neighborhood groups within the commu-

Noble Coucheron's Consolidated Bands, shown about 1914, with musicians from Olivia, Renville, Hector, Bird Island, Delhi, and Belview

nity, an area of roughly 110 square miles, proves that the farmers go to the village for their trading and for their social life. They are drawn there by the general attractiveness of the town, and by the good roads leading to it, as well as by its courthouse and its cooperative creamery. Three-fourths of any average audience at the moving-picture shows and open-air band concerts are country people." Farmers combined business with pleasure in their trips to town. In its frontier period, Ada, platted in 1880, "was undoubtedly a lively little town," wrote economist Weld in 1915. "Dances, card parties, church socials, and home entertainments were of very frequent occurrence. The brass band was in great demand not only in Ada, but in surrounding towns. . . . Roller skating became the rage in 1884 and a 'large new rink' was built in 1885."[42]

When trade fell during the late 1880s, however, this "great social activity" declined. "In 1888 Ada failed to celebrate the Fourth of July for the first time; social events became less frequent; even the band disbanded." Most significant, perhaps, was the development of rural-town tensions and village cliques within the previous few years. "It is said that in the early days there often used to be as many farmers as villagers at the dances in Ada; that the country people frequently drove as much as ten miles with the thermometer well below zero to attend these village functions. The stratification of social groups in the village has undoubtedly had something to do with the change that has come about." Real differences in prosperity and practices emerged between people on farms and in towns, unlike the early days when townspeople and farmers had worked together to build communities.[43] After the 1920s, as farmers gained in prosperity and in their connection with national cultural influences, social gaps narrowed and brought town and country closer together again.

Small-town social life has varied by place as well as time. Weld found that the local Socialist party organization in Ada had more members (thirty-two) than any of the other village lodges and societies except the Modern Woodmen and the Masons. The Socialists had "two or three social meetings during the year. A holiday supper or dance is generally given, and an annual picnic is held during the summer. These functions are exceptional in that the farmers and town people mix freely." One leader commented that "socialism seems to be the only bond that brings country and town people together socially." On the other hand, economist Gustav P. Warber saw little to commend in the socialism that was present in Braham at the same time: "It seems to the writer, that owing to the gradual change wrought by newcomers of different nationalities, and the dissemination of socialistic doctrines with their usual agnostic accompaniments, the church is losing control over the ethical and moral standards and aspirations of the community." Warber's conservative social ethic led him to comment on aspects of town life seldom discussed by other writers. "It was maintained by a person who claims to know," he reported, "that 'practically all illicit sexual relations as well as the increasing number of cases of venereal infection may be traced back to the public dances.' . . . Although it is a sad commentary to make, a common opinion of both young and old men is that 'as a class, the girls who have been working in the cities for a while, are the chief cause for this constantly growing evil.' " And it was at the country "bowery or barn dances" that "the tougher set gathers." Only 15 percent of the families willingly allowed girls to attend such dances.[44]

Moral questions and frictions between town and country did not fade over the decades as automobile ownership gave farm families easy access to different towns. A 1942 study found that three Meeker County towns varied considerably in their reputations on moral questions. Dassel was known as a good family town, where local clergy had managed to prevent public dancing and the sale of beer and had closed a roller-skating rink. An exciting Saturday night was listening to a band concert on the town square. Nearby Darwin had almost no business district except for "several beer parlors and a dance hall" staffed by cowboy bands, from which Dassel mothers tried to keep their daughters. Litchfield had movies and dances at the community center, but the dances were "on a much higher level than those in Darwin." Farmers, it was claimed, preferred Dassel's entertainment.[45]

Churches have been a main focus of town social life. Although few religious groups founded exclusive communities in the state, churches formed an institutional base for early settlement in many Minnesota towns. The religious component of settlement was evident in central Minnesota, especially in Stearns County, where many hamlets were named for saints. Towns like DeGraff and Avoca were promoted by the Catholic Colonization Bureau. To encourage settlement, railroads and town proprietors often donated lots to any congregation that would construct a church. Most communities had a range of congregations, and reflections of ethnicity in Minnesota towns are largely the by-products of nationality-centered religious participation. The community in and around Braham, for example, had nine churches in 1915, serving about a third of the families in the area. Six of these were Swedish denominations, including Baptists and Lutherans. The local territory had no Catholic church. In Litchfield sectarianism was "strongly rooted," according to Brunner in 1927. With a population of 2,850 the town supported twelve churches, representing four Swedish congregations, one German, one Norwegian, five other Protestant congregations, and one Roman Catholic.[46]

Churches have not been an entirely positive influence in the community. Village social life revolved largely around churches, and church affiliation (with nationality playing its part) was a principal factor in stratifying townspeople into social groups. Weld said of Ada in 1915 that "each group is rather self-centered and self-sufficient. In view of the lack of contact with the outside world, a more general social life in the village would undoubtedly aid in developing wider interests." Still, churches provided a social link between townspeople and farmers that otherwise would not have existed. Ada villagers often attended church suppers in the country, and these social ties were strongest among the Norwegians. The Braham study from the same period noted that "newcomers in the community who can understand only English are poorly provided for . . . since services are conducted either in Swedish or German, according to the neighborhood in which the church is located." Churches sponsored social activities, including societies for young people and women. Youth activities were considered an important alternative to secular entertainment. Warber concluded that in Braham "at least two of these organizations are a decided influence for good, in that they give the pleasure-loving youth the right kind of social entertainment."[47] Women's groups combined social interaction with fund raising for the church.

As the century progressed, the increasing use of automobiles and decreasing rural church membership as the countryside lost population led many country churches to merge with those in town. Nonetheless, church affiliation has remained the cultural element least influenced by the centralization of services – such as schools and businesses – into the towns. Despite congregational mergers, churches (and seldom-used township halls) have become the only rural services left in much of the state. Farm-to-town migrants have remained loyal to their congregations, and many townspeople have continued to attend country churches.[48]

Churches and other organizations may have divided people into groups, but small-town schools united entire communities. "Employing nearly one hundred persons as teachers alone," a 1969 study of Benson pointed out, "the Benson public schools exert a major shaping influence on the life of the community. In the fall, on Friday nights, when stores are open for shopping in town, the school plays its home football games to large audiences. . . . Even those who have no children or who are older follow school events." Community support for school sports projected a positive view of the town. But the Benson schools also reflected small-town tensions. The educational mission struck an uneven balance between the needs of the local community and those of the young people who would migrate from the town, between the stated goal of fitting in and a curriculum designed to meet "the needs of youth who are living in a changing world" – that is, being taught to leave.[49] As the Benson schools adjusted to broader cultural demands, the school district absorbed scores of nearby rural schools, leaving one-room country schoolhouses standing empty.

The Benson educational dilemma mirrored concerns that date to the early twentieth century. In 1915, Braham area schools practiced a "formally conscious effort of the community to train its youth for greater efficiency and higher culture for the purpose of better citizenship." Warber discussed the problems of the Braham schools by citing a report for schools in neighboring Kanabec County, which had fifty-one districts with fifty-four schoolhouses. Attempts at consolidation had failed because farmers found that it usually cost more to support a consolidated school than a small, independent district. Few of the schools went past the eighth grade, and teachers with even high-school diplomas were unusual. The benefits of public education were weighed against local and translocal effects. On the one hand, the Braham study concluded that "the standard of living is undoubtedly being raised higher and higher from year to year. Foremost in this work are the public schools, which furnish most of the new ideals." Growing prosperity helped farmers and their families to satisfy ever-increasing wants, but not all thought the trend was to be applauded. Social discontent, especially among the younger generation, was commonly blamed on "too much education," in the words of some older people in the community. "People are getting to have wants which we, forty years ago, regarded as luxuries fit only for kings. That is the reason, too, why so many young people will not get married; they're after only fun in life, and they don't care to settle down to work like good honest people used to."[50]

If the mere fact of education disturbed some farmers in 1915, school consolidation over the years has had profound impacts on the state's small towns and rural areas. Efficiencies in financing, more state intervention in curriculum, compulsory education laws, and increased demands for a better quality of schooling led to the closing of thousands of rural schools; eventually, some small towns lost their schools to nearby larger places. In the late 1970s and early 1980s, Minnesota school districts merged at the rate of one or two a year, and the pace picked up dramatically to ten or more per year in the mid-1980s. Decline of community control of schools has been a serious concern. More keenly felt, however, is the emotional blow of the loss of community identity following a school closing. One need only follow prep sports and remember the highway signs welcoming visitors to the "Home of the 1982 State AA Champions" to glimpse the allegiance given to local schools. Sports rivalries became the biggest stumbling block to school mergers because the towns had set themselves up as competitors, not neighbors. The pain of creating a new identity is reflected in such hyphenated namings as Russell-Tyler-Ruthton, or in the new word Rocori (for Rockville-Cold Spring-Richmond).[51]

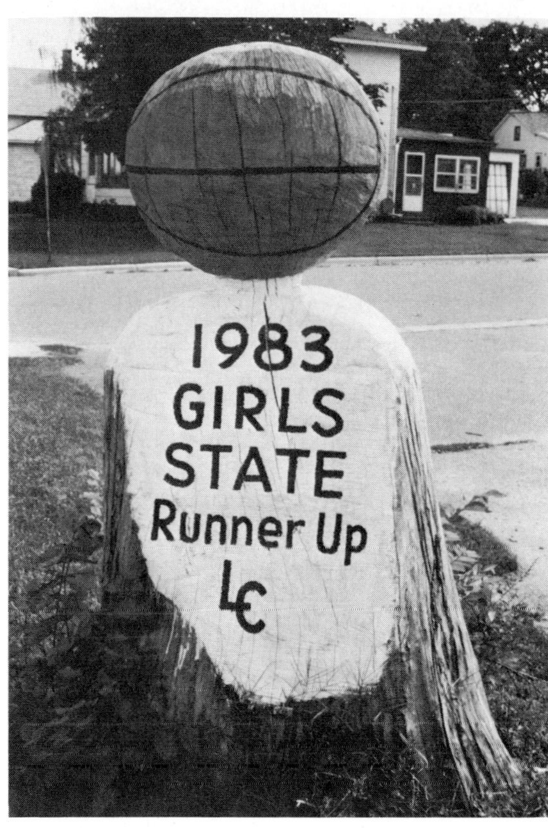

Lake City carving celebrating the town's participation in the 1983 state girls' basketball Class A tournament

Celebrations have also served to distinguish town from country and to provide place identity for individual communities. County fairs, ostensibly agricultural and educational events, have invariably been held at fairgrounds in towns. The Lac Qui Parle County Fair, reportedly the "oldest successive fair in the state," has played a "tremendous part in the growth of Madison," according to town historians. Fairs could even be used to promote nearby towns. In 1916, the *Holdingford Advertiser* publicized an annual auto trip to the Stearns County Fair. "The interest [this year] is more widespread than usual. This may be largely accounted for by the fact that there are twice as many car owners in this vicinity this year compared with any previous year. . . . A hundred automobiles in the procession can be as easily gathered this year as twenty was two years ago. These trips to the county fair has [*sic*] done a lot towards giving Holdingford a reputation for progressiveness, and that is the only kind of reputation that does a town any good." The writer went on to extol the merits of establishing a good "automobile trail" across the north part of the county.[52]

The Chautauqua movement, which was closely related to church activities, spread through the Midwest late in the nineteenth century and lasted to the 1920s. Old Settlers Associations were not, as one might expect, formed years after a town's start to honor its pioneers. Rather, they were founded in the earliest years by older settlers, and only later was the term used to honor pioneer ancestors in community events celebratory of a

Parade on Paul Bunyan Day in Brainerd, about 1935

town having survived for twenty-five, fifty, or one hundred years.[53] These and similar celebrations were later subsumed under "town days," which were developed early in the century and retained their importance into the 1980s. Originally conceived as commercial promotions, these events usually played up a significant happening in a town's history, noted some quirk of ethnic settlement, or glorified a local product. Worthington's "Turkey Days" has perhaps been the most famous, each year drawing state and even national political figures to speak. Seldom, however, were the identity-makers dominant in the actual history of a town. Trivia became the trademark of many a town's celebration. Everything from eelpout to water-skiing has been used to celebrate Minnesota towns.[54]

Paying Attention to Small Towns

Small towns have a greater significance to the people who live there and on nearby farms, as well as to city dwellers, than is reflected in statistics about their population levels and economies. As farm conditions worsened in the 1980s, the entire state seemed to be paying attention to the changes in rural and small-town Minnesota. Twin Cities newspapers provided special reports from Minnesota communities, and their business pages covered bank and industrial openings and closings. Commercial and public radio and television stations aired documentaries and forums on the prospects of small towns. When Minnesota Public Radio broadcast speeches from a 1987 conference on small towns held in Grinnell, Iowa, the request for tapes and transcripts overwhelmed conference sponsors. And the legislature repeatedly discussed the impact of public policy on farms and agricultural towns.[55]

People's interest in small-town Minnesota was typical of reactions in the country as a whole. National residential preference surveys in the

1970s showed that nearly three-quarters of those surveyed wanted to live in a small town or rural area. A "rural turnaround," according to demographer Calvin Beale, showed disproportionately high growth rates for nonmetropolitan counties in the early 1970s. The future seemed to be looking good for smaller places: many people were actually acting on their preferences. A detailed study of these population changes, however, provided a more revealing picture. Retirement and resort counties flourished, as well as counties with a large proportion of land owned by the federal government. Mining and manufacturing areas were growing more slowly – at a rate below the national average – and agricultural counties were growing most slowly. And, in the 1980s, metropolitan growth was once again outstripping nonmetropolitan growth.[56] This national pattern of population change was also true in Minnesota, as the growth of lake communities, decline of mining towns, and stagnation of farm towns made evident.

Hundreds of towns in Minnesota seemed too small and too lacking in public infrastructure – many of them too far from alternative job and service centers – to do more than merely survive, based on the experience of such places in the earlier decades of the twentieth century. Many towns with fewer than 500 people were likely to continue their slow decline, particularly as losses of local services and farm population made it more difficult to compete with larger centers. Towns with 500 to 2,500 people were likely to hold their own but not to grow. Towns with more than 2,500 were continuing to absorb functions from smaller places and to attract some urban commuters and older residents moving from farms. Herberger's, a chain of department stores located mostly in small cities, expanded rapidly after 1975. According to a company executive, the stores benefited from the farm crisis. "It's a serious situation out there, but the impact is more on the smaller communities. Some of that business will gravitate to the next larger area. We're getting the runoff."[57]

Many factors – the health needs of an aging population, continuing farm consolidation, shifts from goods-producing industry to services, and a growing disparity in wages – have worked to the detriment of small towns, at least those outside the metropolitan core extending from St. Cloud through the Twin Cities to Rochester. But the future of any particular town has remained impossible to predict. Special mixes of location and entrepreneurship would assure the viability of some towns, and others would surely survive by inertia. Despite limited services, the built environment of private dwellings and commercial buildings would continue to offer inexpensive rents for retirees, commuters, and start-up or marginal businesses. In Hector, in Renville County, the population fluctuated between 1,150 and 1,300 between 1960 and 1980. Two high-technology companies employed more than 300 people there in the mid-1980s, generating revenues of more than $50 million a year and making Hector a manufacturing success in Minnesota's farming region. The companies had moved their operations into vacant buildings that once housed an International Harvester farm equipment dealership and hardware, grocery, furniture, and clothing stores. A local box factory had replaced the John Deere dealer.[58] Outright abandonment was a slow process, and even Funkley, in Beltrami

County, and Tenney, in Wilkin County, showed signs of surviving, though they had fewer than one hundred residents since 1910 and 1930 respectively.[59]

Minnesotans' perceptions of small towns have slowly been adapting to the actual changes in these communities. The population threshold of full-service small towns has continued to creep upward, and the agricultural connections of town and country have grown weaker. "Small town" is no longer equated with "country town," and the traditional image of Main Street has lost some of its vitality. Too many Main Streets have become scenes of decline, not of public activity. Businesses have continued to move to highway strip locations, either within towns or in larger communities. Away from metropolitan areas, the viable towns – ones that could attract new residents – have been the larger places with true business districts. The small-town image has survived best through a haze of nostalgia in architecturally preserved but hardly typical towns like Northfield or Lanesboro.

The misperception cuts two ways. On the one hand, people have failed to see the many towns that do not fit the ideal image and have failed to understand the real problems that these places face. This collective self-deception – which is shared by many small-town residents – has made planning for the future more difficult.[60] On the other hand, nostalgia has continued to keep the entire state interested and concerned. That could only benefit Minnesota's small towns.

NOTES

This essay draws upon research done by the author at the Minnesota Historical Society (MHS) in 1985–86 in connection with the planning for an exhibit on small towns to be called *Common Places*.

1. Here and below, *Madelia Times-Messenger*, Apr. 30, 1986, p. 2, 14; Region Nine Development Commission, *Madelia: Region Nine Development Commission Report on the City of Madelia to U.S. Senator Dave Durenberger* (Mankato, Nov. 5, 1985); *Minneapolis Star and Tribune*, Nov. 3, 1985, p. 1B, 6B. The other towns were the southwestern Minnesota town of Fulda and a town in west-central Minnesota that was undisclosed because the commission thought less "bad news" would come out if it were identified, according to the account in the Minneapolis newspaper. The reports for the other towns, which were smaller than Madelia and suffered more from the farm crisis, did not provide the depth of the Madelia survey.

2. Chuck Slocum, *Minneapolis Star and Tribune*, Aug. 19, 1986, p. 9A, quoting Madelian Chris Olson Tatman.

3. "Overview" and "Madelia Community Profile," in Region Nine Development Commission, *Madelia; Minneapolis Star and Tribune*, Nov. 3, 1985, p. 1B.

4. The American small town has been studied extensively; see, for example, Lewis Atherton, *Main Street on the Middle Border* (Bloomington: Indiana University Press, 1954), Page Smith, *As a City upon a Hill* (New York: Alfred A. Knopf, 1966), Richard Lingeman, *Small Town America: A Narrative History 1620–Present* (Boston: Houghton Mifflin Co., 1980), and John A. Jakle, *The American Small Town: Twentieth-Century Place Images* (Hamden, Conn.: Shoe String Press, 1982). Lingeman's work is especially useful for its analysis of literature about small towns.

5. Edward Eggleston, *The Mystery of Metropolisville* (New York: Orange Judd and Co., 1873); Laura Ingalls Wilder, *On the Banks of Plum Creek* (New York: Harper and Row, 1953), as well as portions of *By the Shores of Silver Lake* (New York: Harper and Row, 1953); Sinclair Lewis, *Main Street* (New York: Harcourt, Brace and Howe, 1920).

6. Mark Schorer, *Sinclair Lewis: An American Life* (New York: McGraw-Hill Book Co., 1961), 268–69, 299–300; Charles P. Hall, *Sane Street: A Short Story of Minnesota* (Red Wing: Red Wing Advertising Co., 1922). Examples of journalistic accounts of Sauk Centre include James B. Hendryx, "Sauk Centre, Minnesota," *Ford Times* 43 (February 1951): 2–9; Dick Dahl, "Exile on Main Street: The Legacy of Sinclair Lewis," *Minnesota Monthly*, July 1985, p. 22–27; Henry Anatole Grunwald, "Main Street 1947," *Life*, June 23, 1947, p. 100–114; Joel Katz, "The Long Arm of the Small Town" (N.p., ca. 1967), available at MHS.

7. Edmund deS. Brunner, Gwendolyn S. Hughes, and Marjorie Patten, *American Agricultural Villages* (New York: George H. Doran Co., 1927); Edmund deS. Brunner, *Village Communities* (New York: George H. Doran Co., 1927), 182–96; Louis D. H. Weld, *Social and Economic Survey of a Community in the Red River Valley* (Minneapolis: University of Minnesota, 1915); Gustav P. Warber, *Social and Economic Survey of a Community in Northeastern Minnesota* (Minneapolis: University of Minnesota, 1915). The town of Benson was the subject of a later study by two Minnesota sociologists; see Don Martindale and R. Galen Hanson, *Small Town and the Nation: The Conflict of Local and Translocal Forces* (Westport, Conn.: Greenwood Publishing Corp., 1969).

8. *Lake Wobegon Days* (New York: Viking, 1985); Susan Allen Toth and Paul Gruchow, "Romance and Reality of Small Town America: Views of the Writers," in *The Small Town in America*, ed. William Deminoff (Proceedings of a symposium held Mar. 4–7, 1987, at Grinnell College, Grinnell, Iowa), 50–51. The popularity of Lake Wobegon stories probably made possible a more accurate view of small-town Minnesota by Minneota resident Bill Holm entitled *Prairie Days* (Dallas: Saybrook Publishing Co., 1987; originally published as *The Music of Failure* by Plains Press, Marshall, 1985).

9. *Village Communities*, vii.

10. United States, *Census*, 1980, vol. 1, chap. A, part 25, p. 16, 24; Map of Kasota, Minnesota, printed by Holmes, Payte and Buechner, St. Paul, ca. 1855. Estimate of town-lot capacity is based on number of lots and average household size of four people.

11. Two speakers at the 1987 Grinnell symposium pointed out the history of creating disposable towns. In the Midwest, this process was particularly strong because of the dependence on railroads and the fact "that we've made communities . . . that are based on economic convenience and that are as such disposable." See Richard Lingeman, "The American Small Town: Where It Came From, What It Was, What It Is," 34–35, and Paul Gruchow, "Romance and Reality of Small Town America," 44 (quotation), both in *Small Town in America*, ed. Deminoff.

12. Merlin Stonehouse, *John Wesley North and the Reform Frontier* (Minneapolis: University of Minnesota Press, 1965), xii–xiii.

13. "State Puts Some of Them Back on Map," *Minneapolis Tribune*, Jan. 1, 1979, p. 2B, 4B. Viability and a place on the map have varied from region to region in the state. In densely settled southeastern Minnesota, where Willow Creek is located, the map has been too cluttered to retain many place names. In the lightly settled Red River valley, more names have been kept, thus making the area look more "urbanized" than it actually is. In Polk County, Key West was no more than the junction of a railroad and a gravel road in the 1980s; still, it was on the 1987–88 map.

14. Office of State Demographer, *Minnesota Population and Household Estimates, 1986* (St. Paul: Minnesota State Planning Agency, 1987), 8; Adolf W. Link, *Remembrances of Kelliher, Minnesota* (N.p., [1986]), available at MHS.

15. Michael Hibbard and Lori Davis, "When the Going Gets Tough: Economic Reality and the Cultural Myths of Small-Town America," *American Planning Association Journal* 52 (1986): 419; the basic idea is from Page Smith. See also D. W. Meinig, "Symbolic Landscapes: Some Idealizations of American Communities," in *The Interpretation of Ordinary Landscapes*, ed. D. W. Meinig (New York: Oxford University Press, 1979), 167–69.

16. Jackson, *Discovering the Vernacular Landscape* (New Haven: Yale University Press, 1984), 73. Richard Lingeman created a similar image in his essay "The American Small Town," 26.

17. U.S., *Census*, 1980, vol. 1, chap. A, part 25, p. A-2. The definition used in this essay is the same one used by Peirce F. Lewis in his "Small Town in Pennsylvania," in *Regions of the United States*, ed. John Fraser Hart (New York: Harper and Row, 1972), 323–51. In the Midwest, however, a population of less than 15,000 may provide a more acceptable definition – only six nonmetropolitan towns in Minnesota (Albert Lea, Austin, Faribault, Hibbing, Owatonna, and Willmar) had 1980 populations between 15,000 and 25,000.

Small towns are defined and counted herein based primarily on their status in 1980 and are not redefined for previous census periods; thus, those that were urbanized in 1980 are also excluded from 1900 small-town counts. Towns that were once incorporated but that have disincorporated, however, are included. Populations are only recorded for incorporated places, based on census listings (federal census reports for 1890 through 1980). A town added to a decennial census would have incorporated in the prior ten-year period and those dropped would have disincorporated during that time. Towns with less than 25,000 in population but within urbanized areas are identified from the Census Bureau's "component parts" listing of urbanized areas (U.S., *Census*, 1980, vol. 1, chap. A, part 25, p. 42–43). Also defined as urbanized are Dellwood and Pine Springs, which fall within the Metropolitan Council's "developing ring" boundaries for the Twin Cities; Skyline and North Mankato, which are contiguous to Mankato; and Goodview, contiguous to Winona. Free-standing towns such as Stillwater and Sauk Centre are treated as small towns despite their location in census-defined metropolitan statistical areas, which include large portions of counties that are not urbanized.

For census and field-based studies of midwestern towns, see John Fraser Hart and Neil E. Salisbury, "Population Change in Middle Western Villages: A Statistical Approach," *Annals of the Association of American Geographers* 55 (1965): 140–60; John Fraser Hart, Neil E. Salisbury, and Everett G. Smith, Jr., "The Dying Village and Some Notions about Urban Growth," *Economic Geography* 44 (1968): 343–49.

18. Population requirements for incorporation have changed over the years. See Harvey Walker, *Village Laws and Government in Minnesota* (Minneapolis: University of Minnesota Press, 1927), 64, 82.

19. Analysis based on definition of small town as described in n. 17 and federal census reports, as follows: U.S., *Census*, 1900, *Population*, part 1, p. 456–58, 1920, *Population*, vol. 1, p. 236–40, 1940, *Population*, vol. 1, p. 551–53, 1960, *Number of Inhabitants: Minnesota*, p. 27–31, 1980, vol. 1, chap. A, part 25, p. A-2–A-5, 3, 7, 28–38, 41.

20. For more on plat requirements, see Walker, *Village Laws and Government*, 1. Original plats, on file at county recorder offices, list survey date, date of filing with county, proprietor, and surveyor. Plat analysis in the following paragraphs is based on author's participation in field and mail surveys of recorder offices as conducted by the State Historic Preservation Office, MHS, in the early 1980s. The high numbers that have been given in some sources for filings during the early years of speculation may include plats that have been lost or destroyed. Historian William W. Folwell, for example, says that at least seven hundred towns were platted between 1855 and 1857 (*A History of Minnesota*, rev. ed., vol. 1 [St. Paul: Minnesota Historical Society, 1969], 362).

21. The following section draws upon Thomas J. Baerwald, "Minnesota's Cities and Towns," *Architecture Minnesota* 2 (July–August 1976): 19–23; John R. Borchert and Neil C. Gustafson, *Atlas of Minnesota Resources and Settlement* (Minneapolis: Center for Urban and Regional Affairs, University of Minnesota, 1980).

22. Charles E. Lively, *Growth and Decline of Farm Trade Centers in Minnesota, 1905–1930* (University of Minnesota Agricultural Experiment Station, Bulletin 287, July 1932).

23. See also Arnold R. Alanen, "Years of Change on the Iron Range," *this volume*, 160–69.

24. Weld, *Survey in Red River Valley*, 4, 53, 55.

25. President's Subject Files, no. 3773, "Diagrams of Competitive Grain Territory of G.N. Ry.," sheet 7, August 1902, Great Northern Railway Co. Archives, MHS.

26. Arthur J. Larsen, *The Development of the Minnesota Road System* (St. Paul: Minnesota Historical Society, 1966), 399–400, 419–27; Richard S. Prosser, *Rails to the North Star* (Minneapolis: Dillon Press, 1966), 56; "Rail Users Convince Line to Keep Towns on Track," *Minneapolis Star and Tribune*, June 29, 1984, p. 3B, 4B.

27. The quotation is by Wilbur Zelinsky in "The Pennsylvania Town: An Overdue Geographical Account," *Geographical Review* 67 (1977): 138. The following material draws upon Thomas Harvey, "Railroad Towns: Urban Form on the Prairie," *Landscape* 27, no. 3 (1983): 26–34, and "The Making of Railroad Towns in Minnesota's Red River Valley" (Master's thesis, Pennsylvania State University, 1982); John C. Hudson, *Plains Country Towns* (Minneapolis: University of Minnesota Press, 1985), esp. 6, 88–90.

28. For example, see *Main Street*, 35–38. An "Elm Street" alternative is given in Hildegard Binder Johnson, *Order upon the Land: The U.S. Rectangular Land Survey and the Upper Mississippi Country* (New York: Oxford University Press, 1976), 177–84.

29. Johnson, *Order upon the Land*, 90.

30. William T. Morgan, "Strongboxes on Main Street: Prairie-style Banks," *Landscape* 24, no. 2 (1980): 35–40; Larry Millett, *The Curve of the Arch: The Story of Louis Sullivan's Owatonna Bank* (St. Paul: Minnesota Historical Society Press, 1985).

31. Paul J. Ostendorf, "The History of the Public Library Movement in Minnesota from 1849 to 1916" (Ph.D. diss., University of Minnesota, 1984), 160, 181–95.

32. On strip developments see Jackson, *Discovering the Vernacular Landscape*, 79–80; Thomas Harvey, "Main Street and Highway Strip in Southwestern Minnesota" (Paper presented at annual meeting of Association of American Geographers, Philadelphia, April 1979).

33. Brunner, *Village Communities*, 183; Atherton, *Main Street on the Middle Border*, 220; inventory form, Thief River Falls Power Plant, State Historic Preservation Office, MHS.

34. Gerhard A. Gesell, *Minnesota Public Utility Rates* (Minneapolis: University of Minnesota, 1914), 1; League of Minnesota Municipalities, *An Analysis of the Generation and Distribution of Electric Power in Minnesota* (Publication 28; Minneapolis, 1929).

35. Material for this section is drawn from John W. Webb, "Basic Concepts in the Analysis of Small Urban Centers of Minnesota," *Annals of the Association of American Geographers* 49 (1959): 55–72; Robert J. Holloway, *A City Is More than People: A Study of Fifteen Minnesota Communities* (Minneapolis: University of Minnesota Press, 1954).

36. U.S., *Census*, 1920, *State Compendium: Minnesota*, 29–32.

37. Brunner, *Village Communities*, 182; Warber, *Survey in Northeastern Minnesota*, 33–35, 37–38, 41; Weld, *Survey in Red River Valley*, 36.

38. Baerwald, "Minnesota's Cities and Towns," 19–23; John R. Borchert, *America's Northern Heartland* (Minneapolis: University of Minnesota Press, 1987), 166; Holloway, *City Is More than People*, 43.

39. Prosser, *Rails to the North Star*, 17, 27–28; David A. Walker, *Iron Frontier: The Discovery and Early Development of Minnesota's Three Ranges* (St. Paul: Minnesota Historical Society Press, 1979), 48, 57–58.

40. Chisago City Booster Club, *Building Chisago City* (Chisago City, 1981), 26; Brian McGinty, "Mr. Sears and Mr. Roebuck," *American History Illustrated*, June 1986, p. 34–35; *Minneapolis Star and Tribune*, Mar. 9, 1986, p. 19A.

41. Preface to *Main Street*.

42. Brunner, *Village Communities*, 182; here and below, Weld, *Survey in Red River Valley*, 73–74.

43. Hudson, *Plains Country Towns*, 123–30.

44. Weld, *Survey in Red River Valley*, 83; Warber, *Survey in Northeastern Minnesota*, 103, 114.

45. Doris A. Pearson, "Dassel: Past and Present. A Survey of Recent Changes in an Agricultural Community," 1942, p. 24–25; typescript available at MHS.

46. Humphrey Moynihan, "Archbishop Ireland's Colonies," *Acta et dicta* 6 (1934): 215, 217, 225–26; James P. Shannon, *Catholic Colonization on the Western Frontier* (New Haven, Conn.: Yale University Press, 1957), chaps. 3, 4; Warber, *Survey in Northeastern Minnesota*, 84–85; Brunner, *Village Communities*, 191.

47. Weld, *Survey in Red River Valley*, 74–75, 86 (quotation); Warber, *Survey in Northeastern Minnesota*, 83, 88.

48. See also Richard M. Chapman, "Religious Belief and Behavior," *this volume*, 520–23.

49. Martindale and Hanson, *Small Town and the Nation*, 53–54, 116, 118.

50. Warber, *Survey in Northeastern Minnesota*, 75–77, 110, 114.

51. "Rural School Districts Using Selective Mergers to Save Town Identities," *Minneapolis Star and Tribune*, Dec. 4, 1986, p. 1A, 16A; "Mazeppa and Zumbrota Will Merge Their Schools," *Minneapolis Star and Tribune*, Mar. 25, 1987, p. 3B.

52. Madison Centennial Book Committee, *Madison Historical Album* (Madison, [1985]), 87; *Holdingford Advertiser*, Sept. 14, 1916.

53. Lingeman, *Small Town America*, 305–6; Atherton, *Main Street on the Middle Border*, 311.

54. Ann Burckhardt, "Many Summer Festivals Will Offer Local Foods," *Minneapolis Star and Tribune*, May 13, 1987, p. 3T. For a historical perspective, see Works Progress Administration, *The WPA Guide to Minnesota* (New York: Viking Press, 1938; St. Paul: Minnesota Historical Society Press, 1985), xxxix–xl. See also Karal Ann Marling, "Culture and Leisure: 'The Good Life in Minnesota,'" *this volume*, 560–62.

55. The proceedings of the conference were published as Deminoff, ed., *Small Town in America* (see n. 8 above).

56. Lewis, "Small Town in Pennsylvania," 326–27; William Mueller, "Do Americans Really Want to Live in Small Towns?" *American Demographics* 9 (January 1987): 34–37, 60 (reference to Beale on p. 34).

57. "Herberger's Company-as-Family Strategy Pays Off," *St. Paul Pioneer Press and Dispatch*, Jan. 20, 1986, p. 8D.

58. U.S., *Census*, 1980, vol. 1, chap. A, part 25, p. 29; Main Street Radio Team, Minnesota Public Radio, "Against the Grain" (Documentary on Minnesota's rural areas and small towns broadcast on KSJN-FM, Jan. 2, 1988). See also John Fraser Hart, "Small Towns and Manufacturing," *Geographical Review* 78 (1988): 272–87.

59. "Small-Town Life Is Big in Funkley and Tenney," *Minneapolis Star and Tribune*, June 3, 1986, p. 1A, 8A; U.S., *Census*, 1920, *State Compendium: Minnesota*, 30, 33; 1940, *Population: Minnesota*, 17, 19; 1980, vol. 1, chap. A, part 25, p. 10, 24.

60. Hibbard and Davis, "When the Going Gets Tough," 427.

Thomas O'Connor delivering the mail in Le Sueur County, about 1910

DAVID L. NASS

The Rural Experience

While a variety of reasons drew early Minnesotans to the area, the lure of the land was both a recurring and a powerful inducement to settlement. The Homestead Act of 1862 offered 160 acres to would-be farmers, and the prospect of buying a tract of cheap railroad land attracted others. Golden opportunities seemed to beckon European peasants who could only dream of such estates in their homelands. By the end of the century, state-published pamphlets in the English, Norwegian, Swedish, and French languages encouraged new arrivals to the United States to seek out Minnesota and offered information on crops, land prices, credit terms, and other practical matters to potential settlers.[1]

From the 1870s through the 1890s settlers from the more established eastern states and from Iowa, Illinois, and Ohio moved into Minnesota. Official immigration efforts coupled with railroad land-market activities appealed to the restless American farmer and speculator, fueling continuing settlement. By the 1890s southern Minnesota's counties were described as well developed but still offering opportunity for the ambitious. Farms in Olmsted, Waseca, and Redwood counties sold for at least twenty-five dollars an acre. Wheat and small grains were the leading crops; flax was thought to have a great future. Stock raising and dairying increased; roads, schools, and churches were well established, and the counties were optimistic of future growth.[2]

Publicity given to the highly mechanized "bonanza farming" operations of the Red River valley had also stimulated settlement. "The land of the sure crop," as historian Hiram M. Drache labeled it, attracted many willing to invest in large-scale wheat operations, often more than a thousand acres each, in hope of quick profits. By 1890 the bonanza-type farms had declined in importance, but the valley continued with a higher proportion of large farms to small than other areas of the state.[3]

The majority of rural settlers sought profit from farming or land speculation; however, the ratio of those attracted to Minnesota as "move-up" farmers from the East to new settlers looking for a permanent home is not known. Traditional studies, such as Richard Hofstadter's *The Age of Re-*

form, picture the American agriculturalist as a small businessman on the make, moving often to profit from land sales, rather than as a settled farmer. Closer to home Jon Wefald, former Minnesota commissioner of agriculture and chancellor of the state university system, portrayed the immigrant farmer as treasuring the land and pursuing economic self-sufficiency. According to Wefald, the Norwegian-Lutheran farmer, at least, wanted a farm to support the family – not for speculative gain. Whatever the merit of the two approaches, tension between advocates of farming as a business and those viewing it as a way of life dominated public debate on farm policy in the twentieth century.[4]

Although most of the desirable agricultural lands had been cultivated by the 1890s, Minnesotans continued to promote farm development. One method to increase crop acreage was to drain wet land, and by 1902 progress in drainage had benefited many farmers. The increase in hay and pasture land stimulated diversification, encouraging a shift from heavy reliance on wheat to dairying and stock raising.[5]

With machines like the Buckeye Traction Ditcher moving through 160 rods a day, drainage land increased throughout the Red River valley and in southern Minnesota in the first years of the twentieth century. Legislation passed in 1905 extended drainage efforts to state-owned land in northern Minnesota. The state's attorney general, Edward T. Young, decided it was proper to help counties drain marshy areas affecting private land, provided the results benefited public health and utility. Between 1907 and 1913, state- and county-drained ditches improved 6 million acres (estimated at a value of from fifteen to sixty dollars each) at a cost of about $1.50 per acre. In Roseau County, for example, the state drained about 350,000 acres and estimated that 4 million more could be converted to agricultural use. Drainage and building projects were combined, and the soil removed in dredging was used to build roads alongside the ditches. The total drainage effort provided land for more and bigger farms and increased agricultural profits; it also changed the look of the land and eventually affected wildlife and flood-control efforts.[6]

The attempted development of cutover areas of northern Minnesota was another tactic meant to expand croplands and extend profit and the good life to more farmers. In 1921 the Land Clearing Department of the University of Minnesota, in cooperation with northern county farm bureaus, launched a campaign to remove brush and stumps from the land. Crews toured the area in trucks, putting on twenty-seven demonstrations in Cook, St. Louis, Carlton, Pine, Mille Lacs, and Morrison counties. Stumps and stones were blasted with dynamite and picric acid (an explosive made by the government for "war purposes"); experts demonstrated the use of stump pullers and tillage techniques to gatherings of 100 to 175 people. Thirty-four carloads (744,000 pounds) of picric acid were distributed, and plans called for clearing thirty-five thousand acres.[7]

A 1922 land-clearing contest in Koochiching, Crow Wing, St. Louis, Aitkin, Beltrami, and Itasca counties advanced the cause of cutover farming. The average contestant brushed and stumped about fifteen acres, much more than the typical settler's annual rate of three acres a year. Yet despite the amount of energy spent clearing relatively small land areas, the cutover land never really paid off.[8]

Wheat farming and flour milling dominated the Minnesota agricultural scene in the late nineteenth and early twentieth centuries in what historian Theodore C. Blegen labeled the "dual domain." Increasing wheat production was probably a combination of more people planting wheat on new land and of the growth of scientific agriculture. Working in North Dakota and Minnesota, W. M. Hays, assistant secretary of the U.S. Department of Agriculture and international agricultural adviser, and D. N. Harper developed Minnesota No. 163 (Improved Fife). This now-famous wheat strain, released to farmers in 1899, yielded 26.2 bushels per acre, a 21 percent increase over its parent, Scotch Fife. North Dakota farmer L. N. Haynes developed Minnesota No. 169 (Haynes Bluestem), which was released to farmers through the University of Minnesota in 1901. At the same time, plant diseases were being attacked by those like E. M. Freeman, founder and director of one of the nation's first plant pathology divisions, located at the University of Minnesota.[9]

As exclusive wheat production exhausted older land, many farmers had to choose between moving west or north and investing in new equipment or livestock. Reluctant to change their methods, many opted to move. Others began to diversify – to oats, corn, potatoes, barley, flax, and rye, or to dairying and livestock. In 1900 wheat was the dominant crop, accounting for about half (50.69 percent) of cultivated land, but by 1910 acreage had declined to about 25 percent. The largest decrease occurred in southwestern Minnesota, where by 1910 about as much land was devoted to oats as to wheat. The increased production of hay and forage crops reflected the practice of rotation and a growth in dairying and livestock farming.[10]

The development of a strain of alfalfa that would overwinter while providing good yield greatly aided diversification. Wendelin Grimm, a German immigrant, came to Carver County in 1857 with fifteen or twenty pounds of alfalfa seed and each year planted seeds from plants that had survived the winter before. His alfalfa or "everlasting clover" (*ewiger Klee*) provided feed for cattle, dairy cows, and swine, and yielded three or four cuttings annually. It eventually caught the attention of the University of Minnesota Agricultural Experiment Station and later the U.S. Department of Agriculture. In 1910 Minnesota farmers planted about 2,300 acres of alfalfa, mostly in Carver County. With the help of county agents, over six thousand farmers seeded 12,000 acres in 1914; the 1915 estimate was over 25,000 acres.[11]

The North Dakota Grimm Alfalfa Seed Producers' Association incorporated in 1916; a Minnesota group formed in 1924. These organizations required strict testing of seed to keep the variety pure and promoted the use of certified seed. Minnesota farmers believed in "an acre of alfalfa for every cow," and because alfalfa restored fertility, its use won support among farmers interested in soil conservation. In 1924 the seed producers' association placed a bronze marker honoring Grimm's work at his farm.[12]

A farm family stopping for lunch during harvest, Nicollet County, 1907

C. D. Gilfillan of Redwood County, a prominent proponent of diversification, in an 1897 speech before the Minnesota Stock Breeders' Association urged his neighbors to raise livestock and poultry. He emphasized that these activities would improve family life by developing good habits and responsibility. Growing wheat did not encourage intellectual activity, Gilfillan maintained, but caring for animals sharpened observation and exercised reasoning. He concluded that diversification would improve finances *and* make farmers into better thinkers and happier citizens.[13]

Gilfillan's rationale reminds us that the rural experience involves more than crop development. While diversification and technology affected daily work, changes in transportation, electrification, postal service, education, communications, business, finance, and marketing influenced the economic, social, religious, political, family, and recreational lives of twentieth-century farmers, sometimes bringing them closer to life in the cities and sometimes alienating them.

Life on the Farm

Whether a settler sought pastoral splendor or land appreciation, the reality of farming was very different from the romantic vision. The Homestead Act of 1862 offered 160 acres of land only to the settler who could survive on it for five years, cultivate it, and build a permanent dwelling. Many homesteaders succeeded, but many others died or went broke while trying to realize their dreams.[14]

Life on the farm, especially before World War I, was difficult. The Currier and Ives view of the rural homestead does not reveal the tremendous difference between the everyday conveniences in town and the hardship in country homes, where ordinary household chores simply took more time and energy. There was usually no running water, central heat, indoor plumbing, electricity, refrigeration, gas, city sewage, or nearby store. Although mechanization made farm work less tedious after the Civil War, much physical labor was still necessary. Simply taking care of horses, for example, added greatly to daily chores.

In 1908 President Theodore Roosevelt appointed the Country Life Commission to investigate living conditions on the farm. In reviewing the commission's report the next year, the president indicated that country life failed to satisfy the social and intellectual aspirations of the people. This failure, along with the superior business opportunities available in urban areas, was contributing to the movement of rural people to the cities. The commission reported that farmers were prosperous in comparison with those of the past, but that the progress of agriculture could not be compared to that of business.[15]

The country life movement demanded consideration of issues beyond economics. Its goal was to raise the standard of living by promoting modern housing, home conveniences, and farmstead beautification with trees, flowers, shrubs, and attractive, well-laid-out buildings. Social activities, literary clubs, and the revitalization of country schools and churches were the subjects of meetings and forums across the nation. The Minnesota Country Life Conference held in 1916 at the College of Agriculture in St. Paul addressed workers in agricultural instruction, consolidated-school principals, normal-training teachers, Young Men's Christian Association and rural church staff, and lay people interested in educational, social, and religious developments. Among those participating were Gov. Joseph A. A. Burnquist, George Edgar Vincent, president of the University of Minnesota, and Catholic archbishop John Ireland. *The Farmer*, Minnesota's oldest and most influential farm magazine, praised the work of the conference but regretted that only a few farmers attended the meetings.[16]

An obvious purpose of the movement was to make rural life more attractive, thus stemming the flow of young people to the city. Dean H. L. Russell of the University of Wisconsin College of Agriculture encouraged farmers to improve their homes as well as pay off the farm mortgage. Russell reasoned that investing in the home might be an important factor in keeping the boy on the farm.[17]

Water was one of the greatest problems. Most rural homes lacked running water; it had to be hauled from the well to the house for cooking, washing, and bathing. Wells were often placed for convenient feeding of livestock, without domestic consideration. Russell suggested that bringing water into the home be a priority. Windmills and gravity arrangements could provide pressure systems for bathing and removing waste to cesspools.

The pull between spending for the farm and spending on the family was a recurring theme in farm journals and conversations with rural people.

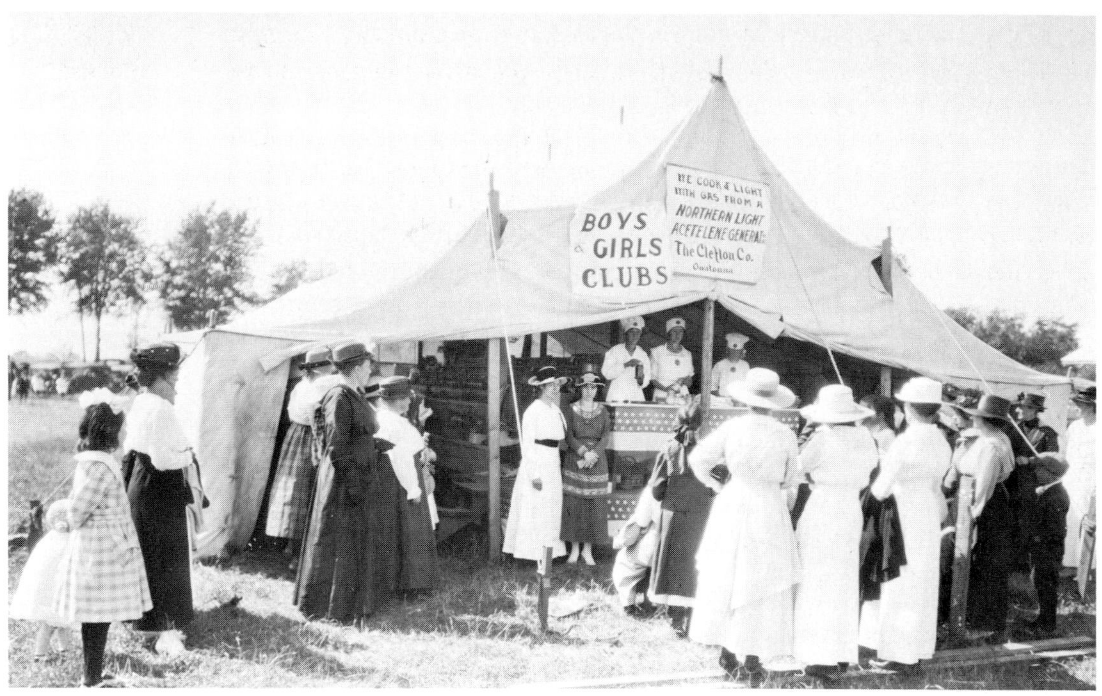

Women watching a demonstration of gas cooking at the University of Minnesota Experiment Station at Crookston, about 1915

In 1914 author May L. Spencer took on the issue directly, claiming the mother was the most overworked person on the farm: women not only cooked, washed, sewed, and cared for the children but also fed chickens and calves, milked cows, and kept vegetable gardens. Using as an analogy the practice of taking good care of cows so they would produce a high percentage of butterfat, she asked, "Is he always careful to see that his wife does not work too hard?"[18]

Spencer suggested several ways to ease the farm woman's burden: A thoughtful husband would see that his wife had one afternoon a week to herself plus the use of a horse and carriage for visits, as a relief from farm and household chores. A convenient and well-arranged kitchen, plumbing, and power laundry equipment would greatly lighten housework. If a community were large enough, a cooperative laundry, such as the one at Chatfield, might be set up at the local creamery. Improvements made to lighten women's work and prolong their lives would be worth the expense even if families had to wait for a new barn.

Farm journals frequently published notices of building plans running the gamut from silos and barns to sheep houses, icehouses, chicken houses, and family dwellings. Writers stressed the need for careful planning of structures that would be attractive as well as functional. They said buildings should be in proportion to the value of the land. Special magazine supplements printed the winning entries in building-plan contests. *The Farmer* offered a book of plans to anyone who sent in four cents postage, and in 1913 the Minnesota State Art Society awarded five hundred dollars to the top six entries in a model farm home contest for architects. Its purpose was to develop and make available modern plans providing the maximum comfort and convenience at the lowest cost.[19]

Those trying to better country life paid much attention to rural churches. Suggestions for improvement ranged from church mergers to special training for pastors. The editor of *The Farmer* wished "to bring about a consciousness in the country that a strong rural church matters much more than any particular denomination or sect." Such urban-based analysts overlooked both the importance of denomination to country parishioners and the social patterns that developed around churches.[20]

Conferences, such as one held at Hamline University in St. Paul in 1921, and agricultural short courses at the University of Minnesota aimed to make pastors more enthusiastic. Under the direction of Dean Albert Z. Mann, Hamline's professor of rural leadership, ministers were offered courses in rural economics, farmers' elevators, tenantry, and farm organizations as well as church administration. The idea was to help them become more knowledgeable about rural practices, as well as highly inspired to promote education, recreation, and social activity. These men could then make their churches into real community centers.[21]

Efforts to improve rural schools focused on bettering the quality of teachers, modernizing school buildings, instilling respect for the rural lifestyle, and effecting consolidation. In the one-room country school, a single teacher taught all the lessons to students of all ages. Professional educators saw this as an unsatisfactory arrangement in comparison to graded urban schools that had specialized, better-trained instructors. In 1910 Henry Wallace, editor of *Wallaces' Farmer,* urged Minnesota county school superintendents to upgrade their institutions. Citing the Country Life Commission finding that rural schools were inefficient and promoted drift from country to towns, he stressed that "farm life is on the whole more satisfying to the average man than the life of the city." Wallace asked the superintendents to add the teaching of two or three specifically agricultural topics to their curricula. He also suggested that the flow from farm to city resulted in high-priced, inefficient farm labor and decreasing production. Schools stressing the virtue of rural life and stimulating interest in agriculture could help remedy the problem.[22]

The Minnesota legislature of 1911 provided funds for increased education in agriculture, home economics, and manual training and required that instructors be graduates of four-year agricultural colleges. In addition, short courses were devised for farmers and country students whose time at school might be limited. State superintendent of schools C. G. Schulz reported thirty-five rural school consolidations in six months that year, concluding that people demanded better schools, buildings, and transportation. Schulz saw a real need for principals who could help create schools with distinctly rural qualities and train children with an interest in and knowledge of farm life.[23]

The trend toward consolidation continued, with 303 occurring between 1911 and 1921. Then, in 1922 the state increased aid (for nonresident student tuition and other needs), making it less advantageous for districts to expand. Between 1922 and 1932 there were 101 consolidations; between 1932 and 1940, only 21.[24]

Ending Rural Isolation

Isolation has always been a problem in the rural Midwest. Some early farm organizations such as the Grange sought to counteract this isolation through meetings and educational activities, but the establishment of Rural Free Delivery (RFD) in 1896 was the first giant step toward opening communication for rural citizens. Before RFD, farmers went to the nearest town perhaps once a week for mail, supplies, and visiting. The small, local post offices became social and political centers that helped attract business to the villages.[25]

Merchants, and especially postmasters, saw RFD as a threat. Mail delivered to farmhouses meant less incentive to go to town, at least a particular town. Some nervous farmers feared their mail and stamps would be stolen. Opponents of RFD argued it would be too expensive, bankrupting the country. It did not, but it did lead to the closing of many fourth-class post offices and the disappearance of some small villages.

The 1890 census showed depopulation of rural districts in several states, and proponents of RFD argued it could stop the drift from the farm by relieving isolation. The U.S. postmaster general supported this position in 1900: "Rural free delivery brings the farm within the daily range of the intellectual and commercial activities of the world, and the isolation and monotony which have been the bane of agricultural life are sensibly mitigated." His report showed that RFD increased correspondence, postal receipts, and the circulation of newspapers and periodical literature; it also stimulated road improvement.[26]

By 1899 Minnesota's only RFD routes were four experimental ones at Farmington. Two years later there were 134 routes serving sixty-seven thousand people, and by 1925 the state's 1,720 routes covered 49,160 miles. Besides the advantages listed in the postmaster general's report, RFD, in conjunction with parcel post and mail-order marketing services, eventually added even greater dimension to rural living.[27]

The period from 1900 to 1918 was one of general prosperity for American farmers. During World War I they continued to thrive, expanding operations to meet an increased demand. After the war, however, crop prices plummeted, and by 1921 American agriculture was in the throes of a depression. Improvements in rural housing slowed during the 1920s and 1930s, and a 1940 survey showed many rural Minnesotans living in substandard dwellings. According to the University of Minnesota's Agricultural Experiment Station, only 34 percent of rural homes had running water, 16 percent had central heating, and 27 percent had electricity. There were significant regional variations in the quality of household living, with the northern half of the state ranking lower than the southern.[28]

Rural life did not improve substantially until the Rural Electrification Administration (REA) brought central station electric power to the countryside. When the REA was established in 1935, only about 10 percent of America's farmhouses had electricity, though power plants had been built in some Minnesota cities as early as the 1880s.[29]

Most people today have some idea of what rural life was like before electricity: People used kerosene lamps and went to bed early. But the lack of electricity had more wide-ranging implications. There was usually no pressurized water system for washing, drinking, and waste disposal. Water was pumped by hand and heated on a wood- or corncob-burning stove for baths, dish washing, and laundry. Women used scrub boards or washing machines with gasoline engines. An outhouse, usually placed back near the grove, served for waste disposal. Water for cattle was supplied by a windmill, and cob heaters were used to keep water from freezing. Although these methods were ecologically sound, they were burdensome.

The rural family without electricity not only went without the comfort and safety of central heating, refrigeration, and running water, but also was denied educational and medical advances. Rural schools had no movies, slides, or other sophisticated audio-visual aids. Small-town doctors treated patients without central station electric service. For example, Dr. R. A. Peterson and Alice Mellquist Peterson, his wife and nurse, practiced in the Redwood County town of Vesta (population 250). They managed with only a community-owned gasoline-powered generator – by scheduling tonsillectomies and circumcisions on Mondays and Wednesdays from 8:00 A.M. to noon, the hours when they had power. The town had electricity from dark until 10:00 P.M. each day.[30]

Farmers demanded electricity long before they all got it. As early as 1914, a group from Stony Run Township in Yellow Medicine County organized a company to distribute electricity. This forerunner of the REA co-ops bought power from the Granite Falls municipal plant and connected twenty-six farms over that many miles of line. Another group in Dawson built its own lines and negotiated a five-year contract with the Otter Tail Power Company in 1926, but other farmers were not so lucky.[31]

In the 1920s the University of Minnesota Division of Agricultural Engineering, in cooperation with Northern States Power Company, equipment manufacturers, the state Committee on the Relation of Electricity to Agriculture, and farmers, developed one of the first experimental farm powerlines in the world. This 6.2-mile stretch served ten farms near Red Wing. (Nine potential farm customers along the route refused service.) The first energy flowed through the lines on Christmas Eve of 1923 to perhaps the best-equipped farms in America. Manufacturers lent equipment, and each item had a separate meter to register usage and efficiency. The project experimented with electrical applications, determined costs, and assessed problems, producing much valuable information. The use of electricity to run milking machines, grain elevators, feed mills, ensilage cutters, and threshing machines was impressive. The convenience of pressurized water systems, electric lights, irons, washing machines, and

Linda Benitt working at the electric refrigerator in her kitchen, Dakota County, 1944

refrigerators was apparent.[32] Still, the extension of central station power to the rest of rural America went slowly. Why?

The fundamental obstacle to electrification was the philosophy of utility companies that each line extension had to pay for itself; as a result, most utilities extended lines only to the next farm or the most promising area. Proponents of rural electrification advocated area development instead. Under such a program, companies would offer service to large blocks of farmers simultaneously, with the idea that increased use and balanced power loads would lower unit costs. The REA eventually adopted this principle.

Upon the creation of REA in 1935, Minnesotans began establishing co-ops to be eligible for distribution loans. Generally, an organizing committee formed, usually with assistance from the county agent, and held a mass meeting to explain the program to farmers. In every community a few men did the bulk of the work. They drove from farm to farm trying to get signatures and five-dollar membership fees, usually receiving no pay but between three and five dollars a day for expenses. Morris L. Cooke, REA's first administrator, attended the 1936 dedication of the first Minnesota REA co-op – Meeker Cooperative Light and Power Association of Litchfield. By 1963 electricity had reached 99 percent of Minnesota's farms, 83 percent of it from REA co-ops. This most successful New Deal program in rural America did much to bridge the gap between rural and urban life.[33]

Minnesotans made major contributions to the rural electrification movement. Ancher Nelsen, born on a farm in Renville County and elected state senator from McLeod County from 1935 to 1949, served as national administrator of the REA from 1953 to 1956. Robert S. (Bob) Bergland, a Roseau farmer and secretary of agriculture in President Jimmy Carter's cabinet, later served as chief executive for the National Rural Electric Cooperative Association.[34]

Another change in rural life rolled in with the automobile. The horseless carriage, over the span of about a generation, also helped to end rural isolation. Although it frightened those who saw it as the "devil wagon," most rural Minnesotans adopted the car with an enthusiasm equal to that of their city cousins. By 1913 about half of the state's more than forty thousand autos were registered in rural areas.[35]

While rural Minnesotans reviewed ads in country magazines for Fords, Overlands, and Hudsons, two men emerged as leaders of the Good Roads movement. Charles M. Babcock of Elk River, an exponent of road improvement, gained appointment to the state highway commission in 1910 and later became commissioner of highways. Robert C. Dunn of Mille Lacs County, founder of the *Princeton Union* and a state legislator, championed laws designed to improve Minnesota's rural highways. In 1913, Dunn authored a law revising the funding of rural roads so that the wealthiest and most populous counties would assist those less fortunate. In 1920 Commissioner Babcock's educational and lobbying efforts culminated in the passage of a constitutional amendment that allowed the state to issue bonds to finance road building. This so-called Babcock Amendment marked the beginning of the modern trunk highway system.[36]

By the late twentieth century, the state was laced with a highway and freeway system – the dreams of the Good Roads pioneers come true. Highways and automobiles together made a tremendous impact on rural life. Improved roads made it easier for farmers to market crops at country elevators; indeed, the farm-to-market road was a common theme for highway boosters. But the changes brought by the auto were as much social as economic. RFD, electricity, and the radio carried the nonagricultural world into the country, creating a whole new set of expectations. The car provided a way of getting to that other world.[37]

Unlike government programs that had imposed changes on rural citizens, owning an auto allowed individuals to make decisions that ultimately altered rural activities and institutions such as schools, churches, medicine, and leisure. People no longer chose pastimes, friends, or family doctors by proximity alone; the auto gave them access to better goods and services. At the same time, many activities within reach by auto were beyond the control of local communities and therefore suspicious. Young peo-

Farmers operating a steam-powered plow in Chippewa County, about 1914

ple driving to nearby church socials or YMCA dances were one thing; their dancing at urban roadhouses was quite another. The auto brought new opportunities, but it also inflicted emotional and economic strain on small towns that had to compete with larger population centers.[38]

Two enterprising Hibbing individuals, Carl Eric Wickman and Andrew G. Anderson, used an open car to transport miners from one site to another in 1914. From this humble beginning their operation developed into the Mesaba Transportation Company, the Northland Transportation Company, and then the Greyhound Corporation. By 1927 buses carried over fifteen million passengers in Minnesota, and the motor bus has since been an important supplement to rural auto and rail service.[39]

The gasoline engine not only made travel easier but also changed the way work was done on the farm. Ever since the J. I. Case Company of Racine, Wisconsin, produced what it called the first steam engine for farm use in 1869, manufacturers had sought to replace human and animal labor with mechanical power. Steam-powered devices were heavy and bulky, and in 1892 Case introduced its first gasoline-driven engine for the farm. Gasoline traction engines soon became "tractors," evolving into lighter, more adaptable machines. By 1917 the first mass-produced tractor, the Fordson, hit the market.[40]

With the introduction of the power take-off, the tractor engine could be used to drive other farm machines such as binders and mowers. International Harvester developed a tricycle-type tractor in 1924 for cultivating row crops like corn. When Allis-Chalmers introduced a rubber-tired model in 1932, the basic elements of the modern tractor were in place. The machine has continued to evolve: diesel and liquefied petroleum gas have joined gasoline as fuels; hydraulics, four-wheel drive, and enclosed cabs with air conditioning and stereos have made operations smoother and more comfortable. Self-propelled combines have further lightened the work of farmers, making their labor far different from that of their early-twentieth-century counterparts.

Wealthier or more progressive farmers led the way with power equipment, but by the late 1920s and early 1930s tractors were common on Minnesota farms. As late as 1941, however, some advocates argued for retaining horses and mules, even while acknowledging that nine of ten farms had tractors. World War II brought new demands for increased production along with shortages of labor and led to the virtual retirement of the Percherons and Belgians that had toiled in an earlier day. By 1974 the average Minnesota farm had 2.6 tractors and no work horses.[41]

Education, as well as new sources of power, sparked changes on the farm. Advertisements, county fairs, and exhibits provided information on seeds, equipment, and techniques but left some individuals confused about finances and management. Early in the century the College of Agriculture at the University of Minnesota began to offer farmers help with the latest scientific and management approaches. Agricultural extension became part of the university's Division of Agriculture in 1909, receiving fifty thousand dollars in state support for the 1910–11 biennium. The 1913 legislature provided matching funds of one thousand dollars per year to any county employing an extension agent.[42]

Minnesota 4-H Club members with their heifers, about 1935

Before an agent was sent to the field, the extension service required that a county have a functioning farmer organization to serve as a local base of support. This policy led to close ties between the extension program and county farm bureaus, a connection some rural people did not like. In Douglas County, for example, the Nonpartisan League (organized to redress farmers' grievances by electing selected candidates to state offices) strongly opposed both extension service and farm bureaus; the county went without an agent from 1918 to 1933. The agricultural depression of the 1920s and 1930s hurt extension funding efforts too, but the work generally prospered as state and federal appropriations increased. The 1953 legislature repealed any official connection between bureau and extension service.[43]

Extension programs addressed subjects beyond farm production. By 1960, seventy-nine counties had home agents conducting programs in food, nutrition, clothing, family life, and economics. The 4-H program, begun in 1914 to train youth in production techniques and equipment handling, broadened its list of classes. By the 1950s, 4-H groups offered students, aged nine to twenty-one, courses in dog care, bicycle maintenance, crafts, entomology, and photography. Although such classes were popular, those for people older than nineteen years were abandoned in 1964.[44]

The Farmers Organize

Despite technical assistance and educational programs, the modernization of commercial agriculture over the past century spawned economic and political conflicts. With expanded mechanization, better seeds, and scientific methods, American farmers produced more and earned less. Faced with greater capital needs and unpredictable world markets, they sometimes struck out in fury at creditors, railroads, middlemen, and the grain "trusts," as big corporations were labeled before World War I. Some groups sought to restructure the American economic system; others wanted reform. Some agrarians were just plain cranks; some businessmen were as unscrupulous as their victims alleged. All were caught in a modern industrial capitalist society where Jeffersonian rhetoric glorifying yeoman farmers no longer fit reality.

In a search for relief from low crop prices, tight credit, and high freight charges, many nineteenth-century Minnesota farmers had flirted with the Greenback (National Independent) party, the antimonopoly movement, the Farmers' Alliance, and the Populist party. Their mistrust of railroads, banks, and grain merchants evident in these movements lived beyond William Jennings Bryan's defeat for the presidency in 1896. The American Society of Equity, devoted to the idea of cooperatives, took up the grievances of spring wheat growers in 1903 when it urged farmers to hold their grain until the price reached a dollar a bushel. Many did just that, and when the price went up the Equity swiftly took credit.[45]

Equity membership quickly increased. In 1908 the Equity Cooperative

Exchange organized to improve prices through terminal marketing. Exchange leaders engaged in a war with railroads, bankers, grain merchants, and the Minnesota State Grading and Inspection Board, denouncing them for low weights, undergrading, and unreasonable dockage for foreign matter in grain. State inspectors were labeled as tools of the "speculators," "thieves," and "crooks" who ran the trade. Some charges were legitimate and some were not; regardless, many farmers believed there was a conspiracy depriving them of just rewards for their gamble and hard labor.

The Minneapolis Chamber of Commerce sought to destroy the young Equity movement by unleashing its secretary, John G. McHugh, who had lobbied to oppose Canadian cooperatives, against the farmers' exchange. In 1913, when the state legislature began to investigate the acrimonious rivalry, Minnesotans were treated to the charges and countercharges of chamber and Equity forces testifying before house and senate committees. The investigation produced no concrete results or resolution, leading scholars of the movement to conclude that "neither group conducted an impartial investigation, but each, with some accuracy, accused the other of being unfair."[46]

During the prosperity of World War I, the Equity exchange grew. Although it never achieved national status, it added stockholders and built new elevators totaling eighty by mid-1922: fifty-two in North Dakota, twenty-six in Minnesota, and two in South Dakota. It managed to promote grain and livestock shipping associations, increased pressure for better grading standards, warehousing, and credit facilities, and generally furthered the cooperative movement. Nevertheless, weaknesses in the organization combined with the depression of 1921 sent it into receivership by 1923; the Minnesota Farmers Union absorbed it, continuing the cooperative movement. Along with its legacy of program and practices, the Equity also produced leaders like Myron W. Thatcher, who later held positions in the strong cooperatives developed by the Farmers Union. Other Equity leaders were active in the Nonpartisan League.[47]

The Nonpartisan League (NPL) was in some ways a political outgrowth of Equity. Originating in North Dakota, it represented farmers who felt exploited by grain companies, railroads, banks, and middlemen. The NPL wanted state-owned terminal elevators, flour mills, packinghouses, and cold-storage plants, state inspection of grain, state hail insurance, nonprofit rural credit banks, and tax exemption for farm improvements. To this, add endorsement of woman suffrage. The NPL platform was enough to make any conservative community shudder.[48]

Under the leadership of fiery orator Arthur C. Townley, former flax farmer and ex-Socialist, the NPL movement spread through North Dakota like wildfire from 1915 to 1918. The league gained complete control of the North Dakota legislature and governor's office in the 1918 elections and, in the famous "Farmers Legislature" of 1919, implemented much of its program. Townley declared the dawning of a new era in American politics. So it seemed, at least in North Dakota.

In 1917 the NPL moved its headquarters from Fargo to St. Paul. Organizers worked in Minnesota, Montana, and South Dakota, as Townley envisioned a swing bloc in Congress. But with U.S. entry into World War I, the league ran into serious trouble. Although it voiced support once the country entered the war, it had close ties with the Socialists, who opposed American involvement. Anti-German hysteria and patriotism were ready-made and effective weapons for those seeking to squelch what they considered dangerous doctrine. The Twin Cities press and the Minnesota Commission of Public Safety led the attack against the NPL, with businessmen and politicians, whose livelihoods the organization threatened, joining in harassment and intimidation. Mobs uncontrolled by local officials broke up meetings and beat organizers. In Rock County a farmer with a German name was "deported" in tar and feathers across the state line with orders never to return; such violence was not unusual. Merchants suspected of league sympathies found their stores painted yellow, and professors at the University of Minnesota had desks searched and listening devices planted in their classrooms. By late 1919 the NPL in Minnesota was in decline, but the movement eventually led to the organization of the Farmer-Labor party, which captured the governorship for Floyd B. Olson in 1930.[49]

As the Great Depression tightened its grip, rural Minnesota suffered and farmers became hard pressed to pay taxes, interest, and principal on land and equipment. After World War I they had coped with falling prices, a rash of foreclosures, and a dramatic drop in land value before improvement in the mid-1920s. But from 1929 to 1933 prices dropped precipitously and thousands of farmers faced bankruptcy. In 1932 frustration, anxiety, and anger led the militants among them to organize the National Farmers' Holiday Association (FHA) in support of a mortgage moratorium. The Farm Holiday, as it was often called, maintained that economic conditions were beyond farmer control and foreclosures should be suspended until a refinancing program could be developed. It also urged federal guarantee of cost of production (plus profit) and threatened a farm strike.[50]

John H. Bosch of Kandiyohi County served as president of the Minnesota FHA and as vice-president to the national leader, Milo Reno from Iowa. Bosch, born in 1898, was the eleventh of fourteen youngsters in a politically conscious household. Family members often recounted the time when a visitor asked three-year-old John his name. He replied "I am a Populist." Although Bosch believed in the passive resistance techniques of Mahatma Gandhi, Farm Holiday members used direct action to stop mortgage sales, sometimes exceeding limits set by their leaders. Many observers considered the FHA a radical organization; they were amazed when farmers mobbed courthouses, pushed sheriffs, and prevented foreclosure sales. After delaying a sale for an hour, thus forcing its readvertisement, they would place a membership card in the sheriff's pocket and go their way. Another tactic, used mainly at chattel mortgage sales of equipment, was the penny auction, through which Holiday members bid pennies for equipment they later returned to the original owner. These activities brought condemnation from conservatives and demands that Governor Olson call out the National Guard. Olson, however, was sympathetic to the association; he refused to call out the troops and told local sheriffs not to hold sales when there was danger of violence.

Grant County farmers joining a Farm Holiday march to the State Capitol, about 1935

The national Farm Holiday Association set September 20, 1932, for a farm strike to enforce its call for a mortgage moratorium and cost-of-production guarantee. Most Minnesota groups went on strike on September 21; the Nobles County group jumped the gun a few days in support of Iowa strikers. West-central and southwestern Minnesota provided the main source of FHA strength, particularly Lac qui Parle, Kandiyohi, Chippewa, and Yellow Medicine counties, and the association claimed success in shutting off produce shipments to county seats. At first the public – even generally conservative groups – was sympathetic, but as incidents of fisticuffs, punctured tires, and broken windows increased, anti-Holiday forces formed for battle. The two most dramatic occurrences were the death of picketer Nordahl Peterson, shot on October 5, 1932, by an enraged neighbor near Canby in Yellow Medicine County and a riot involving about eight hundred people at Howard Lake in Wright County. The violence led the Holiday to pull back its pickets. The strikes were economically ineffective, but they served to dramatize the immense discontent in rural Minnesota, prompting political action.[51]

The FHA was so successful in stopping foreclosure sales in 1933 that lenders in some areas called it for permission before attempting legal action. Overzealous Holiday boosters stopped some sales even though the farmers wanted foreclosure to end their hopeless economic plight. Amidst the turmoil Governor Olson proclaimed a temporary mortgage moratorium late in February 1933. A rally of thousands of farmers at the Capitol the next month may have influenced a reluctant senate to support the

FHA program, and eventually the legislature approved temporary relief to debtors, extending the redemption period for two years.[52]

The New Deal administration of Franklin D. Roosevelt attempted to alleviate the farm crisis with the Agricultural Adjustment Act of 1933 and the Farm Credit Act, which created the Farm Credit Administration (FCA). The FCA suggested that governors appoint special conciliation committees to work out settlements between debtors and lenders. In Minnesota, most members of these committees were chosen by the Holiday and appointed by Governor Olson. Still, Milo Reno and the national association's leaders argued that Roosevelt's proposals did not go far enough and called for a national strike.

The 1933 strike, probably an error in tactics, reflected the desperation prevalent in rural areas. The Minnesota Farm Bureau, discreetly silent earlier, condemned the proposed strike. Communities blockaded in 1932 protested the loss of business to neighboring towns. Although most farmers probably were willing to give the New Deal a chance, militants seized the Montevideo creamery, and on November 10, 1933, thousands marched on Marshall, disarmed the sheriff, cut fire hoses, and forced the temporary closing of the Swift and Company poultry processing plant. Although the Minnesota Farm Holiday Association remained strong until about 1936, it never again attempted this kind of action. In the long run, Holiday activists deserved credit for enforcing the mortgage moratorium and influencing New Deal price and credit policies.[53]

The Great Depression and World War II precipitated trends greatly affecting life in all of rural America. Farm mechanization combined with greater opportunity in the cities led to migration from the countryside. Farmers on marginal land, tenants without a future in agriculture, and young people seeking careers in urban centers moved from the farm. During World War II Minnesota agriculture thrived, but farms got bigger and equipment replaced human labor. After the war there was surplus; prices dropped and farmers banded together again.

In the 1960s the National Farmers Organization (NFO), which was organized in Iowa in 1955 to provide collective bargaining power to its members, began a series of holding actions to force increases in beef, hog, and milk prices. In 1962 three hundred NFO members picketed the St. Paul stockyards, and two dozen shots reportedly were fired at market-bound trucks near Slayton. In 1964 another holding action, intended to discourage livestock-to-market shipments, effectively blockaded a truckload of slaughter cows at Marshall, and an NFO member was sentenced to sixty days in jail for obstructing traffic in another Lyon County incident. In Redwood County four men received ninety-day jail sentences for throwing a large rock at a livestock truck. In Lac qui Parle County, a truck tire was shot out, and damage to the NFO headquarters at Bellingham was reported. By October the organization called a "temporary recess" to its holding action as disputes over its success filled the air.[54]

The NFO staged a twenty-five-state holding action in 1967, seeking higher milk prices. Newspapers reported milk dumpings in Dodge,

Olmsted, and Pipestone counties, among others. Bob Jensen of Farmington personified the dairy farmers' dilemma as he reported clearing only $1,600 on a $175,000 investment after working twelve-hour days. Compared to earlier holding actions this campaign was remarkably peaceful, and the NFO apparently gained support from some politicians for curbing dairy imports and increasing exports. The organization also negotiated contracts with some milk processors, but the economic effectiveness of this action was widely debated.[55]

In the late 1970s, Minnesota farmers joined on another battlefield. Western Minnesota was the scene of a bitter and ironic struggle embroiling rural citizens and their own power cooperatives. In 1973 Cooperative Power Association (CPA) of Edina and United Power Association (UPA) of Elk River announced plans to transmit electricity from a coal-fired generating plant in North Dakota 430 miles east to the Twin Cities. As generating and transmission co-ops, CPA and UPA participated in power-pooling agreements with private companies; the power generated in North Dakota could be used by customers of private companies like Northern States Power. Co-op managers and directors who felt they were making a reasonable decision to fill the future power needs of their members were astounded at the repercussions.[56]

Before the lines were energized, political and legal battles, acts of sabotage, and clashes with highway patrol officers and county sheriffs became front-page news, as co-op members and farmers concerned about the long-term effects of power lines over their land demanded to know how the directors had reached their decision. Suddenly rural electric co-ops, once denounced as socialistic, were perceived as part of the utility establishment by some of their own members. The project went ahead. Observers in the 1980s could not agree whether it was wise, but most believed the method used in pushing it through was in error.

Crisis and Change

It is no wonder farmers protest. By the 1980s Minnesota farmers were among the most proficient producers of food in the world. Because of their efficiency and use of hybrid seeds, advanced fertilizers, herbicides, and pesticides, they produced too much, driving prices so low that only the shrewdest and luckiest among them could survive. The trend toward fewer farms of increased average size accelerated after World War II. The number of Minnesota farms decreased from 179,000 in 1950 to 99,000 in 1974; average size increased from 184 to 280 acres.[57]

New crop specializations emerged as seed, soil, and market conditions dictated. Minnesota farmers in the 1980s raised a wide variety of crops and livestock, but specialization in particular areas was strong. Crop farming tended to dominate southern and southwestern Minnesota, while dairying was strong from the southeast to west-central areas of the state.

Electric irrigation system covering about 110 acres in Dakota County, 1976

Increases in size, mechanization, and specialization resulted in drastically changed capital needs for farmers. Agriculture changed from a labor- to a capital-intensive industry. Family labor contributed about 59 percent of total production requirements as late as 1940. Two decades later labor's share constituted only 30 percent and capital increased to 61 percent, with larger farms generally having greater debt ratios. To big operators, farming was much more a business than a way of life.[58]

After 1930 many rural counties lost population. In others the number of rural residents grew, but the rate lagged behind that of urban areas. In the early 1970s planner Gerald F. Heil conducted a study of eighteen counties in southwestern Minnesota, a major agricultural area in the state and nation. Research showed that from 1940 to 1970 mass migration, primarily of young adults, had left fewer, predominantly older, and poorer residents in the region. Only four counties – Kandiyohi, Lyon, Nobles, and Rock – showed growth, and three of them had significant public institutions such as colleges and state hospitals. The pattern of migration was from the farm and small towns to larger towns in the region and from those to other parts of the state or nation.[59]

Migration from rural Minnesota mirrored the national pattern: In 1940 about 44 percent of all Americans lived on farms or in small towns; by 1970 that figure was only 27 percent. In Minnesota about half the population in 1940 lived in small towns or rural areas, dropping to about 34 percent thirty years later. In southwestern Minnesota the shift was from 81 to 70 percent.[60]

While it is clear that increasing farm size and mechanization resulted in fewer people producing more food, other effects on rural life are harder to see. In a "catch-22," rural communities in the 1970s and 1980s tried to provide roads, schools, libraries, medical service, snow removal, fire and police protection to a rural population that had fewer and fewer taxpayers to support these services. Without such services, however, even more people moved. Consolidation was increasingly necessary to provide state-of-the-art services at affordable prices, but it further weakened small communities as it benefited larger ones. Medical centers and high schools serving entire counties loomed as a possibility for the near future.[61]

After 1980 farm prices declined steadily. Fear and frustration visited rural areas where land values dropped and farmers reached dangerous debt-to-asset ratios. A 1985 report to the legislature showed that farm net worth had dropped 8 percent per year since 1980. Debt load per acre in 1984 was $1,045, compared to $650 in 1978. Some farmers were forced to sell out to programs like the Department of Agriculture's dairy herd buy-out; in Minnesota more than seventy-nine thousand cows were to be slaughtered in this national attempt to limit dairy production. By 1987,

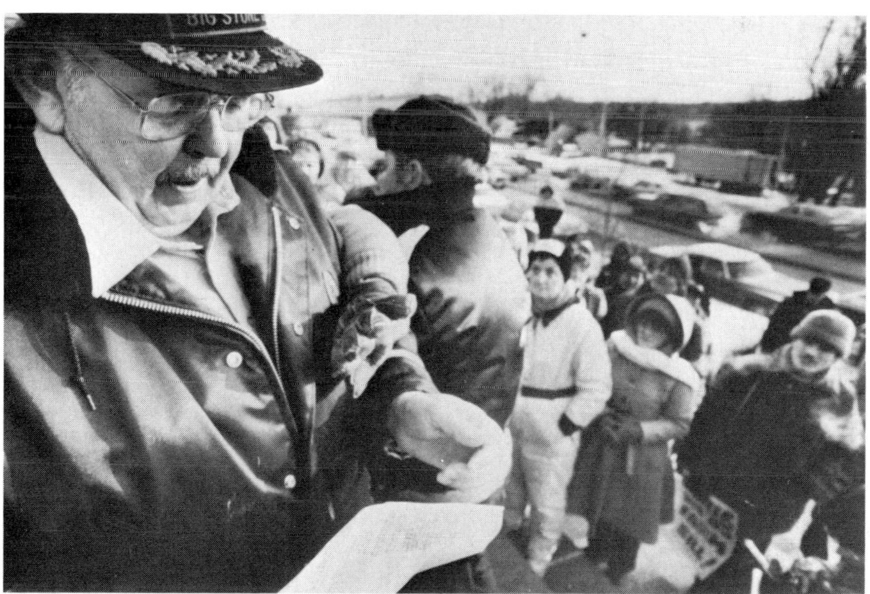

The sheriff of Big Stone County reading a foreclosure notice in Ortonville, 1985, as a protester tries to grab it

A holiday meal in a farmhouse near Chatfield, 1976

land values, the most important farm asset, had dropped almost 50 percent from their peak in 1981.[62]

These difficulties again generated protests against foreclosure sales and support for a mortgage moratorium. Groundswell, a regional protest group with strength in southwestern Minnesota, and the American Agriculture Movement, a national organization, became active during the crises of the 1980s.[63] By the late 1980s support for various extremist views appeared to wane, but the economic problems had reached beyond the farm: Small towns, for instance, lost car and implement dealerships as well as main-street businesses as farmers were forced to the wall. Argument continued between those who believed that a cheap food policy was destroying American agriculture, the small town, and a way of life and those who maintained that the marketplace must drive the economy. While politicians, economists, and ideologues debated, the families of rural Minnesota adjusted to another round of economic dislocation.

In the late 1980s the state legislature provided temporary help in promoting mediation between creditors and lenders as well as an interest buy-down program to help restructure farm debt. These were, however, only stop-gap measures, and the state remained at the mercy of national farm policy. Continuing crisis was likely to shrink further the number of farmers. For the long term, Minnesotans would have to consider public policy changes and development incentives to broaden the base of the rural economy. How well this scheme would be accomplished was impossible to predict. Nevertheless, the rural life continued to appeal to many Minnesotans, and there was good reason to expect the lure of the land to endure in the twenty-first century.

NOTES

The author thanks Deborah Miller, research supervisor at the Minnesota Historical Society (MHS), for her help, use of her office, and encouragement; Clifford Clark for his patience, suggestions, and help with developing this essay; Ellen B. Green for her substantial editorial contributions; Mark Haidet of the MHS, Carla Nass, and Lori Fox for their research assistance; Lucile Kane and Carl Chrislock for their suggestions and ideas. Judy Nass, Dorothy Frisvold, and Joan Taylor provided typing. Southwest State University provided a sabbatical leave, making research possible.

1. See, for example, Commissioner of Statistics, comp., *Minnesota: Its Resources and Progress; Its Beauty, Healthfulness and Fertility; and Its Attractions and Advantages as a Home for Immigrants* (St. Paul, 1870); a German translation was published two years later in Minneapolis. See also William E. Lass, "Minnesota: An American Siberia?" *Minnesota History* 49 (Winter 1984): 149–55; Hiram M. Drache, *The Challenge of the Prairie: Life and Times of Red River Pioneers* (Fargo: North Dakota Institute for Regional Studies, 1970).

2. Northern Pacific Railroad, *Guide to the Lands of the Northern Pacific Railroad in Minnesota* ([St. Paul?], 1872); State Board of World's Fair Managers, *Minnesota: A Brief Sketch of Its History, Resources and Advantages* (St. Paul: Pioneer Press Co., 1893), 103, 107, 115.

3. The most complete account of bonanza farming is Drache, *The Day of the Bonanza: A History of Bonanza Farming in the Red River Valley of the North* (Fargo: North Dakota Institute for Regional Studies, 1964). See also Gilbert C. Fite, *The Farmers' Frontier, 1865–1900* (Albuquerque: University of New Mexico Press, 1974), 93.

4. Joseph Dorfman, *Thorstein Veblen and His America* (New York: Viking Press, 1934), 7; Richard Hofstadter, *The Age of Reform: From Bryan to F.D.R.* (New York: Alfred A. Knopf, 1955), 41–46; Jon Wefald, *A Voice of Protest: Norwegians in American Politics, 1890–1917* (Northfield: Norwegian-American Historical Association, 1971), 15–17; Paul W. Gates, "Research in the History of the Public Lands," *Agricultural History* 48 (January 1974): 31–50. See also Gilbert C. Fite, "'The Only Thing Worth Working For': Land and Its Meaning for Pioneer Dakotans," *South Dakota History* 15 (Spring/Summer 1985): 2–25; Kathleen N. Conzen, "Peasant Pioneers: Generational Succession among German Farmers in Frontier Minnesota," in *The Countryside in the Age of Capitalist Transformation: Essays in the Social History of Rural America*, ed. Steven Hahn and Jonathon Prude (Chapel Hill: University of North Carolina Press, 1985), 259–92. For more on farming as an economic proposition, see D. Jerome Tweton, "The Business of Agriculture," *this volume*, 261–94.

5. *Northwestern Farmer* (St. Paul) 11 (Mar. 15, 1893): 103; *Northwest Magazine* (St. Paul), May 1902, p. 45. The *Northwestern Farmer and Breeder* began publication in Fargo in 1883; in 1890, it moved to St. Paul. In March 1893, its name was changed to the *Northwestern Farmer*, and in 1900 it became *The Farmer*.

6. *Revised Laws of Minnesota, 1905* (St. Paul: State of Minnesota, 1906), 510–13; *The Farmer* 21 (Aug. 1, 1903): 436; *Commercial West* (Minneapolis), Aug. 5, 1905, p. 22; *The Farmer* 23 (Sept. 15, 1905): 569; *Commercial West*, Nov. 7, 1908, p. 10, Oct. 21, 1911, p. 34, Feb. 8, 1913, p. 20. For more on drainage and the landscape, see Thomas J. Baerwald, "Forces at Work on the Landscape," *this volume*, 29–30, 47–48.

7. *The Farmer* 39 (Nov. 19, 1921): 1552.

8. *The Farmer* 41 (Feb. 17, 1923): 222; W. P. Kirkwood, "Practical Lessons from Stump Land Farms," *The Farmer* 39 (Sept. 3, 1921): 1251.

9. Merrill E. Jarchow, *The Earth Brought Forth: A History of Minnesota Agriculture to 1885* (St. Paul: Minnesota Historical Society, 1949), 20–21; Theodore C. Blegen, *Minnesota: A History of the State*, 2d ed. (Minneapolis: University of Minnesota Press, 1975), 346–48; *The Farmer*, Apr. 2, 1949, p. 31–32. On the importance of milling to Minneapolis, see Lucile M. Kane, *The Falls of St. Anthony: The Waterfall That Built Minneapolis* (St. Paul: Minnesota Historical Society Press, 1966, 1987).

10. Blegen, *History of Minnesota*, 346–47; George J. Miller, "Agriculture in Minnesota," *Journal of Geography* 14 (February 1916): 200–201. As an example of the movement from southern Minnesota, see *The Farmer* 28 (Dec. 10, 1910): 1420. For more on diversification see Baerwald, "Forces at Work on the Landscape," 27–28.

11. Blegen, *History of Minnesota*, 395-96; *The Farmer* 33 (Jan. 30, 1915): 147. See also *The Farmer* 42 (June 21, 1924): 857, 864; William E. Lass, *Minnesota: A Bicentennial History* (New York: W. W. Norton, 1977), 140-41.

12. *Commercial West*, Feb. 12, 1927, p. 8, May 10, 1924, p. 47; Everett E. Edwards and Horace H. Russell, "Wendelin Grimm and Alfalfa," *Minnesota History* 19 (March 1933): 30-32.

13. C. D. Gilfillan, "Cattle Feeding in Minnesota," *Northwestern Farmer* 15 (Feb. 1, 1897): 39.

14. See, for a powerful fictional example, Ole Rølvaag, *Giants in the Earth* (New York: Harper and Row, 1927).

15. *Dictionary of American History* (New York: Charles Scribner's Sons, 1976), 6:171. See also William L. Bowers, *The Country Life Movement in America, 1900-1920* (Port Washington, N.Y.: Kennikat Press, 1974).

16. *The Farmer* 34 (July 1, 1916): 1042, and 34 (Aug. 12, 1916): 1180.

17. Here and below, see H. L. Russell, "The Standard of Life in the Country," *The Farmer* 32 (Jan. 17, 1914): 75, 86.

18. Here and below, see May L. Spencer, "A Plea for the Country Wife and Mother," *The Farmer* 32 (Jan. 17, 1914): 78.

19. Material for this paragraph is drawn from *Northwestern Farmer and Breeder*, *Northwestern Farmer*, and *The Farmer* from 1890 through 1914.

20. *The Farmer* 40 (Aug. 19, 1922): 954. For a comprehensive discussion, see James H. Madison, "Reformers and the Rural Church, 1900-1950," *Journal of American History* 73 (December 1986): 645-68. See also Richard M. Chapman, "Religious Belief and Behavior," *this volume*, 520-23.

21. *The Farmer* 39 (July 30, 1921): 1139.

22. Henry Wallace, "The Rural School Problem," *The Farmer* 28 (June 25, 1910): 829.

23. *General Statutes of Minnesota, 1913* (St. Paul: West Publishing Co., 1913), 664-65, 668-69; C. G. Schulz, "Progress in Rural Education through the Extension of Industrial Training and the Establishment of Consolidated Country Schools," *The Farmer* 29 (Dec. 2, 1911): 1400.

24. Mary Klauda, "School Records: The Minnesota Experience" (Paper delivered at MHS staff meeting, 1982), copy in state history papers. Clarke A. Chambers, "Educating for the Future," *this volume*, 475-80, covers educational development in greater depth.

25. Here and below, see Janice A. Louwagie, "The Development of Rural Free Delivery" (Seminar paper, May 1979), on file at Southwest State University, Marshall; Wayne E. Fuller, *RFD: The Changing Face of Rural America* (Bloomington: Indiana University Press, 1964).

26. "Report of the Postmaster-General," in *Annual Reports of the Post-Office Department for the Fiscal Year Ended June 30, 1900* (Washington, D.C.: U.S. Government Printing Office, 1900), 6.

27. C. A. Rasmussen, "Rural Free Delivery," in *Second Annual Meeting of the Postmasters' Association of Minnesota* (St. Paul, 1901), 9; *Commercial West*, Jan. 24, 1925, p. 22.

28. Vernon Davies, *Farm Housing Needs in Minnesota*, University of Minnesota, Agricultural Experiment Station Bulletin no. 393 (St. Paul, March 1947), 8, 14.

29. Richard A. Pence, ed., *The Next Greatest Thing: 50 Years of Rural Electrification in America* (Washington, D.C.: National Rural Electric Cooperative Association, 1984), 64; Jeffrey A. Hess, "Energy in Minnesota," *Roots* 9 (Spring 1981): 24. See also D. Clayton Brown, *Electricity for Rural America: The Fight for the REA* (Westport, Conn.: Greenwood Press, 1980); Jack Doyle, *Lines across the Land* (Washington, D.C.: Environmental Policy Institute, 1979); Harold Severson, *The Night They Turned on the Lights: The Story of the Electric Power Revolution in the North Star State* (N.p.: Midwest Historical Features, 1962).

30. R. A. Peterson and Alice M. Peterson, interview by David L. Nass and Maynard Brass, Feb. 27, 1973, on file at Southwest Minnesota Historical Center (SMHC), Marshall; see also Mr. and Mrs. William Raveling, interview by David L. Nass, Kathy Ramier, and Diane Opp, July 5, 1973, SMHC.

31. *Granite Falls Tribune*, Apr. 20, 1944, p. 5; Oscar Torstenson, interview by Nass and Ramier, Aug. 24, 1973, SMHC; *Electrical World* (New York), May 14, 1921, p. 1087.

32. Robert W. Heinz, "Red Wing Experiment Paved the Way for Powerful Farms," *Edison Electric Institute Bulletin* (New York) 19 (May/June 1965): 1-4; E. A. Stewart, "Report on Red Wing Project" (Paper given at Madison, Wis., June 26, 1925), copy in author's files. For information on a similar project, contemporary to the Red Wing one, see "Rural Electrification on the Renner Trial Line," *South Dakota History* 16 (Summer 1986): 144-54.

33. Rebecca R. Wise, ed., *Rural Electric Fact Book* (Washington, D.C.: National Rural Electric Cooperative Association, 1965), 3; *Willmar Tribune*, July 29, 1936, p. 1; Patrick J. Casey, *The First 100 Years: A History of Meeker County* (N.p.: Patrick Casey, 1968), 183-85; Pence, *Next Greatest Thing;* Severson, *The Night They Turned on the Lights;* Torstenson

interview. Membership fees and organizers' expenses varied slightly among the different co-ops.

34. *Biographical Directory of the American Congress, 1774–1971* (Washington, D.C.: U.S. Government Printing Office, 1971), 1463; *Current Biography* (New York: H. W. Wilson Co., 1977), 51–54.

35. Arthur J. Larsen, "Development of the Minnesota Road System" (Ph.D. diss., University of Minnesota, 1938), 427. Michael L. Berger, *The Devil Wagon in God's Country: The Automobile and Social Change in Rural America, 1893–1929* (Hamden, Conn.: Archon Books, 1979) is an excellent account of the impact of the auto on rural social institutions.

36. Larsen, "Development of Minnesota Road System," 415–27, 448–58; Blegen, *History of Minnesota*, 465.

37. Berger, *Devil Wagon*, 124–26. See also James R. Hayes, "Rural-Urban Interaction in Minnesota," KRSW radio program, Apr. 27, 1974, transcript in SMHC.

38. Berger, *Devil Wagon*, 206–13. For more on the rising and falling fortunes of small towns, see Thomas Harvey, "Small-Town Minnesota," *this volume*, 108–9, 123–24.

39. Blegen, *History of Minnesota*, 465–66. For more on Greyhound, see Margaret Walsh, "Tracing the Hound: The Minnesota Roots of the Greyhound Bus Corporation," *Minnesota History* 49 (Winter 1985): 310–21.

40. Here and below, see *Men, Machines and Land* (Chicago: Farm and Industrial Equipment Institute, 1974), 19–28. For more on transportation, see John R. Borchert, "The Network of Urban Centers," *this volume*, 70–72.

41. *Commercial West*, Dec. 22, 1928, p. 3; *The Farmer*, Jan. 3, 1920, p. 5, Feb. 8, 1941, p. 8, Mar. 22, 1941, p. 38; John R. Borchert and Neil C. Gustafson, *Atlas of Minnesota Resources and Settlement* (Minneapolis: Center for Urban and Regional Affairs, University of Minnesota, 1980), 93.

42. Roland H. Abraham, *Helping People Help Themselves: Agricultural Extension in Minnesota, 1879–1979* (Minneapolis: Minnesota Extension Service, University of Minnesota, 1986), 46, 163.

43. Abraham, *Helping People*, 85–86; *Farm Bureau: A Short History of the Minnesota Farm Bureau and American Farm Bureau Organizations* (Pamphlet published by Minnesota Farm Bureau, n.d.), copy in author's possession.

44. Abraham, *Helping People*, 89–186; *Dictionary of American History* 6:175.

45. Here and below, see Theodore Saloutos and John D. Hicks, *Agricultural Discontent in the Middle West 1900–1939* (Madison: University of Wisconsin Press, 1951), 132–48. For more on the era and its movements, see Edward H. Abrahams, "Ignatius Donnelly and the Apocalyptic Style," *Minnesota History* 46 (Fall 1978): 102–11; John D. Hicks, *The Populist Revolt: A History of the Farmers' Alliance and the People's Party* (Minneapolis: University of Minnesota, 1931), 231–32; Lawrence Goodwyn, *Democratic Promise: The Populist Movement in America* (New York: Oxford University Press, 1976); James M. Youngdale, *Populism: A Psychohistorical Perspective* (Port Washington, N.Y.: Kennikat Press, 1975); Larry Remele, "'Things as They Should Be': Jeffersonian Idealism and Rural Rebellion in Minnesota and North Dakota 1910–1920," *Minnesota History* 51 (Spring 1988): 15–22.

46. Saloutos and Hicks, *Agricultural Discontent*, 138.

47. Saloutos and Hicks, *Agricultural Discontent*, 146–48.

48. Here and below, see Larry Remele, "The Nonpartisan League: The Courage to Stand up for Farmers," in *Plowing up a Storm: The History of Midwestern Farm Activism* (Lincoln: Nebraska Educational Television Network, 1985), 10–15, booklet issued with videotape of the television program of the same title. The most detailed study of the NPL is Robert L. Morlan, *Political Prairie Fire: The Nonpartisan League, 1915–1922* (Minneapolis: University of Minnesota Press, 1955; St. Paul: Minnesota Historical Society Press, 1985). For more on the NPL and Minnesota politics, see John E. Haynes, "Reformers, Radicals, and Conservatives," *this volume*, 368–75.

49. Morlan, *Political Prairie Fire*, 152–83. For more on the hysteria of the period, see Bruce L. Larson, *Lindbergh of Minnesota, A Political Biography* (New York: Harcourt Brace Jovanovich, 1971), and LaVern J. Rippley, "Conflict in the Classroom: Anti-Germanism in Minnesota Schools, 1917–19," *Minnesota History* 47 (Spring 1981): 170–83.

50. Here and below, see Theodore Saloutos, *The American Farmer and the New Deal* (Ames: Iowa State University Press, 1982), 12; David L. Nass, ed., *Holiday: Minnesotans Remember the Farmers' Holiday Association* (Marshall: Plains Press, 1984), xii, xviii, an oral history collection; John L. Shover, *Cornbelt Rebellion: The Farmers' Holiday Association* (Urbana: University of Illinois Press, 1965), the most complete account of the movement. See also Everett E. Luoma, *The Farmer Takes a Holiday* (New York: Exposition Press, 1967); Lowell K. Dyson, *Red Harvest: The Communist Party and American Farmers* (Lincoln: University of Nebraska Press, 1982); Dale Kramer, *The Wild Jackasses: The American Farmer in Revolt* (New York: Hastings House, 1956); Roland A. White, *Milo Reno, Farmers Union Pioneer* (New York: Arno Press, 1975); George H. Mayer, *The Political Career of*

Floyd B. Olson (Minneapolis: University of Minnesota Press, 1951; St. Paul: Minnesota Historical Society Press, 1987), 103–7.

51. Lyndon Johnson, "Minnesota Farmers' Holiday," in *Holiday*, ed. Nass, xix–xx.

52. Johnson, "Farmers' Holiday," xxii–xxiii. See also David L. Nass, ed., "Recollections of Rural Revolt," *Minnesota History* 44 (Winter 1975): 304–8.

53. *Marshall Messenger*, Nov. 10, 1933, p. 3; *New York Times*, Nov. 11, 1933, p. 7; Johnson, "Farmers' Holiday," xxiv–xxvi. On the Minnesota Holiday's sense of accomplishment, see Bosch interview in *Holiday*, ed. Nass, 191–96.

54. George Brandsberg, *The Two Sides of the NFO's Battle* (Ames: Iowa State University Press, 1964), 121–24; *New York Mills Centennial History* (New York Mills: The Centennial Committee, 1984), 104; *Lyon County Independent*, Aug. 26, p. 1A, 6A; Sept. 2, p. 1A; Sept. 9, p. 1A, 2A, 7A; Sept. 16, p. 1A, 2A, 1C; Oct. 7, p. 1A – all 1964.

55. *Minneapolis Tribune*, Mar. 15, p. 11; Mar. 17, p. 30; Mar. 18, p. 9; Mar. 19, p. 14B; Mar. 20, p. 1, 8; Mar. 25, p. 1, 7; Mar. 26, p. 16A; Mar. 28, p. 4, 15; Mar. 30, p. 1, 6; Mar. 31, p. 1, 6 – all 1967. See also *Lyon County Independent*, Mar. 29, p. 1A, 2A, 6A; Apr. 5, p. 1A – both 1967.

56. Here and below, see Barry M. Casper and Paul David Wellstone, *Powerline: The First Battle of America's Energy War* (Amherst: University of Massachusetts Press, 1981), a detailed account frankly sympathetic to the protesters; see also review in *Minnesota History* 47 (Summer 1981): 253–54. The Minnesota Powerline Oral History Project, housed at MHS and the University of Minnesota, Morris, documents all sides of the controversy.

Directors who had pioneered rural electrification found themselves denounced as closed-minded and dictatorial, a bitter reward after years of service. Protesters countered that democracy should guide a co-op, meetings should be open, minutes made available, and full discussion precede major decision making. The author, who participated in separate programs sponsored by management and reformers to give members a sense of their history and help work out a plan for their future, came to see rural co-ops still evolving as they sought to make cable TV, satellite dishes, and computer systems available to members. War between private utilities and co-ops is probably unwise for both, but should the co-op become just another utility, rural Minnesota will have lost a unique institution.

57. Here and below, see Borchert and Gustafson, *1980 Minnesota Atlas*, 61–84; Vic Spadaccini, ed., *Minnesota Pocket Data Book, 1985-1986* (St. Paul: Blue Sky Marketing, 1985), 227.

58. Hiram M. Drache, *Beyond the Furrow: Some Keys to Successful Farming in the Twentieth Century* (Danville, Ill.: Interstate Printers and Publishers, 1976), 462–63; for a full discussion of this topic, see p. 450–95. Management costs accounted for much of the remaining 9 percent.

59. *Worthington Globe*, Oct. 19, 1971, p. 6; [Gerald F. Heil], "Southwest Minnesota Population Study" (Marshall: Southwest Planning, 1971), part 2, p. 9, copy in Southwest State University Library. A summary entitled "Exodus" was published in the *Worthington Globe*, Oct. 18-23, 1971.

60. [Heil], "Southwest Minnesota," part 2, p. 14, 15.

61. For elaboration on the debate over consolidation in schools, see Chambers, "Educating for the Future."

62. "Executive Summary of Interagency Task Force Report on Farm Financial Data Collection," in Farm Financial Data Collection Task Force, *1985 Report to the Minnesota Legislature* ([St. Paul], 1985?), 11; *The Land* (Mankato), Apr. 11, 1986, p. 4; *Minneapolis Tribune*, Sept. 14, 1986, p. 10.

63. William P. Browne and John Dinse, "The Emergence of the American Agriculture Movement, 1977–1979," *Great Plains Quarterly* 5 (Fall 1985): 221–35; *Marshall Independent*, Nov. 12, 1987, p. 8.

ARNOLD R. ALANEN

Years of Change on the Iron Range

Although Minnesota has changed significantly since 1900, no part of the state has experienced more volatile economic, social, and landscape alteration than the northern region commonly known as the Iron Range. Actually comprising three ranges – the Vermilion, Mesabi, and Cuyuna – the Iron Range stretches in a linear band from Ely–Winton at the northeastern tip of the Vermilion to Grand Rapids at the southwestern end of the Mesabi, and it also embraces a small clustering of communities near Crosby–Ironton on the Cuyuna. Throughout the twentieth century, the Iron Range has been caught up in dramatic boom-or-bust cycles created by the development and exploitation of its natural resources.

Mining activities began in northeastern Minnesota during the 1880s and 1890s. By the turn of the century, the range had been transformed from a sparsely populated wilderness into an industrialized landscape inhabited by immigrants from almost every nation of Europe. The Iron Range eventually became the primary source of iron ore for the nation. During this hectic period of growth and prosperity, mining significantly changed the visual landscape throughout the region, especially on the Mesabi Range. Forests, hills, swamps, and lakes were converted into massive open pits, and tax revenues from the rich ore deposits allowed communities to build public facilities seldom equaled in settlements of similar size elsewhere in America. When iron ore production increased dramatically in the early twentieth century, the population of the Iron Range also soared, and the advent of collective bargaining agreements between labor and management during the late 1930s and early 1940s eventually made iron ore miners among the highest paid blue-collar workers in the nation.

Periods of economic decline and depression, on the other hand, have brought disproportionately great hardship to the Iron Range. The finite nature of the iron ore resource ultimately leads to depletion and the abandonment of mine sites. Within this larger reality, however, is the impact of changes in the demand for iron ore, the development of new technologies, and the importation of foreign low-priced ore, steel, and manufactured products. By the mid-1980s, much of the nation had recovered from

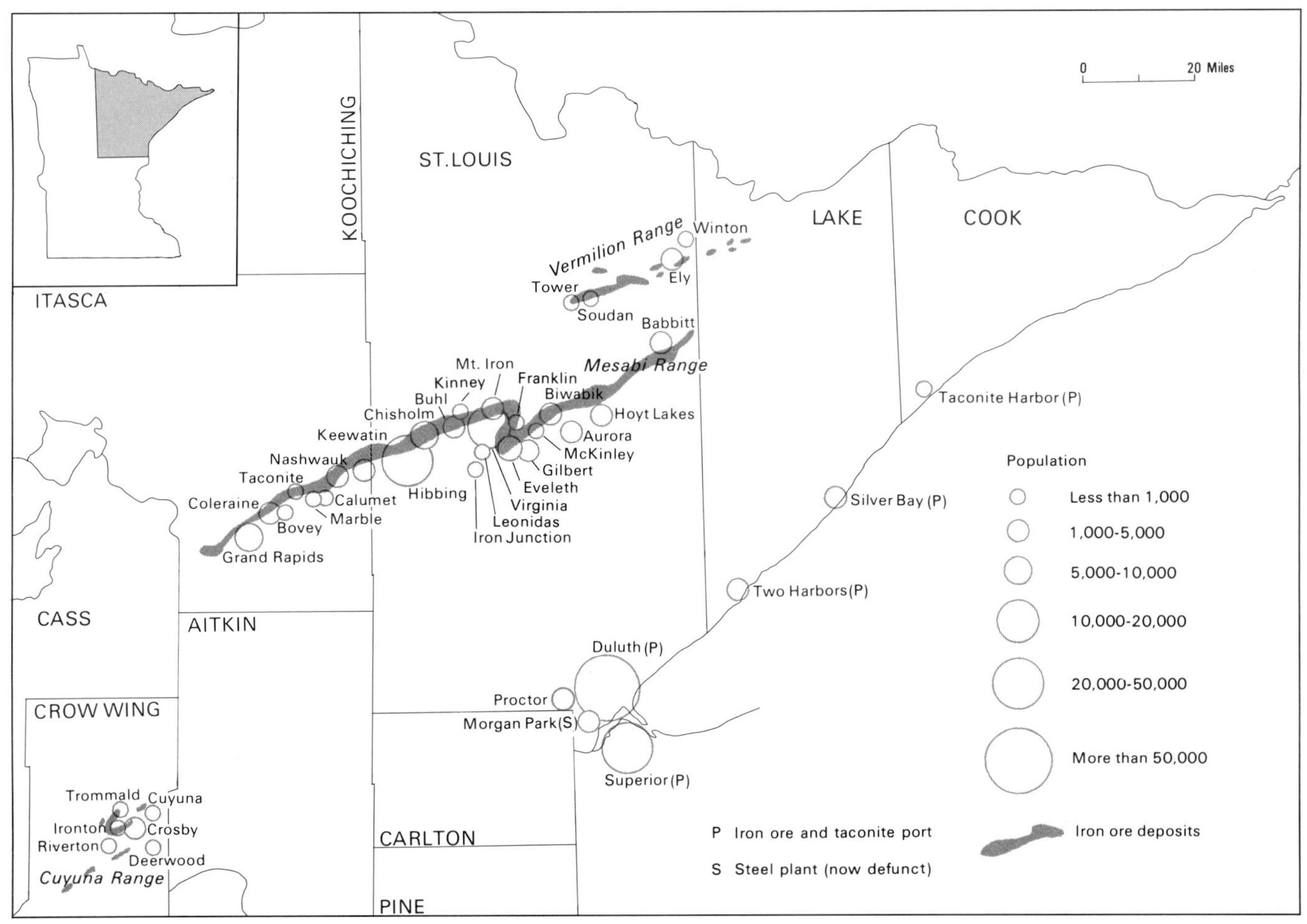

Mining industry communities on the Iron Range and Lake Superior, 1980. Source: *Population size determined from the 1980 census.*

the national recession of 1982, but America's steel industry and Minnesota's iron mines continued to languish. When unemployment rates are relatively high in the U.S. steel-manufacturing enterprise, they are often even higher on the Iron Range.[1]

Two accounts, separated by more than eighty years, capture the dramatic changes that have occurred on the Iron Range. Dwight E. Woodbridge, a northern Minnesota mining authority during the early boom years, reported in the *Hibbing News* in 1900 that economic conditions had seldom been more favorable: "New miners are earning more money than they have ever known; there are as many jobs, perhaps more of them, than men. Money is plenty in the mining towns of the state." A report written by a journalist in 1986 about economic slowdown on the range offered a striking contrast: "In [1981–84], people moved out of the three Iron Range counties [St. Louis, Lake, and Itasca] at four times the rate that Minnesotans in general moved out of the state. . . . Experts predict a smaller, older work force, fewer children in fewer schools, clustering of people and jobs into larger towns."[2]

The reasons for the changes have been varied and complex, but the observations and attitudes mirrored in these accounts highlight the radical transformation of life and labor on the Iron Range in the twentieth century. The immediate impression is that the Iron Range has evolved from a position of socioeconomic health and vitality to one of decline and semiparalysis, a generalization, however, that ignores the intervening time periods and the events that have taken place during the century. This essay, therefore, examines not only the evolution of Minnesota's iron resource region but also the internal dynamics that have accompanied the range's periods of growth and decline.

Production and Population: An Overview

The first iron ore was shipped from the Vermilion Range in 1884, and ore from the Mesabi followed in 1892. Two years later, the Mesabi was producing and shipping more ore on an annual basis than the Vermilion. During the nineteenth century, the total output of the Mesabi Range exceeded that of its older counterpart by ten million tons.[3]

Throughout the twentieth century the Vermilion and Cuyuna ranges, even together, could not begin to approach the massive shipments of the Mesabi. The mines of the Vermilion shut down completely in the 1960s; those of the Cuyuna did so in the next decade, although small amounts of stockpiled ore continued to be shipped from this westernmost of Minnesota's iron ranges through the mid-1980s.[4]

Most of the Vermilion mines and about half of those on the Cuyuna were underground operations, whereas much of the Mesabi's ores lay near the surface and could be removed by strip-mining. The deposits of the Mesabi proved to be so vast that this one range overwhelmed all other ore-producing districts in the country, including the significant deposits of the

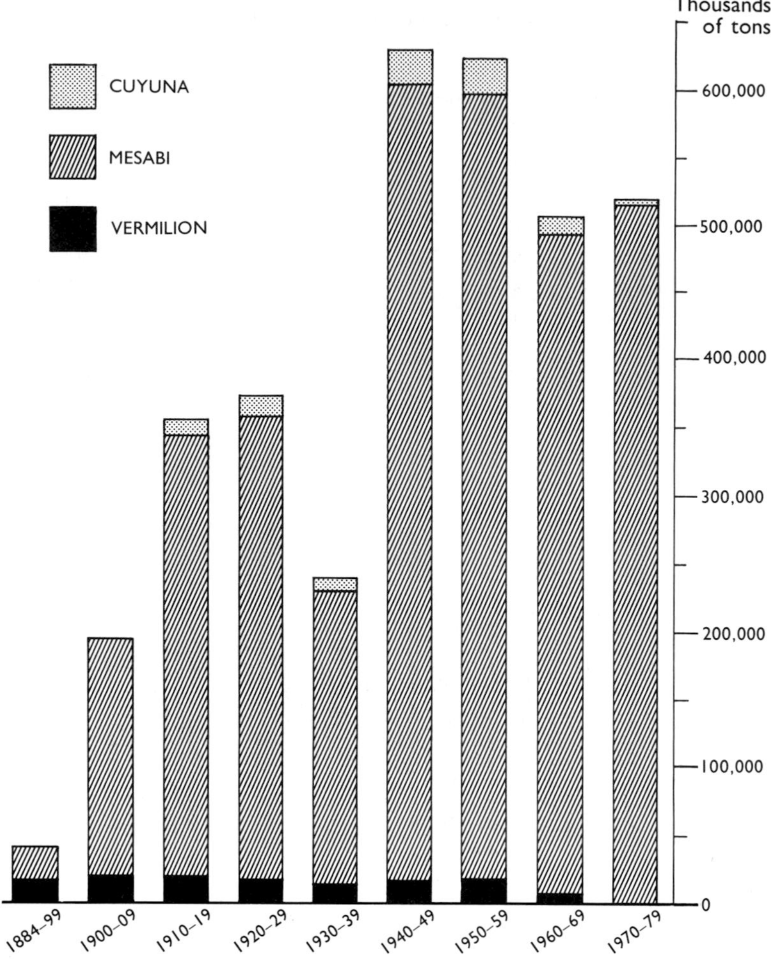

Ore production on Minnesota's iron ranges, 1884–1979. Sources: *See nn. 6–7.*

Lake Superior region in Michigan and Wisconsin (the Marquette, Menominee, and Gogebic ranges). From 1900 to 1980, the Mesabi Range contributed more than 70 percent of the total ores extracted from the mines of the Lake Superior region and produced about 60 percent of the nation's total output.[5]

Minnesota's production of iron ore varied considerably over the decades, often because of calamitous world conditions. Total iron-ore tonnage for the state grew noticeably during the first three decades of the twentieth century, but the depression of the 1930s brought unprecedented cutbacks in virtually all segments of the economy. Mining was no exception. Production fell by some 36 percent during the decade, and in one especially traumatic year – 1932 – mining came to a virtual standstill.[6]

The demands for iron ore during World War II sparked an extraordinary increase in output. Overall production throughout the 1940s exceeded that of the depression decade by two and one-half times. Mining activities continued to expand throughout the 1950s, the decade when

Iron Range Population, 1900-85

Year	Vermilion Range	Mesabi Range	Cuyuna Range	Iron Range Total	Lake Superior Shoreline Communities[a]
1900	7,690	15,800	–	23,490	4,060
1910	7,430	68,120	2,105	77,655	7,235
1920	8,105	84,180	8,100	100,385	9,050
1930	8,180	83,850	7,325	99,355	9,075
1940	8,855	81,510	6,585	96,950	8,515
1950	7,955	79,800	6,320	94,075	9,255
1960	8,740	98,675	6,030	113,445	13,635
1970	8,130	90,340	5,330	103,800	13,525
1980	8,020	93,015	5,835	106,870	12,320
1985	6,915	87,855	5,825	100,595	12,130

Sources: Data are taken from census reports as described in nn. 9-11.

a. Two Harbors (1900-85), Proctor (1900-85), Morgan Park (1920-85), and Silver Bay (1960-85).

taconite concentrates began to be produced from the low-grade ores of the Mesabi Range. Output declined somewhat in the 1960s and 1970s in comparison with that of the war period, but taconite continued to play an important role in the state's iron-ore picture. Taconite pellets made up more than 40 percent of all shipments from the Iron Range in the 1960s, and by the 1970s they had grown to three-fourths of the total.[7]

By the 1980s, taconite clearly was the "iron" of the Iron Range (constituting 95 percent of all Mesabi ores), although total shipments declined from the previous decade. Fifty-two million tons of ore were shipped during an average year in the 1970s, but between 1980 and 1985 the figure fell to thirty-seven million tons. In the recession year of 1982, only twenty-four million tons of ore were shipped – the smallest amount since 1938. Moreover, Minnesota's share of the world's annual iron-ore production fell from a former high of 30 percent to a level of 4 percent by the mid-1980s.[8]

The population of the Iron Range, paralleling the development of the iron mines, grew rapidly during the early decades of the twentieth century (see table). From 1900 to 1920 the range's population rose from 23,500 residents to more than 100,000. Despite the years of high iron-ore production during the 1920s and 1940s and the intervening lethargy of the 1930s, the population then stabilized until the 1950s.[9]

The taconite boom that began after World War II contributed to the second significant period of growth. Between 1950 and 1960, the population of the range increased by 21 percent. Despite a decline in numbers during the next two decades, the census counts for 1970 and 1980 remained above 100,000 and exceeded the totals for any census year before the war. Between 1980 and 1985, however, population estimates revealed a decline of about 1 percent per year. The Cuyuna Range, where mining was no longer a factor in the local economy, maintained a stable population between those years, but figures indicated a loss of about 5,150 residents for the Mesabi and 1,000 for the Vermilion. Reductions in taconite operations have particularly hurt such settlements as Ely, Tower, Aurora, Gilbert,

Downtown Virginia, 1941

Hoyt Lakes, and Babbitt on the Vermilion and eastern Mesabi ranges. On the far western Mesabi (Itasca County), where the economic base has been more diversified, the population estimates revealed slight growth from 1980 to 1985.[10]

Although their populations have fluctuated, five townsites – Hibbing, Virginia, Grand Rapids, Chisholm, and Eveleth – have ranked as the largest urban centers on the Mesabi Range for more than six decades, and Ely and Crosby have played similar roles on the Vermilion and Cuyuna ranges. Population has also shifted in the four Lake Superior shoreline communities that have served as centers for ore shipping, transportation, manufacturing, and processing for varying periods of time: the ore harbor of Two Harbors (in operation since 1884), the rail center of Proctor (1892), the steel-manufacturing complex at Morgan Park (1915), and the taconite production plant at Silver Bay (1955). From 1920 to 1950, the combined populations of the first three shoreline communities remained quite stable; the total count increased noticeably with the addition of Silver Bay to the 1960 census, although a slight decline has been registered in each succeeding census period. Silver Bay itself, however, lost close to 40 percent of its population from 1960 to 1985 (an estimated decline of more than 20 percent was experienced from 1980 to 1985 alone); indeed, no other community in the region with a total population greater than one thousand residents demonstrated a more significant population loss between 1960 and 1985.[11] Despite its status as one of the newest settlements in northeastern Minnesota, Silver Bay was among the communities most directly affected by the social and economic consequences of the crisis in America's iron-ore mining and steel-manufacturing industries.

The Settlements: Townsites, Locations, and Company Towns

A map portraying the communities of the three iron-ore ranges in Minnesota clearly reflects the linear nature of the ore deposits that stretch along the Vermilion and Mesabi ranges and the more dispersed nature of the ore deposits of the Cuyuna. Most settlements on the three ranges have been linked entirely to the extraction of iron ore, although the economic base for a few communities (Virginia and Grand Rapids, for example) has included such industries as timber and pulpwood manufacturing. Some enclaves emerged spontaneously, with little or no forethought given to their physical orientation or layout; but most communities were platted, albeit in a rudimentary and utilitarian manner, before settlement.

Two major community forms typified settlement on Minnesota's Iron Range and in the entire Lake Superior mining region: townsites and locations. Entrepreneurs and firms platted the townsites, generally for speculative purposes, in an effort to capitalize on the booming Iron Range economy. The mining companies often owned land and property within the townsites, but the larger ones that were incorporated legally as villages and cities often emerged as outposts of political independence on the Iron Range. Locations, on the other hand, served as regional versions of the company villages found elsewhere in the United States. Throughout the region, the term referred to the land, mining buildings, and residences that made up an individual mine site. The locations were not incorporated – except under most unusual circumstances – and served strictly as residential enclaves. A few locations had schools and very occasionally a store, but saloons and visible signs of vice were banned outright by corporate decree.[12] Examples of a third community form – the traditional company town – were rare on the Iron Range, but some included design features that made them model villages.

Tower, the first townsite on the Iron Range, was platted in 1882 and saw the beginning of permanent settlement one year later; another site followed a similar chronology along the Lake Superior shoreline at Two Harbors. Both were sponsored by the Minnesota Iron Company. Charlemagne Tower, Sr., president of the firm, issued orders from his home in the eastern United States calling for relatively wide streets and a public square at both new townsites.[13] The careful though paternalistic attention devoted to the planning and development of Tower and Two Harbors was seldom replicated in later Iron Range communities. Other

Moving a church from Hibbing's "North Forty" in 1920

thoroughfares," commented the *Hibbing Tribune* in 1904, "and unless removed before warm weather begins, every sort of disease will find a breeding place therein."[18]

When residents of the Iron Range tried to beautify their communities by planting flowers, lawns, small trees, and gardens, such efforts were likely to be thwarted by cows that wandered freely. Citizens in Hibbing complained that the cows stood "for hours at a time chewing their cuds and sunning themselves and leaving the sidewalks in a dirty shape," while residents in Tower and elsewhere reportedly could not sleep at night because of the noise of cow bells and bellowing cattle.[19] Most communities passed cow-impounding ordinances before 1910, but they had trouble enforcing them. One Eveleth resident was fined in 1915 for keeping cows in the basement of his house. The problem continued in some places into the third decade of the century, and roaming cows were reported as a nuisance as late as 1940 in Buhl.[20]

In addition to problems of sanitation, the early towns were often threatened by fire and the discovery of new ore deposits. When Virginia and Chisholm burned over, they had to be rebuilt. Yet even a well-established settlement was subject to displacement by the inexorable expansion of mining activities, especially on the Mesabi. Eveleth was the first townsite to be vacated, after ore was discovered under a portion of the original plat in the late 1890s.[21] Some years later the mining companies determined that Sparta, a townsite near Eveleth, rested on a major deposit of iron ore. In 1909, they moved the buildings to a new townsite at Gilbert. By 1911, reporters said that the village of Sparta had disappeared and that nothing was left at the former townsite but a large pit.[22]

At Hibbing, however, the magnitude of townsite displacement far exceeded that at any other community on the range. Eveleth and Sparta had been moved in a few years, but problems associated with Hibbing's "North Forty" continued for decades. In 1902, nine years after its founding, rumors began to circulate that iron ore lay beneath the town. By 1909, dynamite blasting and extraction activities had moved so close to the North Forty that buildings were shifting on their foundations. From 1912 to 1914, residents of the beleaguered enclave, now surrounded by "continuous yawning chasms" on three sides of the settlement, filed injunctions against the Oliver Iron Mining Company.[23] They pursued additional legal maneuvers during subsequent years, but in 1919 the company began to move buildings to a site about a mile farther south. Although some structures were razed, many buildings were transplanted to the new area. In addition to the expenses involved in transporting and rehabilitating existing buildings, an estimated $20 million was spent on new improvements to what was then referred to as the Central Addition or "Alice."[24] The primary move was completed in 1921, but many homes and business buildings remained on the old site as lonely, abandoned sentinels for an additional twenty-five years. Not until the late 1930s did the courts and the Minnesota legislature resolve the issues between the remaining property owners and the Oliver Iron Mining Company. The last buildings were razed after World War II. Soon the former site would constitute part of the huge open pit that adjoined Hibbing's northern border.[25]

Living conditions in Iron Range townsites began to improve around 1910 when small groups of individuals – primarily mining officials, professionals, merchants, and school officials – campaigned for the betterment of their communities. They gave special attention to the inspection of water supplies and improved sewage and waste-disposal systems. Although this elite minority "rejoiced in promoting the common good," according to historian Clarke A. Chambers, its benevolence was based upon retaining undisputed control of the community and its operations. By the second decade of the century, however, minority rule began to erode when voters recognized the importance of controlling the potential tax revenues of individual communities. In Hibbing, disgruntled voters elected Victor L. Power as mayor in 1913; he was the first elected official in a major Iron Range community not beholden to the mining companies. Power initially gained notoriety when he represented residents of Hibbing's North Forty in their successful 1912 suit against the Oliver company.[26]

Power's influence was reflected in the startling rise in Hibbing's municipal budget after his election. In 1913, the budget was $275,000, but by 1921 it had risen to $2.4 million. Tax levies on the lucrative mining interests operating within the town and other settlements generated revenues for relief projects that employed out-of-work miners during the off-season; athletic and recreational programs, mothers' clubs, night schools, well-baby clinics, and music and drama organizations; community doctors and nurses; and, above all, school buildings and expanded educational programs. A $4 million school building in Hibbing crowned an educational system that affected virtually every resident of the region in some way.

The second major community form on the Iron Range, the location, existed in three basic types. Squatters' locations, the first type, were unplatted, haphazardly organized enclaves inhabited almost exclusively by eastern and southern European immigrants. These settlements emerged when the miners constructed shacks, hovels, and occasionally more substantial dwellings on leased land. Since there was no preconceived street plan in a squatters' location, the buildings, according to a former resident, were "all in a jumble," with "a house here and house there."[27] One observer wrote in 1928 that the locations appeared "as if they had just been poured out of something into a heap," while another visitor, viewing White City Location by Marble, described the structures as "log huts[,] for they cannot be called houses, underground rooms with no ventilation and with the sheep and pigs a part of the family."[28]

The platted company location, the second type, was the most common settlement form on the Iron Range. Laid out with the precision of a mining engineer's T-square, company locations displayed a rigorous application of the grid plan. Mining firms often constructed housing for their employees in these settlements, although residents sometimes purchased or built houses on company land. The basic intention of the company location was to provide housing for married employees, who were considered the most dependable and stable workers. Although larger, better-designed houses were often constructed for mining superintendents and captains, the housing was usually quite uniform and even monotonous. (One former resident claimed that people who lived in some company locations might walk into the wrong house because all were so similar in appearance.) As late as 1940, sociologist John Syrjamaki described the locations of the Mesabi as standing "stark against an open and drear background of mine shafts, open-pits, dumps, railroad tracks, and tree stumps and boulders."[29]

The model location was the third type. These developments, which offered better housing than the company locations and were more attractively organized, were few in number and intended for the most highly valued personnel at important mine sites like Mahoning, Monroe, and Fraser.[30] Mahoning Location, situated west of the original townsite of Hibbing, was begun in 1894, but several improvements in 1902 reportedly gave the enclave a clean, trim appearance and converted it into a "model" one. Each house was equipped with hot and cold water, an amenity that was not provided in other company locations for many years. As late as 1921, 31 percent of the Oliver Iron Mining Company's two thousand residences in the Lake Superior region did not have piped-in water, and 63 percent were without indoor bathrooms.[31]

Soudan, the oldest and largest location on the entire Iron Range, typified all of the basic features that later would characterize the vast majority of such settlements in northeastern Minnesota. Except for a few squatters' enclaves on state-owned property, all land in Soudan and the other locations was owned by the mining firms. Residents either rented houses built by the companies or paid an annual fee for a ground lease that allowed them to construct their own dwellings. Since commercial establishments were seldom permitted in a location, store owners in the town-

Kerr Location near Hibbing, 1919

sites delivered groceries and other necessities to the smaller enclaves. Location residents who wanted to attend church or a cultural event, to visit a saloon, or simply to experience the excitement of a town had to trek along the roadways and boardwalks that connected the location to a townsite that could be more than a mile distant.[32] In 1913, a streetcar line was opened on the Mesabi Range; bus service began a year later with an enterprise that evolved over the years into the Greyhound Bus Corporation. Both systems connected several townsites and locations along the Mesabi.[33]

In addition to the locations, which served as residential variants of company communities throughout the Lake Superior region, the mining companies built a few company towns on the Iron Range. Coleraine, Marble, and Taconite were established on the far western end of the Mesabi Range at the beginning of the century. A fourth company town, Morgan Park, was constructed between 1913 and 1915 near Duluth, sixty miles south of the Iron Range, when a new steel plant was built there.[34] Two of the company towns, Coleraine and Morgan Park, embraced so many unique planning features that they merit designation as model villages.

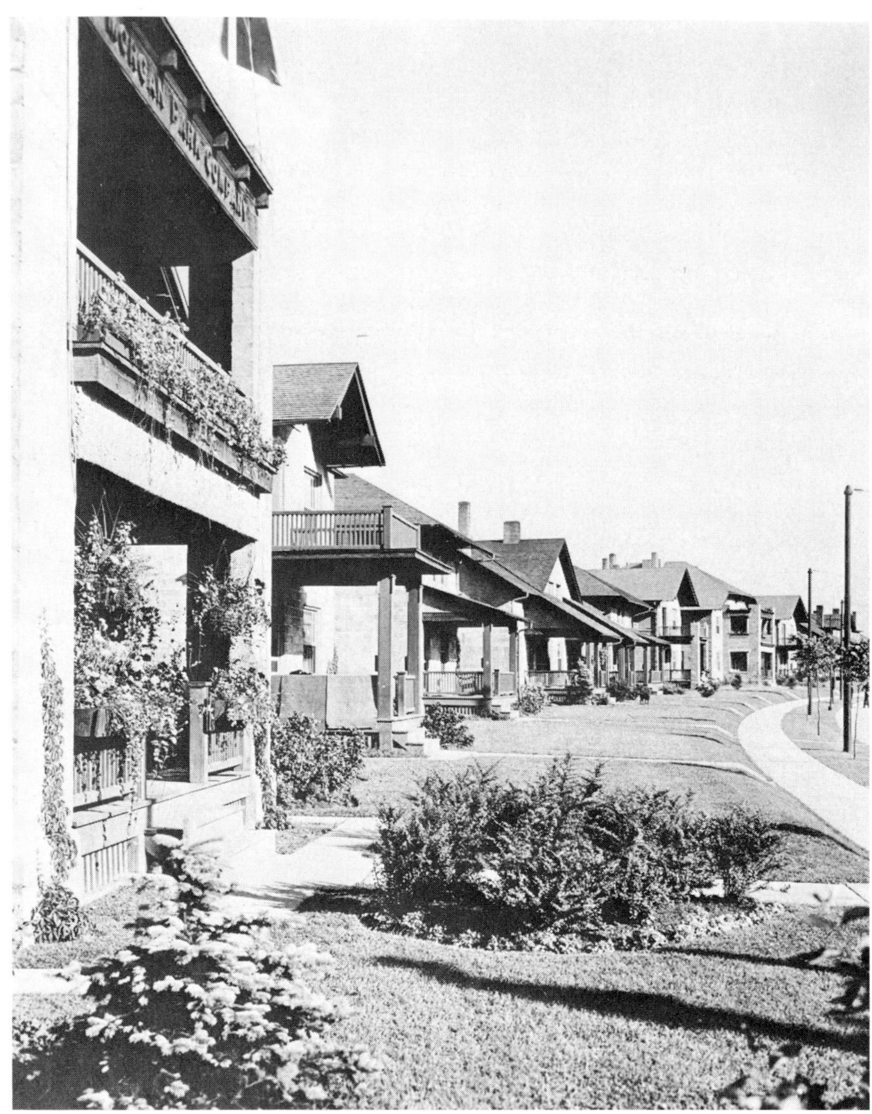

Houses lining a street in Duluth's Morgan Park, 1917

Announcements that appeared early in 1906 for Coleraine envisioned a utopian community.[35] In addition to wide streets, large lots, parks, and public facilities, building regulations ensured the maintenance of certain standards of architectural variety and construction. Nothing, however, received more attention than the efforts of the Oliver Iron Mining Company and its district superintendent, John C. Greenway, to eliminate vice from Coleraine. The plan, which supposedly would prohibit the "saloons, gamblers [and] wantons" that were typical in other mining towns, stressed a concern for promoting "health and happiness and [features] which are beautiful."[36] Citizens constantly contrasted their town with the nearby settlement of Bovey, where twenty-two saloons existed in 1907. (This gave Bovey one saloon per sixty-four residents – the highest per capita figure for any townsite on the western Mesabi at that time; Gilbert had this distinction on the eastern Mesabi.)[37] Superintendent Greenway pointed out that Coleraine allowed only one closely regulated saloon, which sold limited amounts of alcohol to residents "rather than have them follow the present practice of going to Bovey and getting very drunk." Although Bovey's residents initially worried that the strict regulations in Coleraine would hurt their businesses, they eventually came to see Bovey as the "safety valve" that would make an enterprise like Coleraine practical.[38]

By 1908, observers were praising the layout and development of Coleraine, which was situated on a hill overlooking picturesque Trout Lake. Conrad B. Wolf, park superintendent for Hibbing, was hired several years later to develop Longyear Park, a former bog that adjoined the lake. The park, with its flowers, trees, shrubs, lily pond, rustic bridge, and bandstand, emerged as one of the most formally designed landscapes on the entire Iron Range.[39]

The nearby company towns of Marble and Taconite were also built under Greenway's direction during these years. Neither, however, was as ambitious as Coleraine. Both Marble and Taconite had relatively large, comfortable homes with attractive lawns and gardens, but little emphasis was given to the development of a central business district. Although the two communities were more restricted than other Iron Range townsites, they were not as highly controlled and planned as Coleraine.[40]

Morgan Park, situated on the far western side of Duluth, was the premier example of company town planning in northeastern Minnesota. The Morgan Park community was built by United States Steel next to its new plant, which was reportedly constructed in return for the state legislature's decision in 1907 not to impose a tonnage tax on ore shipped out of the state. Although various factors delayed the opening of the plant to late 1915, the adjacent model village began to receive attention in professional and popular journals as soon as construction began in 1913. Unlike the grid plans used in other townsites, the Morgan Park plat was designed by the Minneapolis landscape architectural firm of Morell and Nichols with curvilinear streets, some of which provided views of the ravines and bluffs that bordered the community. The houses, designed by Dean and Dean, a Chicago architectural firm, were somewhat gray and drab but very solidly built; potential visual monotony was avoided by using an array of different gables, eaves, and roof lines.[41]

Overall, Morgan Park was regarded by several experts as one of the best-planned company towns built in early-twentieth-century America. In 1918, a national architectural journal noted that the development of the community "had been along systematic and orderly lines; correct principles of town planning have been followed and the educational and recreative elements necessary in a development of this character have been provided in a most modern and satisfactory manner."[42]

Miners working an underground drift in Sellers Mine near Hibbing, 1906

ginia) was an Italian enclave, Helmer Location (Buhl) was primarily Bulgarian, and Frenchtown Location (Virginia) was French Canadian.[51]

The few locations that catered to the American-born were better designed and planned than others on the Mesabi, since they were constructed to attract highly trained employees. Monroe Location (Chisholm), whose population was three-fourths American, was built as a model enclave for skilled workers and mining supervisors employed by United States Steel. In the Hibbing area, more than three-fourths of the residents in Penobscot, Rust, and Webb locations were American born; English was virtually the sole language used in these locations, since the largest foreign-born groups were the British and British Canadians.

The immigrants who toiled together in the mines communicated with one another by using broken English (termed "mine English") or by speaking a new language that incorporated basic terms from various European tongues and dialects. When a mine timber broke, a piece of equipment malfunctioned, or a shaft suddenly filled with water, men who worked together also died together: death did not discriminate among Slovenian, Finnish, Italian, and Croatian laborers. Mining companies also had a policy of deliberately intermixing employees from many nationalities. Not only were large numbers of workers needed in the region, but representatives from many nations, as reported by the U.S. Immigration Commission in 1911, "naturally prevent[ed] the formation of strong and well-organized labor unions." Similar sentiments were expressed in the *Eveleth Mining News* after a local strike had ended in 1904: "In order to avoid the dangers that come from hiring one nationality predominantly [that is, the Finns]," reported the newspaper, "the management saw to it that the new labor force was mixed as far as that point is concerned."[52]

Certain immigrant groups were highly concentrated in specific mining occupations. A study of Eveleth's 1905 work force revealed that almost 85 percent of the miners were "Austrians" (South Slavs), Finns, and Italians.[53] A sample from the 1910 federal census of 2,125 employed males revealed a similar pattern: almost 75 percent of the 650 miners in the group were of Slovenian, Italian, Finnish, or Croatian origin. While these miners supplied the sweat, muscle, and sometimes even blood to extract the ore of the Iron Range, a host of their compatriots pursued related occupations. The latter individuals, often identified simply as "day laborers," formed the second-largest group of workers in both 1905 and 1910. Some were involved in stripping the glacial overburden that covered the ore deposits, and others were employed as railroad workers, loggers, teamsters, and road builders. In 1905 three-fourths of Eveleth's day laborers were from Finland, the South Slavic countries, and Italy, and the 1910 sample of several Iron Range settlements revealed that Finns, Italians, Swedes, and Slovenes provided the majority of workers in this employment category.[54]

Smaller numbers of immigrants were employed as shopkeepers, saloon operators, clerks, tailors, or in many other occupations unrelated to mining. Virtually every ethnic group had representatives performing these jobs, although some groups, such as the Jews, were almost exclusively employed as shopkeepers, merchants, clerks, and peddlers, and the few Chinese on the range operated or worked in restaurants and laundries.

American-born workers filled many of the jobs – carpenter, blacksmith, mason, machinist, plumber, for example – that required a certain level of skill and training. (Almost all immigrant groups were represented in this category, too, but by much smaller numbers.) Supervisory roles in the mining industry were held largely by American-born men, with those of British origin also playing an important role. Most of the professional and managerial positions that emerged in the booming mining region and that demanded specialized training and English-language abilities – engineer, doctor, newspaper editor, preacher, banker, lawyer – were held by individuals born in the United States. In addition, Americans were the entrepreneurs involved in townsite development, land speculation, and other business and commercial ventures.

As has been true of the formative years of any mining region, men significantly outnumbered women on the Iron Range. Nevertheless, women played essential roles as wives and mothers and in filling the limited number of jobs available to them. A sample from the 1910 census shows that of almost three hundred women employed outside the home, just over half

A Finnish boardinghouse in Ely, about 1910

were American born. Of the women working in such professional and proprietary positions as teacher, nurse, and store owner or operator, more than 90 percent were American born, and Americans were also found in close to 80 percent of all clerical jobs held by women. Of the women who found employment in such domestic and servant occupations as laundry worker, waitress, and chambermaid, however, 70 percent were immigrants.

A special 1918 survey of women workers in Minnesota offers even more telling insights into the burdensome toil that women often faced on the Iron Range. A review of 670 listings from this survey indicates that American-born women of American parentage worked an average of just over fifty-six hours per week, whereas women born in the United States of immigrant parents worked sixty-four hours and foreign-born women worked sixty-seven hours. The first group earned an average wage or salary of $14.00 per week (25 cents an hour), the second $10.85 (17 cents an hour), and the third $9.00 (13 cents an hour).[55]

The most demanding jobs were associated with the operation of boardinghouses. Conditions in 1910 in one of the larger boardinghouses in Gilbert, then a booming mining town only three years old, provide a glimpse into the world within which the cleaning women, dishwashers, waitresses, and cooks worked. Pete Tonia's operation, for example, housed forty-six of his Finnish male compatriots; three young, single women, all recent immigrants from Finland, lived in the boardinghouse and performed the many chores that kept the facility functioning. In Keewatin in 1910, Mary Chachich, a twenty-year-old immigrant from Croatia who had arrived on the Iron Range just months earlier to marry a Croatian miner, ran another boardinghouse. Twenty-seven Croatian men lived with the Chachiches. Like several of her immigrant sisters throughout the Iron Range, Mary Chachich did most of the work that accompanied the operation and management of her boardinghouse. In 1918, women employed in boardinghouses averaged almost seventy-five hours of work per week; some even worked in excess of one hundred hours. All of the female boardinghouse employees listed in the survey worked seven days a week and received, on the average, a weekly wage of $7.55, or 10 cents an hour.[56]

Most immigrant women were limited by the nature of the local economy and by cultural preferences to raising children, managing households, and caring for boarders. Indeed, only 13 percent of the employed women listed in the 1918 survey were married at the time. Given the overall shortage of women on the Iron Range during these early years, few women, especially among immigrant groups, remained single for long. Immigrant women often viewed the creation of a new family as a way to reduce the anguish associated with the breaking of familial relationships in the homeland, and the men, besides responding to emotional and sexual needs, viewed marriage from a pragmatic perspective: "Financial considerations," wrote historian John Bodnar, "also prompted many men to seek a companion who would cook, clean, and care for them for no wages at all."[57]

Accurate data on Iron Range prostitution are difficult to find, for it is likely that women who pursued this occupation were reluctant to disclose it to census takers. Of the state manuscript censuses from 1885 to 1910 that are available for perusal, only the one taken in 1895 lists more than a token number of prostitutes – and then just for Virginia and Hibbing. Of sixty-nine women listed as "demi monde," "sports," or "prostitutes," almost three-fourths were born in America. The twenty immigrant women noted in the 1895 Iron Range census were from Canada, Ireland, Sweden, England, Scotland, and Norway, but a few prostitutes were probably found in most ethnic groups. Women who "went wrong," however, are believed to represent but a small minority of the total immigrant (and native-born) community. (Seventeen men in Virginia were listed as gamblers; of these, seven were immigrants.)[58]

The different immigrant groups that lived on the Iron Range interacted with each other in their communities and workplaces, but certain places – the home, the church, the hall – and holiday celebrations tended to be limited to the family or to people sharing a common cultural heritage and language. Each Iron Range community had its unique personality, even though all were tied into America's industrial and manufacturing complex, and residents of the region maintained their ethnic distinctiveness for decades.

Few American-born residents were able (or inclined) to distinguish among the many ethnic concentrations on the Iron Range. The immigrants strongly disliked the failure of native-born Americans to recognize their cultural and national differences. Novelist Phil Stong, for example, commented that the only insult comparable to calling a Finn a Swede on the range was to term a Serb a Bulgarian. Some immigrant groups were not only identified by such commonly used pejorative terms as "Dago," "Hunky," "Bohunk," and "Finlander," but were further classified as "black" or "white" Europeans. Syrjamaki observed in his 1940 study of Mesabi Range immigrants that southern Europeans were identified as "black," and the U.S. Immigration Commission quoted Minnesota mining officials in 1911 who specifically identified "black" Europeans as Montenegrins, Serbs, South Italians, Greeks, and Croatians. The British and Scandinavians, or the "white" Europeans, were considered to be the best workers. "White Finns" were identified by some people as those Finnish immigrants who did not question corporate practices and who were sober and God-fearing. "Black Finns" were perceived as heavy drinkers, Socialists, and anarchists.[59]

Although language undoubtedly helped to unify an ethnic group, many old-time residents of the Iron Range interviewed in the 1970s and 1980s asserted that religion played the key role. St. Patrick's Catholic Church in Eveleth, for example, was organized in 1904 by Irish and Italian immigrants, but the Italians left the congregation in 1915 to form the Immaculate Conception Church. Our Lady of Lourdes Church in Virginia was formed in 1893 and had Italian, Polish, Slovenian, Croatian, Irish, and English-speaking parishioners; in 1905, however, the Poles separated from the congregation and organized St. John the Baptist Polish Catholic Church.[60] Similar distinctions developed among the Serbs, Montenegrins, and Croatians who shared a similar language (Serbo-Croatian) but who were divided between the Eastern Orthodox (Serbs and Montenegrins) and the Roman Catholic (Croatian) faiths. The latter group, indeed, identified more closely with the Slovenes. These differences were noted by William J. Bell, an early-twentieth-century missionary and social worker for the Presbyterian church, when he said that in Iron Range locations inhabited by South Slavs "the old line of Constantine went down the middle of a location road, and sometimes I suspected the line went right through the middle of a boarding house table."[61]

Finnish was not even remotely similar to the languages used by other immigrant groups on the Iron Range, yet the Finns had their own internal factions. Various religious schisms in the Finnish-American community led to the organization of three separate Lutheran church bodies. Finnish Congregational, Unitarian, and Pentecostal congregations also existed on the range. Unlike the Finnish immigrants of the early nineteenth century, many of these later arrivals professed no more than a lukewarm appreciation of organized religion. Some who joined Socialist groups even expressed an outright disdain. In addition to the eleven thousand foreign-born people on the Iron Range who spoke Finnish, nearly five hundred Swede-Finns – who had been born in Finland – spoke Swedish. These people often found it difficult to associate with either the Finns or the Swedes, a fact that was pointed out to Syrjamaki in 1940 by a Swede-Finn: "We are people without a country. The Swedes high-hat us, and we can't talk to the Finns."[62]

In Franklin Location by Virginia, Italians and other immigrants used the saunas of the Finns on a regular basis; one former Italian resident claimed that the sauna was especially useful and healthful because the location lacked indoor plumbing for many years. Immigrants also learned about different plants and gardening practices from their neighbors. The Italians, acknowledged as the "star" tomato growers on the Iron Range, reportedly introduced this plant to the Finns, who then adopted it as their own garden mainstay. Dances at Finnish halls, whether sponsored by temperance or Socialist organizations, were attended by the children of other immigrants, such as Slovenes and Croatians, although the older South Slavs reportedly would not participate because they found it difficult to understand such a strange concept as temperance. Some of the Scandinavians, on the other hand, looked down upon the way southern and eastern Europeans consumed alcohol.[63]

Newspaper accounts from the early twentieth century reflect the hostile attitudes of Americans toward immigrants, as well as the acrimony that sometimes existed between different immigrant groups. The newspapers often included ethnic slurs in their reports of altercations, especially if the participants were South Slavs, Italians, or Finns. When several Italian laborers argued with a mining foreman in 1904, the report in the *Hibbing Tribune* said that the police entered the camp where the workers were staying and "demanded the unconditional surrender of the Italian forces, together with all the macaroni and garlick [*sic*] on the premises." A few months later an account in the same newspaper made the following statement: "Italy and Finland have declared war. The first engagement occurred on the public highway near the Mahoning mine Monday afternoon. A squad of a dozen or so Italians met four or five Fins [*sic*] and an altercation was begun, then followed a fistic combat, and a Fin sought to even matters by smashing a Dago's face with a rock."[64]

When unmarried men left the Iron Range to return to their homelands in eastern and southern Europe, a Hibbing newspaper editorial posed the question: "What of it? . . . These are not the people that make the pith and back bone of any town or country." An Eveleth schoolteacher wrote in a letter in 1908 that only one-fifth of the residents in and around the community were "civilized folk." Some people in the poorer locations were mistreated by those who lived in better surroundings. One person of Croatian background who lived in Adams Location by Eveleth recalled that classmates termed him and his friends "stump jumpers" and "swamp rats." People living in the small immigrant location of Bruce, adjacent to the larger and more attractive Monroe Location where Americans predominated, rarely crossed the border between the two enclaves; a former inhabitant of Bruce claimed that children who lived there were the victims of taunts, insults, and small objects that were hurled at them by their Monroe counterparts.[65]

Nevertheless, most residents of Iron Range settlements appear to have been content with their homes and communities. The vast majority of individuals interviewed in the 1970s and 1980s by the Iron Range Research Center stated that whether they had resided in a townsite or a location, the people within the enclaves generally got along well together. Living with different ethnic groups, one wife and husband said after residing in locations around Chisholm for some years, was a good lesson for life.[66]

Corporate Welfare and Labor Struggles

The elite group of professional and business leaders who began to work from about 1910 to improve health and sanitary conditions in the mines and mining communities was participating in the corporate welfare or welfare capitalism efforts initiated by many American corporations at the turn of the century. These programs were intended to improve conditions for workers and their families, to forestall strikes and labor unrest, and to head off the reform movements being advocated by governmental agencies and consumers' groups during the progressive era.[67]

The most important facet of corporate welfare was workers' housing, but large corporations like United States Steel also set up safety programs, stock subscription plans, pension and voluntary relief benefits, and sanitation and welfare committees. Labor stability, historian David Brody observed, was the primary objective of these efforts: "Through promotions, housing, bonuses, pensions, and steady work, corps of company retainers were developed. The skilled workmen entered an orbit of dependence, induced to accept without dispute the terms of employment."[68]

Although many of the programs ignored the needs of the recent immigrant worker, mine safety was one area where employers could improve conditions for all the laborers who worked in Iron Range mines. During the early 1900s, miners died or were injured in distressingly large numbers throughout the region. Committees and juries that investigated accidents invariably absolved the companies from any responsibility, usually concluding that the accident was unavoidable or that the victims were to blame because of their ignorance of technology and inability to understand English. John Pengilly, a mining captain in the Ely area, reflected these attitudes in 1902 when he commented that the number of fatalities was deplorable but that most were the result of "the carelessness of [the men] themselves, though sad." Accounts in local newspapers described the mining accidents in graphic detail, with little or no hint of apology given for the deaths or injuries. "Death Reaps a Heavy Harvest," reported a *Hibbing Tribune* headline when announcing an accident that killed six men in 1906; the account appeared in the middle of a story about a series of unrelated violent deaths. Similarly, a 1911 issue of Chisholm's *Tribune-Herald* matter-of-factly commented that three miners had been "blown to atoms" by a premature explosion in the Sellers Mine.[69]

The state began to collect accurate data on mining accidents in 1905 after the legislature approved a mine inspection law. From 1905 to 1910, a total of 386 mining fatalities were recorded on the Iron Range – about 5 per 1,000 workers. Company and state safety programs implemented during subsequent years lowered the total number of fatalities even as the work force expanded: from 1910 to 1915, 272 fatalities occurred, or about 2.5 per 1,000 workers. Thereafter the overall accident death rate generally declined, although 1917 and 1924 were particularly tragic years on the Iron Range.[70] The fatality figure for 1924 was significantly increased by the Milford mine disaster on the Cuyuna Range, when a nearby lake abruptly emptied into an underground mining operation and either drowned or buried in mud 41 miners. The report of a governor's investigating team declared that the mine owners and operators would not be charged with any blame in the tragedy, but several additional regulations concerning mine safety were passed by the Minnesota legislature.[71]

The vast majority of those who died were foreign born. Of the more than 700 miners killed between 1906 and 1916, fully 90 percent were immigrants. Close to 300 of the 700 deaths occurred among South Slavs, and just over 150 Finns and 75 Italians were killed. A total of 125 deaths were spread out among fifteen or so other immigrant groups, and 50 American-born men died.[72]

In addition to improving the safety of their operations, mining companies tried to prevent labor disturbances and strikes. During the formative years of Iron Range history, most strikes were confined to one mine or company or to a group of mines. In the 1890s, for example, several hundred of the Vermilion's South Slavs and Italians refused to work on Corpus Christi Day, one of their major holidays.[73] In 1904, close to 600 men in Ely struck to protest the abusive tactics of a local mining captain, and a wage protest strike by 1,500 miners in Hibbing one year later led to the killing of two Finnish participants.[74]

Finns emerged as major leaders, organizers, and participants in the Mesabi strike of 1907, an event that overshadowed all previous labor conflicts on the Iron Range. Finnish Socialists brought Teofilo Petriella, an Italian immigrant, to the range to organize a local for the Western Federation of Miners. On July 20 at least ten thousand men, three-fourths of them Finns, struck. To combat the widespread work stoppage, the mining companies imported trainloads of Greeks, Italians, Slovenes, Croatians, and Montenegrins, men who "had not yet learned the meaning of labor solidarity," and broke the strike by mid-August.[75] Subsequently, many Finns were blacklisted for their participation, and the Finnish proportion of the Oliver Iron Mining Company's work force on the range quickly shrank from 18 to 8 percent. "This exodus of the Finns from the Range towns and their replacement by Southern Europeans," said Paul H. Landis in his retrospective review of the Mesabi Range in 1938, "did much to change the nationality complexion of the Range, as well as to erect a barrier of animosity between Finns and the mining companies."[76]

Many of the Finns moved to the nearby cutover wilderness of St. Louis County, or elsewhere in the Lake Superior region, to carve out farms and homesteads. But these and other agricultural pioneers encountered difficult conditions. Rocks, stumps, brush, and trees had to be removed, marshes drained, and farm buildings constructed before farming could begin. Despite the poor soils and short growing season, however, farming was often viewed as a favorable alternative to mining. Immigrant newspaper reports and other publications commented on the restorative magic of "clear, cold, sparkling water" and the clear air and simple, invigorating way of life to be found in rural areas; in addition, a Biwabik correspondent noted that "when hard times arrive at a mine, then . . . the farm is a haven of refuge."[77] Land agents, supported by University of Minnesota scientists, promoted the perceived agricultural potential of the region. A. J. McGuire, director of the university's agricultural experiment station at Grand Rapids, declared in 1909 that the cutover area should be advertised widely until "there is a farmer on every eighty acres of land, till every swamp is drained and every needed road is built." Some of these early settlers established successful farming operations, but the marginal agricultural potential of the region forced many to abandon their efforts – especially during periods of economic depression.[78]

In 1916, the Industrial Workers of the World supported another major strike, sending such well-known labor organizers as Elizabeth Gurley Flynn to the Mesabi. Ironically, not only Finns but also South Slavs – including several of the same groups that had been imported as strikebreakers in 1907 – participated in this confrontation. The strike lasted for three months and led to the deaths of three persons, but it ended when the resources of the strikers were depleted in September 1916.[79]

Following this strike, the Oliver company developed a "mutuality plan" to improve relationships between the corporation and its workers. According to the *Ely Miner* in 1918, the new effort was "destined to bring the employe and employer closer together and is a step long needed." Such concerns included improving working conditions and equipment, providing medical services, and upgrading residential living conditions.[80] The most visible program developed during this period was the effort to enhance the appearance of location landscapes by improving yards, lawns, and gardens. Companies conducted contests, gave small cash prizes to participants with the most attractive gardens and yards, and published announcements of winners in company bulletins. Improved appearance was not the only benefit the companies hoped to achieve by implementing their garden programs. United States Steel informed its subsidiary companies in 1914 that gardens helped laborers to use their free time wisely: "The man who has learned to take pride in his garden hurries home from his work, spending little time in loitering and none in the saloon. Therefore, the garden tends to reduce alcoholism. The man's standing in the community is raised; and what is even better, his own self-respect is promoted."[81]

Mining companies initiated visiting nurse programs as another important facet of welfare or mutuality on the range. The programs sought not only to "Americanize" the mining employees and their families, ostensibly by improving health, morals, and living standards, but also to engender "a very kindly feeling toward the company." Some nurses were frustrated by the large number of cases they were expected to handle on the Iron Range. Others were dismayed by the tendencies of immigrant women to follow Old World customs when feeding and caring for children, maintaining households, and prescribing remedies for illness. One nurse noted that in

The children of Frank Zgonc, a Slovenian miner working the Pioneer Mine, in the family's vegetable garden in Ely, 1917

addition to providing health care she served as a seamstress, dietician, sanitarian, home demonstrator, gardener, and mechanic.[82]

The visiting nurse programs did not begin to address all the health and social needs of Iron Range residents. Local school districts also employed nurses and social workers who monitored the well-being of children, and night-school teachers instructed their parents in the English language and American civics.[83] In addition, church organizations sought to serve the spiritual and social needs of Iron Range residents. Especially visible was the nondenominational Iron Range ministry funded by the Presbyterian Home Board and managed locally by William Bell from 1913 to 1931. At first, Bell worked virtually alone to reach the immigrant population of the locations, but he was later aided by a cadre of assistants and volunteers, many of them students from Macalester College in St. Paul who served on the Iron Range during their summer vacations. Bell often used location schools to accommodate various activities that expanded the boundaries of traditional evangelism, including scouting work, story and play hours, children's nurseries, motion pictures, newcomers' receptions, music and drama clubs, baby clinics, pig clubs, and classes for teaching cooking, housekeeping, and immigrant folklore.[84]

The corporate welfare and mutuality programs run by the mining companies doubtless improved the quality of life in the locations, but workers paid a price in the strict regulations that the companies imposed. Oliver's mutuality plan included provisions for discharging an employee for insubordination, instigating disorder or confusion among workers via agitation, soliciting union membership while at work or on community property, serving as a member of an organization that promoted anarchy or violence, or incapacity. Even more intrusive was the spy network or-

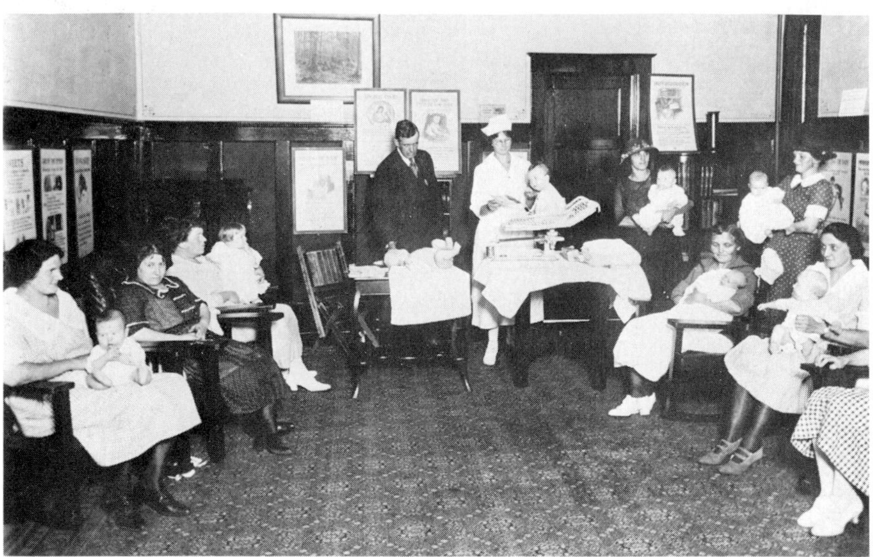

A baby clinic operated by the Oliver Iron Mining Company, Virginia, 1922

ganized by the Oliver company to fight the spread of unionism throughout the 1920s and much of the 1930s.[85]

All the welfare efforts, both private and public, were severely strained during the 1930s when the full impact of the Great Depression came crashing down upon the Iron Range. By 1931, after most mines in the region had shut down, in Hibbing alone close to 3,000 unemployed men registered for relief work. The village could provide local jobs for no more than 250 workers, and officials claimed that thousands of the needy were starving and in danger of losing their homes. The election of Franklin D. Roosevelt to the presidency in late 1932, followed by the rapid implementation of New Deal recovery programs, had an immediate impact upon the range. Indeed, federally sponsored programs soon replaced many of the private and local public-relief efforts that had been offered before. By 1933, thousands of individuals on the Iron Range were being selected from charity lists and put to work, first on local Civil Works Administration projects and later on Works Progress Administration (WPA) jobs that included street and sidewalk repairs, park and cemetery improvements, rural road and telephone line extensions, and state and federal forestry work. Nurses were employed by the WPA to serve the needs of the elderly and of mothers and children, and a facility was provided in Virginia to offer "an eight-week course in all details of household management to girls from needy families who are anxious to earn their living at household work."[86]

Perhaps no federal legislation had greater impact on the Iron Range than did the National Labor Relations (Wagner) Act of 1935. After the constitutionality of the act was affirmed by the U.S. Supreme Court in 1937, workers vigorously pursued efforts to organize unions and establish collective bargaining agreements. Several mining companies signed contracts with the Congress of Industrial Organizations in the late 1930s, but not until 1943 did United States Steel (including its subsidiary, Oliver Iron Mining) agree to terms with the United Steel Workers of America. With this action, the miners of the Iron Range finally gained the major objectives they had struggled for during the preceding half century.[87]

The Taconite Era

By the late 1930s, lawmakers from northeastern Minnesota were looking for ways to improve the economic prospects of the Iron Range. Among several recommendations made to the 1941 session of the Minnesota legislature was a proposal to encourage the mining of low-grade iron ore. The legislative committee that considered the proposal acknowledged that "the relief problem on the Range is acute, and . . . we are confronted with the problem of a stranded population group." The legislature agreed to fund a body that came to be termed the Iron Range Resources and Rehabilitation Board (IRRRB). In subsequent years the IRRRB has supported a large number of projects, many of them designed to bring diversity to the economy of the Iron Range.[88]

The full-scale commitment of the United States to the war effort in late 1941 transformed conditions on the Iron Range virtually overnight: ore production increased dramatically and full employment became the byword. A limited number of women even replaced some of the men who left the mines to serve in the armed forces.[89] But the extraction of massive amounts of the high-grade natural ore, or hematite, only hastened the depletion of Minnesota's major reserves.

The development of a process to convert the low-grade taconite ores of the region into a product for steel-manufacturing purposes prevented a decline in the state's iron-ore mining industry as the hematite was exhausted. During the 1940s, E. W. Davis and his colleagues in the University of Minnesota's Mines Experiment Station continued their long-standing efforts to perfect taconite processing operations. Working in concert with several iron-ore mining and steel-manufacturing companies, the University of Minnesota team succeeded in developing a process that could convert the hard taconite rock (containing no more than 25 to 35 percent iron) into concentrated pellets suitable for shipment on Great Lakes ore carriers. In 1955, the Reserve Mining Company put into operation a mine site and crusher at Babbitt and a concentrator and pelletizing plant at Silver Bay. Two years later the Erie Mining Company opened its taconite plant at Hoyt Lakes.[90]

Had these taconite operations not developed, several existing mining towns on the eastern Mesabi and the Vermilion, such as Aurora, Gilbert, McKinley, and Tower, would have been threatened with extinction. When the new plants opened, the towns converted into Iron Range versions of "commuter suburbs." Since the early taconite units were situated in remote areas, new towns were constructed at Babbitt, Hoyt Lakes, and Silver Bay to provide nearby housing for a portion of the work force. All three communities were post-World War II versions of the company town,

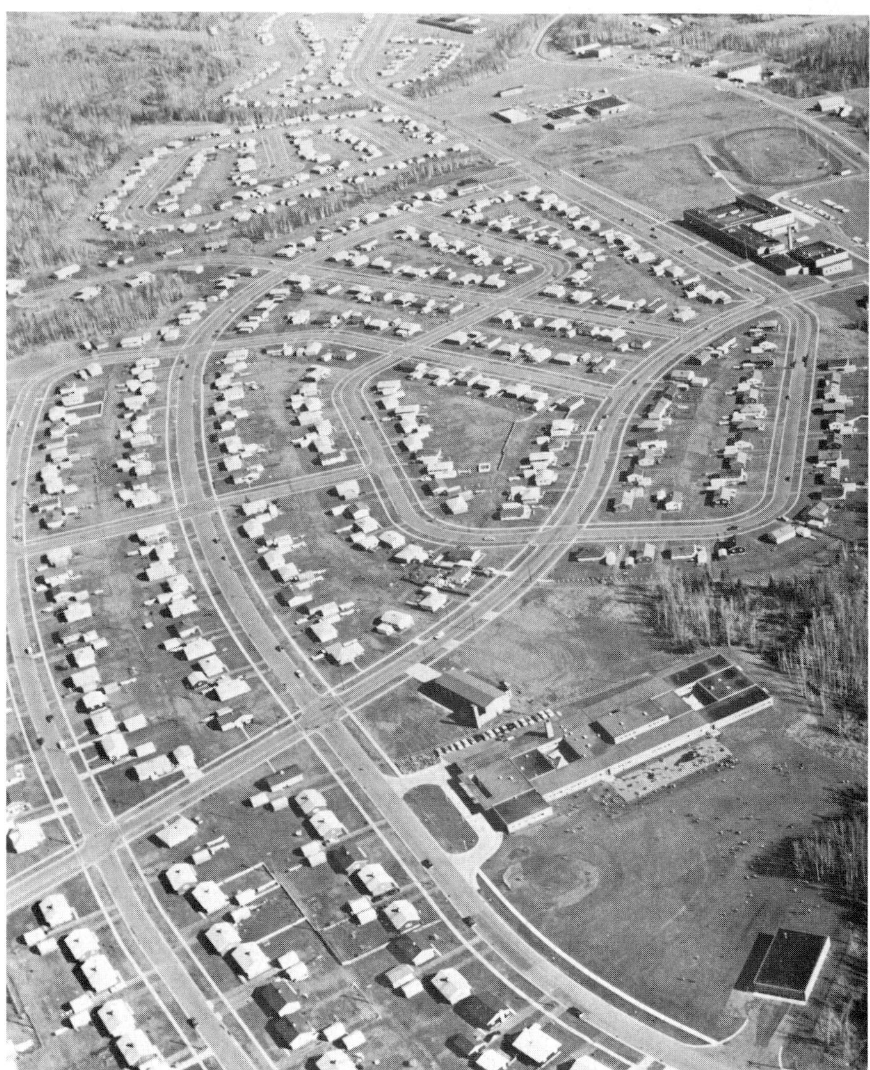

The Lake Superior shoreline town of Silver Bay, about 1960

but the approach to planning and organization was quite different. For example, when earlier company towns were built the mining companies made no effort to assess the preferences of residents; in the 1950s, however, the Chicago consulting firm involved with the planning of Silver Bay and Babbitt commissioned a sociologist to conduct a survey among prospective inhabitants of the two communities. The survey results confirmed that a skilled work force could be assured for the taconite operations only if the communities and residences were "attractive enough to draw people into the area in spite of the climate and lack of amenities."[91]

Although the three towns were built on sites covered with second-growth timber, all vegetation and considerable amounts of soil were removed before construction began. The buildings erected on these barren sites followed the curvilinear outlines characteristic of the suburbs of that era. The availability of large undeveloped land tracts permitted Hoyt Lakes and Babbitt to be situated some distance from the taconite plants and their noise, traffic, and air pollution, but site configurations at Silver Bay limited the facility and community to a concentrated area along the Lake Superior shoreline.

Proposals to construct more taconite plants were accompanied by a long and often rancorous debate throughout Minnesota in the late 1950s and early 1960s. Finally, in 1964 voters of the state passed a constitutional amendment to guarantee taconite processors a twenty-five-year period free of tax increases. This legislation led to the development of additional taconite plants at Eveleth, Nashwauk, Keewatin, Hibbing, and Mountain Iron and the expansion of facilities already in operation. Since these plants were situated near existing communities, there was no need to build new towns to house the workers and their families. However, the additional plants, and especially the expansions that occurred in the 1970s, led to a brief boom in housing construction. A 1977 survey of Iron Range residents revealed that the greatest problem faced in the region was a shortage of affordable housing. A few years later the situation was reversed, with many residents who wished to leave the region having trouble selling their already underpriced homes.[92]

Economics and the Environment: New Issues Emerge

The environmental movement gaining strength nationally and in Minnesota began to have an economic impact on the Iron Range during the relatively prosperous period of the late 1960s and the 1970s. At Morgan Park, environmental groups and government agencies examined the effect of pollution emissions from United States Steel's manufacturing operations. Following several hearings and reviews conducted by the Minnesota Pollution Control Agency, the company decided to close the plant permanently in late 1973. This action, which put 2,500 people out of work, was cited locally as an example of the economic hardships that could result from overly restrictive environmental legislation. The primary reason for the United States Steel decision, however, was tied more closely to its problems with a plant that had become antiquated, was poorly maintained, and had always been isolated geographically from the mainstream of American market activity.[93]

During the debate about Morgan Park, an environmental issue with broader national implications emerged at Silver Bay. Termed by consumer advocate Ralph Nader in 1973 as "the most demonstrable eco-catastrophe in the country," the Silver Bay taconite plant was the subject of controversy for over a decade.[94] The principal issue was the daily dumping of some sixty-four thousand tons of taconite tailings into Lake Superior by the Reserve Mining Company. Concerns over the impact of this dumping upon the lake had been raised in 1947 when Minnesota's Department of Conservation conducted hearings before approving Reserve's application to construct the new plant. Representatives for the cities of Duluth and Superior and the Izaak Walton League had pointed to the visual blight and possible harm to drinking-water supplies and aquatic life that could occur, but economic considerations ultimately prevailed. "The economic phase of the proposal," said O. L. Kaupanger of the Minnesota Emergency Conservation Committee, "outweighs all other consideration." Davis, the scientist who had led the way in developing the technology for taconite processing, testified against on-land disposal of the tailings because of the dust problem and stated that "getting them down under the water in Lake Superior is the most unobjectionable way to deal with them."[95]

By the late 1960s and early 1970s, the disposal method attracted national attention when concerns were raised that carcinogenic asbestos fibers were polluting Lake Superior and endangering the drinking water of several communities. In 1978, after eight years of litigation and hearings that focused upon the proposed transfer of the tailings dump to an on-land site, Reserve Mining agreed to move this facet of its operation away from Lake Superior by 1980.[96] After delays that resulted in the layoff of about half the company's 2,800 employees for a period of up to three months, the new disposal site, termed "Milepost 7," opened in June 1980. The residents of Silver Bay, who served as pawns throughout a controversy that generally failed to address their ultimate fate in a precarious one-industry town, were overjoyed with the news that the new disposal site would open and taconite operations could continue. Early Thanksgiving Day church services were held in October 1980 to commemorate Silver Bay's apparent survival.[97] Only a few years later, however, the community's future once again became clouded as reduced demand for taconite led to further economic hardship on the range.

Until the early 1980s, industry and government officials predicted that the boom in taconite expansion and construction that began in 1974 would continue indefinitely. With the number of highly paid mining jobs on the increase, the composition of the work force also changed as women were hired for permanent positions formerly held exclusively by men.[98] By 1982, however, the national economic recession and a declining demand for domestic iron ore led to unemployment levels that had not been encountered on the Iron Range since the 1930s. As taconite plants shut down and workers were laid off, the Minnesota legislature met in special session to consider emergency relief measures. The $16 million allocated at that session came from the Northeast Minnesota Economic Protection Trust Fund (also referred to as the 2002 Fund), a reserve that had been accumulating revenue since 1977 from a taconite production tax. Although the fund was designed for use in the twenty-first century, the legislature declared an economic emergency that gave the communities of northeastern Minnesota immediate access to some of its resources.[99] Given the enormity of the problems faced on the Iron Range, however, the fund offered only short-term relief.

The IRRRB sought in the 1970s and 1980s to promote greater economic diversification in the region by funding local development projects and facilities to promote recreation and tourism, such as Giants Ridge ski area near Biwabik and the Iron Range Interpretative Center (Ironworld USA) at Chisholm. Other efforts to expand the forest products industry included the development in 1986 of a chopsticks factory at Hibbing.[100]

The magnitude of the problem on the Iron Range was spelled out in a 1984 University of Minnesota report that determined that at least ten thousand people in northeastern Minnesota had lost their jobs since the recession of the early 1980s because of the decline in the steel industry. The outlook for replacing a large portion of the lost jobs with employment opportunities in new industries was said to be remote at best, considering the significant number of people who had been involved in mining operations.[101] Since then, the Butler Taconite Plant near Nashwauk closed permanently in 1985, the Reserve Mining Company's facilities at Babbitt and Silver Bay shut down, and the remaining taconite plants have experienced significant reductions in production and employment. Meanwhile, in 1981–84 an average of thirty-one people per day left the three counties of St. Louis, Lake, and Itasca to search for a new life elsewhere. Those who stayed behind, claimed one Minnesota business leader, were trapped by the anchor of their homes: "They've become prisoners of the Iron Range, chained by their mortgages and no buyers."[102]

Statements of gloom and doom about the range, however, have tended to ignore the resilience of its people. The determination, tenacity, and even stubbornness of Minnesota's "Rangers" have given the northeastern area of the state its unique stamp of identity. This "culture unto itself" combines a harsh, spectacular landscape with a rich mixture of ethnic backgrounds. Diverse styles of cooking, a variety of immigrant music, and the local dialect and vocabulary that people use to "speak Ranger" are some of the distinct aspects of Iron Range culture, and people from the range have held on to the spirit and identity of this culture even when they have moved away to find better job opportunities.[103]

After a century of mining activity, northeastern Minnesota in the mid-1980s still retained a huge supply of taconite ore in reserve. Changes in demand for the raw materials of the region, or new technologies that would support different forms of steel production, could spark a resurgence of economic activity on the Iron Range.[104] As with its past, the future of the range is linked to its natural resources and the skills and adaptability of its people.

NOTES

The author thanks David Zehms, Therese Gripentrog, Carol Ahlgren, Dean Proctor, Carol Chapin, and Susan Haswell for their assistance in gathering and assessing the data on ethnic groups. Archivists and librarians in Iron Range communities, Duluth, and the Twin Cities gave invaluable assistance, and the College of Agricultural and Life Sciences at the University of Wisconsin at Madison provided research support.

1. Barry Bluestone and Bennett Harrison, *The Deindustrialization of America: Plant Closings, Community Abandonment, and the Dismantling of Basic Industry* (New York: Basic Books, 1982), 36–37, 144–45; David Bensman and Roberta Lynch, *Rusted Dreams: Hard Times in a Steel Community* (New York: McGraw-Hill Book Co., 1987), 71–91; D. J. Tice, "The Thing on the Hill," part 1, 2, *Corporate Report Minnesota*, October, November

1982, p. 57–66, 91–99. For keen observations on the Iron Range's social and economic problems in the mid-1980s, see *Range Update*, a newsletter published three times yearly in 1985 and 1986 by the Range Community Fund of Grand Rapids.

2. Woodbridge, "The Mesabi Range," *Hibbing News*, May 26, 1900, p. 4; *Minneapolis Star and Tribune*, Apr. 27, 1986, p. 10A.

3. Here and below, see Lake Superior Iron Ore Association, *Lake Superior Iron Ores* (Cleveland, Ohio: The Association, 1938), 199, 252–66, 276–77.

4. Mildred R. Alm, *Mining Directory Issue: Minnesota, 1965* (Bulletin of the University of Minnesota, Mines Experiment Station, 1965), table 7, p. 238–40; Rodney J. Lipp, ed., *Minnesota Mining Directory: 1985* (Minneapolis: Mineral Resources Research Center, University of Minnesota, 1985), table 7, p. 223–25.

5. Lipp, ed., *Minnesota Mining Directory: 1985*, table 5, 20, p. 219, 240; John R. Borchert and Neil C. Gustafson, *Atlas of Minnesota Resources and Settlement* (Minneapolis: Center for Urban and Regional Affairs, University of Minnesota, 1980), 52.

6. Lake Superior Iron Ore Association, *Lake Superior Iron Ores*, 199, 252–64, 276–77, 308–9.

7. Alm, *Mining Directory Issue: 1963*, table 7, p. 255, and *Mining Directory Issue: 1965*, table 7, p. 238–40; Lipp, ed., *Minnesota Mining Directory: 1985*, table 7, p. 223, 225.

8. Lipp, ed., *Minnesota Mining Directory: 1985*, table 7, 25, p. 223, 244–45; John R. Borchert, *America's Northern Heartland.* (Minneapolis: University of Minnesota Press, 1987), 53.

9. United States, *Census*, 1900, *Population*, vol. 1, part 1; 1910, *Population*, vol. 2; 1920, *Population*, vol. 1; 1930, vol. 3, part 1; 1940, vol. 2, part 4; 1950, vol. 2, part 23. Rather than using county figures to describe population changes on the Iron Range, this study is based on totals derived from census counts for separate mining communities and townships. The population of an individual settlement was only included after the nearby mine or mines had begun producing ore.

10. U.S., *Census*, 1960, *Population*, vol. 1, part 25; 1970, PC (1)-A25; 1980, vol. 1, chap. A, part 25; Office of State Demographer, *1985 Minnesota Population and Household Estimates* (St. Paul: Minnesota State Planning Agency, 1986).

11. Figures for Two Harbors, Proctor, and Silver Bay are derived from U.S. censuses for 1900–80 and from Office of State Demographer, *1985 Minnesota Population Estimates.* Figures for Morgan Park are taken from *Morgan Park Bulletin* 2 (Feb. 13, 1919); U.S., *Census*, 1940, *Population and Housing Statistics for Census Tracts, Duluth, Minnesota;* 1950, *Census Tract Statistics, Duluth, Minnesota*, vol. 3, chap. 18; 1960, *Census Tracts, Duluth-Superior, Minn.-Wis. SMSA*, PHC (1)-41; 1970, *Census Tracts, Duluth-Superior, Minn.-Wis. SMSA*, PHC (1)-60; 1980, *Census Tracts, Duluth-Superior, Minn.-Wis. SMSA*, PHC80-2-142. Because 1920, 1930, and 1985 data for Morgan Park are not available, the local census count taken in 1919 (2,127 residents) was used for both 1920 and 1930, and the 1980 figure (2,186) was adopted for 1985.

Geographer John R. Borchert has noted that "Hibbing and Virginia had just taken their turn as the fastest-growing urban areas in the Upper Midwest" about 1920 (*America's Northern Heartland*, 69).

12. Arnold R. Alanen, "The 'Locations': Company Communities on Minnesota's Iron Ranges," *Minnesota History* 48 (Fall 1982): 95, 96.

13. C. Tower, Jr., to C. Tower, Sr., June 29, 1883; T. Prince to C. Tower, Jr., Nov. 10, 1883; T. Prince to R. H. Lee, Nov. 11, 1883; all in Charlemagne Tower, Sr., Papers, microfilm copy in Minnesota Historical Society (MHS), St. Paul.

14. David A. Walker, *Iron Frontier: The Discovery and Early Development of Minnesota's Three Ranges* (St. Paul: Minnesota Historical Society Press, 1979), 253.

15. *Hibbing News*, May 18, 1901, p. 4; Charles Agnew to G. L. Nute, Mar. 19, 1956, Grace L. Nute Papers, Northeast Minnesota Historical Center, University of Minnesota, Duluth; *Hibbing Tribune*, June 12, 1903, p. 4.

16. *Virginia Enterprise*, July 3, 1903, p. 4; *Eveleth News*, Jan. 25, 1908, p. 1, Feb. 15, 1912, p. 1.

17. *Mesaba Ore and the Hibbing News*, June 4, 1910, p. 2; *Hibbing Sentinel*, July 15, 1899, p. 1; *Hibbing Tribune*, Apr. 7, 1904, p. 4 (quotation).

18. *Hibbing Tribune*, Mar. 17, 1904, p. 1.

19. *Hibbing Tribune*, Apr. 13, 1900, p. 4; *Vermilion Iron Journal* (Tower), June 14, 1894, p. 5; *Tower Weekly News*, June 10, 1904, p. 1.

20. *Eveleth News*, Feb. 25, 1915, p. 1; *Buhl-Kinney Herald*, Oct. 18, 1940, p. 1. Examples of problems with cow-impounding ordinances may be found in the *Virginia Enterprise*, July 20, 1906, p. 1, May 10, 1907, p. 1, July 5, 1907, p. 1, Apr. 30, 1909, p. 1; *Eveleth News*, Sept. 5, 1912, p. 1, May 6, 1915, p. 8, Oct. 19, 1922, p. 4; *Tower Weekly News*, June 10, 1904, p. 1, June 11, 1915, p. 1.

21. *Ely Times*, July 29, 1898, p. 1, Mar. 10, 1899, p. 1, Oct. 20, 1899, p. 8; *Tower Weekly News*, Aug. 6, 1900, p. 1, Oct. 22, 1900, p. 1.

22. *Eveleth Mining News*, Apr. 14, 1906, p. 1; C. F. Bailey to Pentecost Mitchell, May 14, 1907, Materials Relating to the Oliver Iron Mining Co., 1863-1972, James S. Steel, comp., 1963, 1976, MHS; *Eveleth News*, Mar. 27, 1909, p. 1, Apr. 27, 1911, p. 1.

23. *Mesaba Ore and the Hibbing News*, Aug. 2, 1902, p. 4, May 29, 1909, p. 2, Mar. 2, 1912, p. 1, June 29, 1912, p. 1, Aug. 17, 1912, p. 1, 5; *Tribune-Herald* (Chisholm), June 18, 1915, p. 4 (citing *Minneapolis Daily News*).

24. *Mesaba Ore and the Hibbing News*, Oct. 9, 1915, p. 1, 6, Nov. 27, 1915, p. 1, 8, Nov. 7, 1919, p. 1, Nov. 28, 1919, p. 7; *Hibbing Daily News and the Mesaba Ore*, Mar. 5, 1920, p. 6, July 4, 1920, sec. 3, p. 1, 2, June 25, 1921, p. 1.

25. *St. Louis County Independent* (Hibbing), Jan. 20, 1933, p. 2, Nov. 17, 1939, p. 1, June 12, 1942, p. 1, Nov. 6, 1942, p. 6; *Duluth News-Tribune*, Oct. 14, 1945, Pictures section, p. 3.

26. Here and below, see Chambers, "Welfare on Minnesota's Iron Range," *Upper Midwest History* 3 (1983): 4 (quotation), 7, 8, 37.

27. Alanen, "The 'Locations,'" 96–99; Joe Jagunich, interview by David Perry, Sept. 12, 1983, tape in Iron Range Research Center (IRRC), Chisholm.

28. Marguerite Lains, "Six Weeks on the Range, 1928," and Charlotte Anderson, "Report, 1926," both in Daily Vacation Bible School (DVBS) reports, William J. Bell Papers, MHS.

29. Alanen, "The 'Locations,'" 99, 100; Elsa Erickson, interview by Thomas Rukavina, Dec. 29, 1983, tape in IRRC; John Syrjamaki, "Mesabi Communities: A Study of Their Development" (Ph.D. diss., Yale University, 1940), 235.

30. Alanen, "The 'Locations,'" 97, 101.

31. *Virginia Enterprise*, Nov. 23, 1894, p. 1; *Mesaba Ore and the Hibbing News*, Sept. 6, 1902, p. 8; "Sanitation Record," June 30, 1921, Oliver Iron Mining Co. Papers, 1901–30, MHS.

32. Alanen, "The 'Locations,'" 97, 98, 103.

33. *Tribune-Herald*, Jan. 24, 1913, p. 1; Margaret Walsh, "Tracing the Hound: The Minnesota Roots of the Greyhound Bus Corporation," *Minnesota History* 49 (Winter 1985): 312.

34. Donald L. Boese, *John C. Greenway and the Opening of the Western Mesabi* (Bovey: Itasca Community College Foundation, 1975), 85–112, 160–62; Arnold R. Alanen, "Morgan Park: U.S. Steel and a Planned Company Town," in *Duluth: Sketches of the Past*, ed. Ryck Lydecker and Lawrence J. Sommer (Duluth: American Revolution Bicentennial Commission, 1976), 111.

35. See, for example, *Itasca Iron News* (Bovey), Feb. 2, 1906, p. 8, June 16, 1906, p. 10; *Chisholm Herald*, Feb. 23, 1906, p. 4; *Tower Weekly News*, Apr. 6, 1906, p. 1.

36. *Itasca Iron News*, July 11, 1908, p. 1; *Itasca Iron News*, Mar. 9, 1906, p. 4 (quotation).

37. The number of saloons in Bovey was derived from *Range Towns Directory*, vol. 4 (Duluth: R. L. Polk and Co., 1907), 822–28. The per capita figure was determined by using the 1907 saloon data and the 1910 population census.

38. John C. Greenway to George D. Swift, June 12, 1907, Materials Relating to Oliver Iron Mining Co., MHS; *Itasca Iron News*, Feb. 2, 1906, p. 8.

39. *Itasca Iron News*, July 11, 1908, p. 1, *Itasca Iron News* (Coleraine), Dec. 31, 1914, p. 1, Feb. 4, 1915, p. 1, Jan. 13, 1916, p. 1.

40. Boese, *John C. Greenway*, 160, 161.

41. Langdon White and George Primmer, "The Iron and Steel Industry of Duluth: A Study in Locational Maladjustment," *Geographical Review* 27 (January 1937): 83; Alanen, "Morgan Park," 112; James A. Scott, *Duluth's Legacy: Architecture* (Duluth: City of Duluth, 1974), 33.

42. "Morgan Park: An Industrial Suburb for the Minnesota Steel Company," *American Architect* 113 (June 1918): 743.

43. John C. Hudson, "Cultural Geography and the Upper Great Lakes Region," *Journal of Cultural Geography* 5, no. 1 (1984): 20.

44. David Brody, "Labor," in *Harvard Encyclopedia of American Ethnic Groups*, ed. Stephen Thernstrom, Ann Orlov, and Oscar Handlin (Cambridge, Mass.: Harvard University Press, 1980), 609; W. J. Lauck, "Iron Ore Mines on the Mesabi and Vermilion Ranges," *Mining and Engineering Journal* 35 (Dec. 23, 1911): 1269; Introduction to *They Chose Minnesota: A Survey of the State's Ethnic Groups*, ed. June Drenning Holmquist (St. Paul: Minnesota Historical Society Press, 1981), 3.

45. This assessment was derived from the U.S. manuscript census schedules, 1910, for six settlements: Eveleth's First Ward, Fayal Location, Gilbert, Keewatin, McKinley, and Tower.

46. Data in this paragraph and the five that follow are derived from Minnesota manuscript census schedules, 1885; U.S. manuscript census schedules, 1900, 1910. A note is in order regarding data about several of the ethnic groups referred to in this essay. The group described in text and on the graph showing foreign-born populations as "English-speaking Canadians" includes 270 Canadians who identified their heritage as Irish in the 1910 census;

the remaining 1,330 British Canadians were primarily English in origin, with smaller numbers of Scots and Welsh. Also, about 760 South Slavs were identified in the 1910 census simply as "Austrians"; this group is included on the graph with the "Other Europeans."

47. The 1910 U.S. census is also the most recent one for which the original manuscript schedules are available for perusal.

48. Sarah P. Rubinstein, "The British: English, Scots, Welsh, and British Canadians," in *They Chose Minnesota*, ed. Holmquist, 121.

49. In 1910, Grand Rapids was only peripherally affected by mining activities; hence, the ethnic composition of the townsite was quite unlike that of the true mining towns situated some miles to the east.

50. *Itasca Iron News*, Dec. 13, 1923, p. 4-1. Boese, *John C. Greenway*, 85–112, 160–61, stated that Taconite did not display the same population controls as Coleraine; however, when Boese prepared his account in the early 1970s, he did not have access to the manuscript schedules for the 1910 U.S. census.

51. Here and below, see U.S. manuscript census schedules, 1910.

52. Waino Suomi, interview by Joe Drazinovich and Ron Dicklich, Dec. 7, 1974, tape in IRRC; U.S. Immigration Commission, *Reports of the Immigration Commission: Immigrants in Industries, Part 18: Iron Ore Mining*, 61st Cong., 2d sess., 1911, S. Doc. 633 (Serial 5677), 395; *Eveleth Mining News*, June 10, 1904, p. 1.

53. Matti E. Kaups, "The Finns in the Copper and Iron Ore Mines of the Western Great Lakes Region, 1864–1905: Some Preliminary Observations," in *The Finnish Experience in the Western Great Lakes Region: New Perspectives*, ed. Michael G. Karni, Matti E. Kaups, and Douglas J. Ollila, Jr. (Turku, Finland: Institute for Migration, 1975), 80–83.

54. Here and following three paragraphs, see U.S. manuscript census schedules, 1910. For a listing of the settlements that were sampled, refer to n. 45.

55. Data here and below were derived from "Industrial Survey of Women Employed outside the Home," records for St. Louis County, Commission of Public Safety, Committee on Women in Industry in Co-operation with Bureau of Women and Children and Department of Labor, 1918; original files in MHS.

56. U.S. manuscript census schedules, 1910.

57. Commission of Public Safety, "Industrial Survey of Women Employed outside the Home"; Bodnar, *The Transplanted: A History of Immigrants in Urban America* (Bloomington: Indiana University Press, 1985), 75 (quotation), 79.

58. Minnesota manuscript census schedules, 1895; Maxine Schwartz Seller, *Immigrant Women* (Philadelphia: Temple University Press, 1981), 116–17. See also Anne M. Butler, *Daughters of Joy, Sisters of Misery: Prostitutes in the American West, 1865–90* (Urbana: University of Illinois Press, 1985).

59. Phil Stong, *The Iron Mountain* (New York: Farrar and Rinehart, 1942), 48; Syrjamaki, "Mesabi Communities," 257–75; U.S. Immigration Commission, *Reports of the Commission*, 340–41. See also C. Whit Pfeiffer, "From 'Bohunks' to Finns: The Scale of Life among the Ore Strippings of the Northwest," *Survey* 36 (April 1916): 8–14.

60. Catholic Archdiocese of St. Paul and Minneapolis, "Parish Questionnaire and Related Papers," 1948, microfilm copy on file in MHS. For comments that point to religion as the most important factor in uniting ethnic groups, refer to the following tapes on file in the IRRC (all interviews by Thomas Rukavina): Helen Chiabotti, Sept. 21, Sanford Oja, Sept. 8, and Clarence Williams, Sept. 21, 1983.

61. Arnold R. Alanen, "William J. Bell: Reminiscences of a Pioneer Missionary and Social Worker on the Mesabi Range, 1913–1931," *Range History* 8 (Spring 1983): 3.

62. Timo Riippa, "The Finns and Swede-Finns," in *They Chose Minnesota*, ed. Holmquist, 306–9, 314–16; Syrjamaki, "Mesabi Communities," 259. Figures for the Finns and Swede-Finns are derived from the U.S. manuscript census schedules, 1910.

63. Helen Chiabotti, Sept. 21, Elsa Erickson, Dec. 29, Segundo Gentilini, Nov. 10, Leslie and Ellen Karvela, July 28, Sanford Oja, Sept. 8, and Bruno Scipioni, Dec. 1, 1983, all interviews by Thomas Rukavina, tapes in IRRC.

64. *Hibbing Tribune*, Nov. 24, 1904, p. 1, Feb. 23, 1905, p. 3.

65. *Hibbing Tribune*, Nov. 12, 1903, p. 4; Polly C. Bullard to Clara Failing Bullard, Nov. 6, 1908, Polly C. Bullard, "Remembrance of the Past," manuscript at MHS; Joe Jagunich, interview by David Perry, Sept. 12, 1983, Regetta Pagliacetti, interview by Catherine Rukavina, Aug. 24, 1978, tapes in IRRC.

66. Mary and Walter Johnson, interview by David Perry, Dec. 5, 1983, tape in IRRC.

67. Gwendolyn Wright, *Building the Dream: A Social History of Housing in America* (Cambridge, Mass.: MIT Press, 1983), 177–82. See also Stuart D. Brandes, *American Welfare Capitalism, 1880–1940* (Chicago: University of Chicago Press, 1984); Carl H. Chrislock, *The Progressive Era in Minnesota, 1899–1918* (St. Paul: Minnesota Historical Society, 1971).

68. United States Steel Corporation, Bureau of Safety, Relief, Sanitation and Welfare, *Bulletin No. 3* (August 1912), 3–7, *Bulletin No. 8* (December 1920), 6–7, *Bulletin No. 9* (De-

cember 1922), 28; Brody, *Steelworkers in America: The Nonunion Era* (Cambridge, Mass.: Harvard University Press, 1960), 90-91.

69. John Pengilly to C. P. Coffin and Board of Directors, Chandler Iron Co., May 8, 1902, Materials Relating to Oliver Iron Mining Co., MHS; *Hibbing Tribune*, July 5, 1906, p. 1; *Tribune-Herald*, May 26, 1911, p. 3.

70. Minnesota Bureau of Labor, *Tenth Biennial Report* (Minneapolis: Harrison S. Smith Co., 1907), 449, 452; data on fatalities for the years 1898–1920 were derived from Minnesota Bureau of Labor, *Biennial Reports*, and data for 1921–29 were derived from Minnesota Industrial Commission, *Biennial Reports*.

71. *Crosby Courier*, Feb. 8, 1924, p. 1, Dec. 5, 1924, p. 1, 5, Dec. 26, 1924, p. 1.

72. Figures for fatalities among ethnic groups are from Minnesota Bureau of Labor, *Biennial Reports*, 1906–16.

73. *Ely Iron Home*, Sept. 15, 1891, p. 1; D. H. B. to H. H. Porter, June 18, 1892, Materials Relating to Oliver Iron Mining Co., MHS. See also Walker, *Iron Frontier*, 72.

74. *Mesaba Ore and the Hibbing News*, Apr. 23, 1904, p. 8, Apr. 15, 1905, p. 1, 8, Apr. 22, 1905, p. 1.

75. Neil Betten, "Strike on the Mesabi – 1907," *Minnesota History* 40 (Fall 1967): 340–47 (quotation on 347).

76. Hyman Berman, "Education for Work and Labor Solidarity: The Immigrant Miners and Radicalism on the Mesabi Range" (1963), 43–44, available on microfilm, MHS; Michael G. Karni, "Finnish Immigrant Leftists in America: The Golden Years, 1900–1918," in *"Struggle a Hard Battle": Essays on Working-Class Immigrants*, ed. Dirk Hoerder (DeKalb: Northern Illinois University Press, 1986), 211; Landis, *Three Iron Mining Towns: A Study in Cultural Change* (Ann Arbor, Mich.: Edwards Brothers, 1938), 110.

77. J. H. Jasberg, *Maalaiselämän edut* (Hancock, Mich.: Suomalais-Lutherilainen Kustannusliike, 1913), 5; *Päivälehti* (Calumet, Mich.), July 23, 1902, p. 2; *Amerikan Sanomat* (Ashtabula, Ohio), Feb. 3, 1909, p. 7.

78. McGuire, "Report of the Northeast Experiment Farm at Grand Rapids, Minnesota," *University of Minnesota Experiment Station Bulletin 116* (St. Paul: University of Minnesota, 1909), 2; Northern Lakes States Regional Committee, *Regional Planning – Part VIII – Northern Lakes States* (Washington, D.C.: U.S. Government Printing Office, 1939), 24–25.

79. Donald G. Sofchalk, "Organized Labor and the Iron Ore Miners of Northern Minnesota, 1907–1936," *Labor History* 12 (Spring 1971): 229; Neil Betten, "Riot, Revolution, Repression in the Iron Range Strike of 1916," *Minnesota History* 41 (Summer 1968): 82–93; Karni, "Finnish Immigrant Leftists," 218–20. See also Peter Rachleff, "Turning Points in the Labor Movement: Three Key Conflicts," *this volume*, 196–202.

80. *Ely Miner*, May 31, 1918, p. 1; "Oliver Iron Mining Company Adopts Labor Cooperation Policy," *Engineering and Mining Journal* 105 (July 29, 1918): 1166.

81. United States Steel, *Bulletin No. 5* (December 1914), 58.

82. "Proposed Outline of Visiting Nurse Work: Report of Special Committee of the Subcommittee on Sanitation . . . , July 27, 1920," Materials Relating to Oliver Iron Mining Co., MHS; Alma B. Brown to Pentecost Mitchell, "Monthly Report of Visiting Nurse – October," Nov. 16, 1928, Oliver Iron Mining Co. Papers, MHS.

83. R. K. Doe, "Where Melting Pot Melts: Remarkable Work among Toilers of Mesaba Range – 25,000 at Naturalization Night Schools," *New York Times*, Mar. 12, 1922, sec. 7, p. 5.

84. William J. Bell, "From 1913 Diary" (extracts) and "Church Statistics, 1913," both items in Bell Papers, MHS; *St. Paul Sunday Pioneer Press*, Aug. 8, 1920, sec. 3, p. 9; Fred Eastman, "A New Sky Pilot on an Old Trail," *Outlook* 147 (Dec. 21, 1927): 497. See also Richard M. Chapman, "Religious Belief and Behavior," *this volume*, 516–18, 525–27; Alanen, "The 'Locations,'" 102–3; Clarke A. Chambers, "William J. Bell: Disciple of the Social Gospel," *Minnesota History* 49 (Summer 1985): 241-51.

85. "Oliver Iron Mining Company Adopts Labor Co-operation Policy," 1167; Sofchalk, "Organized Labor and Iron Ore Miners," 239–40. See also Frank L. Palmer, *Spies in Steel* (Denver: Labor Press, 1928).

86. *St. Louis County Independent* (Hibbing), Aug. 7, 1931, p. 1, May 6, 1932, p. 1, Jan. 20, 1933, p. 1, Dec. 29, 1933, p. 6, Sept. 27, 1935, p. 1, Oct. 9, 1936, p. 1, Nov. 6, 1936, p. 8.

87. *NLRB: The First 50 Years* (Washington, D.C.: U.S. Government Printing Office, 1986), 18–26; *St. Louis County Independent* (Hibbing), Apr. 23, 1937, p. 1, Aug. 6, 1937, p. 1, Aug. 27, 1937, p. 1, Apr. 21, 1939, p. 1, May 29, 1942, p. 4; Rudolph Pinola, "Labor and Politics on the Iron Range of Northern Minnesota" (Ph.D. diss., University of Wisconsin, 1957), 90.

88. Minnesota Department of Iron Range Resources and Rehabilitation, *Biennial Report, 1960–1962* (St. Paul, 1962), 38–39; Minnesota Interim Commission on Iron Ore Taxation, *Reports* (St. Paul, 1941), 92 (quotation); Department of Iron Range Resources, *Biennial Re-*

port, 1960–1962, 40; Iron Range Resources and Rehabilitation Board (IRRRB), *Biennial Report* (Eveleth, 1984).

89. Interview with Ruth Dolinar, Chisholm, July 24, 1987; notes in possession of author. See also Ruth Dolinar's comments on the videotape entitled "St. Louis County during World War II" (Duluth: St. Louis County Historical Society, 1986).

90. E. W. Davis, *Pioneering with Taconite* (St. Paul: Minnesota Historical Society, 1964), 108–23, 178; Borchert and Gustafson, *1980 Minnesota Atlas,* 52.

91. Here and below, Arnold R. Alanen, "The Planning of Company Communities in the Lake Superior Mining Region," *Journal of the American Planning Association* 45 (July 1979): 270; Pace Associates, *New Towns at Babbitt and Beaver Bay, Minnesota* (Chicago: Pace Associates, 1952), 3.

92. Borchert and Gustafson, *1980 Minnesota Atlas,* 52; Lipp, ed., *Minnesota Mining Directory: 1985,* 254–62; *Duluth News-Tribune,* Nov. 3, 1977, p. 1; Greg Breining, "Century of Iron: Life on the Range," *Minnesota Monthly,* September 1984, p. 12; *Minneapolis Star and Tribune,* Feb. 3, 1985, p. 7C.

93. Arnold R. Alanen, "The Rise and Demise of a Company Town," *Professional Geographer* 22 (February 1977): 32–35.

94. *Duluth News-Tribune,* Aug. 11, 1973, p. 1.

95. Minnesota Department of Conservation, "Transcript of Hearings Re Application of Reserve Mining Company," June 17, 1947, p. 38 (Davis quotation), July 11, 1947, p. 23–37, July 22, 1947, p. 21 (Kaupanger quotation), Minnesota State Archives, MHS; *Duluth News-Tribune,* July 10, 1947, p. 1.

96. For full discussion of the events at Silver Bay during the 1970s, see Frank D. Schaumburg, *Judgment Reserved: A Landmark Environmental Case* (Reston, Va.: Reston Publishing Co., 1976), and Robert V. Bartlett, *The Reserve Mining Controversy: Science, Technology, and Environmental Quality* (Bloomington: Indiana University Press, 1980).

97. *Duluth News-Tribune,* June 18, 1980, p. 1A, 11A, June 25, 1980, p. 1A, 7A, Oct. 13, 1980, p. 1A, 4A.

98. *Duluth News-Tribune,* Sept. 16, 1979, p. 1A, 2A, Oct. 5, 1979, p. 1A, 16A. *Wildrose,* John Hanson's feature-length film of the early 1980s, portrayed the difficulties women encountered when pursuing traditional male jobs on the Iron Range.

99. *Duluth News-Tribune,* May 21, 1982, p. 1A, 4A; *Minneapolis Star and Tribune,* July 10, 1982, p. 1A, 7A, Aug. 3, 1982, p. 3C.

100. IRRRB, *Biennial Report*; *Minneapolis Star and Tribune,* Dec. 6, 1986, p. 1A, 9A, 12A.

101. Dennis A. Ahlburg, *The Decline of the U.S. Steel Industry: Some Labor Market Implications for Northeast Minnesota* (St. Paul: Northeast Minnesota Task Force, Agricultural Extension Service, University of Minnesota, 1984), 3, 8.

102. *Minneapolis Star and Tribune,* Apr. 27, 1986, p. 1A; Wheelock Whitney, "A 'Freedom Fund' to Help Those Trapped by Homes on the Range," *Minneapolis Star and Tribune,* Jan. 7, 1985, p. 11A.

103. *Minneapolis Star and Tribune,* July 5, 1987, p. 1B. For a review of ethnic foods on the Iron Range, see Joan Nathan, "Sarma and Strudel," *New York Times,* Feb. 25, 1987, p. 1C, 6C.

104. An upturn in the taconite and steel industry during 1988 has led to an increased demand for skilled workers on the Iron Range and some stabilization in the outflow of population. See *Duluth News-Tribune,* May 14, 1988, p. 1A, 8A, July 16, 1988, p. 2A.

PETER RACHLEFF

Turning Points in the Labor Movement: Three Key Conflicts

Had a volume like this been compiled in the middle of the twentieth century, it would not have included an essay on the history of labor. Although labor economists and industrial relations specialists studied the institutional history of trade unions, few historians paid much attention to the lives and struggles of working people. When Minnesota marked its centennial in 1958, a group of political radicals formed the People's Centennial Book Committee to publish *The People Together*, a volume that includes writings by Clarence A. Hathaway, Meridel Le Sueur, Thomas McGrath, David Montgomery, Irene Paull, Carl Ross, and others. Poems, oral histories, accounts by farmers and Indians are interspersed with historical studies. The collection stands alone in the labor historiography of Minnesota's first century.[1]

Beginning in the mid-1960s, an intellectual revolution has taken place in labor history. More historians have turned their attention to labor, and they have begun to ask new questions. They have probed the roles of both technology and new management approaches in shaping the workplace. They have examined working-class neighborhoods, social institutions, fraternal and even religious organizations.[2] Minnesota has been in the forefront of these developments. University of Minnesota historians have researched aspects of working-class life, directing dozens of graduate students in studies of key themes in the state's labor history. Individuals at other state institutions, including the University of Minnesota at Duluth and Mankato State University, have made substantial contributions to this storehouse of knowledge, and ethnic historians have shed light on the experiences of their own groups. By the mid-1970s, the Minnesota Historical Society began to reflect and encourage these developments in its conferences and publications, drawing upon its growing collection of materials related to the labor movement.[3]

This essay uses these groundbreaking researches in trying to convey the rich and complex history of labor in the state. It is organized around three major labor conflicts that placed Minnesota in the national spotlight: the northern Minnesota strikes of 1916–17, the Minneapolis teamsters' strikes of 1934, and the Hormel strike of 1985–86. Each conflict represented the social forces and dynamics of an entire period, not just in Minnesota but across the country, and taken together they offer material for an understanding of key developments in twentieth-century labor history.

The Age of Industrial Violence

The first two decades of the twentieth century witnessed an unprecedented level of industrial conflict in the United States. Employers' efforts to introduce scientific management into the workplace were bitterly contested by skilled workers and their unions. Unskilled workers, swamped by wave upon wave of immigrants from southern and eastern Europe, struggled for security. Both kinds of workers built organizations to protect themselves and improve conditions on the job, but the organizations remained separate: skilled workers formed the American Federation of Labor (AFL) and unskilled ones the Industrial Workers of the World (IWW). Divisions between skilled and unskilled workers reinforced differences between ethnic groups, with the craft unions of the AFL dominated by workers of old-stock American or northern and western European backgrounds, and the industrial unions of the IWW consisting largely of recent immigrants.[4]

Divided, workers were seldom a match for their employers, who organized into associations to protect their interests on local and national levels. Most of these organizations dedicated themselves to the eradication of unions, joining in the open-shop drive that swept industry.[5]

America's involvement in World War I altered the dynamics of class conflict within the nation. Industrial conflict was given an explicitly political dimension when the Socialist party was organized on the dual (though poorly connected) bases of immigrant Socialists and American-born skilled workers. Socialists led a vigorous antiwar movement that included isolationists, pacifists, anarchists, German Americans, farmers, and trade unionists. The activities of the Socialist party and the IWW – including the rights to meet, protest, and organize – were severely curtailed by state and federal authorities, and many leaders were jailed.[6] But the conflict did not subside after the war, when industrial America experienced the greatest wave of strikes in its history. Union-organizing drives attracted tens of thousands of people, and a general strike in Seattle in 1919 shut down the entire city. Serving as a backdrop to these events was the unrest that shook the established order around the world, especially the Bolshevik Revolution of 1917.[7]

It was at this time that northern Minnesota became the focus of national attention, with powerful, expanding corporations confronting immigrant workers in a long-term struggle over conditions in the mines and forests. The corporations wanted the lumber and iron ore that would allow them to control their industries from raw materials through finished product. They attracted an unskilled immigrant work force to cut the timber and extract the ores, and they sought the same control over their employees that they exercised over their markets. The network of paternalistic controls included company housing, stores, and schools, as well as workplace spies and private police. Company officials tolerated no independent workplace organizations.[8]

Unity among the workers was elusive. Bringing to Minnesota their diverse ethnic legacies, languages, and values, the immigrants tended to develop separate community institutions – mainly churches and fraternal societies.[9] Within several of the ethnic groups were veterans of peasant, labor, and Socialist movements in their native lands. While organizing on behalf of the movements they had left behind, they helped to build social and political organizations on Minnesota's industrial frontier. Among them were Finnish Socialists who emigrated because of repression following the unsuccessful revolution against the czar in 1905, as well as Croatian and Slovenian veterans of activist political and worker organizations.[10]

For most immigrants, life on the industrial frontier was a daily struggle to survive. Iron mines, lumber camps, and sawmills were among the nation's most hazardous workplaces. Miners and lumberjacks spent long days working for low pay, some in deep mine shafts on slippery footing, others operating heavy machinery or setting explosives. For every 1,000 workers employed in St. Louis County's mines in 1905–06, 7.5 were killed.[11] In July 1907, the miners struck. They were organized into locals within the Western Federation of Miners, under the leadership of experienced immigrant radicals; each local was itself divided into ethnic sections. The strike began at the Mountain Iron site of the Oliver Iron Mining Company (a United States Steel subsidiary) and rapidly spread east across the Mesabi Range. But the corporations responded quickly. They fired strikers, evicted them from company housing, and blacklisted them from all mining employment in northern Minnesota. Thousands of strikebreakers – many recent immigrants themselves – were recruited from outside the state to replace the strikers.[12]

Not all workers in northern Minnesota were immigrant miners or lumberjacks living in mining "locations," lumber camps, or company towns. As larger communities developed – Virginia, Hibbing, Eveleth, and others – local industries grew. Building-trades workers in these communities began to organize on the eve of World War I. Although they were culturally and politically different from the unskilled miners and lumberjacks, their activities eventually had an effect in encouraging those other workers to unionize. In 1914–15, concerted organizing among building-trades workers led to the establishment of the Hibbing Trades and Labor Assembly. The Minnesota State Federation of Labor (the state structure of the AFL) made this organizing drive a top priority. It launched the Labor Forward Movement early in 1916 in Duluth, where four thousand workers were affiliated with the AFL and another one thousand would join by May. The movement extended halfway across the iron ranges to Hibbing, where the state federation planned to hold its 1916 convention to highlight the organizing drive in northern Minnesota towns and cities.[13]

Despite this wave of activity, union organizers and AFL officials demonstrated no interest in immigrant miners and lumber workers. The organizers, who came from Irish, German, or Scandinavian backgrounds, were second- or third-generation Americans, whereas the miners were more likely to be recent Finnish, Slovenian, Italian, and Croatian immigrants. Although miners developed strong ties across ethnic groups in their own ranks by 1916, they had little contact with the skilled building-trades workers who were based in the larger communities of the region. Many of these miners had actually come to the Mesabi Range as strikebreakers in 1907. Over the next decade, however, conditions in the mines and lumber camps had improved little: wages were still low and accident rates were high. Living conditions in many mining locations were abysmal, and underground miners felt exploited by a contract system in which employers manipulated payments based on output and encouraged workers to compete against each other. For an eighty-four-hour week, sawmill workers were paid 25 percent less than similar workers in the Pacific Northwest who were already organized by the IWW.[14]

The Labor Forward Movement helped to ignite union organizing among immigrant miners. In several major communities, the AFL's new strength had led to the election of public officials who were openly sympathetic to the labor movement. Hibbing's mayor, Victor L. Power, told the delegates to the 1916 convention: "As long as God gives me the power to breathe, I will be a friend to labor . . . because I was a laborer once myself in the employ of the U.S. Steel Corporation and I know what it is to work for one dollar and seventy-five cents a day."[15] The drive to unionize also benefited from the wartime expansion in the demand for iron and the accompanying decline in immigration, which brought relatively full employment to the iron ranges in 1916.

Socialist and other radical newspapers – for example, *Työmies* (*The Workman*) among the Finns and *Proletarec* among the Slovenes – urged immigrants to take up the banner of unionism. The IWW sent its top organizers to the Mesabi Range, including Carlo Tresca, an Italian exile; Joe Schmidt, a Lithuanian immigrant; and Sam Scarlett, a Scot. Elizabeth Gurley Flynn, the charismatic IWW speaker who was called the "rebel girl," joined the effort in mid-July after these leaders were jailed in Duluth. Many immigrants were eager to join a labor organization that spoke to them in their own languages, articulated their concerns, and offered them a vision of a better future. IWW activists (called "Wobblies") had little love for the AFL craft unions, but they made intelligent use of AFL organizing successes in their efforts to encourage the miners. They were determined to organize the sixteen thousand miners on the iron ranges, whether the AFL supported them or not. Fanning out across the Mesabi Range, they often operated undercover to avoid the company's spy network. "To make a Union under the steel giant," a Finnish miner's wife recalled, "we met in the woods, everybody coming after dark, laughing past the company stools."[16]

On June 2, 1916, a small group of mine workers struck at the eastern end of the Mesabi Range. Within a week, several hundred miners had joined the strike. The IWW leaders set up a strike committee that included representatives of the different nationality groups, many of whom were already organized into fraternal or religious societies. Worker demands included an end to the contract system and a wage increase. By late June, at least eight thousand miners had pushed the strike to the western edge of the Mesabi Range.[17]

The strikers, who sought the support of range communities, explained their goals in an undated strike bulletin:

> We are demanding more wages, shorter hours, a better standard of living and some measure of protection against a ruthless employer and their [*sic*] dishonest hirelings. . . .
>
> Our work is important work, at the basis of all the steel industry. Machinery, steel rails, great engines, surgical instruments, armor plate, all pass in the raw through our hands. Necessary work, useful work, hard, nerve-racking and body-straining work, – shall we not receive for it a living wage?

Because many range residents viewed corporations like United States Steel as outside powers, their decision makers able to influence the quality of life in the region without having to live there themselves, public opinion

Striking miners organized by the IWW marching down Pine Street in North Hibbing, 1916

was sympathetic to the strikers. Business people extended credit to strikers until their own credit was cut off by Duluth wholesalers.[18]

But the strikers received no support from the state AFL. At the moment of crisis, the organization representing skilled workers turned its back on the unskilled, striking immigrants. On June 17, two weeks into the strike, state AFL president E. George Hall denounced the strike while speaking in Hibbing. When the federation assembled in Hibbing for its convention on July 17, the strike raged all about the city. In his welcome address to the convention, Mayor Power urged the delegates to reach out to the striking miners. Socialist delegates pushed for a discussion of the strike, and a member of the strike committee was invited to address the gathering. After a moving speech from the striker, delegates endorsed the miners' demands and called for an AFL organizing drive. The state leadership dragged its feet about the drive in hopes that the strike would run out of steam, and the AFL ended up providing little assistance to strikers.[19]

Women were a major source of support for the strikers. Many immigrant women brought to the United States their traditions of active involvement in economic and political life, as reflected in the success of Finnish women in gaining the vote in the early twentieth century. These traditions were adapted to life on the American industrial frontier, where women worked to keep their communities united. Early in the miners' strike, on June 16, the IWW held a meeting at the Finnish Socialist Opera in Virginia for the "mothers, wives, and sweethearts" of the strikers, according to a reporter for a Virginia newspaper. Women helped to raise relief funds in a national appeal, and they staffed a relief store in Hibbing and strike kitchens across the range.[20] As IWW organizers and strike leaders were jailed, the role of the women expanded. One Finnish woman, Mrs. Koski, later recalled:

> Then they wouldn't let the men picket, so we formed a line of children a block long with signs. They marched in their fathers' places. "We want milk!" . . . "We are human beings!" And the women went along pushing baby carriages. The priest came out and tried to shame us, but we laughed. . . . Not a steam shovel moved in Hibbing or Chisholm, the flat iron pigs did not move, the iron locos were silent, the pits and shafts, empty.[21]

By late summer, although the strike had spread to the Cuyuna and Vermilion ranges, it had lost ground in its original centers. The steel corporations had outlasted the strikers. On September 17, the Central Strike Committee called the strike off:

> We were compelled to rely upon the labor movement throughout the country for relief to provide bread for our wives and babies. Hundreds of our ranks as well as our organizers and speakers were arrested. . . . We have fought all summer and have grappled with the mighty octopus the Steel Trust with all the power we possessed. But we feel it would be unwise to prolong our battle throughout the terrible cold of a Minnesota winter.[22]

The strike was not a total defeat. To be sure, Metal Mine Workers' Industrial Union No. 490 had failed to win recognition from the employers and, some months later, would collapse altogether. No stable union organization took root among the miners. Nor had bonds been established between the unskilled miners and the skilled workers of the AFL. Yet the miners did not trickle back to work as defeated individuals. After their organization called an end to the strike, the rank and file across the iron ranges returned to the mines as a body. Few strikers suffered the blacklisting that had followed earlier strikes. Soon after the strike ended, the

Finnish Socialist Opera in Virginia, a meeting place for strikers and their supporters during the 1916 miners' strike

corporations raised wages and eliminated some of the abuses of the contract system.[23]

As strike activity ebbed on the iron ranges, unrest flared up among sawmill laborers and lumberjacks. The timber and iron-mining industries had long complemented one another, both having seasonal demands for labor. Thousands of workers spent the summer and fall in the open-pit mines and headed to the lumber camps with the onset of winter. In both settings they faced powerful corporate employers that sought to extract northern Minnesota's minerals and lumber at the lowest possible cost, from the level of wages to spending for food, bedding, and shelter. Moreover, conditions for sawmill laborers and lumberjacks had deteriorated after 1905 as Minnesota's lumber industry began to decline.[24]

In the fall of 1916, thousands of miners carried their strike experiences with them as they entered the lumber camps and sawmills for the industry's busy season. Veterans of recent IWW organizing drives among harvest hands in the Dakotas helped to organize the lumber workers, and ethnic associations provided continuity as well as communications and material assistance.[25] Once again, Virginia's Finnish Socialist Opera was a hub of activity. And, once again, the AFL had little hand in the campaign, leaving the field to the IWW. Branches of the radical organization soon appeared in Bemidji, Gemmell, Virginia, Duluth, and Minneapolis. Late in the fall, IWW activists set their sights on the Virginia and Rainy Lake Lumber Company sawmill – the largest white pine sawmill in the world, with 1,200 workers and fifteen square miles of work and storage space. Workers had long chafed under the lengthy hours (the mill operated around the clock), low pay, and dangerous and dirty working conditions. Inspired by the miners' recent struggle, they began to organize, with IWW help and with Finnish workers in the lead.

Several score of sawmill workers met with an IWW organizer at the Finnish Socialist Opera on December 24, 1916. The list of demands that they compiled included an immediate raise in pay, an eight-hour workday on Saturdays and Sundays, no night work on Sundays, weekly shift changes, and no reprisals against individuals for union activity. They elected a committee to present these demands to management. Company superintendent Chester R. Rogers was not impressed, however. When shown credentials from William D. Haywood himself ("Big Bill," the IWW's best-known agitator), he commented: "I wouldn't piss on Bill Haywood. And I can piss a good bit." The strike was on, and northern Minnesota stayed in the national spotlight.

IWW organizers spread the strike from the sawmill sites to the logging camps, promoting the vision of a union that would encompass all workers in the wood-products industry. "Flying squads" of activists headed to the camps where they found thousands of lumberjacks ("timber beasts," as they were pejoratively called) living and working under miserable and dangerous conditions. Following the sawmill workers' lead, the lumberjacks raised their own demands: a wage increase of ten dollars per month, a nine-hour workday, clean bedding and sanitary food, cleaning of bunkhouses twice a week, and no discrimination against union members. On

Editorial cartoon published in the Industrial Worker, *August 25, 1917*

New Year's Day, 1917, one thousand men struck the logging camps by walking out and heading into the nearest town.

The forces of order acted quickly. Official response in Virginia was typical: the sheriff deputized the superintendent of the Virginia and Rainy Lake sawmill and his hired guards, and the city council banned the distribution of handbills. Local strike leaders and almost one hundred rank-and-file strikers were arrested. The newspapers stirred up anti-Wobbly hysteria with stories of poisoned wells, crippled horses, and hidden arms caches. They decried "terrorism" and endorsed the use of extraordinary police powers. Repression broke the strike, with local sheriffs and company guards effectively ending the walkout by sawmill workers and lumberjacks.

The organizing campaigns and strikes in northern Minnesota were not isolated labor struggles. Industrial and political conflict had also reached the Twin Cities. The Socialist party was a significant force in Minneapolis, where it had citywide and foreign-language locals. The International Association of Machinists and other unions worked closely with the Socialists. Four Socialist party members represented predominantly immigrant, working-class precincts on the city council in 1914, and Socialist Thomas Van Lear was elected mayor in 1916. Party activities included dances, picnics, and rallies, and newspapers published in English and Norwegian were sympathetic to the Socialist cause. In the late fall of 1917, workers campaigned to unionize the Twin City Rapid Transit Company. They engaged in a "button war," defying company bans on wearing union buttons on the job. Fifteen thousand supporters rallied at the St. Paul Auditorium on December 5, and the local labor movement united behind streetcar workers when they struck to protest the firing of union activists.[26]

The Nonpartisan League (NPL), which had moved its headquarters from Fargo, North Dakota, to St. Paul in 1917, represented a similar challenge to established political and economic power in small towns and rural areas of the region. During elections, the league united farmers and workers in an effort to capture key nominations within the primary of the dominant party (at this time, the Republicans) and influence its platform. NPL activists also held discussions with AFL leaders over political alliances and with IWW organizers over relations between farmers and harvest hands.[27]

To be sure, this upsurge of activity included people who disagreed substantially about goals and tactics. Syndicalists and those who favored direct action argued with political socialists about the efficacy of the ballot box. Craft unionists differed with industrial unionists about ways to organize the unskilled work force of the nation's new industrial corporations. Immigrant labor and Socialist organizations built rich subcultures that often remained isolated and self-contained. NPL organizers debated among themselves about running candidates solely within primaries or organizing a new party. So, too, did these political and labor activists clash in their responses to some of the key issues of the day: prohibition, woman suffrage, birth control, U.S. entry into World War I.[28]

The upsurge itself arose from dynamics that were shaping labor relations all over the country, as unskilled immigrants demanded improvements in pay and working conditions. Corporations that opposed the demands were assisted by an increasingly powerful state apparatus. World War I provided an opportunity to repress radical movements in the name of patriotism, and in Minnesota the 1917 legislature passed two measures that were designed to put down the unrest. The Criminal Syndicalism Act, one of a series of laws passed in western states alarmed about radicalism, broadly threatened the ability of unions to organize. The Commission of Public Safety, which was also created in that year, was given sweeping

Streetcar workers at a rally in Rice Park, St. Paul, during their 1917 strike against the Twin City Rapid Transit Company

powers to counter influences that its members considered subversive to the state. German-language newspapers were harassed, and aliens were required to register and declare their property. NPL meetings were banned or broken up, and activists were arrested. Taken together, these measures ultimately fragmented the labor movement and radical political organizations along their multiple fault lines. The pattern of suppression and decline was similar all over the country.[29]

The Rebirth of the Labor Movement

The 1920s was a grim decade for the labor movement. Scientific management and mass-production technologies undermined the position of skilled workers. Commercialized mass culture – movies, radio, amusement parks – threatened the traditional values of the ethnic groups that had been the foundation for working-class unity. The freedom of automobile travel sapped the cohesion of neighborhoods that had once nourished the labor movement, as workers chose to live at a distance from their jobs or to drive away from home for their leisure activities. Some large employers entered this vacuum in working-class life with welfare capitalism, tying their workers to them with the strings of vacations, pensions, and other benefits and co-opting attempts to unionize by providing company organizations that were called "employee representation" plans. AFL unions, which advocated a narrow craft approach to organization and addressed only the shrinking ranks of skilled workers, were little match for this corporate power. Industrial unions were severely repressed during and after World War I, and they remained outside the mainstream of the labor movement. Organized labor shriveled during the 1920s and then dropped sharply as unemployment rose in the first years of the Great Depression. From a 1920 peak of five million, union membership had fallen by 1933 to three million workers.[30]

In Minnesota, militant labor organizations had been driven out of existence. Eager to rid the labor movement of radicals, AFL leaders were fearful of any industrial conflict. When AFL national president William Green visited Minneapolis in 1926, he proudly told the local media: "I know of no other city today where there is as little unrest and agitation."[31] Local employers, linked to major financial institutions through the Minneapolis Citizens' Alliance, made sure that unions mounted no comeback in the 1920s. Nowhere did the labor movement shrink more dramatically than in Minneapolis. Governed by a Socialist mayor only fifteen years earlier, it had become the open-shop citadel of the Midwest. In the political arena, farm and labor activists made progress by joining together in 1924 to form the Farmer-Labor Association. But outside of electoral politics, Minnesota unions remained on the defensive. By 1933, economic hard times, antiunionism among employers, conservatism among skilled workers' organizations, and the continuing isolation of these unions from the mass of unskilled industrial workers had combined to sap the drive of the labor movement.[32]

Between 1934 and 1938, however, the U.S. labor movement saw its most impressive turnaround. Militant activists led new unions into organizing drives across the face of American industry, and workers who were seeking a vehicle to protect their interests responded enthusiastically. Developments in Minnesota were at the heart of this turnaround: the tactic of the modern sit-down strike, which fired the imagination of tens of thousands of workers, originated in a labor conflict at the George A. Hormel and Company meat-packing plant in Austin in 1933.[33]

Union activist Frank W. Schultz later recalled the conditions that prevailed at the Hormel plant:

> The boss was king of his castle, and your continued employment depended upon his good graces and ulcers. Seniority was unknown, job advancements depended upon doing favors for the boss. Wage raises were only granted to the boss's friends, and of course, those with the proper attitude. Overtime payments didn't exist. . . . There were no paid vacations, holidays or sick leave payments. Grievances were unknown. If you had a complaint, it was met with an answer, "If you don't like it, you can

quit. There are 50 guys across the tracks waiting to take your job for less than you are being paid."[34]

In July 1933, long-time Wobbly Frank Ellis, a foreman in the dry sausage department, and hog-kill workers who were veteran labor radicals organized a series of mass meetings in public parks. Hundreds of workers signed pledges at these meetings, leading to the formation of the Independent Union of All Workers (IUAW). The new union sought community support by sponsoring Labor Day festivities (the first in Austin in fifteen years) and by appealing to owners of local small businesses: "How can a merchant expect a man to walk into his store and buy when he is making only $10 a week?" said Harold Harlan, secretary of the IUAW.[35]

In late September, as negotiations for a wage increase dragged on, the IUAW took a strike vote. Hormel extended formal recognition but did not budge on wages or other issues. When another strike vote passed overwhelmingly on November 10, hog-kill activists led a group back to the plant and pulled out the sheep-kill gang that was still at work. They took over the plant in a sit-down strike and held it for three days. Farmer-Labor governor Floyd B. Olson came to Austin to inspect the situation, but he refused to order in the National Guard. Owner Jay C. Hormel then agreed to submit the wage demands to binding arbitration and to negotiate on the other issues. A month later, the Hormel workers received wage increases of three to five cents an hour. The IUAW activists spread unionism to other workers in Austin and to meat-packers in Albert Lea, Minnesota; Cedar Rapids, Ottumwa, Storm Lake, and Waterloo, Iowa; and Mitchell and Sioux Falls, South Dakota. The union expanded from its industrial base (which already made it different from AFL craft unions) to include retail, service, and hotel and restaurant workers; public employees; and even those working in machinery manufacturing.[36]

Among the labor activists outside Austin who watched the strike with interest was a group of Trotskyists in Minneapolis. Many belonged to Local 574, the General Drivers' Union of the International Brotherhood of Teamsters, Chauffeurs, Stablemen, and Helpers. In February 1934, a group of activists in the coal yards organized a brief strike during the busiest season. The action won union recognition and a pay raise. Like the Hormel meat-packers, the Minneapolis teamsters used this victory as a launching pad for more organizing. Long hours, low pay, and job insecurity characterized the entire trucking industry. Local 574 developed a campaign that linked drivers with loading-dock and warehouse workers: union buttons and membership spread from one category of workers to another as committed rank-and-file teamsters recruited workers with whom they came into contact on the job. Teamsters union national president Daniel J. Tobin, long a proponent of AFL craft unionism, objected to this innovation of organizing "outside" and "inside" workers together. Despite Tobin's opposition, Local 574 – which used laid-off coal-yard drivers and workers as organizers – reached workers in such varied settings as transfer companies; building-materials firms; wholesale fruit, produce, and grocery

Soup kitchen operated by the Ladies Auxiliary of Local 574 during the Minneapolis teamsters' strike, 1934

houses; taxi fleets; package and store delivery services; oil companies and filling stations; and oxygen and acetylene suppliers.[37]

In May 1934, in anticipation of a second strike, Local 574 moved its headquarters into a garage on Chicago Avenue and set up a barracks, picket-car assembly, and dispatching post. Mass meetings and entertainments were held in the main section of the garage. This nerve center of communications was also the focal point for the work of the Ladies Auxiliary, which ran a hospital and commissary and provided services for needy families. On May 16, the union struck dozens of local businesses over demands for a closed shop, wage increases, and shorter hours. Most commercial traffic was halted, with cruising squads of pickets playing a major role in keeping the strike solid. Picketers shut gas stations to reduce the use of private cars as substitutes for trucks, occasionally clashing with attendants who tried to keep the stations open. Minneapolis cab drivers also joined the strike. St. Paul truck drivers, who belonged to a different teamsters local, voted to strike but accepted arbitration of their grievances when it was offered. Streetcar workers threatened to strike and then agreed to submit their demands to the Regional Labor Board, a body set up by the federal government to mediate labor disputes.[38]

The local labor movement, particularly at the rank-and-file level, rallied around Local 574. The Central Labor Union (the association of local AFL affiliates) voted its support. The Building Trades Council threatened a sympathy strike, and members of the electrical workers and painters marched to Local 574's headquarters to offer their assistance. On May 21 and 22, strikers fought with police and special deputies in the streets of downtown Minneapolis. Public support for the strikers was high, with more than twenty thousand people filling the market district on May 22 to see the strikers rout their opponents in the Battle of Deputies Run. Two special deputies (including a board member of the Citizens' Alliance) were killed.

With the help of Governor Olson and the Regional Labor Board, Local 574 reached a compromise with employers that included seniority protection for hiring, layoffs, and recall and an agreement to submit wage demands to arbitration. The local had no written contract, however, and no agreement on the union status of inside workers. Because they knew that Teamsters president Tobin did not favor this sort of arrangement, employers were slow to negotiate on the issue, hoping that his opposition would weaken the efforts of Local 574.

During the second half of 1934, Minneapolis – together with San Francisco, Toledo, and areas of New England and the South where the textile industry was strong – became the center of a labor revival. Union activists followed events in Minneapolis closely, attracted by Local 574's militant tactics (its squads of automobile-based pickets, for example); by the industrial, rather than craft, basis of its structure; and by the fighting spirit of its thousands of rank-and-file members.[39] In this atmosphere of national scrutiny, the trucking firms and Local 574 prepared for yet another showdown. The Citizens' Alliance and most Minneapolis business interests backed the trucking companies, and Local 574 was joined by elements from the reawakening labor movement and by unemployed workers, who were increasingly organized. On July 6, Local 574 led an eighteen-block-long parade that featured motorcycle brigades from the May strike, farmers' delegations, members of numerous unions, and two airplanes flying overhead with "574" painted on them.[40]

The third strike began on July 16, under the direction of an elected Committee of 100. *The Organizer,* a union newspaper that had started as a weekly tabloid on June 25, printed as many as ten thousand copies a day. The committee involved unemployed workers in picket duty and enlisted the support of farmers through such organizations as the Farm Holiday Association. In return, the union helped to build the Minneapolis Central Council of Workers, which fought to expand the relief rolls and to improve working conditions and raise wages on relief projects. The union aided small truck farmers within the Twin Cities market district by setting up another area for their stalls and by passing out permits to get them into the city through the roving pickets.

Tensions exploded on July 20 ("Bloody Friday") when police fired on a truck carrying unarmed pickets, killing two and wounding dozens of nearby strikers. The violence increased public support for the strikers. A crowd estimated at fifty thousand to one hundred thousand people attended the funeral for Henry B. Ness, one of the slain strikers. At this point, Governor Olson acted to bring the strike to an end. He called in the National Guard, raided the headquarters of both Local 574 and the Citizens' Alliance, and provided mediators. More important, he turned to Pres. Franklin D. Roosevelt, who used the Reconstruction Finance Corpo-

Mile-long funeral procession in Minneapolis for Henry B. Ness, one of two strikers killed by police fire on "Bloody Friday," July 20, 1934

ration to pressure the Minneapolis bankers who were among the leaders of the Citizens' Alliance. After several weeks, the Citizens' Alliance yielded and agreed to accept the results of elections that were conducted on August 29 by the National Labor Relations Board. Local 574 took 69 percent of the vote in the market district, where the votes of inside workers were included.[41]

This strike, together with similar ones in San Francisco and Toledo, signaled the labor movement's coming to life in 1934. In each case, a group of workers stood up to challenge working conditions and received widespread support from inside and outside the labor movement. Echoes rippled through the textile, steel, and coal industries, and even workers in the automobile industry – long a bastion of management control – were restless. The labor movement that came to life was a new one, however, based on unskilled immigrants and organized along industrial rather than craft lines. Although teamsters were officially part of the AFL, Local 574 typified the new labor movement. Besides growing rapidly itself, the local over the next two years also helped to organize about five thousand workers – jewelry makers, cemetery workers, employees in the breakfast-foods and sash-and-door industries – who joined other unions.[42]

The new labor movement often entered into ferocious combat with the older one represented by the AFL. On a national level, the issue of industrial organization threatened to split the labor movement in two. Delegates to the 1935 AFL convention broke into fisticuffs when John L. Lewis of the United Mine Workers struck William L. Hutcheson of the United Brotherhood of Carpenters. Together with activists from the garment, printing, textile, and oil industries, Lewis launched the Committee for Industrial Organization. In August 1936, the AFL expelled Lewis and his allies, who then formed the separate labor federation that came to be called the Congress of Industrial Organizations (CIO).[43]

The CIO launched an organizing drive that reached into working-class neighborhoods all over the country, a drive that coincided with an explosion of political participation in the Democratic party of Roosevelt and his New Deal. Hundreds of thousands of industrial workers used the sit-down strike to force concessions from employers, and as a result some of the country's chief industrial empires – United States Steel, General Motors, General Electric – were brought to terms between 1935 and 1938. Millions of people joined the unions of the CIO, and millions more were identified with the older unions of the AFL, which underwent a resurgence of their own.[44]

The victories of the Austin meat-packers and Minneapolis teamsters were significant in the region not simply for their symbolic value, but also for the material support and leadership they provided. In Minneapolis alone, thirty-seven local unions were organized between 1934 and 1936,

Workers on strike at American Gas Machine Company in Albert Lea, 1937

bringing as many as fifteen thousand new members into the labor movement. In northern Minnesota, veteran activists renewed their struggle to unionize the iron mines and forest-products industries. They found new vehicles in the Steel Workers Organizing Committee and the International Woodworkers of America, both unions allied with the CIO. The "giant" of the iron ranges – United States Steel – eventually signed a labor contract in 1943.[45]

This second stage in the development of the Minnesota labor movement was built on the very ideas that had been so controversial in the first stage – the participation of unskilled immigrants as equal members of the movement and the development of unions that were structured by industry so that they could deal with the nation's new industrial corporations. But controversy remained. The CIO unions were separate from those in the AFL, and the two organizations frequently fought more with each other than with employers. Conflicts between conservative business unionists and radical activists added to the controversy, as did factional battles between leftist organizations. The new labor movement carried the legacy of the past.

The Fight against Concessions

The labor movement consolidated its position during and after World War II. Unions won recognition from employers and legal protection from the state, thus achieving significant economic security for members. But they also grew to be more like the businesses they bargained with – bureaucratic in structure, reliant on professional advice. According to labor historian David Milton, "The AFL-CIO merger in the mid-fifties officially symbolized the return of American labor to the principles of business unionism."[46] Trading the right to strike for the arbitration of grievances, they worked increasingly through narrow legal channels. Rank-and-file workers, whose dues were automatically withheld from their paychecks, had little to say about rules on the shop floor, bargaining positions, or selection of national leaders.[47]

This interdependence between unions, corporations, and government became harder to maintain, however, as the world economy changed. By the 1970s, the old arrangements were being questioned by workers whose jobs were threatened by new technologies. Corporations found cheaper labor in Latin America or Asia, and the "deindustrialization" of America led to efforts to create a business environment in the United States that would be free of union interference. Among the changes sought by corporations were cuts in wages and benefits; changes in job descriptions and seniority systems, so that managers could have maximum flexibility in job assignment; elimination of past work rules; and the dismantling of steward systems and grievance procedures. The political climate also supported the deregulation of many industries – trucking and airlines, for example – and the weakening of safety and health rules in the workplace.[48]

Minnesota was not immune to these developments. Deindustrialization and reorganization in the meat-packing industry undermined the economic security of thousands of union members in South St. Paul. Farm machinery manufacturers reduced their work forces or closed entirely. The steel industry looked to countries like Brazil for cheaper iron, abandoning its operations in northern Minnesota. Rail workers saw their numbers stagnate, shrink by attrition, and then plummet. Garment and toy manufacturers moved their plants to southern states or Mexico. Some corporations with multiplant operations moved part or all of their Minnesota operations to open-shop states or to nonunion facilities in rural Minnesota.[49]

Beginning in the late 1970s, some unions took steps to resist their employers' demands for concessions. Miners, members of the United Steelworkers of America, fought a lengthy strike on the iron ranges of Minnesota and Upper Michigan in 1977. Minnesota state workers organized by the American Federation of State, County, and Municipal Employees struck for three weeks in the summer of 1981. Members of the Graphic Arts International Union struck eight Twin Cities print shops in the summer of 1983, a struggle that saw angry picket-line confrontations as employers hired "permanent replacements." One hundred twenty printers remained on strike a year later, when replacement workers in seven print shops held elections that successfully decertified the union. During a national strike in the fall of 1983, many unions and local labor activists aided Greyhound bus drivers, members of the Amalgamated Transit Union, in their fight against an aggressive management. Similar help was given in February 1984 during a prolonged strike by Iowa Pork Industries meatpackers in South St. Paul, members of the United Food and Commercial Workers (UFCW). About six thousand members of the Minnesota Nurses Association, nearly all women, struck fifteen Twin Cities hospitals in the summer of 1984. Their unity – and a nursing shortage in the area – led them to an impressive victory.[50]

In Austin, UFCW Local P-9 had been a strong organization since its establishment as the IUAW in 1933. Members maintained a democratic local with an effective presence on the shop floor, and the local frequently extended support to other workers. Wages at Hormel were at the top of the scale for the meat-packing industry. In the decade before 1985, however, Hormel – responding to the pressures of increased competition and changes in consumer buying – moved to reduce its labor costs by winning concessions from employees. When the company threatened in 1978 to build a new plant outside of Austin, the union accepted a five-year wage freeze, pledged not to strike, and arranged for workers to loan their premium or bonus payments to the company at 6 percent interest. The loans, amounting to more than $1 million, and other concessions helped to subsidize the new Austin plant.[51]

When the plant opened in August 1982, it employed less than half the traditional work force. Speeds were set 20 percent above the old plant standard. Problems developed with the new technologies, and injury rates skyrocketed. As veteran workers left, several hundred younger workers were hired, many from farms that had failed or meat-packing plants that had closed elsewhere in the Midwest. In the fall of 1984 Hormel imposed a 23 percent wage cut, arguing that the firm needed the reduction in order to remain competitive. Experienced members of Local P-9 and some of the newer hires began looking for a means to regain the ground they had lost.[52]

The conflict brought together key elements of the American labor scene in the 1980s: a corporation's desire to deal with a cooperative union and to win concessions from workers; the government's efforts, from the federal courts to the NLRB, to support this corporate agenda; a national union's acceptance of its role as a junior partner in management, based on its ability to control the rank and file; and the workers' determination to protect their standard of living and their safety on the job. Around the country, support for Local P-9 grew wherever local unions and labor activists had faced similar pressures.[53]

From the start, rank-and-file workers led the struggle against Hormel. In December 1983 they elected Jim Guyette president of the local, with a mandate to oppose further concessions to the company. Guyette helped to fashion a leadership group within Local P-9 that united the different generations of workers in the plant. The local turned to Ray Rogers and his Corporate Campaign, Inc., a labor consulting firm based in New York City. Rogers was best known for his success in organizing the J. P. Stevens boycott of the late 1970s. His "corporate campaign" strategy called for actions against First Bank System, which held about 15 percent of Hormel's stock and, the local maintained, was the company's prime creditor. When the UFCW International refused to sanction the corporate campaign, the local's rank and file voted an assessment of three dollars a week per worker to hire Rogers.[54]

In July 1985, Hormel proposed a contract that eliminated many of the work rules, grievance procedures, and protections for seniority that employees had traditionally enjoyed. The wage rate that the firm offered was only slightly higher than the one imposed in October. Alarmed by the concessions that the new contract included, workers voted to strike in mid-August when their old contract expired. Soon after the strike began, Hormel appealed to the regional office of the NLRB on the grounds that the corporate campaign against First Bank was an illegal secondary boycott under the Taft-Hartley Act. The NLRB found in the company's favor and obtained a federal injunction on September 24, 1985, to prohibit activities directed against the bank.[55]

As the strike proceeded, the rank and file of the local organized an impressive array of strike-support activities, including a food shelf, clothing exchange, and the "toolbox" – a counseling service for workers under stress that was staffed by co-workers who had been through programs like Alcoholics Anonymous. Strikers also became public speakers, explaining the issues to other union locals and to churches and community groups in the region and then throughout the United States. At the center of these activities was the United Support Group, which started with potluck suppers in the park and came to include more than five hundred family members and friends. Working from the Austin Labor Center, workers and their supporters distributed leaflets at the plant gates and in neighborhoods around the Midwest; demonstrated with banners at First Bank branches; and attended Hormel stockholders' meetings, court hearings, and the state AFL-CIO convention.

Members of Local P-9 drew closer together through rank-and-file meetings, informal rallies, and gatherings to hear from visitors who sympathized with their cause. They heard firsthand about labor and social-justice issues confronting people in other cities. Over time, these Austin workers came to see themselves within a larger context. Their efforts were buoyed by expressions of support from workers, farmers, members of minority groups, feminists, and peace activists in Minnesota and elsewhere who sent material help and distributed boycott leaflets.

On January 3, 1986, the company announced plans to reopen the plant with permanent replacements for workers who continued to strike. When a motor blockade of pickets succeeded in shutting the plant on January 20 (a demonstration staged to coincide with the first observance of Martin Luther King, Jr., Day), Gov. Rudolph G. Perpich dispatched National Guard troops at the request of local officials. The local then sent roving pickets to Hormel plants in Iowa, Nebraska, and Texas. In Ottumwa, hundreds of Hormel workers honored the picket lines and were fired. Support committees were organized in thirty states, and more than three thousand local unions sent help to Local P-9. On April 13, Jesse Jackson came to the Austin jail to hold a prayer service with eighteen union activists who were being held in connection with a picket-line confrontation. According to Jackson, "What Selma, Alabama, was to civil rights in 1965, Austin, Minnesota, has become to collective bargaining in 1986."[56]

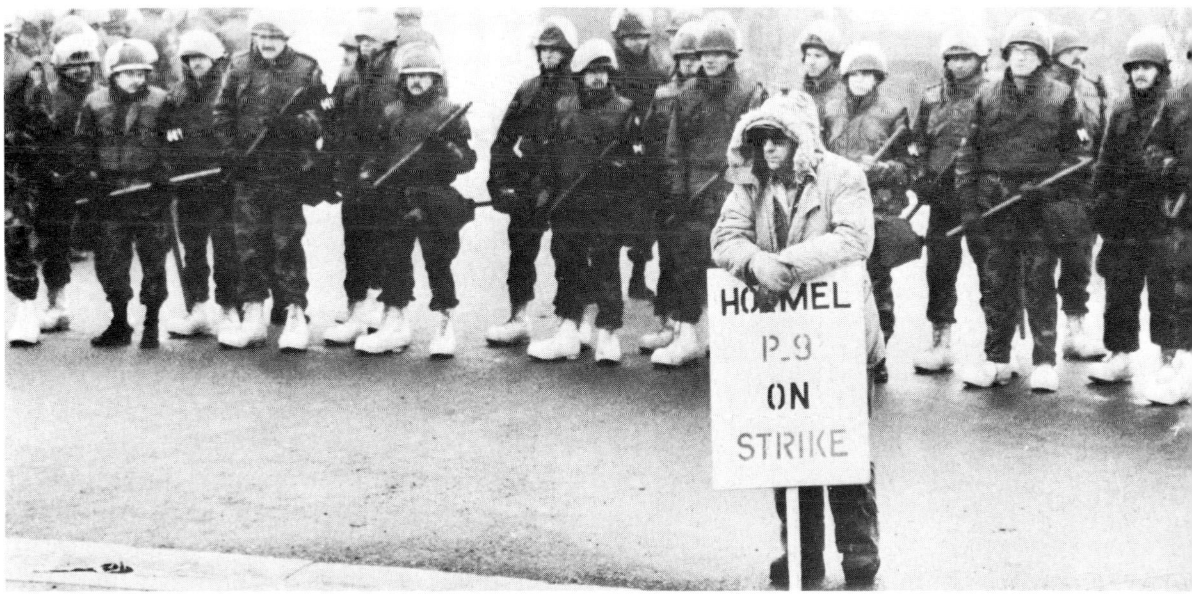

National Guard troops dispatched to the Hormel plant in Austin after pickets forced closing of the plant, January 1986

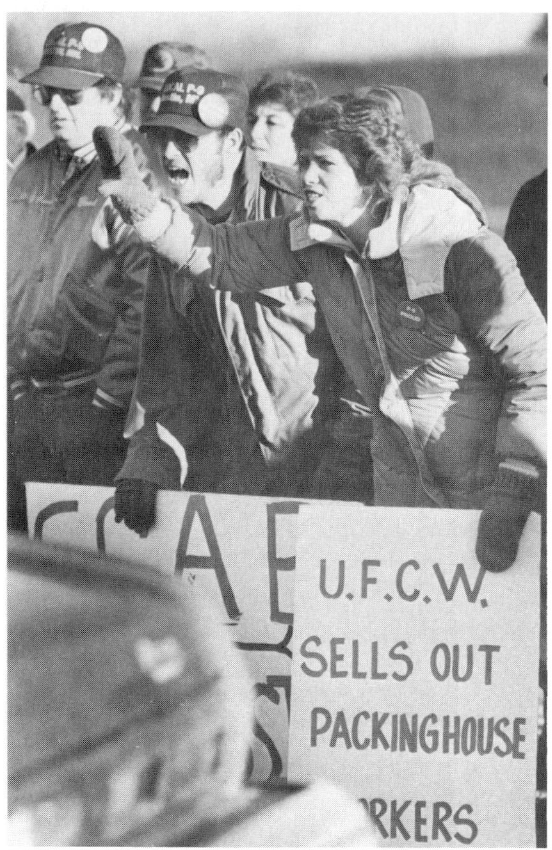

Local P-9 members shouting at replacement workers entering the Hormel plant, April 1986

Opposition to the strike was strong, however. Hormel, one of Minnesota's most profitable corporations, was a powerful presence in Austin. The Hormel Foundation – whose officers included past and current Hormel executives – funded such institutions as the YMCA, the town's only hospital, and a University of Minnesota research institute. The local media presented Hormel's position sympathetically, and Local P-9 was never able to swing its own community solidly behind the strike. First Bank System, the target of the corporate campaign, was one of the Midwest's largest financial institutions. Actions of the NLRB, the courts, and state and local officials also favored the efforts of Hormel to reopen its Austin plant.[57]

The UFCW – Local P-9's international union – opposed the strategy of the corporate campaign from the beginning, maintaining that Rogers was leading the local on a "suicide mission," in the words of union president William H. Wynn. During the strike, UFCW leaders refused to involve other union locals in the struggle or to sanction the presence of roving P-9 pickets at other plants. The international retained $1.2 million that other unions had donated to help Local P-9, charging against the funds those strike benefits that it had paid out. On June 2, 1986, the UFCW received court authorization to place the local in trusteeship. The trustees from the international then evicted the strike organization from union headquarters in Austin and began negotiations with Hormel for a new contract. On September 12, members of the reorganized local ratified a four-year agreement with the company that included most of the features of the contract proposed by the company the year before. The contract also placed the Hormel plant on the staggered schedule of expiration dates that was in effect at the other plants, a strategy that forced the locals to negotiate with Hormel on a plant-by-plant basis.[58]

The opposition of UFCW leadership to the goals and tactics of Local P-9 was another example of the recurring conflict between established unionism and the resurgence of a creative labor movement through the actions of the rank and file. When miners and lumberjacks struck for better pay and safer working conditions in northern Minnesota in 1916–17, an AFL organization that was based on craft unionism offered little support. The striking workers of Local 574 won their strike in Minneapolis in 1934 despite the opposition of their union, the International Brotherhood of Teamsters. Similarly, the UFCW decided that a "controlled retreat" or retrenchment was better, in the face of industry demands for concessions, than an all-out struggle to retain the benefits that had been won in past years. According to UFCW leadership, Hormel was the wrong company to take on in 1985; instead, the union wanted to concentrate its efforts on improving conditions for workers at the low end of the wage scale. Indeed, the 1985–86 strike at Hormel was a turning point for the national labor movement. The particular direction that the movement would take as the twenty-first century approached, however, was not clear.[59]

What do the events, movements, and struggles recounted in this essay suggest about the history of labor in Minnesota? On the one hand, it would be hard to deny the reality of class conflict in the state during the twentieth century. Despite the reputation of Minnesota as a liberal or pro-labor state, these three periods of intense conflict – intellectual and cultural, as much as physical – testify to the depth and intensity of class hostilities. In each case, an immediate conflict was subsumed within a larger context, and major social, economic, and political forces were arrayed against one another. More was at stake than the working conditions of lumberjacks, or the wages of coal-yard workers, or the wage cuts faced by meatpackers. On the other hand, unity eluded the house of labor during these intense periods of class conflict. Skilled workers turned their backs on unskilled ones; the native-born scorned immigrants; craft unionists opposed industrial unionists; international unions strangled their own locals.

Despite the similarities among these three conflicts, however, they were separated by significant developments that took place over the course of the century. Communications exploded, connecting local struggles more closely with national campaigns and enhancing the ability of one conflict to serve as the rallying point for another. But public attitudes toward the labor movement shifted as well, leading to the expectation that community support would fall to the employers rather than to the workers.

The labor movement has also been threatened by deep-seated structural changes within the U.S. economy. Multinational corporations have deindustrialized whole communities or industries as they have shifted

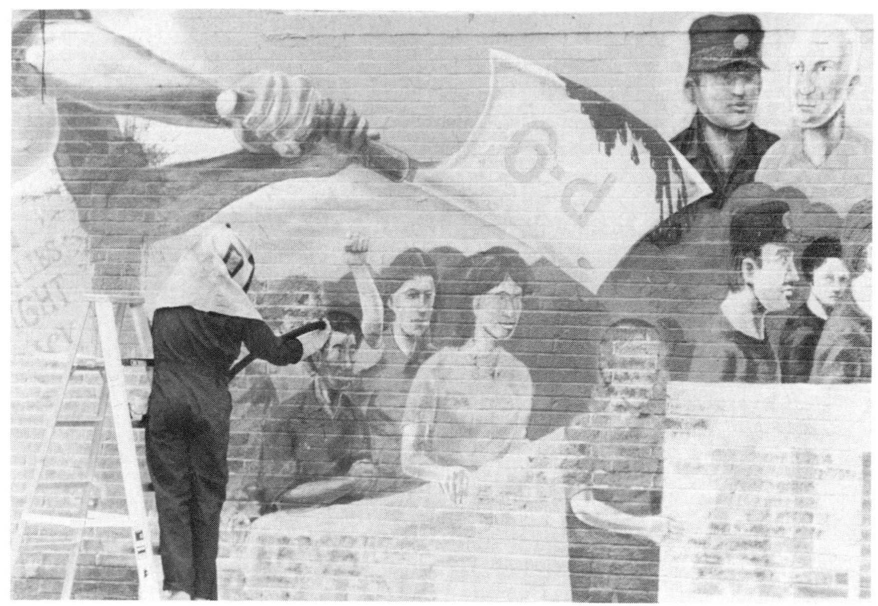

Sandblaster removing the Austin Labor Center mural commemorating Local P-9 strikers after the UFCW leadership took control of the union, October 1986

their profits into other industries or into overseas investments. Where manufacturing has remained, new technologies have eliminated jobs and transformed skilled positions into unskilled ones. Competition from Japan and West Germany and from American multinationals across the globe has pressured domestic manufacturers to cut costs and boost labor productivity. The traditional bases of labor movement strength have become shrinking islands in a sea of low-paying and part-time jobs in the service sector.[60]

The history of the American labor movement has revolved around the central themes of solidarity and disunity. In the early twentieth century, the IWW articulated this principle by proclaiming "an injury to one an injury to all." The past – nationally and in Minnesota – is replete with tales of both unity and division. The future of the labor movement will depend on how these internal dynamics operate within the context of a changing economy and a changing work force.[61]

NOTES

1. Meridel Le Sueur et al., eds., *The People Together: A Century Speaks* (Minneapolis: People's Centennial Book Committee, [1958]); David Montgomery's contribution was published under the pseudonym Amos Flaherty. See also Joseph S. Smolen, *Organized Labor in Minnesota: A Brief History* (St. Paul: Minnesota AFL-CIO Federation of Labor, 1965); George W. Lawson, *History of Labor in Minnesota* ([St. Paul]: Minnesota State Federation of Labor, 1955); "Joining Together: Labor Organization in Minnesota," *Roots* 3 (Spring 1975).

2. Two good examples of the new labor history are James R. Barrett, *Work and Community in the Jungle: Chicago's Packinghouse Workers, 1894–1922* (Urbana: University of Illinois Press, 1987), and Shelton Stromquist, *A Generation of Boomers: The Pattern of Railroad Labor Conflict in Nineteenth-Century America* (Urbana: University of Illinois Press, 1987).

3. Hyman Berman, professor of history at the University of Minnesota, is to be credited with much of the original spadework in locating and researching primary documents. He and his colleagues at the university – Clarke A. Chambers, Rudolph J. Vecoli, David W. Noble, and Sara Evans – have contributed to working-class history and trained many able graduate students. Independent labor historians, often former labor activists like Carl Ross, have also added to the storehouse of labor history knowledge.

4. The classic work on scientific management is Frederick W. Taylor, *Principles of Scientific Management* (New York: Harper and Brothers, 1911). For changes in the workplace in these decades, see Harry Braverman, *Labor and Monopoly Capital: The Degradation of Work in the Twentieth Century* (New York: Monthly Review Press, 1974); David Montgomery, *Fall of the House of Labor: The Workplace, the State, and American Labor Activism, 1865-1925* (New York: Cambridge University Press, 1987).

5. Bruno Ramirez, *When Workers Fight: The Politics of Industrial Relations in the Progressive Era, 1898-1916* (Westport, Conn.: Greenwood Press, 1978); Daniel Nelson, *Managers and Workers: Origins of the New Factory System in the United States, 1880–1920* (Madison: University of Wisconsin Press, 1975).

6. William Millikan, "Defenders of Business: The Minneapolis Civic and Commerce Association versus Labor during World War I," *Minnesota History* 50 (Spring 1986): 2–17; Paul L. Murphy, *World War I and the Origin of Civil Liberties in the United States* (New York: W. W. Norton, 1979), 80, 95–96.

7. Harvey O'Connor, *Revolution in Seattle* (New York: Monthly Review Press, 1964), 125–45; James Hinton, *The First Shop Stewards Movement* (Winchester, Mass.: Allen and Unwin, 1977); Paolo Spriano, *The Occupation of the Factories* (London: Pluto Press, 1975).

8. Arnold R. Alanen, "The Planning of Company Communities in the Lake Superior Mining Region," *Journal of the American Planning Association* 45 (July 1979): 256–78; David A. Walker, *Iron Frontier: The Discovery and Early Development of Minnesota's Three Ranges* (St. Paul: Minnesota Historical Society Press, 1979), 202–30; Clarke A. Chambers, "Welfare on Minnesota's Iron Range," *Upper Midwest History* 3 (1983): 1–40; John Syrjamaki, "Mesabi Communities: A Study of Their Development" (Ph.D. diss., Yale University, 1940), 204–8.

9. For example, Timo Riippa, "The Finns and Swede-Finns," 306–11, June D. Holmquist, Joseph Stipanovich, and Kenneth B. Moss, "The South Slavs," 388–93, and Rudolph J. Vecoli, "The Italians," 462–63, all in *They Chose Minnesota: A Survey of the State's Ethnic Groups*, ed. June Drenning Holmquist (St. Paul: Minnesota Historical Society Press, 1981). See also Arnold R. Alanen, "Years of Change on the Iron Range," *this volume*, 179–80.

10. Carl Ross, *The Finn Factor in American Labor, Culture and Society* (New York Mills: Parta Printers, 1977), 59–72, 106–18; Neil Betten, "The Origins of Ethnic Radicalism in Northern Minnesota, 1900–1920," *International Migration Review* 4 (Spring 1970): 44–46; Joseph Stipanovich, " 'In Unity Is Strength': Immigrant Workers and Immigrant Intellectuals in Progressive America: A History of the South Slav Social Democratic Movement, 1900–1918" (Ph.D. diss., University of Minnesota, 1979), 153–59; Al Gedicks, "Working Class Radicalism among Finnish Immigrants in Minnesota and Michigan Mining Communities" (Ph.D. diss., University of Wisconsin, 1979), 9–12, 141–57; Michael G. Karni et al., eds., *The Finnish Experience in the Western Great Lakes Region: New Perspectives* (Turku, Finland: Institute for Migration, 1975); John I. Kolehmainen, "The Inimitable Marxists: The Finnish Immigrant Socialists," *Michigan History* 36 (December 1952): 395–405.

11. James Barrett, Rob Ruck, and Steve Nelson, *Steve Nelson: American Radical* (Pittsburgh: University of Pittsburgh Press, 1981), 17–32; Betten, "Origins of Ethnic Radicalism," 48. For an impressionistic account of life in a logging camp, see O. E. Rølvaag, *The Boat of Longing* (New York: Harper and Brothers, 1933; St. Paul: Minnesota Historical Society Press, 1985), 162–65.

12. Neil Betten, "Strike on the Mesabi – 1907," *Minnesota History* 40 (Fall 1967): 340–47; Rudolph Pinola, "Labor and Politics on the Iron Range of Northern Minnesota" (Ph.D. diss., University of Wisconsin, 1957), 21–28.

13. Here and below, Donald G. Sofchalk, "Organized Labor and the Iron Ore Miners of Northern Minnesota, 1907-1936," *Labor History* 12 (Spring 1971): 223–28. See also M. M., "Union Comes to Mesabi," in *The People Together*, ed. Le Sueur et al., 27. Researchers into labor history during this period may also consult the E[manuel] George Hall Papers, Minnesota Historical Society (MHS); Hall was president of the state AFL during the range conflicts.

14. Robert M. Eleff, "The 1916 Minnesota Miners' Strike against U.S. Steel," *Minnesota History* 51 (Summer 1988): 67; John E. Haynes, "Revolt of the 'Timber Beasts': IWW Lumber Strike in Minnesota," *Minnesota History* 42 (Spring 1971): 164.

15. Sofchalk, "Organized Labor," 226.

16. Here and following three paragraphs, Sofchalk, "Organized Labor," 227–29, 231–35. See also Elizabeth Gurley Flynn, *The Rebel Girl: An Autobiography – My First Life*

ter access to the raw materials of industry: farm products, lumber, ore. By 1900, responding to the growth of the railroad network and the concentration of population in cities, leaders in business and finance were creating large enterprises in a number of industries.[1] In Minnesota the manufacturing sector was small in 1900, and its comparative advantage lay in resource-intensive products rather than products requiring much skill or advanced technology. In a population of more than 1.7 million, only 77,234 Minnesotans were employed as wage earners in manufacturing in 1900. They produced a great variety of items, from awnings and tents to men's suits and boots, from pickles and sauces to trunks and valises. But two-fifths of the value of Minnesota's manufactured product came from the food industries, with lumber a distant second. Two flour-milling companies were the largest manufacturing firms in the state.[2]

The growth of the food industries was a response to population changes under way in Minnesota and throughout the nation. More and more families, including the millions of immigrant families arriving between 1900 and the outbreak of World War I, lived in cities where they were unable to produce milk, meat, and bread for themselves. Minnesota food-processing firms such as Hormel, Pillsbury, and Minnesota Valley Canning (later renamed Green Giant) increasingly sold packaged products in a national market, employing advertising and brand names to win the loyalty of urban consumers.[3]

At the turn of the century, Minnesota led the nation in flour milling. Two firms, Washburn Crosby and Pillsbury-Washburn Flour Mills Company, dominated this industry by being among the first to adopt mass-production manufacturing. In 1879, Cadwallader C. Washburn opened a continuous-process mill that boasted the most modern machinery for grinding, purifying, and dressing flour from grain. The machines were arranged to ensure a continuous and nearly automatic flow of material through a series of processes all housed under one roof. Washburn's mill thus attained a high output with a reduced number of workers. Other millers around the Falls of St. Anthony in Minneapolis, notably the Pillsbury brothers, rushed to imitate and then surpass Washburn. For two decades Minneapolis became a kind of testing ground for the flour industry as rivals leapfrogged one another in the race to adopt new technology, and output rose enormously.[4]

The "new process" of flour milling brought unit costs down so sharply that the millers who pioneered it were able to expand their market share by underselling less innovative rivals. As large producers, they could buy wheat in quantity at low prices and ship flour at favorable freight rates. They quickly gained an advantage that they never relinquished.[5]

Between 1900 and 1920 flour milling remained the leading industry in Minnesota although the meat-packing, dairy, and bakery-products industries grew at more rapid rates. Under the leadership of James Stroud Bell, Washburn Crosby began even before 1900 to expand its markets around the nation. The company packaged its flour under the Gold Medal brand name and opened its first national advertising campaign; this campaign aimed to persuade the woman consumer to try Gold Medal flour by using the slogan "Eventually – Why Not Now?"[6] Not to be outdone, Pillsbury-Washburn replied on billboards, "Because Pillsbury's Best." This firm had been branding its flour with the label "Pillsbury's Best" and the "XXXX" mark since 1872, but it introduced several new products at the end of the century: Vitos Wheat Food and Flaked Oat Food, two breakfast cereals, and Germos, a health flour. Thereafter the company marketed packaged products directly to the homemaker as well as selling flour in bulk to wholesale grocers.[7]

Washburn Crosby and Pillsbury-Washburn aggressively expanded the scope of their operations because they needed new markets for the flour they were able to produce. When demand for bulk flour leveled off in the 1890s, producers developed new flour-based packaged products. Each company sought to build consumer loyalty by using brand names; if a product gained a reputation as a "premium" item, the company could raise the price and boost its profit margin.[8]

Like flour milling, meat-packing grew with the expansion of the railroad network and the growth of the urban market for processed foods. But meat-packing, Minnesota's fourth-ranking industry by value of product in 1900, differed from milling because the product was more perishable. Gustavus F. Swift, a Chicago meat-packer, had grasped the importance of efficiently transporting and distributing dressed meat in the newly developed refrigerated railroad cars. Instead of sending meat east "on the hoof," Swift and his imitators did their butchering close to the livestock grazing lands of the West and shipped dressed meat to eastern cities. By 1900 a small number of large firms, each with an elaborate distribution network like Swift's, dominated this industry.[9]

The importance of the Twin Cities as a rail center enabled it to become a regional livestock center. Four of the "Big Five" meat-packers (Swift, Armour, Cudahy, and Wilson) eventually established packing plants in South St. Paul. Meat-packing enjoyed more rapid growth than did any other major Minnesota industry in the first two decades of the century.

George A. Hormel and Company, founded in 1891 as a retail butcher shop in Austin, had emerged as the state's leading meat-packer by 1920. Hormel risked losing markets to the Big Five meat-packers and decided to expand to avoid being driven out of business. In the early years of the century, as sales grew year by year, Hormel plowed its profits back into enlarged facilities and new equipment. Desperate for funds for expansion, the company recapitalized four times between 1906 and 1920. Like the flour millers and the larger meat-packers, Hormel began to market its products directly to the homemaker by using brand names and national advertising. Dairy Brand ham and bacon appeared in ads in the *Ladies' Home Journal* in 1911; Hormel also appealed to various immigrant groups by producing several dry sausages: Holsteiner, Di Lusso Genoa Salami, Goteborg.[10]

Beer, like meat, was a perishable product, and the brewing industry followed a similar pattern of development. Minnesota boasted eighty-five breweries in 1900 in such small towns as Brainerd, Little Falls, Perham, Tower, and Northfield, as well as the major brewing centers of St. Paul,

Women making parts for tractors at the Minneapolis Steel and Machinery Company, about 1917

turned out decorative ironwork at a forge: Crown made the wrought-iron balconies and interior columns and the stairs and railings for the Minneapolis City Hall as well as many other public buildings. During World War I, Crown turned its expertise at metal fabrication to the production of steel barbed-wire screwposts for trench warfare and steel girders for cargo ships.[23]

Another metalworking firm, Minneapolis Steel and Machinery Company (1902), began as a fabricator of steel construction beams but did not prosper in that business. In a restless search for the right product line, the company shifted to the manufacture of stationary engines, then added the "Twin City" line of farm tractors and heavy-duty gasoline engines. During World War I, it accepted government contracts to produce machine tools and artillery shells. Other important machinery and implement manufacturers included American Hoist and Derrick, which produced derricks used in large construction projects such as dams, harbors, and bridges; Minneapolis Threshing Machine Company; St. Paul Plow Works; and Monitor Drill Company. But it was not yet clear whether these companies could survive in the farm-implement industry, which was dominated by large, well-capitalized firms like International Harvester and John Deere.[24]

The elaboration of the railroad network connecting all parts of Minnesota to the rest of the nation was a basic prerequisite for the development of these large corporations, since manufacturers needed a regional or national market before their production could grow beyond what would serve local needs. Already by 1910 a number of Minnesota firms in addition to the flour-milling giants were marketing their products in distant places. Northwestern Knitting Company of Minneapolis (later Munsingwear) was the world's leading manufacturer of underwear. Kilgore-Peteler Company produced railroad dump cars, steam shovels, and sawmill machinery for the national market. Minneapolis Steel and Machinery had a network of branch sales offices throughout the western United States and Canada to market its gasoline engines and tractors.[25]

Along with the railroad, an equally significant dynamic force by 1900 was the concentration of population in large cities. In one way or another, Minnesota's major manufacturers all produced for the urban market. The food industries gathered the product of rural areas and sold it, suitably processed and packaged, to urban families. Producers of lumber, doors and window sashes, linseed oil, and fabricated metal items helped to build the houses, office buildings, factories, and bridges of the new cities. Of course, Americans on farms and in small towns also bought many of these products; thanks to the railroad, they too had become part of a national economic system. But the great cities like Chicago and Philadelphia were growing at a more rapid rate than were the rural areas. By 1920 more than one-fourth of the American people lived in cities of one hundred thousand or over.[26]

Many an owner in 1900 had labored alongside employees in a small shop or at a desk in the next room. At Hormel, for example, owner George A. Hormel wore work clothes to his slaughterhouse and spent his days splitting hog carcasses with a cleaver; in 1899 he began wearing a suit and working in the business office next door to the plant. In contrast to the owner-run shop, in late 1915 United States Steel opened the largest manufacturing plant seen in Minnesota to that time: a steel works at Morgan Park outside Duluth that would employ three thousand workers.[27] Morgan Park reflected broader changes in the workplace; by 1919 a substantial proportion of Minnesota's 115,623 industrial wage-earners were working in medium-sized to large workplaces.[28]

Hardly any Minnesota manufacturing firms in 1900 had armies of salaried managers or clerical workers. The ten leading industries of 1900 employed only 3,614 "salaried officials, clerks, etc." In contrast, the top ten industries of 1919 had 13,617 such workers. Predictably, the greatest number was found in the milling industry, where the development of modern corporate enterprise had proceeded the farthest.[29]

Why did Minnesota in 1920 still have few very large manufacturing corporations? Giant firms were usually found in oligopolistic industries, those where a small number of companies controlled most of the production. Several industrial groups with a strong tendency toward oligopoly did not figure significantly in the Minnesota economy before 1920: petroleum, rubber, electrical machinery, tobacco, medical and scientific instruments. One of Minnesota's leading industrial groups, lumber and wood products, showed little tendency toward oligopoly.[30]

In the foods and paper industries, however, production was becoming concentrated in the hands of a few firms by 1920. Minnesota's earliest giant firms appeared in these industries. The reasons for concentration differed. In foods, firms able to make heavy investments in advertising and distribution grew rapidly and gained a larger market share. This is what happened to Washburn Crosby, Pillsbury, and Hormel.

In the paper industry, manufacturing involved expensive continuous-process technology in the form of an amazing device called the fourdrinier machine. Around 1921, according to an economic historian, a state-of-the-art "newsprint fourdrinier cost $600,000, was 375 feet long, weighed 1,200 tons, and required sixty freight cars for transportation." Firms able to afford the technology could produce in high volume, bring down costs, and expand their profit margin. As pulp and paper manufacture came to be concentrated in the hands of fewer companies, Mando and Northwest Paper benefited from capital transplanted from the declining lumber industry and from their excellent manufacturing sites along the Rainy and St. Louis rivers with good access to both raw materials and markets.[31]

Diversification and Research and Development, 1921–45

During the 1920s, major Minnesota corporations in several different industries pursued a strategy of diversification to ensure further growth when traditional markets appeared to be stagnating. A company usually developed a full line of products within its core industry – all manufactured through processes the firm already knew well – and distributed them in its familiar markets.[32] Later, it might add "dissimilar products" for diverse markets. At that point, it ran a risk not often foreseen in the 1920s: if the new venture succeeded and the company became a more diversified manufacturer, the problems of managing its operations and planning for the future increased manyfold. Consequently, diversified firms one by one adopted a decentralized, multidivisional organization. By the time the United States entered World War II, a handful of leading Minnesota companies had changed to the new form. More followed after the war.[33]

If a company decided to diversify its manufacturing activities, how did it find new products to make and sell? Several innovative Minnesota firms began programs of ongoing corporate research and development (R&D) in the 1920s. An effective R&D strategy could develop new products that kept a firm several years ahead of its rivals and put smaller competitors and new entrants at a great disadvantage.[34] Three companies – Minneapolis Heat Regulator Company (later Honeywell), 3M, and Wood Conversion – illustrate the pattern.

Minneapolis Heat Regulator (1885), a manufacturer of thermostats for coal-fired furnaces and boilers, diversified its line of regulator devices through merger during the 1920s. Since its thermostats worked on the feedback principle, Minneapolis Heat Regulator had "stepped off into the great future world of automation," according to a company historian.[35] But the company's happy future was not so evident just after World War I. Many homeowners converted from coal to oil to heat their houses, and Minneapolis Heat Regulator was a novice at using that different technology. During the 1920s the firm was hard pressed by a smaller but aggressive rival, Honeywell Heating Specialties Company of Wabash, Indiana. At the same time a slowdown in housing construction (a warning sign of the coming depression) convinced leaders of both firms that they would prosper by combining efforts instead of competing for the same stagnating market. In 1927, prodded by brokers and investment bankers, they agreed to merge. The product lines and patents of the two companies complemented each other well, and by merging they put an end to a costly

Honeywell round thermostat assembly line in Golden Valley, about 1960

duplication of sales networks. The new company, with headquarters in Minneapolis, took the name Minneapolis-Honeywell Heat Regulator Company.[36]

Honeywell, a journalist reported, "did not regard itself as being in the thermostat business but [as being] in the controls business, which is a broader area." The company planned for growth and diversification through R&D and acquiring other companies to gain their patents and manufacturing expertise.[37] In 1931 Honeywell acquired Time-O-Stat Controls Company, a small firm with a line of heat and refrigeration controls and automatic radiator thermostats. Other acquisitions followed. By the end of the 1930s, Honeywell had become a leading producer of controls for manufacturing processes and of automatic heating and air-conditioning control systems for homes, office and commercial buildings, churches, and schools. Net sales had tripled between 1928 and 1940; the number of employees rose from 1,000 in 1928 to 3,300 in 1936. By diversifying, the firm had protected itself during the housing slump and remained sound with a vigorous R&D program even during the worst of the depression.[38]

During this period, 3M also diversified, but differently from Honeywell. The company continued to expand its line of abrasives with a new sandpaper for wet sanding. Wetordry, introduced in 1921, was the first coated abrasive of its kind; it found a ready market in the automobile industry because wet sanding greatly shortened the time required to finish a car body and reduced the danger of workers' inhaling dust and metal particles. Over the next few years, 3M began marketing Wetordry to the furniture industry and to retail hardware chains for use in home projects.[39] But 3M still had a narrow technological base in coated abrasives, for which there was limited demand in the depressed 1930s.

The executives at 3M strongly encouraged the search for new products by setting up a research laboratory. Organized in 1916 to test the quality of materials after the fiasco of the oil-coated load of garnet, the lab made a major contribution when Richard G. (Dick) Drew, a young technician, developed a masking tape that appealed to car manufacturers because it helped them with two-tone spray-painting. After two years of experimenting with a variety of oils and resins, Drew, assisted by 3M staff, concocted a new adhesive that left no residue; 3M introduced masking tape in 1925.[40]

Five years later, Drew invented a cellophane tape – 3M's famous Scotch brand. By the 1930s it was clear that 3M had developed a second technological strength – adhesives – out of its initial strength in coated abrasives, and that consumer markets were beckoning. From its interest in adhesives, the company moved quite naturally into rubber and resins; and from its work in coated surfaces, it expanded into photographic films and related products. Still another technological area opened up when 3M developed a sun-resistant, artificially colored roofing granule, Colorquartz, in 1931. Research and development, central to the company's strategy of diversifying its technological base, enabled 3M to weather the depression with steadily expanding sales, produce a flow of new products, and make regular dividend payments to shareholders.[41]

Cellulose tape rolling off the machine at 3M, 1931

The Wood Conversion Company was Minnesota's premier example of an R&D-oriented firm in the wood-products field. The firm produced wallboard and an insulating material called Balsam-Wool, which was manufactured out of waste fiber from paper mills. Pressed into a continuous mat and glued to a paper backing, this product was easy to install as an insulating and sound-deadening substance. Nu-Wood (1927), a particle wallboard that the firm manufactured from sawmill waste, sold well from the first, despite competition from rival products such as Mando's Insulite. Wood Conversion also introduced a third product – a refrigerator insulation dubbed K-25 – in 1927. Despite serious financial difficulties due to the collapse of new housing construction during the depression, Wood Conversion managed to avoid bankruptcy through further product diversification: ceiling tile and an industrial cushioning substance, Tufflex, made from sulfite pulp.[42]

In the foods industries such as meat-packing and flour milling, diversification also proved to be an effective strategy. The difference between a 3M and a Washburn Crosby was that the food firms' approach to diversification depended not on R&D but on advertising to establish new brands in the consumer market. Minnesota's two leading flour-milling companies followed strikingly different paths in the 1920s and 1930s. The firm that diversified vigorously also grew and prospered; the firm that hesitated entered a period of decline. To boost stagnating sales of bulk flour consequent on the wheatless days of World War I and changing needs and tastes, James Ford Bell, Washburn Crosby's vice-president, first tried a mass-persuasion approach reminiscent of the war years: an "Eat More Wheat" billboard campaign launched in 1923. When this had mixed results, Washburn Crosby introduced more foods bearing distinctive brand names, advertised them vigorously, and negotiated with grocery firms to ensure that its products would be given prominent shelf locations in the large new chain stores.[43]

In 1923, Bell created a new division, the Gold Medal Food Products Company, to manufacture several new packaged foods including a cake flour – Softasilk – and a ready-to-eat wheat-flake breakfast cereal – Wheaties. Flour sales still accounted for 72 percent of the firm's income in 1932, but this proportion declined steadily over the next two decades as the company introduced and advertised more packaged products, such as Bisquick and Kix (1930s) and Cheerios (1941).[44]

Washburn Crosby adopted the name General Mills in 1928.[45] To drum up business for its traditional product, Gold Medal Flour, the firm used the slogan, "Kitchen-Tested," which supplanted the earlier "Eventually – Why Not Now?" When thousands of women began to write the company requesting recipes and cooking advice, executives at General Mills hit upon the idea of setting up a service bureau to answer letters. All the responses would come from a mythical expert homemaker – Betty Crocker, "the stalwart, reliable essence of the maternal" but also "a woman of large mind and imagination" with an "interest in grace." Every employee who used her name was indoctrinated in the "Betty Crocker idiom," the "Betty Crocker set of values." Later she was fitted out with a portrait that was updated frequently, including a change in image in 1986. By the mid-1930s, Betty Crocker had become the second best-known woman in America, after Eleanor Roosevelt.[46]

Under the leadership of Albert C. Loring, Pillsbury was slower to expand its product line than was its Minneapolis rival. After World War I, as Pillsbury celebrated its fiftieth anniversary, the company carried on a vigorous national advertising campaign for its "Family of Foods": Vitos Wheat Cereal, Health Bran, pancake flour, and of course Pillsbury's Best Flour. In 1929 the company added a new product, Sno Sheen cake flour. But Loring, who had begun his milling career in 1877, was uneasy about making a major strategic shift from bulk flour toward packaged, branded products for the consumer. Concerned about the "enormous" packaging and distribution costs, Loring complained in 1928 that "people are spending too much" and warned that "we are moving too quickly." The product line changed little until after Loring's death in 1932. In 1940 when Philip W. Pillsbury assumed the presidency of the firm his grandfather had founded, Pillsbury Flour Mills Company seemed, according to one historian, "neither a promising nor a progressive organization." It had a limited range of products and in one entire line, grocery products, had failed to keep up with rival firms.[47]

Until the 1920s the typical large business corporation usually had a central office with functional departments such as purchasing, transportation, manufacturing, and sales, each organized on a hierarchical staff-and-line system. Once a firm had begun to diversify its operations, executives often discovered a serious flaw in the functional structure: it tended to overwhelm them with information and responsibility for day-to-day operating decisions.[48] The solution to this organizational crisis, pioneered at General

Motors, Jersey Standard, Du Pont, and Sears, Roebuck in the 1920s, was a new structure of industrial organization, the decentralized firm with a home office and autonomous operating divisions. Each division would carry out all the functions involved in producing a line of products – purchasing, manufacture, sales – almost as if it were a separate firm. The executives of the home office, relieved of month-to-month operating concerns, could evaluate the performance of the divisions and make long-range decisions about where to invest the firm's capital for future growth. Once a company had adopted this new structure, further diversification and even frequent reorganization of the operating divisions became possible.[49]

General Mills was one of the first Minnesota firms to adopt the multidivisional structure. Organized since 1928 as a holding company, General Mills owned some thirty operating units across the country. Since these units often sold competing products in overlapping territories, problems emerged. James Ford Bell, chairman of the board from 1934 to 1948, proposed in 1936 to segregate the various activities into two divisions, each catering to a different market. The Flour and Feed Division would manufacture and sell animal feeds and bakers' flour in bulk, while the Grocery Products Division would handle all the well-known consumer products sold through grocery stores. Each division would handle its own manufacturing and merchandising; each would keep its own books.[50]

Following the path taken by General Mills, 3M created separate divisions for each of its four major businesses by the late 1930s: abrasives, tapes, roofing granules, and adhesives. Each division manufactured products based on a core technology and sold them in a distinct set of markets. Evaluating the divisions and making long-range planning and investment decisions were the responsibilities of executives in the home office in St. Paul.[51]

As the major corporations grew and diversified between the two world wars, the characteristics of their leaders changed too. Some of the founders and early builders of these firms, men like George A. Hormel, James Ford Bell, and William L. McKnight, were now retiring from the scene or would do so just after World War II. Leaders in the new generation tended to define themselves as managers or administrators. Often they had engineering or business-school backgrounds. As observers pointed out in the 1930s, a separation of ownership and control was taking place in the business corporation: ownership was vested in tens of thousands of stockholders, while the new managers who made far-reaching policy decisions were salaried professionals owning only a small proportion of the shares of stock. Descendants of the company founders might still have a place on the board of directors, but typically they played a diminished role in everyday decision making.[52]

This trend was particularly evident in the food industries. Management changes at Hormel following George A. Hormel's retirement in 1927 provide an example. His son Jay became president of the company in 1929, George's younger brother Ben assumed the position of senior vice-president, and other family members held top positions for the next few years. But as Hormel continued to grow, the family could not manage the company unassisted; in the 1930s dozens of younger men joined the firm as sales directors, plant and product managers, or specialists in finance or advertising. In 1946 following the death of George A. Hormel, Jay C. Hormel became chairman of the board of directors, and a nonfamily member, Horace Harold (Tim) Corey, succeeded him as president.[53]

As top management became professionalized, a middle level of managers also grew rapidly. Pioneered at the turn of the century in some of the early giant firms such as General Electric, middle management appeared decisively in Minnesota companies during the interwar years. Typically, middle managers carried out specialized responsibilities such as managing plants or sales districts. Their task was to speed up production and distribution and to expand markets through implementing a myriad detailed, undramatic changes, such as better tracking of raw materials and parts, marginal improvements in production machinery, innovative local advertising campaigns, or more effective training of sales personnel. Evaluated on the basis of return-on-investment data provided by modern accounting methods, middle managers could hope, if they excelled, for eventual promotion to the management of entire divisions within the firm and subsequently to the top executive ranks.[54]

The outcome of this transition toward professional management was that big corporations were better managed in routine operations. But in the long run, they incurred the risk of growing bureaucratized and less able to innovate. In the 1980s, some critics of the American corporation argued that many giant manufacturing firms seemed ponderous and unable to match the competition from abroad. But these same critics often cited 3M as an example of a large company that had managed to build and maintain a corporate culture that encouraged risk taking and innovation.[55]

The depression of the 1930s had an uneven impact on Minnesota manufacturers. For 1931, 61 percent of the manufacturing firms in the state reported operating losses; the following year, 86 percent did so. But an economist at the University of Minnesota, writing in 1933, commented that the capital-goods industries, such as pulp and paper, machinery, and metals, suffered most severely. The slowdown in business use of office paper and newspaper advertising, the drying up of demand for farm equipment and road-building machinery, and the general decline in heavy construction hurt these industries badly. Cutbacks in payrolls came early and were drastic. Still these industries were proportionately less important in Minnesota than in some industrial states. Minnesota's food industries, by contrast, represented a proportionately larger part of the total manufacturing picture and did not suffer nearly as greatly as metals, machinery, and paper. This circumstance buffered the Minnesota economy, to a degree, from the worst of the depression.[56]

Mando had begun to encounter trouble as early as 1927; the company had taken on considerable debt in the mid-1920s to expand capacity and diversify operations and then found itself unable to generate the profits required to pay off the debt. E. W. Backus, desperate for income to service a $5 million bond issue, began shifting millions among his various properties and turned to lawsuits against railroads and others in hopes of winning a big settlement. Production slowed at the Backus plants. When banks refused in 1931 to refinance Mando's indebtedness, the company went into receivership, one of seven large paper firms in the United States and Canada to do so. Forced to resign his executive position, Backus appealed to his "Old Loyal Employees" and accused eastern financiers of "conniving and conspiring to wreck the M and O." While visiting New York in October 1934 to raise money so that he could regain control, Backus died of a heart attack in his hotel room.[57]

Crown Iron Works suffered from the drastic decline in construction during the depression. The firm had completed a number of major projects during the 1920s, both within Minnesota (Northrop Auditorium at the University of Minnesota and the Foshay Tower in Minneapolis among others) and elsewhere. But Crown lost money every year but one during the 1930s. The firm chose to take any work available, even at ridiculously low prices, and to cut wages rather than to close up and wait for better times.[58]

On a more positive note, the end of Prohibition in 1933 brought new opportunities to the twenty-five remaining breweries in Minnesota. Many small brewers in such towns as Glencoe, Long Prairie, and Northfield had shut down for good during the long dry spell; a few, such as Schmidt and August Schell, produced near beer, mineral water, and soft drinks. After repeal, brewing quickly returned to normal. At the Hamm's plant in St. Paul, according to a company historian,

> row upon row of delivery trucks were lined up for half a mile around the brewery, waiting for the 12:01 a.m. zero hour. Thousands of people surrounded the brewery at midnight, and bedlam broke loose as sirens announced it was 12:01. Horns honked, whistles blew, people shouted, the truck drivers revved their motors and pulled away into the night.[59]

The years following repeal saw growing pressure on local breweries as the largest firms installed modern equipment in their plants, purchased fleets of new delivery trucks and thousands of metal kegs, and poured money into advertising. Hamm's, after its expansion program, increased its annual capacity to one million barrels.[60]

Manufacturers moved rapidly from depression to boom conditions in 1940–41 because of the wartime mobilization. They had all the capital they needed for expanding and modernizing, but raw materials and equipment were in short supply, and instead of a labor surplus, they suddenly faced a shortage of workers. Business leaders had to plan major plant expansions and gear up to manufacture unfamiliar products, usually in just a few months. Despite these frustrating conditions, war-production opportunities helped most manufacturers.[61]

Manufacturers large and small made the switch to wartime production. Don W. Larson, in his brief history of business in Minnesota, listed some of these changeovers: Munsingwear, the maker of underwear, manufactured garments for the armed forces. The Ford Motor Company assembly plant in St. Paul converted to production of military vehicles. Crown Iron

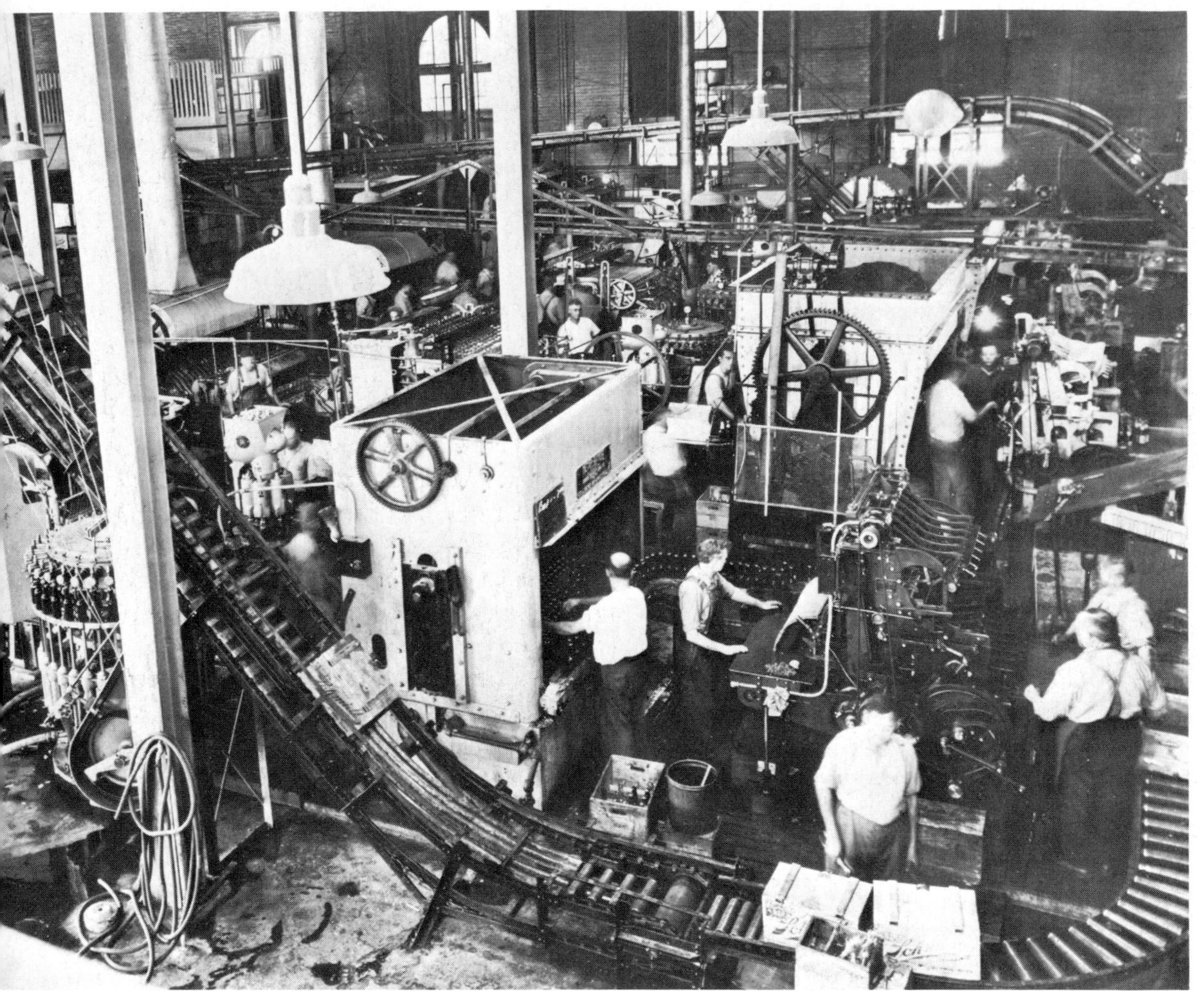

The bottling plant at Jacob Schmidt Brewing Company, 1933

Works expanded its operations to produce portable bridges and pontoons; American Hoist and Derrick manufactured heavy equipment for other defense plants. Andersen Corporation of Bayport, a wood-products firm, turned out prefabricated huts. Mando, its reorganization completed in 1941, produced Insulite panels for prefabricated army barracks; the Mando paper mills manufactured kraft paper for camouflage netting.[62]

Three war contractors – 3M, Northern Pump, and Honeywell – deserve a closer look. At 3M, defense work was well under way even before Pearl Harbor. The firm accelerated production of its standard products and developed some new ones related to its familiar businesses, including roofing granules in camouflage colors for military structures and Safety-Walk, a nonslip sheeting for ship decks and airplane wings. Perhaps 3M's most important product to receive a boost was Scotchlite reflectorized tape, which, among other things, was used for blackout markings along airstrips. The company had been working on the development of Scotchlite since 1938, but use by the military proved the product's effectiveness and positioned it for rapid sales growth after 1945.[63]

No Minnesota manufacturer was more altered by war production than was Northern Pump Company, a small Minneapolis firm founded in 1907 to manufacture pumps for fire engines. Northern Pump landed its first military contract in 1939; the company produced a light-weight submersible pump that became standard equipment on United States Navy ships. The following year, the navy handed Northern Pump the job of building a large defense plant from scratch. John B. Hawley, Jr., Northern's chief executive and owner, acquired a site in Fridley and had the plant built and operating within three months. Northern employed seven thousand workers to produce gun mounts and hydraulic equipment at the Fridley plant, which gained a reputation as "the finest machine shop on the globe"; the company became the largest wartime producer of ordnance for the navy.[64]

Through war contracts, Honeywell developed capabilities in entirely new industries that became central to the company's postwar growth. By 1942 Honeywell was producing precision instruments for the army and navy, especially fire-control devices such as tank periscopes, telescopes, and gunsights. Honeywell pioneered "new methods of tooling, assembly, labor training and inspection" in order to turn out these devices in quantity; eventually the company delivered 3.9 million periscopes and 300,000 telescopes to the armed services. Equally important for the future of the company, war contracts enabled it to apply its specialty in feedback-control instruments to an entirely new area – guidance systems for heavy bombers. A Honeywell automatic pilot became standard equipment on precision bombing planes.[65] This new application proved to be the source

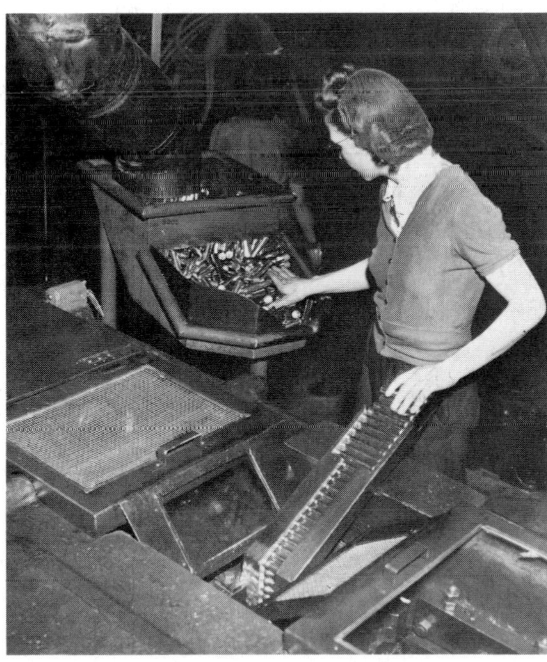

An employee putting cartridges on a conveyor belt at the Twin Cities Ordnance Plant, Federal Cartridge Company, Arden Hills, about 1942

of Honeywell's postwar move into missile guidance systems and its emergence as a major defense contractor in the 1950s.

By World War II, a handful of large corporations, including the leading firms in automobile, chemical, and electrical machinery manufacture and oil refining, dominated American manufacturing. In Minnesota the largest firms appeared in the breakfast-cereals and meat industries (General Mills, Hormel) where there had long been high concentration because new entrants found it difficult to incur the advertising and distribution costs needed to establish their products. Large firms also appeared in paper (3M) and in measuring and controlling devices (Honeywell), although both companies diversified into several other industries during the 1930s and no longer fit neatly into one manufacturing category. These leading-edge firms typically worked with chemical processes, electricity, and precision manufacture, where a successful entrant needed high initial investments in order to achieve economies of scale. Using R&D was a way to erect barriers to the entry by others into such industries. As in the foods group, but for different reasons, the early entrants had imposing advantages.[66]

During World War II major firms in many industries cemented their dominant position through defense contracts, new plants and equipment financed through the Defense Plant Corporation, a wartime federal agency, and "carry-forward" provisions of the tax code that allowed them later to recapture taxes paid on wartime profits.[67]

The Emergence of High-Technology Manufacturing in the Postwar Era

From 1941 onward, Minnesota became a center for high-technology industry, a vague although widely used term. By 1980 four high-technology firms – 3M, Honeywell, Control Data, and the Univac Division of Sperry-Rand – employed more than 50,000 of the state's industrial labor force of about 325,000. These firms were also among the six largest defense contractors in the state.[68] The U.S. Bureau of Labor Statistics definition of high technology included thirty-six industries (out of 977), such as the manufacture of drugs, aircraft, electronic components, computers, and laboratory equipment.[69] The computer and medical-devices industries were important examples of the emergence of high-technology manufacture in Minnesota.

During the war the federal government funded the development of many complex new products embodying advanced scientific knowledge: radar, jet aircraft, atomic weapons, and computers. Afterward several firms developed commercially practical computers, often for a specific federal agency. Former naval officers, including William Norris, founded Engineering Research Associates (ERA) of St. Paul in 1946 to produce computers for U.S. naval intelligence. Remington Rand, manufacturer of the UNIVAC computer, acquired ERA in 1952; three years later, when Remington Rand merged with the Sperry Corporation and became

Sperry-Rand, Norris was named general manager of the company's Univac Division, with headquarters in the Twin Cities.[70]

"We sat there [at Sperry-Rand] with a tremendous technological and sales lead," Norris later recalled, "and watched IBM pass us as if we were standing still." Dissatisfied with their new employer, Norris and a small group of old ERA hands left Sperry-Rand in 1957 to found a new computer firm, Control Data Corporation. Norris said his strategy was "to build large, scientific computers with a lot more bang for the buck" for scientific research laboratories and defense agencies such as the Atomic Energy Commission. Because these users were knowledgeable about computers and would need few frills and little support, Control Data would be able to sell its computers at a low price yet still show an early profit. In the era of the cold war and the space race, Norris recalled, Control Data "took off like a rocket to the moon."[71]

By 1966 Control Data employed more than ten thousand people but faced a crisis. The firm had always been cash poor but was now finding that customers preferred to lease computers rather than purchase them outright, meaning extended payback periods. In response Control Data began to diversify by acquiring manufacturers of peripheral devices, computers for business use, and "information appliances" such as remote theater-ticket printers. The firm completed a stunning acquisition in 1968 when it worked out a merger with Commercial Credit Company of Baltimore, a finance company with assets of $3 billion, or about nine times Control Data's assets. Commercial Credit quickly set up a subsidiary to handle leasing arrangements for Control Data.[72]

By 1969 with Seymour Cray as chief designer, Control Data enjoyed the image of a tough, stripped-down company at the forefront of technological change.[73] Control Data's remarkable growth helped to make the Twin Cities an important center for the computer and electronics industries. By 1970 the metropolitan area was home to more than 175 electronics firms, several founded by entrepreneurs formerly associated with Control Data, including Data Card (machines for encoding and embossing credit cards) in 1967, Data 100 (computer terminal systems and peripherals) in 1969, and Cray Research (supercomputers) in 1972.[74]

Norris was nothing if not aggressive. Control Data sued IBM in 1968, claiming that IBM was trying to monopolize the industry through predatory pricing and premature announcements of new computers. In a 1973 settlement, IBM agreed to a cash payment of $101 million and handed over its Service Bureau Corporation, the IBM subsidiary that handled time-sharing services. Norris, aiming for continued growth through acquisitions and joint ventures, announced that "we're going to become a great, global company."[75]

Control Data had transformed itself from a maker of specialized supercomputers with a limited market into a firm that offered a full line of computers, peripherals, and data services. But the entire history of Control Data illustrated Norris's own adage that "other than IBM, investing in a computer company is taking a sizable risk" because of the immense costs of R&D, the financial burdens of computer leasing, and the overwhelming

Control Data's 7600 computer, about 1968

presence of IBM. One journalist noted in 1972 that as its financial condition worsened, "Control Data can no longer afford to spend heavily on costly future research. Only IBM can afford that." Perhaps because of the research cutback, Control Data in 1972 lost Seymour Cray, the genius who had designed "computers that IBM couldn't touch."[76]

Honeywell's experience as a computer firm was also troubled. After diversifying into advanced military technologies, Honeywell had entered the computer industry in 1955 because computers were becoming a vital aspect of military hardware. Rapid growth and change at Honeywell since World War II had convinced Harold W. Sweatt, Paul Wishart, and other officers that the company possessed the technological competence to compete in the computer industry, but whether it also had the financial resources was an open question. Honeywell began by forming a joint subsidiary called Datamatic with Raytheon Corporation. Two years later Raytheon pulled out. Honeywell proceeded to develop the Datamatic 1000, a first-generation office computer (one using vacuum tubes). A second-generation (transistorized) mainframe, the Honeywell 800, was introduced in 1959.[77]

Honeywell proceeded bravely, trying to establish a foothold in the military, scientific, and business markets. But in the mid-1960s it was not yet showing a profit on annual computer sales of over $100 million. Could any "small" firm succeed over the long run? Honeywell had some cause for hope: the company remained a close-knit firm with many small-company habits, including an informal and rapid flow of ideas across group and division lines.[78] Honeywell made clear its determination in the 1970s by acquiring the computer divisions of General Electric and Xerox. *Forbes* commented ominously, "Honeywell is now too deeply committed to computers to follow RCA's example and get out."[79]

The manufacture of medical devices, notably heart pacemakers, became a second important high-technology industry in Minnesota. By the mid-1980s more than three hundred firms had appeared; most were quite small, but a few ranked among the world leaders. Several factors were involved: the strong computer and electronics industries offered a pool of talented technicians who could readily jump to the medical firms; the University of Minnesota and the Mayo Clinic in Rochester contributed steadily to technological development through research activities; and venture capital was available. Many observers emphasized the role of one firm – Medtronic – in fostering this industry.

Medtronic was founded in 1949 in a garage in northeast Minneapolis. One partner moonlighted as a television repairman; the other mortgaged his lumber business. The little firm began to grow rapidly when founder Earl Bakken developed the first battery-powered external heart pacemaker in 1958. An implantable pacemaker followed two years later. Medtronic later diversified and grew by developing such products as heart valves and pumps and electric pain relievers. Because such products are health-related and often vital to the treatment of life-threatening conditions, their manufacturers enjoy solid profit margins and are sheltered from recession. Medtronic and the other companies also benefited from the continuing inability of the American health-care system to control expenditures.[80]

The history of Medtronic, like that of Control Data, began acquiring the legendary characteristics requisite to the nurturing of nascent entrepreneurs. "Baby Medtronics," as they were nicknamed, proliferated in the 1970s as computer firms had in the 1960s. Cardiac Pacemakers, founded by four Medtronic executives in 1972 to manufacture a lithium-battery-powered heart pacemaker, was the first of the babies. "Growing" a new company has come to be a well-understood process; the founders of Cardiac Pacemakers established explicit goals for R&D expenditures, sales, and profitability and had a detailed plan for obtaining capital. Eli Lilly and Company of Indianapolis acquired the firm in 1979 and operated it as a subsidiary. Other Minnesota companies manufacturing pacemakers and related devices have included St. Jude Medical (artificial heart valves), Bio-Medicus, and Cardio-Pace Medical.[81]

A number of other firms including Dahlberg Electronics, Lang Hearing Instruments, Argosy Electronics, and Starkey Laboratories have specialized in advanced communications devices such as inner-ear hearing aids.

Genetic Laboratories, with headquarters in Roseville, produced a biological bandage called Mediskin. Empi and Medical Devices, Inc., have manufactured transcutaneous electrical nerve stimulators, electrical pain-suppression devices. Two companies, Medicon and Aequitron Medical, have developed systems for monitoring sleep apnea. Some larger companies have also diversified into the industry increasingly known as biotechnology. 3M set up a Medical Products Division and later acquired AVI, a small local firm whose first product was an intravenous infusion system. Control Data's Healthcare Services Group offered computer programs for the specialized management and record-keeping needs of health-care organizations.

Attempts to hold down the cost of Medicare under the Reagan administration profoundly affected Medtronic, since Medicare traditionally paid for two-thirds of all pacemaker implants. Although other factors such as lawsuits over defective wires played a part, this was one cause of a drop in sales and net earnings at Medtronic in 1983–85, a slide in the firm's stock price, and layoffs of employees. The company remained in a strong position, however, because it had entered new product areas such as heart pumps and valves and because worldwide demand for pacemakers continued to grow. Yet all manufacturers in the field of biotechnology faced unsettled conditions due to ongoing technological and demographic change, the "corporatization of health care," and shifts in federal policy toward health care and international trade.[82]

Since the glory days of ERA and Control Data, Minnesota has been home to the world's leading manufacturers of supercomputers, powerful mainframes costing $20 million or more per unit and used in such diverse fields as weather forecasting, automotive design, and oil exploration. Only a few hundred such computers are in operation worldwide; Cray Research, the industry leader with nearly two-thirds of the world market, installed only thirty-five units in 1986. Founded in 1972 by Seymour Cray, this firm employed 2,200 people in 1985 (Honeywell, by comparison, employed just over 94,000).[83]

In the 1980s, while the computer industry as a whole approached maturity, the supercomputer segment was growing at about 30 percent per year. A major new market opened for the advanced machines: corporate research labs at places like General Electric's aircraft engine division where a supercomputer modeled stresses and performance under various conditions and thereby replaced physical tests.[84] But precisely because its business was developing so rapidly, Cray began to face competition. Japanese firms entered the industry (although they were several years behind), and IBM and a few other firms moved to offer "baby Crays," superminicomputers.[85]

According to a business journalist, Seymour Cray used to design and build sailboats for a hobby. "Every fall, he threw a party where he and a few friends would burn the boat he'd built only months before . . . to avoid the temptation to re-use the techniques or design concepts" when planning his next boat. Designing supercomputers required the same willingness to discard past solutions and search for radical new approaches.

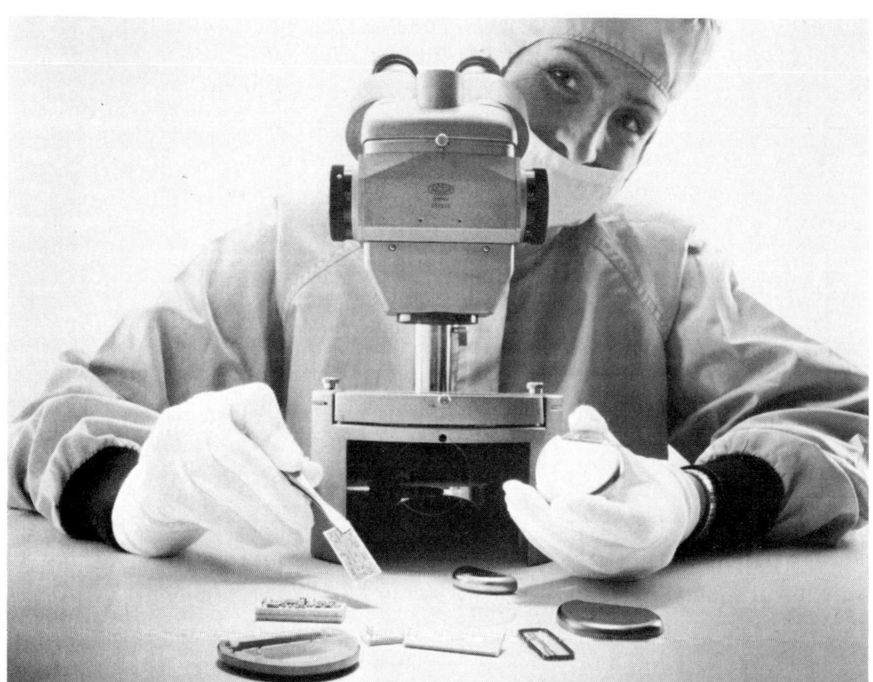

An employee holding the circuitry for a pacemaker in her forceps at Medtronic's manufacturing plant in the Netherlands, 1988

Still a small company in 1988, Cray was succeeding through "the Cray Style," a management philosophy emphasizing informal and democratic relations in the workplace, decentralization, and a willingness to take large risks in computer design.[86]

In the 1980s aggressive competition from Japan and other advanced industrial nations challenged the leadership of American manufacturers in one industry after another. In response, corporate America embarked on a drastic strategy called downsizing, streamlining, or, most often, restructuring. Of the one thousand largest U.S. corporations, more than half reorganized after 1980 in order to focus their resources on their most profitable operations. Frequently restructuring meant retrenchment, pure and simple: selling off unprofitable divisions, closing outmoded plants, and laying off thousands of wage workers and middle managers. So when a big corporation restructured, it affected the economic future of individuals and communities – indeed, of the entire state. One news magazine declared that "it spells farewell to the notion . . . of the corporation as a kind of private-sector welfare state, with unlimited perks and unshakable job security," although some business leaders held out the hope that restructured firms would be more competitive in the world economy and thus better able to grow and provide jobs in the future.[87] In Minnesota most of the largest manufacturing corporations, including 3M, Honeywell, Control Data, Pillsbury, Hormel, and General Mills, went through major restructuring in the 1980s.[88]

The restructuring process was most painful at Control Data. Still searching for an effective strategy of diversification in a rapidly changing industry, Control Data in the 1970s began to emphasize computer services through user time-sharing. The company set up sixteen centers worldwide, each with a giant mainframe computer, and sold computing time to businesses and other customers. It also established some fifty business and technology centers, all linked through PLATO (an advanced computer-based instructional system that the firm had been developing) to a central computer, in hopes that many businesses would purchase computer-based training for their managers and employees through these facilities.[89]

Control Data regularly lost money on its PLATO-based learning centers. Some executives argued that the company should use its capital for R&D in its main businesses – scientific computers and peripherals. Norris, however, predicted that PLATO would become a profit maker for his firm by the mid-1980s and talked of having eight hundred learning centers by 1985.[90] Control Data's huge investment in time-sharing and engineering services was based largely on remote mainframes accessed by telephone. But the 1980s saw the coming-of-age of microcomputers and minicomputers that directly challenged this market. Where PLATO had a real market – notably with business corporations that wanted to retrain workers for new technical jobs – its success depended on customizing and constantly updating the instructional programs. But this, of course, meant ongoing costs to Control Data.[91]

The time-sharing operations involving PLATO continued to lose money; Control Data's highly profitable disk-drives business, starved of R&D funds, faced aggressive competition from Japanese manufacturers and began to falter in the marketplace. By 1984, its products out of date and uncompetitive, Control Data was experiencing a steady decline in earnings, its stock price had dropped by half, and there was talk that it might become a takeover target.[92] In 1985 in default to banks on $309 million of short-term loans and with thousands of employees laid off, Control Data was found to rank among the six least-admired American companies in a survey of four thousand corporate executives.[93]

When William Norris, age seventy-four, announced his retirement early in 1986, he was unrepentant: "We are satisfied that the company's basic strategy is solid." In retrospect, Norris seems a figure out of the American era of self-confidence that began with World War II and ended with the Kennedy-Johnson years of the 1960s. An engineer, he had an outlook shaped by the remarkable achievements of the war and postwar years: nuclear power, the space program, the development of the computer. Norris believed that there must be a technological and managerial solution to each social and economic problem besetting the United States; a utopian at heart, he conveyed a sense of confidence, even euphoria, for years after it had faded from American culture generally.[94]

Robert M. Price, a cofounder of Control Data and Norris's successor as chief executive officer, worked quickly to downsize the firm and focus its talent on its traditional core businesses – large mainframe computers and peripherals. Control Data sold some of its least profitable operations, trimmed its work force further, spun off Commercial Credit, and arranged a long-term debt offering to reduce its burden of short-term debt. The company foresaw a modest profit for 1987.[95]

Honeywell maintained a stubborn presence in the computer industry that was no longer growing at 25 or 30 percent per year in the 1980s; eventually, it altered its marketing strategy by adapting its large computers for special markets, such as airline reservations, and avoiding direct competition with IBM.[96]

In 1982 operating earnings from computers fell 46 percent at Honeywell. "The amount of research and development it takes to be in the large-scale mainframe business is of such a magnitude that it's difficult for companies like Honeywell . . . to keep up," Honeywell vice-chairman James J. Renier explained. The next year the firm embarked on an immense and complex restructuring by announcing that instead of manufacturing large mainframes, it would market computers produced by Nippon Electric (NEC), a leading Japanese manufacturer. The computer division at Honeywell lost five thousand jobs between 1980 and 1986.[97]

Honeywell's computer business still provided almost a third of the firm's total sales revenues in 1985, but the clear strategy was to withdraw from the computer industry and emphasize traditional strengths such as factory control systems and defense electronics. Overall Honeywell profitability remained disappointing enough that in May 1986, Sperry offered to buy the firm with the probable intention of breaking it up and selling it off bit by bit, but Honeywell rejected the Sperry proposal. Later in that momentous year Honeywell agreed to buy the aerospace division of Unisys (a firm created by the merger of Sperry and Burroughs) for $1 billion and also announced that it would sell its shrunken computer division for $250 million below book value in a joint venture with NEC and Compagnie des Machines Bull, France's state-owned computer manufacturer.[98] All of this cost four thousand jobs and brought a $398 million loss, Honeywell's first annual loss since its founding in 1927.[99]

The shocking decline of Control Data and the decision at Honeywell to cut its losses in computers were local signs of an industry marked by rapid technological change and intense competition worldwide. Honeywell chairman Edson Spencer promised a bright future for his leaner firm. But some observers wondered whether the company would become too dependent on defense contracts at a time when the national defense buildup had peaked. Others viewed the restructuring as a disturbing example of American manufacturers' retreat from highly competitive businesses. "The life of a Pentagon contractor is not a harried one," mused Harvard political economist Robert B. Reich. "The Japanese pose no threat. . . . Profits are guaranteed." Military contracts for electronic products such as missile-guidance systems, controls for jet fighters, and antitank weapons would bring in 40 percent of Honeywell revenues in 1987, up from 29 percent in 1985.[100]

The food industries showed a common set of trends in the decades following World War II: greater concentration of production in the hands of a small number of large firms (the two hundred largest national firms had

81 percent of total assets by 1978), further diversification, and the widespread use of a technique known as product differentiation.[101]

Diversification was a key element in growth for the major food companies. For example, Pillsbury diversified energetically after 1952. It first developed refrigerated dough products such as biscuits and cinnamon rolls and later expanded its line of dry packaged mixes by adding new cake mixes, brownie and frosting mixes, and instant potatoes. All of this required new plants and more advertising. Inevitably a major corporate reorganization ensued: in 1958 Pillsbury was restructured into three segments for consumer, industrial, and agricultural products. Proceeding with its diversification strategy, Pillsbury acquired a small manufacturer of artificial sweeteners, thereby positioning itself to move into low-calorie foods and drinks, and a firm that produced frozen desserts such as pies.[102]

In 1967 Pillsbury entered the rapidly growing restaurant industry by acquiring the Burger King chain with its 275 outlets. Eight years later, there were 1,395 Burger King restaurants; their sales came to more than $700 million. Pillsbury opened its first Poppin Fresh Pie Shop in Des Moines in 1969. In the 1970s under chief executive officer William H. Spoor, Pillsbury set out to become a "great company" noted for "quality products" and "quality earnings." Spoor and his successor, Winston R. Wallin, restructured by selling operations with little chance for earnings growth, expanding international operations, acquiring the Steak and Ale restaurant chain in 1976, and opening a new chain, Bennigan's, two years later. Its best-known acquisitions were Green Giant (1979), Totino's and Jeno's frozen pizza (1975 and 1986), and Häagen-Dazs ice cream (1983).[103]

The leading food manufacturers in Minnesota vigorously pursued the strategy of product differentiation, the practice of offering a wide range of brands to appeal to every consumer taste. The activities of General Mills in the ready-to-eat breakfast-cereals industry provide a good example. Techniques of producing ready-to-eat cereals are well known, and the costs of technology and raw materials are not a barrier. To discourage new entrants, established firms relied partly on television advertising (18.5 percent of sales revenue in 1967 was spent on advertising and promotion) and partly on product differentiation. General Mills marketed three brands of breakfast cereal in 1950 and nineteen in 1973. By the 1970s General Mills and three rivals controlled 90 percent of the ready-to-eat breakfast-cereal market. For the established firms fewer new entrants has meant "elevated, supranormal profitability" since they avoid some of the rigors of price competition.[104]

An episode in the early 1970s showed how General Mills and the other major firms dominated the ready-to-eat breakfast-cereals industry. When an unanticipated market niche opened up – the demand for "natural" cereals – some new firms, including Pillsbury, moved quickly to fill it; but then General Mills introduced its own natural product, Nature Valley, in 1973. This maneuver put a stop to the incursion, and some of the new entrants, including Pillsbury, dropped out. By the late 1970s the major cereal producers had regained control of this market niche.[105]

Many economists and social critics had concluded by the 1970s that, in

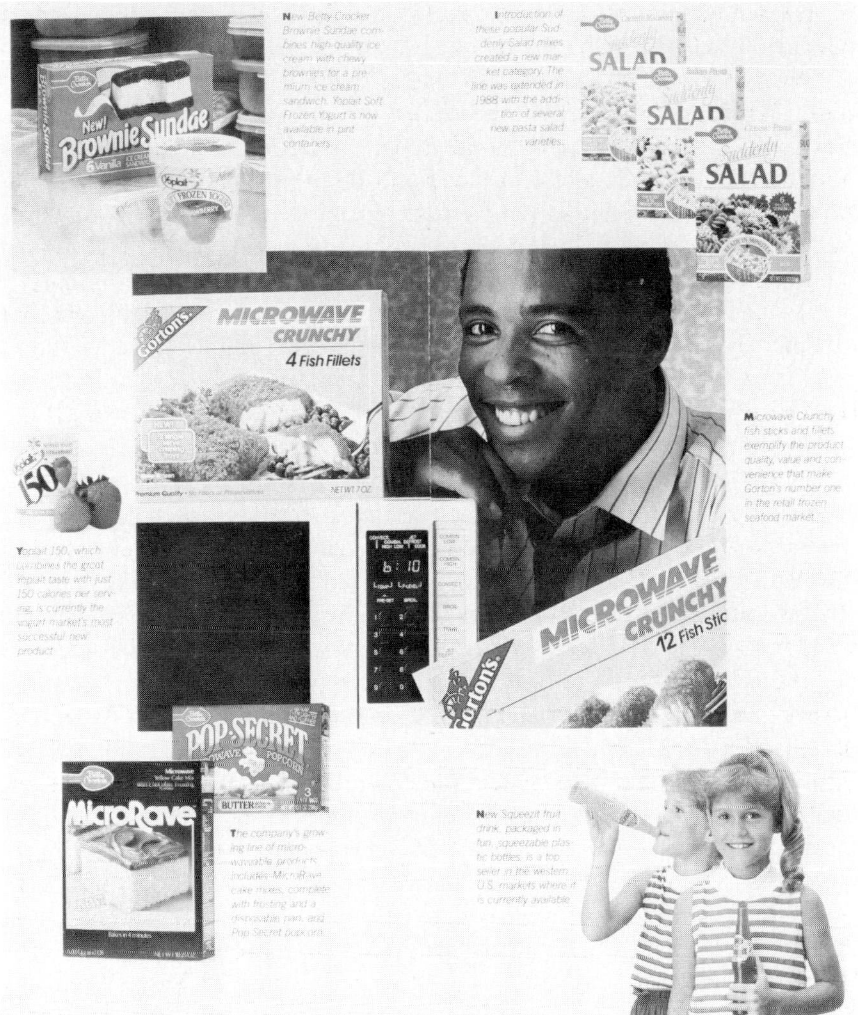

A page in the General Mills annual report for 1988 highlights conveniently packaged foods for time-conscious families.

the words of one economist, "much cereal advertising is . . . a social waste: an expenditure that would not have occurred if price competition had been working." As a result of such concerns, the Federal Trade Commission (FTC) in 1972 brought suit against major food firms including General Mills, Kellogg, and General Foods alleging monopolization of the breakfast-cereals industry. The companies fought the commission's action strenuously and tried to get Congress to pass legislation halting the suit. A September 1981 FTC decision absolved the cereal companies.[106]

An "Age of Discontinuity"

In 1982, out of a state population of just over four million, some 350,000 Minnesotans were employed in manufacturing – a considerably higher proportion of the population than in 1900. (Of these, about 200,000 were production workers.)[107]

Signs of rapid and unsettling change were evident in many of Minnesota's industries, not just computers, throughout the 1970s and 1980s. Paper manufacturing entered a boom period in the late 1970s as Potlatch Paper Company built plants at Cook and Bemidji and Blandin Paper and St. Regis Paper expanded their operations at Grand Rapids and Sartell. But because paper production was highly automated, these mills did not create enough new jobs to compensate for the decline of iron mining in northern Minnesota. The state also remained an important producer of wafer and particle board, boxes, and crates. But a number of major wood-products firms, including Conwed and Hoerner Waldorf, were acquired by larger corporations outside the state.[108]

Brewing in Minnesota continued its long decline. Familiar breweries such as Joseph Hauenstein of New Ulm, Fitger of Duluth, and Jacob Schmidt of St. Paul could not afford to invest heavily in advertising and modern equipment, such as new bottling machines. Undercapitalized and obsolete, they either closed their doors or sold out to larger producers. By 1980 the state had just four breweries, and two of these were owned by large firms with headquarters outside Minnesota. Even Theodore Hamm of St. Paul, the state's largest brewer for decades, saw its market share decline rapidly in the 1960s; in 1965 the Hamm family sold out to Heublein, Inc., of Hartford, Connecticut.[109]

In the metals and machinery industries, American Hoist and Derrick (Amhoist) was badly hurt by the decline in the world oil and nuclear-power industries; the firm has produced large cranes and derricks used to construct offshore oil-drilling rigs and nuclear-power plants. Amhoist's cost-cutting measures included closing its crane-manufacturing plant in St. Paul in 1985 and moving the operation to North Carolina.[110] In Duluth the 1970s saw the closing of United States Steel's plant at Morgan Park. Like many breweries in the state, the steel plant was obsolete and uncompetitive. Rather than invest in new equipment to meet stricter standards for the control of air pollution, the company curtailed and then in 1979 halted production at Morgan Park. While pollution concerns were the proximate cause of the plant's demise, it probably would have closed shortly anyway, one of many victims of the upheaval in the American steel industry.[111]

The old stockyards in South St. Paul, founded in 1886 and among the world's largest by the 1940s, declined rapidly in the 1960s. New beef processors were building smaller, highly automated plants in scattered locations closer to where the animals were raised; they worked directly with feedlot operators rather than buying at major stockyards such as South St. Paul. The two largest packers at South St. Paul, Swift and Armour, closed their outmoded beef-slaughtering operations in the late 1960s, idling thousands of workers. Packing plants also shut down by 1980. Some older packing firms invested heavily in modernizing their operations, but this choice, too, exacted a cost. In 1982 Hormel opened a new, highly automated, $80 million pork plant in Austin, the largest food-processing plant of any kind in the United States. It employed 1,150, about one-quarter the number of Hormel workers at Austin in the late 1940s. Hormel's conflict with Local P-9 of the United Food and Commercial Workers in 1985–86 showed that plant modernization often caused labor strife as the number of jobs declined and the intensity of work rose.[112]

A few Minnesota manufacturers had been involved in overseas sales and manufacturing as early as the 1920s, but international operations grew in significance after World War II. By the mid-1980s, the state's leading exporters, ranked by percentage of revenue from exports, were MTS Systems (computer systems and software), Cray Research, Data Card, CPT (word processors), and Graco (systems and technology for handling fluids). But many other companies with little or no direct export revenue had international activities in the form of overseas divisions, subsidiaries, or joint ventures; these included, for example, Control Data, Hormel, Ecolab (formerly Economics Laboratory; cleaning and sanitation products and systems), and Toro (lawn-care equipment).

Three examples convey a sense of Minnesota's involvement in the world economy. Conwed began in 1961 to license foreign firms to manufacture its mineral ceiling board. Conwed also exported the board and other products directly to the Middle East, Southeast Asia, and Latin America. Donaldson Company, a manufacturer of products such as engine mufflers and hydraulic filters, followed its traditional American customers overseas; when machinery manufacturers set up foreign subsidiaries, Donaldson did so also in order to continue to supply them. Subsequently the firm found new customers among foreign manufacturers. By 1979 Donaldson had eleven subsidiaries in ten foreign countries. Onan Corporation, a producer of industrial engines and electrical generators, first entered international markets in the 1930s by setting up a distributorship in Venezuela. People all over the world learned about Onan generators when the United States armed forces used them during World War II and subsequently when the military turned its bases over to local authorities. By the 1970s Onan had regional sales offices in England, Venezuela, Singapore, and Dubai and more than a hundred distributorships worldwide. The company opened a new R&D center in Minneapolis to develop products suited for various climates, such as that of Saudi Arabia with its high temperatures and dust levels.[113]

If the importance of international operations for many Minnesota manufacturers was one sign of the emerging world economy, another and more unsettling sign was that many state firms, like other U.S. manufacturers, faced significant competition from rivals in other nations, principally those of Western Europe and the Pacific Rim. The United States share of world sales of manufactured goods declined by 23 percent during the 1970s, while the other industrialized nations and the developing nations expanded their share. The American proportionate decline was most precipitous in capital-intensive, high-volume industries, such as automobiles and steel. Observers cited a variety of causes. Some blamed inept corporate management, others mentioned high labor costs or excessive federal regulation of business, and still others pointed to the strong U.S. dollar.[114]

Around the early 1970s, corporate leaders in the state and nationally grew alarmed at signs (in the form of energy crises and stagflation) that the long postwar era of sustained American economic growth was ending. Despite the policies of the Reagan administration and the decline of inflation, troubling evidence mounted that the United States, slow to adapt to foreign competition, was yielding its manufacturing preeminence to other nations.[115]

Business leaders decided that they should speak out more vigorously about the need for a favorable business climate in Minnesota. The Minnesota Business Partnership, founded in 1977 on the model of the Business Roundtable (a national organization), emerged as the chief voice of the major corporations. Comprising chief executive officers of some seventy-five leading firms, the Partnership addressed a variety of issues, including equitable taxation, workers' compensation reform, and improved public education. By sponsoring research reports and engaging in quiet dialogue with public officials, the Partnership helped to focus statewide debate on its key issues.[116] Yet it remained to be seen whether such reforms at the state level could seriously improve the competitive strength of Minnesota's major manufacturing corporations as they girded for business in a world economy marked by rapid and continuing technological change.

NOTES

1. For an overview of industrial growth, see Alfred D. Chandler, Jr., "The Beginnings of 'Big Business' in American Industry," *Business History Review* 33 (Spring 1959): 1–31; Peter George, *The Emergence of Industrial America: Strategic Factors in American Economic Growth since 1870* (Albany: State University of New York Press, 1982).

2. United States, *Census*, 1900, *Manufactures*, part 2, p. 442, 450–54.

3. Other food industries, notably poultry slaughtering and dressing and vegetable canning, also grew rapidly in this period. U.S., *Census*, 1920, *Manufactures*, 9:720.

4. U.S., *Census*, 1900, *Manufactures*, part 2, p. 443; Alfred D. Chandler, Jr., *The Visible Hand: The Managerial Revolution in American Business* (Cambridge, Mass.: Harvard University Press, 1977), 249–53; James Gray, *Business without Boundary: The Story of General Mills* (Minneapolis: University of Minnesota Press, 1954), 20–24, 37–38; William J. Powell, *Pillsbury's BEST: A Company History from 1869* (Minneapolis: Pillsbury Co., 1985), 27–32, 49; Charles Byron Kuhlmann, "The Development of Flour Milling in Minneapolis" (Master's thesis, University of Minnesota, 1920), 65; John Storck and Walter Dorwin Teague, *Flour for Man's Bread: A History of Milling* (Minneapolis: University of Minnesota Press, 1952). Different members of the Washburn family were involved as partners in Washburn Crosby and Pillsbury-Washburn, but the two companies were entirely separate entities.

5. Chandler, *Visible Hand*, 249, 294; Gray, *Business without Boundary*, 38; Kuhlmann, "Development of Flour Milling," 67–68.

6. Gray, *Business without Boundary*, 51–68.

7. Powell, *Pillsbury's BEST*, 32, 54–56.

8. Chandler, *Visible Hand*, 294–95.

9. U.S., *Census*, 1900, *Manufactures*, part 2, p. 444; Chandler, *Visible Hand*, 299–301.

10. Richard J. Arnould, "Changing Patterns of Concentration in American Meat Packing, 1880–1963," *Business History Review* 45 (Spring 1971): 18–34; *St. Paul Pioneer Press*, Dec. 13, 1981, p. 14; Richard Dougherty, *In Quest of Quality: Hormel's First 75 Years* (Austin: Geo. A. Hormel and Co., 1966), 60, 64–69, 77, 80, 87.

11. United States Brewers' Association, *Year Book* (New York: The Association, 1909), 192, *Year Book* (1911), 320; Stanley Baron, *Brewed in America: A History of Beer and Ale in the United States* (Boston: Little, Brown and Co., 1962), 241, 257–60, 272–73; Charles Edwin Dick, "A Geographical Analysis of the Development of the Brewing Industry of Minnesota" (Ph.D. diss., University of Minnesota, 1981), 103, 108–19; Chandler, *Visible Hand*, 301.

12. Agnes M. Larson, *History of the White Pine Industry in Minnesota* (Minneapolis: University of Minnesota Press, 1949), 349–55, 360–61; U.S., *Census*, 1900, *Manufactures*, part 3, p. 876.

13. Ralph W. Hidy, Frank Ernest Hill, and Allan Nevins, *Timber and Men: The Weyerhaeuser Story* (New York: Macmillan Co., 1963), 115–16, 182; Don W. Larson, *Land of the Giants: A History of Minnesota Business* (Minneapolis: Dorn Books, 1979), 36–37; Agnes Larson, *White Pine Industry*, 231–46. Pine Tree Lumber became Pine Tree Manufacturing Company after 1909.

14. Hidy, Hill, and Nevins, *Timber and Men*, 182–93, 197–98; Agnes Larson, *White Pine Industry*, 234–36.

15. Hidy, Hill, and Nevins, *Timber and Men*, 199–200, 354–59.

16. Hidy, Hill, and Nevins, *Timber and Men*, 194–95; for annual operating statistics see Appendix VIII.

17. R. Newell Searle, *Saving Quetico-Superior: A Land Set Apart* (St. Paul: Minnesota Historical Society Press, 1977), 34–42; "Mando's First Forty Years, 1910–1950," *The Mandonian* 4 (September–October 1950): 1–29, available in Minnesota Historical Society (MHS); Alfred D. Chandler, Jr., "The Structure of American Industry in the Twentieth Century: A Historical Overview," *Business History Review* 43 (Autumn 1969): 294. The firm was known as Minnesota and Ontario Power Company until 1918 when it changed its name to that given in the text.

18. Searle, *Saving Quetico-Superior*, 39–41, 92; "Mando's First Forty Years," 28–29; *Moody's Industrials*, 1924, p. 361–62.

19. Virginia Huck, *Brand of the Tartan: The 3M Story* (New York: Appleton-Century-Crofts, 1955), 1–44; Minnesota Mining and Manufacturing Co., *Our Story So Far: Notes from the First 75 Years of 3M Company* (St. Paul: The Company, 1977), 51–52 (quotation on 51). The latter work relies heavily on the former.

20. 3M, *Our Story So Far*, 58–60; Huck, *Brand of the Tartan*, 46–53, 57, 62–71.

21. Huck, *Brand of the Tartan*, 43–60, 72–78, 81–83.

22. E. B. Alderfer and H. E. Michl, *Economics of American Industry* (New York: McGraw-Hill Book Co., 1942), 107; Horace B. Hudson, ed., *A Half Century of Minneapolis* (Minneapolis: Hudson Pub. Co., 1908), 386, 389–90; Chandler, *Visible Hand*, 356–57.

23. Clifford H. Anderson, *Crown Iron Works Centennial, 1878–1978* ([Minneapolis: The Company], 1978), 4, 7–9, 20–21, 26.

24. Hudson, ed., *A Half Century of Minneapolis*, 387–89, 407; Norman Francis Thomas, *Minneapolis-Moline: A History of Its Formation and Operations* (New York: Arno Press, 1976), 230, 284–85; John M. Wickre, "Farm Implements and Tractors," in *A Guide to the Industrial Archeology of the Twin Cities*, ed. Nicholas Westbrook (St. Paul: Society for Industrial Archeology, 1983), 89–90. Railroad-car manufacture and repair, the fifth-leading industry in both 1900 and 1919, is briefly discussed in John M. Wickre, "Railroads," in *Industrial Archeology*, ed. Westbrook, 72–87; *Fourteen Years on Line: Being a Record of Fourteen Years Service by the American Railroad Ditcher* (St. Paul: American Hoist and Derrick Co., 1920).

25. Chandler, "Beginnings of 'Big Business' in American Industry"; Hudson, ed., *A Half Century of Minneapolis*, 390–92, 407; Thomas, *Minneapolis-Moline*, 230–33, 251–56; Wickre, "Farm Implements and Tractors," 89–90.

26. U.S. Department of Commerce, Bureau of the Census, *Historical Statistics of the United States: Colonial Times to 1970* (Washington, D.C.: U.S. Government Printing Office, 1975), part 1, p. 3, 11.

27. Dougherty, *In Quest of Quality*, 56, 59, 60; *Iron Age*, Dec. 30, 1915, p. 1507–19; Charles C. Lynde, "Steel Production at New Minnesota Plant," *Blast Furnace and Steel Plant* 4 (June 1916): 251–60.

28. In the shoe industry, 86 percent of wage earners worked in factories with one hundred or more employees; in flour mills, 64 percent; in meat-packing, 96 percent; in lumber mills, 84 percent; in linseed oil, 61 percent; in paper and pulp mills, 95 percent. Calculated from U.S., *Census*, 1920, *Manufactures*, 9:726. Comparable figures are not available for 1900.

29. Calculated from U.S., *Census*, 1900, *Manufactures*, part 2, p. 441, 450, 452 (quotation on 441), *Census*, 1920, *Manufactures*, 9:740–44. The milling industry employed 4,457 such workers in 1920.

30. Chandler, "Structure of American Industry," 255–98. While paper is a wood product, the Standard Industrial Classification system devised by the federal government separates paper and allied products (group 26) from lumber and wood products (group 24). See U.S. Executive Office of the President, Office of Management and Budget, *Standard Industrial Classification Manual* (Washington, D.C.: U.S. Government Printing Office, 1972).

31. Avi J. Cohen, "Technological Change as Historical Process: The Case of the U.S. Pulp and Paper Industry, 1915–1940," *Journal of Economic History* 44 (September 1984): 775–99

(quotation on 791). On the capital demands made by Northwest Paper's managers for expansion, see Hidy, Hill, and Nevins, *Timber and Men*, 194–95.

32. Jon Didrichsen, "The Development of Diversified and Conglomerate Firms in the United States, 1920–1970," *Business History Review* 46 (Summer 1972): 202–19; Richard E. Caves, "Industrial Organization, Corporate Strategy and Structure," *Journal of Economic Literature* 18 (March 1980): 64–92.

33. Chandler, "Structure of American Industry," 265, 273–74; Didrichsen, "Development of Diversified and Conglomerate Firms," 204; Alfred D. Chandler, Jr., "The Emergence of Managerial Capitalism," *Business History Review* 58 (Winter 1984): 473–503.

34. David A. Hounshell, "The Rise of Industrial Research in the United States" (Paper presented at conference on "The R & D Pioneers" at the Hagley Museum and Library, Wilmington, Del., Oct. 7, 1985), copy in author's possession. The quoted phrase is Hounshell's.

35. Don Larson, *Land of the Giants*, 125–28; *Fortune*, May 1959, p. 113; Judith Yates Borger, *Honeywell: The First 100 Years* (Minneapolis: The Company, 1985).

36. C[larence] W[illard] Nessell, *The Restless Spirit* (Minneapolis: Minneapolis-Honeywell Regulator Co., 1963), 29–76; "All Together Now, Happy Centennial!" *Honeywell World*, Centennial issue, Jan. 7, 1985, available at MHS. The name Minneapolis-Honeywell was not shortened to Honeywell until 1964, but this essay will refer to the firm as Honeywell from here on.

37. "Little Big Honeywell," *Forbes*, Nov. 15, 1964, p. 22–25 (quotation on 23). Minneapolis Heat Regulator's earliest product-development laboratory appears to have dated from 1923; Nessell, *Restless Spirit*, 58–60.

38. "Little Big Honeywell," p. 23; Honeywell annual reports, 1928, 1940, 1952, available at MHS; Nessell, *Restless Spirit*, 69, 77–106; "All Together Now," 12, 16–17.

39. Huck, *Brand of the Tartan*, 92–102; *Our Story So Far*, 62–69. 3M saw itself as essentially a manufacturer of producer goods. The company did almost no consumer advertising until 1932 when it began to market Scotch brand cellophane tape.

40. Huck, *Brand of the Tartan*, 72–75, 131–38.

41. Huck, *Brand of the Tartan*, 139–49, 161–62, 179–80; *Our Story So Far*, 60–74, 101–15; Didrichsen, "Development of Diversified and Conglomerate Firms," 213.

42. Hidy, Hill, and Nevins, *Timber and Men*, 358–61, 442–43.

43. Gray, *Business without Boundary*, 83, 87–88.

44. Gray, *Business without Boundary*, 97–98, 102–3, 210–13, 215, 218.

45. Gray, *Business without Boundary*, 129–42. Technically the creation of General Mills is considered a merger and is often listed as one of the principal mergers of the late 1920s.

46. Gray, *Business without Boundary*, 173–74; *Minneapolis Star and Tribune*, May 23, 1986, p. 1A.

47. Powell, *Pillsbury's BEST*, 97, 101, 106–7, 114–15, 120–21, 131.

48. This is, of course, the central theme of Alfred D. Chandler, Jr., *Strategy and Structure: Chapters in the History of the Industrial Enterprise* (Cambridge, Mass.: MIT Press, 1962), esp. 42–51.

49. Chandler, *Strategy and Structure*, 324–96.

50. Gray, *Business without Boundary*, 218–28; Chandler, *Strategy and Structure*, 346–49. General Mills added further divisions in 1945 and reorganized on several later occasions.

51. Huck, *Brand of the Tartan*, 179–80, 185–86. 3M's Abrasives Division manufactured more than ten thousand products in 1937. Honeywell also created separate manufacturing divisions, but the information is sketchier; see the firm's annual reports for this period.

52. Adolf A. Berle, Jr., and Gardiner C. Means, *The Modern Corporation and Private Property* (New York: Macmillan, 1932; reprint ed., Buffalo, N.Y.: William S. Hein and Co., Inc., 1982); James Burnham, *The Managerial Revolution: What Is Happening in the World* (New York: John Day Co., 1941).

53. Dougherty, *In Quest of Quality*, 122–34, 140–41, 165, 167, 202–3, 222–28.

54. Chandler, *Visible Hand*, 411–14. See also Peter F. Drucker, *Concept of the Corporation* (New York: John Day Co., 1946).

55. Critics from across the ideological spectrum made this charge. The classic statement was Robert H. Hayes and William J. Abernathy, "Managing Our Way to Economic Decline," *Harvard Business Review*, July–August 1980, p. 67–77.

56. Roland S. Vaile, Richard L. Kozelka, and Warren C. Waite, *Impact of the Depression on Business Activity and Real Income in Minnesota*, University of Minnesota Studies in Economics and Business, no. 8 (Minneapolis: University of Minnesota Press, 1933), 15. The ratio of workers in food manufacturing to total workers in the state was three times higher than the ratio for the nation as a whole.

57. Searle, *Saving Quetico-Superior*, 91–94, 102–3; "Mando's First Forty Years," 16–17.

58. Anderson, *Crown Iron Works Centennial*, 23.

59. Dick, "Geographical Analysis," 124–31; Jeri Engh, *Hamm's: The Story of 100 Years in the Land of Sky Blue Waters* (St. Paul: The Company, 1965), 10.

60. Dick, "Geographical Analysis," 60–66, 124–27, 130; Baron, *Brewed in America*, 338–39.
61. Don Larson, *Land of the Giants*, 144.
62. Don Larson, *Land of the Giants*, 145–46; "Mando's First Forty Years," 29.
63. *Our Story So Far*, 109–10; Huck, *Brand of the Tartan*, 173–77, 227–28, 231.
64. Don Larson, *Land of the Giants*, 146–51.
65. See Minneapolis-Honeywell annual reports for 1941–45 (quotation, 1942 report).
66. Chandler, "Structure of American Industry," 267–81.
67. Arthur M. Johnson, "American Business in the Postwar Era," in *Reshaping America: Society and Institutions, 1945–1960*, ed. Robert H. Bremner and Gary W. Reichard (Columbus: Ohio State University Press, 1982), 102–3; Barton J. Bernstein, "America in War and Peace: The Test of Liberalism," in *Towards a New Past: Dissenting Essays in American History*, ed. Bernstein (New York: Random House, 1968), 289–321.
68. For an overview of post-World War II technological development, see Walter A. McDougall, *The Heavens and the Earth: A Political History of the Space Age* (New York: Basic Books, 1985), esp. 4–11, and John Tirman, ed., *The Militarization of High Technology* (Cambridge, Mass.: Ballinger Pub. Co., 1984). See also "Minnesota: Restoring the Entrepreneurial Explosion," *Minnesota Business Journal*, November 1980, p. 63; Minnesota Clergy and Laity Concerned, "Jobs and Peace" (1982), 16–19, available at MHS. The other two defense contractors were Northwest Airlines and the Northern Ordnance Division of FMC Corp., formerly Northern Pump and acquired by FMC in 1964.
69. "America Rushes to High Tech for Growth," *Business Week*, Mar. 28, 1983, p. 85. For 3M's postwar growth as a high-technology manufacturer, see Huck, *Brand of the Tartan*, 236–39, 249; *Our Story So Far*, 104–9; Thomas J. Peters and Robert H. Waterman, Jr., *In Search of Excellence* (New York: Harper and Row, 1982), 224–34; "Sticking It Out: How 3M Almost Scotched Its Best-selling Office Product," *Corporate Report Minnesota*, July 1984, p. 47–52.
70. Franklin M. Fisher, James W. McKie, and Richard B. Mancke, *IBM and the U.S. Data Processing Industry: An Economic History* (New York: Praeger, 1983), 3–6, 9–10; *Minneapolis Star and Tribune*, Sept. 10, 1986, p. 1M, 5M.
71. Robert Sobel, *IBM: Colossus in Transition* (New York: Times Books, 1981), 153–57; "Small, Smart, Sharp," *Business Week*, May 25, 1963, p. 154–66; Fisher, McKie, and Mancke, *IBM*, 38–46, 90–91 (quotations on 91).
72. In 1965, for example, Control Data reported net earnings of $7.9 million on gross revenues of $160.5 million – a profit margin of 12.2 percent – and had just $98 million in working capital, by far the lowest figure for any major computer manufacturer. IBM, by contrast, had a profit margin of 26.4 percent and working capital of $698.7 million. Without the profits of Commercial Credit, Control Data would have lost money in some years. Sobel, *IBM*, 169; "When a Whiz Kid Grows Up," July 30, 1966, p. 30, "CDC Takes Peripheral Road to Growth," Aug. 5, 1967, p. 118, "Marrying for Money," June 22, 1968, p. 37, "Control Data Digs Its Gold Mine," Sept. 28, 1968, p. 59–60 – all *Business Week*; "Can Control Data Make It?" *Forbes*, June 15, 1972, p. 31.
73. "Control Data Tackles the Giant," *Business Week*, June 28, 1969, p. 148–54.
74. *Corporate Report of the Ninth Federal Reserve District*, Feb. 14, 1970, p. 9; "Profiles of Leading Twin Cities Companies," *Greater Minneapolis*, March–April 1976, p. 78; *Minneapolis Star and Tribune*, Jan. 13, 1986, p. 6M.
75. Sobel, *IBM*, 254–61; "Why Bill Norris Is Smiling," *Business Week*, Nov. 10, 1973, p. 188–94; "Windfall for the Little Five," *Forbes*, Oct. 1, 1973, p. 36–44 (quotation on 41).
76. "Control Data Tackles the Giant," 148 (quotation); "Can Control Data Make It?" 30, 32, 34 (quotation on 30). The latter article offers a detailed and skeptical evaluation of Control Data's emerging strategy. See also "Corporate Moby Dick," *Forbes*, Nov. 15, 1974, p. 34–35.
77. "Minneapolis-Honeywell: The Darn Thing Works," *Fortune*, May 1959, p. 112–18, 172, 177–78, 181; "Little Big Honeywell," 22; Honeywell annual reports.
78. "Little Big Honeywell," 22–25; "Honeywell Bets on Automation," *Business Week*, Feb. 5, 1966, p. 60–62, 67.
79. "Progress Report," *Forbes*, Oct. 15, 1971, p. 53. For a more favorable assessment, see Sobel, *IBM*, 295–96.
80. "Left to Their Own Devices," *Minnesota Business Journal*, August 1982, p. 14–22; Carol Pine and Susan Mundale, *Self-Made: The Stories of 12 Minnesota Entrepreneurs* (Minneapolis: Dorn Books, 1982), 38–54.
81. Here and below, *Corporate Report of the Ninth Federal Reserve District*, May 1973, p. 11–12; "Spotlight on a Company: Cardiac Pacemakers, Inc.," *Minnesota Business Journal*, June 1980, p. 54; "Left to Their Own Devices," 14–22; "The Healing Fields," *Corporate Report Minnesota*, May 1985, p. 90–97; "High Tech 100," *Corporate Report Minnesota*, September 1985, p. 62–71; "Minnesota: The State of Health Care" (Edina, 1986), a publication of Minnesota Medical Alley Association, a trade group, copy in author's possession; "Twin Cities Business Scene in Review," *CityBusiness* (Minneapolis-St. Paul), Dec. 17, 1986, p. 19.

82. "Heart Trouble," *Corporate Report Minnesota*, November 1984, p. 52–58; "Left to Their Own Devices," 14; *Minneapolis Star and Tribune*, Apr. 10, 1986, p. 2M, May 8, 1985, p. 1M. For background see Donald W. Light, "Corporate Medicine for Profit," *Scientific American*, December 1986, p. 38–45. The quoted phrase is from "Twin Cities Business Scene in Review," *CityBusiness*, Dec. 17, 1986, p. 19.

83. "Where Three Sales a Year Make You a Superstar," *Business Week*, Feb. 17, 1986, p. 76–77; *Minneapolis Star and Tribune*, Mar. 2, 1986, p. 33A; "Zen and the Art of Building Cathedrals," *Corporate Report Minnesota*, January 1986, p. 47–56, 59–60, 62, 64, 66 (for an explanation of supercomputers, 52); Cray Research annual report, 1986, p. 2.

84. "The Future Is Now," *Forbes*, Jan. 27, 1986, p. 88–89, 92; "Zen and the Art of Building Cathedrals," 60.

85. "The Future Is Now," 88–89, 92 (chips for the first supercomputer at ETA Systems, a Control Data spinoff, were manufactured by Honeywell, the result of a research project into high-speed integrated circuit technology funded by the Department of Defense); "Where Three Sales a Year Make You a Superstar," 76; "Zen and the Art of Building Cathedrals," 59–62.

86. "Zen and the Art of Building Cathedrals," 54–56 (quotation on 56).

87. For journalists' discussions of corporate restructuring, see "The Hollow Corporation," *Business Week*, Mar. 3, 1986, p. 56–85, "The End of Corporate Loyalty?" Aug. 4, 1986, p. 42; "Remaking the American C.E.O.," *New York Times*, Jan. 25, 1987, sec. 3, p. 1; "Rebuilding to Survive," *Time*, Feb. 16, 1987, p. 44–48 (quotation on 44). For background and a broader view, see Michael J. Piore and Charles F. Sabel, *The Second Industrial Divide: Possibilities for Prosperity* (New York: Basic Books, 1984); Peter F. Drucker, "The Changed World Economy," *Foreign Affairs* 64 (Spring 1986): 768–91; Robert B. Reich, *Tales of a New America* (New York: Times Books, 1987).

88. *New York Times*, Sept. 30, 1985, p. 1A, 5D; *Minneapolis Star and Tribune*, Mar. 3, 1986, p. 1M, Mar. 31, 1986, p. 1M; "How Jake Jacobson Is Lighting a Fire under 3M," *Business Week*, July 21, 1986, p. 106–7.

89. "The Dream Turns Sour: Towering Troubles at CDC," *Corporate Report Minnesota*, September 1985, p. 52.

90. "Social Strategy Aimed at Profits," *Business Week*, June 25, 1979, p. 118, 123, "Computerized Training May Finally Be about to Take Off," Mar. 28, 1983, p. 88; "CDC Emerging Strategy," *Datamation*, December 1980, p. 53–54, 56 (quotation on 53). Estimates of Control Data's investment in PLATO have varied between $200 million and $1 billion.

91. "Control Data: Is There Room for Change after Bill Norris?" *Business Week*, Oct. 17, 1983, p. 119–24.

92. "Control Data Starts a Painful Retrenchment," *Business Week*, Oct. 22, 1984, p. 94, 96; *New York Times*, Oct. 29, 1985, p. 5D; "Control Data: Ragged Trousered," *Economist*, Nov. 2, 1985, p. 74–75; *Minneapolis Star and Tribune*, Mar. 8, 1987, p. 1D.

93. *Washington Post*, Jan. 5, 1986, p. 3B; for other analyses of the firm's problems, see *Minneapolis Star and Tribune*, Jan. 13, 1986, p. 1M, 6M; "The Dream Turns Sour," 45–59, 142–46.

94. *Minneapolis Star and Tribune*, Jan. 13, 1986, p. 1M, 6M; "Corporate Culture: Norris at Colonnus," *Corporate Report Minnesota*, February 1986, p. 126; James C. Worthy, *William C. Norris: Portrait of a Maverick* (New York: Ballinger, 1987).

95. "Control Data's Outlook: Partly Cloudy with Possible Clearing," *Business Week*, Aug. 4, 1986, p. 59, 62, "How Bob Price Is Reprogramming Control Data," Feb. 16, 1987, p. 102; "Twin Cities Business Scene in Review," 18; *Minneapolis Star and Tribune*, Mar. 10, 1987, p. 7B.

96. "A Big Push in Minicomputers," *Business Week*, Feb. 2, 1976, p. 20–21, "Honeywell: Betting Minicomputers Will Keep Its Customers," Feb. 15, 1982, p. 84–85.

97. "A Computer Link Boosts Hopes at Honeywell," *Business Week*, Nov. 7, 1983, p. 43–44; "Strategic Withdrawal," *Forbes*, Feb. 10, 1986, p. 34.

98. "Strategic Withdrawal," 34–35; "Can Honeywell Turn around in a Fishbowl?" Oct. 6, 1986, p. 73, "Honeywell May Get a Boss Not a Partner in NEC," Oct. 20, 1986, p. 43, "Honeywell Beats a Retreat from the Computer Wars," Dec. 15, 1986, p. 30 – all *Business Week; New York Times*, Dec. 3, 1986, p. 1D; *Minneapolis Star and Tribune*, Dec. 18, 1986, p. 1A.

99. *Minneapolis Star and Tribune*, Feb. 23, 1987, p. 1M.

100. *Minneapolis Star and Tribune*, Feb. 23, 1987, p. 1M; Reich, *Tales of a New America*, 57, 73–74 (quotation on 74). See also Reich, "High Technology, Defense, and International Trade," in *Militarization of High Technology*, ed. Tirman, 33–43.

101. John M. Connor, "The U.S. Food and Tobacco Manufacturing Industries: Market Structure, Structural Change, and Economic Performance," U.S. Dept. of Agriculture, Economics, Statistics, and Cooperatives Service, Agricultural Economic Report no. 451, March 1980, p. 8–14. Minnesota-based firms in the top two hundred included George A. Hormel,

Land O' Lakes, Green Giant, ConAgra, International Multifoods, Peavey, General Mills, Pillsbury, Cargill, and American Crystal Sugar.

102. Powell, *Pillsbury's BEST*, 151, 153, 158–59, 161–66, 172–73.

103. Powell, *Pillsbury's BEST*, 181–85, 189–213, 219–22; *Minneapolis Star and Tribune*, Mar. 10, 1986, p. 1M. General Mills also restructured in the 1980s; see *Minneapolis Star and Tribune*, Mar. 14, 1987, p. 7B.

104. Connor, "U.S. Food and Tobacco Manufacturing Industries," 24–32, 38, 39 (quotation on 24); Frederic M. Scherer, "The Breakfast Cereal Industry," in *The Structure of American Industry*, ed. Walter Adams, 6th ed. (New York: Macmillan, 1982), 191–217, esp. 196, 198.

105. Scherer, "Breakfast Cereal Industry," 201.

106. Scherer, "Breakfast Cereal Industry," 213–15 (quotation on 215). Scherer (216) also discusses efforts to force cereal manufacturers to fortify their cereals and to disclose ingredients and nutrient content and the celebrated effort of the FTC in 1978 to stop the firms from advertising on television programs directed at children deemed too young to evaluate the ads. Eventually the FTC was pressured to suspend its effort to regulate "kid vid" advertising.

107. U.S., *Census*, 1980, *Population*, vol. 1, p. I-43; U.S., *Census*, 1980, *Manufactures*, Geographical Area Series, *Minnesota*, 3. In 1900 about 5.7 percent of the Minnesota population was employed in manufacturing; in 1982, about 8.75 percent. The subheading for this section comes from Peter F. Drucker, *The Age of Discontinuity: Guidelines to Our Changing Society* (New York: Harper and Row, 1968, 1969).

108. *St. Paul Pioneer Press/Dispatch*, Dec. 27, 1982, p. 1B; "Forest Products: A Vital Minnesota Industry," *Industrial Development News*, January 1975, p. 7–10. Conwed was acquired by Cardiff Equities Corp. in 1985; Hoerner Waldorf by Champion.

109. The two locally owned brewers were Cold Spring and August Schell. Dick, "Geographical Analysis of the Development of the Brewing Industry in Minnesota," 150, 157–73. Hamm's later was purchased by Olympia Brewing Co.

110. "Hoisting the Profit Margins," *Dun's Review*, July 1972, p. 67–68; *Minneapolis Star and Tribune*, Feb. 11, 1987, p. 1M, Feb. 16, 1987, p. 11M.

111. *Duluth News-Tribune*, Feb. 10, 1970, p. 1, 12; *Duluth Herald*, Apr. 27, 1970, p. 1, 2. See also Donald F. Barnett and Louis Schorsch, *Steel: Upheaval in a Basic Industry* (Cambridge, Mass.: Ballinger Pub. Co., 1983), esp. chap. 3.

112. *St. Paul Pioneer Press*, Dec. 13, 1981, p. 14; *St. Paul Pioneer Press/Dispatch*, Sept. 13, 1982, p. 1B. For more on the Hormel strike, see Peter Rachleff, "Turning Points in the Labor Movement: Three Key Conflicts," *this volume*, 213–16.

113. "Minnesota Firms Go National," *Minnesota Business Journal*, November 1979, p. 16–19. Onan was acquired by Studebaker Worthington in 1960; in 1987 it was held by Cummins Engine Co. of Columbus, Ind., and Hawker-Siddeley Group of London, England.

114. "Minnesota's International Companies," *Corporate Report Minnesota*, January 1986, p. 69–79; Reich, *Next American Frontier*, 122; Bruce R. Scott, "U.S. Competitiveness: Concepts, Performances, and Implications," in *U.S. Competitiveness in the World Economy*, ed. Bruce R. Scott and George C. Lodge (Boston: Harvard Business School Press, 1985), 1–70. See also Richard Rosecrance, *The Rise of the Trading State: Commerce and Conquest in the Modern World* (New York: Basic Books, 1986).

115. *New York Times Magazine*, Dec. 7, 1986, part 2, p. 22. For representative critiques see Hayes and Abernathy, "Managing Our Way to Economic Decline," and Reich, *Next American Frontier*. See also *U.S. Competitiveness in the World Economy*, ed. Scott and Lodge.

116. On the Minnesota Business Partnership, see Ken Wakershauser, "MBP Bolsters State Business Climate," *Minnesota Business Journal*, December 1980, p. 30–33; Judson Bemis and John A. Cairns, "In Minnesota, Business Is Part of the Solution," *Harvard Business Review*, July–August 1981, p. 85–93; John A. Cairns, "The Changes in Governance" (Paper presented at policy committee and members meeting of the Minnesota Business Partnership, Dec. 17, 1981), copy in author's possession; *Minneapolis Star and Tribune*, June 29, 1986, p. 1D; David Vogel, "Why Businessmen Distrust Their State: The Political Consciousness of American Corporate Executives," *British Journal of Political Science* 8 (January 1978): 45–78.

Girl working in a sugar beet field in Polk County, 1937

D. JEROME TWETON

The Business of Agriculture

Farming is a precarious business. As producers of raw materials, farmers have no control over the prices that they receive for their crops or livestock. They have become very small pieces in the gigantic and complicated jigsaw puzzle of international trade. What happens in the Soviet Union or Argentina directly, and sometimes immediately, affects the farmer near Blue Earth or Crookston. A drought in the Soviet Union may cause a short supply of wheat and bring unexpectedly good income to the Red River valley; a bumper potato harvest on Canada's Prince Edward Island may lower the income of potato growers north of Minneapolis; a change in Argentina's beef-export policy may endanger profits in the Minnesota beef belt. A strong American dollar may hamper foreign purchases of Minnesota farm produce; a congressional shift in farm policy will result in higher or lower Minnesota farm income.

Nor can the farmer control the weather that helps determine the size and quality of a crop. Too little or too much rain can cut production, lowering farm receipts. A hailstorm can wipe out a season's work in a few minutes. A twist in the weather can mean millions of dollars in farm-income loss. For example, in 1981 during the highly intensive sugar beet harvest a five-day frost in the Red River valley trapped half the crop in the fields. Sugar beet growers lost $50 million.[1]

Agribusiness is, of course, tied to what happens on the farm. During depressed times farmers purchase less new equipment. Farm programs of the 1980s such as Payment-In-Kind, which took land out of production, or a dairy-cow buyout, which reduced herd size, translate into fewer sales of seed, feed, fertilizer, and supplies. When the sugar beets froze in 1981, the American Crystal Sugar Company processed just half a crop, reducing its revenues and employing fewer people for a shorter time. Delicate interrelationships exist among farmers, rural main streets, and processors; all are inextricably linked. For example, in 1984 Wilson Foods Corporation of Oklahoma, which was facing bankruptcy, was on the verge of closing its outdated (1916) Albert Lea hog and lamb packinghouse. The slaughter of 8,100 hogs and 1,800 to 2,000 lambs each day created an extremely important market for Freeborn County's livestock farmers. The annual payroll of $17 million and 1,550 jobs spelled well-being for Albert Lea (population 19,200) and its main-street businesses. Termination of the plant would have meant economic disaster to both farmers and townspeople. That is why all fifteen of the county's banks put together a $2.2 million loan in the search for $17.5 million in financing so that a local businessman could purchase the plant. "Wilson is very important to our pork producers," a bank president in a tiny nearby community declared. "They need that market." The Albert Lea situation tells in microcosm the story of twentieth-century Minnesota agriculture: the interdependence of farming, marketing, and processing.[2]

The Cycles of Minnesota Agriculture

As Minnesota said goodbye to the old century and welcomed in the new, its farmers were entering an era of unprecedented prosperity. Those years between the Spanish American War and World War I were indeed the "good years – the Golden Age of Agriculture." High crop yields accompanied high prices, land values increased rapidly, mortgage indebtedness fell, and farmers achieved a position of parity – farm prices remained in a favorable position to the prices farmers paid for manufactured items. As urban populations mushroomed under the strain of the new immigration and as available farmland disappeared, demand began to overtake supply. By 1900 Minnesota's cultivation frontier had reached maturity; most of the good land was gone. Farms, most of which were 160 to 180 acres, were self-sufficient and relied on horse power. The scientific "New Agriculture" focused attention on the use of fertilizers, improved techniques such as rotation, and diversification. Minnesota's regional farming patterns were established as farmers matched their crops and livestock to the best-suited land. The farm economy reflected diversification – a balanced blend of dairying, livestock, and crops.[3]

World War I further stimulated the farm economy as the government urged – almost demanded – that farmers plow to the fence for defense. American farmers broke 40 million new acres, and in Minnesota they pushed the cultivation line farther north into less productive areas. By 1919 farm prices had skyrocketed: wheat to $2.16 per bushel, hogs to $17.85 per hundred pounds (cwt), corn to $1.51 per bushel, beef to $15.50 cwt. But the war had created only a short-lived demand. Foreign markets shriveled up as Europe recovered and Argentina, Canada, and Australia entered postwar world trade. In 1920 the bubble burst. The nation went into recession, and farm prices skidded sharply downward. By 1921 corn had dropped to $.52 per bushel and wheat to $1.03; hogs were down to $8.51 cwt, beef to $8.20. Milk and poultry declined less severely, about 30 percent and 7 percent, respectively.[4]

Most of the nation pulled out of recession within two years; farmers did not. Prices recovered somewhat but did not approach wartime highs.

Farm debt rose and land values declined; farmers found themselves squeezed as the prices of items they needed to buy did not drop much. And Minnesota farmers had never been in a better position to maintain and even increase production. Although most operators continued to use horses, the tractor allowed increasing numbers of farmers to work twice the crop with the same labor time. Between 1920 and 1940 the percentage of Minnesota farms with tractors increased from about 8 to 49. Disease prevention, better breeding techniques, and improved feeds reduced both pig and calf losses.[5]

The Great Depression forced the collapse of the farm economy. Between 1929 and 1933 farm income fell some 60 percent, and in 1932, the worst of those years, national farm price averages tumbled to bankrupting lows: wheat, $.38 per bushel, corn, $.32; hogs, $3.83 cwt, beef cattle, $6.70 cwt. At many local markets farmers received even less. In 1933 sixty of every one thousand Minnesota farmers went bankrupt. Only the federal government's intervention under the New Deal kept farmers on the land. Production-control, price-support, and commodity-loan programs bolstered and maintained a disabled farm economy throughout the 1930s, forging a new relationship between farmers and the federal government. Diversification and self-sufficiency, however, placed Minnesota farmers in a better position to cope with the depression than their counterparts in the Dakotas who were tethered to the one-crop wheat economy or in Iowa where the corn-hog culture dominated. Diversification softened and the New Deal ameliorated the depression in Minnesota.[6]

World War II again caused agriculture to boom. Good rains, bumper crops, and worldwide demand pulled farmers out of the depression and pushed them into a new era of prosperity. During the war years most crop and livestock prices rose dramatically, surging by 1947 to wheat, $2.29 per bushel, corn, $2.16; beef, $25.83 cwt, hogs, $24.45. Strengthened by the government's price-support system and a fairly strong world market, farm prices remained near or above postwar levels for a decade, providing farmers with a position of parity or near parity in the nation's commerce. In the late 1950s, however, the farm economy moved into a sluggish market. Although some sectors of agriculture experienced an occasional rally, generally the years between 1958 and 1973 placed farmers in an unfavorable position in relation to the total economy. Armed with more sophisticated equipment, new chemical fertilizers, greatly improved hybrids, and protein-loaded feed, Minnesota's farmers, like those across the country, produced much more than the market demanded. They received about the same or less for their crops and livestock – except for beef cattle and dairy products – in 1971 as they had in 1946, and the cost of production had increased significantly. As stagnant as the farm economy became, however, it never approached the calamitous condition of the 1920s.[7]

And then, almost overnight, farming once again became a profitable business. Because of disastrous drought in several parts of the world in 1972 and 1973, demand skyrocketed, and, stimulated by a grain deal with the Soviet Union, so did farm prices, especially crop. Wheat jumped from $1.34 per bushel in 1971 to $4.09 in 1974 (and more than $5.00 on some market days); corn, $1.08 to $3.02; sugar beets, $15.40 to $46.80; soybeans, $3.03 to $6.64; sunflowers, $5.09 to $15.90. Minnesota farmers reaped the golden harvest. Between 1969 and 1974 the value of farm products sold doubled – from $1.7 billion to $3.4 billion. Net income per Minnesota farm increased from $5,900 to $15,700. From Luverne to Hallock, from Ortonville to Center City, farmers enjoyed their greatest era of prosperity, but the peak of the demand cycle was brief. Prices retreated from their record-setting highs of 1973–75 but still remained considerably higher through the early 1980s than the 1971 levels. Even though production stayed high and prices, by 1971 standards, remained good, agriculture fell into a recession. By 1982 Minnesota's net income per farm had fallen to about $10,500.[8]

The farm problems of the 1980s stemmed from the complicated interplay of several factors. High interest rates severely damaged farmers who historically have depended heavily on operational and expansion loans. A grain embargo imposed in 1980 ended sales to the Soviet Union. A strong dollar dried up other markets. Spiraling inflation substantially increased the cost of production. The price of seed, fertilizer, machinery, and supplies rose steadily as farm prices declined. Minnesota's land values, which had risen rapidly during the 1970s when farmers were expanding their operations, fell dramatically during the 1980s from an average price of $1,281 per acre in 1981 to $609 in 1986. The nature of the dilemma is illustrated in the case of Warren Nethring, winner of Stearns County's Outstanding Young Farmer Award in 1974, and his wife Sandy. They began farming in 1963 with beef cattle and a few sows on the 240-acre home farm that they purchased from his father. In 1972 the Nethrings added 180 acres and two years later bought another 180 acres. They built a new house, silos, and barns. In the late 1970s and early 1980s low hog prices and hail damage caused $100,000 in losses. In 1983 the machinery and grain had to go in order to pay off a $400,000 bank loan, and the following year the sheriff auctioned off the farm to carry out the mortgage holder's foreclosure. As of fall 1985 the Nethrings were renting their old farm, hoping to buy it back. That same year the Minnesota Department of Agriculture estimated that 33,000 farm families – one-third of the state's total – would be gone from the land within five years, testimony to the precarious nature of farming.[9]

Except for the immediate postwar era and the 1970s, overproduction was the number-one enemy of farmers after World War II. Technology and science worked a revolution on Minnesota farms. Chickens laid many more eggs, cows gave much more milk, each head of livestock produced substantially more meat, and acres yielded abundantly more crops. Developments in the Minnesota corn belt (the southern tiers of counties), for example, generally reflected what happened to the state's agriculture. Hybrid corn seed doubled and even tripled yields, from below 40 bushels an acre in 1940 to as much as 125 to 150 by the 1980s. Chemical fertilizer replaced barnyard manure; between 1949 and 1969 corn-belt farmers increased their use of fertilizer sixfold. Anhydrous ammonia tanks became part of rural Minnesota's landscape. Greater production demanded larger, more sophisticated machinery. On the eve of World War II only one in three corn-belt farmers owned a tractor. By 1949 almost all had at least one. Vastly greater investment in machinery tended to increase farm size, as farmers sought the most efficient use of their equipment. Between 1949 and 1982 corn-belt farms almost doubled in size; for Minnesota as a whole, the average grew from 184 acres in 1950 to 304 acres in 1984.[10] The post-World War II agricultural revolution considerably altered Minnesota's rural landscape and forever changed the nature of farming. Yet one factor remained constant: farming was still a business in which owners-operators could do almost nothing to control their market.

King Wheat

Although by the mid-1980s wheat ranked far behind dairy products, cattle and calves, corn, soybeans, and hogs as an income producer for Minnesota's farmers, such was not the case during the last decades of the nineteenth century. When Minnesota was young and part of the West's new agricultural frontier, wheat was king of the fields. Minnesotans, of course, grew food staples and kept livestock for subsistence, but for cash they raised spring wheat. By 1880 almost 70 percent of the state's tillable land (4.4 million acres) was planted in it, producing over 34 million bushels. Southern Minnesota and the bonanza farm country of the Red River valley, where one Minnesota wheat farm claimed 33,000 acres, belonged to the domain of the golden grain. Twenty years later the state's farm pattern had changed substantially. Farmers in southern and central Minnesota had shifted toward better-suited beef cattle, corn-hog, and dairy farming. The Red River valley and transitional areas adjacent to it became Minnesota's primary wheat region. In 1900 the state's wheat production stood at about 95 million bushels (greatest in the nation), with about half of farm acres devoted to the crop. Wheat remained an important cash crop (about 121 million bushels in 1984) but was far from dominating the state's economy as it had in the post-Civil War decades.[11]

The reign of King Wheat accounted for Minnesota's ascendancy in two auxiliary businesses: milling and grain handling. Where waterpower and wheat farmers merged, a grinding mill usually sprang up. In Blue Earth County alone over thirty mills had turned wheat into flour by 1878. As early as 1880 Minneapolis had surpassed St. Louis as the nation's leading city in flour production, a position it held until 1930 when Buffalo, New York, outproduced it. Although by 1900 many flour mills had gone out of business or merged, 377 operations produced more than 30 million cwt of flour. Minnesota, and especially Minneapolis, maintained its reputation as the world's milling capital for fifty years not only because of the abundance of spring wheat in the state and its Dakota hinterland but also because of the revolutionary technology (the middlings purifier and the roller mill) that made possible "New Process Flour" which vastly improved uniformity, color, and production.[12]

Hauling wheat to the elevator in Boyd, Lac qui Parle County, about 1910

Even though hundreds of mills shared 1900s flour production, two Minneapolis giants dominated the business and were stretching for national markets. Pillsbury-Washburn Flour Mills, Ltd., created in 1889 when a British syndicate merged C. A. Pillsbury and Company and Washburn Mill Company, had the greatest capacity (29,000 cwt). Washburn-Crosby Company, Inc., maker of Gold Medal Flour, however, surpassed Pillsbury-Washburn in 1909, having greatly increased its Minneapolis output and expanded into Buffalo and Louisville as early as 1903. Both companies reflected the changing structure and nature of the nation's food-centered businesses during the twentieth century. In 1924 Pillsbury Flour Mills Company became publicly owned, after absorbing its British-owned predecessor. In 1928 General Mills was formed as a holding company that assumed ownership of Washburn-Crosby and other related businesses. General Mills and Pillsbury survived the crippling depression of the 1930s by shrewd management and went on during the post-World War II years to become billion-dollar corporations with highly diversified international marketing and processing operations. By the 1980s General Mills had sales exceeding $5 billion and employed over eighty-three thousand people in such diverse business areas as foods, milling, restaurants, toys, and fashion. Pillsbury's almost $4 billion in sales and fifty-six thousand employees represented a broad range of activity, including milling, frozen foods, dough products, grain and feed ingredients, Burger King, and Steak and Ale restaurants.[13]

The diversification that characterized the milling companies after World War I, and especially after World War II, reflected the declining importance of flour production in Minnesota. In 1919 the state's mills turned out products worth over $381 million – more than twice as much as meat-packing, their nearest rival in the manufacturing industries. By 1947 the milling business had fallen off dramatically as pulp and paper, farm machinery, electrical apparatus, and meat-packing surpassed it in production value and number of employees. In 1982 it held fourteenth place, about one-ninth the value of office machines and computers. By then Minneapolis had only two spring wheat flour mills. Pillsbury and General Mills were still the country's leading flour makers, but their mills were elsewhere. Few people used the endearing term for Minneapolis, "the Mill City"; fewer yet remembered seeing the Minneapolis Millers of baseball's American Association.[14]

In the days when flour mills were small, local operations, farmers from the surrounding countryside sold their wagonloads of wheat directly to the miller. With the development of large mills and a railroad network, this procedure was abandoned. Both the Minnesota farmer and the Minnesota miller needed someone to act as a middle agent, someone to buy, store, sell, and ship wheat. At the turn of the century two men dominated the state's grain trade: William Wallace (Will) Cargill and Frank Hutchinson Peavey. When they both opened offices in Minneapolis in the same year, they ensured that it would become the world's leading grain exchange center.

The Cargill grain business had its roots in the small Iowa farm town of Conover where in 1865 young Will Cargill began buying and selling wheat. During the next three years he established four more small warehouses along the McGregor and Western Railroad as its tracks pushed northwestward toward Minnesota. With his brothers Sam, Sylvester, and later James, Will Cargill followed the expanding wheat frontier to Minnesota, setting up headquarters at Albert Lea where the Milwaukee Railroad intersected with the new Southern Minnesota Railroad. In 1884 he established offices and a warehouse in Minneapolis. By 1886 Cargill had established a chain of thirty-one elevators along the Southern from Pipestone, near the South Dakota line, to his headquarters at La Crosse, Wisconsin. In 1910 the Cargill Elevator Company, an 1890 incorporation of several family enterprises, controlled forty-one elevators across southern Minnesota, twenty-eight west of Minneapolis along the Great Northern Railway to Browns Valley, and thirteen in or near the Red River valley. (The family also owned seventy-five in the Dakotas.) In addition Will headed the Cargill Commission Company, the Superior Terminal Elevator Company, which constructed a 2.3-million-bushel terminal at Superior, Wisconsin, and the Terminal Elevator Company, which had a 1-million-bushel facility in Minneapolis. In spite of the apparent strength with which the Cargill enterprise entered the twentieth century, business dealings not related to the grain trade drained financial resources to the point that the successful grain operations (a $2 million business annually by 1909) were in jeopardy. In 1916 the Cargills began a long process of reorganization.[15]

Frank Peavey, like Cargill, began his career buying and selling grain in Iowa, at Sioux City in 1874. He built elevators along the Omaha and the

Wheat pouring from a grain elevator into the hold of a lake freighter in Duluth harbor, about 1935

Chicago–St. Paul–Minneapolis railroads and expanded his business rapidly during the 1870s. When the Minneapolis Millers Association became his largest buyer in 1884, he moved his center of operations to Minneapolis. On March 22, 1894, Peavey sold 3.25 million bushels of wheat to the Pillsbury-Washburn Company – at that time considered to be the largest cash wheat deal ever made in the Northwest and certainly a sign of the magnitude of his business. By the turn of the century he controlled 435 country elevators with 10.25 million bushels capacity and eighteen terminals with storage for 26 million bushels in Minneapolis. Peavey revolutionized the role of the grain middleman. His expansion into Chicago broke the grain buyers' territorial tradition. When boxcars for shipment were in short supply, he organized the Peavey Grain Line Company with five hundred company-owned cars. The quest for world markets led to the Peavey Steamship Company. Disastrous elevator fires prompted experimentation with what would become the accepted construction medium for grain storage: concrete. During the years just before World War I expansion came largely through development of a network of elevators in western Canada – the last wheat frontier. (By 1945 the company owned 373 elevators in Canada.)[16]

The web of elevators that Peavey and Cargill built controlled the lion's share of Minnesota's grain trade in the generation before World War I. In very few areas did the merchants directly compete; both built lucrative empires, and their companies went on to become highly diversified agribusinesses with international markets. During the 1920s Peavey expanded into flour milling (King Midas brand), lumberyards, and feed and fertilizer commerce with the acquisition of Van Dusen Harrington Company. By the 1980s the company had become a subsidiary of Conagra, Inc., which had a sales volume in excess of $3 billion. By 1931 Cargill interests had gone through difficult years of reorganization, placing their operations under a holding company, Cargill, Inc. Half a century later it was Minnesota's largest agribusiness, with revenues of more than $32 billion and a portfolio that included the merchandising and processing of agricultural commodities (among them 300 million bushels of grain in 1983); feed, seed, and fertilizer distribution; feed lots; poultry and beef processing; marketing of industrial products such as steel, resins, and salt; and, in 1987, wholesale petroleum distribution.[17]

The Peavey and Cargill companies must have been apprehensive about the farmers' cooperative movement that began to threaten their positions of supremacy in the grain trade. As early as the 1890s wheat farmers began to organize their own elevators and grain-selling cooperatives in an effort to remedy what they believed to be unfair prices and grading practices. The movement had its roots in North Dakota where growers were weary of their colonial hinterland status. In 1908 the Equity Cooperative Exchange was organized in Minneapolis; three years later it incorporated in North Dakota, hoping to market its grain cooperatively. The Minneapolis Chamber of Commerce, the only market for wheat in the Twin Cities, forbade its members to sell the exchange's grain, so in 1914 it moved across the river, and the St. Paul Grain Exchange came into existence. Three years later the exchange opened a 500,000-bushel terminal in St. Paul, a tiny facility compared to the combined capacities of Cargill and Peavey. By 1918, however, it handled 15 million bushels of wheat from elevators in Minnesota and North Dakota. In 1922 the exchange claimed 17,500 members and owned 80 country elevators, 26 of them in Minnesota. By 1921 Minnesota farmers had built 417 elevators that handled 47 million bushels. Competition with the established grain traders was extremely difficult, however, and in 1923 the exchange went into bankruptcy and operating receivership.[18]

But three years later the Farmers' Union assumed control of the exchange's terminal operations in St. Paul. The Farmers' Union Terminal Association was organized and by 1930 was handling 15 million bushels of wheat, the volume the Equity had marketed in 1918. In 1931 the association sold out to the government's Farmers' National Grain Corporation, an agency established to bolster the sagging farm economy. The national cooperative, however, failed; in 1938 the Farmers' Union organized its second effort at regional cooperative marketing – the Grain Terminal Association (GTA). During the first season GTA handled 17 million bushels, bought 138 rural elevators, and soon began construction of huge terminal elevators in Superior, Minneapolis, and St. Paul. War and postwar farm prosperity stimulated GTA's growth. By the late 1950s it was handling one-fourth (150 million bushels) of the grain that was sold on the Duluth and Minneapolis markets. It owned 148 elevators in Minnesota and the Dakotas, had diversified into lumberyards, and had increased its storage capacity to 20 million bushels. By 1983 when GTA became the Harvest

States Cooperatives after it merged with North Pacific Grain Growers, it had become a diversified agribusiness that handled about 530 million bushels of grain and oil crops annually. Although the farmer-owned cooperative had come a long way from the terrible Thirties, it did only a fraction of the business of Cargill.[19]

Diversification: Dairying, Livestock, and Poultry

A 1900 map that depicts the distribution of dairy cows makes Minnesota look like it has a very bad case of the measles. From it the casual observer might conclude that dairying had become significant to farm income throughout the state. Since most farmers had Bossy or Bessie to produce milk and butter for home use, the pattern is not surprising. An 1896 map that locates creameries, skim stations, and cheese factories more accurately pinpoints those places where farmers had become dependent upon dairy cows as a source of cash. Generally the dairy region stretched from Faribault, Freeborn, and Mower counties on the Iowa border in south-central Minnesota north toward Minneapolis-St. Paul and then west and northwest, north of the Minnesota River valley, up to Otter Tail County. By the 1980s the area of dairy concentration had not changed much. Closely associated with hilly, wooded, less fertile pastureland, the dairy belt in the late twentieth century ranged from extreme southeastern Minnesota (Houston, Fillmore, Winona counties) to the state's west-central region (Otter Tail, Douglas, Stearns counties). Carver County, on the southwest edge of the Twin Cities, was the most intensive dairying county.[20]

Minnesota was a natural agricultural setting for the expansion of dairying. By the 1870s and 1880s the industry was taking on major importance in the southeastern counties; farmers in the southwestern part of the state were slower to turn away from wheat. Technology and new ideas stimulated the process. Oren Gregg, who in 1885 became superintendent of the University of Minnesota's Farmers Institute, came to Minnesota from Vermont. "My grandfather used the cow to turn the grass of the old Green Mountains into butter," he declared. "Why could not I use the cow to turn the grass of the western prairie to butter?" He preached diversification and championed winter dairying, convincing farmers that allowing a cow to freshen in the spring and go dry in the winter was nonsense. Wendelin Grimm, a German immigrant, introduced his "everlasting clover" to Minnesota farms and by the 1920s alfalfa had become a common farmstead word. The centrifugal cream separator, a test for measuring butterfat, the silo – all these innovations promoted the rapid development of dairying.[21]

By 1900 Minnesota farmers had about 754,000 dairy cows that produced 304 million gallons of milk and dairy products valued at over $16 million. A farmer who had ten cows could count on about $220 per year in cash income from their productivity. Ten years later there were more than a million cows in the state and income had doubled. Only wheat and oats brought in more cash. Minnesota had joined Wisconsin, New York, and California as a premier dairy state. Dairy farmers did not experience the tremendous price skids of the 1920s when milk products became the state's top farm-income producer, but the depression of the 1930s did impair that sector's continued growth. Herds peaked at nearly 1.4 million in 1929. During the depression of the 1930s, however, the New Deal's emergency cattle-buying program, supervised by the Department of Agriculture, substantially reduced Minnesota's head count. That, coupled with breed specialization and increased milk production per cow, accounted for the decline of 43 percent between 1929 and 1974. Income per cow as well as statewide dairy income significantly increased, however. In 1982 dairy products continued to lead other farm income with $1.3 billion in sales, about $1,600 annually from each cow. By the late 1980s Minnesota ranked fourth nationally in milk cows and milk production, second in nonfat dry milk, and third in butter production.[22]

Raising beef cattle paralleled the economic growth and geographic development of dairying. Between 1880 and 1900 the numbers of cattle that the census takers classified as primarily for meat production about tripled from 383,505 to more than 1.1 million. The greatest concentrations of beef cattle were quite naturally in the dairy belt, although the far southeastern and southwestern counties, where good grazing land combined with feed crops, tended to lead the state as the twentieth century progressed. Quality increased with breed specialization, feedlots, and the separation of beef from dairy operations. By the 1980s Minnesota had fewer beef cattle than at the turn of the century, but production per animal had tripled. By the 1980s cash receipts for cattle and calves averaged about $1 billion each year, ranking Minnesota tenth nationally.[23]

As spectacularly as dairy and beef cattle numbers increased after 1880, swine statistics grew even more rapidly: from 381,000 in 1880 to 1.4 million in 1900. In the 1800s hog raising was tied to dairying, as farmers fed their skimmed milk to swine. By 1900, however, hog country was established in the state's southern tiers of counties, which had become the northern extension of the nation's corn belt. The grain thrived in the mellowed soil and warm, humid climate of southern Minnesota. Fillmore County, which for many years had led Minnesota in wheat, became the leading corn county by the turn of the century. Used almost entirely as hog feed, corn soared from 14.8 million bushels produced in 1880 to 67.9 in 1910. During that time, in Minnesota as elsewhere in the nation, corn and hogs became inextricably linked in one farming culture. (In the 1930s, when the federal government set up farm programs for individual crops to cut production and raise prices, it organized the corn-hog program, recognizing that reduction of both had to be in tandem.) Although corn cultivation moved northward with the development of shorter-maturing varieties, its heartland remained in the southern counties and the Minnesota River valley. Still used primarily as a feed crop in the mid-1980s, the grain was also sold for starch, oil, and syrup. By 1983 corn production reached 367 million bushels with a cash receipt value of almost $1 billion, placing it as the state's primary crop in value. At the same time, swine numbers ranged around 4 million, representing about $800 million in farm income. Nationally Minnesota ranked third in hog and fourth in corn production.[24]

Sheep and lambs, on the other hand, have significantly declined as important factors in the Minnesota livestock market. In 1910 Minnesotans raised about 600,000 sheep, producing more than 3 million pounds of wool worth about $800,000. Slaughtering generated about $71,000. By 1982 sheep numbers were down to 275,000; the area of concentration had shifted from northern to southwestern Minnesota, although flocks could be found throughout the state. In the mid-1980s farm income from sheep remained fairly constant at about $14.7 million.[25]

Farmers, whether they raised dairy cows, beef cattle, hogs, or sheep, faced a mutual problem – marketing. Cargill and Peavey had developed the concept of the grain handler for wheat, but milk and livestock were quite different matters. The problems of farmers who daily milked their cows were unlike those of farmers who raised cattle, hogs, and sheep. In the mid-1880s the solutions for both groups came about in different ways and through different means. Most dairy farmers turned to farmer-run cooperatives; entrepreneurs in the mold of Cargill and Peavey established centralized marketing for livestock. Not until the twentieth century did livestock raisers band together in a co-op.

Lack of refrigeration and poor roads worked against farmers who wanted to market dairy products on a broader scale. Minnesota dairy farmers solved their problem through the cooperative. The cooperative creamery at Clark's Grove in Freeborn County, organized in 1889–90, quickly became the Minnesota model. It was fashioned after successful operations in Denmark and Iowa, where members delivered milk to their dairy and shared the profits on the basis of the production each generated. The Clark's Grove success (12 million pounds of butter and almost $4 million in profit over forty years) sparked the state's cooperative creamery movement – a movement that the University of Minnesota praised and promoted. Of the state's 664 creameries in 1898, 560 were cooperatives. On the eve of World War I Minnesota's 671 cooperative creameries represented about half of those in the United States.[26]

For the most part, creameries provided milk and butter to a restricted local market. In order to share information and to coordinate marketing as production increased, they organized the Minnesota Co-operative Association in 1911. Dairy farmers, however, needed a statewide network – a large cooperative that could bring Minnesota's dairy products to a broader – perhaps regional, even national – market. Ten years after the marketing co-op began, 320 Minnesota dairy farmers, who represented more than half of the state's cooperative creameries, organized such a statewide venture – Minnesota Cooperative Creameries Association, Inc. The new association hoped to improve and standardize the quality of butter and help market products through existing channels. With a loan of $1,000 and office space from the Farm Bureau, the cooperative orchestrated the pooling of 1,826 carloads of butter, saving the membership more than $215,000. In 1923 the organization began to devise a national marketing strategy, opening sales offices in New York, Chicago, and Philadel-

Cooperative creamery in Milaca, about 1915

phia. In 1924 a contest to find a brand name resulted in "Land O' Lakes" ("Maid O' the West" came in second), and since the brand name soon became better known than that of the co-op, the latter changed its name in 1926 to Land O' Lakes Creameries, Inc. By the end of its first decade Land O' Lakes had opened packaging plants in Duluth and Chicago, had entered the egg and turkey businesses, had posted sales of $52.6 million with assets of almost $7 million, and was handling over 91 million pounds of butter.[27]

Land O' Lakes survived the depression through diversification. In 1929 it established an agricultural service division that provided creamery supplies to member associations and, shortly thereafter, to member farmers. Three large cheese cooperatives that represented ninety-five factories joined in 1934, and a feed and seed division developed a new dry calf meal. After discovering that skim milk retained 70 percent of its food value, the cooperative began converting fluid skim milk to powder. By the end of World War II, it operated twenty-two drying plants and claimed to be the world's largest manufacturer of dry milk. From 1933 to 1940 sales volume grew from under $31 million to nearly $36 million. When the depression ended as America went to war, Land O' Lakes symbolized the success of the cooperative movement.[28]

After World War II Land O' Lakes increased its annual sales from $103 million to well over $2 billion. By 1986 it represented 1,112 member cooperatives and more than nine thousand members to whom $7.6 million in patronage refunds were returned in 1985 alone. Through acquisition and merger, the company entered or expanded its operations in retail milk and ice cream, cheese, dry milk products, meats, fertilizer, seeds, soybean processing, and agricultural supplies. And in 1972, after twenty-two years of cautious deliberation, secret research, and office memoranda that referred only to the "M-72" project, the nation's number-one butter maker announced that it was going to begin production of what for so many years had been a forbidden word around Land O' Lakes – margarine.[29]

By the late twentieth century Land O' Lakes was Minnesota's largest cooperative, but it was not the only one in dairy products. Of Minnesota's

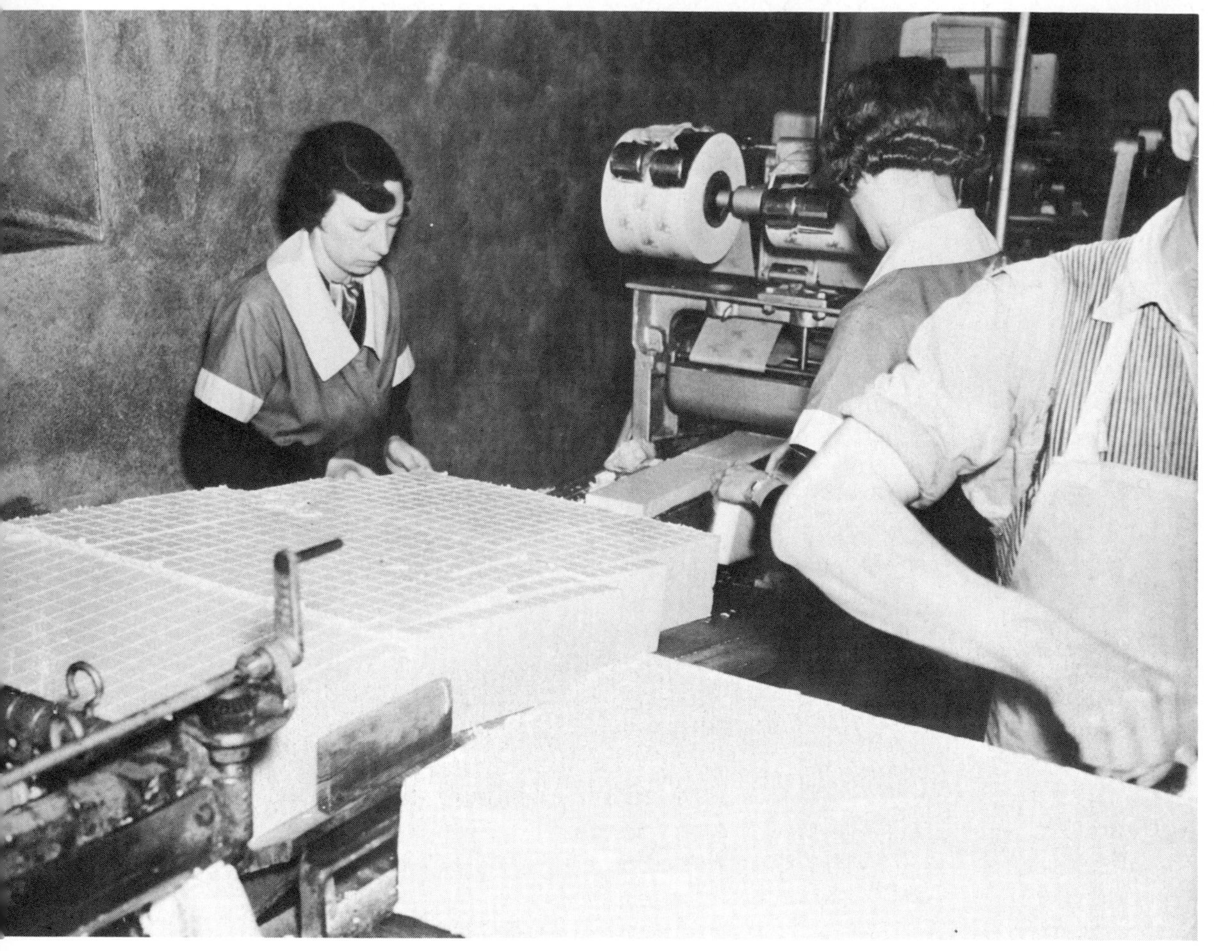

Cutting butter at the Farmers Cooperative Creamery in Fergus Falls, 1937

agribusinesses, American Milk Producers, Inc., Mid-America Dairymen, Inc., and Bongard's Creameries were among the top twenty in sales. Mid-America Dairymen, the nation's second largest dairy cooperative, for example, maintained offices for its northern division in St. Paul, operated a plant in Zumbrota, and had 1,900 member farmers in Minnesota. Noncooperative dairy companies such as the Stroh Brewery Company, Marigold Foods, Inc., Norris Creameries, Inc., Oak Grove Dairy, and the Superior Dairy Fresh Milk Company generated considerably less sales than the farmer-owned cooperatives.[30]

Since the turn of the century the dairy processing industry maintained an important and steady position among the sectors of Minnesota manufacturing. In 1919 it ranked third, behind milling and meat-packing, with $93.6 million in production. Although its standing varied from census to census, largely depending upon the health of the farm economy, by the early 1980s dairy products stood in fifth place, far ahead of milling and one-fourth the size of the state's most productive industry, computers and office machines.[31]

While dairy farmers were moving toward cooperative creameries, beef and hog farmers generally sold their surplus livestock to butcher shops in nearby towns. Large-scale cattle raisers might drive a herd to St. Paul or other railroad centers for shipment to Chicago's Union Stockyards, the terminal market that served the major packinghouses. In 1886 investors, hoping to attract cattle from the Dakotas and Montana as well as Minnesota *and* the large Chicago packing companies, launched the St. Paul Union Stockyards in South St. Paul. The stockyard company provided the facilities and services (food, water, pens, veterinarians, animal managers) for selling and buying livestock. Commission merchants handled sales for a set fee; their task was to strike the best possible price for the producer. At the peak of business after World War II, thirty-six firms worked the yards.[32]

The success of the yards was directly tied to the development of South St. Paul as a meat-packing town. Within a year of the yard's opening Fowler Brothers of Chicago built First Minnesota Provision and Packing Company, and in 1897 Swift and Company entered the competition. Armour and Company completed a $14 million plant that provided thousands of jobs in 1919, testimony to the success of the St. Paul yards. A third Chicago meat giant arrived in 1925 when Cudahy purchased the defunct Farmers Terminal Packing Company, a cooperative that had organized in 1915 but headed for bankruptcy with the collapse of farm prices in the early 1920s.

After the late 1960s the volume and profits of the St. Paul Union Stockyards declined. By the 1980s only seven commission firms operated there due to the drop in volume and a shift toward auction sales. Livestock-order-buying companies handled the purchasing of animals; a single buyer might represent up to thirty packers or processors. The movement of

Union Stockyards in South St. Paul, about 1929

packinghouses to rural areas with lower operating costs left South St. Paul with three: Iowa Pork Industries, Sunstar Beef, and Tan Vo Packing. The rise of trucking and the decline of railroading stimulated the growth of regional auction centers. This decentralization process caused serious problems for the South St. Paul yards – owned in the late 1980s by United Stockyards Corporation, which operated eleven others as well – but it remained a major market. Nearly forty packers from thirteen states bought hogs at the St. Paul stockyards.[33]

Most farmers at the turn of the century were in no position, either in herd size or in finances, to ship their animals to South St. Paul. Their main market remained the local buyer who dealt with them individually, leaving the sellers little bargaining power. As had dairy farmers in the 1880s, many livestock raisers turned to the cooperative concept; in 1908 farmers around Litchfield organized Minnesota's first cooperative shipping association. By the eve of World War I nearly six hundred associations were shipping their cattle, hogs, and sheep to the stockyards for sale in unit lots. In 1917 these groups organized the Minnesota Central Co-Operative Livestock Shippers' Association to look after the welfare of producers in the marketing process. Stock raisers then concluded that they needed a farmer-owned-and-operated commission organization that would ensure fair treatment in the market and patronage refunds to members. With the support of the Farm Bureau, the Equity, and the Grange, the shipping associations in 1921 formed the Central Co-operative Commission Association (later renamed the Central Livestock Association) "to obtain bargaining power through the control of the sale of a large volume." During the first two weeks of operation, the cooperative topped the list of the thirty-five commission firms on volume of sales – a place it still held some sixty years later.[34]

The terminal market represents the end of livestock raising for the farmer/rancher and the beginning of processing for the meat-packer. By luring the large Chicago-based companies to town, the St. Paul Union Stockyards drastically increased the demand for local cattle and hogs. It was, however, in the heart of southern Minnesota's corn-hog country that Minnesota's most enduring and successful meat-packing business developed – George A. Hormel and Company. In 1887 Friedrich and Hormel, "Butchers and Packers," opened its doors in Austin. Four years later the partnership was dissolved and George A. Hormel and Company was born. At the turn of the century Hormel was slaughtering over 32,000 hogs annually, had expanded the plant, and recorded sales of more than seven hundred thousand dollars. It had opened a distribution center in Minneapolis and was preparing to establish several branches including ones at Duluth, Chicago, San Antonio, Atlanta, and Dallas. Hormel's pork products were gaining a national reputation. By 1917 Hormel was slaughtering 476,748 hogs, fifteen times its turn-of-the-century kill.[35]

During the 1920s, in a pioneer venture, the company began marketing canned ham, which took the market by storm. New branches in San Francisco, Seattle, and Mobile helped Hormel become a well-known brand, popularized by national advertising. Contrary to the experiences of most packers during the depression, Hormel sales increased – from $25 million in 1933 to $75 million in 1941. Imaginative, depression-oriented products played a paramount role in that growth. Hormel participated in a federal program to provide surplus food to needy people, making a beef-and-gravy product that was canned in twenty-four-ounce tins. When the program ended, the company was left with millions of empty tins. It filled those tins with its own beef stew (later Dinty Moore). A whole meal in a twenty-four-ounce tin for fifteen cents – a real bargain in the depression days of 1935. The stew's success led to other "poor man's dishes": chili con carne and in 1937 the revolutionary canned spiced ham – SPAM. Three years later 70 percent of the urban American public was eating this economical and handy product. During World War II SPAM became a ubiquitous food for the armed forces, giving rise to its own genre of humor. Cook to mess sergeant: "I've got it. Something really different. We'll slice SPAM lengthwise." After World War II Hormel expanded its products and facilities nationally and internationally, selling frozen, fresh, cured, smoked, and canned meats. Sales moved from $126 million in 1946 to almost $2 billion in 1986.[36]

Although technology, changing life-style, and new approaches to breeding, marketing, and processing had a significant impact on all Minnesota's livestock raising and allied manufacturing, no segment of the farm economy experienced a more revolutionary change than did poultry. "Poultry raising in 1909 was widely distributed in Minnesota," observed an economist at the University of Minnesota in 1915, "being a side industry often carried on by the women." More than forty years later, according to an economic geographer, things had not changed: "Chickens usually are considered the duty of the wife and so become private income for the women in the family." The consumption of poultry, too, followed long-standing, almost ritualistic, eating habits: chicken every Sunday and turkey on Thanksgiving.[37]

By the end of the 1960s the image of the farm woman feeding the chickens and pocketing the egg money had vanished. Instead of having a few chickens on most farms, a few large-scale egg producers that were scattered around the state dominated the market. The numbers of laying hens dropped considerably, but because of highly scientific mass production, the output of eggs increased. By the early 1980s eggs had become a $100 million business.[38]

Chicken on Sunday and turkey on Thanksgiving went the way of the farm wife's egg money. A well-designed national campaign and a growing emphasis on low- or no-fat diets increased substantially the demand for poultry – especially turkey. Minnesota's poultry industry represented about $320 million in farm marketing receipts by 1982 – almost 14 percent of all livestock, including dairy income. That year the state was second in the nation (behind North Carolina) in turkey production, raising slightly more than one out of every six birds. Like the egg business, turkey and meat chicken (broiler) production became the domain of a small number of producers. In 1974, for example, sixty-two farms, each with a half-million dollars in sales, sold over 14 million turkeys, 63 percent of Minnesota's total. During the 1960s both broiler and turkey raising began to concentrate in central and west-central Minnesota.[39]

Willmar in Kandiyohi County, located in the heart of the west-central turkey country, provides a superb case study of agricultural integration, wherein hatching, growing, supply distribution, special feeds, and processing came together to create an intense agribusiness community. After World War II Kandiyohi and adjacent Swift, Meeker, and Stearns counties experienced the greatest increases in turkey count; in the 1980s they led in the state's production. The Willmar Poultry Company began to specialize in hatching poults in 1947. By 1970 it was producing 8 million of them. Supplied by several dozen independent breeder-flock owners, the company, billed as the world's largest turkey hatchery, hatched over 19 million poults in 1986, providing more than half of Minnesota's and North Dakota's gobblers. By the late 1980s the company also operated several large turkey farms and a complete supply division. In 1987, for example, the multimillion-dollar turkey-feed plant of Farm Service Elevator Company, which the owners of Willmar Poultry organized in 1954, turned out a thousand tons of feed per day.[40]

The development of turkey processing in Willmar was a logical outgrowth of these ventures. In 1949 Earl B. Olson, who had made and lost money in turkey growing, established Earl Olson's Farmer's Produce Company. Renamed Jennie-O (for his daughter) to create more popular appeal, the company led the campaign to make turkey an everyday meat. In addition to processing a boneless turkey for the army, Jennie-O developed the concept of packaging turkey breasts, roasts, frozen parts, and wieners. As of 1985 the firm raised 3 million turkeys on its twenty-five farms and also manufactured feed. Its marketing system included twenty-two foreign countries.[41]

Of the agricultural processing industries, meat has held the most consistently significant position among Minnesota manufacturers. By 1919 it ranked only behind milling; after the decline of the flour industry, it became the state's largest employer and greatest generator of business income. Even though the Chicago giants abandoned South St. Paul, smaller, decentralized plants and Minnesota's own giants, Hormel and Jennie-O, kept production high. Only the rise of the computer industry moved meat products into a second-place ranking among the state's manufacturing industries.[42]

The Farmer Plants for Oil

Because flax gained a reputation for being an excellent "breaking crop" on virgin ground, farmers who moved westward to open new agricultural territory devoted acres to the plant. By the early 1800s American farmers primarily planted flax for seed rather than for fiber, since cotton had replaced linen as the most widely used fabric for cloth manufacturing. At the beginning of the twentieth century the most profitable product derived from flaxseed was linseed oil (twenty pounds per fifty-six pound bushel), which was used as a "drying oil vehicle" in items such as paint, varnish, oilcloth, linoleum, lacquer, printing ink, shoe polish, and patent leather. The remaining thirty-six pounds per bushel were processed into protein meal used in livestock feed, much of which was exported to Europe.[43]

A few Minnesota farmers, however, did produce flax for fiber, especially around Meadowlands in St. Louis County. Their market was Duluth's Western Linen Company (later named Western Rug Company and then Klearflax Looms), which was organized in 1909 to make yarn for New England mills. During the life of the business, which stretched into the 1950s, it manufactured napkins, towels, and carpets and heated its sizable factory with flax straw and other manufacturing wastes.[44]

Small processing plants that extracted oil from the flaxseed sprang up adjacent to growing areas. As flax moved west, so did the linseed oil industry. From 1891 to 1899 Minnesota led the nation in flaxseed production; in 1905, although second to North Dakota in production, its five largest linseed oil processing plants did $7 million in business. By 1919 income totaled $33 million.[45]

The state's first plant opened in 1862 at Minneapolis, which later became a major production center. Incorporated as the Minnesota Linseed Oil Company in 1870, it was the state's largest processor during the late nineteenth century. Its companion company, Minnesota Linseed Oil Paint Company (later Minnesota Paints), pioneered in prepared paints. In 1899 Midland Linseed Products Company opened for business, and three years later John Daniels organized the Daniels Linseed Company. In 1905 George A. Archer, who had gained experience with the St. Paul Linseed Works, joined the firm, forming what would soon become an industry giant, Archer-Daniels Linseed Company. Smaller plants developed outside the Twin Cities. In 1902, for example, Red Wing business interests organized the Zumbro Linseed Oil Company in response to flax farmers' needs; the company remained locally owned until 1921 when Pittsburgh Plate Glass Company purchased it.[46]

The thriving industry assured Minnesota as well as Dakota farmers of a market for their flaxseed. Minnesota or North Dakota led the nation in production between 1921 and 1950; the North Star state held first place for eighteen of those years. In 1931, for example, Minnesota farmers harvested 6,027,000 bushels, more than half the national production, and in 1948, 19,100,000 bushels, over a third of the nation's harvest. Although flaxseed was grown throughout the state, the lion's share came from the tiers of counties adjacent to the Dakotas, with the southwestern counties accounting for well over half of the crop.[47]

Until the 1930s Minnesota farmers had little use for flax straw. Because it rotted so slowly, most farmers burned it, enriching the soil as a fertilizer. Archer-Daniels-Midland (Archer-Daniels had acquired Midland in 1923) experimented with the processing of flax for its fiber to be used in the manufacture of paper. The company modernized an old processing plant (likely linseed) in Winona and by the late 1930s was in full operation, adding to the demand for flax. Kimberly-Clark Corporation opened fiber-processing plants in Windom and Breckenridge; the plants shipped most of their production to North Carolina for use in the manufacture of cigarette paper. A by-product of flax straw, "shives," became marketable to wallboard and insulation manufacturers.[48]

The demand for linseed oil, however, began to decrease gradually in the late 1950s and rapidly in the 1960s. Vinyl floors replaced linoleum; quick-drying acrylic paint became popular; new finishes started to edge out varnish. By the 1960s linseed oil production was half what it had been in the 1920s. In 1960 Archer-Daniels-Midland closed its processing plants, arranging to purchase what oil the company needed from its competitors. The decline of the linseed oil industry brought a corresponding decline in flax farming. By 1966 Minnesota production had dipped to just under 4 million bushels, about 16 percent of the national figure and about one-fifth of its peak seasons in the late 1940s. The 1980s witnessed the near-end of the state's linseed processing business. In 1961 GTA had purchased the Minnesota Linseed Oil Company, essentially to give its members a market. In 1986 the plant closed; there was no demand for what once had been a sought-after commodity. That year national flax production was about 11.5 million bushels – little more than half of Minnesota's bumper crops forty years earlier.[49]

As flax and linseed oil profits declined, soybeans and sunflowers became viable alternatives as cash crops. John Evans, who farmed near Montevideo, had experimented with soybeans as early as 1917, and during the 1930s Minnesota farmers, especially in the lower third of the state, planted soybeans as a green manure crop as part of the Agricultural Adjustment Administration's soil building programs. Before 1935 farmers who harvested the beans generally used them for seed or feed. Soybeans were eventually recognized as a protein source of "awesome potential," according to historian Kenneth D. Ruble. The right beans under the right conditions yield a 74 percent protein concentrate, a finding that, by midcentury, dictated the bean's primary uses: meal and oil.[50]

Because of high transportation costs, the development of local processing was essential if soybeans were to be profitable to Minnesota farmers. Livestock raisers provided an excellent market for soybean meal. The oil, until 1951 the most valuable soy product, for the most part was used in foods such as shortening, margarine, and salad oils. The Archer-Daniels-Midland Company pioneered a crushing process at its Minneapolis linseed oil plant during the late 1930s. In 1939 Mankato business people organized and erected a processing plant that could crush forty tons per day. During World War II the plant ran at capacity to meet the nation's demand for fat substitutes, and in 1943 the Cooperative Poultry Association of Washington acquired it to ensure an adequate supply of meal. Wartime pressure fostered two additional plants at Lakeville in Dakota County and Preston in Fillmore.[51]

World War II also had a dramatic impact on the domestic production of soybeans. Because the war disrupted normal channels of trade and created a new home-front demand for soy oil, the processing industry mushroomed. In response to new demand and excellent prices, corn-belt farmers shifted significant acreage from barley and oats to soybeans. Although Minnesota-grown beans contained a lower oil content than those grown farther south, farmers in south-central Minnesota between the Iowa border and the Minnesota River joined the move toward soybeans. By 1949 about 20 percent of Minnesota's farms had acreage devoted to them, producing about 13 million bushels and elevating soybeans to the state's third-ranking cash crop.

The importance of soybean meal to the Minnesota feed industry was made very clear in 1945 when Archer-Daniels-Midland Company cut off its supply to the Hubbard Milling Company of Mankato in order to stock its own new feed-manufacturing plant. Facing a severe crisis and possibly the ruin of its lucrative and prominent feed division, Hubbard in 1946 purchased the Preston Soya Company, which immediately became the company's "brightest spot on the horizon," remembered Charles B. MacLeod, then president. Hubbard saved its feed line and protected itself in what was becoming a fiercely competitive market.[52]

By 1951 farmers and processors had raised Minnesota to sixth among the states in soybean production, about 6 percent of national output. That year Minnesota's eight plants crushed almost 10 million bushels of beans – only 2 million short of their annual capacity. After the 1950s the value of soybeans to farmers, processors, and manufacturers increased substantially. Between 1958 and 1982 the state's soybean production jumped from about 54 million to about 175 million bushels, and its value increased from about $107 million to $943 million. The soybean changed the face of southern Minnesota agriculture. By the 1980s it had become Minnesota's second cash crop, not far behind corn and twice the value of third-place wheat.[53]

Like soybeans, sunflowers became an important Minnesota crop during the years that followed World War II. With the increased demand for sunflower seeds as a source of oil and for use in the confectionery industry, production grew rapidly, especially in the 1970s when tonnage hit 62,000 on its way to 132,000 in the early 1980s. Minnesota farmers in the upper Red River valley, particularly Wilkin and Traverse counties, grew most of the state's sunflowers, finding that the crop rotated well with grains and provided an attractive income in times of sagging wheat prices. In 1982 sunflowers ranked as the state's fifth source of farm income behind corn, soybeans, wheat, and sugar beets. In farm-receipt value, however, sunflowers generated $96 million in 1982 – only about 10 percent of soybean income.[54]

Two agribusinesses developed to handle the crop: oil and seed processing. Much of the crop for oil, the most important product, was crushed at plants in Hastings (Archer-Daniels-Midland) or in North Dakota at West Fargo (Cargill) and Enderlin (Sun Products). The resulting crude oil was sold to food plants, largely for use in salad and cooking oils, shortening, and margarine. The seed meal left after crushing was processed primarily for feed or as an additive to wheat flour. Dahlgren and Company, incorporated in Crookston in 1962, was by the late 1980s Minnesota's leading promoter, processor, and supplier of sunflowers as edible seed, as well as a provider of hybrid seeds to a national market. A subsidiary of Sanofi, Inc., a French firm, Dahlgren maintained research and seed-conditioning facilities in Crookston as well as plants in Fargo and Lisbon, North Dakota. Its rise in the industry was a direct response to the farmer's decision to diversify into sunflowers.[55]

The Variety of the Landscape: Specialty Crops

Throughout the twentieth century, livestock, poultry, dairy products, the oil crops, and wheat accounted for the lion's share of Minnesota's farm income. Yet to farmers and related agribusinesses in various parts of the state, more specialized crops meant economic diversity and well-being. By late in the century commercial apple orchards dotted the southeastern countryside; wild rice – paddy grown and natural – brought a bountiful harvest in the northern lake country; home-grown grapes provided the Alexis Bailly Vineyard near Hastings with quality table wine. Vegetables, potatoes, sugar beets, and malting barley, however, were the most significant specialty crops and supported profitable processing industries.[56]

Vegetables

Vegetable gardens for home use blanketed the state, but the canning industry gave birth to commercial growing. Since the turn of the century, this endeavor has been centered in south-central Minnesota in counties such as Dodge, Steele, Faribault, Le Sueur, and Scott. By the 1980s Minnesota ranked second in the nation in sweet corn production and third in green peas. Sweet corn provided the agricultural economy annually with more than $38 million in farm income and a high return per acre.[57]

The M. A. Gedney Company is a good example of the effects of the factory on the farm. Gedney, which began pickling operations at Minneapolis in 1881, successfully encouraged farmers to grow substantial cucumber crops. The company contracted with growers, many with small plots, for their harvest. Gedney got its cucumbers and the farmers earned a little extra money. By the late 1970s Gedney had contracts with more than two thousand farmers. Similarly, in Le Sueur around the turn of the century, promoter John Silver Hughes talked some people into starting a canning factory. The town needed industry, and the Minnesota River valley was well suited for white sweet corn. The Minnesota Valley Canning Company (Green Giant Company after 1950) packed almost twelve thousand cases of corn in its first year, 1903. Area farmers had an expanding market for their sweet corn and, after 1907, their peas.[58]

The vegetable-canning and -preserving business grew from sixteen plants in 1910 to thirty-seven in 1947, about the time when freezing began to be a factor in vegetable preparation. Three companies, two with regional sales (Gedney and Owatonna Canning Company) and one with national and world sales (Green Giant), reflect the growth of the industry as

Workers at the M. A. Gedney Company pickling and food-packing business, Minneapolis, about 1912

well as its technological and business changes in the twentieth century. In 1893 the *St. Paul Trade Journal* reported that Gedney had packed more than twenty thousand barrels of pickles in five varieties. The company soon expanded from pickles to packing related foods such as peppers, sauerkraut, beets, and vinegar. In 1958 it consolidated its operations into a new plant near Chaska, southwest of Minneapolis in the Minnesota River valley, where eighty-five varieties of pickled vegetables constituted more than 60 percent of its business. Owatonna Canning Company, which began processing vegetables in 1911, operated five canneries throughout southern Minnesota in the late 1980s. It grew its own asparagus, green and wax beans, and pumpkin on company-controlled land but contracted with farmers for about half of its corn and peas. The firm distributed its Festal brand canned goods throughout the Upper Midwest. Because the canning of locally grown fresh vegetables is necessarily seasonal, Owatonna contracted with Hormel to can some of its products (such as Dinty Moore beef stew) in order to operate on a year-round basis. The Minnesota Valley Canning Company stayed with corn and peas for thirty years before branching out rapidly into other vegetables and establishing packing plants outside of Minnesota. As a leader in technology and hybrid development, the company entered the frozen food market in 1961 with revolutionary flavor-tight cooking pouches and inaugurated overseas sales. The Green Giant Company moved in and out of the red-meat and garden-center businesses; first and foremost its reputation and sales rested on vegetable processing, even after its acquisition by Pillsbury in 1979.[59]

Potatoes

Before the 1880s the price for potatoes was so low that farmers could not depend on the crop for much cash income. Most farmers grew potatoes for their own use or to barter in town for kerosene or flour. The rapid popu-

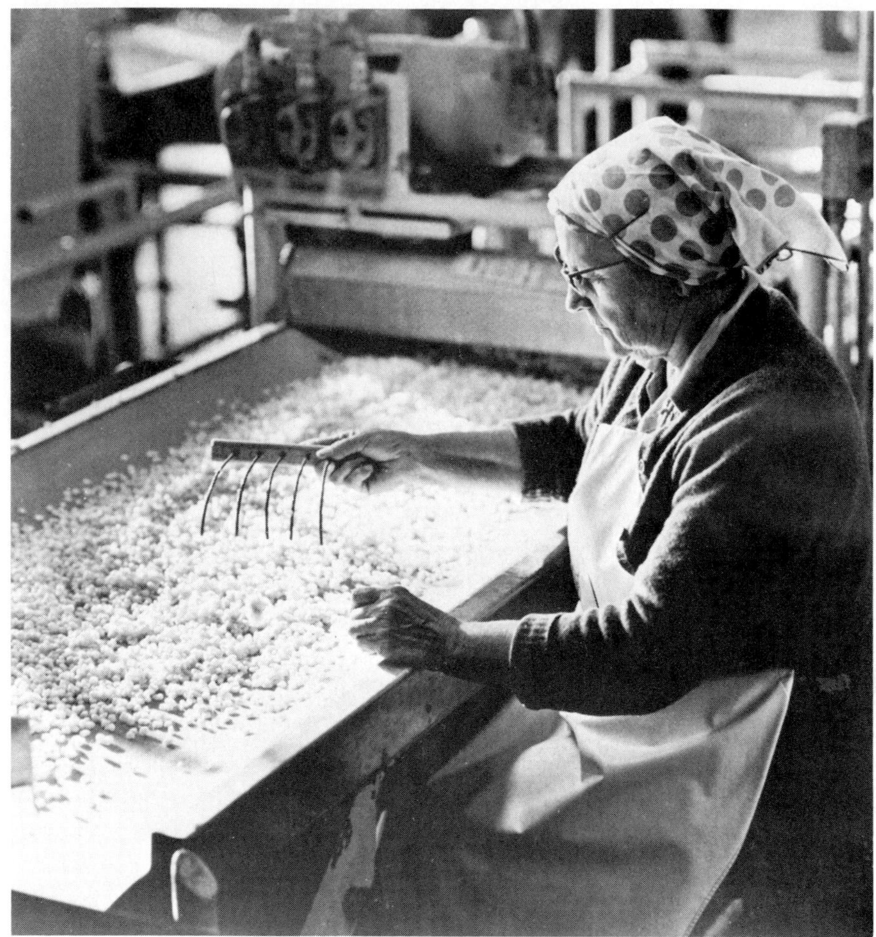

Inspecting corn kernels at the Green Giant Company in Le Sueur, about 1968

lation increase of Minneapolis and St. Paul, however, changed that; as the urban market mushroomed, a specialized potato district developed in the counties (especially Anoka, Isanti, and Chisago) immediately north of the Twin Cities. So fast did potato growing catch on that in 1889 a Minneapolis produce firm shipped one thousand carloads to New England alone. Potato growing remained concentrated near the Twin Cities until after 1900 when farmers in Clay County around Moorhead, in a step toward crop diversification, began raising them as a cash alternative to wheat. (Wheat acreage in that region declined 30 to 40 percent during the century's first decade.) The Red River valley's potato acreage increased phenomenally between 1900 and 1920; for example, in Clay County it jumped from about 3,500 to 31,600 acres, Norman, from 850 to 10,000, and Polk, from 1,600 to 14,600. During World War I potatoes began to reach the limits of their role in the area's diversification scheme when farmers devoted about 55,000 acres to the crop. Between 1980 and 1984 growers there averaged about 51,000 acres per year; Minnesota's total acreage was about 77,000. Outside of the valley, potato growing remained intensive north of the Twin Cities, especially in Sherburne, Isanti, and Anoka counties and spread farther away to Freeborn and Pope. Minnesota's output in the late 1980s translated into about 11.6 million cwt and $60 million in marketing receipts. Compared to the 7.3 million acres in corn or 5.3 million in soybeans, potato's domain was puny, but its economic impact on those counties where potatoes diversified the economy was significant. On the Minnesota side of the Red River, nine wash plants were spread throughout the valley's potato country, and one processing plant in Otter Tail County (along with those in Grand Forks and Grafton, North Dakota) turned potatoes not destined for the retail trade into frozen products and chips.[60]

Barley

The formula, wheat therefore milling, does not follow to barley therefore brewing. In 1880, when the number of Minnesota breweries peaked at 132, the state's farmers produced 3 million bushels of barley, most of which was feed rather than malting quality. Barley production hit 47 million bushels in 1930 during Prohibition and remained generally in the low 40 millions into the 1980s. Although nearby sources of excellent barley for malting were essential to the development of early breweries, other factors loomed more important in the rapid growth of brewing centers and beer production in Minnesota. Cold Spring Brewing and Mineral Water Company, one of the few small brewers that still operated in the late 1980s, is a case in point. Michael Sargel, a German immigrant, founded the brewery in 1874 in Cold Spring, not far from St. Cloud. Although proximity to good barley in the Red River valley kept the cost of raw materials at a minimum, the quality of the natural spring water and the concentration of German-born people in the surrounding countryside were much more important to the success of the venture. For the most part, German immigrants founded breweries in German areas throughout Minnesota. Names like Hamm, Gluek, Hauenstein, Schell, and Fitger dominated Minnesota's brewing business.[61]

By 1900 the number of breweries had declined to ninety-four, closely following the national trend toward consolidation and larger facilities. Production, however, more than doubled during the 1890s to more than 700,000 barrels, almost 2 percent of the national figure, ranking Minnesota thirteenth among the states. Access to capital for modernization and expansion and a transportation system that facilitated marketing allowed Minneapolis and St. Paul to dominate the state's industry. In 1900 Twin Cities brewers had a capacity twice that of actual beer production and accounted for more than half of all beer brewed in Minnesota. The Theodore Hamm Brewing Company alone produced just under one-third of all Minnesota beer at that time. The years between 1900 and the advent of national prohibition in 1919 were difficult for most Minnesota brewers, although production reached a record 1.6 million barrels in 1915. Increased competition within the state and with out-of-state firms sparked price cutting and other cutthroat practices. Less capital-intensive breweries fell by the wayside, reducing the number to fifty-one in 1919. Prohibitionists increasingly attacked the saloon and the beer that it peddled. Local option

Harvest hands shocking bundles of barley on a demonstration farm in Wilkin County, 1938

began "drying up" parts of western Minnesota. Beer production plummeted to less than 500,000 barrels.[62]

In January 1920 the brewing of beer came to an abrupt end. Companies either had to sell their premises or develop alternative products. The small brewers closed; the larger ones kept their corporate structures intact, waiting for the day that the "noble experiment" would end. The Theodore Hamm Company produced near beer, syrups, confectioners supplies, and corncob pipes. Its master brewer took a course on ice-cream making. Cold Spring marketed mineral water, soda pop, and near beer, while August Schell Brewing Company of New Ulm made near beer and jobbed candy and soft drinks.[63]

When Prohibition ended in 1933, twenty-five Minnesota breweries rushed into production, and within two years the peak output of 1915 had been surpassed. In spite of, or perhaps because of, the depression, folks were ready for a brew. The advent of cans worked against the small brewers who lacked the capital for new machinery and expansion into interstate marketing, suddenly feasible because canned beer was relatively light and easy to transport. After World War II the Minnesota brewing industry contributed to the nationwide trend toward consolidation and centralization. In 1945 nineteen breweries produced about 2.5 million barrels; in 1970 six produced 4.5 million. Out-of-state companies began to buy up the Minnesota industry. By 1980 only four Minnesota breweries were in operation, and of those only the small Cold Spring and August Schell businesses remained Minnesota owned. A slight resurgence occurred toward the end of that decade, however, as three "microbreweries"– companies content to produce less than 10,000 barrels per year–opened in the Twin Cities.[64]

For those farmers who specialized in malting barley, the brewing industry meant good income. Because brewers paid a premium price, malting barley doubled in price as beer production soared during the first decade of the century. When commercial brewing once again began during the depression, the industry emphasized the positive impact of beer production in the state: thousands of jobs, millions in tax revenue, and enriched income to farmers. Under headlines such as "Beer Opens Barley Market to Farmers" and "Barley Brings Cash to Farms," newspapers reported that Prof. W. W. Brookins, director of the state university's "Barley Schools," told growers that "the return of beer to Minnesota has opened up a splendid market. . . . Malting grade barley brings a premium of approximately 25¢ a bushel over feed barley." In peak post-World War II production years Minnesota breweries used about 10 percent of the state's total barley crop; the going ratio was one bushel of barley for one barrel of beer.[65]

Sugar Beets

When the state's first sugar beet processing plant was built at St. Louis Park in 1898, no one dreamed that by the 1980s Minnesota would lead the nation in acres devoted to the white beet. Farmers would have to prove that a greater cash return per acre could be made in beets than in the established grain crops and would have to compete with rivals in states such as California, where growers employed a controlled water system through irrigation. Turn-of-the-century efforts to establish a sugar beet industry stumbled when Minnesota's small processing plant burned in 1905, and the salvaged machinery found a new home in California.[66]

The American Beet Sugar Company (after 1934 American Crystal Sugar), a Denver-based corporation, and agricultural experiment station experts were certain, however, that sugar beets could become a cash crop alternative for farmers, especially in the Minnesota and Red River valleys. By 1910 the Carver County Sugar Company (later Minnesota Sugar Company) had a beet plant in operation at Chaska; farmers in that area raised about twenty-four thousand tons that year. When western Minnesota growers incorporated as the Red River Sugar Company in 1924 in order to build the state's second refinery at East Grand Forks under the aegis of the Minnesota Sugar Company, the area's farmers were more than eager to turn from wheat to beets due to depressed grain prices. Meanwhile, American Beet Sugar's interest in the region grew. It bought up several midwestern companies, including Minnesota Sugar, and completed the East Grand Forks plant in 1926. Because of capacity limitations, the

Trucks lined up at a sugar beet processing plant in East Grand Forks, 1937

processing company entered into production contracts with farmers, a practice still in force in the 1980s, establishing a unique farmer-company relationship.[67]

The agricultural boom and worldwide demand for sugar after World War II stimulated the growth of the industry. American Crystal erected two additional plants on the Minnesota side of the Red River valley, in Moorhead (1948) and Crookston (1954); each could handle 4,800 tons per day. Minnesota farmers also contracted with the North Dakota operations at Drayton, Hillsboro, and Wahpeton. The closing of the Chaska plant due to obsolescence and financial difficulties in 1971 created a serious problem for growers along the Minnesota River – from Renville County northwestward to Swift County – the heart of that valley's beet raising. The three hundred farmers who belonged to the Southern Minnesota Beet Growers Association found themselves without a market; they decided to form a cooperative and built their own refinery. Overcoming organizational and financial problems, the Southern Minnesota Beet Sugar Cooperative sliced its first beet in its Renville plant on October 14, 1975. During the next decade the cooperative's 310 members in fifteen counties planted about fifty-seven thousand acres in beets annually, providing about 11,000 cwt of sugar per day. In the meantime the Red River Valley Sugarbeet

Growers Association, worried by a decade of retrenchment and plant closings, took steps to secure its future. In 1973, after several years of negotiation and fundraising, the growers purchased the American Crystal Sugar Company and reincorporated as a cooperative. The new management moved its headquarters to Moorhead and assumed ownership of the East Grand Forks, Crookston, Moorhead, and Drayton plants. In 1975 it merged with the Red River Valley Co-op and acquired its plant at Hillsboro.[68]

Because plant capacity dictated crop acreage, annual production remained fairly constant. By the mid-1980s Minnesota's beet growers planted 260,000 to 278,000 acres, and the state's four processing plants annually refined about 9 million cwt of sugar from about 4.5 million tons. Sugar beets ranked fourth among the crops in farm cash receipts; its $210 million return in 1982 was the highest per acre of any commodity. In addition, two by-products, dried beet pulp for feed and beet molasses for yeast and chemicals, provided revenue for the cooperatives. Sugar officials estimated that the beet industry generated close to $300 million in economic benefits to Minnesota.[69]

The Business of Agriculture

Minnesota's geographic position as a transitional region between the corn-hog and dairying-cattle territory to the east and south and the wheat and flax land to the west assured it a high degree of diversification. For example, in 1984 Minnesota ranked among the top five states in sixteen of nineteen categories of crop, poultry, and livestock production. In total farm cash receipts it stood in fifth place.[70]

In absolute terms farm production steadily increased after the turn of the century, but the growing and processing of food products, especially after World War II, declined in relation to the rest of Minnesota's economy. Although wild swings in farm prices sometimes distorted agricultural statistics, during the 1950s manufacturing clearly surpassed farming as the state's leading generator of wealth and consistently increased its margin of value. By 1982 farming produced income about 20 percent that of manufacturing. The number of people employed in farming dropped over 44 percent between 1955 and 1980, while other sectors showed considerable gains: services, 215 percent; retail-wholesale trade, 95 percent; manufacturing, 70 percent. Although meat-packing and dairy-product making remained significant factors in the manufacturing sector, food processing as a whole gradually declined. Between 1947 and 1982 the number of people who were employed in food processing dropped from 46,600 to 41,000 (from 26 to 12 percent of those employed in all manufacturing). During the same time, the value of food products decreased from 27 to 16 percent of all manufacturing.[71]

The impact of these developments in farming and food processing was, of course, greater than the "statistics of decline" indicate. Farming supported a broad spectrum of agribusinesses that were not involved in processing; in 1985 these included sixteen firms in animal health-care products and breeding, fifteen in custom application of chemicals, thirteen in export services, fourteen in farm structures, seventy-seven in equipment manufacturing, and thirty-five in supply distribution. Some were small and employed few people. American Breeder Service at Forest Lake, for example, paid seven workers. Some were very large, did gigantic business, and employed hundreds. CENEX (Farmers Union Central Exchange, Inc.) handled $1.4 billion in sales and had 1,200 employees. The agribusinesses that served the state's farmers depended upon a healthy farm economy. Agricultural troubles in the 1980s hurt business. According to a Minnesota agricultural economist, one out of five farm-machinery dealerships closed its doors between 1981 and 1986, and one-third of all agribusinesses were "in trouble."[72]

Many Minnesota main streets depended upon the farm economy for survival. Forty percent of Minnesota's counties in 1986 remained almost totally dependent upon farm income. That year State Auditor Arne Carlson stressed that direct link when he ventured to say that "it's not unlikely that one or two Minnesota counties will be facing [the equivalent] of bankruptcy." Agricultural economists in the late 1980s tended to be pessimistic about the future of Minnesota farming. They viewed the prosperous 1970s as a "blip in a long-term adjustment for agriculture and rural communities." Yet hope persisted in rural Minnesota. "It isn't all gloom and doom in the agricultural business," observed Marlyn Buss, the manager of Farmfest '86 in Lake Crystal. Perhaps the owner of a children's clothing store in Windom best summed up rural Minnesota's attitude: "We'll just hang on for awhile, and I'm sure it's going to get better."[73]

Throughout the twentieth century farmers attempted to gain a measure of control over their markets. In spite of processor contracts, cooperative enterprises, and government assistance, however, they made little headway. As producers of raw materials, they have had to take what others determined their produce was worth. When agricultural prices went down, farmers had to harvest more to maintain a stable income, often setting off a supply-demand spiral that was detrimental to themselves. Shifting to new crops provided only short-term solutions to overproduction and low prices. The sunflower and soybean markets, for example, boomed with the demand for oil during and after World War II. But those prices began to sag as more and more farmers moved into production, and by the late 1970s oil-crop growers had no advantage in the marketplace.

On the other hand, most agricultural marketing and processing businesses, although they depended upon the produce of the field and barn, grew and prospered – even during the dark days of the 1930s. Sometimes adversely affected by farm-price swings, corporations such as Hormel, Cargill, and Pillsbury nevertheless held much more control over the business of agriculture than did individual farmers. Corporate structures guaranteed them flexibility and a measure of control over their economic destinies that farmers lacked. As manufacturers of finished products, they were able to adjust to supply and demand and to determine the prices for their processed food items. Pillsbury turned farmers' wheat into a wide variety of new shapes and tastes for the consuming public. Hormel molded and mixed pork into dozens of shapes, textures, and flavors in its competition for supermarket sales. Cargill, once tied to the marketing of wheat, diversified into nonagricultural activities such as steel marketing and wholesale petroleum distribution. The twentieth century brought dramatic and sudden changes to Minnesota agriculture and intensified the interdependence of farming, marketing, and processing. But of the businesses of agriculture, farming remained the most precarious.

NOTES

1. *Minneapolis Star and Tribune*, Oct. 13, 1985, p. 3D.

2. Ann Ryan, "The Logical Choice," *Corporate Report Minnesota*, May 1984, p. 95–97; *Albert Lea Evening Tribune*, Mar. 30, 1984, p. 1C; *Des Moines Register*, Oct. 19, 1986, p. 1F; *Minneapolis Star and Tribune*, Feb. 19, 1984, p. 12A, 13A. For another perspective on this interdependence, see David L. Nass, "The Rural Experience," *this volume*, 129–54.

3. John R. Borchert and Neil C. Gustafson, *Atlas of Minnesota Resources and Settlement* (Minneapolis: Center for Urban and Regional Affairs, University of Minnesota, 1980), 63. See also D. Jerome Tweton, "The Golden Age of Agriculture, 1897–1917," *North Dakota History* 37 (Winter 1970): 41–56.

4. Prices reflect the national average and are based upon U.S. Census Bureau, *Historical Statistics of the United States, Colonial Times to 1957* (Washington, D.C.: U.S. Government Printing Office, 1960), 291–97.

5. James A. Shideler, *Farm Crisis, 1919–1923* (Berkeley: University of California Press, 1957); Theodore Saloutos, *The American Farmer and the New Deal* (Ames: Iowa State University Press, 1982), 5–13; U.S. Census Bureau, *1964 United States Census of Agriculture*, vol. 1, part 15, p. 7; U.S., *Census*, 1940, *Agriculture*, vol. 1, part 2, p. 11.

6. Census Bureau, *Historical Statistics*, 283, 291–97; Saloutos, *American Farmer*, 12. Whereas Saloutos gives 60 percent as the drop in farm income, *Historical Statistics*, 283, reports a 49 percent decline in gross farm income, 55.8 percent in net for the same time period. See also Theodore C. Blegen, *Minnesota: A History of the State*, 2d ed. (Minneapolis: University of Minnesota Press, 1975), 521–49; D. Jerome Tweton, *Depression: Minnesota in the Thirties* (Fargo: North Dakota Institute for Regional Studies, 1981), 7–9.

7. Census Bureau, *Historical Statistics*, 291–97; U.S. Department of Agriculture (USDA), *Agricultural Statistics 1947* (Washington, D.C.: U.S. Government Printing Office, 1948), 11, 39, and *Agricultural Statistics 1974* (1974), 2, 29.

8. USDA, *Agricultural Statistics 1986* (Washington, D.C.: U.S. Government Printing Office, 1986), 1, 30, 76, 124, 130; Borchert and Gustafson, *1980 Minnesota Atlas*, 64; U.S. Census Bureau, *1982 Census of Agriculture*, vol. 1, part 23, p. viii; *Grand Forks Herald*, May 31, 1987, p. 1A, 8A.

9. *Minneapolis Star and Tribune*, Apr. 13, 1986, p. 1D, Nov. 11, 1985, p. 17A; Jay Walljasper, "The Quiet Crisis," *Minnesota Monthly*, October 1985, p. 30.

10. Borchert and Gustafson, *1980 Minnesota Atlas*, 61–62, 84, 88, 93; U.S., *Census*, 1940, *Agriculture*, 3:513; *The 1985 Minnesota Ag Manual* (Minneapolis: Minnesota Agri-Growth Council, 1984), 6; John Fraser Hart, "Change in the Corn Belt," *Geographical Review* 76 (January 1986): 53–55. By 1974 the state average was 3.3 tractors per farmer.

11. Edward Van Dyke Robinson, *Early Economic Conditions and the Development of Agriculture in Minnesota*, University of Minnesota, Studies in the Social Sciences, Bulletin no. 3 (Minneapolis, March 1915), 174; USDA, *Agricultural Statistics 1986*, 5; U.S., *Census*, 1900, *Agriculture*, vol. 6, part 2, p. 92.

12. Vernard E. Lundin, *The Hubbard Milling Company, 1878–1978* (Minneapolis: T. S. Denison and Co., 1978), 24; Herman Steen, *Flour Milling in America* (Minneapolis: T. S. Denison and Co., 1963), 46–49, 258–59.

13. Steen, *Flour Milling*, 273, 285–86, 293; James Gray, *Business without Boundary, the Story of General Mills* (Minneapolis: University of Minnesota Press, 1954), 25–50; *1985 Minnesota Ag Manual*, 11, 162, 285. See also William J. Powell, *Pillsbury's Best: A Company History from 1869* (Minneapolis: Pillsbury Co., 1985).

14. U.S., *Census*, 1920, *Manufactures*, 9:720; U.S., *Census of Manufactures: 1947*, 3:320–22; U.S., *1982 Census of Manufactures*, Geographic Area Series, *Minnesota*, 8–13;

William E. Lass, *Minnesota: A Bicentennial History* (New York: W. W. Norton and Co., 1977), 201–2.

15. John L. Work, *Cargill Beginnings, An Account of Early Years* (Minneapolis: Cargill Inc., 1965), 71–81, 87–96, 114–18, 133–36, 148–53; Don W. Larson, *Land of the Giants, a History of Minnesota Business* (Minneapolis: Dorn Books, 1979), 61–63.

16. Kenneth D. Ruble, *The Peavey Story* (N.p., ca. 1963), 14–16, 23, 28–29, 33–36, 54; Larson, *Land of the Giants*, 63–65.

17. Ruble, *Peavey Story*, 63, 68, 69; *1985 Minnesota Ag Manual*, 11, 83, 99; Terry Brown, "The Cargill Combination," *Corporate Report Minnesota*, May 1983, p. 57; Work, *Cargill*, 153; *Cargill News*, March 1987, p. 8–22.

18. Elwyn B. Robinson, *History of North Dakota* (Lincoln: University of Nebraska Press, 1966), 275–78; Blegen, *History of Minnesota*, 398.

19. Elwyn Robinson, *History of North Dakota*, 388, 449–50; Harvest States Cooperatives, *1983 Annual Report – Financial Report* (St. Paul), 2; John Franklin, Harvest States Cooperatives, telephone conversation with the author, July 15, 1986.

20. Edward Robinson, *Early Economic Conditions*, 140, 156; Borchert and Gustafson, *1980 Minnesota Atlas*, 78–80.

21. Blegen, *History of Minnesota*, 392–94; Lass, *Minnesota*, 139–41.

22. Edward Robinson, *Early Economic Conditions*, 225, 227, 230–31; Borchert and Gustafson, *1980 Minnesota Atlas*, 78; *1985 Minnesota Ag Manual*, 7; *Minnesota Data Book 1985–1986* (St. Paul: Blue Sky Marketing, 1985), 227; Census Bureau, *1982 Census of Agriculture*, vol. 1, part 23, p. 2.

23. Edward Robinson, *Early Economic Conditions*, 170, 280; Borchert and Gustafson, *1980 Minnesota Atlas*, 79; Blegen, *History of Minnesota*, 392; *1985 Minnesota Ag Manual*, 4, 11; *Minnesota Data Book*, 227.

24. Edward Robinson, *Early Economic Conditions*, 108, 111, 141, 225, 229; Borchert and Gustafson, *1980 Minnesota Atlas*, 67–69; *1985 Minnesota Ag Manual*, 6–7.

25. Borchert and Gustafson, *1980 Minnesota Atlas*, 79, 82; *1985 Minnesota Ag Manual*, 6–7; Edward Robinson, *Early Economic Conditions*, 230, 232; USDA, *Agricultural Statistics 1984* (Washington, D.C.: U.S. Government Printing Office, 1984), 287.

26. Blegen, *History of Minnesota*, 397–98; Ann Regan, "The Danes," in *They Chose Minnesota: A Survey of the State's Ethnic Groups*, ed. June Drenning Holmquist (St. Paul: Minnesota Historical Society Press, 1981), 281; Edward Robinson, *Early Economic Conditions*, 141.

27. "Guideposts for the Future," History of Land O' Lakes script, ca. 1980, p. 1–3, on file at Land O' Lakes corporate headquarters, Minneapolis. Blegen, *History of Minnesota*, 398; Kenneth D. Ruble, *Men to Remember: How 100,000 Neighbors Made History* (Chicago: R. R. Donnelley and Sons Co., 1947), 70, 81, 118, 181, 203.

28. Joseph G. Knapp, *The Advance of American Cooperative Enterprise: 1920–1945* (Danville, Ill.: Interstate Printers and Publishers, 1973), 413–15, 612; "Guideposts for the Future," 4–6; Ruble, *Men to Remember*, 207, 257, 260; Kenneth D. Ruble, *Land O' Lakes: Farmers Make It Happen* (N.p.: K. D. Ruble, 1973), 5.

29. Land O' Lakes, Inc., *Nineteen Eighty-Six Annual Report* (Minneapolis, 1986?), 1, 19, 32; Ruble, *Land O' Lakes*, 33–40, 63–72, 77–83, 107–8, 165–71; "Guideposts for the Future," 7–9.

30. *1985 Minnesota Ag Manual*, 11, 226, 235, 255, 267, 338, 344.

31. U.S., *Census*, 1920, *Manufactures*, 9:720; U.S., *1982 Census of Manufactures*, Geographic Area Series, *Minnesota*, 8–13.

32. Here and below, see *Saint Paul Union Stockyards, 1886 Centennial Year 1986* (St. Paul: Fahey and Associates, 1986), [6, 14, 20, 26, 33].

33. *Saint Paul Union Stockyards*, [14, 46, 48]; "Hog the Road to CLA," a publication of the Central Livestock Association, Inc., ca. 1985, p. 4.

34. Lyle Lamphere, *They Charted the Course . . . , The History of Central Livestock Association, Inc.* (N.p.: Central Livestock Assn., Inc., [1971?]), 3–5, 6, 7, 9; "Hog the Road to CLA," 4.

35. Richard Dougherty, *In Quest of Quality, Hormel's First 75 Years* (St. Paul: North Central Publishing Co., 1966), 35, 38, 49, 63–65, 73, 87.

36. Dougherty, *In Quest of Quality*, 118, 136, 158–63, 171; "Hormel," a company publication, ca. 1980, p. 2–4, 10; George A. Hormel and Co., *Annual Report, Fiscal Year Ended Oct. 25, 1986* (Austin, 1987), 1, 4, 9, 46; George A. Hormel and Co., "Annual Report on Form 10-K [to Securities and Exchange Commission], Oct. 25, 1986," 1–3, 7–8.

37. Edward Robinson, *Early Economic Conditions*, 180; Melvin E. Kazeck, *North Dakota, A Human and Economic Geography* (Fargo: North Dakota Institute for Regional Studies, 1956), 73.

38. Borchert and Gustafson, *1980 Minnesota Atlas*, 78, 84; *1985 Minnesota Ag Manual*, 7.

39. Borchert and Gustafson, *1980 Minnesota Atlas*, 84–87; *1985 Minnesota Ag Manual*, 4, 7; USDA, *Agricultural Statistics 1983* (Washington, D.C.: U.S. Government Printing Office, 1983), 376.

40. *West Central Tribune* (Willmar), undated clipping ca. 1980, on file at Willmar Poultry Co., and July 9, 1981, p. 3C, 12C; *Gobbles* (St. Paul), October 1986, p. 14–15; *Feedstuffs* (Minneapolis), Oct. 27, 1986, p. 1–2, 5; Sue Backes, Willmar Poultry Co., to author, Mar. 17, 1987.

41. *Minneapolis Star and Tribune*, June 8, 1986, p. 1A, 14A–15A; *1985 Minnesota Ag Manual*, 197.

42. U.S., *Census*, 1920, *Manufactures*, 9:720; U.S., *1982 Census of Manufactures*, Geographic Area Series, *Minnesota*, 8–13.

43. Whitney Eastman, *The History of the Linseed Oil Industry in the United States* (Minneapolis: T. S. Denison and Co., 1968), 17–18, 21, 25–26, 128, 129.

44. Lawrence J. Sommer, "Forgotten Industries of Duluth," in *Duluth: Sketches of the Past*, ed. Ryck Lydecker and Lawrence J. Sommer (Duluth: American Revolution Bicentennial Commission, 1976), 199.

45. Eastman, *Linseed Oil Industry*, 25–26, 28, 61; U.S., *Special Reports of the Census Office: Manufactures, 1905*, part 2, p. 536, 546–47; U.S., *Census*, 1920, *Manufactures*, 9:720.

46. Eastman, *Linseed Oil Industry*, 40–41, 48, 49.

47. Eastman, *Linseed Oil Industry*, 62; Weber H. Peterson, *Flaxseed in American Farming*, USDA Technical Bulletin 938 (November 1947), 10. See also George H. Primmer, "United States Flax Industry," *Economic Geography* 17 (January 1941): 24.

48. Eastman, *Linseed Oil Industry*, 34, 125–27.

49. Eastman, *Linseed Oil Industry*, 40, 62, 130–33; Franklin, telephone conversation, July 15, 1986.

50. Ray A. Goldberg, *The Soybean Industry, with Special Reference to the Competitive Position of the Minnesota Producer and Processor* (Minneapolis: University of Minnesota Press, 1952), 15–16, 74; Ruble, *Farmers Make It Happen*, 148. A sixty-pound bushel yielded about fifty pounds of meal and ten pounds of oil.

51. Here and below, see Goldberg, *Soybean Industry*, 19, 21–23, 30–34, 42, 53, 64, 74–75.

52. Lundin, *Hubbard Milling Company*, 116–18.

53. Goldberg, *Soybean Industry*, 16, 76, 78; U.S., *1982 Census of Manufactures*, Geographic Area Series, *Minnesota*, 8; USDA, *Agricultural Statistics 1959* (Washington, D.C.: U.S. Government Printing Office, 1960), 137, 139, *Agricultural Statistics 1983* (1983), 131, 132, and *Agricultural Statistics 1987* (1987), 126, 127; *1985 Minnesota Ag Manual*, 7.

54. *1985 Minnesota Ag Manual*, 6–7, 112; Borchert and Gustafson, *1980 Minnesota Atlas*, 68–69, 76–77; Kazeck, *North Dakota*, 67–68.

55. Mary DeVoer, Dahlgren and Co., telephone conversation with the author, July 15, 1986; *Dahlgren Leader*, August 1985, p. 1, 7, 8.

56. *1985 Minnesota Ag Manual*, 40.

57. Borchert and Gustafson, *1980 Minnesota Atlas*, 76–77; *1985 Minnesota Ag Manual*, 4, 7.

58. Charles L. Mundale, "Gedney: King of the Dill," *Corporate Report*, December 1977, p 34–37, 78, 79; "M. A. Gedney Company," a company publication, 1986, p. 1 2; *Memoirs of a Giant: Green Giant Company's First 75 Years, 1903–1978* (N.p.: Green Giant Co., 1978), [4].

59. Edward Robinson, *Early Economic Conditions*, 196; U.S., *Census of Manufactures: 1947*, 3:320; Mundale, "Gedney," 36, 79; "M. A. Gedney Company," 1–2; "Fussy, That's Festal," a publication of the Owatonna Canning Co., 1986, p. 1; *Memoirs of a Giant*, chronology page facing [1]; Powell, *Pillsbury's Best*, 211. Owatonna Canning Co. was first organized in 1904 but ran into financial difficulties; it was reorganized in 1911. See Edgar B. Wesley, *Owatonna: The Social Development of a Minnesota Community* (Minneapolis: University of Minnesota Press, 1938), 91.

60. Edward Robinson, *Early Economic Conditions*, 109–11, 128; Stanley N. Murray, *The Valley Comes of Age: A History of Agriculture in the Valley of the Red River of the North, 1812–1920* (Fargo: North Dakota Institute for Regional Studies, 1967), 203–4; Randal C. Coon, F. Larry Leistritz, and Donald F. Scott, *The Contribution and Impact of the Red River Valley Potato Industry on the Economies of North Dakota and Minnesota*, North Dakota State University Agricultural Experiment Station, Agricultural Economics Miscellaneous Report no. 95 (Fargo, March 1986), 1, 6–9, 31; Borchert and Gustafson, *1980 Minnesota Atlas*, 74, 76; *1985 Minnesota Ag Manual*, 6–7, 412; *Minnesota Data Book*, 231. For more on potatoes, see Frank W. Hussey, *Red River Valley Potato Growers Profile and Economic Concerns*, USDA Farmer Cooperative Service, Service Report 139 (Washington, D.C., 1974).

61. Blegen, *History of Minnesota*, 346, 391–92; *1985 Minnesota Ag Manual*, 6; Charles E. Dick, "A Geographical Analysis of the Development of the Brewing Industry in Minnesota" (Ph.D. diss., University of Minnesota, 1981), 334; Frederick William Salem, *Beer: Its History and Its Economic Value* (1880; reprint, New York: Arno Press, 1972), 219–22; Wil-

liam L. Downard, *Dictionary of the History of the American Brewing and Distilling Industries* (Westport, Conn.: Greenwood Press, 1980), 50.

62. Dick, "Geographical Analysis," 115–18, 184, 188, 192, 237, 241.

63. Jeri Engh, *Hamms: The Story of 100 Years in the Land of Sky Blue Waters* (St. Paul: Theodore Hamm Brewing Co., 1965), 10; "Cold Spring Brewing Company," a company publication, 1986, p. 1; "August Schell Brewing Company, Our Brewery Past and Present," a company publication, ca. 1985, p. 1; Downard, *Dictionary*, 50.

64. Dick, "Geographical Analysis," 65, 137–38, 145–46, 185, 293, 299, 320–22; Stanley Baron, *Brewed in America, A History of Beer and Ale in the United States* (Boston: Little, Brown and Co., 1962), 341; *St. Paul Pioneer Press Dispatch*, May 27, 1987, p. 1B.

65. John E. Siebel and Anton Schwarz, *History of the Brewing Industry and Brewing Science in America* (Chicago: N.p., 1933), 110; *Zumbrota News*, Apr. 15, 1938, p. 1; *Hubbard County Journal*, Apr. 21, 1938, p. 7; Dick, "Geographical Analysis," 146; USDA, *Agricultural Statistics 1949* (Washington, D.C.: U.S. Government Printing Office, 1949), 61.

66. "Sugar: A Fact Sheet," a publication of the Sugar Association, Inc., June 1984, p. 1; Roy M. Gilcrest, *Sugar Beet Production in the Red River Valley* (Fargo: North Dakota Agricultural Experiment Station, 1950), 2–3; *Facts about Sugarbeets and Beet Sugar* (Renville: Southern Minnesota Sugar Cooperative, 1985), 2–3.

67. Edward Robinson, *Early Economic Conditions*, 196, 227; Kazeck, *North Dakota*, 56–58; *Facts about Sugarbeets*, 3. See also *50 Years in the Valley: The Story of East Grand Forks, American Crystal's Flagship Plant* (Moorhead: American Crystal Sugar Co., 1976); David Carmichael et al., comps., *Guide to the Records of the American Crystal Sugar Company* (St. Paul: Minnesota Historical Society, Division of Archives and Manuscripts, 1985), 5.

68. *Facts about Sugarbeets*, 1–3; Carmichael et al., comps., *Guide to the Records*, 6–7.

69. *1985 Minnesota Ag Manual*, 7; "Midwest Agri-Commodities," a publication of Midwest Agri-Commodities (sugar beet by-products), 1986; *Facts about Sugarbeets*, 4.

70. *1985 Minnesota Ag Manual*, 4.

71. Borchert and Gustafson, *1980 Minnesota Atlas*, 118, 119, 233; U.S., *1982 Census of Manufactures*, Geographic Area Series, *Minnesota*, 8.

72. *1985 Minnesota Ag Manual*, 24–32, 45, 86; *Minneapolis–St. Paul CityBusiness*, Apr. 30, 1986, p. 12.

73. *Minneapolis-St. Paul CityBusiness*, Apr. 30, 1986, p. 1, 12; *Minneapolis Star and Tribune*, Aug. 7, 1986, p. 3B. For more on the effects of the farm economy on rural communities, see Thomas Harvey, "Small-Town Minnesota," *this volume*, 122–24.

GEORGE S. HAGE

Evolution and Revolution in the Media: Print and Broadcast Journalism

Newspapers, magazines, and radio and television broadcasts inform and entertain the people they serve; they also reflect and help create their communities' identities. But the process by which the reports and programs themselves are brought to the public is a beat covered by few journalists. Since 1900 that process has changed radically: inventions have altered production methods of print media, and other new technology spawned radio and television. Corporations and families have bought and sold newspapers and broadcasting companies in response to economic changes. Journalists have altered the content and style of writing and reporting to reflect the changing tastes and expectations of the people they served.

The impact of these changes on the lives of Minnesotans can be suggested by a few figures. Foreign-language newspapers numbered in the hundreds at the turn of the century, but there was only one in 1984. The number of newspapers published in the state, both daily and weekly, increased in the first two decades of the century, then declined.[1] In 1900, four copies of daily newspapers were sold for every ten residents of the state over the age of fourteen; in 1979, the figure was three copies. Radio stations began broadcasting in the 1920s, television stations went on the air in the 1940s, and by the 1980s the broadcast media were omnipresent. Ninety-eight percent of households in the United States in 1980 had television sets and 99 percent had radios; there is no reason to believe that Minnesota's proportions were significantly different. The changes brought by broadcasting were especially dramatic. As a writer observed in 1924, "Radio brings the farmer and his family in daily contact with the outside world and makes him a next door neighbor to a hundred cities." Marshall McLuhan's global village was at hand.[2]

Throughout all the changes, Minneapolis and St. Paul maintained dominant positions within the state's media industry. The residents of the metropolitan area represented the state's major media market. The cities' newspapers were sold throughout the state, and their radio and television stations broadcast into a large region. Corporate power, advertising dollars, media families, the newest technology – all have been concentrated in the metropolitan area. Because of the importance of the Twin Cities media, this essay emphasizes their story.

Another constant during these years of great change was the attitude of the media toward freedom of expression. Although the issues changed, the media's responses followed a predictable and not entirely admirable pattern.

The News in Print, 1900–20

In the first two decades of the century, the term "media" was not much used – "mass media" not at all. Only newspapers could make any claim to a mass audience; the few magazines published in the state were selective in their readership. But there were more newspapers than at any other time in the history of the state. Between 1900 and 1910, their number increased from 677, of which 36 were dailies, to 757, of which 37 were dailies. And by 1920 there were 761 newspapers and periodicals, of which 45 were dailies, 622 weeklies, and the balance of varying periodicity.[3]

The state's two largest cities claimed seven major daily newspapers in 1900: the *Minneapolis Journal* (evening, dating from 1878), the *Minneapolis Times* (morning, 1889), the *Minneapolis Tribune* (morning and evening, 1867), the *St. Paul Dispatch* (evening, 1868), the *St. Paul Globe* (morning, 1878), the *St. Paul Pioneer Press* (morning, 1849), and the *St. Paul News* (evening, 1900). Only the *Times* and the *News* declared themselves politically independent, and only the *Globe*, Democratic; the others varied from outright Republican (*Tribune, Dispatch, Pioneer Press*) to independent Republican (*Journal*). In later years the papers would drop their party affiliations, subscribing to a national trend toward less blatant partisanship.[4]

In appearance, these newspapers of 1900 were closer to their predecessors of 1850 than to their successors of the 1980s. Papers were thin – ten pages was a normal size. Because illustrations were expensive and infrequent, the pages gave an overall impression of grayness. Stories were laid out in vertical columns; headlines generally fit within single columns, and for major stories they ran through several decks of diminishing size of type, each revealing more details. For example, a page-one headline of the *Journal* for January 2, 1901, read: "A Famous Man Called Home/ Hon. Ignatius Donnelly Succumbs to Heart Disease/ The End Is Unexpected/ Though His Powers Had Been Failing for Several Months/ An Eventful Career Closes/ He Had Made a Name in Literature as Well as in Politics."

News from abroad was scarce, considering the cities' high proportion

The Minneapolis Journal *stretched a "gridiron" across the street in about 1904 to show a play-by-play account of the University of Minnesota's football games for thousands of spectators.*

of immigrants, and was almost invariably limited to conflict. A markedly local tone ran through much of the news, as shown by the lead of a feature story about the first baby born in Minneapolis in the twentieth century: "What shall we name the baby? Charles Lundeen of 427 Knox avenue No. propounds the question to all of Minneapolis and motherly old Minnie is expected to answer. . . . Address all suggestions: A Name for the Baby, care of the Journal." (The city's daughter was dubbed Alpha Twencentia Minnea Lundeen.)[5]

Foreign or domestic, news was news. Today's reader would look in vain for analysis, interpretive articles, advice columns, consumer service columns, and sports features or columns. Markedly different, too, was the style of writing. The pace at which a story unfolded was, at the least, unhurried. Lead sentences ran interminably, piling detail on detail. An example from the *Journal* of January 2, 1910, is perhaps an extreme, but it is not unique: "A speeding automobile driven by a man whom the police are exerting every effort to capture, about 7 o'clock last night struck John McLeod, 2311 Humboldt Ave. S., head of the Chamber of Commerce firm of John McLeod & Co., as he alighted from a car at Hennepin Avenue and Twenty-fourth street and hurled him thirty feet onto the fender of another car. Late last night physicians had not determined the extent of his injuries."

The owners and editors of these newspapers and others in the state were, for the most part, substantial civic leaders: Joseph A. Wheelock, editor of the *Pioneer Press* (from 1862 to 1906), whose work on behalf of St. Paul's park system was memorialized in Wheelock Parkway; George Thompson, editor of the *Dispatch* (1887–1917) and *Pioneer Press* (1909–17), a prominent Republican; Charles K. Blandin, Thompson's successor (1917–27), who was later to devote his business talents to the Grand Rapids paper mill he had bought as a hedge against rising newsprint costs. In Minneapolis, John Scudder McLain, managing editor, and Lucian Swift, Jr., business manager, had made the *Journal* a force in regional affairs, giving the paper a progressive Republican, antitrust, antirailroad stance until it was purchased in 1908 by Herschel V. Jones, publisher of *Commercial West*, a regional business magazine, and his brother, William S. Jones.[6]

In Winona, the appropriately named Horace Greeley White purchased the *Winona Independent* in 1903 and started a publishing enterprise that was to last through three generations of his family. In Rochester, another family publishing enterprise got under way with the purchase of the *Rochester Daily Bulletin* by Glenn S. Withers in 1916.[7]

More colorful than any of these was William J. Murphy, who became publisher and sole owner of the *Minneapolis Tribune* in 1908. His heirs would control, eighty years later, not the *Tribune*, but WCCO television, WCCO-AM radio, and WLTE-FM radio. Family legend explains that WJ, as the Murphy family called him, came to found a communications dynasty through a fluke. As a young lawyer in Grand Forks, North Dakota, he was approached one evening in a local bar by the almost bankrupt owner of the *Grand Forks Plain Dealer*, who said, "WJ, if you will meet Saturday's payroll, the newspaper is yours." WJ turned the *Plain Dealer* around in short order. But Grand Forks was too small an arena for his talents and ambition; learning that the *Tribune* in Minneapolis might be for sale, he worked out a deal with one of its owners, Thomas Lowry, to become executive editor of the *Tribune* in 1891. By 1908 he had gained complete ownership.[8]

The paper prospered once WJ had steered it through the panic of 1893. He was an autocrat, even in his own family, as well as a sagacious businessman. His son Kingsley recalled that he suggested to his father, after working one sweltering day in the basement pressroom, that a fan be installed there. WJ's response was to call him "a little Socialist" and suggest that he mind his own business. Not all of WJ's decisions were gold-plated, and when he died in October 1918, the *Tribune* carried a heavy load of debt.

While these families built profitable publishing firms by appealing to a general readership, other publishers in the state were selective in their search for readers. Chief among these were two that catered to major industries in the state: *The Farmer*, flagship of the Webb Publishing Company of St. Paul, and the *Northwestern Miller*, pride of the Miller Publishing Company of Minneapolis. *The Farmer* had been founded in 1882 in Fargo, North Dakota, by Edward Allyn Webb, a Congregational minister's son who went west to make his fortune in bonanza wheat farming but started a publishing empire instead. Initially a monthly, *The Farmer* became a biweekly in 1890, and, in 1910, a weekly. In 1890, Webb moved the magazine to St. Paul, where he was near the University of Minnesota's School of Agriculture, whose expertise Webb set about making available to his readers. (Shortly afterward, he bought the *Farmer's Wife*, which had been launched in Winona a few years earlier.) *The Farmer* preached diversification of farming, and its list of subscribers throughout Minnesota, the Dakotas, eastern Montana, Iowa, and Wisconsin continued to grow through good times and bad, until it peaked in 1955 at 276,000 farm homes.[9]

Like *The Farmer*, the *Northwestern Miller* was a publishing success through many decades because it met a need of the region's economy and kept adapting to changes in that economy. Founded in 1873 at La Crosse, Wisconsin, it was intended by its publisher as a marketing device for a machine that dressed millstones. With the development of roller mills, the *Miller* moved to Minneapolis in 1879 and became a journal for millers and flour buyers. The magazine established correspondents in London and New York in 1894, then opened branch offices in the principal milling cities in this country and Canada. Its reputation for service to the milling industry was unmatched, and successive generations of editors took pride in traditions memorialized in the magazine's club room adjacent to the editorial offices.[10]

Publications for another set of specialized audiences, the foreign-language press, received some mortal blows during the 1910s. Although the total number of periodicals in Minnesota continued to increase, the decline in foreign-language newspapers had set in and was accelerated by the wave of patriotic fervor induced by entry of the United States into World War I and by the anti-Red hysteria that followed it. The period was not a proud one for the press. The most severe suppression of speech and press in the nation's history was more than ordinarily harsh in Minnesota, where a state sedition law was passed even before the federal Espionage Act, and the Minnesota Commission of Public Safety was extraordinarily intrusive in regulating both public and private conduct.[11]

Press scholars have postulated from long observation that freedom of expression exists in direct ratio to the stability of government and that threats to national security have often been used to rationalize suppression of speech and press. Critics of the press, moreover, have observed that the mainstream press is more vocal in support of free expression as an abstraction than in its defense in specific instances of suppression.[12]

A study of newspapers in the state during this period has indeed found this to be the case. A researcher examined editorials in nineteen of the state's dailies, including the *Tribune* and *Journal* in Minneapolis and the *Pioneer Press* and *Dispatch* in St. Paul, during four months in 1912, when Socialists and the Industrial Workers of the World were raising free-speech issues; three months in 1918, when the wartime state sedition law was being zealously enforced; and three months in 1920, when the state attorney general's raids against alien radicals made the issues concrete. She found that "overall, editorials in the 19 dailies failed to uphold not only the speech and press rights of unpopular minorities but of commercial newspapers, as well. The editorials unanimously endorsed freedom of expression in principle, but refused to extend such freedom to German-Americans, radicals, and others who were the targets of repression during, after, and, to an extent, before the war. . . . In general, editorial commentary revealed an apparent willingness among members of the press to place national security interests over speech and press freedoms, with little visible concern for the long-term implications of wartime suppression."[13]

Even in years not affected by suppression, the number of daily newspapers was declining. There were 45 evening dailies in 1920, 43 in 1930, and 28 in 1945. The number of periodicals, however, almost doubled in the same period, from 84 to 140.[14]

Radio Fills the Air

The development of commercial radio broadcasting in the first years of the twentieth century was tentative rather than headlong. Nine stations were launched in Minnesota in 1922, several of which signed off before the end of the year. By 1930, there were eleven stations throughout the state, and at the end of the 1930s, only twenty. Operating a radio station was an expensive business, and the potential for advertising revenue was not at first apparent.[15]

Of the nine radio stations established in 1922, three were the stepchildren of newspapers, born of rivalry and the race for prestige: WBAD, founded by the *Minneapolis Journal* and Sterling Electric Company, began operating April 20 atop the Radisson Hotel in Minneapolis; WAAL, established by the *Minneapolis Tribune* and William R. Beamish (who owned a radio parts store), started operating the same evening from the roof of the Tribune annex; and WAAH, launched by the *St. Paul Pioneer Press* and Commonwealth Electric Company, went on the air April 22 from the roof of Commonwealth's building in St. Paul. The extent of the newspapers' commitment to the new medium is suggested by the fact that all three stations went off the air simultaneously, by mutual agreement, in September of that same year.[16]

The newspaper-affiliated stations were preceded by WLB, the University of Minnesota station, which became KUOM in 1945. The station had been broadcasting experimentally since the spring of 1921, but it did not receive its call letters and its license to broadcast at one hundred watts of power until January 13, 1922. The second oldest of the stations that survived is St. Olaf College's WCAL, which went on the air on May 19. Other stations, all of Minneapolis, and their operational dates were: WCE of the Findley Electric Company, with studios in the Curtis Hotel, April 15;

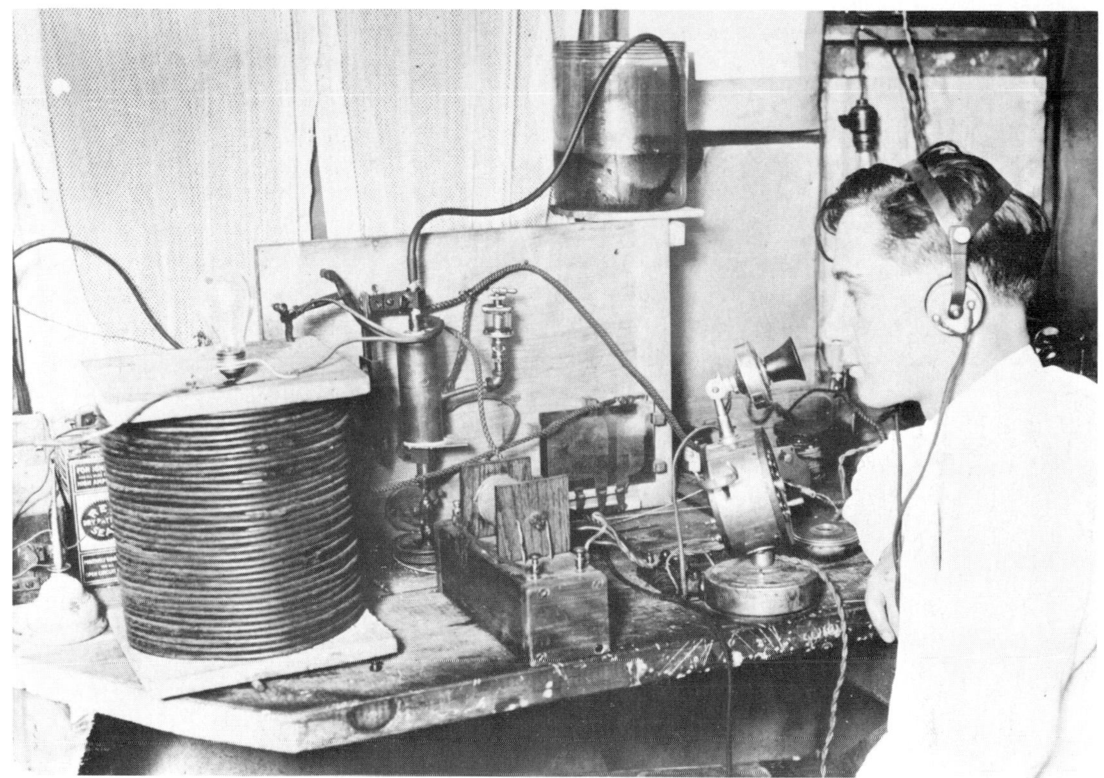

James A. Coles at the microphone of his broadcasting set, Minneapolis, 1914

WBAH of the Dayton Company, with studios in the record department on the second floor of the store, May 11; WCAS of the William Hood Dunwoody Industrial Institute, September 18; and WLAG of the Cutting and Washington Corporation of Minneapolis, with studios in the Oak Grove Hotel, September 4.[17]

The last-named station was more tenacious than most, and it survived to become WCCO, the largest and most powerful radio station in the Upper Midwest in terms of listeners, revenues, and wattage. Credit for its start goes to Walter S. Harris, who became fascinated by the new gadget, "wireless," while growing up in Minneapolis. After World War I, Harris founded and became president of a local outlet for Cutting and Washington Radio Corporation, eastern manufacturers of radio receivers. In order to put a five-hundred-watt station on the air, as required by agreement with Cutting and Washington, Harris solicited funds from local businesses. The budget of thirty-five thousand dollars for the first year did not include fees for performers, who, it was believed, would feel repaid by the privilege of being heard on radio.[18]

Without the faintest idea of how to "program" a radio station, Harris turned to Eleanor Poehler, a locally prominent soprano soloist and voice teacher at MacPhail School of Music and Dramatic Art in Minneapolis. As managing director of the station, she hired one of her students, H. Paul Johnson, to be the first announcer. Poehler, as a classical musician, favored a dead-air interval of at least fifteen seconds to separate the "beauties of classical music" from the "harsh tones" of announcers. Harris opposed the policy. The interval seemed unnecessarily appropriate for a station whose call letters were WLAG.

"WLAG, Your Call of the North Station," at first was heard just two or three days a week, offering weather forecasts, market reports, and some music. Only the marvel of the medium itself can account for listeners staying tuned to lectures with such titles as "Proper Application of Paint," "Where Garden Seeds Come From," and "Bees in April"; these lectures were directed at midwestern farmers and sponsored by *Northwest Farmstead,* a semimonthly magazine published in Minneapolis. A delighted listener wrote, "We have learned a great many helpful things about our every day work. It's such a comfortable way for farmers to sit by the fire and hear all kinds of lectures and concerts."[19]

Doubtless even more riveting were early broadcasts of the University of Minnesota's Gopher football games. Johnny McGovern, a former All-American quarterback, made the first one from old Northrop Field, pulling the microphone "up and down the field on a long cord, but this picked up a lot of noise and was not too successful," as his successor Herb Paul remembered. Paul, a newspaper reporter who had played football in high school, was hired by WLAG and paid $7.50 a game to broadcast football and basketball games and boxing matches.[20]

Not all of the original subscribers were satisfied with the results of the time allotted them for their commercial messages, and when the operating budget for the second year was set at fifty thousand dollars, WLAG was in trouble. Pledges went unredeemed and in July 1924 receivers took over. WLAG signed off for the last time on July 31, 1924. The Dayton Company's WBAH went off the air that same evening, and local set owners, as well as radio dealers and distributors, faced the dismaying prospect of life with two fewer local radio stations.[21]

A promoter for the Northwest Radio Trade Association, seeking funds to save the station, appealed to Donald D. Davis, vice-president of Washburn Crosby Company, who was interested enough to discuss the matter with James Ford Bell, president of the company. The result was a proposal to the Minneapolis Civic and Commerce Association and the St. Paul Association of Commerce: if the associations would raise matching funds, Washburn Crosby would buy the property and assets of WLAG and contribute fifty thousand dollars a year for three years; the station would be known as the Gold Medal Station, the brand name of Washburn Crosby's flour, and it took its new call letters – WCCO – from the company's name. Broadcasts resumed on October 1, 1924. The Twin Cities' trade associations were pleased to be rid of "Call of the North." It was bad for the national image.

Washburn Crosby leased space in 1925 on the twelfth and thirteenth floors of the new Nicollet Hotel in Minneapolis for the station's studios and also purchased land near Anoka for erection of the transmitter building and towers. Davis persuaded Henry A. Bellows, editor of *Northwestern Miller* and former professor of rhetoric at the University of Minnesota, to

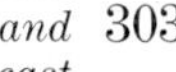

The Red River Valley Gang, master of ceremonies Bob De Haven, and Tom and Eddie Plehal, harmonica players, about 1948

manage the station, a commitment that led to a vice-presidency of the Columbia Broadcasting System (CBS) in 1931. It was Davis, too, who assigned Earl H. Gammons, a former *Tribune* reporter and editor of Washburn Crosby's house organ, to publicize the station; Gammons became station manager when Bellows moved up. And it was Davis who persuaded Washburn Crosby directors to assume sole ownership of WCCO when the trade associations withdrew their support late in 1925.

In the meantime, the station had acquired a rival in the person of Stanley E. Hubbard, founder of yet another communications dynasty, who, with his progeny, was to compete with WCCO for listeners and viewers – to say nothing of advertisers – throughout the succeeding decades. Hubbard had a rare combination of engineering and entrepreneurial genius; as a child he had started tinkering with mechanical things, as well as selling space on the curtain of his miniature theater in Red Wing. He sensed the potential of radio and in 1923 arranged for studio and transmitter space at the Marigold Gardens, a dance hall on upper Nicollet Avenue; WAMD ("Where All Minneapolis Dances") began broadcasting in April 1924.[22]

The call letters of Hubbard's station suggested not only the nature of its programming – ballroom dance bands – but also his disdain for the piano and soprano aired by WLAG. He prowled apartment building hallways many evenings, listening for the sounds from behind closed doors in order to gauge his station's popularity against that of the competition. What he heard helped him in his daily routine of selling advertising in the morning and planning programs in the afternoon. "We were starving," he later recalled. "At one point, I got so discouraged that I called the staff to-

KSTP mobile unit at tournament, Keller Golf Course, Maplewood, 1931

gether and said: 'Here's your paycheck. From now on, if the money comes in, fine – you'll get your next check. If it doesn't, well, I won't be responsible.' " Only one member of the eleven-person staff quit.

In 1928 the station's call letters were changed to KSTP and the main studios were moved to the Hotel St. Paul. Hubbard claimed to have started the first regular radio news program in the country, after persuading the wire services to supply radio stations as well as newspapers. The station was an early broadcaster of live sports events, following a golf tournament by hauling a transmitter around the links in a baby carriage.

In the next few years, KSTP and WCCO had some on-and-off relations with the national networks. The National Broadcasting Company (NBC) was successfully pushing the sale of commercial time on radio, and WCCO had become NBC's key station in the area, carrying such popular network programs as the "Ipana Troubadours," "The Eveready Hour," and "The Cliquot Club Eskimos." Bellows felt he had achieved a coup in selling sponsorship of a Sunday night program by the Minneapolis Symphony to Northwestern National Bank, only to learn that NBC's Chicago office had sold a similar program by the Chicago Symphony to Standard Oil of Indiana and wanted WCCO to carry it just before the Minneapolis orchestra's broadcast. In the dustup that followed, NBC offered the Chicago orchestra program to KSTP, WCCO began taking programs from the newly established CBS, and NBC withdrew network affiliation from WCCO in favor of KSTP.[23]

The head of CBS was William S. Paley, a young cigar salesman from Philadelphia, who traveled to Minneapolis in August 1929 to purchase WCCO for the network. Paley arrived at a good time. A year earlier, Washburn Crosby had become part of General Mills, and General Mills directors had become convinced that the company should get out of broadcasting and concentrate on milling. In September 1929 Paley agreed to pay $150,000 for a one-third interest in WCCO with an option to buy the remainder in three years. Also in 1929, WCCO received one of the country's forty "clear channel" frequencies (meaning only one full-time station could operate on the frequency) established by the Federal Radio Commission. The station's power was increased to fifty thousand watts.

With that power, WCCO – like the other Twin Cities stations – broadcast programs and advertisements into outstate Minnesota. The impact of these radio broadcasts in formerly isolated rural areas wrought a revolution. Instantaneous mass communication made distances shrink and brought information, cultural programming, and advertisements into thousands of homes. Broadcasting was centralized in the Twin Cities in the early years: sixteen of the seventeen stations started outside of the metropolitan area between 1912 and 1930 failed by 1938; five of the seventeen started in the Twin Cities were still on the air in the late 1980s. All eight of the stations started outside the Twin Cities metropolitan area in the 1930s were broadcasting in the 1980s.[24]

The Newspapers Respond to Social Changes

All of this broadcasting activity did not go unobserved in the pages of the newspapers. The *Pioneer Press* was the first of the metropolitan dailies to start a radio column, published in its Sunday edition, and on February 19, 1922, it began publishing a page of news for radio amateurs each Sunday. The *Journal* and *Tribune* were content to publish special sections on how to construct a radio set.[25]

The *Pioneer Press*'s radio column shows how newspapers reflected changes in the society in this period. Perhaps the outstanding development was the formal recognition of special interest groups within the general readership. In the last several decades of the nineteenth century, the daily newspapers had paid increasing attention to business news ("Finance and Trade") with daily market reports consuming more and more column inches. Designation of one page in the Sunday editions as "society" news had been an innovation of the late nineteenth century. Although it was not actually labeled the women's page, the society section generally ran near the fashion, theater, and book pages, and it reflected the assumption that women's interest in news was limited to reports of parties, weddings, and engagements – an assumption that prevailed in many quarters as late as the 1970s.[26]

Sunday editions of the city dailies had begun to cater to sports enthusiasts with special pages ("In the Field of Sport" and "In the Sporting World") as early as 1890. In the 1920s, as sports became institutionalized, the dailies began to allocate space to news of sports, as yet not designated sports sections but readily identifiable as such. "Notes of Sportdom," a modest, one-column heading over one-sentence items about crew at Syracuse or rugby at Toronto or soccer and lacrosse at Chicago, began to appear regularly on an inside page of the *Mankato Daily Free Press*. The *Winona Republican Herald*, the *Rochester Daily Post and Record*, and the *St. Cloud Daily Times* adopted the practice of collecting stories on bowling and boxing and other sports in season on one or more pages, still not designated as "Sports." By the 1930s "Sports Slants," a column by Alan J. Gould, Associated Press sports editor, had become a regular feature on many of these pages. Judged by standards of the 1980s, these sports pages were drab in appearance. Makeup was vertical, headlines were restrained, and pictures – if any – were single-column and posed: hockey player with stick, basketball player with ball, baseball player with bat.[27]

While sports were thus claiming space of their own in the dailies of the 1920s, it was agriculture that was getting special consideration in the news and editorial columns of the *Minneapolis Tribune*, thanks to the accession of Frederick E. Murphy, brother of WJ, to the publisher's post in September 1921. Fred Murphy's passion was agriculture, and the paper became an all-out advocate of diversified farming. "Reporters would have loved him more if he had loved purebred dairy herds less," noted one historian of the paper. "Generally they resented the headline prominence given to such Murphy cows as Sedgland Rosalie Creamelie, a phenomenal producer of butterfat with a name that no reporter with a normal yen for rising in the newsroom hierarchy would dare misspell."[28]

Another historian argued that the paper's support of agricultural diversification overstretched the *Tribune*'s resources. Annual dividends shrank from the seventy-five dollars a share that prevailed in the 1920s to five dollars a share in the 1930s. The Great Depression's blows to both circulation and advertising took their toll, and the paper's finances were once again shaky when Fred died in 1940.[29]

In June 1935, the *Tribune* had suffered a further blow. John and Gardner ("Mike") Cowles, newspapermen from Des Moines, bought the *Minneapolis Star*. "This meant," later noted William J. McNally, Fred Murphy's nephew and heir to his leadership, "that the competition, which had been rugged even when the Journal was the Tribune's only serious rival, must from now on be murderous. For the Cowleses were rich, powerful, intelligent and well-trained newspaper operators. . . . From a newspaper publisher's point of view, practically no break could be worse than a Cowles invasion of your own city."[30]

What made the Cowles's invasion so intimidating was their reputation for success. The brothers had learned the newspaper business at first hand on the *Des Moines Register* and the *Tribune*, newspapers purchased by their father Gardner, an astute and affluent banker in Algona, Iowa. John Cowles's formula for success in Minneapolis was to eliminate the competition by seducing readers with sensation and pursuing aggressive promotion and circulation policies, then to use his monopoly position to publish a responsible newspaper. Admittedly, the *Star* was an easy target. It had been established as the *Minnesota Star* in 1920 by the Nonpartisan League in that organization's brief period of prosperity. After four years, the paper had been sold; the death in 1934 of one of its owners suggested to the Cowles brothers a promising new area of enterprise.

To implement the first part of his formula, John Cowles imported Basil L. ("Stuffy") Walters from Des Moines, where he had been managing editor of the *Register* and *Tribune*, and installed him as editor of the *Star* in 1937. His nickname better described his opinion of the *Journal* and the *Tribune;* stuffy, he was not. Typical of his news philosophy was his adjuration to reporters and editors: "Tell your story. Don't write it." Type, in all its dazzling variety of sizes and styles, was to be used to GET ATTENTION. Under Walters, the *Star* redefined the meaning of news. One issue carried an eight-column banner headline at the top of page one proclaiming, "Mrs. Robin Has Twins," with four accompanying bird photographs to confirm this thrilling natal event. Readers flocked to the *Star*. Between 1935 and 1939, the *Star*'s circulation jumped from 75,770 to 150,056.[31]

Worse news for the *Tribune* was to come. In 1939, John Cowles bought the *Journal* from the Jones family, and the *Tribune* was faced with even tougher, consolidated competition when the papers merged into the *Star Journal* on September 1 of that year. Katherine Connolly Murphy, Fred's widow, had appealed to her nephew, William McNally, to take over the reins, and McNally knew that the paper was in no position to slug it out with the *Star Journal*. The total daily circulation of both Tribune papers, morning and evening, was 185,000, of which the afternoon paper accounted for 115,000, compared with the *Star Journal*'s afternoon circulation of more than 240,000.

On November 18, 1940, McNally invited John Cowles to join him for lunch in his Leamington Hotel apartment. When the dishes had been cleared away, McNally made a bold proposal: merger of the two newspaper properties on a fifty-fifty basis. Cowles was interested, but not eager. Negotiations continued over several months, and on April 29, 1941, the merger was completed – but on a seventy-thirty basis, with Cowles and the *Star-Journal* having the larger share.[32]

Ownership in St. Paul, as in Minneapolis, had undergone change in this period. Leo Owens, another nephew of Fred Murphy and the production manager of the *New York World*, visited St. Paul in 1926 on a search for newsprint and called on C. K. Blandin, owner and publisher of the *Pioneer Press* and *Dispatch*. Blandin surprised Owens by casually suggesting that he buy the St. Paul papers. Owens lacked the capital, but when he returned to New York he mentioned to one of the Ridder brothers during a game of golf that the St. Paul papers might be for sale.[33]

The Ridder brothers were interested. Herman, their father, had founded the *Catholic News* in New York in 1875, and, a quarter of a century later, purchased one of New York's German-language newspapers, *Die Staats-Zeitung*. Sons Bernard H., Joseph E., and Victor F. had joined the enterprise and maintained the *Staats-Zeitung* throughout the anti-German hysteria of the World War I period. Their success so impressed financiers that they had no trouble getting backing for a series of purchases of newspapers, including the *Pioneer Press* and *Dispatch* in 1927, the *Grand Forks Herald* in 1929, and the *Duluth Herald* and *News-*

Tribune in 1936. The Ridders included Owens in the deal for the St. Paul papers, and for ten years he was publisher.

The Ridders came on the St. Paul scene at a time when the city was not enjoying the best of reputations. The police chief, John J. O'Connor, had devised a system for keeping his city free of serious crime by guaranteeing safe haven for criminals from other cities as long as they committed their crimes elsewhere. Such public enemies as Baby Face Nelson, John Dillinger, Alvin Karpis, and Ma and Fred Barker were in and out of the city, and accounts of bank robberies around the state and region too often concluded: "The robbers' car was last seen fleeing toward St. Paul." It was bad for civic pride but good for newsstand sales. The covenant between police and criminals became inoperative in 1933 with the kidnapping of William Hamm, heir to a brewing and banking fortune, which was closely followed in 1934 by the kidnapping of Edward Bremer, another banking family scion, for an even larger ransom. That was too much. Editor Howard Kahn of the *St. Paul News* (purchased by the Ridders in 1933) launched an anticrime campaign and the *Pioneer Press* and *Dispatch* both followed suit.[34]

Although the major Twin Cities daily papers were bought and sold during this period, ownership and direction of nonmetropolitan dailies in the state were more stable. In Winona, Maxwell H. White succeeded his father as publisher in 1934; in Rochester, Glenn S. Withers continued as editor-publisher; in St. Cloud, Frederick Schilplin, Jr., after advancing from reporter to city editor to business manager of the *Times-Journal*, in 1919 began a thirty-year career as owner and publisher of the *Daily Times*. Another multidecade career of owning and publishing, this one by a husband-wife team, was begun in 1920 when Harry E. and Geraldine Rasmussen bought a partnership in the *Austin Daily Herald*. In Fergus Falls, the second and third generations of Underwood and Adams families continued a publishing partnership in the *Daily Journal* that dated from 1884.[35]

While the St. Paul newspapers dealt with the aftermath of the O'Connor system, the Minneapolis newspapers had another type of violence to deal with, and the dealing was not to their credit. It is only in reading historical accounts of the teamsters' strikes of 1934 that one learns of an organization called the Citizens' Alliance. One cannot learn about it by reading the newspaper accounts of the strikes – actually, a series of confrontations in that year – and the bloody battles that ensued. The Citizens' Alliance was an organization of more than eight hundred Minneapolis businessmen whose purpose was to keep Minneapolis an open-shop city. It had broken nearly every strike in Minneapolis since its founding in 1903. Until it crumbled under pressure from the federal government, exerted on local banks through the Reconstruction Finance Corporation, it was the immovable force opposing the teamsters' demands.[36]

Tribune and *Journal* accounts refer to "the employers" and "the employers' advisory committee," and they tell of "425 special officers [who] went into action to break the truck drivers' strike." The committee placed advertisements calling itself the "General Advisory Committee of employees." But nowhere is the Citizens' Alliance named.[37]

It was in reporting the battle of July 20, during which two strikers were killed, that antistriker bias became most apparent. The accounts emphasized that police armed with shotguns were "literally fighting for their lives" against attacking strikers "laying about them strenuously with fists and clubs"; they asserted that police fired into the air before the attack and into the ground as strikers broke and ran. The reports did not mention that most of the injured strikers were wounded in the back.[38]

While the truck drivers were fighting to ensure that labor's right to organize would be recognized in Minneapolis, newspaper employees themselves were organizing. In the fourth year of the depression decade, college graduates lucky enough to be hired were paid sixty-five to seventy-five dollars a month, and seasoned reporters were not much better off. They welcomed the National Industrial Recovery Act's guarantee of labor's right to bargain collectively, and in 1934 a group in the Twin Cities responded to liberal columnist Heywood Broun's call to unionize.[39]

It was not an easy decision to make. In the Twin Cities, as elsewhere, the argument persisted: union membership would compromise the newspaper worker's integrity. Some claimed professional status and believed that they would be demeaning themselves if they joined a union. But for many, the economic issue won out. The Twin Cities local of the American Newspaper Guild was granted the second charter in the country (the Cleveland Guild beat it by twenty-four hours), signed by Broun himself. Membership swelled quickly from the ninety charter members to nearly two hundred. Contract negotiation began in 1935, and the first contract was signed the following year with the *Tribune*. Contracts with the *Star*, the *Pioneer Press*, and the *Dispatch* were signed in 1937. Those contracts were not hailed in the news and editorial columns of any of the local newspapers, however; newspapers have always been notoriously loath to report or discuss their own immediate involvement in economic issues.[40]

The First Amendment on Trial

More surprising than the newspapers' silence on unionization was their response to a philosophical and legal issue: the government's right to forbid publication of material that might be obscene or libelous. Events in Minnesota were to precipitate a major national First Amendment case on this issue, known as prior restraint. In 1925 the Minnesota legislature passed the Public Nuisance Law, better known as the gag law, which provided that "Any person who . . . shall be engaged in the business of regularly or customarily producing, publishing or circulating, having in possession, selling or giving away (a) an obscene, lewd and lascivious newspaper, magazine, or other periodical, or (b) a malicious, scandalous and defamatory newspaper . . . is guilty of a nuisance, and all persons guilty of such nuisance may be enjoined, as hereinafter provided."[41] Representative George Lommen, one of the bill's authors and its sponsor in the house of representatives, claimed that the Minnesota Editorial Association

TO ALL NEWS DEALERS! Our hour of "passive resistance" has passed. Display Saturday Press exactly as you do other papers or magazines in your place of business. If you are molested in their sale by the police, refuse to remove them from your display stands and we will furnish the legal talent necessary for a "show down" in the courts. In brief, we will stand back of your Saturday Press sales and will carry your case to the court at our expense. If Brunskill still wants a fight, we'll give it to him. Let's force him into court.
---The Editors.

The Saturday Press

Vol. 1, No. 9 — Minneapolis, Minn., Nov. 19, 1927 — Price 5 Cents

A "Close-Up" View Of the City Hall

"Big Mose" Tries to "Smart-up" the Chief, But Found No Brains; Chief Claims He Saved Mayor From Jail and Mayor's Buddy Tries to Find a New Chief. How the Lice Swarmed as in the Days of Egypt, Until They Over-ran the Fixer's Patience. And Some Fodder for Floyd's Mental Silo.

Dawn—and the deep purple of the firmament melted, and gave way to the irresistible rays of Old Sol. The sombre colors of night faded out to make room for the colors of a new day—the gold and silver Brunskill, to show his undying appreciation to Mose for keeping bank robbers from robbing banks in Minneapolis, had cut Mose in on protected gambling. And Mose, to show his undying appreciation to Brunskill for cutting him in on gambling

Demoralizing Our Police Force

Mayor Leach Suspends Patrolman for Tagging Mayor's Car, Then Reinstates and "Delivers Lecture on Courtesy." Is Leach Immune From the Law Bill Jones Is Forced to Obey? Can a Hans Schmit Be Fined and a Leach Feted for Violation of the Same Law? If so, Why?

In other issues, I have called attention to the demoralization of the rank and file of our police department. I have rial stadium during a football game was instructed to tag every car left in a nonparking zone. He wasn't given orders to tag this car and slip that

Saturday Press, *November 19, 1927*

helped him draft it. None of the newspapers in Minneapolis, St. Paul, or Duluth editorialized against the bill.

The law was intended to silence a particularly noisome type of scandal sheet that dealt in anti-Semitism as well as in charges of corruption by public officials. Such scandal sheets flourished in many cities in the age of Prohibition, precisely because the establishment press failed to perform its role as watchdog of government. Duluth for a time had the *Rip-Saw*, published by John L. Morrison, who was variously described as a scandalmonger and a crusading muckraker. Minneapolis and St. Paul had a succession of *Reporters*, dating from 1913, and, beginning in 1927, the *Saturday Press*, published in Minneapolis by Howard A. Guilford and Jay M. Near. Its regular targets were Jews, Minneapolis Mayor George Leach, and Chief Frank Brunskill of the police department.

The first effort to enforce the gag law was a temporary restraining order issued against Morrison in 1926 by a state district court judge in Duluth. Morrison, suddenly stricken ill, fled to a hospital in Superior, Wisconsin, and died of a stroke. The *Rip-Saw* died with him.[42]

The second effort was to have no such swift termination. On November 21, 1927, Hennepin County Attorney Floyd B. Olson filed a complaint against Guilford's and Near's *Saturday Press*, describing it as a "malicious, scandalous, and defamatory publication" and asking for a restraining order under the Public Nuisance Law. It was granted. Thomas Latimer, a lawyer who was no admirer of the *Saturday Press* but who believed the gag law unconstitutional, was attorney for the defense. The Minnesota Supreme Court, asked to certify the law's constitutionality, upheld it unanimously, thus clearing the way for the lower court to make the injunction permanent.[43]

The case might have died there: Near was destitute, and Guilford had lost interest. But someone suggested to Near that he write to a new organization in New York, the American Civil Liberties Union (ACLU). Its founder, Roger Baldwin, came to Near's aid with $150 and the decision to appeal the gag law to the United States Supreme Court. "We see in this new device for previous restraint of publication a menace to the whole principle of the freedom of the press," the ACLU announced.

Minnesota newspapers did not welcome the ACLU's interest. "The Civil Liberties Union will no doubt make a great pother about the freedom of the press, but the legitimate newspapers will be rather bored than excited about it," the *Minneapolis Tribune* declared in an editorial dripping disdain.[44]

A less strange bedfellow for Near than the ACLU, and a more financially powerful one, was Robert R. McCormick, publisher of the *Chicago Tribune* and, like Near, a man of strong prejudices. But he was also a demon defender of First Amendment rights for the press, and when Near appealed to him, he swung into action. Weymouth Kirkland, McCormick's friend and the *Chicago Tribune*'s own lawyer, prepared the appeal and argued the first freedom-of-the-press case of prior restraint before the United States Supreme Court.

On July 1, 1931, more than two and a half years after federal court action was initiated, the Supreme Court ruled, five to four, that the gag law was unconstitutional. Chief Justice Charles Evans Hughes himself wrote the majority opinion. Its essence: "The fact that the liberty of the press may be abused by miscreant purveyors of scandal does not make any the less necessary the immunity of the press from previous restraint in dealing with official misconduct. Subsequent punishment for such abuses as may exist is the appropriate remedy consistent with constitutional privilege."[45] The minority opinion, written by Associate Justice Pierce Butler of Minnesota, regretted that the majority opinion "exposes the peace and good order of every community" to "malicious assaults of any insolvent publisher who may have . . . sufficient capacity to contrive and put into effect a scheme or program for oppression, blackmail or extortion."[46]

Of the Twin Cities dailies, only the *Pioneer Press* and the *Dispatch* gave the decision extended editorial approval. Under the heading, "Good Riddance," the editorial called the decision "highly gratifying" and discussed both majority and minority opinions at some length before concluding, "It is needless to say that the Pioneer Press and Dispatch are greatly pleased by the deserved execution of the vicious law."[47]

The *Journal* devoted most of its editorial paragraphs on the decision to chiding "liberals, so-called, that are forever railing against the justice of permitting five to four Supreme Court decisions . . . but this time they won't rail." The *Tribune* noted that enthusiasm for the decision would be greater outside Minnesota than in, and concluded, "Thus it is that our satisfaction over the vindication by the supreme court of the right of the press to a free existence is diluted by the knowledge that the scandal sheets will quickly revive in Minnesota."[48]

Legal scholars have valued the decision more insightfully. "Even after fifty years, *Near v Minnesota* remains the Supreme Court's most important opinion on this subject," Vincent Blasi wrote in 1981. And constitutional historian Paul L. Murphy affirmed that "contemporaries saw *Near* as a landmark, with one legal commentator on freedom of the press characterizing the case as 'the most important decision rendered since the adoption of the first amendment.' Subsequent authorities continue to view it in a similar light."[49]

The Age of Television

Near was not the only event that distinguished 1931 in the evolution of the media in Minnesota. That year saw Minnesota's first television transmission: George W. Young, who owned and operated radio station WDGY in Minneapolis, experimented with a crude television device to transmit to a receiver in city hall a picture of Mayor William F. Kunze shaking hands with a staff announcer.[50]

The first commercially licensed station in the country, WNBT-TV in New York City, did not go on the air until 1941; Minnesota's first was Stanley Hubbard's KSTP-TV, which began broadcasting on Channel 5 in April 1948. From the outset it provided newscasts. Soon there was announcer Bill Ingram sitting behind a desk, reading the news without benefit of either stills or film: "a radio newscast on camera," in the words of Don Betzold, a historian of WCCO-TV. That same year, KSTP became the first NBC-TV network affiliate.[51]

KSTP was not alone in the field for long, however. Minnesota's television industry grew rapidly in the Twin Cities, where the concentration of affluent households seemed to offer a market to adventurous advertisers. In addition, from 1947 to 1950, the Twin City Television Lab trained producers, directors, camera operators, and talent in its Minneapolis facility. WTCN had applied for a television license in 1946, and in July 1949 it became operational as Channel 4. It was a poor second to KSTP-TV in equipment and staff. WTCN-TV's owner, the Minnesota Broadcasting Corporation, was reluctant to spend money; in 1949, the country's television stations lost more than $25 million. But KSTP's Stanley Hubbard was a plunger. He built new quarters on University Avenue, halfway between the two cities' downtowns, and his station's news operation, staffed by four news photographers and equipped with two radio-dispatched panel trucks – nifty for chasing fire trucks – was the despair of WTCN-TV.[52]

WTCN-TV began operations with a staff of twenty-six, one studio, one studio camera, one film camera, one projector, and two mobile unit

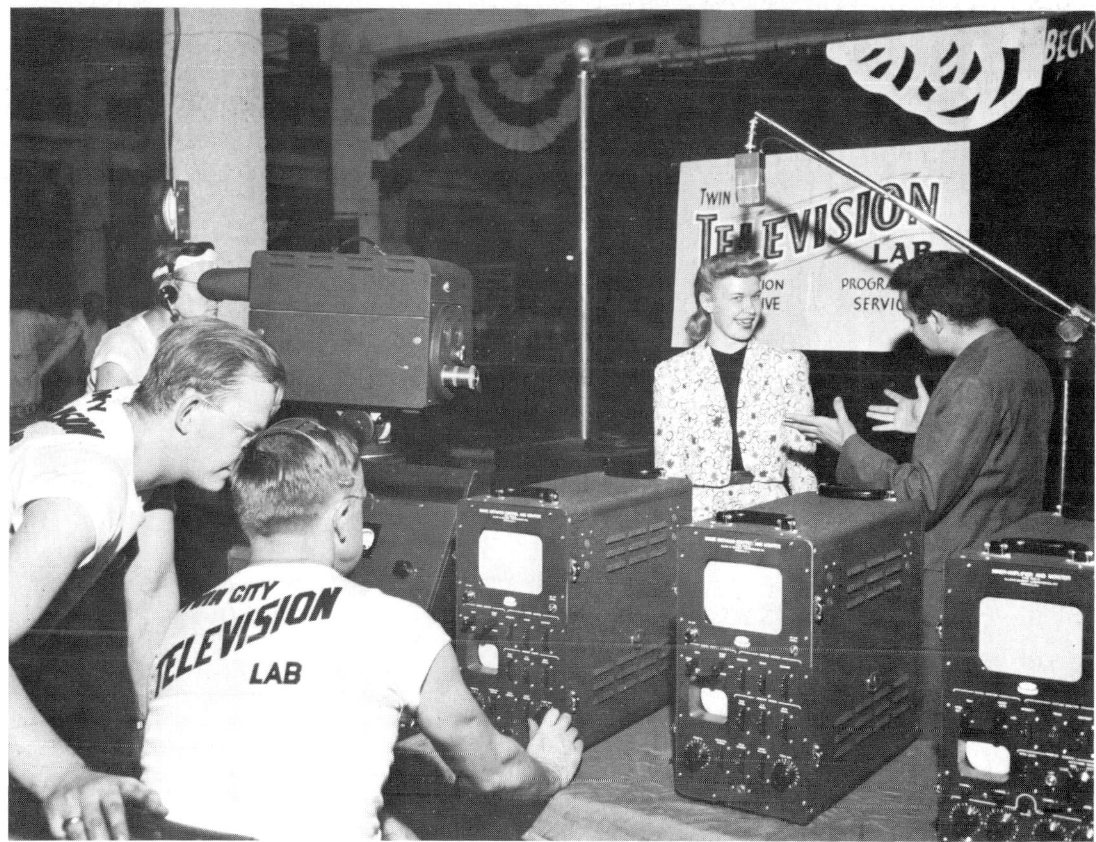

The Twin City Television Lab conducting closed circuit demonstrations of the new technology at the Minnesota State Fair, 1947

cameras – but no news photographer and no newscasts. To compete, its staff improvised: a weekly International News Service newsreel, flown out from New York, supplemented a leased wirephoto machine and the hiring of newscaster Charles ("Chick") McCuen from KRNT radio in Des Moines. His first newsroom was described by detractors as a basement broom closet, with just enough room for a couple of teletype machines and a desk. When McCuen was hired, WTCN-TV began a ratings war with KSTP-TV. McCuen tried a variety of news program formats and newscast lengths. The audience stayed with Bill Ingram at Channel 5. One evening, some inspired writer for Ingram's 10:00 P.M. show had written into his sign-off, "Wink left eye." Ingram complied and it caught on. People talked about "the Wink" and kept tuning to Channel 5.[53]

But changes came swiftly in television land. In 1950 the coaxial cable reached Minnesota, and network programs became directly available. WTCN-TV merged with WCCO radio and was renamed WCCO-TV in August 1952, and on February 9, 1953, its power leaped from 28,500 to 100,000 watts, the maximum under Federal Communications Commission (FCC) rules.[54]

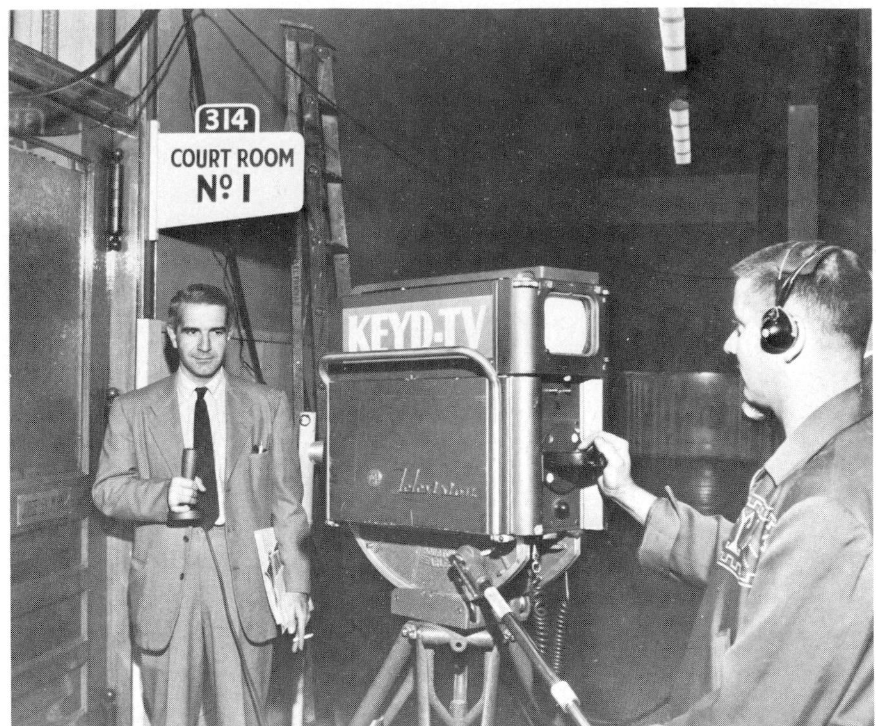

Harry Reasoner, television news reporter, and Tom Carlyon, cameraman, in 1955. KEYD-TV, Minneapolis, became KMSP-TV; Reasoner was hired by CBS and moved to New York City in 1956.

The metro area gained two more television stations in less than a year and a half: a new WTCN-TV (later KARE-TV) aired on Channel 11 in September 1953; KEYD-TV (later American Broadcasting Company affiliate KMSP-TV) was licensed for Channel 9 in January 1955. And in September 1957 KTCA-TV claimed Channel 2, reserved by the FCC for noncommercial, educational broadcasting. It was the culmination of a two-year fundraising effort by local civic leaders.[55]

Technology, too, brought rapid change in the industry. In 1958, the videotape recorder invaded local newsrooms. It reduced processing time by as much as half an hour and enabled live, on-the-scene coverage. Moreover, tape was reusable and cheaper than film. Satellite broadcasts began in July 1962, when WCCO participated in the first international live satellite telecast. A more dramatic change for viewers, however, was KSTP-TV's switch to color newscasts on October 6, 1963.[56]

WCCO-TV did not adopt full color until November 1966, holding back until CBS switched to color and until color cameras were improved. The station's delay cost it points in the ratings war with KSTP-TV. Not even Cedric Adams, the enormously popular columnist for the *Star* and newscaster for WCCO radio, could turn the war around for Channel 4. (Was it true that an airline pilot claimed to know when it was 10:15 P.M. because the lights all over rural Minnesota went out at the end of Adams's 10:00 newscast? Or was the legend created by some smart public relations agency?) Adams broadcast the news for WCCO-TV from 1953 to 1959, but television just was not his medium. WCCO-TV was not to match KSTP-TV's 10:00 P.M. ratings until after 1959, when WCCO hired Dave Moore – a pleasant, intelligent, young man trained as an actor and proven by his versatility in several assignments at the station – as broadcaster. In 1968 WCCO's new format, "The Scene Tonight," integrated news, weather, and sports broadcasts into a single, flexible program. It gave WCCO-TV a strong lead in the ratings and was copied by stations around the country.[57]

Viewers outside the range of metropolitan stations had access to other television programming. Stations in Rochester and Austin went on the air in 1953, followed the next year by the first of three stations in Duluth, and a station in Alexandria in 1958. Mankato, Appleton, Hibbing, and Walker got stations in the 1960s and Bemidji, Brainerd, Redwood Falls, St. Cloud, and Thief River Falls in the 1980s. Eighteen stations outside the metropolitan area served Minnesota in 1988. Television signals from communities in surrounding states were broadcast into Minnesota, pulling trade and workers across the borders. And by 1984, 325 cable television systems, which had reached Minnesota at Lanesboro in 1953, operated in the state.[58]

The invasion of cable into the metropolitan area was less successful. In the mid-1960s, enthusiasts predicted that viewers would line up to subscribe for hundreds of television channels, providing an infinite variety of communication services in addition to more conventional entertainment fare. The reality proved otherwise. By 1986, the state's 480,000 subscribers were only about a third of the potential where the service was available, considerably less than the national rate of 42 percent – and even that figure was below initial projections. As for the wealth of offerings, the St. Paul and Minneapolis franchisees carried fewer than half of the ninety channels they were capable of showing.[59]

Explanations for the shortfall varied: some program services failed to materialize, others failed to win sufficient audience support. Industry observers speculated that the sudden great popularity of video cassette recorders in the 1980s cut into the market for cable and would probably continue to do so.

Broadcast Markets Adjust

WCCO-AM radio, physically separate from WCCO-TV but connected to it by corporate bonds, dominated the metropolitan area from the 1920s through the 1980s. For years it captured an overwhelming 20 percent of the audience in the nation's fourteenth largest market, leaving some forty other AM and FM stations in the metropolitan area to scramble for the rest. WCCO's ratings, however, began slipping in the late 1970s, perhaps because its audience was aging; young adults were listening to other stations. AM and FM stations that targeted specific segments of the population also increased their audience share at the expense of WCCO.[60]

The stations of Minnesota Public Radio (MPR), for example, enjoyed a weekly audience of about 234,000 people throughout the state in the late 1980s; those listeners may have found it hard to believe that as recently as 1966 there was no MPR. On January 22, 1967, a few radio listeners within twenty miles of St. John's University at Collegeville, perhaps seeking relief from the ubiquitous beat of rock and roll, picked up strains of a Cleveland Orchestra concert. KSJR, classical music and fine arts station, modern instrument of the ancient Benedictine tradition of spreading culture in the community, was on the air. The idea was that of Father Colman J. Barry, history professor and later president of St. John's. The implementation was that of St. John's alumnus William H. Kling. Both men were committed to quality.[61]

Kling stressed quality in programming as well as in his appeals to potential funders. And his approach worked. From a single station in central Minnesota grew a network, established as Minnesota Educational Radio in 1971 and renamed MPR in 1974. In 1989 the network included fourteen stations, both AM and FM, including one in South Dakota and one in Michigan. Its contributing membership of over sixty thousand was the largest of any network in public radio; KSJN-AM and FM had the largest of any station in the country.

Although the network owed much of its supporters' loyalty to satellite broadcasts of National Public Radio's news programming, MPR's own news programming has won many awards, including three George Foster Peabody Awards. In 1989 MPR transmitted more than sixty hours of programming a week for national broadcast. From 1974 to 1987, it broadcast storyteller Garrison Keillor's phenomenally popular "Prairie Home Companion," a variety show modeled on the radio programs of the 1940s.

In 1982 MPR and four other producing stations founded American Public Radio (APR), a network with headquarters in St. Paul and 319 affiliates in 1989. It emphasized cultural and performance programming, complementing National Public Radio's news and information focus. Bill Kling, the network's builder, has not been without detractors: some employees have asserted that he is inconsiderate with his own people; other noncommercial station managers have called him ruthless. Even his critics, however, concede that his has been a brilliant achievement.

While Kling was building MPR and APR, that other noncommercial broadcaster, KTCA-TV, was pulling up its socks. In 1965 it received Minnesota's first ultra-high frequency (UHF) license and public station KTCI-TV was born. Spurred by widespread dissatisfaction with the blandness of KTCA's programming and its emphasis on structured educational broadcasting, the stations began upgrading facilities and operations and expanding and improving programming in public affairs and performing arts in the mid-1970s. Since 1974 the station's membership has swelled from 5,000 to more than 110,000 members. "Almanac," its lively local public affairs show hosted by Jan Smaby and Eric Eskola, was seen weekly in some 95,000 households in the metro area. Two innovative national programs that originated with the station, "Alive from Off Center" and "Newton's Apple," were broadcast by more than two hundred other public television stations throughout the country. In 1989 the stations planned a move to new, expanded facilities in downtown St. Paul.[62]

Garrison Keillor and the Powdermilk Biscuit Band (Judy Larson, Dakota Dave Hull, Bill Hinkley, and Peter Ostroushko) signing off a Prairie Home Show, November 21, 1974

Newspapers and Magazines Specialize

Although the broadcast media showed the greatest changes in the middle of the twentieth century, publishing was not static. Changes in the Twin Cities print media show interesting examples of publishers' responses to specialized audiences. A number of new magazines appeared, and newspapers took some interesting new directions.

Under the leadership of Reuel D. Harmon, Webb Company's fourth president, the St. Paul firm launched new agriculture magazines (*National Hog Farmer, BEEF, Farm Industry News*); printed other magazines (*Modern Medicine, TV Guide, Catholic Digest*) and books (for example, 1.25 million copies of the *Living Bible* for the Billy Graham Evangelistic Association in 1972); and custom-made magazines for three airlines and eight other corporate clients.[63]

Change was less fortuitous over at Miller Publishing in Minneapolis. *Feedstuffs*, the company's weekly newspaper for the emerging feed industry, was launched in 1929 and grew in circulation and advertising income even as the *Northwestern Miller*, responding to increasing concentration in the milling industry, shifted from a news weekly to a monthly magazine emphasizing milling technology. By the time the *Miller* suspended publication in 1973, its one hundredth year, contraction of the milling industry had largely eliminated its audience. Its parent company had adapted to diversified agribusiness in the 1950s by introducing a succession of specialized publications: *Feedlot, Hog Farm Management, Dairy Herd Management, Farm Store Merchandiser, Tack'n Togs Merchandising,* and *Home & Garden Supply Merchandiser.* Each was intended for the top management in a specialized area of agriculture. In the 1960s the Miller firm was publishing as many as seventeen magazines from its handsome headquarters on Wayzata Boulevard.[64]

Miller Publishing's stock was owned by its employees, and the company had earned a reputation for pride in employee ownership as well as for pride in a tradition of excellence. Neither, however, was proof against forces of change when the American Broadcasting Company, seeking to diversify and attracted by Miller's impressive profit record, came buying. ABC purchased Miller Publishing in April 1978, just as the agricultural economy once again entered difficult years, and used the publishing profits to sustain its broadcast programming. In 1984, it merged Miller with another publishing firm, Farm Progress of Chicago, and the company's proud traditions were ended.

While Webb and Miller were meeting the information needs of a predominantly rural society, more recent entrants in the state's periodicals mix have appealed to the interests of an urban audience. In 1972 William J. Dorn, a former employee of Miller, introduced a news tabloid called *Corporate Report* and almost immediately changed its format to that of a slick monthly magazine. Lively and well edited, it found an audience in executives and would-be executives of the regional business community (roughly equivalent to the Ninth Federal Reserve District) by profiling corporations and their chief executive officers. By 1978 Dorn was seeking to expand his magazine string (which included *Northliner* and *Architecture Minnesota,* among others) and was looking with particular interest at a floundering city magazine, *MPLS.* So, too, was Burton Cohen, who had recently sold his family's Modern Medicine Publications to the *New York Times.* Dorn, who denied having made a firm offer for *MPLS,* announced publication of a new city magazine, *Twin Cities.* Cohen purchased *MPLS* and promptly changed its name to *MPLS/St. Paul.* Both publishers insisted at the time that there was room for only one city magazine in the Twins, but in the decade that followed they offered disparate fare to the urban reader. *MPLS/St. Paul* provided trendy guidance to dining, entertainment, and Minnesota life-style for a teens-to-forties readership; *Twin Cities,* lush with fine color photography and with a partially free circulation, told a somewhat older audience about the elegant interiors of the area's splashier homes – and the activities of their owners. Both city magazines leavened the fluff with occasional serious articles. The March 1989 issue of *MPLS/St. Paul* announced the purchase of both city magazines and their merger by Stephen Adams, a son of Cedric Adams, whose Wayzata-based Adams Communications Corporation, founded in 1982, owned *Chicago* magazine, *Trailer Life* magazine, and newspaper and broadcasting properties in eleven states.[65]

Two newspapers were directed to black readers in the Twin Cities: the *Minneapolis Spokesman* and the *St. Paul Recorder*, both founded in 1934 by Cecil E. Newman. Their significance grew as the black community expanded during and after World War II. The papers combined news of blacks in both cities with national news of special interest to blacks and an editorial voice that spoke eloquently, but never stridently, for human rights. Newman was proud that more than a third of the two papers' combined circulation of twenty thousand went to white subscribers, and equally proud that journalist Carl Rowan and photographer and writer Gordon Parks began their distinguished careers on his newspapers.

Starting in the late 1970s, a pair of free weekly tabloids, *City Pages* and the *Twin Cities Reader*, served another specialized audience. Both offered a lively survey of the entertainment scene and made occasional forays into investigative reporting. In appealing to a youthful audience as alternative newspapers, they enjoyed attacking the metropolitan dailies as establishment monopolies.[66]

Suburban weeklies and neighborhood newspapers also grew impressively in the metropolitan area after World War II. Suburban weeklies were not new: T. R. Lillie's *Ramsey County Review*, for example, began in 1887 as the *North St. Paul Sentinel*. But their proliferation paralleled that of suburbia. Suburban merchants needed an advertising medium that would reach a limited, local audience, and the new suburbanites needed information about their communities. Almost as soon as they came on the scene, these weeklies were collected into groups, the economic advantage of central printing and central business management and even central editing being too great for independence to be sustained.[67]

Unlike the suburban press, the neighborhood papers of the Twin Cities were an innovation, a development of the late 1960s promoted by the federal government's policies to encourage participation of citizens. Neighborhood associations started and sponsored as many as thirteen of twenty-three such nonprofit papers operating in 1976. Most were staffed by volunteers. The newspapers, which were intended to serve their communities and influence their development, emphasized public affairs, thus meeting needs that were neglected by the major dailies or weeklies.[68]

Reporting the News Objectively

Social changes nurtured the suburban weeklies and the neighborhood press. But it was a change in political climate that effected changes in daily papers' definitions of news and how it should be handled. A shock ran through newsrooms in the early 1950s in the wake of Sen. Joseph R. McCarthy's sensational charges of Communist infiltration of the State Department. Reporters and editors alike realized that the news policy of objectivity, idealized since the decline of partisan journalism earlier in the century, often made them tools of demagogues who knew how to exploit them. Is the public statement of a public figure necessarily news just because public figures are deemed newsworthy? What if the statement is false?

"Objectivity is all right if it is really objective, if it conveys as accurate an impression of the truth as can be obtained," CBS newscaster Elmer Davis told a Newspaper Guild Memorial Lecture audience one evening in 1951. "But to let demonstrably false statements stand with no warning of their falsity is not what I would call objectivity."[69] Others argued that any attempt to warn the reader ran the risk of injecting opinion into a news account and that opinion belonged only on the editorial page. Still others insisted that objectivity, an ideal, was unattainable inasmuch as every reporter's perception of an event is influenced by personal experience and sensibility; the most that the reporter can achieve is an attempt to be fair.

The argument was further animated by insistence that traditional concepts of news were inadequate to mirror an increasingly complex society – that reporting lacked significance unless the reporter dug below the surface to explain the "why" of the event and to give it background and context. More and more, the conventional news account shared the news hole (the space available for news once the advertisements were laid out) with investigative and interpretive articles, enterprisers (articles initiated by reporters or editors rather than news sources or events), backgrounders, and articles earmarked "Analysis." Social science methodology and the techniques of the novelist and dramatist invaded the newsroom to add new dimensions to news reporting. The *Tribune*'s highly respected Minnesota Poll surveyed Minnesotans' opinions on social and political issues and candidates, and New Journalism guru Tom Wolfe had local emulators. Altogether, the newsroom had become a heady place to work.[70]

This was especially true of the separate and competitive news staffs at the *Minneapolis Tribune* and the *Minneapolis Star*, where John Cowles's formula for success (eliminate the opposition, then publish a responsible newspaper) had begun to work. "The primary obligation of a newspaper is to give its readers news, all the news, without bias or slant or distortion or suppression in the news columns," Cowles said in dedicating a new plant in 1949. The news staffs knew he read the papers with care: pages with errors circled in red or queries initialed "J. C." were returned to the newsrooms from his office. Cowles himself was considered a Republican, but his liberal views on social issues and his opposition to traditional Midwest isolationism pervaded the editorial pages of his papers. Under Carroll Binder, editorials in both papers spoke strongly for international organization, civil rights, and population control.[71]

But an era ended in 1968 when Cowles's son, John Cowles, Jr., became publisher, president, and chief executive officer. The next two decades were unsettling ones. Aside from the general factors of inflation and recession, national trends for newspapers – shrinking profits, sharply rising labor and newsprint costs, declining circulations, intensified competition for the advertising dollar – were all reflected locally. Acquisitions of other communications properties (the change in 1982 in corporate name from Star and Tribune Company to Cowles Media Company reflected the expansion) proved unwise in several instances, burdening the corporation

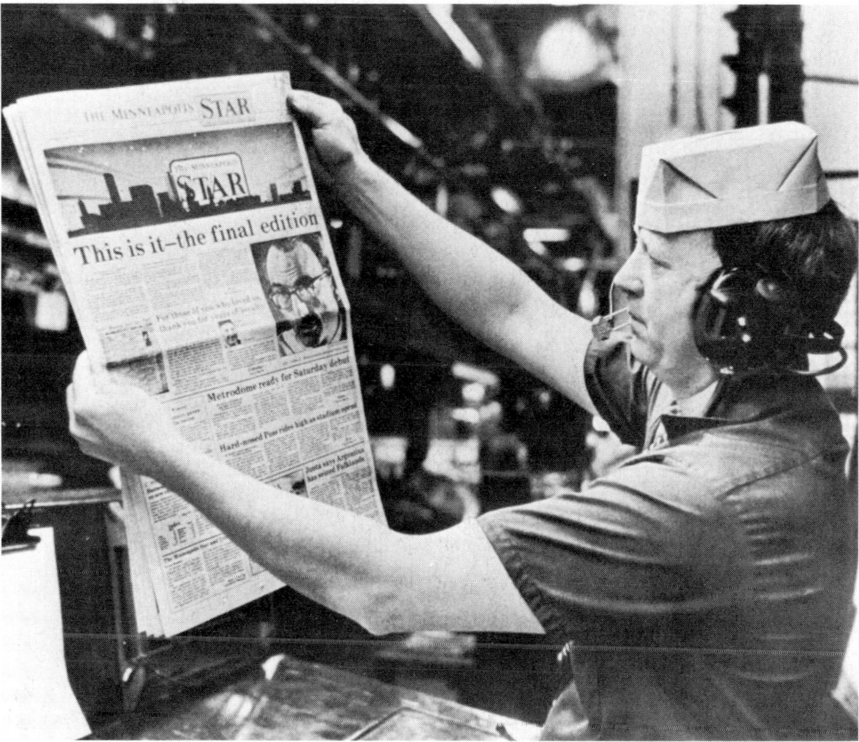

The Minneapolis Star*'s pressroom foreman, Dick Carlson, inspecting the paper's last edition, April 2, 1982*

with heavy debt at a time of high interest rates. In an effort to stem circulation losses, a decline it shared especially with other evening papers around the country, the *Star* underwent a radical change in content, emphasizing in-depth articles and "service" features. The changes did not solve the problems, however, and the *Star* was folded into the *Tribune* in 1982; in 1987 the paper became the *Star Tribune, Newspaper of the Twin Cities,* with separate editions for Minneapolis and St. Paul.[72]

In St. Paul and Duluth, the Ridder chain followed the same national trends by merging in 1974 with Knight Newspapers, Inc., to form Knight-Ridder Newspapers, Inc., which was then the country's largest newspaper enterprise in total daily circulation (3.75 million). In 1985 the St. Paul operation became a single newspaper, the *Pioneer Press Dispatch.*[73]

While the metropolitan dailies were coping with economic pressures by mergers, both of papers and corporate ownership, smaller dailies around the state were passing from tightly held family ownerships to chains, or as they preferred to be called, groups. Thomson Newspapers, Inc., Midwest Newspapers, Inc., Lee Newspapers, Inc., Dow Jones Newspapers, Inc., Stauffer Communications, Inc., Gannett Newspapers, Inc. – these became the owners' names, instead of Adams, Rasmussen, Schilplin, Underwood, Vance, White, Withers. Of the state's twenty-five dailies in 1989, only one – the *Faribault Daily News* – was independently owned. Reasons given for the sales varied: the new generation of a family lacked interest;

incredibly inflated values imposed impossible inheritance taxes; owners could get larger returns, with less stress, by selling than by operating. Opinions of the consequences of this change varied, as well: the greater resources of the group permitted improvement of the paper; where group policy encouraged autonomy of editorial expression, that expression gained vigor because it was less vulnerable to social pressure of the community; diversity suffered; leadership was lost because management was less committed to the community than to advancement in the chain.[74] A former owner, third generation, said regretfully of the new management, "They'll never share the town's concerns the way I've shared them."[75]

A similar but less marked trend was overtaking the weeklies in the state in the late 1980s. Only about a third were owned by groups, and many of those were pairs. But the apparent trend in ownership of weeklies was less significant than the decline in numbers, which continued despite the launching of papers serving suburban communities. In 1980 there were 276 weeklies, not including the 70 that were distributed without charge. The end of the erosion was not in sight. As family farms continued to go under, sapping the vitality of Main Street, the struggle for survival became the newspaper's, too. Many a weekly that regularly published twelve- and fourteen-page issues was reduced as regularly to ten.[76]

Ironically, the decline came after the improvement, in many respects, of the product. A team of researchers at the University of Minnesota, comparing a random sample of fifty-nine weeklies and semiweeklies in 1965 with the same sample in 1985, found that news staffs were somewhat larger and production staffs somewhat smaller in 1985. They also found marked increases in news content of weeklies and increasing emphasis on the watchdog role of the press. Without exception, the weeklies shifted from letterpress to offset production. Many were printed in central printing plants, of which there were nineteen around the state in 1986.[77]

Improvement was fostered, too, by the Minnesota Newspaper Association (MNA), one of the oldest (dating from 1867) and most vital in the country. In 1965 the MNA established its Better Newspaper Contest, an annual competition that drew hundreds of entries in dozens of categories. A consistent winner in many categories, including "state's best weekly," has been the *Monticello Times*, whose former editor-publisher, Lynn R. Smith, started a nationwide movement in 1974 by initiating Don't Smoke Day. Smith's son Donald Q. has continued the observance, as well as the paper's tradition of excellence.[78]

In 1980 the MNA established the Minnesota Newspaper Foundation, a nonprofit service organization to conduct educational seminars and conferences for newspaper personnel. But more innovative was the MNA's sponsorship in 1971 of the Minnesota News Council. The brainchild of the MNA's executive secretary, Robert M. Shaw, it had models in the British Press Council and councils in other European countries. Its purpose was twofold: to hear and evaluate complaints against the media and to improve the public's understanding and appreciation of a free press.[79]

The council, consisting of twelve members of the public and twelve journalists, was set up to hear grievances and responses from the media in question and to render determinations upholding or denying the validity of the complaint. It was not to impose sanctions, but rather to report its findings in news releases and to depend on the general willingness of the media to publish them. Before a complaint could be scheduled for hearing, the complainant was required to waive recourse to the courts or FCC.

The council has received an average of fifty-three complaints a year, most of which have been settled or dropped prior to public hearing. In its first fifteen years the council held hearings on sixty-two complaints. (As if to challenge the council's integrity, the first complaint it heard was brought by a state legislator against Gordon Spielman, then editor of the *Union Advocate.* Spielman was a founding member of the council, which ruled against him.) Research conducted in 1985 supported the concept of the news council: a study of eight hundred libel cases tried nationwide between 1974 and 1984 found that plaintiffs were more concerned with clearing their names than winning damage awards.[80]

Despite the respect it has earned, the council has not enjoyed unanimous support from media institutions. Broadcasters were reluctant to come aboard (the council did not extend its purview to electronic media until 1977), and efforts in other states to follow its example have come to naught. The National News Council, which *did* follow Minnesota's lead, expired after only eleven years (1973–84) despite prestigious membership, largely because the *New York Times* and the *Washington Post* denied it their essential cooperation. The media are notoriously sensitive to criticism, and despite the handwringing that goes on at press association meetings over loss of credibility and charges of media arrogance, Minnesota media have been alone in their support of one of the few agencies designed to improve the public's understanding and appreciation of a free press.

That the Minnesota News Council has survived at all (its meager annual budget of sixty-five thousand dollars depends on gifts) is due in part to support from the *Star Tribune* and in larger part to the sound guidance and dedication of Associate Justice C. Donald Peterson of the Minnesota Supreme Court, who chaired the council through its first decade. But survive it has, and it must be counted a major plus in any toting up of debits and credits in a media balance sheet for the state. On the minus side of such a balance sheet has been the continuing failure of many media people to understand the true meaning of the First Amendment. A major news story of 1979 provided an excellent example.

In the firestorm of protest that followed publication of the outrageous Finals Edition of the *Minnesota Daily* on June 4, 1979, many a publication joined in the clamorous demand for punishment of the University of Minnesota student paper. Prof. Donald M. Gillmor of the university's School of Journalism and Mass Communication, who subsequently examined the communications on the subject, has written: "But only the *Star and Tribune,* the Worthington *Daily Globe,* and the Shakopee *Valley News* saw clearly from the beginning the first amendment significance of what was to follow." As the campaign to deprive the *Daily* of mandatory fee support grew, the school's director, F. Gerald Kline, sought to counter the campaign by enlisting support from newspaper editors throughout the state.

"By more than a five-to-one margin, those editors who responded rejected the first amendment arguments that were being made in anticipation of Regent action to change the *Daily*'s fee structure." In the minority were the *Austin Daily Herald*, which warned against "overkill," and the *Waseca Daily Journal*, which "reminded its readers that publications we detest must be tolerated because freedom of the press exists 'to protect the rights of those we disagree with to publish without censorship.' " Gillmor concluded that "the lesson to be learned is that when vocal segments of the public are aroused the first amendment has few defenders," and he asked: "Why did so much time and effort need to be expended explaining . . . that the first amendment is designed to protect unpopular speech, minority speech, unorthodox speech, abhorrent speech? We are obviously dealing with a fragile freedom, a fragile first amendment."[81]

The *Daily* sued for restoration of its original fee support and won its case against the president and regents of the University, but only on appeal to the federal circuit court. Its supporters should not have been surprised that they were so few and so exposed, had they reflected on media history in this century: on the failure of newspapers to defend radical expression in 1912 and 1918 and 1920, and on their willingness to see the Minnesota gag law enforced against Jay M. Near's *Saturday Press* in 1928.

In other respects, media history in Minnesota in the twentieth century has been one of radical change: introduction and ubiquitous growth first of radio, then of television; decline in numbers, if not circulation, of the newspapers, both daily and weekly; and an increased emphasis on entertainment in all of the media. What has not changed, apparently, is the media's own failure to understand the meaning – in the concrete instance – of the First Amendment, on which all of them ultimately depend.

NOTES

1. For figures that show newspaper growth and decline, see n. 3, below. Of the foreign-language papers, the last was the Finnish *Amerikan Uutiset*, which was sold to a Florida publisher in 1984. For other examples, see June D. Holmquist, ed., *They Chose Minnesota: A Survey of the State's Ethnic Groups* (St. Paul: Minnesota Historical Society Press, 1981), 235, 266, 278, 286, 302.

2. U.S. Bureau of the Census, *Statistical Abstract of the United States: 1980* (Washington, D.C.: Government Printing Office, 1980), 589, 592; *This Is WLAG, the Twin City Radio Central* (Minneapolis: Northwest Farmstead, 1924), 1, pamphlet at Minnesota Historical Society (MHS); McLuhan and Quentin Fiore, *The Medium Is the Massage* (New York: Bantam Books, 1967). Figures for 1900 newspaper circulation are calculated from U.S., *Census*, 1900, *Population*, vol. 2, table 2, p. 54, and *Ayer Directory of Newspapers, Magazines and Trade Publications* (Philadelphia: N. W. Ayer and Son, Inc.), 1900, p. 412–38.

3. *Ayer Directory*, 1900, p. 412, 426, 427, 432, 433; 1910, p. 422; 1920, p. 457; and 1930, p. 479.

4. Here and in following paragraph, see inventories, MHS newspaper library, and *Ayer Directory*, 1900–20.

5. *Minneapolis Journal*, Jan. 1, 1901, p. 1, Jan. 9, 1901, p. 6.

6. For biographical information, see Minnesota Biographies Project files, MHS reference library; Ted Curtis Smythe, "A History of the Minneapolis *Journal*, 1878–1939" (Ph.D. diss., University of Minnesota, 1967).

7. White's paper became the *Winona Republican-Herald* in 1919. He was followed as publisher successively by his son, Maxwell H., and grandson, William F. The Rochester paper became the *Post-Bulletin* in 1925 through a consolidation with the *Post and Record.* Sons

Charles H. and Robert Withers became editor and publisher, respectively, two years after the death of the senior Withers in 1960. See Minnesota Biographies Project files, MHS.

8. Here and below, see C. J. Mulrooney, *Recollections: The Story of the James Murphy Family and Its Association with the Minnesota Tribune Company and Related Events* (Minneapolis: MTC Properties, Inc., 1978), 7–11, 48.

9. Robert O. Baker, *The Webb Company: The First Hundred Years* (St. Paul: The Company, 1982), 3–20, 69.

10. Robert M. Frame III, "The Progressive Millers: A Cultural and Intellectual Portrait of the Flour Milling Industry, 1870–1930" (Ph.D. diss., University of Minnesota, 1980), 132–50.

11. "At least 20 German-language journals went out of circulation" in Minnesota between 1890 and 1910, according to Hildegard Binder Johnson, "The Germans," in *They Chose Minnesota*, ed. Holmquist, 174. The same authority cites 19 German newspapers published in Minnesota in 1917, but only seven in 1920. On repressive legislation and the actions of the commission, see Minnesota, *Statutes*, 1917, ch. 463, H.F. no. 1270; H. C. Peterson and Gilbert C. Fite, *Opponents of War, 1917–1919* (Madison: University of Wisconsin Press, 1968), 17; La Vern J. Rippley, "Conflict in the Classroom: Germanism in Minnesota Schools, 1917–19," *Minnesota History* 47 (Spring 1981): 171–83.

12. See, for example, John Lofton, *The Press as Guardian of the First Amendment* (Columbia: University of South Carolina Press, 1980); John D. Stevens, *Shaping the First Amendment: The Development of Free Expression* (Beverly Hills, Calif.: Sage Publications, 1982).

13. Victoria Marie Smith, "Newspapers and Freedom of Expression: Minnesota Press Reaction to Suppression during the World War I Era, 1912–1920" (Master's thesis, University of Minnesota, 1986), 91–115, 159–60 (quotations). John D. Stevens found similar results in his study of Wisconsin dailies during World War I, "Press and Community Toleration: Wisconsin in World War I," *Journalism Quarterly* 46 (Summer 1969): 255–59.

14. *Ayer Directory*, 1920, p. 457; 1930, p. 479; 1940, p. 447; and 1945, p. 441.

15. Information on early stations is available at the Broadcast Pioneers Library, Washington, D.C.

16. Ted Curtis Smythe, "The Birth of Twin Cities' Commercial Radio," *Minnesota History* 41 (Fall 1969): 328–29, 332–34. Smythe says that, in order to save face, the newspapers asked Gov. J. A. O. Preus to request publicly that they consider "a plan for centering radio broadcasting in the twin cities in the University of Minnesota and under its control."

17. Charles W. Ingersoll, *Minnesota Airwaves 1912 through 1939 and Radio Trivia* (Cloquet: The Author, [1986]), [7, 11]; S. E. Frost, Jr., *Education's Own Stations* (New York: Arno Press, 1971), 387; Smythe, "Birth of Radio," 327; *WCAL, 1918–1953* ([Northfield: The Station, 1953]), [3]; Charles F. Sarjeant, ed., *The First Forty: The Story of WCCO Radio* (Minneapolis: WCCO Radio, 1964), 67–68, 69.

18. Here and in the following two paragraphs, see Sarjeant, ed., *First Forty*, 66–69; Larry Haeg, Jr., *Sixty Years Strong: The Story of One of America's Great Radio Stations, 1924–1984* (Minneapolis-St. Paul: WCCO Radio, 1984), 11–14.

19. *This Is WLAG*, 1, 3, 10, 11.

20. Herb Paul, "When Radio Was Young," *Greater Minneapolis*, March 1962, p. 16, 17.

21. Here and in following two paragraphs, see Sarjeant, ed., *First Forty*, 68–70, 73–78.

22. Here and in following three paragraphs, see William Swanson, "Inside the House of Hubbard: A Visit with the First Family of Twin Cities Broadcasting," in *Corporate Report*, August 1976, p. 27; Ingersoll, *Minnesota Airwaves*, [32–33]; *Broadcasting/Cablecasting Yearbook* (Washington, D.C.: Broadcasting Publications, Inc., 1988), B-151.

23. Here and in following paragraph, see Sarjeant, ed., *First Forty*, 76–77.

24. Figures on radio stations were compiled from Ingersoll, *Minnesota Airwaves*.

25. *St. Paul Pioneer Press*, Feb. 12, 1922, sec. 2, p. 2, Feb. 19, 1922, sec. 2, p. 2. On columns, see *Minneapolis Journal*, Apr. 20, 1922, p. 25; *Minneapolis Tribune*, Apr. 18, 1922, p. 2, as cited in Smythe, "Birth of Radio," 329.

26. For examples, see *Minneapolis Tribune*, Apr. 2, 1890, p. 6 (business news); *Minneapolis Tribune*, Apr. 6, 1890, p. 10, Apr. 11, 1897, p. 34, and *St. Paul Pioneer Press*, Nov. 11, 1898, p. 18 (society). For an example of women's pages, see *Minneapolis Tribune*, Apr. 2, 1970, p. 1.

27. For examples, see *Minneapolis Tribune*, July 6, 1890, and July 24, 1934, p. 13; *St. Paul Pioneer Press*, Sept. 21, 1890; *Rochester Daily Post and Record*, July 24, 1934, p. 8.

28. Bradley L. Morison, *Sunlight on Your Doorstep: The Minneapolis Tribune's First Hundred Years* (Minneapolis: Ross and Haines, Inc., 1966), 29–30.

29. Morison, *Sunlight*, 30; Mulrooney, *Recollections*, 68–69.

30. On the Cowleses, here and below, see William J. McNally, *Tale of an Assignment: Being a History of Minnesota Tribune Company from February 14, 1940, to May 31, 1956* (Minneapolis: MTC Properties, Inc., 1956), 3; Morison, *Sunlight*, 55–56. On the *Minnesota Star*,

see Harold L. Nelson, "A History of *The Minnesota Daily Star*" (Master's thesis, University of Minnesota, 1950).

31. Morison, *Sunlight*, 69–70 (quotes headline); *Ayer Directory*, 1935, p. 456, and 1939, p. 459.

32. Actually, McNally proposed a 49.5/49.5 division with an independent third party holding the swing 1 percent. McNally reasoned that *Tribune* subsidiaries (the paper mill and the farm) would balance the *Star Journal*'s more modern plant, but Cowles had no interest in the subsidiaries. McNally, *Tale of an Assignment*, 13–27.

33. On the Ridder acquisitions, here and below, see Donald J. O'Grady, *The Pioneer Press and Dispatch: History at Your Door, 1849–1983* (St. Paul: Northwest Publications, 1983), 77–78; Mulrooney, *Recollections*, 64. Dates of acquisitions of Grand Forks and Duluth papers were confirmed in author's conversations with staff at the newspapers and Knight-Ridder Newspapers, Inc.

34. On the O'Connor system, here and below, see O'Grady, *Pioneer Press and Dispatch*, 78–82; for an example of the *News*'s campaign, see "The Life of Dick O'Connor," a series of articles written by George C. Rogers and published from Jan. 2 to Feb. 2, 1933.

35. On White and Elmer E. Adams, see Minnesota Biographies Project files, MHS; on Withers, see Val Björnson, *The History of Minnesota* (West Palm Beach, Fla.: Lewis Historical Publishing Co., 1969), 4:842; on Schilplin, see Joseph A. A. Burnquist, ed., *Minnesota and Its People* (Chicago: S. J. Clarke Publishing Co., 1924), 4:561; on Rasmussen, see *Minnesota Press* 41 (June 1968): 1, 3; on Underwood, see *Minnesota Press* 40 (April 1976): 5.

36. George H. Mayer, *The Political Career of Floyd B. Olson* (Minneapolis: University of Minnesota Press, 1951), 221. For a detailed account of the strike and newspaper coverage, see p. 192–222; on the Citizens' Alliance, see Lois Quam and Peter J. Rachleff, "Keeping Minneapolis an Open-Shop Town: The Citizens' Alliance in the 1930s," *Minnesota History* 50 (Fall 1986): 105–17. On the strikes, see Peter Rachleff, "Turning Points in the Labor Movement: Three Key Conflicts," *this volume*, 207–11.

37. *Minneapolis Tribune*, July 21, 1934, p. 1; *Minneapolis Journal*, May 19, 1934, p. 1.

38. *Minneapolis Journal*, July 21, 1934, p. 1; Eric Sevareid, *Not So Wild a Dream* (New York: Alfred A. Knopf, 1946), 58.

39. On newspaper organizing, here and in following paragraph, see O'Grady, *Pioneer Press and Dispatch*, 85; Newspaper Guild of the Twin Cities, Records, 1926–82, Historical Information, MHS Manuscripts Department.

40. An exception was the vocal opposition of the American Newspaper Publishers Association to Section 7a of the National Industrial Recovery Act code proposed for newspapers; its ban on child labor threatened the newspaper carrier system. Edwin Emery and Michael Emery, *The Press and America: An Interpretive History of the Mass Media* (Englewood Cliffs, N.J.: Prentice-Hall, Inc., 1984), 695.

41. Here and in the following two paragraphs, see Minnesota, *Statutes*, 1927, ch. 97, sec. 10123-1; Fred W. Friendly, *Minnesota Rag* (New York: Random House, 1981), 4, 21–22, 29–39.

42. Friendly, *Minnesota Rag*, 23–27.

43. On *Near v Minnesota*, here and below, see Friendly, *Minnesota Rag*, 43, 49–53, 60–70, 75, 91. Olson, too, had been a target of *Saturday Press* charges of corruption. Friendly, *Minnesota Rag*, 78–79.

44. *Minneapolis Tribune*, July 21, 1928, p. 16. The ACLU was later eased out of the appeal.

45. As quoted in Friendly, *Minnesota Rag*, 151.

46. As quoted in Friendly, *Minnesota Rag*, 155.

47. *St. Paul Pioneer Press*, June 2, 1931, p. 8.

48. *Minneapolis Journal*, June 2, 1931, p. 18; *Minneapolis Tribune*, June 2, 1931, p. 10. The *Saturday Press* did indeed resume publication in 1932, and other scandal sheets appeared in Minneapolis and were regularly confiscated by police. Sometime publisher Guilford was gunned down driving in south Minneapolis one autumn day in 1934; his was one of three unsolved murders of scandal sheet publishers, the others being Walter W. Liggett, editor of *Mid-West American*, and Arthur Kasherman, publisher of the *Public Press*. Friendly, *Minnesota Rag*, 163, 165–66.

49. Blasi, "Toward a Theory of Prior Restraint: The Central Linkage," and Murphy, "*Near v Minnesota* in the Context of Historical Developments," *Minnesota Law Review* 66 (November 1981): 11, 97. These articles were papers prepared for a conference observing the fiftieth anniversary of *Near v Minnesota*, sponsored by the School of Journalism and Mass Communication of the University of Minnesota.

50. "TV and How It Grew," *Greater Minneapolis*, May 1982, p. 11.

51. [WCCO-TV], *The Growth of WCCO Television* (N.p.: [WCCO-TV, 1962]), [1–3]; *Broadcasting/Cablecasting Yearbook 1988*, C-37; Lawrence Ingrassia, "Minnesota's Hubbards, TV Pioneers, Dream up Plan for New Network," *Wall Street Journal*, Sept. 22, 1981, p. 1, 15;

Don Betzold, "Racing toward Tonight: The History of a TV Newsroom" (Unpublished summa thesis, University of Minnesota, 1972), 4, available at MHS.

52. Joe Beck, "Pioneering in Television in the Twin Cities," *Minnesota History* 46 (Fall 1979): 279; [WCCO-TV], *Since 1949* ([Minneapolis: WCCO-TV, 1979]), [2]. Minnesota Broadcasting Corporation (later Mid Continent Radio-Television, Inc.) had been formed in 1933 by the Minneapolis Tribune Co. and Northwest Publications, Inc., publishers of the *Pioneer Press* and *Dispatch*.

53. Betzold, "Racing," 3–10, 18, 21. Ultimately Ingram overreached in 1959 and there came one of those abruptly climactic separations from Hubbard employment that were to characterize termination of many a career at KSTP-TV (Betzold, "Racing," 57–58).

54. When the stations merged, a new company, Midwest Radio-Television, Inc., was formed to own WCCO-TV. CBS sold its majority interest in WCCO radio in order to gain 47 percent interest in the new company; the other 53 percent was held by Mid Continent Radio-Television, Inc. (see n. 52). The CBS connection was short-lived, however. In November 1954, in compliance with a new FCC multiple ownership rule, CBS sold its interest in WCCO-TV to the Minneapolis Star and Tribune Company. For the next twenty-two years, the owners and corporate structure of WCCO-TV and WCCO AM and FM (launched in 1973; later WLTE-FM) remained unchanged. Then, in 1976, MTC Properties, Inc. (formerly Minnesota Tribune Company), owner of 50 percent of Mid Continent, bought the Ridders' 50 percent interest in Mid Continent. In 1979 Mid Continent was merged into Midwest Radio-Television, Inc.; in 1982 its name was changed to Midwest Communications, Inc.; and in 1988 the company put itself on the market. Betzold, "Racing," 17; *Since 1949*, [3]; "Midwest Communications, Inc." (Typescript from corporate records dated Aug. 13, 1986, in author's possession).

55. Betzold, "Racing," 21, 30; *The Tenth Anniversary of KTCA-TV* ([St. Paul: KTCA-TV, 1967]).

56. Betzold, "Racing," 47, 77; *Growth of WCCO*, [17].

57. *Alumni News* 72 (March 1973): 28; Betzold, "Racing," 40–41, 55–56, 77, 80–92.

58. *Broadcasting/Cablecasting Yearbook*, C-36, 37, 38; Vic Spadaccini, ed., *Minnesota Pocket Data Book 1985–1986* (Minneapolis: Blue Sky Marketing, 1985), 62.

59. Interview with Chris Donaldson, Feb. 10, 1987. Donaldson had been a member of the state Cable Communications Board, which the legislature discontinued in 1985; Jim Dawson, "Cable TV Firms Plan for a Leaner Future," and Colin Covert, "Cable TV Failing to Live up to Expectations It Would Become an Electronic Wonderland," *Minneapolis Star and Tribune*, Sept. 29, 1986, p. 1A, 5A.

60. Judith Yates Borger, "Making Waves," *Corporate Report*, October 1983, p. 76–77.

61. On MPR, here and in following three paragraphs, see Patricia Weaver Francisco, "The Life and Times of MPR," *Minnesota Monthly*, January 1987, p. 50–57; Steve Berg, "MPR Gunslinger Ready for Commercial Radio Showdown," *Minneapolis Tribune*, June 27, 1980, p. 1C; *Ten Years: The Official Souvenir Anniversary Program for A Prairie Home Companion* ([St. Paul: MPR, 1984]); Lynda McDonnell, "Life after Lake Wobegon: Battling Bill Kling Fights On," *Washington Journalism Review*, May 1987, p. 25–29.

62. *It Takes Two: Twin Cities Public Television, 1986/87* ([St. Paul, 1987]). Additional information was supplied by Bill Handley, executive producer, and Georgia Gould, public information manager.

63. Robert Baker, *The Webb Company: The First Hundred Years* (St. Paul: The Company, 1982), 70–74, 78–82, 86. The company dropped "Publishing" from its title in 1973. A magazine that Webb did *not* publish was DeWitt Wallace's *Reader's Digest*. Young Wallace, son of Macalester College's president and a former employee of Webb, offered his idea for a magazine that would condense articles from other magazines to Webb for one thousand dollars, but one of Webb's co-owners dismissed it as "a crackpot idea," according to Baker, 28. At least a dozen Manhattan publishers turned it down, too, before Wallace decided to undertake publication himself.

64. Here and in following paragraph, see Bruce Rubenstein, "What Ever Happened to Miller Publishing?" *Twin Cities*, March 1987, p. 39–46; "The History," *Northwestern Miller*, July 1973, p. 45–47, 82–83.

65. Steve Berg, "The Great Metropolitan Magazine Battle," *Minneapolis Tribune*, May 5, 1978, p. 1C; Dan Wascoe, Jr., and David Phelps, "A Look at Two Self-Made Media Barons," *Star Tribune* (Minneapolis), Feb. 20, 1989, p. 1D. *Corporate Report* became *Corporate Report Minnesota* in 1981.

66. The *Twin Cities Reader* began publication in 1976 as *The Entertainer* and changed its name in 1977; *City Pages* began as *Sweet Potato* in 1979 and changed its name in 1981.

67. Dennis McGrath, "Sun Rise? Sun Set?" *Corporate Report*, February 1975, p. 41–54. In 1987 Guy Gannett of Portland, Maine, collected the Sun, Current, Sailor, and Post groups in a string of some twenty different publications ringing the Twin Cities with a total circulation of a half million.

68. Jean Ward and Cecilie Gaziano, "A New Variety of Urban Press: Neighborhood Public-Affairs Publications," *Journalism Quarterly* 53 (Spring 1976): 61-67, 116.

69. Elmer Davis, "Must We Mislead the Public?" in *The Press in Perspective*, ed. Ralph D. Casey (Baton Rouge: Louisiana State University Press, 1963), 66.

70. Morison, *Sunlight*, 141; Sydney S. Goldish, "The Minnesota Poll and the Undecided Voter" (Master's thesis, University of Minnesota, 1951), 38. Goldish was the poll's second director.

71. *St. Paul Pioneer Press/Dispatch*, June 26, 1983, p. 1A. From 1944 to 1952, under executive editor Gideon D. Seymour, the *Tribune*, especially, built a strong local staff with specialists on medical science (Victor Cohn), labor (Sam Romer), education (Richard P. Kleeman), and race relations (Carl T. Rowan, the paper's first black reporter), as well as foreign correspondents Graham Hovey in London and Robert Hewett in the Middle East (Morison, *Sunlight*, 79–85, 95, 117–19).

72. David Carr, "Des Moines R&T growth brought debt, criticism," *Citibusiness*, July 7, 1983, p. 10–12; John Kostouros, "Rebound at Cowles Media," *Citibusiness*, Sept. 12, 1984, p. 1, 15–16; *Minneapolis Star and Tribune*, Feb. 3, 1985, p. 1A, 13A–15A; Adam Platt, "The Little Paper That Could (Or Can It)," *Twin Cities Reader*, Nov. 16–22, 1988; Cheryl Arvidson, "The Price That Broke *The Register:* Gannett's Bid and the Family Fallout," *Washington Journalism Review*, April 1985, p. 21–26. For the corporate name change, see *St. Paul Pioneer Press*, Apr. 21, 1982, p. 6B.

73. *Minneapolis Star*, Sept. 4, 1975, p. 8B. This article was part of a series called "The News Machines: An Inside Look at the Twin Cities Media," published from Aug. 25 through Sept. 6, 1975, and republished in a special section titled *Tearing down the Paper Curtain* (Minneapolis: Minneapolis Star, [1975]).

74. Mark Plenke, "Who Owns Minnesota Newspapers?" *The Observer*, Spring 1986, p. 17. After this article was published, one of the two independents that it names was sold to a newspaper chain.

75. Conversation of the author with Charles Underwood, former owner of the *Fergus Falls Daily Journal*.

76. Plenke, "Who Owns Minnesota Newspapers?" 17; *Ayer Directory*, 1980, p. 474.

77. G. A. Donohue, C. N. Olien, and P. J. Tichenor, "How Community Editors See Their Job and Organizations," *Sociology of Rural Life* (University of Minnesota) 8 (Spring/Summer 1986): 1–2, 7. The Minnesota Newspaper Association holds information on newspapers in the state, including the number of printing plants. For a sensitive discussion of the balance between reporting news and providing a medium for retail advertising, see Richard Ousky, "Small Town Papers," *North Country Anvil*, Spring 1985, p. 20–22.

78. On the early history of the MNA, see Thomas F. Barnhart, "History of Minnesota Editorial Association" (Master's thesis, University of Minnesota, 1937).

79. Here and in the following five paragraphs, see Nancy How Girouard, "The Minnesota Newspaper Foundation Is Coming into Its Own," and C. Donald Peterson, " 'The Father of the Minnesota News Council' Looks Back," *The Observer* (Winter 1985–86): 10–11, 12–14.

80. Randall Bezanson, Gilbert Cranberg, and John Soloski, "Libel in the Press: Setting the Record Straight" (Lecture presented at the Silha Center for the Study of Media Ethics and Law, University of Minnesota, Minneapolis, 1985).

81. Donald M. Gillmor, "The Fragile 'First,' " *Hamline Law Review* 8 (May 1985): 278, 288, 289, 305, 306.

DANIEL J. ELAZAR

A Model of Moralism in Government

In 1905 Minnesotans acquired a new State Capitol and a state highway department. Each in its own way symbolized the state's entry into the twentieth century. The new building stood alone on Capitol Hill, a sign of how small Minnesota's state government was in those days in contrast to the 1980s when the Capitol presided over a park stretching nearly half a mile toward downtown St. Paul and nearly half a mile wide at its broadest.[1] Not until World War I was a second building, housing the Minnesota Historical Society, added to the site. The third, the State Office Building, was occupied in 1932. The park below the crest of the hill emerged only after World War II. Construction resumed in the 1950s according to a new master plan that cleared the slums surrounding the Capitol and transformed the area into an architectural expression of the majesty and extent of contemporary state government.[2]

The result was a Capitol complex whose development mirrored the process by which the state government in Minnesota expanded in the twentieth century – orderly and open, classic, an integration of lawns and buildings linked to St. Paul's extensive parkway system, reflecting the character of settlement in Minnesota, which had always blended rural and urban elements. The prominent position of the State Capitol also symbolized the degree to which Minnesota was a civil society, its citizens linked through its polity more than in any other single way.[3]

Minnesota, like most other states established after the original thirteen, did not emerge by organic development but from deliberate acts of founders, resulting in political institutions that were designed to create and order political societies of newcomers. In 1849 Congress established Minnesota Territory. Minnesota was given full form when it was admitted to the Union on May 11, 1858. Its constitution, drafted by separate Republican and Democratic conventions because of intense partisan acrimony and existing as two separate documents, defined the state as a civil society.[4] The different peoples who settled in Minnesota in the nineteenth century formed their links with the land, the state, and each other through its political subdivisions.

The Minnesota State Capitol area, St. Paul, 1987. Shown are (A) *the State Capitol,* (B) *State Office,* (C) *Transportation,* (D) *Veterans Service,* (E) *Capitol Square,* (F) *Centennial Office,* (G) *Historical Society, and* (H) *Administration buildings.*

Minnesota's rural-land frontier came to an end sometime between 1907 when railroads spanned the state from border to border and 1918 when homesteading ceased in the state. The principal industries of lumbering, flour milling, and iron mining, which developed between 1870 and 1920, used the resources of land and water to open the urban-industrial frontier. Urbanization and industrialization continued in the 1920s and 1930s, albeit slowly, perhaps because of the state's location at the northwestern edge of the nation's urban-industrial belt.[5]

After 1945 corporations like Minnesota Mining and Manufacturing, Honeywell, and various computer firms generated the new technology associated with yet a third frontier stage, the metropolitan-technological frontier. The rapid expansion of electronics and cybernetics stimulated the growth of metropolitan Minnesota and the transformation of the Twin Cities from two urban centers into a metropolitan region, with a concomitant decline in the populations of Minneapolis and St. Paul and the growth of suburban population.[6]

By the mid-1970s the metropolitan frontier had reached its end nationwide. While metropolitanization continued, it was no longer at the cutting edge of socioeconomic development. In Minnesota, however, the state's metropolitan areas were distant enough from the rest of metropolitan America to permit continued growth of the metropolitan circle. At the same time there began to emerge a fourth frontier, a new rurban or citybelt-cybernetic frontier, which mixed strips of urban and rural settlement so that no cities were more central than any others and no rural areas were outside the orbit of the emerging Twin Cities-based megalopolis.[7]

State and local governments in Minnesota have had to respond to these frontier stages from the establishment of the first counties in the 1830s in what was still Wisconsin Territory to the organization of the Twin Cities Metropolitan Council in 1967 to serve the state's metropolitan heart. In their structure and in the work they have performed, Minnesota's units of government have been shaped by the demands of the evolving economic and social fabric. This historical relationship can be traced by looking at any of a number of roles that government has played in the state in the twentieth century, especially those that have assumed priority in terms of funding. After surveying the state's constitution and three branches of government, this essay focuses upon the work of government in terms of taxation and finance, conservation, transportation, and welfare and health. The function that has long taken the greatest share of government resources – education – is treated more fully in another essay.[8]

The Structure of Government

The Constitution

The Minnesota constitution basically provides the frame of state government and state protections of individual rights. It has a populist tinge but not overly much. To the extent that they are conscious of its existence, Minnesotans have been satisfied with their constitution (despite its unusual origins) and, for the most part, have not sought to achieve ordinary political change through major constitutional revision. There have been periodic proposals for calling a constitutional convention; all have been rejected in the proposal stage. Instead, such major change as has been deemed necessary has come through the work of two constitutional commissions.[9]

Minnesota's 1857 constitution – both versions – had the easiest amending clause of any state constitution. A proposed amendment had to be passed by simple majorities in both houses of the legislature in one session and ratified by a simple majority of the voters who voted on the proposition in the next general election. In 1898, believing amendment to be too easy, the legislature proposed and the voters approved a constitutional amendment requiring that voter approval involve a majority of the total votes cast in the general election, a much more difficult goal to achieve. The results were immediate – a substantial decline in the number of amendments approved.[10]

Commissions twice attempted to revise the constitution. As part of the effort to "modernize" Minnesota's government, the legislature established the Minnesota Constitutional Commission of 1948, which recommended calling a constitutional convention. Convention proponents tried several times to get the legislature to act but failed because the senate opposed legislative reapportionment, which was a mandated adjunct of a convention. To undercut support for a convention, the legislative leaders initiated extensive constitutional reform through the amendment process. Those favoring constitutional change, realizing that this was the best they would get, worked hard to secure adoption of the amendments; as a result a good part of the commission's report found its way into the constitution.[11]

In the 1950s, 50 percent of all amendments proposed were passed, and in the 1960s the figure rose to 78 percent. Still most of the amendments were fairly narrow in scope, and some people thought that a more far-reaching constitutional revision was necessary. Gov. Wendell R. Anderson took the lead in reopening the issue in 1971, calling for a constitutional convention on the grounds that it was crucial for state government to "reassert its assigned role in the federal system." The governor sought annual flexible legislative sessions, a reduction in legislative size, party designation for legislators, elimination of special tax provisions in the constitution, empowerment of the legislature with total tax responsibility, introduction of an environmental bill of rights, and reexamination of dedicated funds so as to give the legislature "the broadest possible discretion in the appropriation of state funds." Finally he called for an easier method of constitutional revision.

In response the legislature established the Minnesota Constitutional Study Commission of 1972. Governor Anderson appointed former-governor Elmer L. Andersen, a Republican, as chairman; another former governor, Democratic-Farmer-Laborite Karl F. Rolvaag, was elected as vice-chairman by the commission and its steering committee. David F. Durenberger, later U.S. senator, became the commission's executive secretary. The commission reported that "the original document as amended since adoption is an adequate statement of the relationship between the people of this State and their government." All that was needed was a series of amendments that would simplify the language, make amendment easier, and specifically alter the reapportionment and finance articles to transfer reapportionment power from the legislature to a bipartisan redistricting commission, allow the state to levy income taxes computed as a percentage of federal income tax, repeal the gross earnings tax paid by railroads in lieu of other taxes, and allow the legislature to set the rate of taxation on railroads as it did for other industries.

The state adopted a revised constitution with simplified language in 1974. The document was rearranged, rewritten, and shortened, dropping schedules, boundary lists, and lists of highways, so as to make it more readable. Although the new text became the one in general use, the meaning of the constitution was not altered, and in constitutional law cases the 1858 documents remained the final authority. In other words, Minnesota has three constitutional documents saying essentially the same thing.[12]

The Court System

Article Six of Minnesota's constitution established four sets of courts – supreme, district, probate, and justice of the peace – and authorized the legislature to establish other courts as necessary. The supreme court stands at the apex of the state's court system. It is both a constitutional and an appellate court. That is to say, it interprets the state constitution, reviews acts of the executive and legislative branches and of local governments, and is the state court of final appeal in civil and criminal cases.

Between 1867 and 1937 the legislature established at least one hundred municipal courts, each by special act. In the latter year it passed the Municipal Court Act, which provided for automatic establishment of municipal courts in every city and incorporated village having a population of one thousand or more; further, the court was to have jurisdiction over the entire county in which it was located. While this legislation was helpful in less populated counties that had only one eligible municipality, in most counties it instituted overlapping municipal and justice of the peace courts.[13]

The legislature also created a Judicial Council in 1937 to study the court system and suggest changes in biennial reports to the governor and the legislature. In 1941 the council recommended a unified court system, entirely staffed by full-time judges trained in the law and having rule-making powers; the judges would be chosen in a statewide system of judicial selection and have their tenure controlled by lawyers rather than election by the people. Fifteen years later the voters approved a constitutional amendment empowering the legislature to reorganize the judiciary. Provisions for justice of the peace courts were removed from the constitution. As a result of legislative action in 1963, the chief justice of the supreme court was to oversee and plan the work of the courts in the state's ten judicial districts (reduced from nineteen). The chief judge of each district was to supervise the work of the courts within that district. Although many justices of the peace were still being elected to office as late as 1972, their duties were limited to handling guilty pleas, levying fines, and performing marriages. The Court Reorganization Act of 1971, more popularly known as the County Court Act, replaced the jumble of lower courts with one county court having broad local jurisdiction. Counties were to have courts that were continuously in session with a full-time, salaried judge. County courts were organized into three divisions: family, probate, and civil and criminal. The county courts could also include a conciliation court and a traffic and ordinance violations bureau. Ramsey, Hennepin, and St. Louis counties retained their municipal courts.[14]

In the early 1960s court reform took a different direction, one of guaranteeing the right of counsel in criminal cases. In part as a result of U.S. Supreme Court decisions, the legislature established the offices of state and district public defenders in 1965. The state was also moving toward a more integrated court system. In 1971 the legislature established the Commission of Judicial Standards to recommend action to the state supreme court on suspension or removal of local judges shown to be incapable of exercising their duties. A constitutional amendment adopted in 1972 extended the commission's power to include discipline of supreme and district court judges. The following year another amendment created an administrative council, consisting of the chief justice as chairman and two representatives, a lawyer and a layperson, from each court in the state to formulate administrative policies to be carried out by the chief justice.

In a major reorganization in 1982 an intermediate court of appeals was established by constitutional amendment to reduce the burdens on the state supreme court (which had thirteen judges in 1988). Also in 1982, the legislature merged the county and district courts, creating a single district court for the entire state with ten judicial districts and establishing one general trial court. The act was amended in 1984 and 1986, and the merger finally took place in 1986. All of the former municipal, county, probate, and conciliation courts disappeared; all civil and criminal jurisdiction rested with the district court.

The Legislature

Legislative apportionment was a major issue throughout the twentieth century. The number of senators and representatives in the bicameral legislature was constitutionally determined by act of the legislature itself. At the turn of the century the state senate had 63 members, one per district, and the house of representatives had 119, apportioned according to population among senatorial districts so that there were between one and four per district. According to the state constitution, the legislature was to be regularly reapportioned after each federal census. There was no reapportionment between 1913 and 1959, however – the period during which Minnesota changed from a rural to an urban state – because legislators simply ignored constitutional provisions for decennial reapportionment. Dominated by rural and small-town representatives, the legislature opposed increasing the power of the urban areas, which would have meant loss of many individual legislative seats and perhaps a shift in political control as well.[15]

This phenomenon was not unusual among the states in those years. Indeed it can be shown that once a third of a state's population was urban, conflicts of transition set in, becoming severe after the urban population reached the 40 percent mark and not beginning to subside until the population became 60 percent urban. With Minnesota precisely at balance in the 1950s, the conflict was at its most intense. In 1959 the legislature finally surrendered and provided for a reapportionment to take place for the 1962 elections. Thus Minnesota anticipated such U.S. Supreme Court rulings as *Baker* v. *Carr* and began to put its own house in order rather than be required to do so by the federal courts. The 1962 redistricting provided that five and one-half senate seats and eleven house seats move from rural areas to the Twin Cities suburbs.

Redistricting followed the federal censuses of 1970 and 1980, but the legislature deadlocked over the reallocation of seats from lightly populated rural areas to growing urban ones. Both times the state resorted to a redistricting formula ordered by a federal court. In 1988 there were 134 representatives and 67 senators, making the Minnesota legislature the twelfth largest in the United States and its senate the largest.[16]

The legislature met annually until 1877, when it changed to biennial sessions. Initially, sessions had no time limit. A maximum of 60 days was approved in 1860 and subsequently extended to 90 days in 1888. By the 1950s the failure of legislatures to finish their sessions within the 90-day constitutional limit led to the practice of "covering the clock," whereby the legislature could extend its session for several days to finish its work in one final rush. The 1957 legislature, for example, covered the clock for five additional days. At that the governor had to call a one-day special session to finish up the work. Only in 1953 did the legislature adjourn on time. In 1962 the constitution was amended to extend the length of biennial legislative sessions to 120 days.[17]

To ease its problems with the flow of work, the legislature introduced interim committees and commissions to study state problems and draft legislation to deal with them. Commissions were joint senate-house bodies with equal membership from each. By 1957 this arrangement had been regularized through permanent, interim, and standing committees, of which there were twelve in 1988.[18]

In 1913, at the height of the progressive movement, the legislature passed a bill providing for nonpartisan election of legislators. Thereafter, the legislature developed the custom of dividing into conservative and liberal caucuses for purposes of organization. The larger caucus in each house became responsible for organizing that house, controlled legislative expenditures, hired legislative employees, and generally dominated legislative action. Under the nonpartisan system, the speaker of the house – elected by a contest between the caucuses – was especially strong because that person controlled committee assignments. In the senate a powerful Committee on Committees named senators to committee membership. Partisan designation of legislators was reintroduced in 1973, and since 1974 the legislature has been formally organized by party caucuses.[19]

The Minnesota legislature has grown stronger in many respects. Through the 1950s it held its own even with aggressive governors, in great part because it had expert leadership, particularly in the state senate. In the late 1960s the locus of effective leadership was shared between senate and house, which strengthened both bodies. In the 1970s, however, the locus of leadership shifted to the house because of redistricting and the change to party identification of legislators.

The Executive Branch

In Minnesota, as in its sister states and the United States as a whole, the power of the executive branch has grown substantially in the twentieth century. This surge has been especially true since the 1930s and even more so in Minnesota since the 1950s. The great expansion in the size of government, with the resultant increase in governmental complexity, has required more advanced planning, more sophisticated budgeting, and more administrative responsibility for implementation – all of which tend to increase executive power. Fortunately, in the American system of government it has been possible to have a growth in the powers of the governor and executive branch without a corresponding reduction in the powers of the legislature or judiciary, since the separation-of-powers system makes each independent and more likely to generate counterforce against force.

Most Minnesotans accept as an article of faith that the executive branch should have a single head. In fact, Minnesota's constitution was based on a different theory of government. It provided for a six-headed executive department with each of the elected constitutional officers independent in his or her own sphere. Thus every board, commission, and department could be entrusted with substantial power within its own realm because it could not exercise power in any other. The executive branch functioned as a unit only through committees such as the Executive Council in which all sat to make joint decisions.[20]

At the beginning of the century the executive branch consisted of the offices of governor, lieutenant governor, secretary of state, auditor, treasurer, and attorney general. The secretary of state, who also served as commissioner of statistics, had the responsibility for conducting elections. The state auditor, the only officer elected for four years rather than two, reviewed state expenditures and checked land records, which included federal land grants to the state. The treasurer and the attorney general oversaw incoming funds and legal matters involving units of government, respectively. In 1901 state government had a total of 107 employees from the governor through the secretaries in eighteen different agencies. Several hundred more were employed by such state institutions as hospitals and schools.[21]

The office of governor in Minnesota has been strengthened in a variety of ways. The development of more sophisticated planning and budgeting mechanisms in state government and the expansion of the governor's own office and staff have provided the tools. The first step in that direction occurred under Gov. Adolph O. Eberhart, who attempted in 1911 and again in 1913 to reform the state administration. The commission he appointed recommended that the executive branch be reorganized, some form of civil service instituted, and a budget system adopted; however, no action was taken at that time. Gov. Theodore Christianson was the first to succeed in 1925. Among other revisions, he secured the creation of executive branch reorganization, a three-member Commission of Administration and Finance to gain control of expenditures by state government.[22]

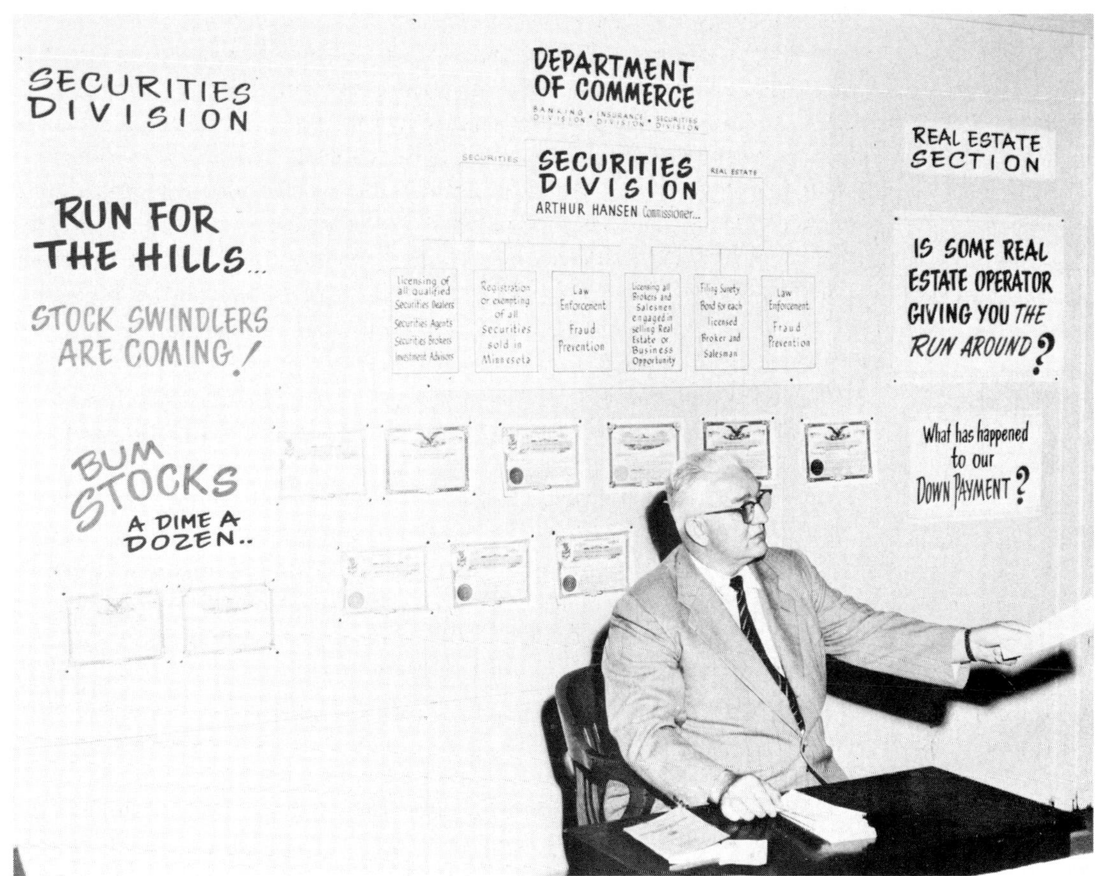

Arthur Hansen, commissioner of securities for the Department of Commerce, conducting a public information session, 1957

Gov. Harold E. Stassen implemented a comprehensive restructuring of the executive branch. The key feature of his 1939 reorganization was the establishment of a Department of Administration under a single commissioner, formally a staff agency of the governor, to deal with budgeting and finances, purchasing and contracting, and care and custody of state properties. The commissioner was made responsible for preparing a comprehensive budget and approving actual expenditure of departmental budgets on a quarterly basis, with the decision to be binding. For the first time, the governor had the equivalent of the federal Bureau of the Budget – a means to assert at least a modicum of management and budgetary control over the other departments of the state. It took very little time for the commissioner of administration, a gubernatorial appointee, to become the governor's administrative alter ego. Such administrative reorganization began to transform the governor into the chief executive officer of the state, a process that continued into the 1980s. Stassen also oversaw the formation of a civil-service system for state employees. What Eberhart had proposed was finally in place twenty-six years later.[23]

One of Gov. Orville L. Freeman's first acts after taking office in 1955 was to pursue another major reorganization of state government. The 1955 Reorganization Act further reduced the number of departments reporting directly to the governor, introduced centralized records control and machine accounting, changed the terms of many appointed officers to coincide with that of the governor, and increased the authority and powers of the commissioner of administration. All of this strengthened the power of the governor as chief executive officer. As a counterbalance the attorney general was given authority to appoint the chief of the Bureau of Criminal Apprehension, a power previously vested in the governor. A new Department of Commerce embraced all of the state's economic regulation and development functions.[24]

By the 1980s there were hundreds of agencies within the executive branch. The governor appointed the heads of the twenty departments and named some of the members of the agencies. In addition there were advisory task forces, advisory councils and committees, authorities, boards, commissions, committees, councils, and governor's agencies. Some had definite termination dates; others were permanent. Some tackled specific problems, such as race relations; others had specific functions, such as the licensing of barbers. Members were legislators, interested members of the public, professional staff, and laypersons with particular expertise. Some were salaried; others received a per diem allowance for expenses; still others worked for the satisfaction that came with public service. Beyond any doubt, the executive branch through the growth of these bodies had reached into nearly every aspect of the lives of the citizens of the state.[25]

The strong governors since Floyd B. Olson in the 1930s have dominated their issue-oriented parties and have been able to use the party as a political resource. This suggests another point, namely, that with all the institutional aspects of the growth of gubernatorial power, the personal abilities of the incumbents make a major difference. Lengthening the term of office to four years, as approved by the voters in 1962, also increased the governor's influence. Since Olson, talented standouts have included Harold Stassen, Luther W. Youngdahl, Orville Freeman, and Wendell Anderson.[26]

Wendell Anderson as governor was an effective leader, and he gained in popularity as a result. He was the first governor to develop a sophisticated staff and a television-oriented public communications program. He emphasized noncontroversial issues in building public support and then turned his popularity into political capital. By and large, in dealing with the legislature on policy issues, he relied upon thorough staff work rather than the mobilization of public opinion. Anderson succeeded in getting better than 82 percent of his programs through the legislature for most of his term, the best record of any of the postwar governors.

The Work of Government

Taxation and Finance

For the fiscal year ending July 31, 1901, the state of Minnesota disbursed $6.9 million against receipts of $6.7 million. More than half went into the general revenue fund and almost a third into school funds.[27] In the 1985–87 biennium the state budget had increased to $15.8 billion, which included $3.7 billion in federal funds.[28]

Finance has been one of the few areas in which the Minnesota constitution has little flexibility. Among other things the constitution deliberately prohibited the state from spending money on internal improvements as distinct from public buildings. Over the years constitutional amendments have been adopted to enable the state to spend money on highways, forest fire prevention, and airports. More recently, broad judicial interpretation has limited the definition of what constitutes internal improvements to allow state funding for construction of sewage systems. Also the Minnesota Supreme Court has held that the internal improvements limitation does not apply to local units of government: they can expend funds for any "public purpose."

In 1906 Minnesota voters ratified a constitutional amendment known as the "Wide Open Amendment" that greatly enlarged the legislature's taxing powers. Thus armed, it soon passed an inheritance tax, a mortgage registry tax, and, in 1913, a classified property tax establishing four classes at different rates. The Minnesota Tax Commission, created in 1907, exercised general supervision over the administration of the assessment and taxation laws of the state and local subdivisions other than municipalities.[29]

Scouts planting trees as part of a program sponsored by the Iron Range Resources and Rehabilitation Board, Nashwauk, 1988

With the onslaught of the Great Depression in the 1930s, Minnesota's tax system underwent major revisions. The reasons were twofold: declining revenue and increased expenses. Income from the property tax dropped precipitously; 55 percent of property taxpayers became delinquent in 1933, and assessed valuations plummeted. Motor vehicle and gasoline tax revenues fell sharply as people spent less on new cars or on recreational driving. Demands for state dollars rose with matching speed as townships and counties lost their ability to cope with caring for the unemployed. In 1933 the state revamped its property tax classification system to give relief to the financially strapped and to shift the tax burden to the more affluent. That same session of the legislature also passed the much-debated income tax on personal and corporate incomes. Taking advantage of the repeal of Prohibition, a special session of the legislature also enacted a tax on alcoholic beverages. The property tax would never again be the chief source of state-generated revenue.[30]

One of the major issues in Minnesota politics for a century was state taxation of mining. Taxed at one penny per ton since 1881, mine output was subject after 1897 to the same ad valorem tax that applied to property elsewhere in the state, leading to increased revenue. Measures designed to recapture some of the losses from mineral extraction were vetoed by the governor in 1909 and 1919. The voters approved a constitutional amendment in 1922, authorizing an occupation tax described as a "modified severance tax on income" and levied on the value of the iron ore mined or produced. A year later a 6 percent royalty tax was added that, in effect, taxed the rent paid by operators to private landowners. Until 1956, 40 percent of the money collected from these taxes went into the permanent trust fund for elementary and secondary schools, just as all the royalties paid to the State of Minnesota by the operators from mining on state lands went into permanent trust funds that provided more than a quarter of a billion dollars by 1961. In 1956 another constitutional amendment authorized the allocation of the funds directly to the schools and the University of Minnesota as current revenue. Ninety-three percent of the revenues from the ad valorem taxes have gone to local government. In the 1960s the state once again shifted its policy to offer special tax incentives to mining companies for taconite production. They served to stimulate the taconite industry for another fifteen years until world economic conditions made it unprofitable.[31]

In the 1975–76 fiscal year, federal, state, and local taxes equaled 34 percent of Minnesota's gross state product, about 95 percent of which was returned to the state income stream through government salaries and other expenditures within the state. Another point of comparison is that in 1902, Minnesota state and local government revenues equaled 6.9 percent of personal income and in 1973–74 they equaled 17.1 percent.[32] Minnesota, always a high-tax state, became slightly more so over the century. In 1902 Minnesota's taxes were 115 percent of the national average; in 1974, 119 percent. The largest share of the state budget in the latter year went to local schools. Tax relief and local government aids formed the second largest item in the general fund budget. In third place was welfare, after which came highways.[33]

Financing government programs has continued to require changes in the tax system. In 1961 the state began to withhold personal income taxes. A sales tax, which Minnesotans had long opposed as regressive, was finally enacted by the Republican-dominated legislature over the Republican governor's veto in 1967. While formally opposing the tax, the DFL party leadership was actually relieved to have it on the books and has never made a serious effort to repeal it.[34]

In 1971 Governor Anderson and the legislature restructured state fiscal policy toward local government, resulting in the so-called Minnesota Miracle. The legislature assumed more control over local tax levies, including the school mill levy, and implemented a state aid formula based upon strong equalization measures. As a result state aid for schools rose from 43 percent to 65 percent of their total operating funds. This newly assumed state responsibility led the state to place spending restraints on local government units. The legislature set limits on budget increases enacted by local government units at 6 percent per year, with anything above that limit being deducted from the state per-capita aid on a percentage basis.[35]

In enacting the reform, the legislature's overall goal was to give owners a property tax relief of 15 to 20 percent. Revenues were forecast to jump by 23 percent through such changes as increasing the income tax, sales tax, and cigarette, beer, and alcoholic beverage tax rates. The legislature also abolished the personal property tax for businesses, reworked the property tax classification system, and revised the credits for property taxes paid by renters and low-income elderly. The legislature preempted sales and income taxes, forbidding local governments to levy either, but provided a limited pledge of the state's full faith and credit to support local general-obligation bonds.

From August 1980 through December 1982, legislative sessions had to grapple with revenue shortfalls as a result of changes in the tax system and the economy during a nationwide recession. The 1981 legislature froze state aid to local government, reduced the property tax relief, and provided for the smallest increase in aid to the state's schools in a decade. The key to the change was the legislative enactment of Gov. Albert H. Quie's proposals to index the state income tax in 1979. Between 1971 and 1979, state revenues increased because income tax collections grew as wage earners were pushed into higher tax brackets as a result of inflation. This led to strong public protests, and in 1979 the governor and legislature introduced the indexing measures to counteract these automatic tax increases. Also by 1981 responsible voices in the state were saying that many homeowners' property taxes had sunk lower than they should have for a balanced tax package, while the cost of property tax relief payments had increased greatly. The 1981 shift was also a critical one. During the rest of the decade Minnesota sought to simplify the mushrooming property-tax classification system and to revise the state tax formulas to reflect changes in the federal tax law; it also pursued the goal of equalizing tax burdens while providing the same level of services throughout the state.[36]

Congressional party during a trip to inspect a proposed national forest at Cass Lake, 1899

Conservation

The Minnesota constitution was virtually silent on the subject of conservation, with the exception of encouraging the forestation or reforestation of both public and private lands. Gradually the thrust of managing Minnesota's lands, wildlife, fish, forests, waters, minerals, and other natural resources changed in the twentieth century from commercial exploitation of resources by private companies to state stewardship of them.[37]

The regulation of wildlife and fish started with the appointment in 1874 of three fish commissioners, who were succeeded by the Board of Game and Fish Commissioners in 1891 when a wildlife and fish conservation code was passed. The first state park, Itasca, was established in 1891 at the headwaters of the Mississippi River. Lumbering and forest clearance produced the tinder and conditions that led to several disastrous forest fires, bringing recognition of the need for first a chief fire warden for the state in 1895 and then a State Forestry Board in 1899. A State Drainage Commission was set up in 1897 "to have the care, custody, control, and supervision of all drainage ditches in the state" at a time when water was generally thought of as an enemy to be subdued and eliminated; a Department of Drainage and Waters followed in 1919. The state auditor's office handled the leasing rights of minerals, including iron ore, on state-owned lands until 1907, when this duty was assigned to another agency; it was returned, with revisions, in 1921.

Responsibility for many of these varied areas was finally centralized when the Department of Conservation, with a commissioner and a five-member commission, was formed in 1931 during the governorship of Floyd Olson. For the first time it was possible for the state to have control through a single agency over its natural resources. The purpose of the new department was well described by the governor when he declared, "Commercial exploitation in the past has despoiled our forests, marred our landscapes, and dissipated our resources. It has robbed our people of the greater part of their heritage of natural resources. Let us guard what is left diligently and zealously."[38]

Born at the time of the depression, the Department of Conservation benefited from the relief programs that the federal government created to provide employment. Forests and state parks, for example, were improved by Civilian Conservation Corps members and other workers who planted trees, cleared land, rivers, and fire breaks, designed and built parks, made roads and trails, strung telephone lines, and constructed buildings for staff and public use. Visitors in particular were to become an increasingly important audience for the department, especially after the Division of State Parks was added in 1932 for "the purpose of public recreation" and "the preservation of natural beauty or natural features possessing historic value." By 1936 the commissioner of conservation reported that the relief programs had spent more than $55 million in the state since the spring of 1933, employing forty-five thousand conservation corps workers and five thousand technical and supervisory persons.[39]

In a major administrative change the conservation commission was replaced with a commissioner who was in sole charge. The department also entered the 1940s with a fresh appreciation of the state's resources of water and wetlands – now considered more as capital to be studied and managed than as nuisances to be drained away. A law passed in 1937 had declared that all navigable waters were public and under the jurisdiction of the Department of Conservation. A broader redefinition in 1946 included rivers, lakes, and other waters.[40]

Employee of the Department of Conservation posting a sign in a state game refuge, 1943

The department furthered its control of the environment through legislation passed in 1951 that permitted endangered wetlands to be purchased and used as game refuges for the purpose of maintaining animal and bird populations. The stocking of rainbow trout in North Shore streams and the improvement of trout streams in southeastern Minnesota, begun in the 1950s, were also cases where the Department of Conservation played a leading role in replenishment. Some thirty years later, more than five hundred thousand acres had been preserved and about sixty miles of streams were being improved annually.

Such broadening fields of responsibility and many structural changes resulted in a key renaming of the agency in 1971 as the Department of Natural Resources. By the 1980s the department's divisions of Parks and Recreation, Fish and Wildlife, Forestry, Waters, Minerals, Enforcement, and a Trails and Waterways Unit had about 1,500 full-time and up to 2,500 part-time employees at some 350 offices across Minnesota. These employees handled the management of sixty-four state parks and seventeen waysides, fish and wildlife for recreational purposes, twenty-six thousand square miles of forest, both surface and underground public waters – including more than twelve thousand lakes and tens of thousands of boatable rivers – the mineral rights of ten million acres of state-owned land, enforcement of state resource statutes, and public trails and waterways, among other duties. The department continued its mission "to perpetuate and enhance the state's rich heritage of lands, waters, timber, minerals, fish, wildlife and other natural resources for the benefit of present and future generations."[41]

Transportation

The creation in 1905 of the Minnesota State Highway Commission signaled the growing involvement of state government in one of the twentieth century's most vital concerns – good roads as part of an efficient and widespread public transportation system. It had become apparent that the county and township roads of the nineteenth century could not handle the increasing traffic demands of the developing state and that improved thoroughfares would be of great benefit to Minnesota. "A perfect highway is a thing of beauty and a joy forever. It blesses every home by which it passes," declared a speaker at a statewide convention of the Good Roads movement in 1893. Similar sentiments led to the passage of the greatly needed constitutional amendment of 1898 that authorized both the formation of the highway commission and a road and bridge fund.[42]

When the three nonsalaried, nonprofessional members of the highway commission were appointed by the governor in 1906, they became the first leaders of an agency that gradually gained in importance until it became one of state government's most influential departments and had responsibilities for all forms of transportation. The commission initially dispensed about sixty thousand dollars among the counties to aid in building state roads, running an educational campaign for good roads, and studying the work of other state highway commissions.[43]

The legislature sought both to regulate motor vehicle traffic and to gain new sources of revenue. A license law for vehicles was passed in 1908. In the next year seven thousand automobiles and four thousand motorcycles were licensed; there were twelve thousand automobiles in Minnesota in 1910 and almost eighteen thousand in 1911.[44] More vehicles increased the demand for more and better roads. By 1913 the state had three classes, with funding based mostly on property taxes: township roads for which township boards were responsible; county roads, built by county boards and maintained by township boards; and state roads, built and maintained by county boards with state aid. Widespread federal assistance was provided nationally through the Federal Aid Road Act of 1916. The State Highway Commission planned for 6,200 miles of roads to be constructed.[45]

Rapid changes in transportation also led to a more professional style of administration. The State Highway Commission was abolished in 1917 and replaced by the office of state commissioner of highways. Charles M. Babcock, an energetic commission member since 1910, was the first person appointed to this post. He served until 1932 and had a great impact on the state, most notably with the Babcock Amendment of 1920. This lengthy and detailed addition to the constitution finally eliminated the prohibition against engaging in internal improvements with regard to roads and highways. Its main purpose was to lay out a fourth class of roads – a state trunk-highway network to be improved and maintained with revenue from state motor-vehicle taxes and with federal highway aid. The network continued to be the basis of Minnesota's transportation system. Originally consisting of 70 numbered routes totaling 6,877 miles and connecting all county seats and other significant population centers, the system increased in fifty years to 335 routes and 12,102 miles. Other modifications that took place during Babcock's tenure as commissioner included the use of revenue from state gasoline taxes for the construction and maintenance of roads. The commissioner gained the right to appoint two assistant commissioners, including a highway engineer. The Babcock Amendment had provided that the highway system might be added to when 75 percent of it was constructed and "permanently improved." This goal was reached in 1932, permitting the legislature to add 4,500 miles of "legislative routes" the next year.[46]

The depression of the 1930s and the consequent money pinch affected the three areas from which the Department of Highways drew its financing: motor vehicle license fees, gasoline taxes, and federal aid. The state reduced charges for licenses and increased gasoline taxes to raise funds for distribution to a county-aid road system and to the trunk highway fund. Aid from the National Recovery Act was substituted for regular federal aid to highways. In 1935 the state authorized $12 million worth of highway bonds in order to meet requirements for federal aid, but only $8 million worth was issued.[47]

The 1940s brought three federal highway acts – in 1940, 1941, and 1944. According to these acts, federal funds were to be used for roads necessary for national defense. The Federal Aid Highway Act of 1944 allotted funds for a postwar program of planning and constructing secondary rural roads

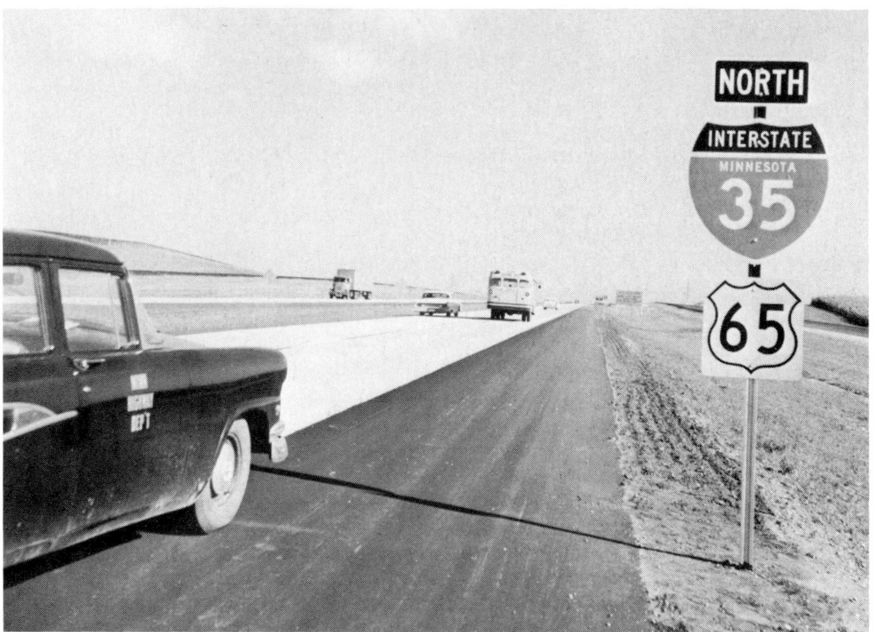

A completed portion of the Interstate and Defense Highway system, 1958

and urban roads; the states, which were to maintain the roads, were required to match the federal funds. Minnesota was awarded $12.4 million in each of three postwar years under the latter act. Minnesota continued to feel the influence of the federal government and the national transportation situation, especially in 1956 when laws authorizing first-construction funds for the National System of Interstate and Defense Highways were enacted by Congress. This scheme for building freeways across the country became part of Minnesota's trunk highway system the following year by legislative action. The first section of interstate highway in the state was opened in 1958 near Owatonna; by 1968 there were 914 interstate miles available to motorists.[48]

Highways and other aspects of transportation administered by the state were drawn together in 1976 when the Minnesota Department of Transportation (Mn/DOT) was organized to handle the duties of the departments of highways and aeronautics as well as the transportation-related activities of the State Planning Agency and the Public Service Department (which had already assumed the functions of the former Railroad and Warehouse Commission). By the 1980s Mn/DOT had varying responsibilities affecting the state's 140 public airports and six thousand registered airplanes, 12,200 miles of state and interstate highways, 2.5 million licensed drivers and 3.3 million registered vehicles, 2.5 million bicycle owners and 5,100 miles of bike routes along state highways, four major ports on Lake Superior, fifty active river terminals, 230 miles of navigable waterways, and 5,100 miles of railroad tracks with 5,700 crossings. In the words of an agency spokesperson, the department sought "to provide a balanced transportation system for the state and [to develop and implement] policies, plans, and programs for aeronautics, highways, motor carriers, pipelines, ports, public transit, and railroads."[49]

Public Welfare and Health

The state began its role in public welfare as the regulator of public institutions for persons with physical or mental handicaps. In 1883 this duty was vested in the Board of Corrections and Charities, which was replaced by the Board of Control in 1901. The new board was composed of three paid members appointed by the governor to manage the state's various institutions and welfare agencies. By 1902 there were three state hospitals, schools for the blind and mentally handicapped, a reformatory, a prison, and an asylum for the insane.[50]

From the 1860s to the 1930s direct public assistance for Minnesotans was the responsibility of county commissions, city councils, and township boards. From 1889 to 1973 Minnesota counties were able to choose, by popular vote, between two systems of providing assistance – the county system or the township system. Under the township system township boards and village councils were responsible for providing assistance to those they determined to be in need. Until the late 1920s the monetary burden on town governments was usually minimal, and public relief expenses were offset by a property tax. In the case of Otter Tail County in the 1930s, direct relief was administered by 62 township boards, 17 village councils, and one city council.[51]

In the county system the county board of commissioners handled all public assistance and supervised the operation of poor farms and poorhouses. As with the township system, poor relief was supported by a tax on property. In 1926–27, fifty-nine of the state's eighty-seven counties

The Board of Corrections and Charities, about 1900

were operating under the county system. Of the twenty-eight under the township system, nine levied a countywide poor tax to supplement township taxes. In 1900 Minnesota county boards operated thirty-four poor farms; by 1927 that number had increased to forty-four.[52]

Minnesotans first received federal direct-relief funds in 1933 through the Federal Emergency Relief Administration. In October 1935, 44,127 families and individuals in the state were receiving unemployment relief. The federal government required that each county board establish a countywide administration to oversee township and village relief activities that used federal dollars.[53] This centralized county structure, in basic form, remained in place in the 1980s.

The passage of the Social Security Act in 1935 substantially changed the way federal relief aid was dispensed as the federal relief effort was turned toward such programs as the Works Progress Administration. General direct relief from the federal government was eliminated and instead returned to local agencies. The resulting burden on local systems was alleviated in part by federal Old Age Assistance, which was administered at the state level through the Division of Old Age Assistance under the Board of Control. In 1936, 42,861 elderly Minnesotans were receiving Old Age Assistance.[54]

From 1935 to 1939 the welfare system underwent further modifications. In 1937 each county was obliged to establish a welfare board to qualify for federal funds. With the creation of the county welfare boards, all welfare-related functions were placed in one authority. The boards received applications for Old Age Assistance, judged the eligibility of recipients, and decided what amount of assistance was needed. One-half of the funds granted were from the federal government, one-third came from the state, and the remainder was usually provided by the county. As part of Governor Stassen's 1939 reorganization of the executive branch, the Board of Control was overhauled and renamed the Department of Social Security; its three divisions were Public Institutions, Employment and Security, and Social Welfare.[55]

By 1971 only twelve counties still operated under the township system of poor relief. Two years later the legislature passed the Human Services Act, which abolished the township system.[56] The act also made it possible for one or more neighboring counties to establish joint Human Services Boards to supervise public assistance, corrections, mental health, and other services. This attempt at multicounty cooperation to cut costs and avoid duplication was largely experimental; only seven Human Service Boards were in operation in 1988.[57] Prompted by the Social Services Act of 1979, many county commissions chose to create social-service centers where people could have access to supportive and rehabilitative services. These centers also came under the supervision of the Department of Public Welfare, in 1984 renamed the Department of Human Services.[58]

After decades of expansion of services at the county level, Minnesota counties in 1971 were responsible for only 25.2 percent of their total welfare expenditures, of which more than 50 percent came from federal sources. By 1984 the county share had shrunk to only 16.7 percent. Meanwhile welfare represented the second largest category of appropriations in the state budget.[59]

In 1987 the Minnesota Department of Human Services was the state's largest agency, having control over a biennial budget of about $4 billion. State allocations amounted to $2.1 billion; the remainder came from the federal government. The department, much as it had in the 1950s, administered public assistance in cooperation with county agencies. Among the programs were Aid to Families with Dependent Children, Emergency Assistance, Food Stamps, General Assistance, and Work Readiness. The Department of Human Services also operated eight state-owned regional treatment centers and two nursing homes that offered treatment and rehabilitative programs for individuals who were mentally ill, chemically dependent, or aged.[60]

When Minnesota established the Board of Health and Vital Statistics in 1872, it became the fourth state in the Union to have such an agency. During its early years the board's role was primarily advisory, but by the turn of the century it had been given power to issue regulations, which were enacted by municipal boards of health throughout the state. Some of the board's early concerns included control of diphtheria, tuberculosis, food and water contamination, and diseases among farm animals.[61]

By 1933 the board had expanded its investigative focus to include water pollution, sewage disposal, all communicable diseases, sanitation at public institutions, inspection and regulation of hotels and tourist camps, vital statistics, and the licensing of embalmers. The Board of Health also became a health-service organization, administering, advising, and funding local services around the state. For example, high infant mortality rates and recent outbreaks of influenza and poliomyelitis prompted the provision for public health nurses in 1919.[62]

In 1935 the Department of Health, which was governed by the board, used federal aid to begin a Rural District Health Unit program to provide general health services. Eight district units were in place by 1948, each serving a multicounty area. By the mid-1960s the Division of Local Health Administration, which implemented its programs through the district units, was receiving 80 to 90 percent of its funding from the federal government.[63]

In 1975 eighty counties had public health nursing services, and sixty-seven had home health-care services, which included disease prevention and control, family planning, nutrition, dental public health, emergency medical assistance, health education, and environmental health. Up to this time, however, administrative relations between local health authorities and the Board of Health were unclear, and state aid to local agencies was given only through short-term grants for special projects. The passage of the Community Health Services Act of 1976 established a system of cooperation between the Department of Health and local governments. The act also encouraged the formation of multicounty Community Health Boards in an attempt to centralize local health administration. By 1987 sixty-nine counties had united in twenty-two multicounty Community Health Boards, and eighteen operated individually in the same capacity.

The State Department of Health itself was restructured in 1977 when the Board of Health was abolished and the department came under the authority of a commissioner appointed by the governor. By 1987 all counties in Minnesota were receiving state subsidies through the Community Health Services program.[64]

The Changing Shape of Government

Local government in Minnesota at the turn of the century was primarily county government. By 1922 Minnesota had eighty-seven counties. County government was relatively simple, with a board comprised of five county commissioners (except Ramsey and St. Louis counties, which had seven) and eleven elected county officers – an auditor, treasurer, superintendent of schools, register of deeds, sheriff, attorney, judge of probate, surveyor, coroner, clerk of the district court, and court commissioner. County government replicated in the local arena the developments already noted in state government. The board of county commissioners formed a multiheaded executive; as needed they appointed committees with specific duties, such as overseeing roads and bridges, which reported to the board as a whole with their recommendations. The board hired other officers as county responsibilities grew. Health and welfare officers, mine inspectors, ditch surveyors, county farm superintendents, and weed control officials were just some of the county employees. The county commissioners also appointed special boards, especially for managing property like courthouses or poor farms or for carrying out such state-mandated functions as child welfare or mosquito control.[65]

In 1973 the legislature passed the Optional Forms of Government Act, which enabled counties to hire people to fill offices that had been elective. Over the next fifteen years, the offices of superintendent of schools, surveyor or engineer, and coroner or medical examiner became appointive. Judicial reform eliminated other county offices. The county budget remained split almost evenly between two major items – roads and bridges, and welfare.[66]

After World War II local government units either were consolidated (as were school districts) or lost functions (as did townships). Between 1950 and 1960, the number of governmental units in the state dropped from more than nine thousand to slightly more than six thousand, principally through school district consolidation, which remained a major activity during the 1960s.[67]

Many of the changes in local government functions were caused by population shifts between rural and urban townships or counties, and central to these changes was the emergence of the Twin Cities as the state's metropolis. Minneapolis and St. Paul underwent a final period of population growth between 1940 and 1950, then their populations began to decline as a result of suburbanization, even as their common metropolitan area grew larger. The number of municipalities in Hennepin and Ramsey

Dakota County Courthouse, Hastings, 1968

counties grew from 28 to 61, while the percentage of the county's population that actually lived in the cities of Minneapolis and St. Paul fell from 90 to 58 percent in the years 1940–70.[68]

In 1959 the legislature established the Minnesota Municipal Commission to prevent the unrestricted incorporation of new municipalities and to encourage annexation of newly urbanized areas by existing cities. To circumvent this limitation, townships could become urban towns under a 1907 act of the legislature, thereby acquiring many of the powers of cities. Several townships in the metropolitan area did so, continuing as townships until their populations were large enough to qualify them for full city status. By 1974 the Twin Cities metropolitan area included 139 separate municipalities and 52 townships. Independent municipal status, rather than incorporation into a larger city, was still the desired goal in suburban areas. Mergers of local governments were almost impossible unless mandated by state statute. Only six have occurred in Minnesota, two of them in the Twin Cities metropolitan area.[69]

Counties in urban areas also acquired a new role as providers of municipal services, thereby enabling the suburbs to exist as independent entities while benefiting from economies of scale. During the 1960s the legislature authorized basic changes in the government of Hennepin County, which became the prototype for other counties in the 1970s. The county board was authorized to hire a county administrator, and many of the independently elected county offices were eliminated and their functions transferred to the county board and administrator. Hennepin County acquired a municipal court system, expanded the general hospital, and increased its park and library systems.[70]

By the early 1960s the Twin Cities metropolitan area had grown to a region the size of Delaware. In 1967 the state legislature established the Metropolitan Council to provide areawide planning and to coordinate the administration of functional authorities that had previously been established. Since the metropolitan area embraced just under 50 percent of the state's population, the legislature continued to take a direct interest in metropolitan affairs in opposition to the demands of certain local interests that the Metropolitan Council be elected by local voters and thus more independent of state government. The Metropolitan Council was hailed throughout the United States as one of the great innovations in local government. Areawide planning and coordination of regional services became its principal functions. One of its major achievements was to implement a tax-sharing plan whereby 40 percent of the taxes generated by metropolitan economic growth were distributed to the region's municipalities on a per capita basis.[71]

During the postwar period, local governments became more dependent upon intergovernmental revenue sources. Between 1945 and 1972, the share of total municipal government revenue from local taxes dropped from 64.6 percent to 31.8 percent, while intergovernmental revenue rose from 4.8 percent to 35.1 percent. Sources such as fees, fines, and assessments remained at about a constant one-third during that period. This meant that overall own-source revenues dropped from 96.2 percent in 1945 to 64.9 percent in 1972. At that, municipalities were receiving 26.8 percent of their total revenue from the state and federal governments in 1970, while special districts received 48 percent, school districts 49.7 percent, towns 51.6 percent, and counties 60.5 percent.[72]

The situation was compounded as a result of the 1971 fiscal reform, which limited local tax levies, provided property tax relief, and prohibited local sales and income taxes. Thus, intergovernmental revenues had to play an increasingly larger role. Although in the 1970s federal aid to localities increased greatly, state aid was still the most important intergovernmental revenue source. With the cutback in federal aid by the end of that decade, the role of state aid became even more important. Fiscally, at least, Minnesotans have seen a substantial centralization of power from the localities to the state since World War II.[73]

The legislature, especially since the 1970s, has followed an active policy of setting standards for specific local government services. In practice, the legislature establishes statewide standards or a minimum service level for a particular function and formally delegates to local governments the responsibility for implementing the state policy. Examples of this include the state building code, shoreland management, and floodplain management. It has been particularly prevalent in environmental matters.

By 1985 Minnesota had the equivalent of 113 full-time employees for every 10,000 of its population, or over 45,463 state employees all told, an in-

Election judges in front of the Town Hall, the voting site for residents of Bridgewater Township in Rice County, 1980

crease of 1,195 since 1975. At that, Minnesota ranked forty-first among the states in the Union in the total number of state employees per 10,000 population. If all state and local employees including those in education are considered, Minnesota had 412 per 10,000 population in 1985 for a total of nearly 171,144, and ranked forty-third in the Union.[74]

In 1988 the state had nearly 19,000 elected officials – local, state, and federal – or about the population of Owatonna; put in other terms, there was approximately one elected official for every 220 Minnesotans. Among them were 9,000 township officers, 4,400 city officials, 2,820 elected school board members, 885 county officials, 460 soil and water conservation district supervisors, 251 judges, 201 state legislators, 8 U.S. representatives, 6 state constitutional officers including the governor, 2 U.S. senators, and 175 elected trustees of the sixteen hospital districts in operation in outstate areas.[75]

Minnesota as a Civil Society

The importance of government in shaping Minnesotans' self-image has been reaffirmed through the 1970s and 1980s by their state's prominent national image as a model of American achievement in "quality of life" matters. To a large extent, these images involve perceptions of the high quality of state and local government. They have been strengthened by the prominence in national public affairs of many Minnesotans, most of whom began their public careers in state or local government. Author Neal Peirce, dubbing Minnesota "The Successful Society," summed it up:

> Its leaders . . . have played [a] . . . role in national life, far out of proportion to the state's modest 2 percent of the national population. Its political structure remains open, issue-oriented, responsible. Its state government has been a leader in services for people, even though citizens and corporations alike have had to pay a high tax bill for those services. Few states exceed Minnesota in the quality and extent of the education offered its citizens; none appears to provide health care of comparable quality. Economic growth has been strong and steady, encompassing the brainpower industries of the electronic era along with traditional farming, milling, and mining. And Minnesota maintains a clear focus of economic and cultural leadership in her Twin Cities, towns whose great industries have resisted the siren call of the national conglomerates. . . . But why successful? . . . These people appear to have control of their own destiny.[76]

John Fischer, long-time editor of *Harper's Magazine,* considered Minnesota to be "the best-governed state in America. It also is the most imaginative, farsighted, and ambitious. Its people have known this all along."[77] Fischer, like so many others, suggested that this was so because of the state's unique political tradition and a common political culture. Minnesota's movers and shakers had a high level of commitment to public service. This plus clean, patronage-free government in which the political parties have tended to be quite open and dominated by amateurs has given the state a particular quality.

Political tradition and culture have had an impact in three ways: by molding citizens', politicians', and public officials' perceptions of the nature and purposes of politics; by influencing the recruitment of specific kinds of people to become active in government and politics; and by subtly directing the way in which the art of government is practiced in the light of those perceptions. These cultural components are manifest in a civic behavior dictated by conscience and internalized moral standards.[78]

Minnesota has been the archetypical moralistic state, more so than any other in the Union or perhaps in the world. When Minnesota gained statehood just before the Civil War, it confronted the most ideologically intense cleavage in American history: the struggle that pitted antislavery Republicans, mostly Yankees, and popular sovereignty Democrats, mostly from the Middle States, against the slaveholding South. The state's development was shaped by the highly moralistic, issue-oriented politics brought by the Yankees and their descendants and later reinforced by settlers from Scandinavia and, to a lesser extent, Germany.[79]

The growth of home-owned industry, and a strong, ideologically based labor movement also strengthened this issue-oriented trend. In contrast to the state's homogeneous political culture, its economic base has been extremely heterogeneous, so that no single industry has ever dominated the state. Members of the academic community and the professions who participated in civic and political affairs vigorously and successfully added another reinforcing element.

Political debate in Minnesota has focused on questions of how large a role government should play in society, not whether government should have a significant role to play. The state's pioneering efforts in railroad and utility regulation, conservation of natural resources, public ownership of utilities, development of a progressive system of taxation, and fostering of a strong cooperative movement are well known. Minnesotans have a nationally acknowledged record for communitarian activities. Although after 1945 there was a relatively high level of growth of government, Minnesota's widespread communal concern was nongovernmental as well.

Early in the century Minnesota political culture encouraged local communities to foster public morality. Municipally owned liquor stores and tight liquor regulation, limitations on Sunday sales, and similar forms of local law enforcement were long-time features of the Minnesota scene. Gambling and various forms of racing were prohibited in the state. This mood changed in the years after World War II for the same moralistic reasons that brought about such regulation in the first place. When Minnesotans reached the conclusion that it was immoral to use government to restrict individual activity in these spheres, their governments abandoned such regulations.

The New England tradition prized local self-government while the Scandinavian and German traditions encouraged statewide action. The result was the development of strong, positive state involvement in most governmental activities, from education to municipal reorganization to law enforcement, but with the preservation of a high degree of local control within the framework of state standard-setting or fiscal assistance. Correspondingly, no important civil community developed its political life outside the state's political culture.

A central feature of Minnesota's moralistic political culture has been its implicit acceptance of the legitimacy, efficacy, and desirability of politics. Where their counterparts in other environments might seek apolitical solutions to political problems and avoid personal involvement in partisan activity, people in Minnesota have been more likely to utilize the political system. The belief that politics can be honest has remained strong among a majority of the population – with good reason.

NOTES

The author thanks Deborah Miller for advice and assistance that made the writing of this essay possible; Sarah P. Rubinstein for substantial editorial help; and Deborah Swanson and James A. Roe for research assistance.

1. For the history of the Minnesota State Capitol, see Neil B. Thompson, *Minnesota's State Capitol: The Art and Politics of a Public Building,* Minnesota Historic Sites Pamphlet Series no. 9 (St. Paul: Minnesota Historical Society, 1974).

2. Virginia Brainard Kunz, *St. Paul: Saga of an American City* (Woodland Hills, Calif.: Windsor Publications, Inc., 1977), 165, 167. In addition to the Capitol complex, state offices are scattered throughout the Twin Cities. Since the 1950s there has been a trend for each major agency to have its own building.

3. Every state as well as the United States as a whole is a civil society, organized and defined politically, to (1) pursue a particular conception of justice that it makes its own; (2) encompass a wide variety of social and economic interests; (3) assume considerable responsibility for satisfying the social, economic, and political needs of its people; and (4) authoritatively mobilize the resources necessary to do so in a manner sufficient to ensure its own maintenance. Every state exists as a society because it is defined or delineated politically or civilly; hence the term "civil society." Using less technical imagery, a civil society is one that in common sense terms could stand alone as a politically sovereign state. Obviously the American states do not, but if by some quirk of fate it were to become necessary, most of them could carry out the functions of full political sovereignty with little adjustment of their political institutions and almost all of them could do better than the bulk of the new "sovereign states" of the post-World War II era.

4. On the curious history of Minnesota's constitution, see William Anderson and Albert J. Lobb, *A History of the Constitution of Minnesota, with the First Verified Text,* Studies in the Social Sciences no. 15 (Minneapolis: University of Minnesota, 1921). See also Millard L. Gieske, "Ideal and Practice in a State Constitution: The Case of Minnesota," *Minnesota Academy of Science Journal* 32 (1964): 51-59.

5. Daniel J. Elazar, *Cities of the Prairie: The Metropolitan Frontier and American Politics* (New York: Basic Books, 1970), 23-65, and Elazar et al., *Cities of the Prairie Revisited: The Closing of the Metropolitan Frontier* (Lincoln: University of Nebraska Press, 1986).

6. Elazar, *Cities,* 327-28; Theodore C. Blegen, *Minnesota: A History of the State* (Minneapolis: University of Minnesota Press, 1975), 557-60, 719-21.

7. Elazar, *Cities Revisited,* 78-81, 158-60. Jean Gottmann, *Megalopolis: The Urbanized Northeastern Seaboard of the United States* (Cambridge: MIT Press, 1961), is the standard work on the subject. See also John Herbers, *The New Heartland, America's Flight beyond the Suburbs and How It Is Changing Our Future* (New York: Times Books, 1986).

8. For more on education, see Clarke A. Chambers, "Educating for the Future," *this volume,* 473-506, esp. 475-77, 482-84, 496-500.

9. Anderson and Lobb, *History of the Constitution of Minnesota.*

10. Anderson and Lobb, *History of the Constitution of Minnesota,* 147-49; G. Theodore Mitau, "Constitutional Reforms in Minnesota – Change by Amendments, 1947-1977," in *Perspectives on Minnesota Government and Politics,* ed. Millard L. Gieske and Edward R. Brandt (Dubuque, Iowa: Kendall/Hunt Pub. Co., 1977), 56-57; Minnesota, Secretary of State, *Legislative Manual,* 1987-1988, p. 38-44.

11. On the 1948 constitutional commission and its achievements, see Mitau, "Constitutional Reforms," in *Minnesota Government and Politics*, ed. Gieske and Brandt, 55–85; Minnesota Constitutional Commission, *Report of the Constitutional Commission of Minnesota* (St. Paul: The Commission, 1948).

12. Minnesota Constitutional Study Commission, *Final Report* ([St. Paul]: The Commission, [1973?]) (quotations, 6, [i]); Mitau, "Constitutional Reforms in Minnesota," in *Minnesota Government and Politics*, ed. Gieske and Brandt, 55–85.

13. Blegen, *Minnesota*, 580; Merle M. Price, "The Municipal Court in Minnesota" (Master's thesis, University of Minnesota, 1929).

14. Here and two paragraphs below, William Anderson, "Reorganizing Minnesota's Judiciary: A Layman's View," *Minnesota Law Review* 27 (March 1943): 383-98; Blegen, *Minnesota*, 581; Donald Leavitt, "Minnesota's Legal System and Its Reform," in *Minnesota Government and Politics*, ed. Gieske and Brandt, 273–82; Minnesota League of Women Voters, *Minnesota Judiciary: Structures and Procedures* (St. Paul: The League, 1972); William E. Haugh, Jr., *The Judicial System in Minnesota, 1972* (St. Paul: West Pub. Co., 1972); Minnesota, Legislature, Senate, Office of Senate Counsel, *The Judicial System in Minnesota: A Comprehensive Analysis* (1969); Minnesota, Department of Administration, *Minnesota Guidebook to State Agency Services, 1987–1990* (1987), 486–93; Minnesota, Secretary of State, *Legislative Manual*, 1987-1988, p. 207-26; Minnesota, *Laws*, 1982, ch. 398, 1984, ch. 494, 1986, 1st Spec. Sess., ch. 3, art. 2, sec. 42. On the formation of the Court of Appeals, see Peter S. Popovich, *Beginning a Judicial Tradition: Formative Years of the Minnesota Court of Appeals, 1983–1987* (St. Paul: The Court of Appeals, 1987).

15. Here and below, Blegen, *Minnesota*, 224, 581; Minnesota, Secretary of State, *Legislative Manual*, 1901, p. 125, 1957-1958, p. 20; Gieske, "Ideal and Practice in a State Constitution," 32:51–59. For more information on state politics, see John E. Haynes, "Reformers, Radicals, and Conservatives," *this volume*, 361–96.

16. Minnesota, Secretary of State, *Legislative Manual*, 1973-1974, p. 130–50, 1987-1988, p. 56; Citizens League, *Power to the Process: Making Minnesota's Legislature Work Better* (Minneapolis: The League, 1985).

17. Blegen, *Minnesota*, 224-25; Joseph Kise, *Minnesota's Government* (Philadelphia: John C. Winston Co., 1953), 70–71; Minnesota, Secretary of State, *Legislative Manual*, 1957–1958, p. 21–22, 1987–1988, p. 65. A 1972 amendment to the constitution "authorized the legislature to meet in regular session in both years of the biennium for a total of 120 legislative days. . . . The temporary adjournment between the session of the first year and the second year of the biennium is not a final adjournment as the biennial session is considered as one continuous session"; Minnesota, Secretary of State, *Legislative Manual*, 1985-1986, p. 65.

18. Minnesota, Secretary of State, *Legislative Manual*, 1953–1954, p. 62, 1957–1958, p. 88–101, 1987–1988, p. 139–43.

19. Here and below, Steven Thomas Seitz and L. Earl Shaw, Jr., "Partisanship in a Nonpartisan Legislature: Minnesota," in *Minnesota Government and Politics*, ed. Gieske and Brandt, 177–84; Citizens League, *Power to the Process*, 11.

20. Homer Williamson, "The Growth of Power of the Minnesota Governor," in *Minnesota Government and Politics*, ed. Gieske and Brandt, 242–44; Minnesota, Department of Administration, *Guidebook to State Agency Services*, 130.

21. Minnesota, Secretary of State, *Legislative Manual*, 1901, p. 374–94.

22. J[eremiah] S. Young, "Reorganization of the Administrative Branch of the Minnesota Government," *Minnesota Law Review* 10 (December 1925): 40–47.

23. Lloyd M. Short and Carl W. Tiller, *The Minnesota Commission of Administration and Finance, 1925-1939: An Administrative History* (Minneapolis: University of Minnesota Press, 1942); Leslie M. Gravlin, "The Commissioner of Administration in Minnesota," in *The Book of the States: 1941-1942* (Chicago: The Council of State Governments, 1941), 4:71–74; T. G. Driscoll, "The Commissioner of Administration in Minnesota," in *The Book of the States: 1945-1946* (Chicago: The Council of State Governments, 1945), 6:145-50.

24. Minnesota, *Laws*, 1955, ch. 856; Minnesota, Self-Survey Policy Committee, *The Minnesota Self-Survey: Reports of the Functional Task Forces and Summary Review* (1956).

25. See Minnesota, Department of Administration, *Guidebook to State Agency Services*, for a full description of the various executive offices.

26. Here and below, Williamson, "Power of the Minnesota Governor," in *Minnesota Government and Politics*, ed. Gieske and Brandt, 242–58.

27. Minnesota, Secretary of State, *Legislative Manual*, 1903, p. 573; Daniel J. Elazar, *The American Partnership: Intergovernmental Co-operation in the Nineteenth-Century United States* (Chicago: University of Chicago Press, 1962), 278–93.

28. Minnesota Senate, *A Fiscal Review of the 1986 Legislative Sessions* (1986), 9.

29. Kathleen A. Gaylord and Susan Chianelli Jacobson, *History of Taxation in Minnesota*, 2d ed., rev., Staff Research Report – Minnesota Tax Study Commission no. 2 (St. Paul: Minnesota Tax Study Commission, 1979), 11–19; Lloyd M. Short, Clara Penniman, and Floyd O.

Flom, *The Minnesota Department of Taxation: An Administrative History,* Public Administration Training Center, University of Minnesota, Studies in Administration no. 8 (Minneapolis: University of Minnesota Press, 1955).

30. Gaylord and Jacobson, *Taxation in Minnesota,* 23–35.

31. Blegen, *Minnesota,* 378–79; William W. Folwell, *A History of Minnesota,* rev. ed., vol. 4 (St. Paul: Minnesota Historical Society, 1969), 53–59.

32. John R. Borchert, *Taxes and the Minnesota Community,* Publication no. 79-3 (Minneapolis: Center for Urban and Regional Affairs, University of Minnesota, 1979), 3.

33. Borchert, *Taxes and the Minnesota Community,* 3; James Cecil, "The Minnesota State Budget," in *Minnesota Government and Politics,* ed. Gieske and Brandt, 357.

34. Gaylord and Jacobson, *Taxation in Minnesota,* 26–28, 55; Cecil, "Minnesota State Budget," 361; Blegen, *Minnesota,* 584, 594.

35. Here and below, United States, Advisory Commission on Intergovernmental Relations, *Federalism in 1971: The Crisis Continues,* 13th annual report (1972), 5–6.

36. *Minneapolis Tribune,* May 31, 1981, p. 1A, 9A; Citizens League, *A First Class Property Tax System* (Minneapolis: The League, 1987); Thomas R. Peek and Douglas S. Wilson, *Local Perspectives on Minnesota's Intergovernmental System* (Minneapolis: Center for Urban and Regional Affairs, University of Minnesota, 1984); James Cecil, "The Minnesota Budget and Inflation," *Minnesota Academy of Science Journal* 49 (1983–84): 3–6.

37. Here and below, see Julius Wolfe, "Minnesotans Protect Their Environment," *Roots* 1 (Winter 1973): 11–13; Alfred L. Nelson, "Department of Conservation: The History behind Minnesota's Resource Management," *Conservation Volunteer* (Minnesota Department of Conservation) 12 (March-April 1949): 1–14 (quotation on 13), Greg Breining, *Managing Minnesota's Natural Resources: The DNR's First 50 Years, 1931–1981* (St. Paul: Minnesota Department of Natural Resources, 1981); Minnesota, Secretary of State, *Legislative Manual,* 1876, p. 100, 1893, p. 285–89, 206–7, 1897, p. 331–32, 1899, p. 342–44, 1901, p. 342–45, 1921, p. 248, 300.

38. Minnesota, Secretary of State, *Legislative Manual,* 1933, p. 446; Breining, *Managing Minnesota's Natural Resources,* 2 (quotation).

39. Breining, *Managing Minnesota's Natural Resources,* 3, 5, 6, 7 (quotation on 5); Blegen, *Minnesota,* 527.

40. Here and below, Breining, *Managing Minnesota's Natural Resources,* 3, 8–9, 15; Minnesota, Secretary of State, *Legislative Manual,* 1943, p. 136.

41. Minnesota, Secretary of State, *Legislative Manual,* 1987-1988, p. 185–86 (quotation on 186); Minnesota, Department of Administration, *Guidebook to State Agency Services,* 261–62.

42. Blegen, *Minnesota,* 463–65 (quotation on 464); Minnesota, Department of Highways, Office of Public Information, *50th Anniversary: 1921–1971* (1971), 5–11; R. A. Gomez, *Intergovernmental Relations in Highways,* Intergovernmental Relations in the United States, Research Monograph no. 2 (Minneapolis: University of Minnesota Press, 1950), 12–13.

43. Gomez, *Intergovernmental Relations,* 13; Minnesota, Secretary of State, *Legislative Manual,* 1907, p. 289–90.

44. A driver's license law was first passed in 1933, allowing the head of a family to buy a license for the whole family for twenty-five cents; there was no examination until 1948. Blegen, *Minnesota,* 464; Minnesota, Department of Highways, *50th Anniversary,* 18, 19, 20–21, 7; Minnesota, Department of Administration, *Guidebook to State Agency Services,* 321.

45. Gomez, *Intergovernmental Relations,* 13.

46. Minnesota, Department of Highways, *50th Anniversary,* 23, 25, 30, 7; Minnesota, Secretary of State, *Legislative Manual,* 1907, p. 289–90, 1919, p. 402, 462, 720, 1931, p. 442, 471; Gomez, *Intergovernmental Relations,* 13–15; Minnesota, Department of Administration, *Guidebook to State Agency Services,* 372–73.

47. Roy C. Blakey and Gladys C. Blakey, *Taxation in Minnesota: 1939 Supplement* (Minneapolis: University of Minnesota Press, 1939), 23; Minnesota, Department of Highways, *50th Anniversary,* 7, 27; Gomez, *Intergovernmental Relations,* 14–15.

48. Minnesota, Department of Highways, *50th Anniversary,* 7, 8, 10, 11; Gomez, *Intergovernmental Relations,* 9–10.

49. Minnesota, Department of Administration, *Guidebook to State Agency Services,* 372, 373; Minnesota, Secretary of State, *Legislative Manual,* 1987-1988, p. 189 (quotation); Bill Farmer and Ellen B. Green, "Movin' Right Along," *Roots* 15 (Winter 1987): 32.

50. Esther Benson, "Organization of Public Welfare Activities in Minnesota" (Master's thesis, University of Minnesota, 1941), 60–64, 75; Minnesota, Department of Administration, *Guidebook to State Agency Services,* 174.

51. William Anderson and Bryce E. Lehman, *An Outline of County Government in Minnesota* (Minneapolis: University of Minnesota Press, 1927), 70–71; D. Jerome Tweton, *The New Deal at the Grass Roots: Programs for the People in Otter Tail County, Minnesota* (St. Paul: Minnesota Historical Society Press, 1988), 40.

52. Anderson and Lehman, *Outline of County Government*, 72-75; Ethel McClure, *More Than a Roof: The Development of Minnesota Poor Farms and Homes for the Aged* (St. Paul: Minnesota Historical Society, 1968), 92.

53. Tweton, *New Deal at the Grass Roots*, 43-46; Benson, "Organization of Public Welfare," 96-102.

54. McClure, *More Than a Roof*, 163-66; Tweton, *New Deal at the Grass Roots*, 46; Benson, "Organization of Public Welfare," 110-14.

55. Benson, "Organization of Public Welfare," 83-85, 117-20, 124, 132-45.

56. James Banovetz, *A Handbook for Minnesota Villages*, 2d ed., rev. (Minneapolis: League of Minnesota Municipalities, 1971), 232-33; Minnesota, *Statutes*, 1973, ch. 261.001.

57. Telephone conversation with Betty Carlson, Department of Human Services, Oct. 26, 1988; Minnesota, *Statutes*, 1986, ch. 402; Minnesota, Office of Human Services, *Human Services Evaluation Project* ([Minneapolis]: Touche Ross and Co., 1976), p. I-1-I-2.

58. Minnesota, *Statutes*, 1986, ch. 256E; Minnesota, Department of Administration, *Guidebook to State Agency Services*, 190-92; Minnesota, *Laws*, 1984, ch. 2162.

59. Minnesota Taxpayers Association, *Fiscal Facts for Minnesotans, 1973: A Concise Background of Pertinent Information about Your State and Its Government* (St. Paul: The Association, 1972), 85, *Fiscal Facts for Minnesotans: A Compendium of Pertinent Statistical Information about Your State and Its Government* (St.Paul: The Association, 1987), 135, and *A Fiscal Review of the 1973 Minnesota Legislative Session: Where the Money Comes from and Where It Goes* (St. Paul: The Association, 1973), 5, 11.

60. Minnesota, Department of Administration, *Guidebook to State Agency Services*, 174, 182; Minnesota, Senate, Senate Counsel and Research, *Fiscal Review of the 1986 Legislative Sessions* (1986), 12.

61. Minnesota, Board of Health and Vital Statistics, *Report of the Minnesota State Board of Health and Vital Statistics, 1922-1943* (1944), 9, 17. In 1873 all incorporated municipalities were required to establish boards of health; see Minnesota, *Laws*, 1873, ch. 8; A. J. Chesley, *The Minnesota State Board of Health: Organization and Functions* (St. Paul: Minnesota Department of Health, 1939), 13-14.

62. League of Minnesota Municipalities, *The Department of Health of the State of Minnesota: Organization, Duties, Statistics* (Minneapolis: The League, 1933), 1; Philip D. Jordan, *The People's Health: A History of Public Health in Minnesota to 1948* (St. Paul: Minnesota Historical Society Press, 1953), 186-87; Minnesota, Department of Health, *Community Health Services in Minnesota: A Report to the 1987 Legislature* (1987), 1-2.

63. Minnesota, Board of Health and Vital Statistics, *Report*, 1922-1943, p. 18; Minnesota, Board of Health, *Biennial Report*, 1965-66, p. 20-21, 52.

64. Minnesota, Department of Health, *Community Health Services*, 2-3, 7, 10; Minnesota, Board of Health, *Biennial Report*, 1973-74, p. 7, 9; Minnesota, *Statutes*, 1986, ch. 144.

65. Anderson and Lehman, *Outline of County Government*, 30-38.

66. M. Harry Lease, Jr., "County Government: Structure, Problems and Reform," in *Minnesota Government and Politics*, ed. Gieske and Brandt, 341-50.

67. Blegen, *Minnesota*, 591; Minnesota, Department of Education, *The ABC's of Minnesota School Finance: Paying for the Public Schools in 1987-88 and 1988-89* (1987), 2-3.

68. Citizens League, *Local Government in a Time of Transition* (Minneapolis: The League, 1974), 17.

69. Citizens League, *Local Government*, 18, 20; Arthur Naftalin, *Making One Community out of Many: Perspectives on the Metropolitan Council of the Twin Cities Area* (St. Paul: The Council, 1986), 13, 4. Mound and Island Park consolidated in the 1950s and Edina and Morningside in the 1960s.

70. Citizens League, *Local Government*, 19-20.

71. Naftalin, *Making One Community*, 11-20, 76n10.

72. Citizens League, *Local Government*, 33.

73. Here and below, Citizens League, *Local Government*, 34.

74. Minnesota Taxpayers Association, *Fiscal Facts for Minnesotans* (1987), 152-53.

75. Data computed from Minnesota, Secretary of State, *Legislative Manual*, 1987-1988; telephone conversations with Minnesota School Boards Association, Nov. 1, 1988, League of Minnesota Cities, Nov. 2, 1988, Secretary of State, Office of Elections, Nov. 2, 1988.

76. Neal R. Peirce, *The Great Plains States of America: People, Politics, and Power in the Nine Great Plains States* (New York: W. W. Norton and Co., 1972, 1973), 110-50 (quotation on 110).

77. John Fischer, "The Minnesota Experiment: How to Make a Big City Fit to Live In," *Harper's Magazine*, April 1969, p. 12, 17-18, 20, 24, 26, 28, 30, 32 (quotation on 12).

78. For a general discussion of American political culture and its subcultures, see Daniel J. Elazar, *American Federalism: A View from the States*, 3d ed. (New York: Harper and Row, 1984), chapters 5-6.

79. On Minnesota's political culture, see Elazar, *Cities*, 323-37.

Poster from Jacob A. O. Preus's successful campaign for governor, 1920

JOHN E. HAYNES

Reformers, Radicals, and Conservatives

Historians have long argued about the degree of continuity between the largely unsuccessful agrarian political protests of the early 1890s and the triumph of progressivism in the first decades of the twentieth century. In Minnesota, the link was clear.

In 1890, farmers elected a number of their own to the Minnesota legislature under the leadership of the militant Farmers' Alliance, and this success was followed by the formation of a lively People's party. In the 1894 gubernatorial contest, a "Populist," the usual term for an adherent of the People's party, came in second behind Republican Knute Nelson but ahead of the Democratic nominee. This revolt against the normal partisan alignment culminated in the 1896 gubernatorial candidacy of John Lind, who had served several terms as a Republican congressman. Lind left his party in 1896 to head a fusion ticket under the Democratic label but with the support of both the People's party and Silver Republicans. The Populists, Democrats, and Silver Republicans were united in 1896 in their support for adopting silver as backing for the dollar at a ratio of sixteen to one with gold. This "monetizing" of silver would inflate the currency, increase prices for farm products, and relieve farmers of their debt burden. Lind and his agrarian coalition lost narrowly.[1]

Lind returned for a second try at the governor's office in 1898, again as a Democrat, but not, this time, as the head of an agrarian crusade. The return of farm prosperity had ended the desperation that had driven so many farmers into the Populist movement. Without disavowing his former position, Lind adjusted his thinking to a new era and won the election. His inaugural address set forth a progressive agenda that would dominate politics until 1917 and remain a powerful force for decades thereafter.[2]

The Progressive Era

John Lind's progressivism contained a significant legacy from the Populist era, such as the shifting of taxes from farms to railroads. But to agrarian grievances, Lind added the concerns of small-town business people and professionals, particularly the reform of politics through the use of direct primaries, referenda, and ballot initiatives. More important, Lind presented this program in a new context. Populism's rhetoric had a divisive quality to it: it defended the "people" against the "interests," but it defined the people in a way that seemed to include farmers and virtually no one else. Progressivism expanded the "people" to include a far broader segment of the population. Farmers, certainly, were of the "people," but so were the leaders and solid citizens of the many hundreds of small towns that dotted Minnesota. And, indeed, these small towns and their lawyers, doctors, journalists, and business people would provide most of the leaders of progressivism. The "interests" that progressives denounced with much fervor had also changed from the Populist variety. No longer were all banks and all bankers the enemy; attention now was focused more narrowly on big banks, particularly large eastern banks. Minnesota progressivism thus expressed provincial resentment against increasing domination of the nation's economy by eastern banks and corporations. Provincial resentment allowed farmers, local bankers, and local merchants to put aside their local conflicts and turn toward a common enemy.

Minnesota progressives were also bound together by moral commitment. They thought of themselves, and usually were, "good" men and women who believed in honesty, fairness, and responsibility and who argued that public life should reflect those same values. The strong partisanship, and sometimes equally strong corruption, of late-nineteenth-century politics appalled many middle-class citizens. They believed that public life should reflect the same moral standards they sought to uphold in their private lives. From these sentiments came the progressive commitment for reform of the political process itself.

Religiously derived values resonated in progressive rhetoric, the legacy of the Protestantism of the late nineteenth century, particularly its mainstream evangelical wing. The vision of the good society seen and often experienced by many Americans was one of farmers, shopkeepers, craftsmen, and professionals living in small towns with strong families under conditions of neighborliness and earning their livelihoods with a large measure of economic independence. This bourgeois, semirural "peaceable kingdom" found itself threatened as the twentieth century got under way. The rise of industrialism with its concentrations of economic power and the expansion of markets to national and international scope threatened the economic autonomy of rural and small-town America. The rise of big cities similarly threatened to dominate cultural life.

Progressivism, like the Protestant culture from which it came, believed in the perfectibility of humanity. In progressivism, the Christian belief in sin and evil had been secularized and externalized. Sin was no longer an

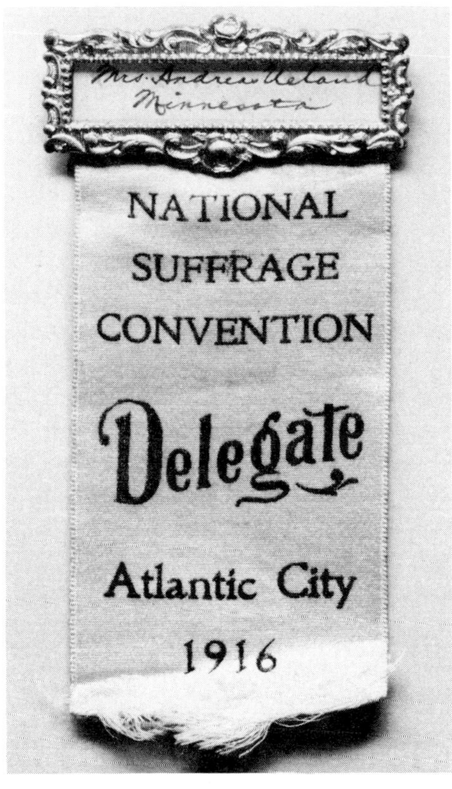

Badge worn by Minnesotan Clara H. Ueland at the National Suffrage Convention, 1916

internal problem of the soul; rather, it was an external problem of society. Perfecting the soul was a difficult problem, but perfecting society – where problems could be traced to readily identified, external sources – appeared much easier. Two issues on the progressive agenda, woman suffrage and prohibition, exemplified this strong moral element.

In part, progressive support for woman suffrage was a straightforward consequence of commitment to the full extension of political equality. But this support also rested on a belief that women were different. Middle-class Americans of the late nineteenth century tended to assign to women a special role as the guardians of morality, and progressives commonly assumed that the inclusion of women in the political process would raise the moral tone of public life. Of all the items on the progressive agenda, however, woman suffrage was the one on which Minnesota progressivism achieved the least success. Before the Nineteenth Amendment enfranchised women in 1920, a number of states acted on their own to extend political equality. In Minnesota, such attempts failed. After gaining the vote, women soon came to be about half the electorate; their voting patterns did not differ significantly from those of men, however. Minnesota elected a few women to public office, but the number of women candidates and elected officials remained minuscule for decades. In the first ten years after the extension of the vote to women, only seven women won election to the legislature.[3] It was not until 1954 that a woman, Democratic-Farmer-Laborite Cornelia G. ("Coya") Knutson, won election to Congress.

(Knutson, a former state legislator, held her rural congressional seat in northwestern Minnesota for two terms before defeat in a vituperative and controversial campaign in 1958.)[4]

The control of alcohol consumption was an integral part of Minnesota progressivism in early decades of the twentieth century. Not every Minnesota progressive was a "dry," but most favored some measure of public restraint of alcohol consumption. The reason for progressive hostility to alcohol was simple: the family was the rock of late-nineteenth-century civilization, and rampant alcohol abuse threatened that foundation, creating anchorless men and abandoned women and children. Progressivism's answer to this threat was also simple: pass a law and prohibit the sale of alcoholic beverages. Although prohibition would in time become discredited, it is important to recognize that prohibitionists were grappling with a genuine problem. Alcoholism was a menace that had ruined the lives of thousands of Minnesotans, and the progressive remedy, prohibition, was a rational (if ultimately unsuccessful) way to deal with the problem. Progressives, in typical fashion, also defined the cause of the problem as one external to the individual – the *sale* of alcohol – and blamed alcohol abuse on an external menace – the saloon interests. Prohibitionists saw the problem as one of supply, which could be addressed by direct social control, rather than of demand, a more difficult problem of cultural and moral discipline that could not be solved through the use of state power.

The most common antialcohol measure supported by progressives was county option, a state law allowing each of Minnesota's counties to prohibit the sale of alcohol. This law passed the legislature in 1915, and within five years forty-six of the state's eighty-six counties had adopted prohibition. Although attempts to pass statewide prohibition failed, Minnesota quickly ratified the national prohibition amendment when the legislature met in session in January 1919. The federal law implementing national prohibition (the Volstead Act) was authored by and named for Congressman Andrew J. Volstead of Minnesota's Seventh District, a progressive Republican and ardent prohibitionist.[5]

Woman suffrage and prohibition were two aspects of the progressive agenda that became an active force in Minnesota politics after the 1898 election of Lind as governor. Despite the praise from legislators for his 1899 inaugural address and the favorable reception for his recommendations, however, Lind's actual record of enacted legislation was short. The legislature's Republican majority, although sympathetic to many of Lind's recommendations, was not inclined to rush enactment of his program and strengthen his political stature. This tactic met success in the election of 1900 when Samuel R. Van Sant narrowly defeated Lind, but his victory was no defeat for progressivism. Van Sant ran as a progressive Republican on a platform that differed little from Lind's. With partisan considerations eliminated, the Republican-controlled legislature hastened to enact a number of progressive measures, including increased railroad taxation and primaries for all except statewide offices. In addition, progressivism became fully respectable under Van Sant, whose reputation for rectitude and flamboyant oratory stressing traditional values removed the last taint of agrarian radicalism.

Van Sant won reelection easily in 1902, but troublesome internal Republican factionalism kept him from running in 1904. Republicans splintered badly over choosing a successor, and progressive Democrat John A. Johnson won the 1904 contest as well as those in 1906 and 1908. He died in office in September 1909 because of complications after surgery. During his tenure, much of the progressive agenda became law: a new inheritance tax; stronger insurance, bank, and railroad regulation; constitutional liberalization of the legislature's taxing authority; and controls over natural resource exploitation. Johnson was a skilled spokesman for the progressive point of view, friendly and sincere in his manner, and rarely divisive. Progressivism's domination of politics is illustrated by the nature of Republican attempts to unseat him. In both 1906 and 1908, Republicans chose candidates whose campaigns came down to promises to be more effective progressives than Johnson.[6]

There were, of course, those who dissented. Both political parties had significant conservative factions, and a sizable segment of legislators voted against most progressive measures. But these dissenters were conservative in the simple sense of the term: they liked things the way they were and saw no pressing need for change. Most were not philosophical conservatives or laissez-faire ideologues; they represented more simply the status quo. Not surprisingly, they tended to receive support from those interests attacked by progressives: railroads, banks, and big corporations. Even big business, however, was not monolithic in its attitude. Many Twin Cities business leaders sided with the progressives on a number of issues. The corruption of Minneapolis city government offended business people, and they often supported reform campaigns. Others, who shared with progressives a resentment against the financial power of eastern banks and industrial corporations, supported progressive assaults on these institutions.

Governor Johnson's actions during the 1907 strike on the iron ranges showed something of the relationship between progressivism and the labor movement. On the one hand, the humanitarianism that permeated progressivism tended to make progressives sympathetic to grievances of industrial workers. On the other hand, organized labor – with its institutional antagonism toward employers – did not fit well into the progressive vision of the peaceable kingdom of small-town Minnesota. When the radical Western Federation of Miners struck the iron mines of northern Minnesota, Johnson refused pleas by the mining companies to send in state troops to break the strike. Instead, he toured the strike areas, speaking with strikers and urging conciliation. But he also made it clear that he would use state troops if the miners used violence or attempted to keep strikebreakers from entering the mines. Nor did he press the mining companies to settle. In the end, the strike was broken.

Johnson's death in 1909 elevated Republican Lt. Gov. Adolph O. Eberhart to the governorship (at that time, the governor and lieutenant governor were elected independently and were often of opposite parties).

Eberhart allied himself with the "standpat" wing of the Republican party, then led by Edward E. Smith, a highly skilled political tactician. Most progressives regarded Smith's political organization as a "plunderbund" uniting the greed of the railroads, the United States Steel Corporation, the brewers, and the purveyors of liquor. Defeating Eberhart quickly became a chief progressive goal, but one that proved difficult despite the progressive tide. Eberhart's incumbency and Smith's skills were sufficient to secure Eberhart the Republican nomination in 1910, and Democratic disarray was sufficient to hand him the election as well.[7]

The election of 1912 was one of the most complex in Minnesota history. In the state's Republican party, progressivism was so strong that the fight over presidential delegates was between progressives who supported Sen. Robert M. La Follette, Sr. (Wisconsin) for the presidency and those who wanted former president Theodore Roosevelt. The "regulars" who supported Pres. William Howard Taft were a weak third. Eberhart, however, carried off a political coup of extraordinary skill. He called an unexpected special session of the legislature to ask for enactment of a primary for statewide offices and other progressive reforms, thus allowing him to claim a progressive label and avoid a Republican convention he was sure to lose. The legislature enacted the primary he requested, ratified the constitutional amendments for a federal income tax and direct election of U.S. senators, strengthened clean election laws, raised railroad taxes, and restricted child labor. Eberhart, wrapping himself in the progressive mantle, defeated a divided primary opposition.

Meanwhile, when the national Republican convention nominated Taft, the majority of Minnesota delegates bolted the party to back Roosevelt's hastily organized Bull Moose Progressive party campaign. Democrats fielded a solid progressive ticket with Woodrow Wilson for president and Peter M. Ringdal, a former Populist state senator, for governor. Roosevelt won the state's popular votes by a plurality, with Wilson a close second, Taft a distant third, and Socialist Eugene V. Debs taking nearly 10 percent of the vote. Eberhart won the governorship with equally complex voting. His coolness toward county option allowed him to take part of the German-American vote, which tended Democratic but was irritated by the strong support for prohibition by most progressive Democrats. Meanwhile, a Prohibition party candidate took 10 percent of the vote and thereby cut into Ringdal's "dry" support. The vote was further split by a Socialist and a Bull Moose Progressive who each received about 10 percent of the vote. Eberhart consequently won, with barely more than 40 percent of the total vote. Eberhart's reelection, however, was about the only setback progressivism sustained in Minnesota. Minnesota's largely Republican congressional delegation was solidly progressive, as were the majority of the legislature, the state's leading newspapers, and most of its statewide officials. Eberhart and the 1913 legislature, however, were unable to agree on most new legislation except for a notable law making state legislators officially nonpartisan.

In 1914, progressive William E. Lee defeated Eberhart in the Republican primary and a fractious Democratic party nominated Congressman

Winfield S. Hammond for the governorship. Both campaigned as progressives, with Hammond eking out a narrow victory. The 1915 legislature under Hammond's governorship was the crest of Minnesota progressivism. Besides securing passage of the measure establishing county option on prohibition, the session enacted laws covering regulation of fire insurance, telephone and utility service, public-school teacher pensions, and an improved workers compensation system. Hammond died unexpectedly on December 30, 1915, and Lt. Gov. Joseph A. A. Burnquist, a Republican with a progressive reputation, became governor.

Progressivism Splits Apart

Tensions within Minnesota progressivism that had been tolerable when the movement was young became less so as it matured. Norwegian Americans had played a prominent role in the movement from its origins, finding in progressivism an expression of some of the hostility toward established political and religious authority that they had brought over from a Norway with rigid class lines and a state church. But this hostility to established elites sometimes carried over to resentment against those of old-stock (Anglo-Saxon) background, a stratum that also produced many progressive leaders and that furnished progressivism with much of its support from higher business and professional circles.[8]

Few German Americans were prominent in Minnesota politics, but they constituted, in fact, the state's largest ethnic group. Although they had tended to vote Democratic, progressivism jolted Germans from their accustomed habits. Particularly, German Americans tended to be unsympathetic to prohibition, and the largely "dry" leadership of progressivism had sent German-American voters back and forth between the two parties in search of candidates least offensive to their beer-drinking heritage. Many of them were also Roman Catholic, and they did not fail to notice the strong Protestant overtones of progressive rhetoric. Some suspected that Roman Catholicism was numbered among the threats that progressives perceived to their ideal of the harmonious society.[9]

Minnesota business leaders had always been divided in their attitude toward progressivism. Many sympathized with the progressive drive against political corruption, and many joined in the attack on the arrogance of eastern financial and industrial power. But Minnesota's business elite also worried that progressivism could get out of hand and that its indictment of the special interests could change into a general indictment of private property. From another direction, the Minnesota labor movement, which resented the paternalism of progressive leaders, was increasingly a source of divisiveness within the progressive coalition. Minnesota unions of the American Federation of Labor (AFL) had made impressive strides in organizing workers in the 1910s. Union leaders were pressing for a measure of political recognition, a status that many progressive leaders, with their small-town political base, were not inclined to grant. Among unionists, a militant minority had abandoned progressivism for socialism. In 1914 Socialists won four seats on the Minneapolis City Council, and in 1916 Socialist Thomas Van Lear was elected mayor. Progressives to whom a defense of the values of small-town and rural America was a high priority saw the growth of unions as another threat to a cherished way of life. Business leaders also saw the rise of the unions and the birth of Socialist political strength as signs that progressivism was, after all, getting out of hand.[10]

Even more disturbing to the progressive coalition was the rise of the farmers' Nonpartisan League (NPL), which threatened to undo the political unity of farmers and small-town elites. The NPL began in 1915 in North Dakota, and a year later league candidates – after having first won in Republican primaries – won the governorship and control of the lower house of the legislature. The league used its power to create a state-owned bank, state-owned grain elevators, and strict regulation of the grain trade. In 1917, the NPL moved its headquarters to Minnesota and sought to repeat its rapid rise to power. The league's program did not differ radically from that advocated by many progressives, but the league charged that mainstream progressive politicians were long on rhetoric and short on results that actually benefited farmers. It demanded that candidates pledge immediate enactment of league programs without compromise.[11]

The NPL was foremost a farmers' organization that insisted on the primacy of farmers' interests. In NPL rhetoric, the "producers," usually defined strictly as farmers and workers, were the only truly worthy classes. Small-town merchants and professionals were not accorded equal standing. In addition, as the NPL rhetorically devalued small-town elites, it also threatened their economic survival by promising to set up competing cooperative enterprises. Rural newspapers found themselves faced with a choice of endorsing NPL doctrines or seeing league newspapers established to compete for their readers. Established politicians also faced a choice of accepting league leadership or seeing league candidates challenge them in their own party primaries.

In North Dakota, a largely agrarian state, these tactics had been successful. Minnesota, however, was a more difficult prospect for the league. Although grain farmers in northwest and west-central Minnesota welcomed the league with enthusiasm, the more diversified dairy, corn, and hog producers of central and southern Minnesota regarded the league's program of state-owned banks and grain elevators as less relevant to their needs. Minnesota also possessed large urban centers, powerful nonagricultural economic interests, and a large number of voters to whom farm problems were of secondary interest. The league was conscious of its need for allies, and it sought to attract support from the labor movement. This appeal broadened the league's political base, but it also heightened the pressure on the progressive coalition. The worst fears of small-town merchants and professionals would be realized if radical agrarians joined hands with Socialist proletarians to threaten established institutions. These small-town elites found that they and the business elites of the Twin Cities were being driven toward an embrace as each was repelled by the dual threats of militant farmers and radicalized labor.

To this mixture brewing within progressivism of class, ethnic, and interest-group conflict was added the yeast of war and patriotism. When fighting began in Europe in 1914, progressives reacted with common shock and distaste. Minnesotans, like most Americans, were initially determined that the United States remain aloof and neutral. The NPL was also firmly neutralist, and its organizers exploited its opposition to intervention as a theme that allowed the league to reach out to farmers, particularly German-American farmers in central and southern Minnesota where the league was weakest.

As the war in Europe grew more desperate, however, Americans' support for neutralism began to splinter. Many began to reevaluate the moral meaning of the conflict. Instead of seeing it as an irrational clash of nationalisms, many Americans reinterpreted the fight as one of German militarism against democracy as embodied in the French republic and the British parliament. And, after war finally came, the Wilson administration portrayed it as a crusade for democracy. This interpretation allowed the moral strain of progressivism to be fully mobilized in support of the war effort.

The progressive vision of the peaceable kingdom – of a harmonious America threatened by the alien influences of big cities, big business, and special interests – was transformed under the influence of the war into a vision of an America under threat from a new direction. The external enemy now was German autocracy and the internal one was aliens, those who subverted the war effort by disturbing the social order and thus aiding the external enemy.

This progressivism-turned-patriotism allowed several constituencies to resolve the tension they had felt as progressivism reached its peak in 1915–16. First, it provided an alternative political stance that was both politically viable and respectable. Second, it allowed the elites of the small towns to make common cause with the business leadership of the Twin Cities. The merchants and professionals of small-town Minnesota were already inclined to view the NPL as a threat to their way of life. The league's hostility to the war allowed these small-town elites to sharpen their perception of the league's threat into one of national disloyalty, an interpretation that business leaders readily endorsed.[12]

Third, progressive patriotism gave those uneasy with the rise of labor unions a way to relieve their anxiety. The labor movement's Socialist minority and those who spoke for the Socialist party in the Twin Cities were militantly hostile to intervention. In addition, there was a limited presence in Minnesota of a truly radical labor organization. In 1916 the Industrial Workers of the World (IWW), a revolutionary, anticapitalist, syndicalist organization, took control of a strike by miners on the iron ranges. The miners' strike was followed in late 1916 by an IWW-led walkout by northern Minnesota lumberjacks.[13] Both strikes were unsuccessful, but the sight of thousands of workers following an explicitly revolutionary organization frightened many Minnesotans. Consequently, many progressives-turned-patriots came to see the labor movement as the same kind of disloyal threat as the NPL.

After America entered the war, most Minnesota progressives, including those who had opposed intervention, shifted to a position of firm support for the war effort. Many adopted Wilson's interpretation of the war as a progressive crusade for democracy on a worldwide basis. This support did not, however, save progressivism from the taint of disloyalty. The memory of the prominent role of progressives in opposing intervention remained strong, and most of the limited opposition to the war that remained visible was led by progressives. Patriotic emotions were further inflamed by the lack of enthusiasm for the war among many German Americans. After American entry, most German-American leaders abandoned their opposition to intervention and supported the war effort. There was not, however, much enthusiasm in their endorsement of the war. In New Ulm, for example, German-American local officials supported the war effort and called for compliance with the draft, but they also called for modification of the law to exempt draftees from fighting in Europe and asked for a national referendum on declaring war. These views did not constitute overt disloyalty, but in the heated atmosphere of the times they were interpreted in that light. The mayor and city attorney of New Ulm were removed from office by state order.[14]

In 1917 the majorities of the Minnesota legislature were, by the standards of prewar days, progressive in orientation. Indeed, one of the chief products of the 1917 legislature was the comprehensive Minnesota Children's Code improving services for neglected children. Among the leading advocates of this type of legislation was Catheryne Cooke Gilman, a prominent member of the Minnesota Child Welfare Commission that wrote the code. Gilman spoke and agitated for various progressive causes throughout the 1920s and into the 1930s as the head of the Women's Co-operative Alliance.[15]

The 1917 legislature also created an extraordinary body, the Minnesota Commission of Public Safety. Consisting of the governor, the attorney general, and five gubernatorial appointees, this commission was given the power to do almost anything it thought necessary for public safety and the war effort. The commission proceeded to use both legal coercion and heavy-handed propaganda in an attempt to crush those it regarded as threats to society. As might be expected, the commission moved quickly against the IWW and those Socialists who denounced the war and the draft. It infiltrated the IWW organization and encouraged local officials to jail and harass IWW organizers. Within a short time, the IWW was eliminated as a serious presence in Minnesota. The commission also saturated German-American communities with propaganda calling for loyalty and denouncing German culture and civilization in brutal terms.[16]

The NPL had shifted its official position to one of endorsement of the war after the United States entered the conflict. Knowing the suspicion with which the league was regarded, NPL orators usually avoided criticizing the war and made a point of supporting the sale of war bonds and other measures that were the staples of civilian support. The Commission of

Public Safety, however, regarded the league as a menace, and its agents harassed league organizers at every turn. In more than a score of Minnesota counties, local officials, with commission support, prevented public meetings of the league.

A key element in the commission's assault on the NPL was the extent to which the attacks paralleled the political needs of Governor Burnquist. Running as a progressive, Burnquist had won the 1916 election by a huge margin against a Democratic nominee beset by severe internal party divisions. But he faced a tougher fight with the NPL in 1918. The league had made no secret about its plans to repeat its North Dakota tactic of running candidates in the Republican primary. In 1918 the league endorsed a slate for the primary with former Republican congressman Charles A. Lindbergh, Sr., a veteran progressive who had firmly opposed intervention, as the gubernatorial candidate.[17]

Burnquist campaigned on a platform of loyalty and presented himself as the man who had saved Minnesota from pro-Germanism. The Republican party also united behind Burnquist because both its "standpat" faction and most of its progressive wing feared they would be cast aside in the wake of a league victory. Lindbergh and the league ticket thus found themselves facing both the bulk of the Republican party and the official weight of the Commission of Public Safety. Even so, Burnquist's victory over Lindbergh was not impressive.

After Lindbergh's defeat, the NPL faced a dilemma. It was not inclined to support the Democratic candidate, Fred E. Wheaton, who was unsympathetic to the league. Indeed, in 1918 the Minnesota Democratic party, whose factional problems had been growing for years, was well on its way to disintegration. (In 1916, arguments between various factions had produced a brawl on the train carrying delegates to the Democratic national convention.)[18] The Minnesota party's various factions supported Wilson's war policies, but this loyalty to the national party damaged its base. Normally, Democrats could count on a substantial German-American vote; for the duration of the war, however, those voters were inclined to avoid candidates associated with Wilson's policies.

The league had the option of running an independent ticket in the general election, a course of action that even offered the chance of expanding the league's base beyond militant grain farmers and discontented Germans. Burnquist and the Commission of Public Safety had created the option by their harassment of the mainstream labor movement as well as the radical IWW. In the summer of 1917, the AFL had sponsored the organization of the workers of the Twin City Rapid Transit Company. The struggle over the streetcar union quickly became a major confrontation between Minnesota's growing labor movement and a business community determined to reassert the existence of the open shop. Minnesota's AFL unions, with few exceptions, firmly supported the war effort. The commission and Governor Burnquist, however, saw things differently. On the grounds of protecting war production, they intervened in the streetcar strike in a manner that helped to defeat the strikers. It was a serious setback for labor, and the AFL burned for revenge against the governor. The Socialist minority in the labor movement strongly urged action, seeing an opportunity to move unions into an overtly political role. Consequently, the AFL responded positively when approached by the NPL about an independent ticket. In a hastily arranged effort, the farmers' Nonpartisan League and the Minnesota AFL held simultaneous conventions and endorsed a common ticket for the general election. According to election law, an independent ticket had to have a label, and the name picked – "Farmer-Labor" – reflected the organizational origins of the ticket.[19]

In the fall campaign, Burnquist used the same loyalty themes that he had used in the primary. The Farmer-Labor ticket, however, was less vulnerable to disloyalty accusations than the league slate had been in the primary. David H. Evans, the Farmer-Labor candidate for governor, was a progressive Democrat with a record of firm support for Wilson's war policies. Burnquist also faced a measure of criticism from those who believed that the Commission of Public Safety had abused its authority. In the election, Burnquist won unimpressively with Evans a respectable second and Democrat Wheaton a distant third.

With the 1918 election, the progressive era came to an end. The bipartisan coalition of farmers, small-town voters, and moral reformers was shattered. One part of the coalition moved into what would become the Farmer-Labor party, keeping much of the old progressive rhetoric but with a definite leftward tilt. Another part joined with business leaders and conservatives to remake the Republican party into a voice of circumspect progressivism and moderate conservatism.[20]

The 1920s and the Establishment of the Farmer-Labor Party

The Nonpartisan League and its labor allies could derive some satisfaction from the 1918 election. Although they had lost, their candidates had done well in the Republican primary and, considering the ad hoc nature of the ticket, well in the general election. Many league leaders favored staying with the strategy of running candidates in Republican primaries. Others, however, saw the strong showing of the independent Farmer-Labor ticket as a new opportunity.

In particular, those union leaders who had engineered the 1918 alliance with the NPL worked to create a new institution. Socialist unionists who were active in AFL locals in St. Paul and Minneapolis had seen the prospects of a strong Socialist party destroyed: the national party had split over America's entrance into World War I, was subjected to government suppression because of its antiwar stance, and then split again over bolshevism. Reluctantly, St. Paul union leader William Mahoney and other Socialists turned away from their party and created the Working People's Nonpartisan Political League as the labor equivalent of the NPL. The labor league, headed by Mahoney, was controlled by delegates from AFL unions.[21]

In the 1920 election, the farmers' Nonpartisan League once again entered a slate in the Republican primary and was beaten. Once again, it arranged an independent slate in the general election with the Working People's Nonpartisan Political League as its partner. And, once again, in the gubernatorial race the Farmer-Labor candidate came in second and pushed the Democrat into a humiliating third place. In 1922 the two leagues went directly to the general election with a Farmer-Labor ticket. This time victory came when Henrik Shipstead defeated incumbent Republican U.S. Sen. Frank B. Kellogg and Farmer-Labor candidates won two rural congressional seats.[22] Anna Dickie Olesen, the first woman nominated for a major state office, was the Democratic candidate for the U.S. Senate in this election. Olesen, a talented orator, was a prominent leader of the progressive, "dry" wing of the party. She came in third, with 18 percent of the vote.[23] Farmer-Labor victories in this election solidified the shift of the alliance from an ad hoc arrangement to a permanent political party. The final step in creating a new institution came in 1924 when the two leagues merged to create the Farmer-Labor Association.[24]

By American standards, the Farmer-Labor Association was an unusual political body.[25] In rural areas, a county association met each year in a convention of all dues-paying members to endorse candidates and select county leaders and delegates to higher conventions. In populous areas, the county convention consisted of delegates from separate Farmer-Labor clubs. These clubs, usually organized on a ward basis, were open only to dues-paying members. The association also allowed union locals, cooperatives, and certain other fraternal, youth, and women's organizations to affiliate directly with a county association and select their own delegates to conventions. In the 1920s and early 1930s, many AFL unions joined, providing the association with most of its funds and its single most influential bloc.

The ideology of the Farmer-Labor movement was ambiguous. One can see a genuinely radical movement, or one can see a movement that was militant but stayed well within Minnesota's progressive tradition. One can see both because both were there. In the history of the Farmer-Labor party are statements that can be read with a radical and a reformist meaning, as well as unambiguously radical declarations followed by backhanded repudiations of radical intent. This ambiguity stemmed from the desire of most Farmer-Labor leaders to gloss over the divisions within their own ranks and to maintain a sometimes precarious balance between the movement's reformist and radical tendencies.

In their radical mode, Farmer-Laborites disavowed capitalism and called for a "Cooperative Commonwealth" where economic democracy would be joined to political democracy. They talked of "Production for Use – Not for Profit" and spoke of public or cooperative ownership of utilities, transportation, and basic industries. In its more militant moods, the Farmer-Labor party scorned liberal programs as mere reformism, and the state's first Farmer-Labor governor, Floyd B. Olson, thundered while in office, "I am not a liberal. . . . I am a radical."[26] The radical wing of the Farmer-Labor party – led by people like Mahoney who came out of the Socialist faction of the labor movement – was strongest among Farmer-Labor clubs in urban areas.

Most of the Farmer-Labor party's successful politicians, however, came from the movement's reformist wing. This moderate bloc, strongest among rural Farmer-Laborites, regarded the politics of Senator Shipstead as the model for the party. Shipstead, a small-town dentist who was elected in 1922 and reelected in 1928 and 1934, projected the image of a progressive statesman and avoided the rhetoric of class conflict. He called for limited government intervention in the economy to support farm income and tame the business cycle, advocated legal protection of workers' rights to join unions, and urged government aid to cooperatives. In many ways, Shipstead's views echoed those of the progressive movement at high tide and foreshadowed the programs of Franklin D. Roosevelt's New Deal.

Another link to progressivism in the moderate wing of the Farmer-Labor movement was its provincialism. There was a strong tone in much Farmer-Labor rhetoric of rural, provincial resentment against national economic forces. Many rural Farmer-Laborites were reluctant to generalize their grievances onto a national stage. They were able to see some common bond between farmers in rural Minnesota and workers in Minneapolis and Duluth, but they did not see their particular complaints as having any kinship with those of industrial workers in Detroit or even with sharecroppers in the South.[27]

If the Farmer-Labor party of the 1920s was progressivism with a left wing, the Republican party of that period was progressivism with a right wing. Republicans sensed that Burnquist's unimpressive plurality in 1918 suggested electoral trouble if his harsh policies were continued. Consequently, when the war ended the Commission of Public Safety was dissolved and Burnquist dropped out of the 1920 gubernatorial campaign. Republicans chose a moderate, Jacob A. O. Preus, as their candidate for governor. Preus accused the NPL of dangerous radicalism, but he put more emphasis on a progressive program that called for increased taxes from the iron-mining companies, support for farmers' cooperatives, and assistance to farmers. After he won election, Preus backed legislation forcing the Minneapolis grain exchange to accept farm cooperatives as members and backing a constitutional amendment authorizing state assistance for farm debt. Under Preus, the Republican party was able to keep many rural voters who were oriented toward progressivism but frightened by the radical potential of the Farmer-Labor movement.

Preus narrowly defeated his Farmer-Labor opponent in 1922, and in 1923 he moved his program even more firmly in a progressive direction. He asked for and got a new tax on iron ore royalties, but the legislature rejected his request for an individual income tax. On the basis of a just-adopted state constitutional amendment, Preus set up a highly popular rural-credit agency to lend money directly to farmers to refinance farm debt. Preus's Republican successor, Theodore Christianson, was a former La Follette progressive turned moderate conservative. Christianson won the gubernatorial election of 1924 with a narrow margin, but he went on to win easily in 1926 and 1928.[28]

Minnesota politics saw two outstanding developments during the 1920s. One, of course, was the establishment of the Farmer-Labor party as a close rival to the dominant Republican party. The second was the continued influence of progressivism and the related gravitation of both Farmer-Laborites and Republicans toward the political center. The election of 1918 had suggested the development of a sharp clash between the Right, gathered behind Burnquist's loyalty crusade, and the Left, led by radical farmers and Socialist unionists. Both the new Farmer-Laborites and established Republicans, however, pulled back from such a confrontation.

Farmer-Labor Ascendancy

The Great Depression shifted enough voters to tip the balance between the parties, and in 1930 Minnesotans elected Floyd Olson to the governorship. Although on good terms with the Farmer-Labor party's radical wing, Olson had been associated with its moderate faction throughout the 1920s. In his 1930 campaign Olson emphasized immediate state issues and hardly mentioned the distant goal of the Cooperative Commonwealth. His supporters formed an "all-party" unit of liberal Democrats, Republicans, and independents as a vehicle for the expansion of his campaign beyond its Farmer-Labor base.[29]

Olson won by a large margin in 1930 and by a similar one in 1932. The immensity of the disarray of economic activity overwhelmed many state governments, but Olson mobilized Minnesota government for relief and enacted an impressive array of economic reforms. He used the new medium of radio to establish a personal rapport with the electorate, shaped his programs to meet political realities, outmaneuvered the state's Republican establishment, and skillfully used his magnetic personal appeal to persuade an often hostile legislature to adopt his program. In addition to unemployment relief, among the significant laws of Olson's era were the enactment of a state income tax and a moratorium on farm foreclosures.[30] Olson could not overcome the limitations of state government in dealing with a national catastrophe, but within those confines his administration responded more swiftly and with greater humanity than most state governments.

Olson also linked Minnesota's Farmer-Labor party to Franklin Roosevelt's New Deal. The governor appeared with Roosevelt during a state campaign stop in 1932 and discouraged attempts by radicals to commit the Farmer-Labor Association to a third-party presidential ticket. After the election, President Roosevelt listened respectfully to Olson's suggestions for federal legislation to relieve farm bankruptcy and urban unemployment. Olson, for his part, endorsed most of Roosevelt's national legislative program. Roosevelt consulted Olson on federal patronage, and

Gov. Floyd B. Olson speaking at the dedication ceremony for the Columbus statue on the State Capitol grounds, 1931

the governor included Democrats in the distribution of state jobs. By 1936 the political understanding between the two had evolved into a firm, informal alliance. The White House used its influence to persuade Minnesota Democrats to defer to Farmer-Laborites in state politics; in exchange, Olson derailed the attempts of radicals to pledge the Farmer-Labor Association to a national third-party ticket in 1936.[31]

Olson and the Farmer-Labor party changed in several ways as the depression persisted. In the early years of his tenure, Olson had used his patronage power with restraint. (Minnesota had no system of civil service for state employees.) Loyal Farmer-Laborites received jobs, but so did many Democrats, Republicans, and independents who had cooperated with the Olson campaign. As the depression continued, however, the value of state jobs rose in the face of continued mass unemployment. By Olson's third term, most state jobs were awarded on the basis of recommendation by Farmer-Labor political leaders. These patronage holders and their families flooded into Farmer-Labor clubs and carried out the political orders of the state administration. Almost all state employees were also required to contribute a percentage of their salary to a political fund controlled by Olson's lieutenants. By the mid-1930s, the state patronage apparatus had displaced trade unions as the single most powerful element in the Farmer-Labor Association.

Olson's rhetoric also gained a more radical tone, and he began to question the viability of capitalism. Olson's "I am a radical" speech to the 1934 Farmer-Labor state convention led the group to push aside the mild reformism of past conventions and proclaim the death of capitalism and the coming of the Cooperative Commonwealth. For a time it appeared that the Farmer-Labor radicals, with Olson's support, had taken control of the movement. Olson's more radical stance was also brought home to Minnesotans by his conduct during the Minneapolis truckers' strike of 1934. This strike, one of the decisive labor conflicts of the 1930s, pitted a Minneapolis teamsters union led by radical Trotskyists against a business community determined to protect the nonunion environment of Minneapolis. After several lengthy work stoppages, a great deal of violence, several killings, and the imposition of martial law, the truckers won. Olson's conduct during the strike did not always please the Trotskyists, but it almost always displeased the business community. His obvious sympathy for the strikers and his refusal to use the state guard to break the strike contributed to the eventual union victory.[32]

Olson sensed, however, that the truckers' strike and the radical manifestos of the 1934 Farmer-Labor convention were unsettling to many voters. Abruptly, he reversed the radical course of the 1934 Farmer-Labor campaign. The radical platform was disingenuously reinterpreted as a reform document safely within the progressive tradition, and rhetorical class conflict was put on the back burner. Even so, Olson's plurality in 1934 plummeted in comparison with that in 1932 as rural and small-town voters deserted the Farmer-Labor camp.

Olson moderated his tactics thereafter, and by 1936 he appeared to be the most popular political figure in the state. His rhetoric and program identified him as a militant New Deal liberal and not as a radical. Olson

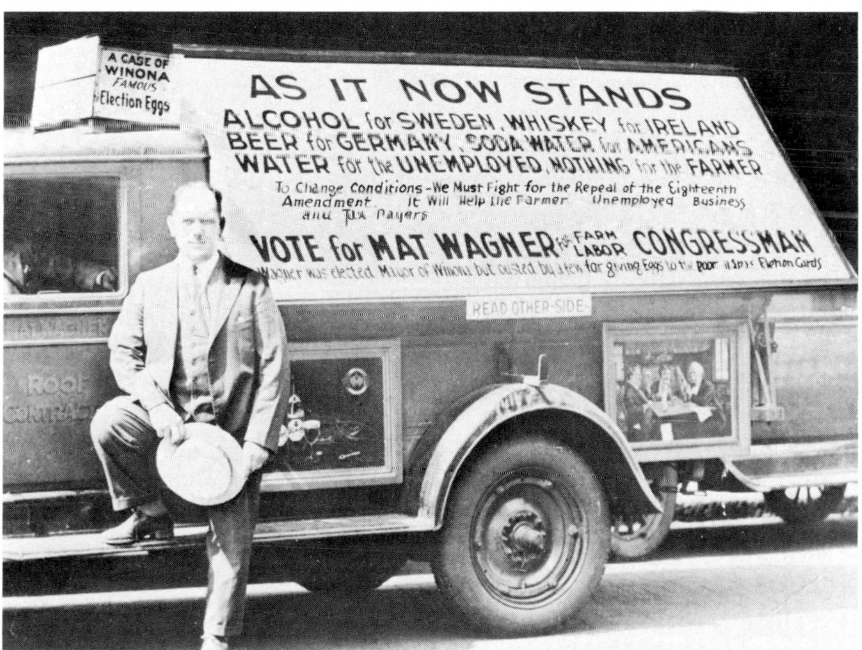

Farmer-Laborite Mat Wagner of Winona campaigning in the 1932 congressional primary

looked to be the certain winner in his bid for a U.S. Senate seat in the fall election, but he died of cancer in August 1936. The Farmer-Labor party, with U.S. Sen. Elmer A. Benson as its gubernatorial candidate, made the election a referendum on Olson's memory and carried nearly everything in the 1936 election.

At the time of Olson's death, the Farmer-Labor movement was a more conventional organization than it had been in the 1920s. Its domination by a patronage machine was more "normal," in a sense, than its prior status as a dues-paying membership organization in which the strongest element was delegates chosen by union locals. Its political stance was also more conventional. By 1936, the Farmer-Labor party presented itself as Minnesota's New Deal party. It no longer exemplified either provincial progressivism or prairie radicalism, and most of its leaders felt at home in some part of the broad, national, center-left New Deal coalition.

The long-standing split between Farmer-Labor moderates and radicals had also ended, but in a curious way. The cleavage along moderate-radical lines was first overlaid and then replaced by a split between anti-Communist Farmer-Laborites and those who supported cooperation with communism. In the mid-1930s, American Communists put aside their revolutionary rhetoric and adopted a new stance that was generally called their "Popular Front" strategy. Responding to the exigencies of American politics, but even more to a new political direction in Moscow, Communists called for an alliance of all liberals and radicals against the threat of fascism.[33] In Minnesota the Communist party had gained some recruits in the early years of the depression, but its greatest growth came in the mid- and late-1930s when Communists provided the leaders of a number of rapidly growing locals of the Congress of Industrial Organizations (CIO). Communists dominated the state leadership of the CIO, led several large and powerful locals of the United Electrical Workers in the Twin Cities, controlled the International Woodworkers of America in northern Minnesota, and had a strong presence in several United Steelworkers locals in Duluth and on the iron ranges.[34]

Olson and other Farmer-Labor leaders, accepting the shift of Communist strategy to the Popular Front at face value, allowed Communists to enter the Farmer-Labor party in 1936. In several ways Communists became a distinctly moderate force in the Farmer-Labor Association, shunning class-conflict politics and urging Farmer-Laborites to avoid radical rhetoric. Communists encouraged the expansion of the Farmer-Labor movement to include middle-class professionals in addition to workers and farmers, a policy that coincided with the view of Farmer-Labor moderates that the movement's radical goals should be dropped for the reformist liberalism of Roosevelt's New Deal. Communists also reconciled many Farmer-Labor radicals to a moderate program by arguing that the threat of nazism made a moderate stance a necessary expedience. A special task that Communists in the Farmer-Labor movement took on was the discrediting of isolationism. The Farmer-Labor movement of the 1920s and early 1930s had been overwhelmingly hostile to American involvement in foreign conflicts and looked back on American intervention in World War I as a mistake. Communists and their Popular Front allies sought to break down this attitude, arguing that the Nazi threat required the United States to ally itself with Great Britain, France, the Union of Soviet Socialist Republics (USSR), and others against Nazi aggression.[35]

Under Governor Benson, supporters of a Popular Front stance took the leadership of the Farmer-Labor Association, and Benson himself became a nationally known spokesman for Popular Front liberalism.[36] Although an effective orator, Benson was not a skilled politician. He irritated many "wet" voters with his continued support for strict state regulation of liquor sales after the repeal of national prohibition. He presented the legislature with an ambitious package of New Deal reforms, but his uncompromising tactics produced a raucous battle that alienated many of the governor's allies and turned his opponents into implacable enemies. His favoritism for the new CIO also angered AFL unions, and many AFL locals dropped out of the association. Benson also continued the policy of allowing Communists into the Farmer-Labor Association. The presence of several Communists in Benson's administration caused considerable complaint from offended Farmer-Labor anti-Communists.

The Farmer-Labor Association, like other Minnesota political parties, had large and active women's organizations by the 1930s. Control of these organizations, which offered a pool of effective workers, became a prize in factional conflicts and maneuvering between rival candidates for party office or nomination. In the late 1930s, the state Farmer-Labor Women's Federation was led by women aligned to the party's anti Communist faction, and the rival Popular Front Farmer-Labor faction promoted instead the Popular Front-aligned Hennepin County Farmer-Labor Women's Club as an alternative organization.[37]

By 1938, public discontent with divisive legislative battles and disgust with the power of the Farmer-Labor patronage machine – as well as disquiet about the role of Communists in the Farmer-Labor party – rendered Benson highly vulnerable. He barely survived a hard-fought primary challenge from Hjalmar Petersen, who had been lieutenant governor under Olson and had become governor for the final months of Olson's term. Petersen flailed away at Benson with emotional denunciations of corruption, machine politics, and Communist subversion, and he also slyly took advantage of anti-Semitic overtones that crept into his campaign. (During the 1930s, Minnesota emerged as one of the nation's centers of popular anti-Semitism.)[38]

Harold Stassen and the Rise of Modern Republicanism

In the general election campaign of 1938, Harold E. Stassen, the Republican nominee, emphasized the issues Petersen had raised in the primary – Farmer-Labor patronage abuse and the role of Communists in the Farmer-Labor movement – and he also covertly exploited the state's anti-Semitism. Benson, who had been elected by a sizable majority in 1936,

The New Leader Minnesota Needs
HAROLD E.
STASSEN
for
GOVERNOR
(OVER)

Campaign literature from Stassen's successful race for governor, 1938

was defeated by an equally sizable majority in 1938. Stassen's election inaugurated an era of Republican domination of politics that would not be seriously challenged until Hubert H. Humphrey's election to the U.S. Senate in 1948. Even after Humphrey's victory, the Republican grip on the governor's office was not loosened until 1954.[39]

Stassen's victory was achieved on more than Benson's vulnerabilities. Since Olson's election in 1930, Republicans had been thrown on the defensive and driven back to their conservative bastions, unable to do much more than act as naysayers to Olson's Farmer-Labor party and Roosevelt's New Deal. Stassen changed that, and changed it decisively. Elected at the age of thirty-one, Stassen offered a new, fresh, progressive Republicanism and asserted that the major difference between his administration and Benson's would be the absence of corruption and communism.

Stassen Republicans were typically young, honest, sincere, middle-class professional or business people who regarded themselves as thoroughly modern. They had no truck with either "standpat" conservatism or with what they perceived as a demagogic New Deal liberalism. One can see in progressive Republicanism a rebirth in a modern cosmopolitan form of the strong religious moralism of progressivism. In the campaign literature of progressive Republicans, one is struck by the frequency with which candidates made sure that a Lutheran church was pictured on brochures. One is tempted to see progressive Republicanism as a sort of secularized Scandinavian Lutheranism: earnest, moralistic, well meaning, and moderate.

This new progressive Republicanism had several elements. One was its acceptance of the changes wrought by the New Deal. There was no covert longing to return to the days before Social Security, minimum wage, income tax, and unemployment compensation. Rather, Stassen and his allies argued that they could manage these policies with greater efficiency, prune away excesses, and even expand the programs where the need was manifest. Progressive Republicanism promised to see that the New Deal welfare state served the general interest and was not used either as an engine of political vote buying or as a weapon in a class struggle against business.

One of the major contributions of Stassen Republicanism to Minnesota was the modernization of government. The exigencies first of the depression and then World War II left state and local governments in an organizational shambles, with jerry-built and obsolete institutional arrangements. Minnesota's progressive Republicans rationalized and modernized much of this structure. Governor Stassen destroyed the basis for patronage machine politics by instituting an all-pervasive civil-service/merit system for state government.[40] Another progressive Republican, Gov. Luther W. Youngdahl (1947–51), reformed the poorly managed system of state hospitals and homes for the mentally ill, handicapped, and retarded, changing them into far more humane institutions. Progressive Republicans also deserve much of the credit for the rapid expansion, modernization, and relatively high quality of public education in Minnesota in the 1950s and 1960s. In particular, Gov. Elmer L. Andersen (1961–63) was identified with the promotion of higher education.[41]

One of the clearest differences between progressive Republicanism and New Deal liberalism was the attitude toward the labor movement. Progressive Republicans accepted the right of workers to organize unions, but most regarded the rights extended to unions under the National Labor Relations Act as excessive and one-sided. They believed that many unions had abused their power and that many union leaders were corrupt. Minnesota's Republican senator Joseph H. Ball, a close ally of Stassen, spearheaded the 1940s congressional drive to change the act, a campaign that culminated in the passage of the Taft-Hartley Act in 1947 over the enraged objections of labor.[42]

Ball's attack on union power had the enthusiastic support, of course, of business. But the concern with labor power was more than just an excuse for carrying out the will of the business community. Disgust with corruption and abuse of power was a major element in the motivation of Stassen

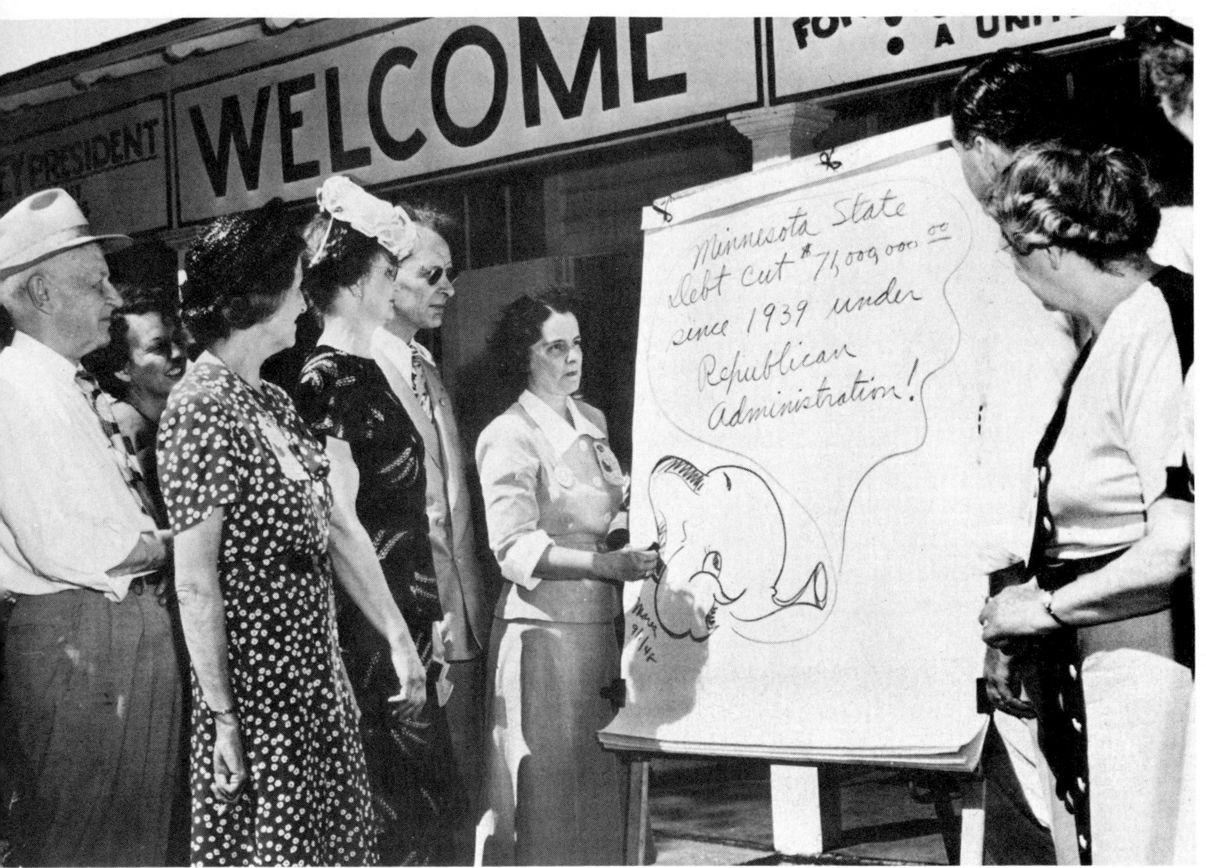

Republican political headquarters at the 1948 Minnesota State Fair

Republicanism and in its attraction to voters. Many elements contributed to the Farmer-Labor party's fall from favor, but none was stronger than voter revulsion at the patronage machine that came to control the Farmer-Labor Association. Linked with rejection of political corruption was public fear of the violent, class-conflict overtones of the truckers' strike and the rapid expansion of union power in Minnesota in the late 1930s. Minneapolis city politics, both Farmer-Labor and Republican, had been marred by corruption, labor violence, and racketeering in the 1930s and 1940s. Stassen's supporters in Minneapolis were prominent among those trying to rid city politics of its chronic corruption. Gambling had become widespread in many areas of the state in the 1930s and early 1940s, with the acquiescence, often corrupt, of public officials. Progressive Republicans led a long struggle that eliminated most official toleration of illegal gambling.[43]

Stassen Republicanism was also ardently internationalist in its outlook. After war came again to Europe in 1939, Stassen worked in parallel with the Roosevelt administration to shift the weight of public opinion toward support for those nations fighting the Nazis. The struggle over intervention and nonintervention in 1939, 1940, and 1941 was difficult in Minnesota, although the issue was not as viciously contested as in World War I. Stassen weakened the strong isolationist bloc in the U.S. Senate after Sen. Ernest Lundeen, a Farmer-Laborite and rigid isolationist, died in an airplane crash in late 1940. Stassen appointed Joseph Ball, a journalist and internationalist, to replace Lundeen.[44]

Much of the debate in Minnesota between internationalism and anti-interventionism also took place within Republican ranks because neither the Farmer-Labor nor the Democratic party was a serious threat to Republican control. During World War II, some of the more energetic political battles took place in Republican primaries, as hard-core conservatives and isolationists fought with progressive and internationalist Stassen Republicans. One of the last of these fights came in 1946 when Senator Shipstead, an undeviating isolationist, was defeated in the Republican primary by Gov. Edward J. Thye, a close ally of Stassen. (In 1940, after having won three terms to the U.S. Senate as a Farmer-Laborite, Shipstead, dismayed with the fate of the Farmer-Labor party, shifted his allegiance and won election to a fourth term as a Republican. Shipstead's progressive domestic views were compatible with those of Stassen Republicanism, but he remained firm in his isolationism.)[45]

Stassen's career after he left state politics revolved around his commitment to internationalism. He resigned the governorship after his reelection in 1942 to take a commission in the United States Navy. (He was replaced by Thye, his lieutenant governor.) After the war Stassen was a prominent national spokesman for the United Nations, and he contributed strongly to the bipartisan acceptance of a U.S. role in that organization. He was a serious contender for the Republican nomination for the presidency in 1952 and later served the administration of Dwight D. Eisenhower in several high diplomatic posts.[46]

The DFL, Hubert Humphrey, and Modern Minnesota Liberalism

After Stassen's election in 1938, the Farmer-Labor party entered a decline from which it never recovered. Many Farmer-Laborites had intensely disliked the entrance of Communists into the movement, but they held their peace during Elmer Benson's governorship. Once he left office, however, anti-Communist Farmer-Laborites took control of the state leadership of the Farmer-Labor Association. They regarded the role of Communists in the Popular Front wing of the movement as both a political liability and a betrayal of the democratic principles of the movement. Anti-Communists controlled the Farmer-Labor Association state conventions in 1939 and 1940, but they lost the leadership in a close vote in 1941.[47] Popular Front supporters, led by former governor Benson, held the leadership from 1941 until the merger with the Democratic party in 1944.

The coordinator of Benson's Popular Front faction was Viena P. Johnson, the first woman to exercise considerable statewide organization power in a major political party outside of a party's women's organization. When Benson became state chairman of the Farmer-Labor Association in

1942, he devoted only a portion of his time to the task. The day-to-day direction of the party fell to Johnson, the state party secretary. After the merger of the Farmer-Labor party with the Democratic party in 1944, Johnson's work was rewarded by Pres. Harry S. Truman with a patronage appointment as U.S. collector of customs for the port of Duluth.

Despite the factionalism within the Farmer-Labor party after Benson's defeat in 1938, its nominees – although losing to Republicans by large margins – still managed to outpoll Democratic candidates. Democrats had hoped that Benson's overwhelming defeat would lead to their emergence as the only significant rival to the Republicans, but they continued to damage themselves with obscure factional contests and to limp along as the "also-rans" of Minnesota politics. A measure of internal unity among Democrats was finally achieved in 1942 under state party chairman Elmer F. Kelm. (Kelm was notable as one of the first German Americans to break the near monopoly of Minnesota Democratic party leadership that had been held by Irish Americans.) The Roosevelt administration strongly wanted a merger between the Democratic and Farmer-Labor parties in Minnesota. Roosevelt's political aides regarded Minnesota as a swing state, and they feared that continued division between the two liberal parties might allow it to fall to the Republican presidential nominee in 1944.

A strange set of circumstances also rendered the Farmer-Labor party ready for merger. In the period between the German-Soviet Treaty of Nonaggression in August 1939 and the Nazi invasion of the USSR in June 1941, the Popular Front faction had opposed cooperation with the Democrats with fanatical vigor. After that period, however, Popular Front views changed. In particular, Communists concluded that their policy of all-out support of Roosevelt's war policies would best be served by a merger. Meanwhile, the Roosevelt administration, which knew of the power of the CIO in the Farmer-Labor party, asked national CIO leaders to urge their Minnesota affiliates to back merger. Elmer Benson initially resisted when the Roosevelt administration and Kelm raised the question of merger in 1943, but pressure from his closest allies, the CIO and the Communists, caused him to shift his views. Negotiations got under way in the late summer of 1943 and resulted in formal merger in April 1944. The new party, with Kelm as its first chairman, proclaimed the merger with its new name, the Democratic-Farmer-Labor (DFL) party.

Although its gubernatorial candidate was trounced by Republican Edward Thye, the new party did reasonably well in 1944 by picking up two congressional seats. The DFL party received a second boost in 1945 when young Hubert Humphrey was elected mayor of Minneapolis.[48] Humphrey proved to be a highly successful and popular mayor, and his obvious electoral appeal gave the party hope that it might be able to challenge the Republicans on a statewide basis.

Before it could do so, however, the DFL party went through a tumultuous factional fight that shaped liberal politics for decades. When World War II ended, the party split into factions reflecting divisions linked to the emerging cold war. In 1946 the DFL's Popular Front wing, still led by Elmer Benson, took control of the party's state leadership. This faction, with a significant Communist presence, called for a reassertion of New Deal domestic programs at home and a foreign policy that sought accommodation with the USSR. When Henry A. Wallace (Roosevelt's vice-president, 1941–44) announced his opposition to President Truman's anti-Communist foreign policy, Benson led his faction into the Wallace camp. After Wallace decided to contest the presidency in 1948, Benson became national chairman of Wallace's new national Progressive party. In Minnesota, Benson announced that his faction would take the DFL out of the Democratic party and affiliate with the Progressive party.[49]

The fight against Benson within the DFL party was led by a new anti-Communist faction headed by Hubert Humphrey. Humphrey and a group of young liberals who formed around him welded those opposed to the Popular Front into a cohesive faction that possessed leadership, organization, and a political program. After a vicious factional brawl that lasted throughout 1947 and 1948, Humphrey's anti-Communists won and established the hegemony of anti-Communist liberalism over the DFL party and Minnesota's labor movement.[50]

Humphrey, the leader of the victorious anti-Communists, won the DFL party's senatorial nomination and the subsequent election in 1948 (defeating Republican Joseph Ball). In the Senate, Humphrey established himself as a national liberal leader, championing civil rights for black Americans and authoring many of the major liberal legislative initiatives of the 1960s. In addition to his long tenure as senator, Humphrey served as vice-president of the United States and contended seriously for the Democratic party's presidential nomination on four occasions, winning the nomination in 1968 and losing the election to Richard M. Nixon by less than 1 percent of the popular vote. Humphrey's liberalism was not unusual in content, although he articulated it with unusual vigor and clarity. He accepted the moderate reform program and interest-group liberalism of the New Deal at face value. He was not a covert radical who found liberalism a flag of political convenience or who saw liberal programs as steps toward a more thoroughgoing political agenda. He did not wish to destroy capitalism, but rather to create a welfare system to share capitalism's abundance with those in need. Humphrey did not believe in class conflict, and he always sought to present liberalism as a program that middle-class voters could support without fear. Humphrey's most significant contribution to liberalism was his key role in moving equal rights for black Americans from the periphery of the New Deal agenda of the 1930s to the center of the liberal agenda of the 1950s and 1960s.[51]

Other important political careers also were born in the 1948 campaign. Eugene J. McCarthy vaulted from obscurity into the U.S. House through his leadership of the anti-Communist bloc of the Ramsey County DFL party. McCarthy joined Humphrey in the Senate in 1958, an election that was also noteworthy because many people thought that Minnesota's Protestant majority would not elect a Catholic to a major statewide office. In 1968 McCarthy became the leader of those opposed to involvement in the Vietnam War, and his campaign for the Democratic nomination convinced Pres. Lyndon B. Johnson to retire from the race.[52]

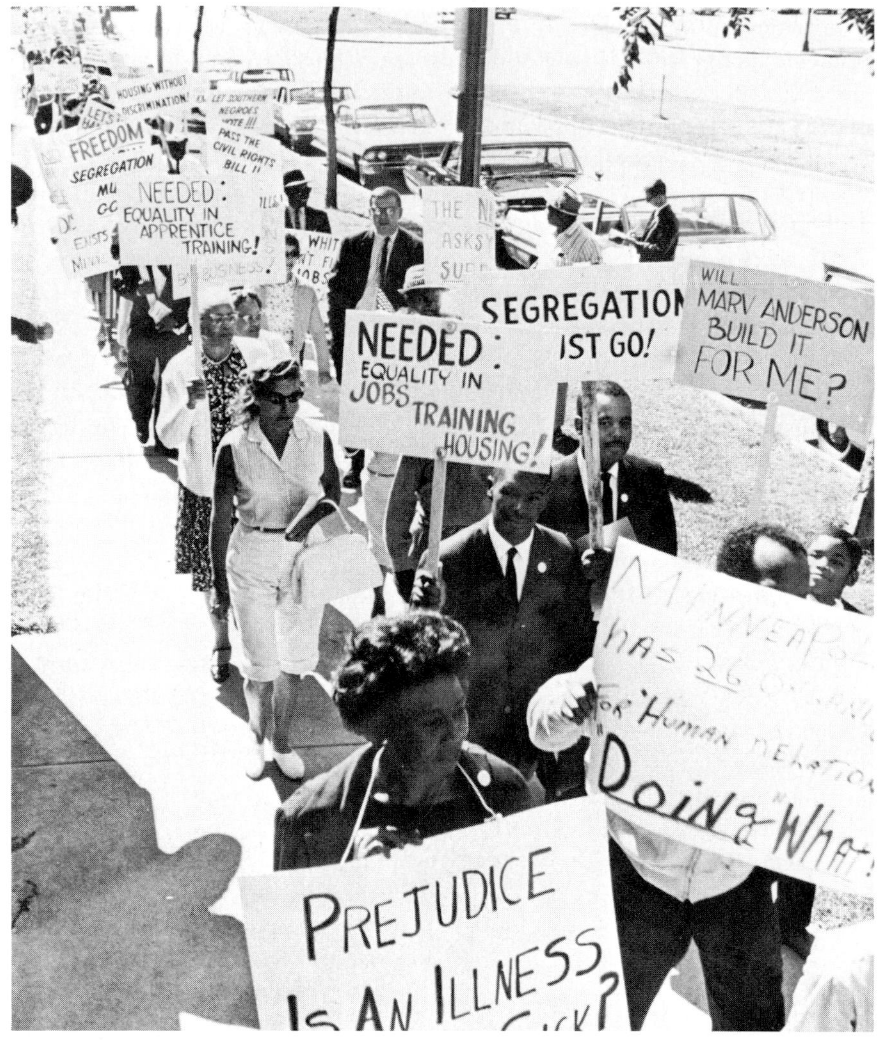

Proponents of civil rights legislation marching to the State Capitol, 1963

Orville L. Freeman, who organized the anti-Communist campaign and who became chairman of the DFL party in 1948, later won election as governor of Minnesota for three terms (1955–61). Humphrey's election had elevated the party to a position of close rivalry with the dominant Republicans, but Freeman's election made the DFL a match. Freeman was an able governor who proved that the DFL could manage state government. After the election, the two parties would remain nearly evenly balanced until the 1970s. Walter F. Mondale, while a student at St. Paul's Macalester College, took part in the anti-Communist takeover of the Young Democratic-Farmer-Labor organization in 1947 and was Freeman's organizer in southern Minnesota in 1948. Mondale later became the attorney general of Minnesota, was appointed to fill out Humphrey's term in the Senate in 1964, won election twice in his own right, and became vice-president of the United States in 1977. In 1984 he won the Democratic presidential nomination, but he was badly defeated by Ronald W. Reagan. Other prominent politicians whose origins date from the postwar anti-Communist struggle in the DFL include Eugenie M. Anderson, who became one of the first women to hold a significant U.S. diplomatic post when she was named ambassador to Denmark in 1949, and Donald M. Fraser, a seven-term member of the U.S. House, a leading figure in the national Democratic party's liberal wing during the 1960s and 1970s, and mayor of Minneapolis in the 1980s.[53]

The struggle for control of the DFL party completed the "nationalization" of Minnesota politics. By the 1950s, both the Republican and the DFL parties were dominated by factions that were part of similar national alignments. Minnesota Republicans were contented members of the moderate, "Eisenhower" wing of the national Republican party, and the DFL thrived on its leadership role in the liberal wing of the national Democratic party.[54] Within Minnesota, the two parties fought for control of the center. Republicans offered themselves as a clean government, center-right coalition led by moderate progressives who were sensitive to the needs of modern society. DFL party members presented themselves as a center-left coalition led by unabashed liberals, but liberals who were safe and sane. This approach by the two parties produced a number of close elections, including one remarkable gubernatorial contest. In 1962,

Elmer L. Andersen speaking to a political gathering, 1959

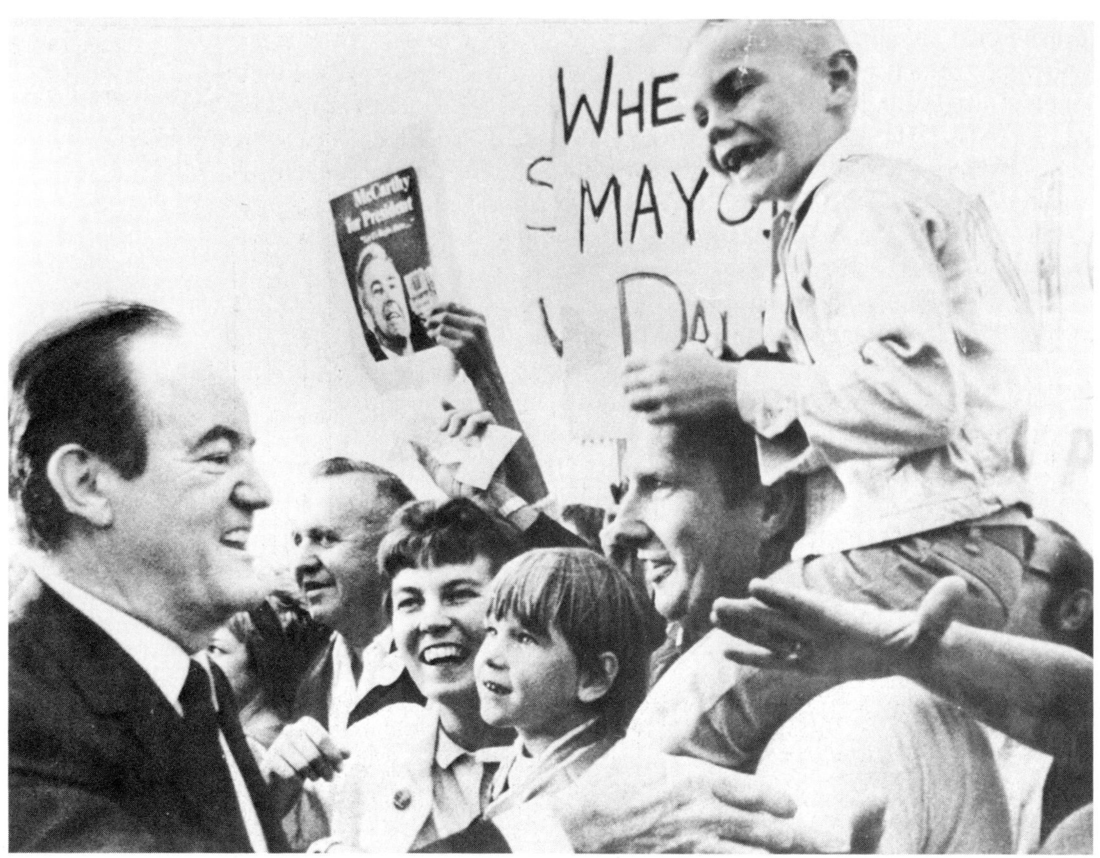

Vice-President Hubert H. Humphrey returning to Minnesota as the Democratic presidential nominee, 1968

DFL candidate Karl F. Rolvaag defeated incumbent Gov. Elmer Andersen by a vote of 619,842 to 619,751. The margin was not only close – it was not clear. Immediately after the election, both candidates claimed victory, beginning months of uncertainty as courts sorted out the results. During the recount, Andersen occupied the governor's office while Rolvaag was relegated to a room in the Capitol basement. It was several months into the term before the courts declared Rolvaag the winner by ninety-one votes.[55]

The DFL party went through two serious factional fights in the latter half of the 1960s. In 1966 the DFL organization ripped itself apart over Governor Rolvaag's renomination, a bloodletting sufficient to allow Republican Harold LeVander an easy victory in the general election. Under LeVander, Republicans achieved a long-sought goal, the diversification of the state's revenue sources, by enacting a general sales tax.[56] The sales tax relieved pressure to increase Minnesota's high, and highly progressive, income tax and was used to reduce local property taxes through a system of state aids to local government.

A second DFL civil war erupted in 1968 when the party split between those loyal to Hubert Humphrey and those who backed Eugene McCarthy and his opposition to the Vietnam War.[57] Humphrey retained control of the Minnesota party, but only by a narrow margin. The antiwar activists who entered the DFL party ended its anti-Communist consensus and initiated a process of change in the nature of liberalism, paralleling the influence of "New Politics" and "New Left" attitudes on liberals all across the United States. In those years, every DFL convention saw clashes between the "regular" liberals and the new "movement" liberals and their radical allies, who supported, variously, gay rights, amnesty for draft resisters and evaders, the legalization of marijuana, an end to cold-war policies, drastically reduced military spending, accommodation with the USSR, a variety of environmental causes, militant feminism, and a "pro-choice" stand favoring legalized abortion. In response to the last, a strong "pro-life" or antiabortion DFL faction developed.

Even though the 1970s were years of considerable internal turbulence for the DFL party, its electoral power reached its peak. The process started in 1970 when Wendell R. Anderson, the first prominent DFL officeholder who was not linked in a direct fashion to the 1948 DFL contest, won the governorship. In 1971 Anderson faced a legislature with both houses controlled by conservative caucuses. (Until 1973, Minnesota's legislature was officially nonpartisan, with Republicans organizing as the Conservative Caucus and DFL members forming the Liberal Caucus.) Even so, Anderson presented a far-reaching tax and school-finance reform plan that convulsed the legislature and led to three special sessions. The final outcome was a victory for Anderson.

Partly as a result of the popularity of Anderson's program (which lowered property taxes by shifting school finance to state income and sales taxes), the DFL party, for the first time, won control of both houses of the legislature in 1972. Anderson won reelection by a huge margin in 1974, and the DFL retained legislative control in both the 1974 and 1976 elections. In this environment, DFL legislators passed virtually the entire liberal agenda: tax reform, equalization of school finance, tough environmental laws, partial public financing of political campaigns, generous expansions of workers compensation and unemployment compensation, broad unionization rights for public employees, and restoration of official legislative partisanship.[58]

The participation of women in Minnesota politics had grown steadily since the early decades of the century. During the progressive era, women had been most prominent as advocates for alcohol control, children's legislation, and educational issues. A similar pattern was apparent in later decades in their work as lobbyists on abortion (on both sides), ratification of the Equal Rights Amendment, and various antidiscrimination proposals. But women were also active within party organizations. By the 1970s, both of the state's major parties had had women leaders, and in the 1980s most party leaders and political candidates avoided the appearance of slighting women voters or women's issues. The DFL party even required that most party offices be allocated on an equal basis between women and men.

The Republican Party: From Progressivism to Conservatism

A major factor in DFL success was the precipitous decline in the organizational strength and morale of Minnesota Republicans. Anderson's victory and the subsequent popularity of his tax and school-finance program were major blows to Republicans, but what shattered Republican morale was the Watergate scandal that led to the resignation of President Nixon. Minnesota Republicans, particularly the dominant progressive wing, took great pride in their reputation as the party of clean government, and they were humiliated by the revelations of the Nixon presidency. In 1975, Minnesota Republican leaders symbolically separated themselves from the tainted national party by renaming the state organization the Independent Republican (IR) party.[59]

To compound progressive Republican troubles, the party's long-quiescent conservative wing awoke. As in the rest of the nation, political conservatism had been slowly gathering vigor in the late 1960s and 1970s. This new conservatism was nourished from several sources: evangelical and fundamentalist Christian reaction to liberal attacks on traditional moral values, resentment against liberal cultural elitism, nationalist and anti-Communist objections to détente with the USSR, pro-life revulsion at legalized abortion, and widespread resistance to high taxes. With progressive Republicans demoralized, conservatives began to flex their muscles, and in 1976 Minnesota's delegation to the national Republican convention contained a sizable conservative, pro-Reagan contingent.[60]

The new Republican conservatism was further encouraged by IR electoral victories. In 1978, the DFL party suffered a massive electoral defeat. DFL adherents had grown complacent with their success and indulged in more than the usual internal factional fighting. Movement liberals had won control of increasingly larger segments of the DFL organization and had pressed candidates for public office to openly support homosexual rights, abortion, militant feminism, and other controversial causes. Further, the DFL party as a whole became increasingly identified with certain constituencies, particularly public employees, teacher organizations, and labor unions.

Wendell Anderson, who had been reelected to the governorship by a landslide in 1974, was in political trouble by 1978. When Walter Mondale vacated his U.S. Senate seat to take the vice-presidency, Anderson resigned the governorship and took the seat on appointment from Rudolph G. Perpich, the new governor and Anderson's lieutenant governor. Many voters regarded the arrangement as unfair, and Anderson faced an uphill battle to retain his seat. The second Senate seat was also up for election after Hubert Humphrey died. (Muriel B. Humphrey, the widow of Hubert, held the seat on appointment until the election.) The DFL party endorsed Rep. Donald Fraser for the position, who at that time was a leading national spokesman for liberal causes and had adopted many of the positions advocated by movement liberals. He was challenged and beaten in the

DFL primary by Robert E. Short, a DFL veteran with a maverick record who appealed to rural voters, antiabortion activists, and older, regular liberals.

In the general election, IR candidates for both U.S. Senate seats and for the governorship won easily. The Senate candidates – David F. Durenberger, from the IR progressive wing, and Rudolph E. Boschwitz, who had conservative support – were ethnic innovations for the Minnesota Republican party. Republicans almost invariably had run Scandinavian Lutherans for statewide office, leaving Catholics largely to the DFL party. Durenberger, however, was of German-Catholic background. Boschwitz was even more unusual: a millionaire entrepreneur, he was Jewish and had been born in Germany. Indifferent to established Republican habits and coming from diverse backgrounds themselves (many were former DFL voters), fundamentalist Christian and New Right conservatives were in part responsible for the greater ethnic variety of Republican candidates. The successful IR gubernatorial candidate was more usual: Albert H. Quie, a veteran IR congressman associated with IR progressives and identified as a close friend of public education.[61]

Governor Quie quickly moved to reduce taxes, particularly income taxes. Generally, however, he acted within the tradition of progressive Republicanism, to the frustration of a number of newly elected conservative legislators. State government finance soon reached a crisis due to a combination of adverse economic circumstances and Quie's overly optimistic management. The state underwent a series of financial crises, special sessions, emergency tax increases, and budget reductions.

The DFL party, confident of victory in the 1982 gubernatorial contest, nominated Warren R. Spannaus, the state attorney general and a party stalwart who got on well with most DFL factions. Former governor Perpich contested, however, and won the primary. Perpich, in essence, ran against the DFL party organization and campaigned as an independent. He picked up support from rural DFL voters and fellow iron-range natives who resented the domination of the DFL party by "Twin Cities liberals." He also received the support of pro-life DFL voters. Perpich won the general election without difficulty. Under a 1972 constitutional amendment, the governor and lieutenant governor ran on a joint ticket, and Perpich's election brought in the state's first woman lieutenant governor, Marlene M. Johnson. Perpich's election was an ethnic milestone. After a long line of Protestant, northern European, usually Scandinavian governors, Perpich was a Catholic and a second-generation Croatian American. Republicans took some comfort from the 1982 election when Senator Durenberger easily defeated Mark B. Dayton, a well-financed DFL opponent.

In Governor Perpich's second term, the state's fiscal stability was restored, to some degree at the cost of higher taxes. Partly in response to the tax increases, voters elected a narrow Republican majority to the state house of representatives in 1984. Prominent among the new IR legislators were a number identified with the Christian Right. The new majority elected a firm conservative to the speakership and demanded massive tax cuts and slashes in welfare spending. Republicans were also encouraged in the 1984 election by their good showing in the Minnesota vote for the presidency. The DFL party's own Walter Mondale was the national Democratic candidate, but he barely won his home state. Minnesota voters also kept Republican Boschwitz in the U.S. Senate. Boschwitz overwhelmed his DFL opponent, state Secretary of State Joan Anderson Growe, and thereby disappointed liberal feminists who had hoped that the state was ready to elect one of their own to a key office.[62] That Mondale, a popular native son, only narrowly defeated Ronald Reagan in Minnesota also demonstrated the increasingly powerful influence of national trends on Minnesota politics.

Governor Perpich's idiosyncratic approach to politics confused partisan divisions in the state. He developed a reputation as a militant liberal in the 1970s, but in his second governorship he won the support of many normally Republican business people. He attempted to meet many business objections to the state's tax system and welcomed business advice on a variety of subjects. Still, he remained an orthodox liberal on many welfare policies and retained close links to the labor movement. After having run against the DFL party organization in 1982, he welcomed its support in 1986. He also easily defeated a major primary challenge in 1986 from George Latimer, the mayor of St. Paul and a favorite of movement liberals.

The 1986 Republican state convention fight over the gubernatorial endorsement was a three-way struggle between different varieties of conservatism. The once-dominant progressive Republicans had to be content to align themselves with one of the conservative alternatives. Cal R. Ludeman, the convention's final choice, brushed aside a primary challenge from a moderate Republican but had trouble finding a vulnerable flank in Perpich's unsystematic mixture of liberal and conservative programs. Perpich won easily, and the DFL party won a resounding majority in the state house of representatives and increased its majority in the state senate.

Minnesota politics as the state entered the late 1980s was in a process of transition. The DFL party remained a thoroughly liberal institution, but it was an institution beset by divisions between regular liberals of Humphrey's generation and younger, movement liberals with a bewildering array of causes. Like liberalism everywhere, Minnesota liberalism showed signs of intellectual exhaustion. Serious divisions also separated pro-life and pro-choice liberals. Furthermore, regional tensions between rural and iron-range DFL voters and Twin Cities voters were clear in a number of DFL primary contests. Many DFL officeholders also increasingly regarded the DFL party organization as irrelevant to their local campaign needs, instead depending on organized constituencies such as public employees and public-school teachers for support. On top of this confusion was the electoral success of DFL Governor Perpich and his eclectic policies.

On the Republican side, the IR conservative wing, which had its own internal divisions between evangelical Christians and other varieties of conservatism, controlled the state party organization. The loss of control

Nine-member subcaucus at a DFL precinct caucus at St. Cloud State University, 1980

of the state house of representatives in 1986, however, caused critics to charge that IR conservatism with its Christian Right aura was losing the political center to the DFL. Progressive Republicans, although a minority in the party organization, retained considerable leadership talent and had the support of much of the business community. In the wake of the 1986 losses, the house Republican caucus chose a moderate as its minority leader; the conservative state party chairman also resigned his position and was replaced by a more moderate figure. Despite the 1986 election setbacks, Republicans had broken out of their Scandinavian-Lutheran heartland and demonstrated the ability to appeal to a far wider range of Minnesotans than was once their habit.

In the twentieth century, Minnesota politics has drawn closer to national political trends, and its future path may well reflect broader national movements rather than unique Minnesota characteristics.[63]

NOTES

1. The campaigns of 1890–96 are described in Carl H. Chrislock, "The Politics of Protest in Minnesota, 1890–1901: From Populism to Progressivism" (Ph.D. diss., University of Minnesota, 1954), 100–314. For statistical information about Minnesota elections from 1857 to 1977, see Bruce M. White et al., comps., *Minnesota Votes: Election Returns by County for Presidents, Senators, Congressmen, and Governors, 1857–1977* (St. Paul: Minnesota Historical Society, 1977). Information about subsequent elections can be found in Minnesota's *Legislative Manual,* issued every two years by the Minnesota secretary of state. For an overview of the development of Minnesota's government, see Daniel J. Elazar, "A Model of Moral Government," *this volume,* 329–59.

2. George M. Stephenson, *John Lind of Minnesota* (Minneapolis: University of Minnesota Press, 1935), 83–190, follows Lind from 1892 (when he was a congressman) through his term as governor and his unsuccessful gubernatorial campaign of 1900. Progressivism in Minnesota from its rise to World War I is discussed in Carl H. Chrislock, *The Progressive Era in Minnesota: 1898–1918* (St. Paul: Minnesota Historical Society, 1971), 9–65.

3. For an essay by Arvonne S. Fraser and Sue E. Holbert entitled "Women in the Minnesota Legislature," see *Women of Minnesota: Selected Biographical Essays,* ed. Barbara Stuhler and Gretchen Kreuter (St. Paul: Minnesota Historical Society Press, 1977), 247–83. The 1975–76 volume of the *Legislative Manual* includes a special section on "Women in Min-

nesota's History," by Gretchen Kreuter and Rhoda R. Gilman, 2–24. See also Marjorie Bingham, "Keeping at It: Minnesota Women," *this volume*, 433–71.

4. Knutson's career is mentioned in a useful short history of the Democratic-Farmer-Labor party by Laura K. Auerbach, *Worthy to Be Remembered: A Political History of the Minnesota Democratic-Farmer-Labor Party: 1944–1984* (Minneapolis: Democratic-Farmer-Labor Party of Minnesota, 1984), 37.

5. Here and below, Chrislock, *Progressive Era*, 14–15, 17, 31–32, 79, 86, 87.

6. For Johnson's gubernatorial career, see Winifred G. Helmes, *John A. Johnson, The People's Governor: A Political Biography* (Minneapolis: University of Minnesota Press, 1949), 136–225, 266–308.

7. Here and following three paragraphs, Chrislock, *Progressive Era*, 37–39, 47–58, 61–65, 77–88, 119–20.

8. Jon Wefald, *A Voice of Protest: Norwegians in American Politics, 1890–1917* (Northfield: Norwegian-American Historical Association, 1971), 45–78, discusses Norwegian-American participation in progressivism. For the experience of Norwegians in Minnesota, see Carlton C. Qualey and Jon A. Gjerde, "The Norwegians," in *They Chose Minnesota: A Survey of the State's Ethnic Groups*, ed. June Drenning Holmquist (St. Paul: Minnesota Historical Society Press, 1981), 220–47.

9. Hildegard Binder Johnson, "The Germans," in *They Chose Minnesota*, ed. Holmquist, 153–84, describes the history of Germans in the state; see also John C. Massmann, "German Immigration to Minnesota, 1850–1890" (Ph.D. diss., University of Minnesota, 1966).

10. Chrislock, *Progressive Era*, 113–16. See also Peter Rachleff, "Turning Points in the Labor Movement: Three Key Conflicts," *this volume*, 204–5.

11. For the 1916 campaign, the influence of the NPL in the North Dakota legislature, and the league's move to Minnesota, see Robert L. Morlan, *Political Prairie Fire: The Nonpartisan League, 1915–1922* (Minneapolis: University of Minnesota Press, 1955; St. Paul: Minnesota Historical Society Press, 1985), 60–108, 125–29.

12. Willis H. Raff, "Coercion and Freedom in a War Situation: A Critical Analysis of Minnesota Culture during World War One" (Ph.D. diss., University of Minnesota, 1957), is an attempt to capture "the real flavor and essence of life in Minnesota" during World War I (quotation on 3).

13. Neil Betten, "Riot, Revolution, Repression in the Iron Range Strike of 1916," *Minnesota History* 41 (Summer 1968): 82–94; Robert M. Eleff, "The 1916 Minnesota Miners' Strike against U.S. Steel," *Minnesota History* 51 (Summer 1988): 63–74; John E. Haynes, "Revolt of the 'Timber Beasts': IWW Lumber Strike in Minnesota," *Minnesota History* 42 (Spring 1971): 162–74.

14. Sister John Christine Wolkerstorfer, "Nativism in Minnesota in World War I: A Comparative Study of Brown, Ramsey, and Stearns Counties, 1914–1918" (Ph.D. diss., University of Minnesota, 1973), 35–74, 177–210, deals with the situation in New Ulm and surrounding Brown County and with the German-American vote in the gubernatorial elections of 1914, 1916, and 1918.

15. The work of Gilman with the commission and the alliance is depicted in Elizabeth Gilman, "Catheryne Cooke Gilman: Social Worker," in *Women of Minnesota*, ed. Stuhler and Kreuter, 192–201.

16. Here and below, Chrislock, *Progressive Era*, 131–33, 140–44, 161–63.

17. Carol Elizabeth Jenson, "Agrarian Pioneer in Civil Liberties: The Nonpartisan League in Minnesota during World War I" (Ph.D. diss., University of Minnesota, 1968), 60–202, focuses on NPL activities during the election campaign of 1918. For Lindbergh's opposition to intervention and his primary campaign of 1918, see Bruce L. Larson, *Lindbergh of Minnesota: A Political Biography* (New York: Harcourt Brace Jovanovich, 1973), 179–249.

18. Here and below, Chrislock, *Progressive Era*, 121–22, 157–60.

19. Millard L. Gieske, *Minnesota Farmer-Laborism: The Third-Party Alternative* (Minneapolis: University of Minnesota Press, 1979), 34–35, 44–47.

20. The campaign of 1918 is covered in Chrislock, *Progressive Era*, 164–81.

21. Here and below, Gieske, *Farmer-Laborism*, 52–64, 69–77.

22. Sister Mary René Lorentz, "Henrik Shipstead: Minnesota Independent, 1923-1946" (Ph.D. diss., Catholic University of America, 1963), 10–35, 66–112, 141–47, outlines Shipstead's 1918–28 congressional campaigns, his major domestic policies, and his involvement with labor issues.

23. Dolores De Bower Johnson, "Anna Dickie Olesen: Senate Candidate," in *Women of Minnesota*, ed. Stuhler and Kreuter, 247–83.

24. For the history of the Farmer-Labor party from its early days to its gubernatorial victory of 1936 and defeat of 1938, see Gieske, *Farmer-Laborism*, 32–232, and Arthur E. Naftalin, "A History of the Farmer-Labor Party of Minnesota" (Ph.D. diss., University of Minnesota, 1948), 64–382.

25. Paul S. Holbo, "The Farmer-Labor Association: Minnesota's Party within a Party," *Minnesota History* 38 (September 1963): 301–9.

26. Gieske, *Farmer-Laborism*, 187–89, 202–3.

27. Steven J. Keillor, *Hjalmar Petersen of Minnesota: The Politics of Provincial Independence* (St. Paul: Minnesota Historical Society Press, 1987), 1–3, 258–60.

28. Chrislock, *Progressive Era*, 185–89. See also John Earl Haynes, "Applied History or Propaganda? The Influence of History on Farm Credit Legislation in Minnesota," *Public Historian* 10 (Winter 1988): 21–33.

29. For Olson's early relations with the Farmer-Labor party, his 1930 gubernatorial campaign, and his first legislature, see George H. Mayer, *The Political Career of Floyd B. Olson* (Minneapolis: University of Minnesota Press, 1951; St. Paul: Minnesota Historical Society Press, 1987), 17–77.

30. Here and below, Mayer, *Floyd B. Olson*, 97–98, 122, 125–27, 131–34, 139, 163–64, 266–68.

31. An evaluation of the Farmer-Labor party's political economy, leadership, labor politics, crisis, and collapse is provided in Richard Martin Valelly, "State-Level Radicalism and the Nationalization of American Politics: The Case of the Minnesota Farmer-Labor Party" (Ph.D. diss., Harvard University, 1984), 122–294.

32. George Dimitri Tselos, "The Minneapolis Labor Movement in the 1930's" (Ph.D. diss., University of Minnesota, 1970), 114–321, gives an overview of the period from 1930 to 1935.

33. John Earl Haynes, *Dubious Alliance: The Making of Minnesota's DFL Party* (Minneapolis: University of Minnesota Press, 1984), 3–46.

34. John E. Haynes, "Communists and Anti-Communists in the Northern Minnesota CIO, 1936–1949," *Upper Midwest History* 1 (1981): 55–73.

35. For communism in Minnesota during the period of the Popular Front, see Harvey Klehr, *The Heyday of American Communism: The Depression Decade* (New York: Basic Books, 1984), 257–65. See also John E. Haynes, "The New History of the Communist Party in State Politics: The Implications for Mainstream Political History," review essay, *Labor History* 27 (Winter 1986): 549–63.

36. Benson's gubernatorial career is covered in James M. Shields, *Mr. Progressive: A Biography of Elmer Austin Benson* (Minneapolis: T. S. Denison and Co., 1971), 83-216.

37. Gieske, *Farmer-Laborism*, 257–58, 286–87.

38. Keillor, *Hjalmar Petersen*, 143–69. See also Hyman Berman, "Political Antisemitism in Minnesota during the Great Depression," *Jewish Social Studies* 38 (Summer-Fall 1976): 247–64; Michael Gerald Rapp, "A Historical Overview of Anti-Semitism in Minnesota, 1920–1960 – With Particular Emphasis on Minneapolis and St. Paul" (Ph.D. diss., University of Minnesota, 1977), 39–109.

39. For a detailed examination of the 1938 gubernatorial campaign and the "revitalized" Republican party, see Ivan Hinderaker, "Harold Stassen and Developments in the Republican Party in Minnesota, 1937–1943" (Ph.D. diss., University of Minnesota, 1949), 198–366.

40. Hinderaker, "Harold Stassen," 410–16, 425–26.

41. The accomplishments of Youngdahl and Andersen are mentioned in Theodore C. Blegen, *Minnesota: A History of the State*, 2d ed. (Minneapolis: University of Minnesota Press, 1975), 552–55, 583–85.

42. Hinderaker, "Harold Stassen," 620–23.

43. Blegen, *History of Minnesota*, 553.

44. Hinderaker, "Harold Stassen," 605–20.

45. Lorentz, "Henrik Shipstead," 53–65.

46. Hinderaker, "Harold Stassen," 668–70, 716–19; Carl Solberg, *Hubert Humphrey: A Biography* (New York: W. W. Norton and Co., 1984), 82–83, 173, 185–86.

47. Here and following three paragraphs, Haynes, *Dubious Alliance*, 36–43, 72–74, 77–78, 110–16, 125.

48. Humphrey's mayoral career is treated in Solberg, *Hubert Humphrey*, 99–110, and Albert Eisele, *Almost to the Presidency: A Biography of Two American Politicians* (Blue Earth: Piper Co., 1972), 49–59.

49. Haynes, *Dubious Alliance*, 168–72.

50. Solberg, *Hubert Humphrey*, 111–23; Hubert H. Humphrey, *The Education of a Public Man: My Life and Politics* (Garden City, N.Y.: Doubleday and Co., 1976), 81-117.

51. For an assessment of Humphrey's legacy, see Solberg, *Hubert Humphrey*, 457–70; the presidential nominating convention of 1968 is described on pages 355–71.

52. Eisele, *Almost to the Presidency*, 71–84, 283–98.

53. Finlay Lewis, *Mondale: Portrait of an American Politician* (New York: Harper and Row, 1980), 48–64, 93–95, 144, 161, 230; Patricia C. Harpole, "Brief Biographies of Other Minnesota Women," in *Women of Minnesota*, ed. Stuhler and Kreuter, 325.

54. Robert Agranoff, "The Minnesota Democratic-Farmer-Labor Party Organization: A Study of the 'Character' of a Programatic Party Organization" (Ph.D. diss., University of

Pittsburgh, 1967), 55–85, 357–412, contains a short organizational history of this "programmatic" party, an analysis of its relations with elected officials, and an overview of its characteristics.

55. See Ronald F. Stinnett and Charles H. Backstrom, *Recount* (Washington, D.C.: National Document Publishers, 1964), for a detailed examination of the recount. Rolvaag also had the distinction of becoming the first Minnesota governor with a four-year term, the voters having approved a constitutional amendment extending the term.

56. David Lebedoff, *The 21st Ballot: A Political Party Struggle in Minnesota* (Minneapolis: University of Minnesota Press, 1969), 43–192, continues the story of the consequences of the recount through Rolvaag's term of office and LeVander's victory in 1966.

57. Auerbach, *Worthy to Be Remembered,* 52. For a memoir of the Democratic presidential nominating campaigns of 1968 from local Minnesota ward to national convention, see David Lebedoff, *Ward Number Six* (New York: Charles Scribner's Sons, 1972).

58. Auerbach, *Worthy to Be Remembered,* 54–55, 57.

59. *Minneapolis Tribune,* Nov. 16, 1975, p. 1A.

60. William L. Hathaway, "Changing Correlates of Conservatism in a Minnesota Political Party" (Paper presented before the Minnesota Academy of Science, May 2, 1986, St. Cloud State University, St. Cloud).

61. Auerbach, *Worthy to Be Remembered,* 60–61.

62. Growe's campaign is covered in Barbara Stuhler, *No Regrets: Minnesota Women and the Joan Growe Senatorial Campaign* (St. Paul: Braemar Press, 1986), 23–77.

63. Additional recommended publications about Minnesota politics include G. Theodore Mitau, *Politics in Minnesota,* rev. ed. (Minneapolis: University of Minnesota Press, 1970), and William L. Hathaway, *Minnesota Politics and Parties Today* (St. Paul: Carter and Locey Publications, 1978).

DAVID BEAULIEU

A Place Among Nations: Experiences of Indian People

Albert E. Jenks did not have much hope for the American Indian in the twentieth century. The anthropology professor at the University of Minnesota explained to a *Minneapolis Journal* reporter in 1916 that Indians most likely would not make it to the twenty-first century. According to Jenks, all but one in every thousand were and wanted to be paupers. "Now the hunting is largely gone, the government cares for them and they get no exercise. . . . As a result two or three generations will see the last of them." [1]

The professor's views of an Indian future were both common and convenient. If Indians did not vanish because of pampering or lack of exercise, as Jenks predicted, or become extinct through racial amalgamation, as his research seemed to indicate, they certainly would disappear, being swallowed up by American civilization.

At the beginning of the twentieth century, options for independence and self-determination were rapidly disappearing for Minnesota's Indians. Thirty-five years earlier, as a result of the Dakota Conflict of 1862, most Dakota (Sioux) had been expelled from the state by the military or by congressional action, scattering to isolated reservations and communities in Dakota Territory, Nebraska, and Canada. Some families, who had not participated in the conflict or had assisted whites, or who had never left the region of their traditional villages after the 1851 treaties of Traverse des Sioux and Mendota, remained in Minnesota and were joined by other families and individuals to form small Dakota settlements.[2]

In this way, the Dakota tribe gradually reestablished itself in Minnesota. The communities that were the state's major Dakota settlements by the late twentieth century – Prairie Island, Lower Sioux, Shakopee-Mdewakanton, and Upper Sioux – had arisen from this combination of attachment to traditional sites and historical circumstance. For example, a few Dakota remained near their village at Shakopee after the conflict, somewhat under the protection of the Pond family of missionaries, who

Isabel Roberts, a Dakota woman from Granite Falls, using a hidescraper, 1934

had been invited by Shakopee (the elder chief by that name) to build a mission and school there in 1846. The Lower Sioux community consisted mostly of Santee Sioux families who had been removed to Crow Creek, Dakota Territory, in 1863 and some of whom had returned to the growing Dakota community near Morton and Redwood Falls during the 1870s and 1880s. About 1887 another group of Dakota founded a community at Granite Falls around the ruins of the old Upper Sioux Indian agency.

The dominant Indian tribe in Minnesota in 1900 was the Ojibway (Chippewa), comprising nearly all of the state's more than nine thousand Indians. As the century began, Ojibway Indians were facing an aggressive campaign by government and timber interests to deprive them of their remaining lands and resources. The effect of the campaign on the Ojibway reservations at Fond du Lac, Grand Portage, Leech Lake, Mille Lacs, Nett Lake (Bois Fort), Red Lake, and particularly White Earth was a condition of poverty unparalleled in the history of the tribe.[3]

Another outcome of the campaign, however, was the start of an intense period of Indian political activity, both internal and external. In the years that followed, this activism laid the foundation for the development of modern tribal government and of significant court cases that secured and maintained treaty rights and established the authority and jurisdiction of tribal governments. Because of this tradition of activism, Minnesota Indians have been involved in the creation and development of nearly every American Indian organization, thereby influencing the political agenda for Indians at the national level.

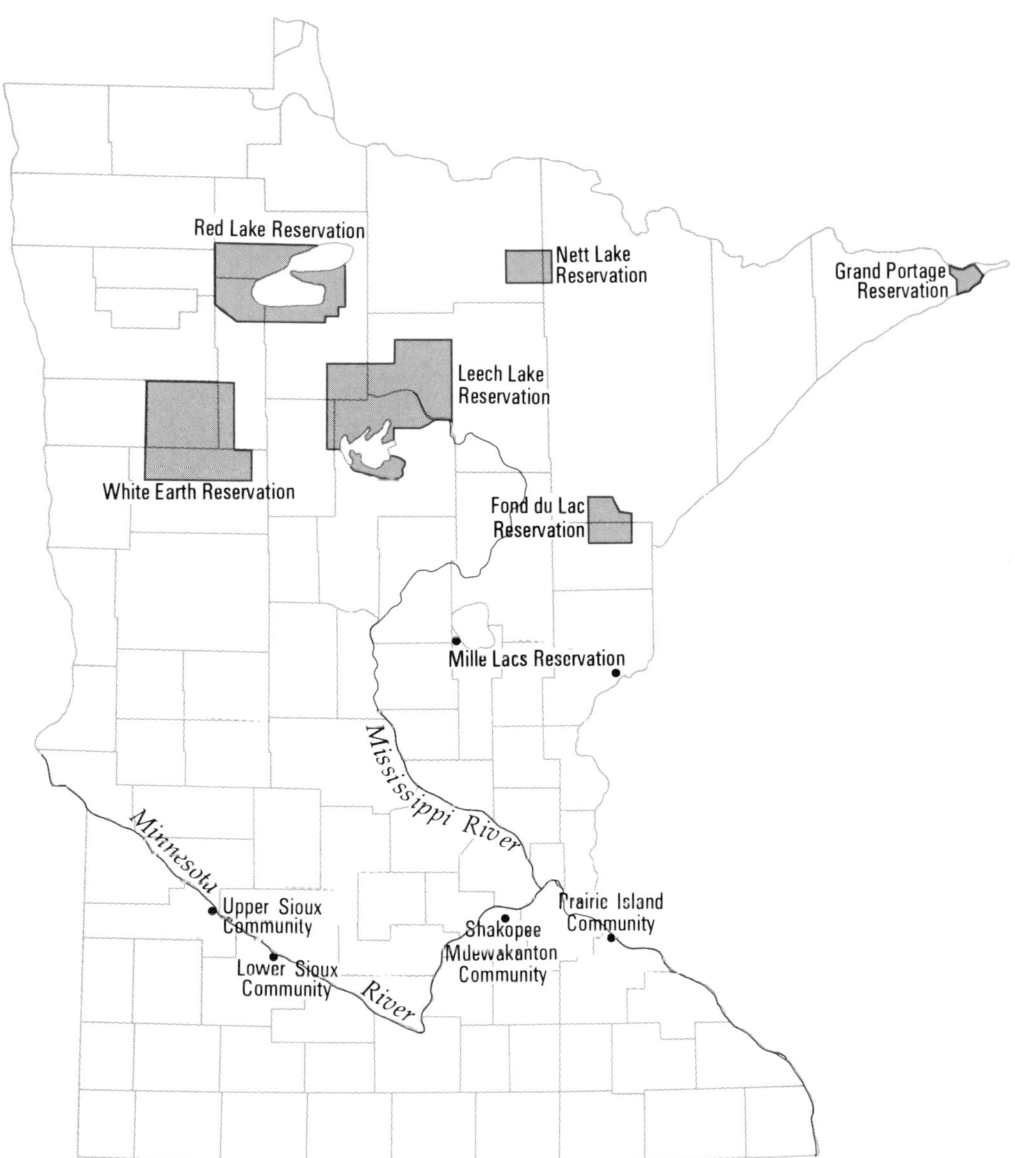

Indian reservations and communities in Minnesota, 1980

The Taking of the Land

Public policy toward American Indians at the end of the nineteenth century had as its central purpose the acquisition of Indian lands and resources, while also attempting to reflect a familiar charitable response to the realities of the poverty and dependency that were caused by the policy. The total assimilation of the American Indian "was a goal that combined concern for native suffering with faith in the promise of America," said historian Frederick E. Hoxie. That the Indian policy created the poverty and dependency was a contradiction that policy makers were able to ignore by resorting to the rationalizations provided by cultural ethnocentrism. "Once the tribes were brought into 'civilized society' there would be no reason for them to 'usurp' vast tracts of underdeveloped land."[4]

In Minnesota the cornerstone of the policy was the federal Nelson Act of 1889 – "An act for the relief and civilization of the Chippewa Indians in the State of Minnesota" – which was designed mainly to assist lumber interests of Minnesota in "developing" vast tracts of Ojibway land. Promising the "benefits" of assimilation through private property, citizenship, and education, the act provided for the forced concentration of the state's Ojibway Indians on individual allotments to be granted to each adult and child on his or her reservation, land that was to be held in trust – safeguarded from sale to outsiders – for twenty-five years. The unallotted land was to be ceded to the U.S. government and then surveyed and sold as "pine and agricultural lands." Proceeds from the sale of the land, after deductions for the costs involved, were to be deposited for fifty years into a permanent, inviolable fund for the Ojibway. Interest from the fund was to be divided among tribal members and also used for Indian schools. After the fifty years, the fund itself was to be divided among "all Chippewa Indians and their issue then living." The Nelson Act anticipated the dissolution of the affairs of the Ojibway as a tribe after fifty years.[5]

As the specific agreements that government-appointed commissioners made with the Ojibway bands to implement the act were broken, however, the Indians felt a deepening sense of betrayal and loss. For example, the White Earth band was promised 160 acres for each individual allotment, but the government reduced the figure to 80 acres. Mille Lacs Indians were promised that they would not have to leave their ancestral land to be removed to another reservation, but the government later withheld their annuities in order to force them off. Other bands were promised blacksmith shops, sawmills, and schools, which were not provided. According to the account of Joseph A. Gilfillan, who served as an Episcopal missionary at White Earth Reservation from 1872 to 1898:

> As one of the Commissioners was a Christian bishop, the Indians thought that his oath would be very binding on him, and his promises carried out. . . .
>
> All of the above broken promises, however, might have been passed over, . . . but that the Indians saw . . . that their money coming to

George Lufkin and his family at White Earth Reservation, about 1900. The original caption reads: "Each one in the group except the baby is entitled to 80 acres of fine land."

> them, the proceeds of their pine, was being absorbed by white men, and that they would finally have everything stolen from them.[6]

Ojibway fears were realized as Minnesota's congressional delegation secured legislation to obtain the lands that had been set aside. In 1902 the Morris Act provided that lands inherited from an allottee could be sold, and a 1904 rider to the land appropriation bill allowed Indians to sell timber on their allotments (increased for that purpose through the 1904 Steenerson Act back to 160 acres). Finally, the Clapp Rider of 1906 removed all restrictions on the sale of White Earth lands held by mixed-bloods, who were defined as "competent" to handle their own affairs. Full-bloods, along with minors, were not considered competent to sell or transfer their allotments.[7]

"What followed was a land-grab orgy so outrageous that to this day local people, regardless of ethnic heritage, speak of it with a sense of bewildered shame," wrote novelists Louise Erdrich and Michael Dorris more than eighty years later. "Threatened, duped or plied with drink, many Chippewa signed away their deeds with an X or a thumb print and received as payment tin money, ancient horses, harnesses and sleighs, used pianos, gramophones and other worthless junk." In 1911 a congressional committee that was charged to investigate the matter blamed "great and greedy lumber concerns and anxious speculators in farming lands, the march of settlement, and the great influence such interests could wield with the Government" for the fraud that ensued at White Earth.[8]

Charles C. Daniels, the U.S. attorney in charge of the land-allotment fraud cases that had been filed on behalf of Indians at White Earth, laid the blame in a 1913 memorandum specifically on "the republican political machine of Minnesota" through its interconnections with government officials, directors of lumber companies, trust companies, and banks. "Every phase of White Earth matters is surrounded with politics," he said, "and political manipulation has been the chief means by which the great injustice done the Indians on this reservation has been accomplished." A year earlier Warren K. Moorehead, a member of the U.S. Board of Indian Commissioners, had given a different interpretation to the injustice at White Earth. Calling it "a black page in American history," he declared: "I have cast about earnestly to find some extenuating circumstances, but there are none. We are responsible for what has happened – all of us." However sincere, it was a view that had the effect of drawing attention from the actual fraudulent activities that had resulted in the loss of the Indian lands. From Moorehead also came the report that the Ojibway people were able to respond with sardonic humor to the betrayal. "Numbers take the position that there is nothing more deliciously ironical than that same sentence beginning, *'For the Relief and Civilization.'* The Indians were certainly *relieved* in short order of their property, and doubtless the white men became better *civilized*."[9]

The Red Lake band of Ojibway Indians formed the important exception to this story of loss of land. Refusing to negotiate an agreement under the Nelson Act of 1889, band members struggled to maintain their independence against significant pressure to cede their aboriginal homeland to the U.S. government, divide their land through allotment, and sell their land and pine resources. By 1918 the Red Lake band had established a constitution and had withdrawn from the Grand Council of Chippewa Indians, which had been established in 1913 to represent the various bands that were party to the Nelson Act. Although the Red Lake band had lost significant lands at the perimeter of the reservation, it steadfastly refused to allot its remaining holdings or to cede the band's vast resources.[10]

Because of its tradition of independence, the Red Lake band came to symbolize a basic truth about tribal sovereignty. During the twentieth century, tribal governments developed an array of governmental institutions and structures to allow them to conduct the affairs of tribal members. Yet what remained fundamental about tribal sovereignty was the relationship of a tribe to an aboriginal homeland. Peter Graves, the longtime secretary-treasurer of the Red Lake band's general council, spoke out in 1953 at a conference about treaty rights and resources. At a time when the federal government was preparing to withdraw from Indian affairs, Graves offered a reminder to those who would abolish the federal government's trustee relationship with Indian tribes:

> There are many . . . who would "clean" that Reservation, if it weren't for the Indian Bureau. We'd use it for individual purposes; we'd divide it

up and get its value in dollars; that way we'd get ready cash instead of keeping a home.

There is a Council at Red Lake who want to keep it for a home. It's the reason for the Council. To recognize that fact doesn't make me a wise Indian. Some people think I'm so "wise" you know, that they can't reason with me – Oh no, you can't reason with me, if you want to destroy my home; you should have a home, if you have nothing else.[11]

Poverty was evident everywhere among Minnesota Indians in the early 1900s, but nowhere was this condition more disturbing to the parade of official investigators than in the district around the settlement of Pine Point in the southeastern corner of White Earth Reservation. About five hundred Indians lived in this district, and a U.S. congressional subcommittee reported in 1911–12 that "nearly every man, woman, and child is afflicted with trachoma, and many are totally blind from its ravages. Twenty-five per cent of these people suffer from tuberculosis and 40 per cent from other dread diseases." Describing each visited "hut" as a "chamber of horrors," subcommittee members found that "10 or more Indians were huddled together at night in a single room, trying in vain to keep out the intense cold." They included "little children, almost naked, aged women, blind and helpless, men, once strong but now broken by disease, [living] a life without hope. . . . Their demeanor eloquently voiced the belief that they had no rights left except the right to suffer in silence." Realizing the contradiction presented by the poverty of Minnesota Indians and the hopeful rhetoric of government policy, the subcommittee said:

It is indeed a sad commentary upon the administration of the Interior Department, and more particularly upon the Indian Bureau, that notwithstanding the fact that they have about $4,000,000 in the United States Treasury, and that millions of dollars of their own money have already been spent, ostensibly for their relief and civilization, the condition of a very large part of the tribe is far worse than when the first treaty was concluded with it at Fort McIntosh, in 1785. When one considers their present condition and reflects on the treatment they have received, he is forcibly reminded of the words of Thomas Jefferson: "When I reflect that there is a just God, I tremble for the future of my country."[12]

Migration from the Reservations

Beginning in the early 1900s, Minnesota Indians began to leave their rural reservation communities in increasing numbers. Their experience in boarding schools far from home, or their service in World War I, led large numbers of Indians to leave their communities for good. The migration had other causes, as well. Poverty, dependency, and a lack of opportunity forced some Indians to look for work of any type elsewhere. Bureaucratic control by the government over the details of personal or family life, as well as the increasing politicization of nearly every aspect of community and tribal affairs, caused many to seek that old sense of Indian indepen-

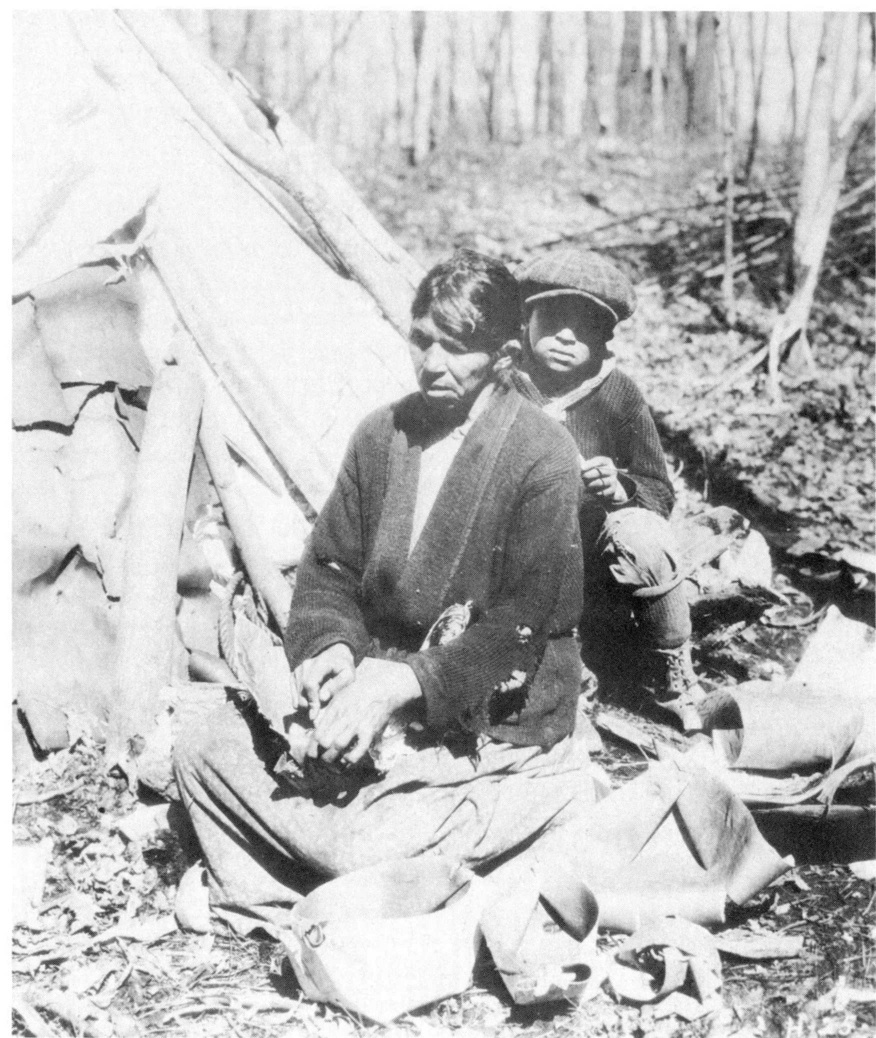

Cecelia Dorr and her son Jess making birch-bark containers for maple sap, Wigwam Bay, Mille Lacs, 1925

dence and freedom in cities far from reservation communities controlled by the Bureau of Indian Affairs (BIA).

William Madison, an Ojibway born on White Earth Reservation, was living in Independence, Missouri, in 1928 when he testified before a congressional committee debating a bill to classify Ojibway Indians as competent or incompetent for the purpose of allowing distributions from the Ojibway fund. "You can go into any large city such as Chicago, St. Louis, Kansas City or any others and you will always find a bunch of Chippewas belonging in Minnesota." On a recent visit to Tulsa, Oklahoma, Madison "got in touch with about 15 Chippewas belonging to the same tribe" as himself.[13]

Many of the Indians who lived in the Twin Cities in the 1920s had experiences similar to those of George C. Peake, a Minnesota Ojibway who was born about 1883 between Mille Lacs Lake and the town of Aitkin. Peake had been sent to Philadelphia to the Educational Home, a part of the Lincoln Institute, when he was ten years old, along with more than twenty other Ojibway boys. He then went to Carlisle Indian Industrial School, also in Pennsylvania, from which he graduated. He continued his studies at Haskell Institute in Lawrence, Kansas. Despite his education Peake found himself unprepared to "meet the battles of life":

> Wholly unskilled, I was neither afoot nor on horseback.
>
> Having received sufficient education to make me desire the comforts and conveniences of the white man's life, and to realize a distaste for the emptiness and idleness of life on the reservation, it was not possible for me to be happy in one, and I had not the wherewithal to procure the other.
>
> And so I drifted to the harvest fields of the Dakotas, and from there to the lumber camps of Minnesota. Here I experienced all the hazards and the wild thrill of log-driving down some rushing turbulent stream.
>
> But at last I wearied of this. . . . I went to the "Twin Cities" in quest of a livelihood and the advantage that cities have to offer in the way of night schools.
>
> Knowing nothing of any trade but not afraid of hard work, I secured employment with the "pick and shovel brigade," spending my evenings studying law at a night school.[14]

His studies were interrupted by World War I, whereupon he enlisted in the army and went to France. After the war he abandoned the idea of becoming a lawyer, instead studying dramatic reading at the MacPhail School of Music and Dramatic Art in Minneapolis. This popular form of entertainment at conferences, club meetings, and other social gatherings of the time provided Peake with a career. He served in leadership positions in Indian organizations, including the Indian Council Fire and the Indian Confederation of America.

Peake's enlistment in the armed forces during World War I was a decision common among young Indian men in Minnesota. "To the everlasting credit of the Indians they were the most forward among the people of America in volunteering for military service," said historian Jennings C. Wise. Although not subject to the draft because they were not citizens, more than seventeen thousand Indians volunteered for service in the U.S. armed forces. Fifty-five percent of all those who registered were inducted, a percentage twice as high as the average for all registrants. Some went north to join the Canadian army's 107th regiment, an all-Indian unit with a distinguished record. Thirty-five members of the Decorah family, Winnebago Indians from Wisconsin, volunteered in a company that was formed in Mauston. Henry Decorah, who later lived in St. Paul, returned to France in 1982 to visit the grave of his father, Foster Decorah, who had been killed there during the war.[15]

Charles A. Bender, a Minnesota Ojibway, was in George Peake's class of 103 Indian students at the Educational Home in Philadelphia. After his return to Minnesota, Bender decided to run away from home and go back to Pennsylvania to attend the Carlisle boarding school. He reported that the best training he received was from "the good Quaker folks of Bucks county" through an outing system that placed Carlisle Indian students in work positions with non-Indian families during the summers. Bender played baseball at Carlisle, and after graduation in 1902 he joined the Harrisburg Athletic Club; he later signed a contract as a pitcher with the Philadelphia Athletics of the American League. Despite his success in professional baseball, which attracted other Indian athletes as well, Bender said that he "wouldn't advise any of the students at Carlisle to become a professional baseball player." He warned that it was "a hard road to travel. Many temptations along the wayside." Bender became one of the great pitchers in major league baseball, with one of the best World Series strikeout records. He was elected to the National Baseball Hall of Fame in 1953.[16]

Two of Charles Bender's sisters also did most of their growing up in boarding schools far from home. Anna Bender traveled to Philadelphia about 1891 at the age of six to attend the Lincoln Institute. When she returned to her parents in Minnesota seven years later, Anna considered the Lincoln Institute the only home she could remember. She went to Pipestone Boarding School in Minnesota for three years and then to Hampton Normal and Agricultural Institute in Virginia, where she became the first Ojibway woman to graduate. Elizabeth Bender also attended Hampton Institute, working after graduation as a teacher in Montana and at the Carlisle school, as well as attending universities in Kansas. She was active in the Society of American Indians and was one of the few Indians in this organization to have also been involved in the National Congress of American Indians, which was founded in 1944. She helped her husband, Henry Roe Cloud, in the work of the Roe Institute, a school founded in 1915 in Wichita, Kansas, that prepared Indian boys for college in an era when Indian education focused on vocational subjects.[17]

George Peake's attendance at the Minneapolis College of Law had been supported by a grant set aside for Indian higher education from the Chippewa fund. Promising students from White Earth Reservation received grants to such schools as the Pillsbury Academy in Owatonna, the Minnesota College of Law, and the Chicago University Medical Department. *The Tomahawk*, the newspaper published at White Earth Reservation, noted in 1918 that "all of these young men made good, decidedly so. . . . Six . . . [are] commissioned officers in the military and one in [the] aviation branch of the government war service and all are fighting on the French front." The newspaper challenged the BIA to match this record of accomplishment through the boarding schools.[18]

Organizing to Protect Indian Interests

One consequence of Indian migration to the cities was the creation of a climate that favored organized political activity around Indian interests. In 1928 the Meriam Report, a major study of Indian affairs that was commissioned by the Interior Department, estimated that about six hundred American Indians lived in Minneapolis and St. Paul and about three hundred to four hundred in Duluth and Superior. "The fact that migrated Indians are often bitter in their criticism of the field employees of the Indian Service is both understandable and regrettable," said the report. Recognizing that this bitterness was more prevalent among urban Indians than among those living on reservations, the report explained that many urban Indians had left their homes because of difficulties with government policies or employees and that they then had an opportunity in the cities to contrast government treatment of Indians with that of other citizens.[19]

The opportunity to speak out against the Indian agency system without fear of retaliation was an important factor in the seemingly more militant disposition of urban Indians. "The present situation, unfortunately, leaves the migrated Indian in a frame of mind which leads him to follow almost anyone who will vigorously attack the Indian Service."[20] Despite this implication that urban Indians were somewhat mindless in their choice of leadership, the Meriam Report was accurate in identifying factors that led to the development of spontaneous and organized Indian political activism in Minnesota, particularly within the Minneapolis Indian community.

In May 1919 a group representing the Society of American Indians, the first national Indian organization, visited the University of Minnesota as part of a speaking tour to support the Indian cause, and one outcome of that visit was an invitation by the university's regents to hold the society's eighth annual convention in Minneapolis. The members of the speaking tour – Dakota physician Charles A. Eastman; Father Philip B. Gordon, Ojibway Catholic priest from Reserve, Wisconsin; and Carlos Montezuma, an Apache physician – had met with mixed results on their trip. The federal agent at the Menominee reservation in Wisconsin had denied the group admittance when he learned that the topic of their presentation was democracy and freedom for Indians.[21]

The society gathered in Minneapolis on October 2 for its three-day convention. As the *Minneapolis Journal* noted, the opening day was by coincidence the anniversary of the day that "whites began scalping Indians" in 1862:

> Fifty-seven years ago to a day the first hunting parties left Minneapolis. The edict of Governor Alexander Ramsey was issued late in September. Hunting parties, however, were not organized and provisioned until the first week in October. The first of these set out with 15 men Oct. 2, which will be the first day of the annual convention of the Society of American Indians in Minneapolis.[22]

The newspaper responded in stereotypic amazement at the prospect of a convention of American Indians being held at the Hotel St. James and elsewhere in Minneapolis. "But the 'full bloods' are not going to parade Minneapolis streets dressed in skins and wampum, smeared with red warpaint, and armed with poison arrows. Their hair and high cheek bones are the only two features that give them away. Several of the visitors are noted professional men."[23]

Charles Eastman, who was born in Minnesota and had escaped with his uncle to Canada following the Dakota conflict, became the focus of the

Journal's amazement. "Born in an Indian tepee near Redwood Falls, Minn., a full-blood Sioux Indian is revisiting Minnesota today. He is Dr. Charles A. Eastman, professor at Amherst college and author of almost a score of books." In his address as president of the society, Eastman described the moral and historical contradictions presented by the case of the Indian who was not yet a citizen. "We Indians started the whole basis of Americanism," he said, echoing the language of the patriotic fervor that was sweeping the nation at the time.

> The Indians stand staunch and when he was called to arms in defense of this country, when this country was in danger, our boys, like their fathers of old, needed no urging. . . . Indians have a power in their hands to get citizenship. We must stand on our treaty rights. We must stand on our constitutional rights and force the Bureau to cease its shameless bluffing.[24]

Father Gordon continued Eastman's attack on the BIA: "We must eliminate the Bureau once and for all. . . . There are many Indians who do not believe in abolishing the Bureau. This number includes the 3000 Indians who are working for the Bureau. . . . It is not right that the Indian, who has fought for his country in France, should go back to his tribe without the right to vote."[25]

As the members of the Society of American Indians debated these issues, Theodore D. Beaulieu of White Earth Reservation reported on the success of the Minnesota Ojibway Indians in organizing to protect their rights. "When our General Council was organized [in 1913], our people were divided. It was hard to get them together. The full blood mistrusted the mixed blood. We had to overcome this and two years ago we united into one big general council on a good working basis. . . . [I]f you want to be successful, you must organize the same as the Chippewas of Minnesota have done."[26]

During the convention, fifty Minnesota Ojibway as well as Indians from other tribes organized a Minneapolis chapter of the society, "proposing to act as missionaries in the twin cities in behalf of their fellow redmen 'imprisoned' on reservations" – reflecting the views of those who sought the abolition of the BIA. The group elected O. DeForrest Davis and Clarence R. Beaulieu – both Ojibway – as president and vice-president, respectively, and De Witt Hare, a Dakota, as secretary-treasurer. The membership committee submitted a list of three hundred to four hundred prospective members in the Twin Cities area. At a chapter meeting on November 19, 1919, Charles E. Drew said that it was the hope of the organization "to abolish the government Indian agency and the reservation system, which are yokes on the neck of the Indian." In the summer of 1920 the group presented a program at West High School auditorium to raise money "for use in improving conditions among reservation Indians through the nation." The program featured Indian music, dance, and songs, both traditional and contemporary. The organization hoped to stage an annual moonlight pageant at Minnehaha Park in Minneapolis, but despite support from city officials there is no record that the pageant was held.[27]

The Society of American Indians faded out of existence as a national organization in the mid-1920s, with the last convention being held in Chicago in 1923. The organization had been formed in 1911 during the reformist climate of the progressive era, and its members had seen some of the national zeal for Indian reform begin to wane as attention shifted to Europe during World War I. Factionalism among the group's leaders also intensified over such issues as the use of peyote and abolition of the BIA. "The conflict in the Society over the 'race loyalty' of Indian Bureau Indians had virtually eliminated one of the Society's major constituencies," wrote historian Hazel W. Hertzberg, "while the fight over peyote eliminated a minor one."

> But the division over the immediate abolition of the Bureau cut the Society to a small band of true believers. In the end most middle-class Indians, much as they resented the Bureau, could not reconcile themselves to a policy which they feared would deliver older Indians into the hands of rapacious enemies and destroy forever the possibility of protecting the Indian land base.[28]

Several years before the demise of the society, in 1917, an organization called the Grand Council of American Indians was formed in Washington, D.C., "without fond glances at the Indian Office and with a constitution that admitted to membership only those of Indian blood," according to the account in *The Tomahawk*. It established an office in Washington to lobby Congress directly on specific Indian issues. Among its "leading spirits" were Minnesotans Charles Eastman and Gus H. Beaulieu. "Surely these gentlemen knew what is necessary for the Indians, and were men able to formulate their views and to carry them out without the aid of bureaucratic office sentimentalists of the Fennimore Cooper school," said the newspaper. Some Indians believed that the Society of American Indians had been too close to the BIA – "too much of the Damon and Pythias attitude between the Indian office and some of the officials of the Society." The newspaper writer expressed the view that a commission should take the place of the BIA; if this could not be done, however, Carlos Montezuma and others should be supported in their efforts to "annihilate" the Indian office.[29]

In 1926 – two years after the passage of the Indian Citizenship Act – Gertrude L. Bonnin, a former leader of the Society of American Indians, founded the National Council of American Indians. A primary purpose of the council was to organize Indian voters, and as part of that work it participated in political campaigns in Oklahoma and South Dakota in 1926. Because it was unable to attract much support from Indian tribes or educated Indian individuals as it attempted to represent their interests in Washington, the council never had a large membership, and it ended by the mid-1930s. It was not until 1944, with the founding of the National Congress of American Indians, that a national Indian organization was again formed.[30]

In the 1920s and 1930s, national development and action on behalf of the American Indian were primarily undertaken by what have been called Indian defense organizations. These voluntary associations of non-Indians tended to emphasize the positive value in tribal cultures while still seeking "the elimination of poverty and illiteracy and the fuller integration of Indians into the national life," according to anthropologist Edward H. Spicer. One was the National Association on Indian Affairs (formerly the Eastern Association), whose leading spirit was Oliver La Farge; his book *Laughing Boy* was awarded the Pulitzer Prize in 1930. Another, the American Indian Defense Association, was led by John Collier, who was appointed by Franklin D. Roosevelt to be commissioner of Indian affairs in 1933.[31]

Before 1924, when Congress passed the Indian Citizenship Act, citizenship was the issue that drew attention to the political and legal no-man's-land in which American Indians lived. In 1916 Arthur C. Parker, a Seneca anthropologist and leader in Indian organizations, posed the question: "Who today, we may well inquire, is the Indian? . . . He is not an alien, he is not a foreigner, he is not a citizen." Parker stated that Indians had "the right of an assured status." Individual Indians might be recognized as citizens by virtue of specific statutes or treaties that were likely to stress criteria related to the individual's social and cultural assimilation, but Indians as a people were not considered U.S. citizens. The centerpiece of this approach to Indian citizenship was a provision of the Dawes Act of 1887 specifying that "every Indian . . . who has voluntarily taken up . . . his residence, separate and apart from any tribe of Indians . . . , and has adopted the habits of civilized life is hereby declared to be a citizen of the United States." Other methods of obtaining citizenship – private ownership of land, marriage of an Indian woman to a white man, or being born to Indian parents who were citizens – reflected the view that an Indian who wanted to be a citizen was required to stop living as an Indian.[32]

When Indian men across the country came forward in 1917 to enlist for war service, the citizenship dilemma led to unique problems. In Philadelphia, an Indian carrying a suitcase presented himself at the registration booth and was asked: "Are you an alien?"

> No; I was born in the United States. Then you are a citizen, he was informed. No, I am not a citizen. I am not an alien. What are you then? I am an American Indian. I have neither the rights of an alien nor of a citizen, yet I was born in the United States. My father is a full-blood Sioux Chiefta[i]n. I am between 21 and 31, and must offer myself for military service.

The registration board was initially confused but eventually registered him as "Big Face, carrying suit case, born in the U.S., but not a citizen." After the war, Congress declared that every Indian who was honorably discharged could apply to a court for citizenship.[33]

The cause of citizenship became symbolically important for such organizations as the Society of American Indians, given the number of Indian people in some states and the political implications of enfranchising them. But the grant of citizenship in 1924 did not change the reality of federal management and guardianship over the land and property of Indians, nor did it automatically confer all of the rights and privileges one would assume to belong to a U.S. citizen. In many states Indians could not vote until well after World War II, and federal law forbade the sale of alcohol to Indians until 1953. Parker's concern that Indians have an assured civic status was thus not solved by U.S. citizenship – that status was to come from the drive by American Indians to create a definite and enduring tribal citizenship in addition to their federal and state citizenship. It was tribal governments, having political relations with the U.S. government as defined by treaties, that laid the foundation for an assured civic status for Indians.[34]

Through the Great Depression and the 1940s Indians continued to migrate from reservations to urban areas, which brought about further changes in federal policy. The Indian population of the Twin Cities grew from about six hundred in 1928 to between four thousand and six thousand by 1952, although about half of the Indians in the latter year were described as temporary winter residents.[35]

One of the first self-help Indian organizations to be formed in the Twin Cities was American Indians, Incorporated, which was created in 1950. It was aided in its formative stages by Daisuke Kitagawa, an Episcopal priest who had come to Minnesota during World War II to work with Japanese Americans assigned to the Military Intelligence Service Language School near the Twin Cities. A member of the Minneapolis Mayor's Council on Human Relations, Kitagawa worked with other religious leaders, social agencies, and Indians to alleviate problems related to Indian involvement in "skid row" crimes. The ideas that emerged – establishment of a community center, creation of a favorable social climate for Indians, and referrals to other agencies – became the mainstay of other urban Indian organizations, including the Minneapolis Regional Native American Center. American Indians, Incorporated, limited membership to American Indians and described itself as "independent of any agency of government, federal or state." The organization sought to secure for Indians the rights and privileges enjoyed by all other citizens and to work for fair play and equality. In order to meet its goals the group worked closely with the Mayor's Council on Human Relations, the Fair Employment Practices Commission, the Governor's Human Rights Commission, and other civic organizations. Members met once a month at the Japanese American Community Center for discussions and for such activities as potluck suppers, Christmas parties, and dancing in both traditional Indian and other styles. The group contributed to the Minnesota Indian scholarship fund and provided speakers for civic groups.[36]

The Upper Midwest American Indian Center, which was established in Minneapolis in 1954, sought many of the same goals as American Indians, Incorporated, working to promote fellowship among American Indians and understanding between Indians and non-Indians. The Chippewa Tomahawk Band, which was established in 1949, published the *New Tomahawk* between 1950 and 1953; this newsletter focused on the need to enlighten the American public and to preserve Indian culture and treaty rights. William Madison, the group's principal leader, was actively involved in efforts addressing Indian issues. Organizations were also formed

Ojibway women, some wearing jingle dresses, and children at a powwow in the gymnasium of the Minneapolis American Indian Center, 1978

to meet the cultural needs of Indians. The Ojibwe-Dakota Research Society (originally the Ojibway Research Society), which was active from the 1940s, worked to preserve native language. The St. Paul Indian Dance Club, which was renamed the St. Paul Indian Club in 1960, sponsored monthly powwows. Early urban Indian organizations focusing on specific issues or needs included the Indian squad of Alcoholics Anonymous and the American Indian Student Committee of the Twin Cities.[37]

The Policy Debate

"Children become adults and grow old while altruists urge, Congress debates, and the bureau administers its laws, while the Indian wastes his patrimony through inexperience and his life in idleness," declared Secretary of the Interior Hubert Work in 1924.[38] His frustration was a common reaction to the cycles of policy debate that have characterized government relations with Indians in the twentieth century.

A significant fixture of that debate by the 1920s was the belief that one could "gain real knowledge of Indian life and problems by systematic observation and study," according to Spicer. The first major attempt to apply this principle was the massive study entitled *The Problem of Indian Administration* – also known as the Meriam Report – which was issued by the Interior Department in 1928. Although the study guided Indian policy through the 1950s, it "fell short of giving any clear idea of Indian aspirations at the time, since its orientation was chiefly that of social welfare within the framework of the dominant culture." Until Indian organizations began to challenge this perspective in the early 1960s, Indian policy development after the Meriam Report was increasingly dependent upon the interpretations of anthropologists and other social scientists.[39]

Work had initiated this major review of Indian policy in 1923 by organizing the Advisory Council on Indian Affairs. Its conclusions laid the foundation for the evolution of public policy for American Indians in the years that followed, and it set precedent by involving Indians in the deliberations. This Committee of One Hundred constituted a cross section of experts and interest groups concerned with Indian affairs at the time, including the philanthropist George G. Heye and anthropologists Frederick W. Hodge and Alfred L. Kroeber, as well as Warren Moorehead, who had deplored the land-grab at White Earth in 1912. Representatives from Minnesota were Albert Jenks of the university and Blanche L. La Du of the Minnesota State Board of Control, which oversaw state welfare programs; Father Philip Gordon from Wisconsin was also a member.[40]

The council recommended a significant, temporary increase in financial support for the BIA so that the bureau could "speed up" its work and thereby bring an end to "many, if not all, of the Government activities for Indian welfare." Secretary Work, who called the effort of the council "a landmark in the history of the Government's efforts to handle the Indian question successfully," agreed, proposing that the states take over this responsibility as a step toward the ultimate goal of assimilation of Indians into American society:

> State governments complain that the Indian pays no taxes, anticipating with forebodings the time when he may be a public charge.
>
> The time to prepare against this melancholy fate is now, before the resources from the Indian's land have been exhausted, before individual ownership so essential to self-respect is beyond his reach, and before a paternalistic policy compelling continuance of primeval communism has overcome his possible initiative.

To make possible the early withdrawal of the federal government from Indian affairs, the council urged the recruitment of better qualified – and better paid – Indian service workers, particularly teachers and doctors. States were urged to cooperate with federal agencies in the areas of education and health by admitting Indians to public schools and by helping to solve public health problems.[41]

The council also recommended that Indian legal cases regarding violations of treaties and agreements be admitted to the U.S. Court of Claims. Although reasonable on the surface, this recommendation rested on the assumption that the government could get out of Indian affairs once it had settled its claims with individual American Indians. The missing element in these discussions of state versus federal responsibility was the drive by Indians to establish and develop tribal government on a firm footing. For the council, tribal government did not exist as an option for the transfer of government activities.[42]

In Minnesota, state Indian policy reflected the national debate. Gov. Theodore Christianson appointed a commission in 1926 to negotiate with Congress for the transfer of Indian trust funds and lands to the state. But the commission opposed negotiations at that time because such a transfer "would involve Congress, the Bureau of Indian Affairs, and the State of Minnesota in a series of long, difficult and complicated legal problems." It would also "necessitate the establishment . . . of a department or bureau of Indian affairs, and would necessitate the expenditure of a large sum of money." The original motivation behind the initiative had disappeared when Congress passed a bill allowing Indian tribes to sue the U.S. government for claims.[43]

The governor's commission, which met as a group only once, was composed of Granville G. Bennett, the Episcopal bishop of Duluth; Edward L. Rogers, an Ojibway attorney from Walker; and Blanche La Du, who had served on Secretary Work's advisory council. Its principal recommendation was that the governor appoint an advisory committee made up of representatives of the state boards of health, education, and control that would develop better relations between the state and federal governments and coordinate Indian programs in Minnesota. Improved health services became a special focus of the committee's work, which also included programs in education, employment, and general welfare.[44]

When the National Conference of Social Work held its annual conference in Minneapolis in 1931, the presentations on American Indians showed the strong impact of the Meriam Report. Lewis Meriam, the survey's technical director, advocated state, local, and federal government cooperation in the social and educational work for Indians. "The ward Indians will be held back if we continue to provide for their social and educational advancement through special segregated institutions and service agencies maintained exclusively for them. They need training and experience in getting government services from the same agencies that serve their white fellow citizens." Yet, "Indians cannot at present carry the average or normal tax burden and they will for years to come require more educational and social service than the state and county normally provides for its white citizens." Minnesota was cited as an excellent example of the attitude that Indians would eventually "become participating citizens of the state and local community." According to W. Carson Ryan, Jr., director of education for the U.S. Indian Service, "Minnesota just naturally assumes that Indians are citizens and are to be included in any and all plans the state has for its citizenry."[45]

It was the eloquence of Ruth Muskrat Bronson, a Cherokee Indian and guidance officer for the U.S. Indian Service in Kansas City, that offered a glimpse into the responses of individual Indians to the transitions that had marked the early decades of the twentieth century. Indian communities were at a unique milestone in the 1930s, and never before had reservation communities contained individuals with such discontinuous experiences:

> There is the old Indian, like my grandmother, who lives in the past, who clings to the old ways and cherishes the old customs; her days are filled with brooding over old wrongs and nursing old wounds that refuse to heal. In reality, she is much nearer "The Trail of Tears" than she can ever be to the Citizenship Act of 1924. She turns a hopeless face toward the struggles of this new order. . . .
>
> In many respects the second type of Indian might easily be my father. He is anxious to accept the standards of living of the white people. He has turned away from the old Indian ways. His clan life and all the old social controls of the ancient Indian life have broken down. Even his language has lost its intimacy for him. He talks Cherokee very rarely now; and he does not know a great deal about English. Frustrated and inarticulate he does not know where to turn for security and balance; he is drifting. . . .
>
> The third type of Indian is increasing with every graduating class from government schools and mission schools. . . . This type of Indian does not stay on the reservation for long. He gets out, as I did, where there is promise of something better than the starvation which faces him at home. . . . He is young and strong and adventurous. He migrates to the city for that is where the jobs are to be found. Sometimes he finds a good job. More often, because of lack of training and discrimination, he does not. . . . He ekes out the barest existence in the city until he becomes overwhelmed by increasing burdens and responsibilities and so returns to the reservation, to be even more unhappy and discouraged.[46]

During Franklin Roosevelt's administration, federal Indian policy underwent a significant reversal. The Indian Reorganization Act (IRA) of 1934 provided a mechanism for self-government by allowing reservations to organize federal corporations, adopt constitutions and bylaws, and implement economic development projects. Allotment also came to a formal end as a policy. The IRA and other New Deal Indian programs stressed direct involvement of Indians in projects designed to benefit Indian reservation communities.[47]

In 1937 the Minnesota Chippewa Tribe – comprising all the Ojibway reservations except Red Lake – was established through a referendum vote, and two years later tribal members approved subcharters that enabled self-government at the reservation level. The creation of the constitution was controversial among Minnesota Ojibway Indians, many of whom believed that the process happened too fast or that the form of government that was adopted favored the interests of the federal government and the BIA. Some urged repeal of the IRA on the grounds that it co-opted and limited tribal sovereignty and diverted attention from long-standing complaints. The constitution of the tribe was amended in 1963 and 1972 to ensure more direct representation of tribal members in determining the makeup of the tribal executive committee and to give more autonomy at the reservation level.[48]

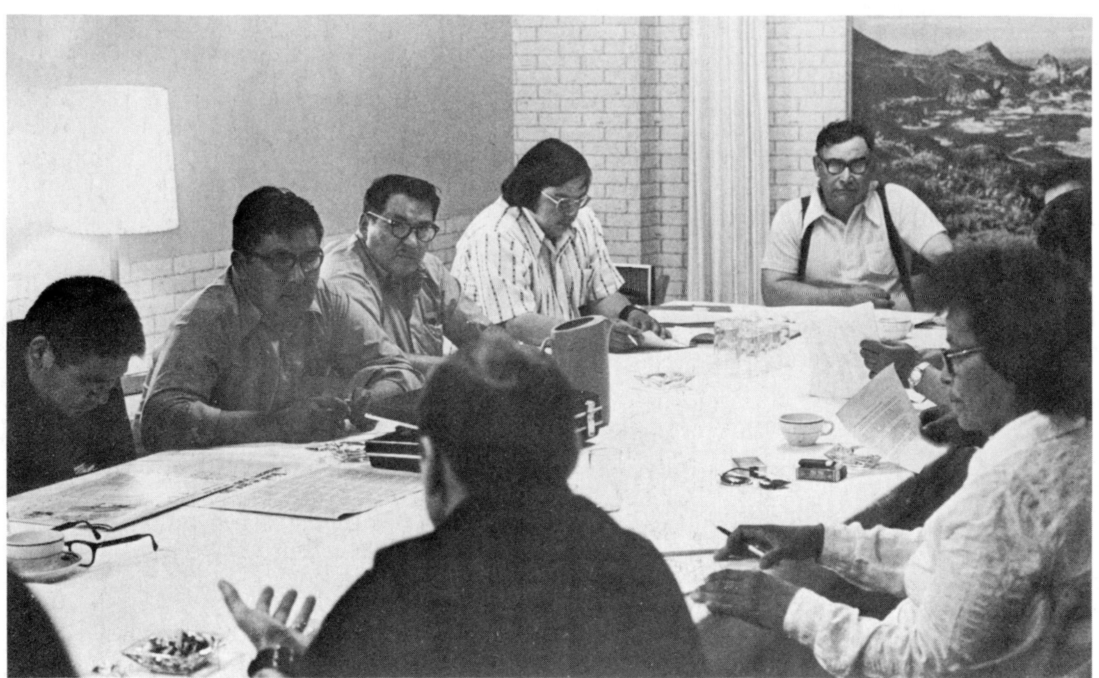

Executive Committee of the Minnesota Chippewa Tribe meeting in May 1973

In the years following the New Deal shift in federal policy, tribal governments evolved structures that were increasingly representative of their constituencies and that provided better services to members. They also increased their role in protecting and defending the rights that were guaranteed by treaty. This evolution of tribal government was dynamic, taking place within the context of significant debate among members. Sometimes the debate echoed the earlier one between the mixed-blood and full-blood factions, as well as the controversy surrounding the establishment of the Chippewa General Council. The issues included the merits of traditional and representative government, development or preservation of natural resources, resolution of past claims against the government, negotiations affecting the implementation of treaty-guaranteed hunting and fishing rights, relationship of tribal and state governments, and relationship of tribal government to its urban members.[49]

John Collier, the architect of the IRA and commissioner of Indian affairs throughout the Roosevelt administration, warned in 1942 that the postwar period would bring many new problems to American Indians. "Unless the industrial world can keep up its pace," he maintained, "there will be a strong trend of migration from industrial areas back to reservations upon the termination of the war" – a migration complicated by the wave of returning soldiers. But the reservations were "in general inadequate to support the Indians who live on them and seek to derive their livelihood therefrom." Because Indians needed to obtain more land, they were faced with the problem of "working out a solution to the heirship problem" to allow efficient land use and of finding ways to refinance returning Indians "who must start over again as farmers and livestock operators."[50]

According to Collier, the dilemma of federal Indian policy reflected a larger concern. Within the context of World War II, Collier linked the dilemma to a worldwide problem "which must be solved if we are to achieve any ordered stability in the international and internal relations of states."

> It is the problem of reconciling the rights of small groups of people to cultural independence with the necessity for larger economic units demanded by modern methods of production and distribution.
>
> This is the problem of small states and small cultural groups everywhere. If here in the United States with our Indian groups we can show a solution to this problem we shall have made a material contribution to the maintenance of world peace.

By the 1950s, however, congressional opposition to the policies embodied in the IRA led to yet another reversal of federal Indian policy. The federal government abandoned its previous emphasis on the economic development of Indian reservations through individual and tribal activities and returned to a stress on the rapid assimilation of Indians into American society. It sought to end the federal trustee relationship to Indian tribes and to extend state civil and criminal jurisdictions over Indian reservations. Public Law 280, which was passed by Congress in 1953, transferred civil and criminal jurisdiction over Indian lands in five states from federal to state government; except for Red Lake Reservation, Indian lands in Minnesota were covered by this measure. Other legislation in the mid-1950s transferred responsibility for Indian education programs to the states and for health programs to the U.S. Public Health Service. In place of reservation economic development, the government encouraged Indians to resettle in urban areas and seek work there. During this same period the BIA increased its efforts to help Indians relocate to urban areas for employment, and voluntary relocation became a primary focus of BIA policy. Minneapolis was the site of an Indian employment and placement center that operated between 1950 and 1954.[51]

In November 1944 more than a hundred Indians from around the United States met in Denver, Colorado, to form the National Congress of American Indians (NCAI). The organization, which was open to both tribal and individual Indian membership, was initially directed by Ruth Muskrat Bronson. Its goal was to fight for pro-Indian legislation and to establish and protect legal rights affecting voting, welfare, and other issues. One leader of the NCAI was Minnesota Ojibway Edward Rogers, who had distinguished himself as a student and athlete at Carlisle boarding school and the University of Minnesota. Rogers practiced law in Walker and served at different times as probate judge in Mahnomen County and Cass County attorney.[52]

By 1951, when the NCAI met in St. Paul for its annual convention, the organization reported a significant advance in the tribal membership of the organization. The group advocated such measures as greater emphasis on

Indian education and accreditation of Indian schools, Indian involvement in national and state legislation affecting Indians, enhancement of the power of reservation superintendents, and extension of time for filing claims with the Indian Claims Commission, which had been established in 1946. Elizabeth Bender Roe Cloud, who was chairman of Indian welfare in the General Federation of Women's Clubs, urged Indians to be individually responsible partners in democracy in order to solve some of the problems confronting Indians as a group. "We are American Indians but, even more, we are Americans," she said. Throughout the 1950s the NCAI led a fight that was successful in slowing and then halting continued implementation of the government's efforts to terminate or end the unique political and legal status of Indian tribes.[53]

During the convention the Minnesota Chippewa Tribe sponsored a powwow for the purpose of adopting Gov. Luther W. Youngdahl into the tribe. In 1947, citing a world view affected by "the shadow of atomic fission," Youngdahl had proclaimed that "all races must quickly learn to cooperate according to principles of justice or perish," and he challenged "the dominant white group" in Minnesota to "set the example by correcting wrongs done to the Indian." But Youngdahl's solutions were reminiscent of late-nineteenth-century public policy toward Indians: he stressed the need to "devote serious effort in correcting those conditions which tend to retard their assimilation into our way of life" and to "help them take their rightful places as citizens, with all accompanying privileges and responsibilities."[54]

According to Robert Esbjornson, Youngdahl's biographer, the Indian problem of the 1950s had two parts: "The short-term problem involves the assumption of responsibility for determining that Indians receive proper treatment from a humanitarian viewpoint. The long-term problem is to fully assimilate the Indian into a new culture." What this meant in real terms was that state and local governments wanted to be compensated by the federal government for providing government services to Indians. Despite the citizenship status of Indians, state and local governments were reluctant or unwilling to provide education, medical care, and other services to indigent Indians because reservation lands were tax exempt and government services were tied to property taxes.[55]

It was an economic view that was politically motivated and that failed to recognize the historical context of Indian poverty. Minnesota Indians were never fully compensated for millions of dollars worth of land and natural resources, a transfer of wealth that added directly to the economic strength of the country at the same time as it impoverished the Indians from whom it was taken. Even the government services that Indians had received from the federal government were largely deducted from the trust accounts established for the tribe upon the sale of land and resources. Further, many Indian individuals did indeed pay taxes. But the presumption that Indians could not receive government public services because reservation lands were tax exempt had a significant effect upon the reception that Indians received from social service agencies in urban areas.[56]

Red Lake Elementary School, 1953

By 1949, the federal government was actively laying the foundation for a policy of withdrawal from Indian affairs. In that year, the Commission on Organization of the Executive Branch of the Government (the Hoover Commission) recommended that the administration of social programs for Indians be progressively transferred to state governments, which would be compensated by the federal government until Indian taxes could carry the load. Tribal property would be transferred to Indian-owned corporations, and Indian lands would lose their tax exemption. The Minnesota legislature and governor considered the implications of such a policy for the state. Through the initiative of Governor Youngdahl, the state acted quickly to consult with Indians and to plan for what was perceived to be the inevitable day when the federal government would get out of the Indian business. The first Governors' Interstate Indian Conference, held at the University of Minnesota in March 1950, included representatives from seven states having large Indian populations. Participants agreed on such measures as providing training for Indian children, utilizing the special talents and skills of Indians, providing employment on and off the reservation, and permitting a full measure of self-government.[57]

At a conference held in Bemidji immediately after the interstate conference, Minnesota Indians offered many ideas about the way in which government should be involved in the solution of Indian problems. Paul LeGarde of Grand Portage emphasized the need for federal, state, and local governments to participate with Indians in creating workable economic and social programs. Peter Graves of Red Lake singled out education as "the only real salvation for the Indians"; he also urged continuation of the BIA. William Madison, representing the Chippewa Tomahawk Band, favored the abolition of the BIA and repeal of the IRA. William Morrell of Leech Lake recommended support of a ten-year program that the Minnesota Chippewa Tribe had proposed to Congress, including such measures as immediate adjudication of claims, improvements in education and health services, and control of timber operations on tribal lands. Reflecting the perspective of the period, Edward Rogers and Chief Little White Cloud of White Earth Reservation denounced the BIA and suggested that its budget be given to the states, with the governors becoming Indian commissioners. For Little White Cloud, this conclusion was reinforced by his opinion of Governor Youngdahl. "For over 100 years the Indian has been carrying a lantern around looking for an honest man. . . . At last that search is ended. We have found that honest man in Governor Youngdahl."[58]

Honesty aside, Youngdahl's policies were consistent with a movement to withdraw federal government services and protection to Indians and to terminate Indian tribes. By 1953, the federal government had introduced a number of termination bills, including bills that terminated the Menominee and Klamath tribes. Attorney Richard Schifter of Washington, D.C., pointed out in that year that groups supporting federal withdrawal and termination were "aided and abetted in their drive by many well-meaning citizens who sincerely believe that they are participating in a campaign to 'set the Indian free', to 'liberate him from the bonds of reservation existence'. . . . [T]his Indian liberation movement is in many respects a movement to liberate the Indian from his land." Indian leader D'Arcy McNickle likened Indian affairs at the beginning of the 1950s to sitting at the bedside of a friend who has been shot by an "unloaded" gun: one could get shot just as fatally unintentionally as by intention.[59]

Emergence of the New Indian Activism

The debate about Indian policy underwent a major shift in emphasis beginning about 1960, a shift that led eventually to a new Indian agenda and a new spirit of activism. One element in the shift was the work of Sol Tax, an anthropology professor at the University of Chicago, who began in that year to explore ways in which to update the Meriam Report of 1928. As a result of discussions with NCAI leaders in Denver, Tax committed himself to the development of a document in which social scientists would take a back seat, only facilitating a process whereby Indians would discuss and formalize their own points of view. This simple yet radical idea set into motion an Indian response to problems posed by the condition and status of Indians, generating ideas for change that have profoundly affected every Indian.[60]

The event that marked the shift was the American Indian Chicago Conference, which was organized in cooperation with the NCAI and was held at the University of Chicago in 1961. Twenty-one Minnesota Indians attended, including members of the Dakota, Ojibway, and Winnebago tribes. The modern Indian movement could well be dated from the publication at this conference of the Declaration of Indian Purpose, which was based on a memorandum by Tax that expressed the consensus of Indians with whom he had been involved in discussions. The memorandum included eight points:

> (1) Indian ways are the right ways for Indians. (2) The traditional rights of Indian nations have never been lost and must not be jeopardized. (3) Indians whose economic resources have been taken away need help but want to manage their own affairs. (4) Knowing that their culture discourages avaricious behavior, Indians will always want special protection against loss of communities and resources. (5) Indians want access to education and to take advantage of the resources of the modern world but believe that they can get these without necessarily adopting the values of the white man's world. (6) The wrongs of the past must be undone wherever possible. (7) Present wrongs must be ended at once. And (8) measures must be taken immediately to protect from now on all Indians' rights as they have never been protected before and to help Indian people achieve better health, education, and economic well-being.

These eight points, as faithfully recorded and articulated by Sol Tax, have ever since represented the principal agenda of American Indians.

In Minnesota the pattern of Indian involvement was set in the late 1950s by the Governor's Human Rights Commission, whose membership included Ellen McIntire, John L. Pemberton, George A. Smith, and Edward M. Wilson. The commission sponsored Indian conferences that focused on a range of socioeconomic and educational issues, giving Indians an opportunity to interact directly with state policy makers and representatives of government agencies. In the year of the Chicago conference, the Indian Committee of the commission issued a report that came to shape state policy toward Indians. Members of the committee included Simon Howard, a former leader of the Minnesota Chippewa Tribe, and Roger Jourdain, longtime chairman of the Red Lake band. After acknowledging the uniqueness of Indian culture and values, the report stressed the legitimacy of tribal governments. It called for "an end to government behavior which arbitrarily demands Indian conformity to edicts and regulations in whose formulation the Indian has had no voice. . . . The right of an Indian to have a voice in his own destiny must be accepted" and the "functions and authority of tribal councils must be understood and respected as important aspects of government." Indians must be given the reasonable choice of living on or off reservations. The goal of educational and other programs must be to give every Indian "an honorable choice to live as a self-reliant, self-supporting individual either in company with his tribal groups or in the world outside."[61]

Another outgrowth of the work of the commission was the creation in 1963 of the Minnesota Indian Affairs Commission, which served as a liaison between the state and tribal governments; it was the first agency of its kind in any state. In 1983 the agency was renamed the Indian Affairs Council. State and tribal government relations have been dynamic in Min-

Indian boys bringing in wild rice for payment, Leech Lake, about 1970

nesota, and cooperation in this sphere has resulted in a distinct effort by state government to meet the needs of Indians in such areas as housing and education.[62]

Across the nation, the Chicago conference had an enduring effect on the direction of Indian policy after 1961. In particular, it served as a catalyst for efforts by two significant Indian constituencies – young people, especially a growing number of college-educated youth, and urban Indians – to seek to develop and represent a national Indian program. As a result of the conference a group of young Indians, mostly from the Southwest, established the National Indian Youth Council (NIYC) in 1961. According to Vine Deloria, Jr., the organization "provided for the radical position in Indian Affairs by always seeking a more liberal and activist position with respect to issues than did the older NCAI. The young Indians thus opened up Indian Affairs as it had never been opened, dividing the traditional government by consensus into a progressive movement with a majority and dissenting philosophy always opposing one another." The NIYC set the stage and style for later Indian activism through its programs of "fish-ins" in defense of Indian treaty fishing rights in the Pacific Northwest.[63]

The social, economic, and educational issues that urban Indians faced and that urban Indian organizations attempted to address demanded increasing national attention during this period. Because of the government policy promoting relocation and the poverty and economic neglect that characterized Indian reservations, Indians continued to migrate to urban areas through the 1950s and early 1960s. The year 1968 saw an unsuccessful attempt to develop a national Indian organization to represent urban Indians. American Indians United, which was initiated in Seattle, was first convened in Chicago and held a national conference in San Francisco in 1969, but the organization then faded from view. Delegates to the San Francisco conference included many Indians from Minneapolis – among them Dennis Banks and Clyde Bellecourt representing the American Indian Movement, which was formed in Minneapolis in 1968.[64]

The American Indian Movement (AIM), as described in a *Black Scholar* interview with Dennis Banks in 1976, was formed to combat racist discrimination in urban areas of Minneapolis and St. Paul, including police brutality and discrimination in housing, employment, and the courts. In its first year AIM organized the Indian Patrol to focus on the issue of police brutality and harassment of Indians in the Minneapolis community. The organization established Indian alternative schools to draw attention to the failure of the public schools and to redefine and provide for the educational needs of Indian young people. AIM also sought to ensure Indian control of Indian organizations and programs.[65]

What distinguished AIM from other Indian organizations, indeed overshadowing historically the significant accomplishments of other organizations in the Twin Cities, was the focus on what Gerald Vizenor called "symbolic confrontation." He defined this controversial focus in the following way: "The confrontation idiom means punching out the symbolic adversary of racism and oppression at the front door, with the press present, and walking out the back door. The negotiation idiom means punching out the adversary at the front door with the press present, but waiting around for an invitation to return and grind out some changes." Between 1968 and 1972 AIM used tactics and held demonstrations that led to confrontations and that offered contradictions to the accepted American thinking about

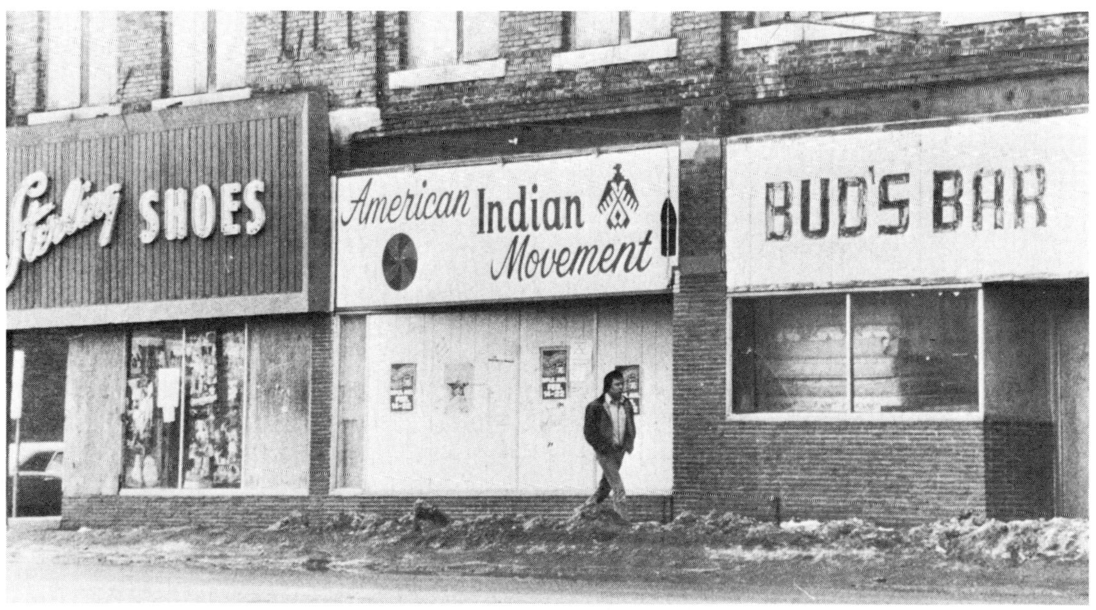

American Indian Movement headquarters on Franklin Avenue in Minneapolis, 1976

Indians. By forming the Indian Patrol, handing out old clothes to welfare workers at a meeting, walking the "Trail of Broken Treaties" – a reverse movement of Indians from the West Coast to the nation's Capitol – or occupying the land at Wounded Knee, AIM not only publicized Indian issues but also provoked a significant reexamination of Indians in American society. Attention from the media was necessary if the organization was to communicate the themes that underlay the demonstrations and tactics.[66]

During this period, Indians were working in other settings and other ways to address the agenda of significant Indian issues, including education. Following a national study of Indian education and hearings held by the U.S. Senate Subcommittee on Indian Education, a group of Minnesota Indians – including Rosemary Christensen and Wilfred (Will) Antell, who had testified at the hearings – organized the National Indian Education Association in 1970. The association, which held a preliminary meeting in Minneapolis in 1969, lobbied successfully for passage of the Indian Education Act of 1972. This act strengthened the involvement of Indian parents in their children's education and provided money to develop programs for Indian children in public schools throughout the United States.[67]

By the 1980s Indian tribal governments controlled and operated their own schools and colleges, with the goal not only of doing a more effective job but also of giving Indian young people a sense of the future that would be connected with their own unique past. Up to the 1920s, as many as 70 percent of Ojibway children had no place to go to school; in 1980 about 25 percent of all Minnesota Indians between twenty-five and forty-four years of age had had at least one year of college education. The Minnesota Indian Scholarship Program, established by the state legislature in 1955, provided assistance to ten Indian students for postsecondary education in its first year. By 1987 more than two thousand students requested assistance from the program annually and about four thousand had graduated from their programs. Seventy percent of these graduates had completed their postsecondary education in the previous decade.[68]

Restoring Indian Rights

"The Indians have a right to know that their name as a people is not hidden forever from its place among the nations of the earth," wrote Arthur Parker in 1916. Characterizing the loss of land and resources as "minor" in comparison, he listed a series of rights, "essential to the life of a man or a nation," that had been stolen from the American Indian.[69]

The seven rights, as they were eloquently described by Parker, were *an intellectual life* ("Civilization . . . by destroying their relationship to nature . . . left a group of people mentally confused. . . . The Indians must have a thought-world given back"); *social organization* (Indians "had associations, societies, fraternities, and pastimes. . . . Every man must have the right to be an exponent of a certain ideal or group of ideals"); *economic independence* ("In his native state the Indian needed no govern-

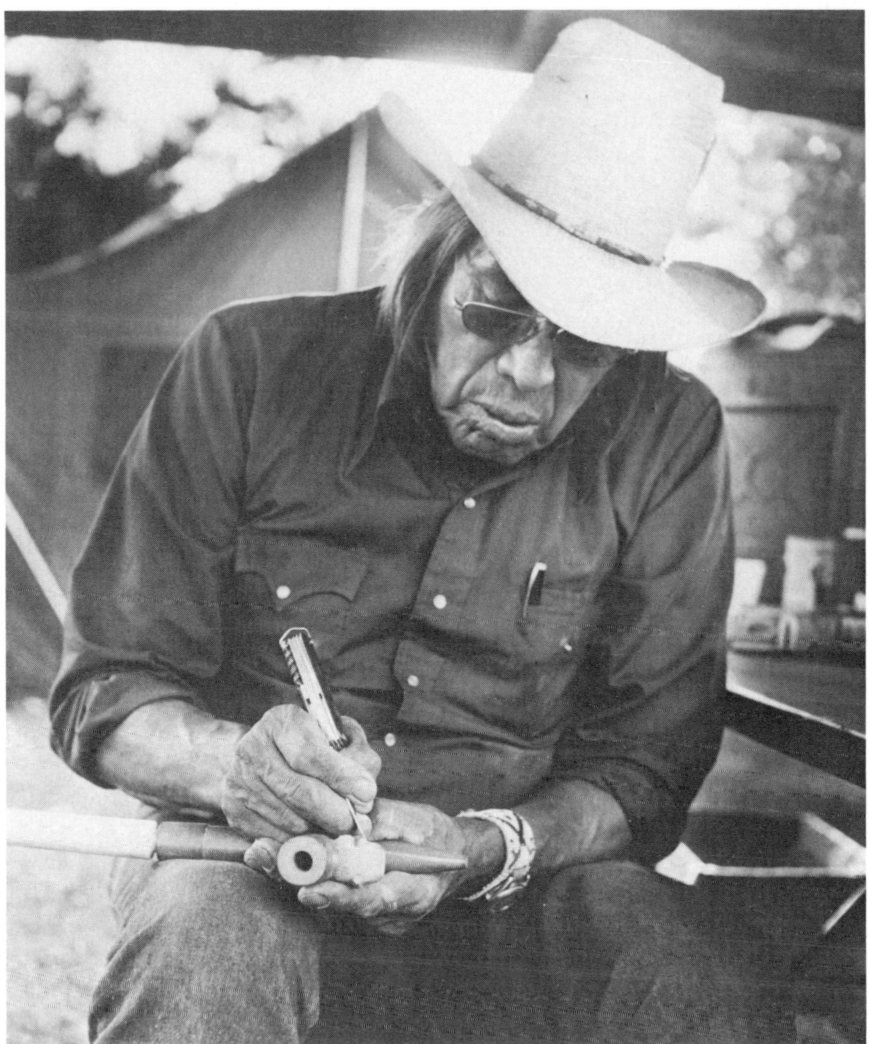

Amos Owen, Dakota spiritual leader from Prairie Island, carving a pipe at Pipestone National Monument, 1978

ment warehouses. . . . Today the reservation Indian has neither the freedom, the capacity, nor oftentimes the desire to create or control his own economic life"); *freedom* ("The first and greatest love of the American Indian was his freedom"); *the God of nations* ("A weak and hypocritical Christianity will make the red man of today what his ancestors never were – an atheist"); *a good name among nations* ("No race of men has been more unjustly misrepresented by popular historians. . . . They have a right to ask that their children know the history of their fathers"); and *an assured status* ("With the whole of his social, economic, and political life and organization taken from him, with his relations to things, persons, and groups completely broken, who today . . . is the Indian?").

Each of the rights identified by Parker was a principal theme of Indian social and political activism in Minnesota in the twentieth century, an activism that has been furthered by Indians and Indian communities in different ways. Indian writers and artists have contributed to the vitality of contemporary Indian culture in unprecedented numbers. Indian religious and ceremonial practices, many of which were not protected by federal law until the American Indian Religious Freedom Act of 1978, have been revived in Indian communities. Many Christian churches have formed ecumenical connections with Indian religions and have come to see Indian spirituality as one of the cultural and religious treasures of the world, with Indian Episcopal and Catholic churches serving as a significant bridge between the traditions. Indians have challenged historians, as well as the educators who select the textbooks and curricula of Minnesota's public schools, to tell the stories of American history truthfully. Some have also demanded that racist images of American Indians be eliminated as trademarks identifying sports teams and commercial products.[70]

The Dakota Conflict of 1862 – the "Sioux Uprising" – was the historical event that Minnesota Indians believed most needed truthful retelling. As the 125th anniversary of the conflict approached in 1987, members of the Dakota communities called for a year of reconciliation; some groups requested formal apologies from institutions that they charged with perpetuating division and hostility between Indians and non-Indians in the state. For many of the Dakota, misrepresentation of the 1862 conflict and its aftermath was symbolized by the years of disrespect that had been shown to the remains of Little Crow, the Dakota leader in that war. His scalp had been among the first to be turned in to the state for a bounty payment in 1863, after he was killed while picking raspberries with his son in the Big Woods near Hutchinson. By 1896 Little Crow's skull, scalp, and arm bones were placed together on exhibit in the museum of the Minnesota Historical Society. After protests from the family of Little Crow, the society eventually removed the remains of the Dakota leader from display in September 1915 and placed them in a vault. Little Crow biographer Gary Clayton Anderson noted: "As the frontier closed and Minnesota entered a new era, the curiosities became an embarrassment." In 1971 the physical remains of Little Crow were finally returned to his family for burial in Flandreau, South Dakota, where descendants of the Dakota leader were living.[71]

In 1924, when he surveyed the difficulties facing Indian people, Secretary of the Interior Work said, "Certainly, if real progress is to be made, it must come through an aroused public interest."[72] But this prediction about arousing the public interest was misplaced: In the twentieth century, it was American Indians who organized to represent and protect their interests; specifically, in Minnesota, it was the aggressive actions of tribal governments. No condition or state of being could have demanded more from a people's leaders. Hampered since the beginning of the century with significant external challenges to their legitimacy and with intense internal factionalism, tribal governments have fought desperately to represent Indian people and to develop the structure and resources to meet their needs.

Mike Oker, Dakota/Ojibway flute maker and sculptor, and Robert Rose-Bear, Ojibway pipe maker and pipestone carver, Minneapolis, 1978

Throughout the first half of the twentieth century, the sovereignty and unique legal status of modern tribal governments were continually threatened by federal and state government institutions. Especially damaging was the incompetence and irresponsibility of an apathetic federal government, whose failures led policy makers repeatedly to propose the abandonment of the trustee relationship with Indian tribes. Ultimately, the faith of American Indians in the honor of words spoken and agreements made according to the treaty provisions of the U.S. Constitution carried the concept of tribal sovereignty through the federal courts and Congress. In the course of this struggle the Indians also strengthened, however inadvertently, every American's faith in the Constitution.

Anthropologist Ward Hunt Goodenough remarked that economic depression is not the only promoter of revolution among peoples. "It would be more accurate to say that revolutionary movements have their roots in human frustration, in the feeling that one's major wants for oneself, whatever they may be, are unfulfilled and without any prospect of fulfillment under existing circumstances. . . . The frustrations arising out of compromised integrity or that accompany feelings of personal worthlessness also carry great revolutionary potential." The "symbolic confrontation" of

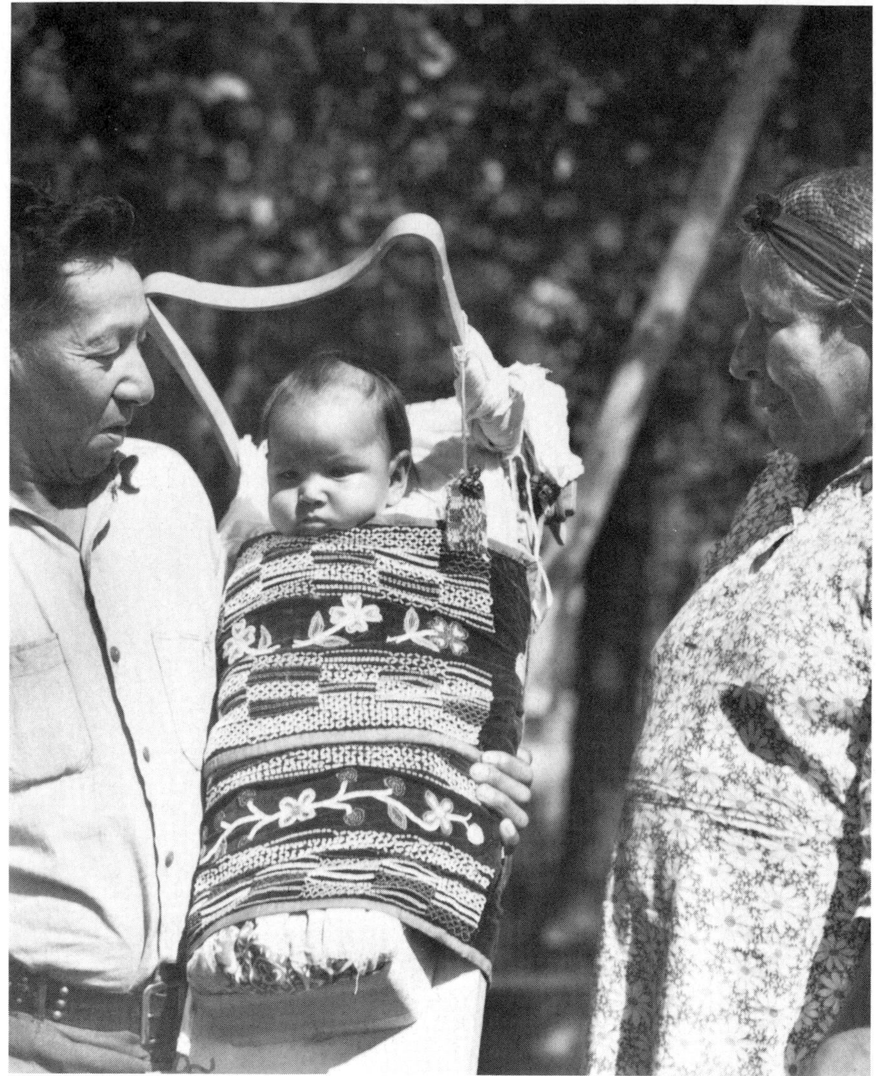

Gerald Wayne Chicog (four months old) with his grandparents at Nett Lake Reservation, 1946. His Indian name is Was sēgi sek (Lightning Sky).

AIM and other organizations with the historical and contemporary American treatment of the Indian was both the result of and a catalyst for a major social revolution among Indians. Nationwide, Indians also saw the creation of organizations like the National Indian Education Association and experienced the benefits of their effective lobbying for legislation. Tribal governments, especially in the West, established colleges that received accreditation. In Minnesota, tribal governments founded successful elementary and secondary schools and business enterprises.[73]

Through the 1970s, the collective experience of American Indians was being transformed. There was a growing sense of pride in being Indian, and there was also something in the air suggesting that nothing was ever going to be quite the same again. Among the Ojibway, the changing of the seasons from winter to spring is traditionally heralded by the arrival of the first crow as the sign that winter is over. "When an Indian sees the crow," Joseph Gilfillan wrote in 1897, "he knows that he has survived the starving time, winter, and that he will live; for he can always find abundant food during the spring and summer and fall months."[74] Sometime in the years after 1960, the first crow arrived among Minnesota Indians. Something in the air says that winter is over. Indians have survived, and there is a great deal of work to do.

NOTES

1. "Indian Vanishing Due to Pampering," *Minneapolis Journal*, Jan. 20, 1916, p. 12 (quotation).

2. Roy W. Meyer, *History of the Santee Sioux: United States Indian Policy on Trial* (1967; reprint, Lincoln: University of Nebraska Press, 1980), 133–54; William W. Folwell, *A History of Minnesota*, rev. ed., vol. 1 (St. Paul: Minnesota Historical Society, 1969), 197–98; Elizabeth Ebbott for the League of Women Voters of Minnesota, *Indians in Minnesota*, 4th ed. (Minneapolis: University of Minnesota Press, 1985), 20–22, 31–32.

3. Ebbott, *Indians in Minnesota*, 40, 24–31.

4. Frederick E. Hoxie, *A Final Promise: The Campaign to Assimilate the Indians, 1880–1920* (Lincoln: University of Nebraska Press, 1984), 15.

5. Folwell, *History of Minnesota*, vol. 4, 219–26 (quotation on 221); *United States Statutes at Large* 25:642–6 (quotations on 642, 644).

6. J[oseph] A. Gilfillan, "The Minnesota Trouble," in *Proceedings of the Sixteenth Annual Meeting of the Lake Mohonk Conference of Friends of the Indian* (Mohonk Lake, N.Y.: The Conference, 1898), 18–27 (quotation on 20). See also David L. Beaulieu, "Curly Hair and Big Feet: Physical Anthropology and the Implementation of Land Allotment on the White Earth Chippewa Reservation," *American Indian Quarterly* 8 (Fall 1984): 281–314.

7. *United States Statutes at Large* 32(1):275; 33(1):204, 359; 34(1):353 (quotation), 1034; Folwell, *History of Minnesota*, vol. 4, 266–67.

8. Louise Erdrich and Michael Dorris, "Who Owns the Land?" *New York Times Magazine*, Sept. 4, 1988, p. 35 (quotation); U.S. Congress, House, *Report in the Matter of the Investigation of the White Earth Reservation*, 62d Cong., 3d sess., 1913, H. Rep. 1336, Serial 6336, 1:v (quotation) – this publication is sometimes known as the Graham Report for James M. Graham, chairman of the House committee responsible for the investigation; Folwell, *History of Minnesota*, vol. 4, 241n 42n.

9. C[harles] C. Daniels, "Memorandum for the Attorney General Relative to White Earth Indian Matters as Affected by Politics and the Ramifications of the Business of Those Whose Financial Interests May Be Antagonistic to the Government," Dec. 20, 1913, Records of the Office of Indian Affairs, Record Group 75, National Archives – photocopy in author's possession; Warren K. Moorehead, "The Lesson of White Earth," in *Report of the Thirtieth Annual Lake Mohonk Conference of Friends of the Indian and Other Dependent Peoples* (Mohonk Lake, N.Y.: The Conference, 1912), 53, 54 (quotations); Folwell, *History of Minnesota*, vol. 4, 288–90; Beaulieu, "Curly Hair and Big Feet," 294–95.

10. Folwell, *History of Minnesota*, vol. 4, 297; Erwin F. Mittelholtz, *Historical Review of the Red Lake Indian Reservation* (Bemidji: General Council of the Red Lake Band of Chippewa Indians and Beltrami County Historical Society, 1957), 83–85.

11. University of Minnesota, Center for Continuation Study, *Proceedings of the Conference on Indian Rights and Resources* (Minneapolis: University of Minnesota, 1953), v, 105 (quotation); Marion E. Gridley, ed. and comp., *Indians of Today* (Chicago: [Millar Publishing Company], 1947), 41.

12. U.S. Congress, House, *Investigation of the White Earth Reservation*, xix, xx.

13. U.S. Congress, House, Committee on Indian Affairs, *Classification of the Chippewa Indians of Minnesota: Hearings before the Subcommittee of the Committee on Indian Affairs . . . on H.R. 461* (Washington, D.C.: Government Printing Office, 1928), 24–26 (quotations on 24); "Chief Madison, Former Indian Lobbyist, Dies," *Minneapolis Morning Tribune*, Dec. 11, 1959, p. 26.

14. Here and below, see George C. Peake, "The Ojibwas Used Firearms in Their Many Skirmishes," *American Indian*, November 1928, p. 13 (quotations); *Twenty-second Annual Report of the Educational Home* (Philadelphia: The Home, 1894), 36–39 – photocopy in author's possession; Marion E. Gridley, ed. and comp., *Indians of Today* (Chicago, 1936), 97.

15. Jennings C. Wise, *The Red Man in the New World Drama: A Politico-Legal Study with a Pageantry of American Indian History*, edited and revised by Vine Deloria, Jr. (New York: Macmillan Company, 1971), 320 (quotation); Duane Kendall Hale, "Hero Development in the 20th Century by White Historians: American Indians in World War I" (Paper presented at National Indian Education Conference, Nov. 20, 1982), 4, 14–15, 10 – photocopy in author's possession; "Old Warrior Returns to France to Find His Father's Grave" and "Mission Accomplished" – both in Oliver Towne column, *St. Paul Dispatch*, Nov. 11, 1981, p. 2B, and Feb. 2, 1982, p. 12A; Dorothy Lewis, " 'Last Warrior' Son Honors Father," *St. Paul Dispatch*, May 28, 1982, p. 1-2A.

16. Here and below, see *Twenty-second Annual Report of the Educational Home*, 37, 39; Robert Tholkes, "Chief Bender – The Early Years" (quotations), copy of article in author's possession; J. G. Taylor Spink, two-part column about Bender published in *Sporting News*, Dec. 31, 1942, and Jan. 7, 1943, in author's possession. See also *Dictionary of American Biography*, s.v. "Bender, Charles Albert ('Chief')."

17. Paulette Fairbanks Molin, " 'Training the Hand, the Head, and the Heart': Indian Education at Hampton Institute," *Minnesota History* 51 (Fall 1988): 90, 94–98; "Mrs. Henry Roe Cloud, American Mother of 1950," *Washington Bulletin* (National Congress of American Indians), June–July 1950, p. 1-3; Hazel W. Hertzberg, *The Search for an American Indian Identity: Modern Pan-Indian Movements* (Syracuse, N.Y.: Syracuse University Press, 1971), 47–48.

18. "Higher Education," *The Tomahawk* (White Earth Indian Reservation), Aug. 15, 1918, p. 1.

19. Institute for Government Research [Brookings Institution], *The Problem of Indian Administration: Report of a Survey Made at the Request of Honorable Hubert Work, Secretary of the Interior, and Submitted to Him, February 21, 1928*, Studies in Administration (Baltimore: Johns Hopkins Press, 1928), 727, 671 (quotation). This publication is called the Meriam Report for Lewis Meriam, the technical director of the survey staff.

20. Institute for Government Research, *Problem of Indian Administration*, 671–72 (quotation on 672).

21. "Indian Convention Is Invited to University," *Minneapolis Journal*, May 28, 1919, p. 16; "Annual Convention," *American Indian Magazine* (Society of American Indians), Fall 1919, p. 153.

22. "Indians Will Meet Here on Anniversary of Day Whites Began Scalping," *Minneapolis Journal*, Sept. 28, 1919, General News section, 18. The newspaper was wrong about the date of the first white hunting parties, which were formed in October 1863; see Walter N. Trenerry, "The Shooting of Little Crow: Heroism or Murder?" *Minnesota History* 38 (September 1962): 152–53. For a discussion of the convention and its slogan, "American Citizenship for the Indians," see Hertzberg, *Search for American Indian Identity*, 184–88.

23. "Indians Will Meet Here," *Minneapolis Journal*.

24. "Indian, Born in Tepee, Revisits Minnesota as College Teacher," *Minneapolis Journal*, Sept. 28, 1919, General News section, 1 (quotation); "Annual Convention," *American Indian Magazine*, 146–47, 150 (quotations on 146, 147, 150).

25. "Annual Convention," *American Indian Magazine*, 153.

26. "Annual Convention," *American Indian Magazine*, 176.

27. "Indians Propose Legal War on U.S. to Escape Bonds of Ward System," *Minneapolis Journal*, Oct. 4, 1919, p. 1; "Indians Organize to Aid Tribesmen," *Minneapolis Journal*, Oct. 24, 1919, p. 33 (quotation); "Indians of City Elect Officers," *Minneapolis Journal*, Nov. 7, 1919, p. 24; "200 Indians Plan to Assist Tribesmen," *Minneapolis Journal*, Nov. 20, 1919, p. 8 (quotation); Daniel F. Littlefield, Jr., and James W. Parins, *A Biobibliography of Native American Writers, 1772–1924*, Native American Bibliography Series, no. 2 (Metuchen, N.J.: Scarecrow Press, 1981), 211, 230, 246; 1919 Minneapolis City Directory, 241, 271, 782; "Indians to Present Songs and Dances," *Minneapolis Journal*, June 4, 1920, p. 28 (quotation); "Indian Fete Visitors Will Discuss Pageant," *Minneapolis Journal*, June 13, 1920, City Life section, 7; "Moonlight Pageant of Indians Planned," *Minneapolis Journal*, July 25, 1920, General News section, 9.

28. Hertzberg, *Search for American Indian Identity*, 59, 177 (quotation), 197–200.

29. "The Society of North American Indians," *The Tomahawk*, Jan. 17, 1918, p. 1.

30. Hertzberg, *Search for American Indian Identity*, 207–8, 289–90.

31. Edward H. Spicer, "Indigenismo in the United States: 1870–1960," *América Indígena* 24 (October 1966): 356 (quotation), 357; D'Arcy McNickle, *Indian Man: A Life of Oliver La Farge* (Bloomington: Indiana University Press, 1971), 50–59, 89–90.

32. Hertzberg, *Search for American Indian Identity*, 48; Arthur C. Parker, "The Social Elements of the Indian Problem," *American Journal of Sociology* 22 (July 1916): 263 (quotations); "Indian Citizenship," Office of Indian Affairs Bulletin 20 (1922), in author's possession; Ebbott, *Indians in Minnesota*, 267–68.

33. Hale, "Hero Development," 2, 3–4 (quotations).

34. Ebbott, *Indians in Minnesota*, 220; Vine Deloria, Jr., ed., *American Indian Policy in the Twentieth Century* (Norman: University of Oklahoma Press, 1985), 105–16.

35. Here and below, G. E. E. Lindquist, *Indians of Minnesota: A Survey of Social and Religious Conditions among Tribes in Transition* (New York: Division of Home Missions, National Council of Churches of Christ in the U.S.A., 1952), 10–11, 28–29.

36. "A Booklet by American Indians, Incorporated" (Issued in cooperation with Minnesota Governor's Human Rights Commission, 1957), pamphlet available at the Minnesota Historical Society (MHS).

37. Pauline Burnette, "Relocation, Termination Mark Indian Life in the 1950's," *The Circle* (Minneapolis American Indian Center), March 1989, p. 15; "Chief Madison, Former Indian Lobbyist, Dies," p. 26; "News and Comments," *Minnesota History* 25 (September 1944): 304. Issues of the *New Tomahawk* are available at MHS.

38. Hubert Work, *Indian Policies: Comments on the Resolutions of the Advisory Council on Indian Affairs*, U.S. Department of the Interior (Washington, D.C.: Government Printing Office, 1924), 2.

39. Spicer, "Indigenismo," 358 (quotations), 359.

40. Work, *Indian Policies*, iv, v; Gridley, *Indians of Today* (1947), 39–40; Inter-County Leader, *Outline for Biography of a Chippewa Indian Who Became a Catholic Priest: Rev. Philip Gordon, LL.D.: "Ti-Bish-Ko-Gi-Jik"* ([Frederic, Wis., 1944]), 25.

41. Work, *Indian Policies*, iv, 1–9 (quotations on v, 1, 2).

42. Work, *Indian Policies*, 11.

43. Here and below, Minnesota, Commission on Indian Affairs, *Report* ([St. Paul, 1927]), [1]-4 (quotations on 3, 4).

44. Blanche L. La Du, "What Minnesota Is Doing for the Indians," in National Conference of Social Work, *Proceedings of the National Conference of Social Work*, 59th annual sess., Minneapolis, June 14–20, 1931 (Chicago: University of Chicago Press, 1931), 626–36.

45. Lewis Meriam, "Statement of the Problem," in National Conference of Social Work, *Proceedings*, 613 (quotations); W. Carson Ryan, Jr., "Cooperation in Indian Education," in National Conference of Social Work, *Proceedings*, 617–18 (quotations).

46. Ruth Muskrat Bronson, "The Indians' Attitude toward Cooperation," in National Conference of Social Work, *Proceedings*, 637–40 (quotation on 638–40).

47. Wise, *Red Man*, 357–58; Ebbott, *Indians in Minnesota*, 12.

48. Minnesota Chippewa Tribe, *Minnesota Chippewa Tribal Government: Student Handbook* (Cass Lake: The Tribe, 1978), 85–90; Ebbott, *Indians in Minnesota*, 54–55.

49. Wise, *Red Man*, 359–61; Ebbott, *Indians in Minnesota*, 53.

50. Here and below, see John Collier, "The Indian in a Wartime Nation," *Annals of the American Academy of Political and Social Science* 223 (September 1942): 34, 35.

51. Felix S. Cohen, *Handbook of Federal Indian Law*, 1982 ed. (Charlottesville, Va.: Michie Company, 1982), 152–53, 169, 175–80; Burnette, "Relocation, Termination Mark Indian Life," 15.

52. Wise, *Red Man*, 372–73; Gridley, ed. and comp., *Indians of Today* (1947), 77.

53. "Great Membership Gains Highlight 1951 Convention," *Washington Bulletin*, June–July 1951, p. 1, 5 (quotation); Wise, *Red Man*, 373–74.

54. "Great Membership Gains," 1; Minnesota, Governor's Interracial Commission, *The Indian in Minnesota: A Report to Governor Luther W. Youngdahl of Minnesota by the Governor's Interracial Commission* (St. Paul?, 1947), [3]-[4].

55. Robert Esbjornson, *A Christian in Politics: Luther W. Youngdahl: A Story of a Christian's Faith at Work in a Modern World* (Minneapolis: T. S. Denison and Co., 1955), 184–85 (quotation on 185).

56. Ebbott, *Indians in Minnesota*, 163.

57. Minnesota, Legislative Research Committee, *Minnesota Indians: Research Report Pursuant to Proposal No. 28 . . .* ([St. Paul]: The Committee, 1950), 116–18; "Indian Edition" of *Minnesota Welfare* (Minnesota State Division of Social Welfare) 5 (April 1950): 1.

58. "Indians – Minnesota Moves Ahead," *Minnesota Welfare* 5 (May 1950): 6–13 (quotations on 7, 9).

59. Wise, *Red Man*, 363–68; University of Minnesota, Center for Continuation Study, *Proceedings of the Conference on Indian Rights and Resources*, 1, 3, 16 (quotations on 3, 16).

60. Here and below, see Carl Tjerandsen, *Education for Citizenship: A Foundation's Experience* (Santa Cruz, Calif.: Emil Schwarzhaupt Foundation, 1980), 64–67 (quotation on 64–65). The registration list for the 1961 Chicago conference included the following names from Minnesota: Mrs. Pearl Blue, Norman R. Campbell, Mrs. Chris Cavender, Amos A. Owen, Mrs. Elsie Peters, and Mrs. Peter Warhol from the Dakota tribe; Roger A. Jourdain (member of the drafting committee that developed the Declaration of Indian Purpose), Andrew L. Sigana, and Louis F. Stately from the Red Lake band of Ojibway Indians; Charles Ackley, George B. Artishon, Mr. and Mrs. Charles Belgarde, Mrs. Frances Charette, Pearl and Vonda Dauphinais, Mrs. Rose Foss, Mrs. C. A. Jourdain, and Larry Martin, also from

the Ojibway tribe; and Peter La Point and Josephine White Eagle from the Winnebago tribe. See *The Voice of the American Indian: Declaration of Indian Purpose* (Issued by the American Indian Chicago Conference, University of Chicago, June 13-20, 1961), 41-49.

61. Minnesota, Governor's Human Rights Commission, *State-wide Conference on Indian Affairs*, June 1, 1956, *Proceedings of the Second Statewide Conference on Indian Affairs*, May 31-June 1, 1957, *Summary of Proceedings: Third Governor's Statewide Indian Conference*, Sept. 11-12, 1959 (all [St. Paul]: The Commission), and *A Five Year Plan for Economic Improvement of Minnesota Indians* ([St. Paul]: The Commission, 1961), [i], 2-3, [15] (quotations on [i], 2-3).

62. Ebbott, *Indians in Minnesota*, 66-67.

63. Here and below, see Wise, *Red Man*, 375-76.

64. Wise, *Red Man*, 376-77; *AIU*, pamphlet issued by American Indians-United, Chicago, and "Conference of American Indians United," typescript proceedings of conference held in San Francisco, October 1969, both in Church Federation of Greater Chicago papers, Chicago Historical Society. Others from Minneapolis included Margaret Smith, Chippewa Tribal Council; Peggy Bellecourt, Indian Citizens' Community Center; Mary Jane Wilson, Indian Women's League; Diane Pike, Indian American Youth Center; William Craig, American Indian Students Association, University of Minnesota, and Indian Advisory Committee, Minneapolis Public Schools; Delores Snook, Department of American Indian Studies, University of Minnesota; Angeline Clark, Project Stairs; and John Red Horse, Indian Upward Bound.

65. William H. McClendon, "The Black Scholar Interviews: Dennis Banks," *Black Scholar* 7 (June 1976): 29-36.

66. Gerald Vizenor, *Tribal Scenes and Ceremonies* (Minneapolis: Nodin Press, 1976), 51-55 (quotation on 52). See also Vine Deloria, Jr., *Behind the Trail of Broken Treaties: An Indian Declaration of Independence* (New York: Dell Publishing Co., 1974).

67. *Indian Education, 1969*, Hearings before the Subcommittee on Indian Education of the Committee on Labor and Public Welfare, U.S. Senate (Washington, D.C.: U.S. Government Printing Office, 1969), part 1, iii; "Registrant List, First National Indian Education Conference" (University of Minnesota, Minneapolis, Nov. 20-21, 1969), in author's possession; *Focus: Indian Education* (Minnesota Department of Education, Indian Education Section, St. Paul), Jan. 31, 1971, May-June, 1971, Oct. 30, 1971, all p. 1; Ebbott, *Indians in Minnesota*, 57.

68. David Beaulieu, "American Indian Higher Education: The Role of Higher Education in Minority Communities," *Briefing* (Commission on Institutions of Higher Education), July 1987, p. 1.

69. Here and below, see Parker, "Social Elements of the Indian Problem," 258-63 (quotations on 258-59, 260, 261, 263).

70. Ebbott, *Indians in Minnesota*, 50-51.

71. David Beaulieu, "The Fate of Little Crow, 1863-1970" (1970), typescript available at MHS, part 4, p. 2-7, 13-14; "Skull Exhibit Banished," *Minneapolis Journal*, Sept. 8, 1915, p. 11; Gary Clayton Anderson, *Little Crow: Spokesman for the Sioux* (St. Paul: Minnesota Historical Society Press, 1986), 181 (quotation). Heirs of Little Crow also came to the Twin Cities in 1916 in an attempt to recover $1,500 that the Dakota leader had deposited in a St. Paul bank in 1860. According to newspaper accounts, these family members included Jane Williams, Little Crow's daughter; Rebecca Quinn, "a brighteyed graduate of Carlisle," Williams's daughter; and Hannah Rede[a]rth, also a daughter of Little Crow, and her two sons. See "Five Heirs of Little Crow Meet Here . . . ," *Minneapolis Tribune*, Dec. 6, 1916, p. 1 (quotation), and "Little Crow Heirs Ask Chief's $1,500," *St. Paul Pioneer Press*, Dec. 7, 1916, p. 14.

72. Work, *Indian Policies*, iv.

73. Ward Hunt Goodenough, *Cooperation in Change: An Anthropological Approach to Community Development* (New York: Russell Sage Foundation, 1963), 287.

74. Joseph A. Gilfillan, "The Ojibways in Minnesota," *Collections of the Minnesota Historical Society* 9 (St. Paul: The Society, 1901), 70.

MARJORIE BINGHAM

Keeping at It: Minnesota Women

At the beginning of the twentieth century, few Minnesota women had achieved national recognition. The state did not have a leader in social work like Illinois's Jane Addams or a suffrage campaigner like Iowa's Carrie Chapman Catt or a major writer like Nebraska's Willa Cather. Neither was Minnesota a leader in suffrage: fifteen states preceded it in granting women the vote. Yet by 1985 Minnesota would be called a "kind of feminist laboratory" in a *Ms.* magazine article entitled "From Minnesota: Recipe for Homemade Revolution."[1]

The "revolution" of the 1980s, when Minnesota took the lead in such programs as battered women's shelters and comparable worth, was the culmination of a long process of network-building by women. If there was one quality that distinguished Minnesota women during the twentieth century, it was this emphasis on group involvement. The Local Council of Women of Minneapolis in 1902 was, according to observers, "one of the strongest associations of the kind in the United States . . . composed of nearly one hundred different organizations in the city."[2] By 1987, the Minnesota Women's Consortium, with its 168 member organizations, was a national model for women's alliances. Why did Minnesota have so many strong women's organizations and so few nationally recognized women?

Four factors contributed to this situation. Two strong religions in the state, the Roman Catholic and Lutheran, stressed roles of motherhood and subordinate service in the church. Minnesota's higher-education system, more than some other states, had a low percentage of women faculty members, and the state lost talented educators. The state's radical reform tradition, though generally supporting women's rights, stressed group activity and not individual visibility. Lastly, Scandinavian immigrants brought with them a belief in the cooperative movement as a way of surviving and creating change. Minnesota women, therefore, often saw reform as a group process, and showed remarkable success in holding groups together for cohesive action.[3]

Organizing for Change: 1900–17

According to the prevailing social mores of the nineteenth century, a woman's main responsibility was to be a good wife and mother in the "separate sphere" of the home. As one Minnesota antisuffrage tract put it, "A racial instinct lies beneath the general division of duty between child-rearing and home-making on the one hand [for women], and the management of business and government on the other [for men]."[4] This outlook was challenged in the nineteenth century by reformers who stressed the need for equity in pay, education, suffrage, and property rights. In Minnesota, where working conditions were particularly diverse, the spheres of home and business so often intertwined that the distinctions had little reality.

Maude Kegg, an Ojibway child growing up around Rice Lake, viewed women's sphere as one of strong physical labor and precise knowledge of nature. She described how she and her grandmother would fish all day and carry the fish to market to sell. They moved from fishing to ricing to garden areas, to spring maple sugaring, and berry picking. "That's how they made their living, selling berries and then buying lard, flour and sugar . . . whatever they need. That's the way the Indians made their living, always working on their own. After we got through picking berries, we'd go home and the garden would be almost ready then." Maude Kegg characterized her grandmother's generation by saying, "Those ladies were such hard workers."[5]

The frontier still existed in early-twentieth-century Minnesota, particularly in the north. Minnesota still had homestead land available; widows and single women, as well as families, established claims. Conditions could be primitive; farmers near Bigfork about 1902 told the tale of how sisters Dena and Mayme Luiten drove off a bear with a homemade rolling pin. In more settled areas like rural Edina, a farm woman in 1900 could expect to buy food at the store; yet her gardening, canning, butter-making, and berry picking might provide the cash margin between keeping the farm and losing it.[6]

For many immigrant women who came to Minnesota, few divisions existed between business and home. Immigrant women ran dairies, did laundry, and even culled logs from the Mississippi to support their families. A high proportion ran boardinghouses – for example, 30 percent of the Italian families in St. Paul in 1917.[7] On the iron ranges, where men worked in the mines around the clock, a boardinghouse keeper had an especially difficult time. One boarder described sleeping over the kitchen of her Finnish landlady while "directly under my room, Hanna baked bread and cake, rattled pans, and at frequent intervals brewed and drank unnumbered cups of vile strong coffee. . . . When Hanna slept, I never knew." Hard work in America had a particular irony for Finnish women, since they lost their right to vote by immigrating.[8]

It was not just immigrant women who did not fit the nineteenth-century stereotype of women in the home, men in business. In 1900, Min-

Maude Kegg making twine from the inner bark of basswood at Mille Lacs, 1947

nesota led all states in the number of young women working away from home. In Minneapolis, 28.1 percent were "breadwinners." In St. Paul the figure was 29.6 percent. As the Twin Cities grew into a major manufacturing center, especially in textiles, an "endless stream of young girls" entered its labor force.[9] Their wages were often so low that researchers wondered how they survived. Some lived with their families. But in Minneapolis more than half of the female labor force – nine thousand women – lived away from home.[10] Mrs. Perry Starkweather, the state's assistant commissioner of labor, described their living conditions:

> Usually, two, three and sometimes four, girls earning $5.00, $6.00 or $7.00 a week, working usually at the same place, rent a room together. For this they pay from $9.00 to $12.00 per month. . . . The girls pool a common purse for food, and by dint of strict economy they frequently bring expenses down so that for four girls it amounts to $2.00 to $2.50 per week. . . . The evening meal is usually . . . purchased on the way home from work and is apt to consist of a bit of meat, a loaf of bread, cakes and pies from the nearest bakery. . . . If she pays $1.00 to $1.50 for rent, allows $1.00 for lunches, puts $2.50 into the common purse for food at home and walks to and from her work, she has from 50¢ to $1.00 or $2.00 left for clothing. . . . There is as a rule no provision for sickness. . . . As for amusements, they are almost entirely lacking.[11]

Besides supporting themselves, some young women sent funds back to help their families. A Danish woman farming near Askov remembered, "Our girls, like so many others, went out to work and they sent home all they could spare from their small wages. That helped a great deal during the difficult times we had. The income was small and we were many to be fed and clothed."[12] Young women who lived at home also contributed to the family income. Some would later speak bitterly of having to leave school and be "buried in a factory" to give their brothers a chance to finish high school and college.[13]

The working and living conditions for domestic servants, of which there were many in 1900, were somewhat better. The Swedish maids living on the top floors of mansions in Kenwood in Minneapolis or on Summit Avenue in St. Paul could at least expect proper food, subsidized clothing, and clean living conditions. But the upstairs rooms were often drafty in winter and hot in summer. The endless round of washing, ironing, and cooking was only bearable, as one Swedish maid put it, "if you only can happen to find decent folks to work for" and have "good humor . . . wherever you go." For some young women the job security was not worth the subservience of being at the beck and call of a family. A factory inspector in 1904, dismayed at the bloody floors of the slaughterhouse where some women worked, asked the foreman what "would induce these girls to turn away from domestic employment to the sickening sights, disgusting odors and small compensation of packing house employment?" He replied, "But you see it's the freedom that the girls have in the evening."[14]

Few professional opportunities for women existed, except in teaching and nursing. Because it seemed like an extension of a woman's child-rearing role, teaching was considered "respectable" for unmarried middle-class women. In actuality, teachers in the one-room schoolhouses of Minnesota or in the impoverished sections of Minneapolis had to do more than child care. Rural teachers scrubbed floors, built fires, and chopped wood. One recalled that she "faced blizzards, waded through deep snows to ice-cold schoolhouses where I built my own fires, and while the fire was getting started and the room warming up a bit before the children arrived, I danced jigs to keep my blood from congealing." Edna I. Murphy, school supervisor for Itasca County, got to one school by duckboat on a nearly frozen lake, then walked along a narrow forest path, one time trailed by wolves.[15]

Teaching often took women to remote areas or ethnic communities that were far different from their middle-class homes. There, they learned about the poverty of other classes and ethnic groups. Watching her students break up peppermint sticks to take part home to brothers and sisters, one teacher "had to swallow hard" to keep the tears from coming. Two of Minnesota's first women legislators, Mabeth Hurd Paige and Hannah Kempfer, were former schoolteachers who retained a lifelong interest in child welfare and other social reforms.[16]

Medicine also brought women into contact with social causes. Though there were few women doctors in Minnesota at the turn of the century, they had considerable impact. Dr. Martha G. Ripley helped found Maternity Hospital in Minneapolis to provide health care for both wed and unwed mothers; she and Dr. Ethel Hurd were also early leaders in the Minnesota suffrage movement.[17] But most women in the medical profession were nurses. Their training was difficult and their hours long. A

Legislators Hannah Kempfer and Mabeth Hurd Paige in the Minnesota House of Representatives, 1941

brochure describing life at the Swedish Hospital School of Nursing in Minneapolis warned, "All nurses are required to be sober, honest, truthful, trustworthy, punctual, quiet, orderly, cleanly, neat, patient, kind, cheerful, and obedient to the rules. Hours of duty, day nurses are from 7 A.M. to 7 P.M.; night nurses 7 P.M. to 7:30 A.M. Leisure hours, when possible, one hour every day; one afternoon a week, and half of Sundays."[18]

Minnesota became a national leader in the professionalization of nursing, in 1907 joining two other states in establishing minimum standards for registered nurses. But hospitals often hired few professional nurses, relying instead on students. As one woman put it, a student on probation was "a glorified cleaning lady and chorewoman," while later she might be the sole ward nurse, with considerable responsibility.[19]

With such long hours and low pay, it is not surprising that some women chose not to be part of the labor force. For middle-class and upper-class women who depended primarily on their husbands' or fathers' incomes, the theory of "separate spheres" might have seemed plausible. Suffrage workers at the turn of the century reported that in various towns they found women in a "lethargic state of mind" or "very unenlightened" about changing their conditions. Yet even in middle-class families women wanted more control of the family income and expanded responsibilities. In one middle-class black family, the mother asked to give up her maid in exchange for the maid's wages so she could have some discretionary income.[20] Other women quarreled, contrived, or cajoled to get some financial control. Because Minnesota was one of the "enlightened" western states to pass "woman laws," Minnesota women – unlike their southern sisters – could control their own wages and the property they brought into marriage. Widows could be guardians for their own children. But financial restrictions still existed. Courts generally held that property gained during marriage was the result of the husband's efforts.[21]

Minnesota novelist Frances Sterrett clearly depicted the dilemma of the middle-class woman contemplating marriage. Not to marry meant surviving on low wages. In one novel, a character stated that "Jane Austen was exactly right when she said unmarried women have a dreadful tendency to be poor." On the other hand, as another character found, "Marriage to me is a many-headed dragon. It eats up a girl's individuality, her ambitions, her talents."[22]

Yet married, middle-class women found ways to use their talents outside the home. Between the spheres of home and business lay a gray area of community involvement in religious, children's, and charitable causes that was seen as a legitimate part of "woman's sphere." Three major types of organizations acted to expand women's involvement in the community – the Woman's Christian Temperance Union (WCTU), women's clubs, and women's rights groups. Many women joined all three, but the groups' aims were not necessarily the same.

The WCTU was the largest women's group in the nineteenth century. Led nationally by Frances E. Willard, it fought not only for prohibition, but also for improvements in child welfare, women's working conditions, health, equal pay for equal work, and international peace. In 1881 women's suffrage became a part of the Minnesota WCTU's platform. The vote was needed, they thought, to obtain the reform measures – particularly prohibition – that men would not pass. The WCTU became both an aid and a liability to the suffrage movement. On the one hand, Minnesota suffrage organizers found a welcome at WCTU meetings. As one said, "I never failed to obtain a Suffrage signature from each one."[23] But the prohibition issue became linked to women's suffrage. Many suffragists believed that their major opposition came from liquor interests, led in the state legislature by Sen. W. W. Dunn, attorney for the Hamm Brewing Company of St. Paul. In the general atmosphere of the progressive movement, however, ties with the WCTU were of more benefit than harm, and often reassured those frightened by the radical image of feminists painted by suffrage foes.[24]

Another type of women's organization, largely middle class, was the women's club. These clubs, devoted to community betterment and self-improvement, became increasingly important from 1900 to 1930. At first they were seen as threats to the proper division of the sexes. In 1905 former president Grover Cleveland warned against women's clubs menacing "the integrity of our homes." Women ought to join "merely one [club]," added Edward Bok, editor of the *Ladies' Home Journal*, and "not place its interests, in importance, before the higher duties of the home." Bok and Cleveland would have been truly dismayed by Twin Cities women. For example, the group that founded the Woman's Club of Minneapolis in 1907 was already involved in libraries, art commissions, kindergarten associations, visiting nurses, the Red Cross, and church groups.[25]

Women picketing for prohibition in Madison, about 1917

Women's clubs often started with small projects and moved on to major endeavors that benefited the entire community. The first women's club in Minnesota, the Ladies' Floral Club of Austin, organized in 1869, followed this pattern. Despite its mild-sounding title, its underlying aim was "to make Austin a better place in which to live." Starting with a few flower shows and a traveling library in members' homes, the women eventually gathered 3,500 books that they helped turn into a town library. Then their interests expanded into child welfare and they helped obtain a rural nurse for the community.[26] What Austin women did was duplicated in towns and cities throughout the state. Women helped found the Minneapolis Institute of Arts, the Schubert Club, the Edyth Bush Theatre, and hotels run by the Woman's Christian Association of Minneapolis.

Often, upper-class club members used family connections to force through change, even against major opposition. One such case was the creation of the Chippewa National Forest. The Minnesota Federation of Women's Clubs, founded in 1894, protested indiscriminate logging on Minnesota Indian reservations between 1898 and 1901. By lobbying Congress and mobilizing public opinion the group got 225,000 acres around Cass and Leech lakes designated as a national forest, a feat that Gifford Pinchot, chief of the U.S. Forestry Bureau, said "would have been impossible" without their help. One historian concluded that Florence Bramhall, chair of the federation's forest reserve committee, used her social position to move congressmen to support the bill. Others used their social positions to support even more controversial activities. One group of well-off Twin Cities women, concerned that the poor had little access to birth control information, provided money for two doctors and a staff to operate an illegal birth-control clinic in St. Paul. They used their husbands' positions to scare off newspaper exposure.[27]

Other women's groups followed more traditional lines of service to their churches, synagogues, and communities. For example, the ladies' aid society of the Kviteseid Lutheran congregation of Milan offered to "stand the expenses" of installing a new church furnace. Box socials, bake sales, and craft displays were sure to follow. Ladies' aid societies and auxiliaries provided a "safety net" in a world without social security, health benefits, or sick leave. The minutes of the black Pilgrim Baptist Church Ladies Aid Society in St. Paul note small contributions made to a Mrs. Hawkins, "who is in destitute circumstances," and detail the creation of quilts to be given or sold for two Brothers of the church, who were "both very grateful to the Ladies Aid." Ladies' auxiliaries of veterans' organizations like the Grand Army of the Republic visited hospitals, supported veterans' homes, and aided the poor, like the "helpless" daughter of a veteran who, placed in the GAR home, expressed "her gratitude at having found a real House."[28] Such groups put their members in touch with economic and social problems and gave women a sense of contribution, action, and leadership.

Nuns took on various projects within the Roman Catholic and Episcopal churches. In the years before World War I, the Benedictines built schools and a hospital in the St. Cloud area; the Sisters of St. Francis helped establish St. Marys Hospital in Rochester. Episcopal Sister Annette Relf helped found St. Barnabas Hospital and the Sheltering Arms orphanage in Minneapolis. These activities fit the traditional missions of charity and religious education. But Sister Antonia McHugh wanted more. With the support of Archbishop John Ireland and his sister Ellen, she founded the College of St. Catherine in St. Paul to provide rigorous academic training to young Catholic women. Some of her order, the Sisters of St. Joseph of Carondelet, objected that the teaching nuns "would be tempted to pride if they held academic degrees." But Sister Antonia thought it "terrible to have a stagnant mind" and sent sisters off "with factory-like speed" to get their doctorates.[29] Sister Mary A. Molloy at Winona's College of St. Teresa also pushed for higher educational standards and announced that "the knell has struck for the finishing school" and "parlor courses." Minnesota became known as a leader in "providing full collegiate training for Catholic women."[30]

Women's rights began to gain serious consideration in Minnesota at the turn of the century. Not all supported suffrage, and it was a frequent debate topic in schools and clubs. Wanda Gág, later a noted artist and writer, wrote in her diary in 1910, "Last Monday we had Current Topics. I had an idea that Mr. Doom thought we were all suffragettes so I decided to take a subject for woman's suffrage. When he called on me I got up and talked of the English suffragettes, their riots and also about their going to jail with their knitting. . . . When I was done, he asked, 'Do you approve or disapprove?' I thought for a while and then with a laugh I said, 'Disapprove.' . . . He said, 'So you are not a suffragette?' and I said, 'No Sir!' He said, 'Good!' and gave me my mark. If I didn't get 100 that time I miss my guess."[31] Later, away from the pressure of male teachers, Gág would be more sympathetic to women's rights.

The minutes of women's clubs recorded numerous debates over women's rights. The St. Paul Thursday Club discussed the topic in 1912; the recording secretary editorialized in her notes that "the time when . . . half the people – the feminine half – was under[dev]eloped, crippled . . . is fast passing away." Other groups, notably the Woman's Club of Minneapolis, did not endorse suffrage, even after the Nineteenth Amendment passed Congress with support from two of the club's founders, Clara H. Ueland and Alice Ames Winter. The names of the wives of Minneapolis mill owners Pillsbury, Washburn, and Bell were prominent on antisuffrage flyers.[32]

The history of the women's suffrage movement in Minnesota has not been written, but several generalizations can be made about it. Until about 1914 it seems to have found support primarily among a circle of professional women led by the teacher Sarah Burger Stearns and the physician Martha Ripley, the latter a personal friend of Susan B. Anthony. In Hennepin County, its growth was impeded by competition between the Minnesota Woman Suffrage Association and the Equal Franchise League. In St. Paul, according to one observer, "misfortune always seemed to attend all attempts to maintain a suffrage club."[33]

Efforts were made almost yearly to introduce a bill for women's suffrage into the state legislature. In 1875, Minnesota women had gotten the right to vote in school board elections, presumably because male voters agreed they had an interest in their children's education. In 1898, women were allowed to vote for and serve on library boards. Yet on even "as harmless an amendment" as the library vote, one suffragist noted, 43,600 men cast ballots against the measure.[34]

Men like Ole Sageng and Ignatius Donnelly lobbied for taxpaying women to vote in municipal elections and on the issue of temperance. All bills were defeated, sometimes by margins as small as one or two votes. In 1909 one Minnesota woman said that "we would wake up some day and find the Turkish women voting before the Minnesotans" – a prophecy that came true when seventy-eight Turkish women voted in the election of 1910.[35] To influence the legislature, women held suffrage parades, arranged lectures by learned women like Frances Squire Potter of the University of Minnesota, and collected names on petitions at the state fair. In 1894 they got Theodore Roosevelt, Gen. Nelson Miles, and Archbishop John Ireland to sign the suffrage register, but nothing seemed to push the Minnesota state legislature into action.[36]

Still, there were signs of change. Under Carrie Chapman Catt's leadership, the National American Woman Suffrage Association began to focus less on state-by-state campaigns and more on a federal amendment. Over twenty thousand names appeared on a "Monster Petition" sent to Congress from Minnesota in 1910.[37] In 1914, when Clara Ueland became president of the Minnesota Woman Suffrage Association, the organization developed a new effectiveness. An excellent fund-raiser, Ueland increased dues and expanded membership. When others were reluctant to ask for funds, she held a huge lawn party and raised money herself. These funds helped pay for professional organizers to campaign throughout the state.

Perhaps Ueland's greatest talent was her ability, as wife of a prominent Norwegian-American judge, to play the role of the gracious upper-class woman, allaying fears of man-hating feminists.[38]

The Minnesota suffrage movement became more united. Hundreds of enrollment blanks were sent out and cities were canvassed for sympathizers. Traveling organizers Rene E. H. Stevens and Bertha B. Moller sent back reports of their progress. Even before Sinclair Lewis immortalized Sauk Centre in the novel *Main Street,* they found it full of gossip and "narrow people." In Faribault, 150 men and women attended a luncheon for legislators. The men furnished the club rooms and speakers, the women (of course) the refreshments. In Minneapolis, black women formed the Everywoman Suffrage Club, led by social reformer Millie Griswold Francis, who impressed Ueland as a *"star"* because "her spirit is a flame."[39]

Money came in to pay for traveling libraries on women's rights, for booths at county fairs, and for dolls dressed in the costumes of nations where women could already vote. But even those who sent in their checks sometimes debated with themselves. Moller wrote, "I am wondering whether I am a real loyal suffragist or not, as I find, after a severe mental tussle with myself, that I simply *can't* give up one single item of feminine vanity . . . in order to make the enclosed check a little larger."[40] Yet enough women did choose suffrage over new hats to make the organization more professional. Minnesota joined other states to put pressure on Congress and Pres. Woodrow Wilson for a suffrage amendment.

Congress finally passed the Nineteenth Amendment on June 4, 1919. When Minnesota's turn came to ratify, the legislature did so relatively easily – 120 to 6 in the house of representatives, 60 to 5 in the senate. Three thousand people turned up at the State Capitol and, as one woman put it, "we had a parade and a jollification." Two hundred fifty automobiles in the parade were decorated in yellow flowers; suffragists sang "The Battle Hymn of the Republic," with lyrics by suffragist Julia Ward Howe, served a chicken dinner to the state legislature, and then had a big sit-down banquet for themselves. The next day a suffragist wrote, "Yesterday [was] such a day to remember! It seems almost too good to be true that our cause has at last been crowned with success. We are used to defeat and know how to face it. But victory?"[41] That uncertain note would echo in women's minds after suffrage, after the war.

World War I: 1914–19

World War I had a divisive effect on women's political groups. Those who supported Jane Addams's Woman's Peace party or the Socialist Party of America found themselves under suspicion for their antiwar stands. The suffrage movement itself was split between Anna Shaw's group, which supported the war, and Alice Paul's National Woman's Party, which picketed the White House to protest sending soldiers overseas to "make the world safe for democracy" when the United States itself lacked a

Workers in the Liberty Loan Department of a Minneapolis bank wearing middy uniforms to encourage enlistments during World War I

democratic franchise.[42] Members of the Minnesota Woman Suffrage Association generally supported the war, though their opponents made attempts to link them to antiwar Socialists.[43]

World War I also brought widened opportunities. Jobs formerly closed to women now opened, ranging from street sprinklers to telegraph operators. Women's organizations used their networks to recruit nurses and defense workers. About a thousand nurses from Minnesota served in the war. Unlike some who had served during the Spanish-American War, World War I nurses were generally well received by male army doctors.[44] For many, the trip off to war was a major adventure. Letters home began cheerfully with descriptions of the sights; but as the war went on, they described the "jaw" wards full of patients with damaged faces, the shock wards, and the gangrene and mustard gas victims. Nevertheless, nurses' letters reflected a sense of increased professional opportunities and responsibility. One who wrote home about her duties concluded, "I will be in the operating next I suppose."[45]

Women served not only on the western front, but also in Greece, Poland, Siberia, and Turkey. They cut their hair because of lice and typhus; they shortened their skirts because of mud and filth. They came back knowing that they had undergone shelling and gunfire, that they had helped to save lives. They also came back to stress more professional training for future nurses.[46]

Back in Minnesota, women supported the war effort by volunteer work with the Red Cross, knitting sweaters and rolling bandages. Most women's clubs met on particular days to perform Red Cross work, though they may have grumbled some about the strict instructions from the Red Cross about what to knit, how to knit, and what colors to use – "no pinks" or "red checks" for French refugees. Minnesota women also raised money for war bonds by canvassing their neighborhoods and holding sales of crafts and baked goods. The YWCA started a Hostess House where military men could entertain families and friends, and when the flu epidemic hit in 1918, volunteers turned the house into a hospital.[47] Thousands of volunteer hours were put into war work, a figure not included in the official economic costs of the war. Minnesota women earned praise for having one of the best-organized and "well executed" volunteer systems in the country. An army engineer, impressed by the many thousands of "comfort kits" given to soldiers, admitted, "I am sure that their work will never be sufficiently understood or appreciated."[48]

Although women in other states performed similar services, what distinguished Minnesota women was their ability to continue their social reform agendas as part of their war work. Women who went out to canvass neighborhoods for savings bonds came in contact with social welfare problems – a crippled child left unattended all day, children sick from eating raw potatoes, or an old man unable to care for himself. These cases were referred to social workers or visiting nurses. To help married working women, the North East Neighborhood House set up a day-care center and started a "Little Mothers League" to teach siblings how to care for infants. When handing out Hoover Pledges to encourage housewives to save wheat and meat, volunteers also used the occasion to give nutrition tips. Sometimes the slogans for these campaigns got silly and shrill, as when Minnesotans were told to "Eat Onions to Finish the Fiendish Hun."[49] Patriotism and women's purity were often linked, giving war propaganda the tone of a moral crusade. The *Minneapolis Evening Tribune* headlined one story, "Safety Committee Bans Trysting Places in Minnehaha Park: Women's Auxiliary Appeals to Parents to Keep Daughters from Meeting Soldiers." At St. Olaf College, women signed pledges to join the food savers, help the Red Cross, and uphold "the highest standards of womanhood." The Minnesota WCTU not only sent two ambulances to France, but also "stereomotorgraphs showing temperance slides."[50]

The most controversial part of Minnesota women's activities during World War I was their role in the Americanization campaign of the Minnesota Commission of Public Safety. Concerned that Minnesota had a high percentage of foreign-born residents who opposed the war, the commission encouraged repression of ethnic values. Ethnic women, as well as men, became the victims of this campaign. A teacher in the St. Paul schools was dismissed for pro-German statements she had made in 1915; another in Wabasha County was forced to resign because pupils claimed she had praised Germany and the kaiser. Ethnic organizations that had encouraged equality between the sexes, like the Finnish Työvän Opisto

(Work People's College) suffered "a disastrous effect."[51] Teachers had to fight to keep foreign languages, including Norwegian, in the schools.

In this atmosphere, the Woman's Committee of the Commission of Public Safety, led by Alice Ames Winter, began its Americanization programs. Some of these programs reached out to communities of women who had been isolated before. Spurred by the Woman's Committee, Red Cross workers translated knitting instructions into Danish and found the immigrant women of Tyler anxious to become part of an America from which they had been excluded. Red Cross meetings and English classes sometimes were the first opportunities foreign women had to gain a sense of their rights under American law, and the classes often started them on the way to naturalization. To some extent, the war broke down the ethnic divisions between women. But the emphasis on Americanization put families under pressure and made ethnic identity suspect. Woman's Committee field workers found "that the young women are not joining the lodges of their mothers," and old ethnic networks were breaking down.[52]

New Ideas, Old Problems: 1920s–30s

In the era of World War I, many women's organizations changed their names. Groups for "woman" became "women's" groups. The Minnesota Woman Suffrage Association made its transition to the League of Women Voters. The change was not just semantic. There seemed less and less to be one set of criteria for "woman" and, instead, many definitions of "women."

In the 1920s, women's groups tried to continue their earlier agenda of social welfare and world peace. The Minnesota League of Women Voters, for example, supported a constitutional amendment banning child labor, more funding for the federal Maternity and Infancy Act, and expansion of compulsory school attendance laws. Like many other women's groups, it did not support the Equal Rights Amendment proposed by the National Woman's Party in the early 1920s, for fear of losing protective laws for women workers.[53] The Women's Co-operative Alliance, a Minneapolis coalition of women's organizations formed in 1915–17 and led by Catheryne Cooke Gilman, continued to work toward better child care, sex education, and nutrition. But as the decade wore on, the League of Women Voters distanced itself from women's issues to focus on "good government" and the Women's Co-operative Alliance turned to a "decency" issue, becoming involved in movie regulation. Though Wisconsin passed an Equal Rights Act in 1921, Minnesota did not.[54]

In the 1920s and 1930s there was a sense that since women were now voters, it was up to them to prove themselves. The daughter of one suffrage leader wrote that women's limitations "are most of them our own making and not imposed on us, as the old-fashioned, aggrieved feminists like to think." As a Norwegian-American woman put it, "The woman of today

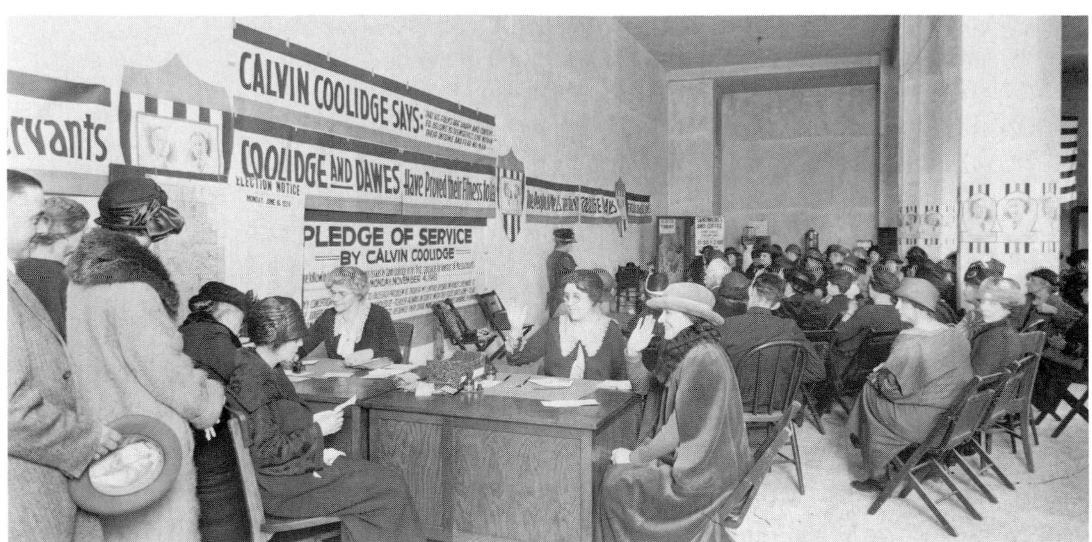

Women registering to vote at the Calvin Coolidge Campaign Headquarters in Minneapolis, 1924

meets a fresh challenge with every new morning. In whatever direction she looks a new invitation beckons to her."[55] The number of women Ph.D.s from the University of Minnesota more than doubled, and women nationally began to make up 40 percent of college classes. While the percentage of women in the labor force declined from its World War I peak, women still made up 20 to 22 percent of Minnesota workers in the 1920s and 1930s. Laborsaving devices like refrigerators, stoves, and washing machines, though used primarily by urban women who had access to electricity, lightened household tasks. New clothing styles gave more physical freedom. One woman remembered later what pride and bravery it took for her to be the first woman in a small town both to cut her hair and learn to drive a car.[56]

Women exercised their new political freedom. They began to serve on juries, and citizenship classes prepared them to vote. Four were elected to the state legislature in 1922, and Anna Dickie Olesen, Democrat from Cloquet, was the first woman nominated for the U.S. Senate by a major party. In smaller towns women were elected to local posts, such as Elizabeth K. Ries, who served as mayor of Shakopee from 1925 to 1929.[57]

Women also influenced international affairs. Fanny Brin became a national leader on disarmament issues, heading the National Council of Jewish Women. In 1935 she expressed the view of many women's groups when she said, "A nation which spends four-fifths of its income on war and preparation for war cannot advance the civilized arts of life."[58] The Minnesota League of Women Voters and other groups supported peace measures such as the World Court, the Kellogg-Briand Pact, and the Washington Conference, each of which elicited a petition – one containing a "Mile of Signatures" – to Minnesota's senators and Pres. Warren G. Harding. The percentage of Minnesota women who actively canvassed for petitions and distributed disarmament pamphlets for the league exceeded those of other states.[59]

Despite their gains, Minnesota women remained limited by employment restrictions. The 1920s saw a kind of "brain drain" as talented Minnesota women left the state for more promising positions elsewhere. Mary Ellen Chase, writer and later professor at Smith College, left her instructorship at the University of Minnesota when "I was forced to acknowledge that a full or even an associate professorship in English would probably be denied me on the ground of my sex."[60] Ada Comstock Notestein also left the university and became a national leader in women's education as president of Radcliffe College. Louise Mathilde Powell, who had begun the state's first five-year nursing course leading to an R.N. degree at the university, became head of nursing at Western Reserve University in 1926. Though historian Agnes Larson remained in Minnesota at St. Olaf College, her sister Henrietta went to Harvard to edit the *Journal of Economic and Business History* and later to become a professor at the Harvard business school. Artist Wanda Gág and Alice Ames Winter, president of the General Federation of Women's Clubs, also found opportunities elsewhere. The old networks became difficult to maintain as individual advancement beckoned women out of the state.[61]

But others were tied to the land. During the 1920s farm problems worsened. Just as rural women had earlier been part of agrarian reform movements such as the Grange and Nonpartisan League, so they joined

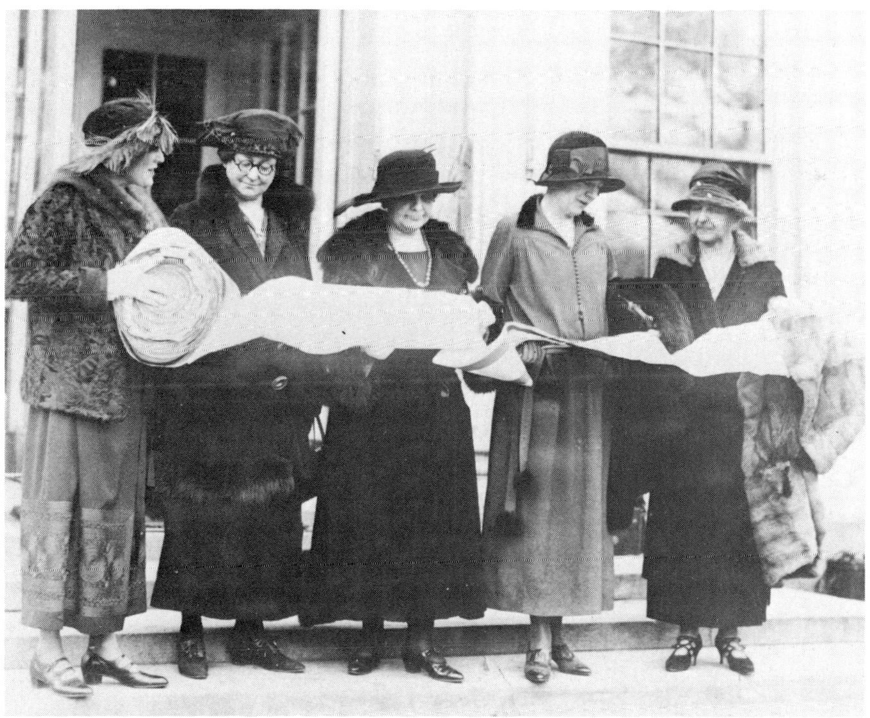

Members of the Ramsey County League of Women Voters with a peace petition in Washington, D.C., 1923

Production worker at Munsingwear Knitting Mills on Glenwood Avenue in Minneapolis in the 1920s

the Farmer-Labor party. Susie W. Stageberg, one of the founders of the Farmer-Labor party, reminisced in a speech about how the women of Otrey-Odessa sold handwork, canned fruit, live chickens, and a goose at an early campaign fund-raiser. In the reports of Farmer-Labor women's clubs the note of worry increased as the 1920s passed. "We have to do something now to save our homes," urged one woman. "Farms are being lost by the dozens."[62]

Not only were economic conditions hard; the sheer physical work of farm life was still extremely demanding. Agricultural extension researchers in 1924 and 1925 found that 53.3 percent of Minnesota women carried water from outside wells to their kitchens. Besides housework, women helped with milking, cleaned dairy utensils, raised poultry, and did fieldwork. The lower the family's income, the more likely it was that women worked in the fields. Without electricity, farm women still washed laundry by hand, cleaned kerosene lamps, and tended wood stoves. While the researchers tried to maintain a neutral tone, by the end of the report they admitted that "women work too hard at farm work [and] housekeeping or other activities more worth while . . . are sacrificed in order to help with the farm." Some farm women felt the sacrifice was worth making. One stated, "We would never any of us get rich. But, oh, the blessedness of independence and the security of the soil."[63] However, the soil of the 1920s and 1930s was not always secure.

Working women in the cities also faced insecurity. Labor unions tried to protect them. Before World War I the largest Twin Cities union for women was the United Garment Workers. Not only did it press for higher wages and better working conditions; it paid sick benefits and kept members informed about national issues. In the 1920s and 1930s women helped start several other unions, notably the Minnesota Federation of Teachers and the Retail Clerks International Association Local No. 2. Women also took part in some of the bitterest strikes of the era, as auxiliaries in the Minneapolis teamsters' strike of 1934 and as workers in the Work Projects Administration (WPA) strikes of 1939.[64]

A major issue in these years was discrimination against married women workers. A survey done in Minneapolis in the 1920s found that over 56 percent of employers preferred unmarried women for clerical jobs. In 1926 the St. Louis Park schools, following a common trend, dropped three married women from the payroll. Other school districts discouraged the hiring of married women. The Minneapolis superintendent of schools gave five reasons for this policy, including that "the employment of both husband and wife results in shiftless and frivolous habits of living" and "because of marriage, no woman is able to perform satisfactorily in the field of teaching."[65] This policy also served to keep wages down, as inexperienced, low-paid teachers replaced married women forced to resign. Such discrimination rapidly increased in the 1930s as the depression deepened and jobs became scarce. Laws prevented both husband and wife from holding federal jobs.

A YWCA study of St. Paul employers in the 1920s also found considerable prejudice against Jewish and black women. Employers stated that they preferred "Americans," Germans, and Scandinavians. In order to teach in the Minneapolis public schools, some black women teachers "passed for white." When a noticeably black woman who had graduated with high marks from the University of Minnesota applied for a teaching job in Minneapolis, she was told, "We don't hire Negroes." Ironically, some black domestic workers had more job security because of the lack of competition for their jobs.[66] So, too, did some Mexican-American women who

Women participating in a WPA sewing project at the Phyllis Wheatley House in Minneapolis, 1936

worked in the sugar beet fields of the Red River valley, and later in the meat-packing plants of South St. Paul. Convinced that their children would do better in Minnesota, they took marginal jobs and faced cold houses, outdoor water pumps, and crowded living conditions. One woman described her work: "I cut meat, packed pigs feet in jars, turned smoked hams, and worked with frozen meats without knowing any English. . . . What I did to learn was to watch someone else do it and then I would be able to do it."[67]

For American Indian women the 1930s were a turning point, but an ambiguous one. As a result of the Indian Reorganization Act of 1934, women received tribal voting rights for the first time. New Deal legislation also included them in social welfare programs, some of which allowed racial discrimination. At Cass Lake in 1936, local pressures forced a segregation of Indian and white WPA sewing projects. White resentment also surfaced because some Indian women held jobs while white women were still on waiting lists. To counteract such attitudes, in 1932 Alice L. Sickels, head of the International Institute of St. Paul, organized the Festival of Nations to celebrate cultural diversity instead of suppressing it.[68]

Whatever their marital status or ethnicity, women's economic problems were intensified by the depression. Mabel Ulrich, head of the Federal Writers' Project of the Minnesota WPA, found that women eligible for WPA jobs were generally stuck in sewing projects regardless of their other skills; she "lifted" several to do village surveys.[69] Minnesota writer Meridel Le Sueur described the women in the unemployment office of the Minneapolis YWCA in the 1930s: "We sit looking at the floor. No one dares think of the coming winter. There are only a few more days of summer. Everyone is anxious to get work to lay up something for that long siege of bitter cold. But there is no work. Sitting in the room we all know it. . . . There is a kind of humiliation in it. We look away from each other.

We look at the floor. It's too terrible to see this animal terror in each other's eyes."[70]

Ironically, the sex segregation among low-paid clerical positions may have allowed a slight increase of women in the labor force. More hurt were professional women, as graduate schools enforced quotas and married professionals found it hard to get work. Women who might have pursued these occupations had to make other choices. As one black woman put it, "I was always very interested in chemistry. It was beginning to get into the heart of the Depression and jobs weren't too easy to find and it kind of curtailed my going to school."[71]

To some extent, the image of women was enhanced by their prominent roles in the New Deal. National black leader Mary McLeod Bethune, head of the Office of Negro Affairs in the National Youth Administration, made sure that when Eleanor Roosevelt came to Minneapolis and St. Paul, black women were represented in the groups that met her. But the New Deal also gave double messages in its sex-segregated jobs and discouragement of married women. Historian Susan Ware characterized women in the 1930s as "holding their own"; it was an apt phrase for Minnesota also.[72]

Watershed Era: World War II and the 1940s

When it looked as if the United States was going to become involved in another world war, the national League of Women Voters tried to gain support for Franklin Roosevelt's 1941 Lend-Lease Bill providing American military support to Britain. But in a generally isolationist Minnesota, the Minnesota league officers reported, "There are not very many here who wholeheartedly support the lease-lend bill."[73] It took the attack on Pearl Harbor in 1941 to get Minnesota women more actively involved.

In comparison with World War I, women's role in the war was very businesslike. The newsletters of the county war committees' women's divisions read almost like those of any other fund-raising organization, with news of a war stamp tea at Clara City or news that "twelve year old Mary Helen Spillane of Backus has purchased a $25.00 War Bond each month since Pearl Harbor. War Bonds will put Helen through college. (Lucky Helen!)" The St. Paul Red Cross noted that "knitters and sewers busied themselves again, as they had done 25 years before."[74] Designers at the Minneapolis Young-Quinlan store made a dress out of war bonds for display. The Daughters of the British Empire in Minnesota brought British children to safety in Minneapolis for the war's duration, and on the queen's birthday gave blood to show solidarity with the British people. When recruitment of women into the armed services lagged in 1943, the Women's City Club of St. Paul sponsored a rally to help the state fill its enlistment quotas, which it did.[75] The University of Minnesota had the largest center for the U.S. Cadet Nurse Corps, training more than one thousand. At the Swedish Hospital School of Nursing, 83 percent of 1943 graduates joined the nurse corps; in 1944 the number had risen to 90 percent. Unlike women in World War I, nurses went overseas with full veterans' rights, thanks largely to pressure put on the government by the American Association of University Women and the General Federation of Women's Clubs.[76]

In an abrupt about-face, the government recruited women workers by arguing that it was their duty to work outside the home. Defense plants like Minneapolis-Moline Power Implement Company published brochures citing "Equal Pay for Equal Work" and pledging that "we do not have the slightest doubt that as a woman you will receive the courtesy and respect you deserve from all of our male employees." In St. Paul so many women worked the night shifts that the YWCA organized dances that began at 1:00 A.M. Married teachers were welcomed back, and medical schools increased their female student ratio from 5 to 12 percent. Analysts calculated that in 1944, 31.5 percent of eligible women were employed nationwide.[77]

Other than Japanese Americans, ethnic groups did not feel as much pressure as during World War I, but some felt uncomfortable. The Hungarian Ladies Benevolent Society decided to place "American" in its title before "Hungarian" because "it doesn't sound so good being called Hungarian." Italian women debated pulling out of the Festival of Nations for fear that their participating children might be booed or harmed. They did take part, however, and received applause.[78] Somewhat ironically, considering its World War I record on ethnic tolerance, Minnesota was selected as an area for Japanese Americans to relocate from the concentration camps in which they had been placed. Some women came to perform Japanese language translation for the army at Fort Snelling, some as wives of servicemen, and some as single women to work or attend school. When Japanese-American women tried to rent rooms in the Twin Cities and were turned down, they appealed to federal agencies in Minneapolis, which intervened to make their entrance into the community easier.[79]

Even while they worked as air-raid spotters or welders, women began to prepare for peace. In 1943, in the midst of headlines about fierce battles in Europe and Asia, the Virginia, Minnesota, chapter of the American Association of University Women was already discussing "The U.S. in the post-war world" and the "Baltic Riddle," and urging postwar economic planning. The League of Women Voters began to support the idea of a United Nations. The Minnesota league was to distribute eleven pamphlets on the U.N. per member – a higher proportion than many other state chapters.[80] But other women were concerned about whether they would have a job after the war. A survey of Duluth women workers in 1945 found that 74 percent wished to keep their jobs. The federal government, which had been using posters and films to propagandize in favor of women working, now began a campaign to get women back into the home. Women were urged to "turn in that work identity badge." Many did, but many did not. World War II was a watershed, particularly in the employment of married women. In spite of government campaigns and the baby boom of the 1950s, the number of women in the labor force continued to increase. By 1950 the percentage of Minnesota women working was 28.8 and rising.[81]

Despite the loss of some jobs, the last years of the 1940s saw breakthroughs for Minnesota women. The Federation of Women Teachers and the Men Teachers Federation of St. Paul joined in 1946 to hold the first organized teachers' strike in the United States. Protesting merit pay based on the superintendent's favoritism, unequal salaries between women and men and between elementary and secondary women teachers, the strikers had a national impact. "It was felt in every little school and every little community," said one teacher, "and nearly all the schools in all these areas were having the same type of problems." Two years later a Minneapolis Federation of Teachers strike, again with women leaders involved, confirmed their assertive role in one of the largest occupations for women.[82]

In the late 1940s Minnesota achieved another first when Eugenie M. Anderson became America's first woman ambassador, first to Denmark and later to Bulgaria. Though the Danes did not quite know what her husband's diplomatic status was, Anderson herself made close contact with the Danish people, even giving a Mother's Day speech in Danish on the radio. The newly formed Democratic-Farmer-Labor (DFL) party also offered changes, and Nellie Stone Johnson, a black labor leader, was one of its early organizers.[83] Yet, despite these achievements, when Mabeth Hurd Paige looked back in the mid-1940s at her own long legislative career, she said, "It has been a deep disappointment to me that more women have not actively evinced their acceptance of legislative work as a definite responsibility." The postwar years had a quality of uncertainty. A Duluth survey asked, "What are the postwar plans of the woman in industry? . . . Will Duluth be able to find the answers to the problems of its hundreds of working women who . . . find themselves the family breadwinners?"[84] The 1950s would provide few satisfactory answers to these questions.

The Rhetoric of Helpmate: 1950s

In a history of the University of Minnesota written in the 1950s, James Gray described the typical graduate student on commencement day: "His wife will be there to see his investiture and along with her there may be a son or daughter."[85] The wife standing by with the children, watching the husband achieve, was very much the image of women in the 1950s.

In the late 1950s the percentage of women students in college was actually less (35.2 percent) than it had been in the 1920s (47 percent). While one in six doctorates in the 1920s had gone to women, Ph.D.s for women fell below 10 percent in the 1950s. Part of the reason was the G.I. Bill, which gave financial aid to veterans, mainly men, and also granted "veteran's preference" in admission to colleges and jobs. As a result, schools tightened quotas for women and shuffled them into secretarial and home economics courses. One woman said, "We married what we wanted to *be*. . . . If we wanted to be a lawyer or doctor we married one."[86]

By the 1950s many women's groups no longer retained an interest in women's rights. As the program chair of the Woman's Club of Minneapolis said, "With the world in political, economic and social dislocation, it is hard to avoid a heavy, ponderous type of program and discussion. But if we were to do that, one half of the membership would cry 'Bravo!' and the other half would stay home." Their 1955–60 series, "The Workshop for Modern Women," included sessions on "Table Settings," "Fashion Trends," and "The New You" (grooming). The League of Women Voters also distanced itself from the women's movement by changing the name of its newsletter from *The Woman Voter* to *The Minnesota Voter*.[87]

During the Korean War, unlike the two world wars, women's organizations were not asked to participate in volunteer activities. Instead, the tensions of the cold war and McCarthy era created a fear of the outside world, and the media stressed the image of women as guardians of the home. "The Donna Reed Show," a television program starring a Minnesota actress, became one of many portraying the sympathetic, if sometimes confused, 1950s housewife. It was the era of the suburb, a housing pattern and life-style that often isolated women in communities with few organized women's networks. The fertility rate rose higher than in the 1920s, but few child-care centers existed for working women. Until the late 1960s the Minneapolis grade schools had no lunchroom facilities because school officials expected mothers to be home to prepare their child's noon meal. Though the popular press argued that women were content in the home, in reality women made up an increasing percentage of the Minnesota work force in the 1950s, rising during that decade from 28.8 to 34.4 percent.[88]

The more women were educated, the more they participated in the work force. Though the percentage of women in colleges and the professions declined, the actual number of professional women increased. In 1959 the University of Minnesota, prodded by Elizabeth L. Cless and Virginia L. Senders, began what one historian called a "revolutionary program," Continuing Education for Women, to encourage older women – "usually in their thirties" – to get degrees.[89]

Meanwhile, volunteer activities continued. The Women's Association of the Minneapolis Symphony Orchestra was created to raise funds for the orchestra. Volunteers like Jewish women in the B'nai B'rith auxiliary and Greek Orthodox women in the Daughters of Penelope focused on serving the community, not just themselves as women. Since many middle-class volunteers thought women sought employment only as a temporary measure, they did not involve themselves in job equity issues. A Minneapolis Jewish mother spoke for a whole decade when she commented on her daughter-in-law: "What's wrong with her working? My son loves her even if he hasn't got a million dollars. So they say they'll both work . . . and then after a few years they'll be able to buy the things they want. Then they will settle down and be happy."[90] It was difficult for some in the 1950s to see working women as happy.

Minnesota women, like others nationwide, faced puzzling messages from society. Unlike their mothers and grandmothers, who tackled the world's social problems with the moral force of "enlightened motherhood," or the "new woman" of the 1920s, or the surviving, country-saving women of the wartime years, women of the 1950s were restricted by the rhetoric of "helpmate."

The New Women's Movement: 1960s

During the late 1950s and the 1960s some signs of change appeared. It came from two directions. One was traditional women's groups and the other was the anti-Vietnam War movement. Groups like the American Association of University Women (AAUW) and the National Federation of Business and Professional Women's Clubs (BPW) had gained Pres. Harry S. Truman's support for an Equal Rights Amendment in the 1940s but had been unable to get the measure passed. Joined by other groups, they now persuaded Pres. John F. Kennedy to form a national commission on women and began, with congressional leaders like Martha Griffiths, to work on a bill mandating equal pay for equal work. During the early 1960s, the President's Commission on the Status of Women, the Equal Pay Act of 1963, the Civil Rights Act of 1964 (which banned discrimination on the basis of sex), and the publication of Betty Friedan's book *The Feminine Mystique* spelled out the disjunction of the 1950s. President Kennedy and the commission urged states to look more closely into the status of women in their regions.[91]

In 1965, Minnesota Gov. Karl F. Rolvaag, urged by Edna Schwartz of the Minnesota BPW, set up the Commission on the Status of Women. The commission, chaired by Viola H. Hymes, found a general pattern of discrimination. There was not a single woman school superintendent, and only 4 percent of members of the Minnesota Association of Secondary School Principals were women; 25 percent of Minnesota schools paid extra to heads of households (usually men); 74 of the state's 173 vocational schools reported little interest in new programs for women; maternity benefits were rare. One employer reported that pregnancy leaves were of no concern because a woman was "automatically terminated" from her job when she married.[92]

Discrimination was particularly apparent in the University of Minnesota professional schools. If one researcher's preliminary figures are correct, the university had been granting doctorates to women at an overall rate of 10 percent throughout its history, while the national average (except in the 1950s) was about 13 percent.[93] In the medical school, women made up 5.6 percent of the students, and a married woman had to pass a special interview before acceptance. The law school graduated 3 percent women, and the consensus was that they had to be "brighter than the average male student." The school of dentistry was the most startling. Though women made up 25 percent of dentists in Scandinavian countries, 40 percent in Latin America, and 80 percent in the USSR, the university's school of dentistry had only one woman student in 1964.[94]

The commission's report issued in 1965 suggested that Minnesota women were "going through a revolution" and that much reform was needed. The commission proposed bills to establish equal pay, overcome discrimination, and set a minimum wage. Yet two years later a supplemental report found, "If the work of the Committee [commission] . . . is to be measured by effort, the members would receive an 'A.' If measured by legislative results, the mark would be 'Fail.' "[95] But the commission was eventually aided by other forces. The Equal Pay for Equal Work Law was passed in 1969 and the Equal Rights Amendment (ERA) ratified in 1973.

Groups of professional women like the AAUW and BPW increased their membership by more than 200 percent between 1940 and 1960. But the older women's groups generally lost membership. The Women's City Club of St. Paul found itself in financial difficulty and in 1971 sold its downtown building. In Minneapolis, a woman asked to run for president of the Woman's Club replied, "Do you want me to preside at the wake?" The League of Women Voters seemed unsure where to lead its members: a 1962 league study found discrimination against women workers, but its conclusions were vague: "The issue is clouded by the fact that women do lead different kinds of lives from men."[96] It took other factors to provide the push for what came to be called "the new women's movement."

One of these new forces was the National Organization for Women (NOW), formed in 1966 to organize support for an Equal Rights Amendment, pay equity, and better access to education. When the Minnesota chapter of NOW was founded in 1970, it also pushed for a Sex Bias Task Force in the Minnesota Department of Education and supported reproductive rights for women. In 1969 the Abortion Rights Council of Minnesota was founded, a bill to reform Minnesota's anti-abortion law was introduced into the legislature, and – in response – the anti-abortion Minnesota Citizens Concerned for Life was created.[97] Abortion would remain a controversial issue for years.

The black civil-rights movement of the 1960s also influenced the debate over women's rights. Black women participated in marches and demonstrations; they served on the boards of the Urban League and National Association for the Advancement of Colored People; they went to Mississippi to help register voters. But most acted as individuals and did not focus on women's issues. Sara Evans, later to become a history professor at the University of Minnesota, noted that young women in the civil rights and other protest movements began to see themselves subordinated to the typewriter, ditto machine, and coffee pot, and even endured sexual harassment within a group working for "equal rights." In the late 1960s women began to use some of the skills and networks they had developed to pursue their own goals. As Evans said, "By 1967–8 hundreds of thousands of young women had been to a march, a meeting, a sit-in, a rally."[98]

Protests against the Vietnam War served as a further training ground for the women's movement. At first the protests followed old patterns. Because women were not drafted, they were often relegated to less visible positions. When Minnesota women marched in the 1960s, they generally did so as part of traditional groups. Typical of such groups was the Minnesota Chapter of the Women's International League for Peace and Freedom, organized in 1922. It had supported humanitarian aid in World War II, but came out openly against the Vietnam War. Members distributed pamphlets, raised bail for war protesters, and assisted draft resisters going to Canada.[99] To the league, opposition to the war was part of its old stand against violence; but younger women in the early 1970s began to see war in the context of feminist ideology, as a male-domineering activity, and began to march in women's contingents. The Vietnam War meant "a constant stream of men going and coming back, all infected with killing." In 1970, the *Female Liberation Newsletter* declared that American males had involved the country in a mess "which gives women nothing, and takes everything, and it is in our [women's] self-interest to stop it."[100]

Some of the women who set out to stop it held positions within the major political parties, like Mary Shepard of the GOP Task Force on Vietnam. Women in the Democratic-Farmer-Labor party were particularly notable in the antiwar movement. Esther Wattenberg, Alpha Smaby, Sally Luther, and Nellie Stone Johnson created support for antiwar candidate Eugene McCarthy's challenge to Lyndon B. Johnson in 1968. McCarthy supporter Patricia Hillmeyer would say later, "I decided no son of mine was ever going to look at me and ask why I hadn't the guts to oppose a war where young men and boys were being destroyed."[101]

During the 1960s, discrimination against women did not change; but women's rights again became the focus for the formation of groups, and the women's movement began to move.

Turnaround Decades: 1970s–80s

The 1970s brought a major upheaval in attitudes toward women. Although Minnesota men and women still married at the same rate as in the 1960s (57 percent), the patterns within marriage changed. *Sexual Politics*, a book by Minnesota writer Kate Millett, became part of a national debate on gender roles. Cleaning the bathroom became as much a part of gender politics as the ERA. Women who had talked about "my husband letting me work" began taking evening courses on "assertiveness training." Employment rates for women rose from 34.4 percent in 1960 to 54 percent by 1980. Some who had married in the 1950s found their marriages renegotiated. The apprehension created by this shift in expectations made Minnesota women in the early 1970s "more critical of the [women's] movement than are men," according to one poll. But that same poll included the comment of one Bloomington woman, "Men are finding out that it's not going to kill them to help out around the house."[102] Some marriages adjusted well, with men relieved of the full financial burden and women challenged by new jobs. Other marriages could not stand the strain, and the divorce rate rose.

For the 25 percent or more of Minnesota women who did not marry, life-styles also changed. To have a child without marriage became more acceptable, and single women had to answer less the perennial question of the 1950s, "Why isn't a nice girl like you married?" Lesbians, for the first time in American history, were able to organize openly, found businesses like the Amazon Bookstore in Minneapolis, and challenge the mainstream women's groups to recognize their contributions.[103]

Consciousness-raising sessions, usually informally organized, spread throughout Minnesota in the early 1970s. Women shared repressed feelings of anger at discrimination and respect for strong female members of their families – those who kept the family together in the depression or worked in factories during World War II. For many it was "an exhilarating time." The invention of such words as "sexism" and "male chauvinism" helped to identify complex phenomena felt but not clearly expressed before. Often, the result of consciousness raising was formation of an action group to work on a specific issue. Among the groups formed from 1970 to 1974 were the Women's Equity Action League (education), the Emma Willard Task Force (education), the Minnesota Women's Political Caucus, Women's Advocates (a shelter for battered women), Women Historians of the Midwest, DFL and GOP Feminist Caucuses, and the Women's Art Registry of Minnesota (WARM). Four feminist theaters were started (of which At the Foot of the Mountain still survived in 1987) to produce entertaining but consciousness-raising plays.[104]

Although the founders of these groups shared experience and trust, their feelings were tinged with concern over failure. Looking back at those early days, the authors of a history of WARM described their questions about opening a women's art gallery; they might have been speaking for many of the organizations created in the 1970s: "There needed to be a time to build trust. Can she do that? Can I do this? Do you think that will work? Build a what? . . . And what are you crazy girls doing down here. A what? Well, good luck. Don't you think you should do it this way? And there was a controversy about men and babies and other suspect intruders. . . . And what about the families and friends who wondered what on earth had happened to us. Poof. Disappeared."[105]

Women artists were not the only ones who disappeared from their usual circles. A Minnesota NOW president said that "some are growing weary of . . . too many meetings. In place of some of the many NOW meetings . . . we need to start going to some meetings of our political party, of our church, of our union, of our children's school, of special interest groups."[106] When they did make it to all those other meetings they challenged old patterns and created new ones.

In the 1970s Minnesota became a national innovator on many fronts. A coalition of women's groups got the legislature to ratify the ERA in 1973, before a nationwide campaign was organized against it. The DFL and GOP Feminist Caucuses helped elect increasing numbers of women legislators. By 1987, women made up 15.4 percent of the legislature, slightly more than the national average. Often, candidates pursued women's issues. Rep. Phyllis Kahn, for example, tackled discrimination in school sports. Male coaches were not pleased at sharing court time and money with women's teams, so it took prodding from Kahn to enforce federal guidelines that outlawed discrimination.[107]

Women began to serve in statewide office. In 1975 Joan A. Growe became secretary of state. Local officials moved along the path to higher positions. For example, Sally Olsen and Phyllis McQuaid served on local school boards before being elected to the state legislature. Minnesota women also became visible at the national level: Muriel B. Humphrey filled out the senate term of Hubert H. Humphrey after his death in 1978; Koryne E. Horbal, a leader in Minnesota's ratification of the ERA, became U.S. delegate to the U.N. Commission on the Status of Women; and Arvonne S. Fraser headed the Office of Women's Development for the U.S. Agency for International Development. Rosalie E. Wahl was the first woman appointed to the Minnesota Supreme Court. Politically active women became public role models.[108]

The presence of women in these positions was a mark of their talents, but it was also the mark of the networks who supported the ideas these leaders represented. Minnesota became known for the creation of battered women's shelters and police programs on domestic violence. The Emma Willard Task Force and the Minnesota Department of Education's Sex Equity Advisory Committee made the state an innovator in nonsexist school curriculum.[109] In religion, two Minnesotans, Jeannette R. Piccard and Alla Bozarth-Campbell, were among the first women priests ordained in the Episcopal church. The "Willmar 8" became the first women to strike for equal rights in the banking industry. Though the strike failed in its immediate goals, it publicized discrimination in banking throughout the country. A second strike, that of Minnesota nurses in 1984, helped to bring national attention to issues of professionalism and wages in a traditionally female occupation.[110]

Why was Minnesota so active in the women's movement of the early 1970s? The state had several advantages: a progressive attitude toward reform; strong "traditional" women's groups that provided networks and experience; a large university located in a metropolitan area; a high level of women's education; economic prosperity; and several private foundations, like the Northwest Area and Amherst H. Wilder foundations, which provided funding for innovative programs.

Much was accomplished in the 1970s. In the 1960s female high-school athletes had to participate in leagues outside of school, if they could find them; in the 1970s they had their own school teams. In the early 1960s St. Olaf and other colleges restricted hours in women's dormitories but not men's; in the 1970s such restrictions disappeared. In the 1960s graduate schools had female quotas; in the 1970s these were dropped. In the 1960s a married woman could not establish her own credit rating or keep her birth name; in the 1970s she could. In the 1960s some of the best universities were closed to women; in the 1970s they were not. In the 1960s abortion was illegal; in the 1970s it was legal. In the 1960s women could not eat lunch in the Oak Grill at Dayton's department store in Minneapolis unless accompanied by a man; in the 1970s they could. In the 1960s women went into the Minnesota Club in St. Paul by back doors; in the 1970s Sen. Muriel Humphrey became the first woman member, and the front doors were reluctantly opened to women. In the 1960s employers could fire women be-

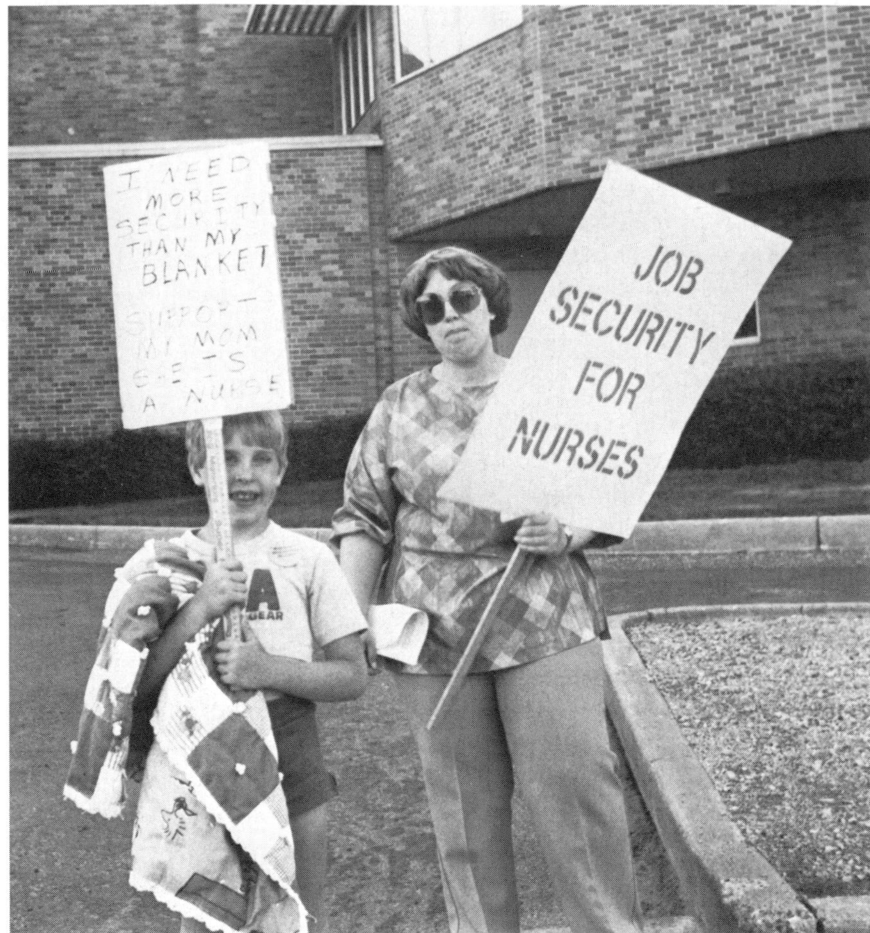

Pickets at St. John's Hospital in St. Paul during the 1984 nurses strike

cause of marital status or sexual preference; in the 1970s they could not. For women, 1970–80 was a remarkable decade.[111]

In many ways the momentum of the 1970s carried over to the 1980s. NOW ranked Minnesota tenth in the nation for supporting women's rights in 1986. One reason was Minnesota's leadership in offering parental leaves and enforcing child support. Another was the comparable worth system for local governments spearheaded by Nina Rothchild, commissioner of employee relations, and state Sen. Linda Berglin. Under this system, female-dominated jobs were paid comparably to male-dominated jobs that demanded similar training and responsibility. It was not an entirely popular measure, and it cost the state money, but a coalition of women's groups helped to convince the legislature of its fairness. Few other states chose to follow Minnesota's lead.[112]

In politics, the Minneapolis City Council came to have a female majority and a female president. In his unsuccessful 1984 presidential campaign, Minnesotan Walter F. Mondale chose Geraldine Ferraro as the first woman vice-presidential candidate of a major party. In the same year a network of women helped to finance senatorial candidate Joan Growe's losing campaign with the largest fund-raisers in DFL history. Marlene Johnson was elected lieutenant governor in 1982, and was challenged by Arvonne Fraser in the 1986 DFL primary. Connie Levi, an Independent-Republican, was house majority leader in 1985–86.[113] By the end of the decade, only the offices of governor and mayor of a major city had never yet been filled by a woman.

But women's issues also became more complex in the 1980s. The abortion issue divided "pro-life" and "pro-choice" women. The controversy shaped elections and caused bitter demonstrations and even violence at abortion clinics. Another divisive issue was the attempt by some feminists to pass an antipornography ordinance in Minneapolis. The proposed ordinance defined pornography as a violation of human rights because it promoted bigotry and contempt. While many feminists supported it, others agreed when Mayor Donald M. Fraser vetoed it on grounds of freedom of speech.[114]

The women's movement of the 1980s was also divided along the lines of ethnicity and special interests. Minority women often found that their greater loyalty lay with their ethnic group; new organizations like the American Indian Women's Resource Center began focusing on their interests. Although women served in few positions of tribal leadership in Minnesota, Indian women rose to positions of authority in education, social services, and business. Interest increased in Indian women's artistic traditions, which formed the focus of exhibitions in Duluth and Minneapolis.[115] It was not easy to recreate the world of Maude Kegg's childhood once the fishing, berrying, ricing, and sugaring places were gone. "Now," Kegg said, "all you see is 'No Trespassing' signs." Still, Indian women in the Twin Cities tried to pass on tribal stories – though, as one woman put it, "I had a feeling that they [the children] listened the same as when I read a story about the Bobbsey Twins or Marco Polo." For some, their role as storyteller or teacher within their own culture was more crucial than the wider women's movement.[116]

Though Minnesota black women have had several strong organizations – the Civic and Cultural Club, Alpha Kappa Alpha, the Links, Inc., Delta Sigma Theta, and local chapters of the National Council for Negro Women and the National Political Congress of Black Women – in 1984 they also formed the Black Women's Political Caucus to support more black women for political office.[117]

New women's groups also grew up in response to the issues of nuclear war and disarmament. One, Women against Military Madness, was particularly concerned about the great size of the federal defense budget as compared with social services. In 1983 an informally organized group of women began the Women's Peace Encampment near the Sperry Corporation, a defense contractor in St. Paul. The live-in protest was modeled after ones in New York and Greenham Common, England. These groups differed from other peace and justice groups because they saw war as a women's issue and preferred consensus styles of leadership.[118]

But whether or not women's groups began to "splinter" or "expand," depending on the point of view, women's opportunities did open up in the 1980s. Women made up over half of college undergraduates and increased their numbers in law school. Rosalie Wahl commented, "I used to count the number of women [admitted to the bar] every year, but their increasing numbers make it no longer necessary to count." Other professions showed similar gains, though older women wondered if the new professional women cared more about "dressing for success" than women's issues. In 1987 the third and sixth congressional districts (the southern suburbs of Minneapolis and the northern suburbs of Minneapolis and St. Paul) led the nation in families with more than one member working – 68.1 percent and 67.7 percent respectively. Minnesota women also appeared in unexpected places: in 1986 Ann Bancroft was the first woman to reach the North Pole overland and Wendy Krupp was the state's first female high-school football player. It took rigor to be a "first" in the 1980s when so many Minnesota women had broken through political, professional, and social doors before.[119]

Yet the 1980s saw several troubling signs for women. In these years of agricultural crisis, Minnesota farm women often found it necessary to work part time in service jobs to keep the family farm going. While many of them loved farm life for its sense of wholeness and connection to a natural pattern, life could be very difficult. One farm-management agent said that more women than men called for assistance because wives often kept the books and answered the bill collectors' calls. Farm women are often portrayed as tough and supportive. But Jeanine Henneman spoke for many about the constant battle to survive; it "does something to you after a while. After you go year after year after year losing money, no matter how hard you work or how much better you get at your operation – you're still losing money – that does something to a person's self-esteem." As farm prices continued to drop, concerned women founded a Minnesota chapter of Women Involved in Farm Economics (WIFE).[120]

Some Minnesota women still lived in poverty. Despite educational and political gains, women still predominated in the ten lowest-paid major occupations. The average female college graduate in 1979 could expect to make less than a male high-school dropout. Buttons worn by feminists of the 1970s and 1980s proclaimed, "56 cents" – the amount women earned for every dollar made by men. In Minnesota, as in the rest of the world, there was a "feminization of poverty." In 1985, over one-third of poor persons lived in female-headed families. In Minnesota, women were a greater portion of the poverty population than they were nationally. When legislative proposals threatened to cut government funds for Aid to Families with Dependent Children in the mid-1980s, these figures united women's groups and church groups, who succeeded in blocking the cuts. But the problem remained unsolved.[121]

In 1985 a group of more than sixty Minnesota women went to Nairobi, Kenya, for the closing of the U.N. Decade for Women. Among them was writer and activist Meridel Le Sueur, whose poem "Solidarity" was read in Swahili at the meeting. Later, Le Sueur said about that moment, "I felt

A woman farmer plowing a field near Albert Lea, 1952

the communication between us all silencing the dread annihilation of the bomb." At another meeting in 1977, Rosalie Wahl spoke of a similar feeling of communication with the early suffragists Anthony, Stanton, and "all those brave, unnamed, unremembered women who gave so much that we might have the freedom and opportunity that is ours."[122]

These quotations illustrate two themes about Minnesota women in the twentieth century: a sense of the networks among women and of women as active agents for change. If Minnesota goes into history without many *great* women, it is perhaps because it had so many *good* ones, active and involved. Along the way, some of their actions may have been misguided or controversial, but considering the educational, political, and social restrictions, the wonder is that they had the courage to act at all. As poet Carol Bly has written – only half teasing – about the earnestness of Minnesota women, "Nearly all of us women feel it our job to keep up civilization; we have an ancient conviction that if we don't keep it up the men will ease backward through evolution."[123]

Minnesota women kept at it.

NOTES

The author would like to acknowledge the support of Valerie Hauch in locating and evaluating sources.

1. Richard N. Current, T. Harry Williams, and Frank Freidel, *American History: A Survey*, 2d ed. (New York: Alfred A. Knopf, 1966), 716; Mary Kay Blakeley, "From Minnesota," *Ms.*, July 1985, 55–60, 110–11. Of the 1,359 women described in Edward T. James, Janet Wilson James, and Paul S. Boyer, eds., *Notable American Women 1607–1950: A Biographical Dictionary* (Cambridge, Mass.: Harvard University Press, 1971), there are eight Minnesota women. As Barbara Stuhler and Gretchen Kreuter point out, many of these either were not raised in Minnesota or else moved out of the state. See their introduction to *Women of Minnesota: Selected Biographical Essays*, ed. Barbara Stuhler and Gretchen Kreuter (St. Paul: Minnesota Historical Society Press, 1977), 2–3. See Mary Christine Pruitt, " 'Women Unite!' The Modern Women's Movement in Minnesota" (Ph.D. diss., University of Minnesota, 1988), for leaders within the state, though less nationally known.

2. Julia B. Nelson, "Minnesota," in *The History of Woman Suffrage*, vol. 4, 1883–1900, ed. Susan B. Anthony and Ida Husted Harper (Rochester, N.Y.: Susan B. Anthony, 1902), 782.

3. This cohesion may be due in part to an emphasis on cooperatives in Minnesota. The number of non-native Minnesotans who led organizations may also suggest that leaders were chosen from outside local factions. Women leaders raised elsewhere include Martha G. Ripley and Clara H. Ueland of the suffrage movement; Alice Ames Winter of the Woman's Committee of the Minnesota Commission of Public Safety; Catheryne Cooke Gilman of the Women's Co-operative Alliance; left-wing activist Meridel Le Sueur; Josie R. Johnson, first black regent of the University of Minnesota (1971–73); and Mabeth Hurd Paige and Hannah J. Kempfer, who served in the state legislature from the 1920s to the 1940s. Arvonne S. Fraser and Sue E. Holbert, "Women in the Minnesota Legislature," and Patricia C. Harpole, "Brief Biographies of Other Minnesota Women," in *Women of Minnesota*, 247, 325–43. On Winter and Gilman, see notes 52, 54, below.

4. Mrs. Elbert L. Carpenter, *A Fair Share for Women* ([Minneapolis]: Minneapolis Association Opposed to the Further Extension of Suffrage to Women, n.d.), roll 14, frames 252–56, in Minnesota Woman Suffrage Association Records, microfilm edition, Minnesota Historical Society (MHS). See also, in the same collection, Mrs. Edmund Pennington, *Woman the Helpmate*, roll 14, frames 232–40.

5. Maude Kegg, *Gabekanaansing/At the End of the Trail: Memories of Chippewa Childhood in Minnesota with Texts in Ojibwe and English*, ed. John Nichols, *Occasional Publications in Anthropology*, Linguistics Series, no. 4 (Greeley, Colo.: Museum of Anthropology, University of Northern Colorado, 1978), 39, and *Gii-Ikwezensiwiyaan/When I Was a Little Girl: Memories of Indian Childhood in Minnesota, Written in Ojibwe (Chippewa) and English*, ed. John Nichols (Onamia: N.p., 1976), 11.

6. Anne B. Webb, "Forgotten Persephones: Women Farmers on the Frontier," *Minnesota History* 50 (Winter 1986): 134–48; James K. Knight, *We Homesteaded* (New Brighton: Printcraft, 1975), 52; Sarah G. Gates Baird, diary, July 8, 1900, Sarah G. Gates and George W. Baird Papers, MHS. For more on the economic contributions of farm women see Deborah Fink, *Open Country, Iowa: Rural Women, Tradition and Change* (Albany: State University of New York Press, 1986).

7. Rudolph J. Vecoli, "The Italians," in *They Chose Minnesota: A Survey of the State's Ethnic Groups*, ed. June Drenning Holmquist (St. Paul: Minnesota Historical Society Press, 1981), 454. One Jewish landlady used the profits from her boardinghouse to bring other relatives to America; see Miriam Blechman, "The House My Mother Built," in *Every Woman Has a Story*, ed. Gayla Wadnizak Ellis (Minneapolis: Midwest Villages and Voices, 1982), 62–64. For other immigrant occupations see Work Projects Administration (WPA), *The Bohemian Flats* (Minneapolis: University of Minnesota Press, 1941; St. Paul: Minnesota Historical Society Press, 1986), 15, 19.

8. Polly Bullard, "Iron Range Schoolmarm," *Minnesota History* 32 (December 1951): 196. Finland granted women the right to vote in 1906. For more on Finnish women see K. Marianne Wargelin Brown, "Trailblazers in Finland for Women's Rights: A Brief History of Feminism in Finland," and "Ida Pasanen: Socialist Agitator and Women's Advocate," in *Women Who Dared: The History of Finnish American Women*, ed. Carl Ross and K. Marianne Wargelin Brown (St. Paul: Immigration History Research Center, University of Minnesota, 1986), 1–13, 136–42.

9. Minnesota Bureau of Labor, Commerce and Industry, Woman's Department, *First Biennial Report . . . 1907–1908* (St. Paul: Willwerscheid and Roith, 1909), 8, 13, 14 (quotation).

10. Lynn Weiner, " 'Our Sister's Keepers': The Minneapolis Woman's Christian Association and Housing for Working Women," *Minnesota History* 46 (Spring 1979): 190.

11. [Mrs. Perry Starkweather], "Department of Women and Children," in Minnesota Bureau of Labor, Industries and Commerce, *Twelfth Biennial Report . . . 1909–1910* (St. Paul: N.p., 1910), 607.

12. Mrs. Jorgen Paulsen, "Pioneering," in *From Partridge to Askov* (Askov: Danish Ladies' Aid, [1946?]), 56.

13. Sarah Cohen, quoted in Rhoda Greene Lewin, "Some New Perspectives on the Jewish Immigrant Experience in Minneapolis: An Experiment in Oral History" (Ph.D. diss., University of Minnesota, 1978), 167.

14. H. Arnold Barton, *Letters from the Promised Land: Swedes in America 1840–1914* (Minneapolis: University of Minnesota Press, 1975), 197; Minnesota Bureau of Labor, *Ninth Biennial Report 1903–1904*, vol. 1 (St. Paul: Great Western Printing, 1904), 113.

15. Mary Etta Hoople Ackerman, "Staking a Claim on the Cannon – 1855," in *Continuum: Threads in the Community Fabric of Northfield, Minnesota*, ed. Lynn Carlin (Northfield: City of Northfield, 1976), 46; Research Committee on Pioneer Women, "Supplement to the Biographical Sketch of Edna Isabelle Murphy," p. 3, Delta Kappa Gamma Papers, MHS.

16. Bullard, "Iron Range Schoolmarm," 197; Fraser and Holbert, "Women in the Minnesota Legislature," 252–62.

17. Nellie N. Barsness, "Highlights in Careers of Woman Physicians in Pioneer Minnesota," *Journal of the American Medical Women's Association* 13 (January 1958): 19–22.

18. Quoted in Pat Gaarder and Tracey Baker, *From Stripes to Whites: A History of the Swedish Hospital School of Nursing 1899–1973* (Minneapolis: Swedish Hospital Alumnae Association, 1980), 7.

19. Gaarder and Baker, *Stripes to Whites*, 5 (quotation), 12, 13.

20. Mrs. H. J. Leigh to Mrs. A. [Clara] Ueland, Sept. 9, 1915 (roll 1, frame 305), Rene E. H. Stevens to Mrs. Briggs, Mar. 25, 1916 (roll 1, frame 436), Minnesota Woman Suffrage Association Records; Adina Gibbs, interview by David V. Taylor, Minneapolis, Dec. 18, 1970, p. 50, transcript available at MHS. The Gibbs family did a great deal of entertaining; since blacks were not allowed in St. Paul restaurants and hotels, they entertained visitors in their homes.

21. Carrie Chapman Catt and Nettie Rogers Shuler, *Woman Suffrage and Politics: The Inner Story of the Suffrage Movement* (New York: Charles Scribner's Sons, 1923), 29. For more on Minnesota laws see Essie W. Williams, *Legal Status of Women and Children in Minnesota* (St. Paul: Review Publishing Co., 1911).

22. Frances R. Sterrett, *William and Williamina* (New York: Grosset and Dunlap, 1917), 15; *Mary Rose of Mifflin* (New York: D. Appleton and Co., 1916), 39. Sterrett generally "solved" the dilemmas in her books by having the heroine marry happily, but she herself remained single.

23. Bessie Lathe Scovell, *A Brief History of the Minnesota Woman's Christian Temperance Union from Its Organization, September 6, 1877 to 1939* (St. Paul: Bruce Publishing, 1939), 116–17, 220; "Report of the First Vice-President for the Year 1916," roll 2, frame 326, Minnesota Woman Suffrage Association Records (quotation).

24. Maud C. Stockwell, "Minnesota," in *The History of Woman Suffrage*, vol. 6, 1900–1920, ed. Ida Husted Harper (New York: J. J. Little and Ives, 1922), 325n. Antisuffrage publications often portrayed feminists as antimale, free-love Socialists, out to destroy the home. See, for example, the undated poem "The Feminist," issued by the Massachusetts Association Opposed to the Further Extension of Suffrage to Women, in which a "feminist" says, "We're like the female spider/Who is known to eat her mate." Roll 14, frame 304, Minnesota Woman Suffrage Association Records.

25. Karen J. Blair, *The Clubwoman as Feminist: True Womanhood Redefined, 1868–1914* (New York: Holmes and Meir Publishers, 1980), 105 (quotation); Jeanette Ludcke, *You've Come a Long Way, Lady! The Seventy-Five Year History of the Woman's Club of Minneapolis* ([Minneapolis]: N.p., [1982]), 416–18.

26. Gertrude Sherwood Catherwood, "Historical Sketch of the Ladies' Floral Club of Austin, 1869–1934," 2–7 (quotation on 6), manuscript available at MHS. For woman's club activities in early-twentieth-century Minnesota, see also Margaret Lansing Oakey, "Woman's Club Movement in Minnesota," 1931, typescript available at MHS.

27. Newell Searle, "Minnesota National Forest: The Politics of Compromise, 1898–1908," *Minnesota History* 42 (Fall 1971): 242–57 (quotation on 250); Sherna Gluck, ed., *From Parlor to Prison: Five American Suffragists Talk about Their Lives* (New York: Octagon Books, 1976), 48–53.

28. Margery Burns, *A Diary of Milan: 1870–1965* (Milan: The Standard Print, [1965]), 28; minutes for Jan. 12 and 26, 1911, vol. 1 (1910–15), Pilgrim Baptist Church, Ladies Aid Society Records, MHS; minutes of the Twenty-fifth Annual Convention, Department of Minnesota, St. Paul, June 5–6, 1917, p. 92–93, Ladies of the GAR Records, MHS.

29. Sister Grace McDonald, "The Benedictine Sisters and the St. Cloud Hospital," *Minnesota History* 33 (Autumn 1953): 291–97; McDonald, *With Lamps Burning* (St. Joseph: St.

Benedict's Priory Press, 1957); Catherine Gaines Boehlke, "Profiles of Twenty-five Episcopalian Women," 1985, p. 5–8, typescript available at MHS; Patricia Condon Johnston, "Reflected Glory: The Story of Ellen Ireland," *Minnesota History* 48 (Spring 1982): 13–23; Sister Helen Angela Hurley, *On Good Ground: The Story of the Sisters of St. Joseph in St. Paul* (Minneapolis: University of Minnesota Press, 1951), 233, 240 (quotation), 245 (quotation).

30. Mary A. Molloy, *Catholic Colleges for Women* (Winona: College of St. Teresa, 1918), 7–8; Mary Mariella Bowler, *A History of Catholic Colleges for Women in the United States of America* (Washington, D.C.: Catholic University of America, 1933), 65. In the 1980s nuns were still creating institutions; Sister Mary Giovanni of St. Paul's West Side founded the Guadalupe Area Project, a school for teenagers. Richard Meryhew, "St. Paul Nun, 71, Combines Fast Talk and Hard Prayer to Make Her School Work," *Minneapolis Star and Tribune*, July 6, 1986, p. 1A, 8A.

31. Wanda Gág, *Growing Pains: Diaries and Drawings for the Years 1908–1917* (New York: Coward McCann, 1940; St. Paul: Minnesota Historical Society Press, 1984), 99.

32. Eva L. Sylvester, "The Eighteenth Annual Report," Apr. 18, 1912, Thursday Club Records, MHS; Ludcke, *You've Come a Long Way*, 52; Minnesota Association Opposed to Woman Suffrage et al., *Some of the Women in Minnesota Opposed to Woman Suffrage* (N.p., n.d.), roll 14, frame 333, Minnesota Woman Suffrage Association Records.

33. Ethel Edgerton Hurd, *Woman Suffrage in Minnesota: A Record of the Activities in Its Behalf since 1847* (Minneapolis: Inland Press, 1916), 7–14 (quotation on 12). Pruitt, "Women Unite!" 44–87, has an excellent chapter on the suffrage movement, particularly as it relates to the National Women's party and its Washington activities.

34. Nelson, "Minnesota," 778–79 (quotation on 779).

35. Emily E. Dobbin, "Reports from Auxiliary States: Minnesota," 1911, roll 1, frame 78, Minnesota Woman Suffrage Association Records.

36. Hurd, *Woman Suffrage*, 29–30, 47.

37. Pruitt, "Women Unite!" 44, 50–51; Hurd, *Woman Suffrage*, 25.

38. Clarke A. Chambers, "Ueland, Clara Hampson," in *Notable American Women* 3:498–99. Historian Theodore C. Blegen wrote that Ueland "brilliantly championed" women's suffrage. Blegen, *Minnesota: A History of the State*, 2d ed. (Minneapolis: University of Minnesota Press, 1975), 467. According to her daughter, Ueland claimed that she never learned to sew because "she would be stuck in it forever." She also told her daughter, "Never be meek" and said it over and over "in a pleasant, but very, very definite way." Brenda Ueland, *Me* (New York: G. P. Putnam's Sons, 1939; St. Paul: North Central Publishing Co., 1983), 91. A plaque in the rotunda at the Minnesota State Capitol commemorates Clara Ueland's quiet forcefulness. It reads, "May her memory save us from all pettiness, all unworthy ambition, all narrowness of vision, all mean and sordid aims, as there was no weakness in her words, no weariness on her brow, no wavering in her loyalties, so may there be none in us. As she fought ever without malice and without hatred, so may we fight."

39. Moller to Ueland, July 13, 1917 (roll 2, frames 591–92), Alice J. Mott to Ueland, Feb. 8, 1915 (roll 1, frames 227–29), Minnesota Woman Suffrage Association Records; Brenda Ueland, "Clara Ueland of Minnesota," 105, 399, typescript available at MHS.

40. Moller to Ueland, Apr. 20, 1916 (roll 1, frame 522), Minnesota Woman Suffrage Association Records. Moller later became a suffrage organizer.

41. L. Chalmers, "A Brief Sketch of the Transformation of the Woman's Suffrage Association into the League of Women Voters," 1, typescript available at MHS; William W. Folwell, *A History of Minnesota*, rev. ed., vol. 4 (St. Paul: Minnesota Historical Society, 1969), 336–37; Fanny B. Ames to Ueland, Sept. 9, 1919 (roll 7, frame 381), Minnesota Woman Suffrage Association Records.

42. Several Minnesota women were prominent among those arrested for civil disobedience: Sarah Tarleton Colvin, Rhoda Kellogg, Bertha Berglin Moller, Gertrude Murphy, and Mary Short. Doris Stevens, *Jailed for Freedom* (New York: Boni and Liveright, 1920), 354–71; Pruitt, "Women Unite!" 53–54.

43. Antisuffrage campaign literature pictured Socialist women with suffrage banners. In a debate held before the Minnesota Academy of Social Studies, Lavinia Coppock Gilfillan argued that the suffrage movement included the "Socialist Suffragist" who "hopes to overturn the governmental and property rights that she finds harassing." Another argument was that if immigrant women could vote, they would constitute a menace to American homogeneity. Gilfillan, "The Disadvantages of Equal Suffrage," in *Papers and Proceedings of the Eighth Annual Meeting of the Minnesota Academy of Social Studies*, ed. J. F. Ebersole (Minneapolis: Free Press Printing, 1915), 175, 178. Perhaps one goal of the Americanization campaign of the Woman's Committee, Commission of Public Safety, was to defuse the argument against immigrant women voting.

44. Franklin F. Holbrook and Livia Appel, *Minnesota in the War with Germany*, vol. 1 (St. Paul: Minnesota Historical Society, 1928), 332. For the experiences of one nurse during

the Spanish-American War see Shiela C. Robertson and Kathleen Ann O'Brien, "A Social History of Women: Theresa Ericksen," 6–8, 1982, photocopied curriculum material available at Upper Midwest Women's History Center for Teachers, St. Louis Park.

45. Marion Azella Backus to "Folks," June 10, 1918, Marion Azella Backus Papers, MHS.

46. Back in the United States, nursing superintendents were still trying to convince supervisors that floor scrubbing was not necessary to a nurse's education. For this and a good description of nursing in Poland during the typhus epidemic of 1920, see Leila Halverson, "Reminiscences of a Registered Nurse, 1907-1948," interview by Lila M. Johnson and Leonora J. Collatz, St. Paul, Sept. 6, 1967, p. 17-25, 27–47, transcript available at MHS. World War I nurses were not considered officers and did not receive equal pay or military benefits. See Susan M. Hartmann, *The Home Front and Beyond: American Women in the 1940's* (Boston: Twayne Publishers, 1982), 32.

47. Wellesley Club Records, MHS; Holbrook and Appel, *Minnesota in the War* 1:228–29.

48. Ida Clyde Clarke, *American Women and the World War* (New York: D. Appleton and Co., 1918), 294; George W. McCree, "Recruiting Engineer for the World War in Minnesota," *Minnesota History Bulletin* 3 (May 1920): 341. At Hamline University, 144 women instructors and students contributed 255 eight-hour working days to the war effort. Henry L. Osborn, *Hamline University in the World War* (St. Paul: [Hamline University], 1920), 23.

49. Minnesota Commission of Public Safety (MCPS), Woman's Committee, "Twelfth Ward Report," MCPS Records, MHS; Winifred D. Bolin, "North East Neighborhood House: The Process of Americanization in a Midwestern Urban Community" (M.A. thesis, University of Minnesota, 1969), 43–46; Holbrook and Appel, *Minnesota in the War* 2:158.

50. *Minneapolis Evening Tribune*, June 15, 1917; Woman's Committee, scrapbooks, 1917-19, MCPS Records; Scovell, *Brief History*, 95.

51. Franklin Holbrook, ed., *St. Paul and Ramsey County in the War of 1917–18* (St. Paul: Ramsey County War Records Commission, 1929), 230; La Vern J. Rippley, "Conflict in the Classroom," *Minnesota History* 47 (Spring 1981): 180; Edith Koivisto, untitled typescript, June 1975, p. 2, Immigration History Research Center, University of Minnesota, Minneapolis.

52. Clarke A. Chambers, "Welfare on Minnesota's Iron Range," *Upper Midwest History* 3 (1983): 11; Woman's Committee, "Americanization Report of Minnesota Woman's Committee," June 1917–November 1918, and "Reports of Director, Committee Chairmen and County Chairmen," November-December 1917 (quotation), both in MCPS Records. On Winter, see Dorothy E. Johnson, "Winter, Alice Vivian Ames," in *Notable American Women* 3:632–33.

53. Edna Honoria Akre, "League of Women Voters: Its Organization and Work" (M.A. thesis, University of Minnesota, 1926), 47–53.

54. Mrs. Robbins [Catheryne] Gilman, "Final Report of the Women's Co-operative Alliance," Dec. 15, 1932, Robbins Gilman and Family Papers, MHS; Elizabeth Gilman, "Catheryne Cooke Gilman: Social Worker," in *Women of Minnesota*, 190–207; Susan D. Becker, *The Origins of the Equal Rights Amendment: American Feminism between the Wars* (Westport, Conn.: Greenwood Press, 1981), 19.

55. Ueland, *Me*, 5; Mrs. M. A. Christensen, "Women's Mission," in *Souvenir: "Norse-American Women" 1825–1925*, ed. Alma Guttersen and Regina Hilleboe Christensen (St. Paul: Lutheran Free Church Publishing Co., 1926), 64.

56. Kathleen R. Hauser, "Eighty Years of University of Minnesota Doctorates, 1887–1967," photocopied typescript available at MHS; Myra Marx Ferree and Beth B. Hess, *Controversy and Coalition: The New Feminist Movement* (Boston: Twayne Publishers, 1985), 7; United States, *Census*, 1930, *Population*, vol. 3, part 1, 1223; Jean E. Johnson, "From Linen to Homespun," in *Every Woman Has a Story*, 195.

57. Dolores De Bower Johnson, "Anna Dickie Olesen: Senate Candidate," and Fraser and Holbert, "Women in the Minnesota Legislature," in *Women of Minnesota*, 226–46, 247–83. Minnesota was one of about twenty states where women could serve on juries. Women in some states – Virginia, for example – did not receive that right until after the 1964 Civil Rights Act.

58. Jacob R. Marcus, *The American Jewish Woman 1654–1980* (New York: KTAV Publishing House, 1981), 144. Brin was later to change her views as Hitler came into power. For more on Brin, see Barbara Stuhler, "Fanny Brin: Woman of Peace," in *Women of Minnesota*, 284–300; Ruth F. Brin, "She Heard Another Drummer: The Life of Fanny Brin, and Its Implications for the Sociology of Religion" (M.A. Plan B paper, University of Minnesota, 1972).

59. Akre, "League of Women Voters," 47; Betty Goetz Lall, "The Foreign Policy Program of the League of Women Voters of the United States" (Ph.D. diss., University of Minnesota, 1964), 29. The Minnesota WCTU also had international connections; Madame Yajima, president of the Japanese WCTU, stopped in St. Paul after presenting a petition to President Harding. American troops who landed in Japan in World War II were startled to be greeted by Japanese women wearing the familiar WCTU white ribbon. Scovell, *Brief History*, 99.

60. Mary Ellen Chase, *A Goodly Fellowship* (New York: Macmillan, 1939), 285.

61. Susan Margot Smith, "Ada Comstock Notestein: Educator," Carol Jenson, "The Larson Sisters: Three Careers in Contrast," and Harpole, "Brief Biographies," all in *Women of Minnesota*, 208–25, 301–24, 339. For Winter and Gág, see Johnson, "Winter," 3:632–33; Karen Nelson Hoyle, "Introduction," in Gág, *Growing Pains*, xiii-xxiii.

62. Stageberg, "Contribution of Women to the Building of the Farmer-Labor Party," Sept. 1, 1940, typescript, and *Report of the Sixth State Convention, Farmer-Labor Women's Clubs of Minnesota* (St. Paul: Willmar Tribune Print, 1932), 4, both in Stageberg Papers, MHS. For women's roles in the Nonpartisan League, see Karen Starr, "Fighting for a Future: Farm Women of the Nonpartisan League," *Minnesota History* 48 (Summer 1983): 255–62.

63. Carl C. Zimmerman and John D. Black, *How Minnesota Farm Family Incomes Are Spent: An Interpretation of a One Year's Study 1924–1925*, University of Minnesota Agricultural Experiment Station, *Bulletin*, no. 234 (June 1927), 20–49 (quotation on 48–49); Shiela C. Robertson and Kathleen Ann O'Brien, "A Social History of Women: Linda James Benitt," 1981, p. 28, photocopied curriculum material available at Upper Midwest Women's History Center for Teachers, St. Louis Park.

64. The United Garment Workers and Retail Clerks International Association Records are available at MHS. For more on the strikes mentioned, see Marjorie Penn Lasky, " 'Where I Was a Person': The Ladies' Auxiliary in the 1934 Minneapolis Teamsters' Strikes," in *Women, Work and Protest: A Century of U.S. Women's Labor History*, ed. Ruth Milkman (Boston: Routledge and Kegan Paul, 1985), 181–205; Meridel Le Sueur, *Salute to Spring* (New York: International Publications, 1940), 177–91; Herman Erickson, "WPA Strikes and the Trials of 1939," *Minnesota History* 42 (Summer 1971): 203–14.

65. M. C. Elmer, *A Study of Women in Clerical and Secretarial Work in Minneapolis, Minnesota* ([Minneapolis]: Minneapolis Occupational Bureau, 1925), 6, 39; Steven Trimble, *Education and Democracy: A History of the Minneapolis Federation of Teachers* (Minneapolis: Minneapolis Federation of Teachers, 1979), 20; *The Years of Depression 1930–35: Report of the Superintendent of Schools to the Board of Education* (Minneapolis: Minneapolis Board of Education, 1935), 47–48 (quotation).

66. M. C. Elmer, *A Cooperative Study of Women in Industry in Saint Paul, Minnesota* (St. Paul: St. Paul Association of Public and Business Affairs, [1924]), 5, 16; John S. Wright Family, interview by John Wright, Minneapolis, May 5, 1974, p. 22, transcript available at MHS (quotation); Carrie L. Dozier, interview by Musa Foster, Malik Simba, and Seitu Jones, Duluth, July 30, 1975, p. 17, transcript available at MHS.

67. Felicitas Herrera, interview by Victor Barela, St. Paul, Aug. 5, 1975, p. 12, transcript available at MHS.

68. Alison Bernstein, "A Mixed Record: The Political Enfranchisement of American Indian Women during the Indian New Deal," *Journal of the West* 23, no. 3 (July 1984): 13–20; U.S. WPA, Division of Women's Professional and Service Projects, Monthly Newsletter, September 1936, p. 4; Alice L. Sickels, *Around the World in St. Paul* (Minneapolis: University of Minnesota Press, 1945), 71–75.

69. Mabel S. Ulrich, "Salvaging Culture for the WPA," *Harper's Magazine*, May 1939, 653–64. Of the WPA relief projects, by far the largest was the sewing project, which employed 3,611 women in 1936. Minnesota WPA, Division of Women's Professional and Service Projects, Monthly Newsletter, July 1936.

70. Le Sueur, "Women on the Breadlines," *New Masses*, January 1932, 5–7. Another literary description of Minnesotans' declining fortunes during the depression is Mary Hedin, "Places We Lost," in *The Minnesota Experience: An Anthology*, ed. Jean Ervin (Minneapolis: Adams Press, 1979), 284–301.

71. Susan Ware, *Holding Their Own: American Women in the 1930's* (Boston: Twayne Publishers, 1982), 28; Hauser, "Eighty Years"; Nellie Stone Johnson, interview by David V. Taylor, Minneapolis, July 15, 1975, p. 86, transcript available at MHS.

72. Eva Neal, interview by David V. Taylor, St. Paul, Jan. 3, 1971, p. 12–15, transcript available at MHS; Ware, *Holding Their Own*.

73. Lall, "Foreign Policy Program," 84.

74. *Minnesota Memo to Women*, March 1943, 2, Hennepin County War Finance Committee, Women's Division Records, MHS; *World War II and the Red Cross* ([St. Paul]: American Red Cross, St. Paul Chapter, [1946]), 2. By contrast, women in World War I wrote poems about the kaiser being "the German Nero." See Eugenia B. Farmer, "God Speed Our Boys," May 1918, manuscript available at MHS.

75. *Minnesota Memo to Women*, August 1943, 7, Hennepin County War Finance Committee, Women's Division Records; minutes of the Patricia Chapter, May 20, 1943, vol. 25, National Society, Daughters of the British Empire in Minnesota Records, MHS; Betty Roney, "City Club Move Shakes Area," *St. Paul Pioneer Press*, Feb. 28, 1971, Family Life section, p. 7.

76. Carol Brink, *The Twin Cities* (New York: Macmillan, 1961), 115; Gaarder and Baker, *From Stripes to Whites*, 18; Hartmann, *Home Front and Beyond*, 35–36. Some Minnesota

women served in unusual capacities, for instance as secretary-technician at the atomic bomb development site in Los Alamos. See Frances Jacob, " 'Nervous in the Service' or 'Up and Atom,' " undated typescript available at MHS.

77. *Women Production Workers, Welcome to Minneapolis Moline* ([Minneapolis]: Minneapolis-Moline Power Implement Company, [1940]), 4, 9; Virginia Brainard Kunz, *St. Paul: Saga of an American City* (Woodland Hills, Calif.: Windsor Publications, 1977), 157; Hartmann, *Home Front and Beyond,* 77; "Women in Industry," *Monthly Labor Review* 59 (November 1944): 1029.

78. Minutes, Jan. 9, 1942, vol. 1, American Hungarian Ladies Benevolent Society Records, MHS; Sickels, *Around the World,* 156–66.

79. Masaharu Ano, "Loyal Linguists: Nisei of World War II Learned Japanese in Minnesota," *Minnesota History* 45 (Fall 1977): 273–87; Michael Albert, "The Japanese," in *They Chose Minnesota,* ed. Holmquist, 560–63. Two women who were particularly helpful to the Japanese-American community were Genevieve F. Steefel and Ruth Gage Colby.

80. Historian's Report of the Virginia Branch, 1943–44, p. 3-4, AAUW, Minnesota Division Papers, MHS; Lall, "Foreign Policy Program," 119.

81. Young Women's Christian Association of Duluth, Industrial Committee, *Women at Work: A Survey of Industrial Workers in Duluth* (Duluth: YWCA, 1945), 18; Leila J. Rupp, *Mobilizing Women for War: German and American Propaganda, 1939–1945* (Princeton, N.J.: Princeton University Press, 1978); Maureen Honey, *Creating Rosie the Riveter: Class, Gender, and Propaganda during World War II* (Amherst: University of Massachusetts Press, 1984); Commission on the Economic Status of Women, *Women in Minnesota* (St. Paul: The Commission and the Hubert H. Humphrey Institute of Public Affairs, 1984), 14.

82. Michael J. McDonough, *St. Paul Federation of Teachers: Fifty Years of Service, 1918–1968* ([St. Paul]: N.p., [1968?]), 11–27; Margaret Kelley in St. Paul teachers' union interview by Jim Dooley, St. Paul, Aug. 12, 1974, p. 4, transcript available at MHS. Among the women leaders of the strike were Mabel Colter, Florence Rood, and Mary McGough.

83. "Address by the Honorable Eugenie Anderson," May 14, 1950, Eugenie Anderson Papers, MHS.

84. Darragh Aldrich, *Lady in Law: A Biography of Mabeth Hurd Paige* (Chicago: Ralph Fletcher Seymour, 1950), 14; YWCA Industrial Committee, *Women at Work,* 2.

85. James Gray, *The University of Minnesota* (Minneapolis: University of Minnesota Press, 1951), 504.

86. Eugenia Kaledin, *Mothers and More: American Women in the 1950s* (Boston: Twayne Publishers, 1984), 43 (quotation), 53; Governor's Commission on the Status of Women, *Minnesota Women* ([St. Paul?]: The Commission, 1965), B-15.

87. Ludcke, *You've Come a Long Way,* 191 (quotation), 241, 260. By contrast, a typical program when the club was founded was "Minneapolis and the Working Girl." In the late 1940s, the Internal Revenue Service began to question the club's tax-exempt status as a charitable organization when it seemed to be primarily a social club.

88. Commission on the Economic Status of Women, *Women in Minnesota,* 14.

89. Ferree and Hess, *Controversy and Coalition,* 7; Theodore C. Blegen, "Introduction," in Vera M. Schletzer et al., *Continuing Education for Women: A Five-Year Report of the Minnesota Plan* (Minneapolis: University of Minnesota, 1967), ii iv; Kaledin, *Mothers and More,* 37 (quotation).

90. John K. Sherman, *Music and Maestros: The Story of the Minneapolis Symphony Orchestra* (Minneapolis: University of Minnesota Press, 1952), 297; Albert I. Gordon, *Jews in Transition* (Minneapolis: University of Minnesota Press, 1949), 200.

91. Hartmann, *Home Front and Beyond,* 131; Ferree and Hess, *Controversy and Coalition,* 51–53.

92. Governor's Commission on the Status of Women, *Minnesota Women* (1965), A-4, B-5, B-6 (quotation), B-11.

93. Hauser, "Eighty Years"; for national figures, see Ferree and Hess, *Controversy and Coalition,* 7.

94. Governor's Commission on the Status of Women, *Minnesota Women* (1965), A-17, A-18 (quotation), A-19. Mary Howell, later associate dean at Harvard Medical School, went through a special admission interview for married women at the University of Minnesota medical school in which the dean told her that the state was reluctant to waste money on women's education. Kaledin, *Mothers and More,* 187. As late as the 1980s, Minnesota, Idaho, and Utah had the lowest percentages of full-time female faculty – 19–21.9 percent. Anne Gibson and Timothy Fast, *The Women's Atlas of the United States* (New York: Facts on File Publications, 1986), 47. Idaho and Utah have strong Mormon populations, but why Minnesota's percentage is so low is not clear. Discrimination against women faculty may perhaps be seen as early as the attempt to remove Prof. Maria Sanford from the University of Minnesota in 1899–1900. The Women's Council of Minneapolis supported her efforts to remain and, not incidentally, the placement of her statue in the Capitol in Washington, D.C. Helen

Whitney, *Maria Sanford* (Minneapolis: University of Minnesota, 1922), 181–82. A more contemporary example is the Shyamala Rajender case of 1973, in which the University of Minnesota paid damages for sex discrimination. See "U Settles '73 Bias Lawsuit," *St. Paul Dispatch*, Apr. 21, 1980, p. 7. For a view that the number of female administrative appointments at the university is "not particularly impressive," see Marcia E. Hanson, "Women in Leadership Roles at the University of Minnesota" (M.A. Plan B paper, University of Minnesota, 1972), 22, available at MHS.

95. Governor's Commission on the Status of Women, *Minnesota Women* (1965), 1, and (1967), 10–13 (quotation on 13).

96. Catherine East, *American Women: 1963, 1983, 2003* (Washington, D.C.: National Federation of Business and Professional Women's Clubs, 1983), 7 (Mary Pruitt called this source to my attention); Roney, "City Club Move," p. 1; Ludcke, *You've Come a Long Way*, 316; League of Women Voters of Minnesota, *Women in the Labor Force* (Minneapolis: League of Women Voters, 1962), 11.

97. National Organization for Women, Minnesota Chapter Records, MHS. The abortion reform bill was introduced by Helen E. McMillan, one of the two women members of the house of representatives at the time; see "New Abortion Law Try Planned Again," *St. Paul Dispatch*, Apr. 10, 1970, p. 7. Among its supporters was Jane Hodgson, a Minnesota physician who publicly announced that she had performed abortions. Minnesota Citizens Concerned for Life was instrumental in forming the National Right to Life Committee.

98. Sara Evans, *Personal Politics: The Roots of Women's Liberation in the Civil Rights Movement and the New Left* (New York: Alfred A. Knopf, 1979), 156–92 (quotation on 170).

99. Becky Swanson Kroll, "Rhetoric and Organizing: The Twin Cities Women's Movement, 1969–1976" (Ph.D. diss., University of Minnesota, 1981), 56, 104–5, 423; Margaret Thomson, interview by Gloria Thompson, Minneapolis, Oct. 15, 1972, p. 1, 11–13, transcript available at MHS.

100. *Female Liberation Newsletter* (Minneapolis and St. Paul), Apr. 16, 1970, available at MHS.

101. Alpha Smaby, "The Minnesota Conference of Concerned Democrats and the Anti-Vietnam Crusade" (M.A. thesis, University of Minnesota, 1982), 39–42 (quotation on 41).

102. Kate Millett, *Sexual Politics* (Garden City, N.Y.: Doubleday and Co., 1970); Commission on the Economic Status of Women, *Women in Minnesota*, 14, 29; "Minnesota Poll: More Men Than Women Approve Women's Lib," *Minneapolis Tribune*, Jan. 21, 1973, p. 13E. Men were more sympathetic – 41 percent as opposed to 30 percent of women – but 70 percent of women (as opposed to 59 percent of men) believed women would "make significant gains in the next five years."

103. Commission on the Economic Status of Women, *Women in Minnesota*, 8; Kroll, "Rhetoric and Organizing," 317–67, 412. In 1972, lesbians protested Betty Friedan's speech before the Minnesota Women's Political Caucus to draw attention to gay rights. Toni McNaron, English professor at the University of Minnesota, was generally recognized as a national leader in lesbian rights.

104. Mary Ziegenhagen to Arvonne Fraser, Aug. 24, 1971, Fraser Papers, MHS (quotation); Dinah Luise Leavitt, *Feminist Theatre Groups* (Jefferson, N.C.: McFarland and Co., 1980). Other theaters were the Alive and Trucking Theatre Company, the Lavender Cellar Theatre, and Circle of the Witch.

105. M. Ampe et al., "State of the Organization 1978," p. 2–3, WARM Records, MHS.

106. Twin Cities Chapter, *NOW Newsletter*, February 1973, p. 4, Fraser Papers, MHS.

107. Steven Dornfeld, "Minnesota Ratifies Women's Amendment," *Minneapolis Tribune*, Feb. 9, 1973, p. 1A, 5A; Robert Whereatt, "Influence of Women Has Grown, Changed in the Legislature," *Minneapolis Star and Tribune*, Feb. 2, 1987, p. 15A; Kahn Papers, MHS. For a list of women in the state legislature from 1923 to 1986, see Commission on the Economic Status of Women, *Newsletter*, December 1986, 3–4.

108. Biographical data on these women can be found under their names in the Library Biography Files, MHS.

109. On women's shelters, see *Women's Advocates: The Story of a Shelter* (St. Paul: Women's Advocates, 1980). Among curriculum projects promoted by the two education groups were Minneapolis Public Schools, Women's Studies Dept., "Eliminating Sex Bias in Education," 1979; St. Paul Public Schools, Urban Affairs Dept., "America's Women of Color," ca. 1979; Northfield Public Schools, "Women in American Culture," 1983; and St. Louis Park Public Schools and Robbinsdale Public Schools, "Women in World Area Studies," 1980–87; all available at Upper Midwest Women's History Center for Teachers, St. Louis Park. The Learn Me bookstore in St. Paul became known for its nonsexist books for children. University of Minnesota professors Andrea Hinding and Clarke A. Chambers organized the Women's History Sources Survey, a research project that aided historians nationwide in finding women's history collections.

110. Alla Bozarth-Campbell, *Womanpriest: A Personal Odyssey* (New York: Paulist Press, 1978), 125. Suzanne Hiatt, another of the original female Episcopal priests, was born and raised in Minnesota. The "Willmar 8" were Doris Boshart, Sylvia Erickson, Jane Harguth, Terren Novotny, Shirley Solyntjes, Glennis Ter Wisscha, Sandi Treml, and Irene Wallin. Mary Ann Grossman, "7 Female Strikers Picket Willmar Bank," *St. Paul Dispatch,* Dec. 16, 1977, p. 1, 2. Though two films of the strike were made, the best is Lee Grant (director), *The Willmar Eight* (San Francisco: California Newsreel/Media at Work, 1979). On the nurses' strike see Gordon Slovut, Lewis Cope, and Josephine Marcetty, "6,000 Nurses Go on Strike," *Minneapolis Star and Tribune,* June 2, 1984, p. 1A, 6A, 7A.

111. A good source for the activity in the Twin Cities during the 1970s is Kroll, "Rhetoric and Organizing," which includes a chronology of events (p. 418–52).

112. "NOW's Guide Ranks States on Women's Rights," *Minneapolis Star and Tribune,* Dec. 11, 1986, p. 27A; NOW Legal Defense and Education Fund and Dr. Renée Cherow-O'Leary, *The State-by-State Guide to Women's Legal Rights* (New York: McGraw-Hill Book Co., 1987), 282–87. The information on comparable worth is from a conversation with Nina Rothchild, May 25, 1988. On Minnesota's parental leave law, see "Minnesota Orders Employers to Offer New Parents Leaves," *New York Times,* June 18, 1987, p. 20A.

113. Barbara Stuhler, *No Regrets: Minnesota Women and the Joan Growe Senatorial Campaign* (St. Paul: Braemar Press, 1986); Bruce Benidt and Martha Sawyer Allen, "Arvonne Fraser: Candidacy Offers Chance to Stump for Women, Reality," *Minneapolis Star and Tribune,* July 7, 1986, p. 1C, 2C.

114. Martha S. Allen, "Pornography Law Vetoed: Mayor Cites Doubts on Constitutionality," *Minneapolis Star and Tribune,* Jan. 6, 1984, p. 1A, 9A, 10A. The Minneapolis proposal led to the adoption of a similar ordinance in Indianapolis, which was struck down by the courts.

115. *Contemporary American Indian Women: Careers and Contributions* (Cass Lake: Minnesota Chippewa Tribe, 1983); Edna Garte, *Circle of Life: Cultural Continuity in Ojibwe Crafts* (Duluth: St. Louis County Historical Society, Chisholm Museum, and Duluth Art Institute, 1984). The Minneapolis American Indian Center also hosted exhibits of women artists.

116. Roger Buffalohead and Priscilla Buffalohead, *Against the Tide of History: The Story of the Mille Lacs Anishinabe* (Cass Lake: Minnesota Chippewa Tribe, 1985), 138; Ignatia Broker, *Night Flying Woman: An Ojibway Narrative* (St. Paul: Minnesota Historical Society Press, 1983), 2.

117. Carol Lacey, "Black Women Determined to Keep Gains," and "Groups' Aims Well-Focused," *St. Paul Pioneer Press,* Oct. 12, 1986, p. 1G, 3G, 4G.

118. In a conversation with the author, Valerie Hauch, a member of the Peace Encampment, said that the protest lasted from Oct. 1, 1983, to Oct. 1, 1984, and carried on various acts of civil disobedience against Sperry that resulted in some arrests. After the closing of the camp, members continued to work in peace and justice organizations and traveled to Britain to make international contacts. See also Kevin Diaz, "Year-long Sperry Vigil Ends in 17 Arrests," *Minneapolis Star and Tribune,* Oct. 1, 1984, p. 1B.

119. Blakely, "From Minnesota," 60 (quotation); Jean Hopfensperger, "Area Suburbs Lead in U.S. Income Statistic," *Minneapolis Star and Tribune,* Feb. 23, 1987, p. 15A, 20A. For Bancroft, see Sharon Schmickle, "She Feared Failure More Than Death," *Minneapolis Star and Tribune,* July 6, 1986, Sunday Magazine, p. 4–9, 19. For Krupp, see Doug Grow, "Female Wide Receiver Isn't about to Drop Her Dream," *Minneapolis Star and Tribune,* Aug. 31, 1986, p. 1C, 5C.

120. Anne Ostberg, "Farm Women Show Their Strengths as Crisis in Agriculture Deepens," *Minnesota Women's Press,* Nov. 11–24, 1986, 1 (quotation), 6–7. For an expression of connection to the land, see Carol Bly, *Letters from the Country* (New York: Harper and Row, 1981), 8–13.

121. Commission on the Economic Status of Women, *Women in Minnesota,* 20, and *Minnesota Women and Poverty* (St. Paul: The Commission, 1985), 1–2; Jeann Linsley, "Women's Coalition Rallies against Aid Cuts," *St. Paul Pioneer Press and Dispatch,* Feb. 23, 1986, p. 4A; Gene Lahammer, "Bishops Condemn Welfare Cuts," *St. Paul Pioneer Press and Dispatch,* Feb. 28, 1986, p. 1C.

122. Meridel Le Sueur, "A Comet, a Child; A Comet, a Woman," *Minneapolis Star and Tribune,* Nov. 24, 1985, Sunday Magazine, p. 12; "Woman of the Year: Minnesota's First Woman Supreme Court Justice Rosalie Wahl," in *Minnesota Woman's Yearbook 1978-'79,* ed. Julianne Corty (Minneapolis: Sprague Publications, 1978), 102.

123. Bly, *Letters from the Country,* 53. For a view of woman as "civilizer," see Gordon, *Jews in Transition,* 197–98. "If it weren't for our wives, I believe that most of us men would stay away from these things which my wife calls 'cultural.' When I get home from the office, I don't like to go gallivanting around, but my wife keeps on insisting, so we go. I suppose that's why I go to the concerts of the Minneapolis symphony orchestra . . . and I've even had to go to the ballet with her."

Singing class at Whittier School, Minneapolis, about 1925

CLARKE A. CHAMBERS

Educating for the Future

Vida Squier traveled from her home in Pennsylvania to Ely, Minnesota, in 1890 to teach school. "I knew I was at the end of the railroad," she said of her first morning in the new iron-mining town on the Vermilion Range, "but I felt I was at the end of the world." Years later she described her six years of teaching immigrant children as "the happiest time of my life." In her "infant class" in 1890 she had seventy children between the ages of five and eight. "The rooms were very meager and there were no supplies," she recalled. "In my room there was a teacher's desk, some small desks and several long benches. Children had to be placed wherever there was any space. An old fashioned coal burner stood in the corner and a movable blackboard in front of the room. There were no books. Reading was taught from a large chart." Few of the children spoke English but they were obedient and loved to come to school, which was "the one bright spot in their lives."[1]

More than twenty years earlier, when William Watts Folwell was appointed the first president of the University of Minnesota, he proclaimed the benefits of a university education to citizen and community. The university, he said, was an agent of popular will; it derived from the people and it ultimately served the people, even if its benefits could not always be measured in immediate or direct economic gain. Higher education "will put bread into no man's mouth directly, nor money in his palm. Neither the rains nor the sunshine do that, but they warm and nourish the spring grass, and ripen the harvest. So higher education, generous culture, scholarship, literature, inform, inspire, and elevate communities."[2]

Out of nineteenth-century American experience arose a faith both in the practical utility of education for daily life and the immeasurable benefits that flowed to the community from learning. This faith moved early settlers in new communities to turn at once to the building of a common school, and it encouraged later immigrants to see education as the way for their children to enter the new society; it also inspired the territorial legislature to found a university as early as 1851. When combined with the desire to preserve ethnic and sectarian loyalties, this faith impelled religious

First graduates of an English-language class for Hmong immigrants at Lao Family Community, St. Paul, 1981

groups to create parochial school systems and to build colleges in which spiritual life would be nourished and teachers of future generations would be trained.

However simple the fundamental beliefs of this faith in education, the enterprises that it set in motion – both public and private – became astoundingly complex over the decades in Minnesota: elementary schools that taught boys and girls the three Rs, along with habits of punctuality, industry, and honesty; junior and senior high schools that taught citizenship and useful occupations, as well as preparing some students for higher education; normal schools and teachers colleges that trained women and men for careers in education; vocational and technical schools in which high school graduates learned occupational skills in environments supportive of general education; community or junior colleges that offered entry into higher education; a university system that awarded baccalaureate and graduate degrees in hundreds of academic disciplines. In addition, the state created special schools for children with handicaps and reform schools for the education and correction of youths determined by the courts to be "delinquent."

By the 1980s there was hardly a formal agency of education in Minnesota that had not initiated "outreach," "extension," or "continuing" programs of learning for children and adults as well. Sunday schools, confirmation classes, and Bible study courses were sponsored by every congregation, parish, and synagogue. Education became the chief mission of a myriad voluntary associations – the Red Cross, Tuberculosis Association, Girl and Boy Scouts, YMCA and YWCA, 4-H clubs, settlement houses, Jewish community centers, and Great Books discussion groups, to name just a few. The Minnesota Humanities Commission, after its founding in 1971, brought scholars and citizens together to explore intellectual and cultural issues much as the Chautauqua and Lyceum had done two generations earlier. All agents of education, whether formal or informal, have their own special histories. This essay cannot detail the dazzling array of stories – it can only strive to shed light on the significant processes that have characterized Minnesota education in the twentieth century.

Teaching Basics to Youngsters

By 1900 the pattern of elementary education in Minnesota had become clear. In every rural community, village, town, and city, citizens had

Children playing outside a public school in Redwood Falls, about 1904

created school districts that were governed by an elected school board having the authority to levy taxes on local property to finance the common schools. Other units of local government raised and expended funds for roads and bridges, courthouses and village halls, sewers and water mains; civil servants were employed to register deeds, audit the books, survey the land, enforce the law, and render justice – but schooling consumed a large proportion of the budgets of Minnesota's communities. In 1906, with a statewide enrollment of 432,000 students, the districts spent a total of $9.8 million on public education.[3]

In isolated rural communities, the ungraded, one-room schoolhouse that is cherished in myth and memory as the cradle of democracy still dominated the educational landscape. There the schoolteacher, usually a woman who was not much older than her rambunctious charges, labored to maintain order so that the fundamentals of reading, writing, and calculation could be taught to eager – or resistant – young minds. There, also, parents and neighbors gathered to discuss community affairs, celebrate holidays, sing and pray and stage Christmas pageants (unconcerned with issues of separation of church and state), or just socialize on a weekend evening. The local schoolhouse thus served as an all-purpose community center. There as well the ambitious politicians met their constituents, "home talent" entertained with music and readings, and women's and farmers' clubs assembled.[4]

The schools' chief function was to teach basics to young pupils, and in that task local school board members had the first and final say. They hired and fired the teachers, set the calendar, authorized books and supplies, made up the budget, set the millage tax, and supervised the course of instruction. To qualify for the financial subsidies that the state provided – until 1915 these were modest, flat grants from the Permanent School Fund – rural schools had to meet minimum standards concerning length of sessions and teacher qualifications. In the early years of the century, observed Folwell in his *History of Minnesota*, "the inspection of the rural schools was left to busy county superintendents, who were often incompetent and indifferent."[5]

On most matters, local boards enjoyed ample elbowroom to make their own decisions. They preferred women teachers in the elementary grades, a view that persisted throughout the century: women were considered more flexible, less rule-bound, closer to young children and therefore more caring. Moreover, young women – many from the same farm neighborhoods that they served as teachers – could be hired at salaries substantially lower than those their male peers could command. Eighty-five percent of the teachers in Minnesota districts in 1906 were women, earning an average of thirty-nine dollars a month; the average for men was forty-nine dollars. Some educators of the period were alarmed about the "feminization" of teaching, especially for its effects on the young boys in the classroom: "If the whole national civilization should receive the feminine stamp, it would become powerless, and without decisive influence on the world's progress." The turnover of women teachers was high, of course, as marriage called them away to families of their own.[6]

Despite features that were common to all of Minnesota's elementary schools in the early 1900s, there were major differences between rural and urban schools. Most important, perhaps, the larger populations of towns and cities allowed separation of students according to grade, so that each teacher commanded a room of students of theoretically the same age and ability. In practice, as many a harried teacher knew, the level of abilities ranged enormously, especially in the higher grades: eagerness and quickness to learn were not uniformly shared among age-peers. Urban schools, in addition, could afford better textbooks and teaching aids, libraries, and special teachers for music and art, and they had the resources to attract teachers with more formal training.[7] As the state grew in population and wealth the investment in elementary education grew apace, especially in larger towns and cities and on the iron ranges, where steady increases in the value of taxable properties provided a broader base to exploit for the common good. By about 1920, spending for schools in mining towns was "lavish beyond comparison," said Folwell. "Chisholm expended $275,000 for a high school building [and] $300,000 for a grade school building. . . . The city of Hibbing outdid all the towns on the Mesabi Range, putting $350,000 into a building for its grade schools and $3,800,000 into one for its high school and junior college."[8]

Although no region of the state could compete with this spending, other districts replaced buildings of simple clapboard construction with schoolhouses of stone or brick and turned adjoining land into playgrounds with swings, giant slides, seesaws, and playing fields. Gymnasiums, auditoriums, and even simple shops were added to classroom facilities. Superintendents employed teachers having normal-school training or (when that option became available) those who had completed a four-year teachers college course. Sixty percent of all elementary teachers in Minnesota in 1904 did not even hold a high school diploma, but less than 10 percent fell into that category by 1926. By the mid-1920s, according to W. E. Peik of the University of Minnesota, the more progressive elementary schools in the state, inspired by a vision of the expanded social role of the schools, had moved toward the development of a "child-centered, child-active, socialized school" in which teachers and principals hoped to cultivate "the open, tolerant mind, and the scientific outlook that are fundamental traits of good citizenship in a democracy."[9]

Preparing Adolescents for Work and Citizenship

The move to extend the number of years that young people spent in school was well under way by the end of the nineteenth century. People of means had always been able to provide private secondary education for their children, and advocates of public high schools wanted to open this opportunity to all capable students. The rapid expansion of adolescent education in the United States came between 1900 and 1940, when the proportion of young people enrolled in classes above the eighth grade increased from roughly 10 to 67 percent; by 1967, the figure had reached nearly 90 percent. About 1,500 students graduated from Minnesota high schools in 1900; in 1988 the number was an estimated 58,000.[10]

The motives behind the extension of education were several from the beginning. It prepared adolescents for the working life that awaited them when they became adults. Education was intended to inculcate the values and habits deemed essential to the efficiency of industry and commerce in the modern world – punctuality, self-discipline, deference to authority, the ability and will to follow rules, initiative, and a competitive spirit within a context of teamwork. In addition, it was expected to advance the political sophistication and patriotism of future citizens of the republic, promote a worthy use of leisure time, and provide a solid academic base for the growing number of students that planned to attend institutions of higher learning.

Intermediate schooling was shaped to fit the psychological and social needs of adolescents as they passed from childhood to young adulthood. They were encouraged to participate in extracurricular programs in music and sports and in organized activities like debate and 4-H clubs. These programs consumed the energies of boys and girls in after-school hours, often on school property and with the guidance of selected teachers. Students were able to explore new interests and to try out new aptitudes while honing their skills in basic subjects. English, science, and social studies were cited in 1934 as the major course offerings, with languages and advanced science and mathematics available for students preparing for college; offerings for students preparing to work after graduation included commercial subjects, home economics, industrial arts, and agriculture.[11]

In Minnesota, as in the nation, these developments made manifest the dramatic ways in which the public schools had became a primary agent in the complicated drive toward modernization. Industry required a body of common laborers, with at least rudimentary skills in communication and computation, who would show up at mine or factory on time and prepared to put in a fair day's work for a fair day's wage. Industry also needed a cadre of skilled technicians able to design and operate complex production systems. As the modern corporation became increasingly bureaucratic and hierarchical, it added a demand for large clerical and managerial staffs to manipulate the flow of paper, money and credit, and natural and human resources that constituted the productive materials of contemporary enterprise. Corporations, governments, department stores, banks, churches, trade unions, the schools themselves – all needed people who were trained in various crafts and skills and schooled to reliability and order.

The schools were expected to play a crucial role in the sorting and selecting of people to fulfill these diverse social and economic functions. Within high schools, the dichotomy between so-called terminal education and the college-preparatory curriculum was one reflection of the difficulties associated with this enlarged educational mission. Fred Engelhardt, a professor in education at the University of Minnesota, wrote in 1934 that "the focus of attention [in high schools] on preparation for college entrance is no longer what it was three decades ago" at the beginning of the century. "Many of the high school pupils are being prepared to enter business and to assume responsibilities in the home, the shop, and the farm." But in 1967 educators were referring to the "breakdown of the clear and simple distinction between academic and vocational or terminal education," identifying such causes as the increased proportion of young people enrolled in high school and the complexity of the jobs for which they were preparing. (By 1988, the return to the early purpose of secondary schooling – preparation for college – was clear in the decision of state evaluators to use college entrance standards in assessing Minnesota's high schools. "Between 1979 and 1988, the proportion of high school juniors planning to complete at least four years of college increased from 41 to 64 percent," the evaluators said, while acknowledging that the schools also fulfilled "other objectives, including vocational training, art performance, and citizenship preparation.")[12]

The Emerging Consensus

After a generation of experience, Minnesota educators settled upon a consensus regarding the role of the public schools in the twentieth century. Teachers and principals came together in Minneapolis in 1935 to draft a statement of purpose, and although their report reflected some concerns peculiar to life in the Great Depression and the bias of a large urban school system, it contained broad agreement about the mission of education. The public schools could not "build a new social order," but they could train students to "think clearly about social problems" and teach "tolerance for other people's opinions, cooperation in worth while tasks, fair play, and honesty both in school and out." Evidence of the continuing influence of John Dewey and other progressive educators was the observation that "the effectiveness of a person depends upon his ability to adjust himself to his social order. . . . [T]his is not a static order but a dynamic and changing one. The schools are the most powerful force in making sure that the change is an improvement."[13]

Moreover, the schools were obliged to recognize the differences among students "in order that each individual may develop to his fullest capacity for living a happy and effective life." All students should be able to participate in "purposeful activity," a goal that required attention to emotional as well as intellectual interests. Well along in the report came the simple declaration that the schools tutored students in fundamental skills essential to effective social and economic activity.

The grand consensus expressed in this report had evolved slowly in Minnesota, and it persisted for decades. In 1951, for example, the state Department of Education set down the criteria by which a "good school" could be measured. The basic ingredients were all there: "training in the fine and practical arts as well as in the academic subjects"; "effective habits of study"; recognition of individual differences, both social and intellectual, so that all aspects of personality would be advanced; "health, social growth, character development, academic proficiency, training in motor skills, and appreciation of the fine arts"; and "preparation for life and citizenship in a complex society." That the schools were believed to function as agencies for social stability and order was reflected in the declaration that *all* young persons, as future citizens, had to be led to an "understanding of the problems of modern life" without which the republic risked the development of "class distinctions which will undermine the stability of American democracy."[14]

Fundamental discrepancies in the implementation of these principles persisted between rural and urban school districts, between the relatively poor and the relatively affluent. Rural and small-town schools often lacked the financial resources to offer a range of college-preparatory courses, and they were sometimes unable to provide enriched extracurricular programs in sports and the arts. Rural teenagers were also more likely to drop out of formal schooling before their age-peers in urban districts. According to the 1940 federal census, high percentages of sixteen- and seventeen-year-olds in Minnesota's farm districts were not attending school – 56 percent of the boys and 37 percent of the girls. Nonetheless, over the years thousands of students from rural schools continued their education beyond high school, made outstanding academic records, and subsequently pursued productive careers. In statewide competitions, individuals and teams from districts that were judged by standard criteria to be "inferior" proved their quality when it came to music, declamation, and sports.[15]

Teaching the Teachers

Before the 1860s schooling was largely a rural and village affair, and most teachers worked in the elementary grades. The young women hired by local school boards were trained by elected county superintendents who represented the interests and disposition of their constituents more than of the profession. School boards in rural areas, moreover, tended to be skeptical (often with sound cause) of the expertise claimed by certified – and distant – educators. Why did presumably intelligent young people, familiar with their community and its families, have to be taught how to teach?

In time, however, resistance weakened and the state established normal schools – at Winona, Mankato, and St. Cloud in the 1860s, Moorhead in 1888, Duluth in 1902, and Bemidji in 1913. These schools, which were intended to serve their own regional clientele, offered similar two-year curricula that included introductory courses in substantive areas, courses in psychology and methods, and practice teaching. Summer schools and institutes were inaugurated in 1891 to upgrade the skills of teachers already on the job. In 1909 the normal schools introduced special courses to prepare teachers of manual training, agriculture, home economics, art, and music.[16]

Teachers and administrators of Lincoln School, St. Paul, about 1900

At the turn of the century the Minnesota Education Association (MEA), a professional organization of teachers and administrators founded in 1861, cited "the increasing demand upon the high schools of the state" in calling for better preparation of teachers. Responding to calls for certified teachers, especially at the secondary level, the state high school board enacted a requirement in 1913 that high school teachers hold a baccalaureate degree. As part of this drive to raise standards, the 1921 legislature upgraded the six normal schools to four-year state teachers colleges that would offer baccalaureate degrees with a concentration in education.[17]

About half of the teachers in Minnesota's public schools between 1900 and 1950 were trained in normal schools or state teachers colleges, and the rest entered teaching by other educational routes. The University of Minnesota's College of Education, which was established in 1905, provided training for teachers and, increasingly, for principals and superintendents. A substantial number of graduates of private secular and church-affiliated liberal arts colleges also turned to careers in teaching. By midcentury, public high school teachers came in almost equal proportions (20 to 30 percent each) from the state teachers college system, the University of Minnesota, the state's four-year private liberal arts colleges, and institutions outside of Minnesota.[18]

In Minnesota, as in other states, women teachers continued to predominate in the elementary grades and outnumbered men (by varying margins) among high school teachers in most areas of learning; of the new teachers hired in 1930, men were the majority only in commercial subjects, general science, industrial and manual training, physical education for boys, and physics. In the 1980s, 77 percent of the teachers in elementary schools and 36 percent of those in secondary schools were women; men held 86 percent of the administrative positions.[19]

As more students attended public schools for longer periods of time, and as the schools were expected to perform more social and educational functions, the teacher in the classroom was joined in the 1920s by school employees who offered other services. Visiting teachers, later called school social workers, mediated between the families of troubled pupils and the schools and helped the "acting-out" child adjust to the social realities of the school environment. Counseling staffs "tracked" students into courses deemed appropriate to their talents, interests, and likely careers. They were also responsible for identifying and guiding students who had emotional or psychological problems and for steering students into educational or employment programs after graduation.[20]

Indeed, counseling services made such rapid strides that a proponent could proclaim enthusiastically in 1930 that progressive urban schools compiled records on every pupil, "giving his physical history, his attendance, his achievement in school subjects, his intelligence quotient, his achievement in special activities, his social and recreational life outside of school, and like data. We have come to a place," he rejoiced, "where diagnosis and guidance are based upon something more than the chance insight of a well-intentioned counselor." Not all schools adopted such comprehensive and invasive systems, but progressive educators agreed that professional guidance constituted an indispensable part of sound education for the life of the whole person.

Governing the Local Schools

Budgets rose sharply in the twentieth century as the schools grew and expanded their services. Between 1900 and 1925 total annual expenditures of Minnesota's public elementary and secondary schools soared from $5.6 million to $56.3 million, while the costs per pupil increased from $14.14 to $106.10. Until the formula for state aid to public education was sharply adjusted in the 1970s, most of these costs fell on local property owners – 80 percent in 1915, 75 percent in 1932, more than 50 percent through the 1960s. Understandably, the sums that any school district could invest depended upon the size of the local tax base and the willingness of taxpayers to tap that reservoir, leading to concern about the inequality of schooling in different parts of the state.[21]

School boards, which were subject to regular election by each district's citizens – solid, *tax-paying* citizens, in common parlance – determined annual budgets and thereby the tax millage for education. In most rural and small-town districts, control of the boards gravitated naturally to people of standing in the community, typically influential men on Main Street and

Ungraded classroom in Lac qui Parle County, 1956

their wives. The boards looked to the superintendents they hired to manage resources and personnel within such broad guidelines as board members chose to lay down. The wise and effective superintendent made certain that he stayed within budget, quieted teachers who threatened to rock the boat, managed difficult students with firm but benign discipline, and maintained good relations in the community by regular participation in Kiwanis, the Junior Chamber of Commerce, and church. He strove to preserve the fact (or the appearance) of a stable and happy family life. If luck was with him he could boast of at least one winning team among the seasons of football, basketball, hockey, and track. To him, because the school was the chief embodiment of civic pride and virtue, the community looked for progressive and sound leadership. Whether the times were prosperous or depressed, community morale in rural Minnesota depended heavily on popular perceptions of how well the school was doing.

Until the pace of centralization and consolidation increased in the 1950s, school districts enjoyed a large degree of autonomy in the running of the schools. Local boards had broad latitude in hiring and firing personnel, setting salary schedules, and defining job expectations (number of class periods, number of students per class, hall and lunchroom duty, and like conditions). State superintendents of public instruction – a position created in 1849 – were often men of some professional distinction, but the office they occupied had little authority and the influence they exerted had to be indirect. The legislature created the State Board of Education and the Department of Education in 1919 to provide general oversight over public elementary and secondary education; a decade later the legislature gave the state board authority over teacher certification. Nearly a half century passed, however, before the department's influence on curriculum, textbooks and teaching materials, special services, and administration became effective.[22]

Another source of influence on public education was the MEA, which labored to raise educational standards, increase state aid to local districts, improve teaching methods, attract able young people into the profession, and advance the social (and financial) status of teachers. The influence of parents was exercised through local units of the Parent-Teacher Association (PTA), which was organized on a statewide basis in 1922; this organization contributed substantially to public understanding of schooling and helped to close the distance between the family and the school. More effective in shaping year-to-year district policies were the coordinating efforts of the Minnesota School Boards Association, organized in 1921, which also came to exercise considerable clout as a lobbying agency with state government. The first and final authority, however, rested with the board that managed the local school district, and most boards vigorously resisted the impulse toward consolidation and centralization. Established traditions of governance came under challenge beginning at midcentury, as pressures favoring consolidation of the state's many districts (7,657 in 1945) gathered strength, but until then the system continued along accustomed paths.[23]

Private Schools and Special Public Schools

Private schools, both secular and parochial, evolved parallel to Minnesota's public school system. Although Protestant denominations founded scattered schools in the state, Roman Catholic schools accounted for a majority of all students in private schools – 90 percent in 1940. The motive for Catholic education in Minnesota, as in the nation, was a determination to maintain religious loyalty in a predominantly Protestant society. Catholics recognized that the public schools represented forceful agencies for socialization to American (in other words, to secular or Protestant) norms. Immigrant communities, primarily Irish and German but including Polish and Bohemian nationals as well, sought through their own schools to preserve cherished beliefs and customs. A Catholic diocese could call on the willing service of various orders of nuns or of lay teachers trained in Catholic normal schools and colleges.[24]

In 1940, about 13 percent of all elementary and secondary pupils in Minnesota attended parochial or other private schools; in 1987 the figure was about 10 percent. Parochial schools have been especially strong in such heavily Catholic urban centers as St. Paul and St. Cloud. And families who chose parochial schools for their children were also likely to encourage them to attend Catholic colleges – the Colleges of St. Thomas and St. Catherine in St. Paul, St. John's University and the College of St. Benedict in Stearns County, or St. Mary's College and the College of St. Teresa in

Winona, for example. Graduates of these colleges, in turn, went back into the parochial system as teachers.[25]

Other private schools were founded in the mid-nineteenth and early twentieth centuries, largely to prepare the children of affluent families for elite colleges and universities, many of them in the East. Some, like Breck School (originally established by Episcopalians at Wilder in 1886), received funding and oversight through the church; St. Mary's Hall (1866) and Shattuck School (1867) in Faribault, also founded by the Episcopal church, were residential campuses. Among the secular institutions were Oak Hall and Summit School for girls and St. Paul Academy for boys in St. Paul and Northrop Collegiate and Blake in Minneapolis; all were governed by free-standing boards. Because most graduates of these schools continued on to college, their courses of study stressed academic subjects. Like Catholic schools, the Protestant academies typically offered daily worship services and stressed the moral as well as the intellectual and social growth of their students.[26]

From its origins in the nineteenth century, education for Minnesota's Indian children took the path of replacing Indian culture with the values and manners of white society. It was a policy "based on the well-known inferiority of the great mass of Indians in religion, intelligence, morals, and home life," said the U.S. commissioner of Indian affairs in 1899. Boarding schools, which removed the child from the influence of the home, were the model for Indian education into the 1920s; they were operated by religious denominations or by the federal government. Students in these schools were forbidden to speak in their native language and were required to follow "American" values, habits, and dress styles; the daily routine was ordered and inflexible and discipline was severe. Girls were trained in home economics and domestic crafts, boys in agricultural and industrial trades.[27]

In 1928 a critical national survey of Indian affairs known as the Meriam Report revealed the poor conditions present in most Indian boarding schools, leading finally to their abandonment. The state assumed full responsibility for Indian education in 1936, with the help of extra funding supplied by the federal government. But even before this time, Minnesota's public schools had included many Indian children: 65 percent of the state's Ojibway students were in public schools in 1926, as opposed to 23 percent in government day and boarding schools and the rest in two mission schools.

Other boarding schools in the state served a quite different clientele. The Minnesota School for the Deaf was founded in Faribault in 1863; an 1896 information circular proclaimed the school "not an asylum or a public charity, any more than our normal schools or universities." Rather, it was an educational institution whose aim was to prepare boys and girls with handicaps for lives of economic independence. In line with that goal, boys were trained in useful trades – printing, tailoring, cooperage, cabinet-making, and baking; girls were trained for marriage and motherhood or domestic service in the homes of others. Sensitive to developments in other educational settings, the staff saw to it that students had access to a range of activities outside the classrooms and shops – sports, scouting, girls' clubs, and even a drum corps. State schools for children who were blind or retarded followed much the same pattern of programs and expectations.[28]

The state also provided "homes" or "schools" for youths deemed to be dependent, neglected, or delinquent. Conditions varied from one protected institutional environment to another, but in their essentials they followed similar lines. The philosophy set down in the beginning for the State Training School for Boys and Girls, for example, guided policy there for many years. The school, which opened in 1891 at Red Wing, was designed "to counteract the results of idleness and evil companionship by moral and intellectual instruction, and by training to habits of industry through useful and remunerative occupations."[29]

Vocational and Technical Education

Most secondary schools added training in manual, technical, or agricultural skills to the curriculum in the early decades of the century. In this development, part of a national trend, Minnesota neither lagged nor pioneered. Proponents of applied training hoped to rationalize the entrance of youths into the labor market. Young women trained in commercial courses – stenography, typing, bookkeeping – could command better entry-level jobs in clerical occupations when certified by the schools. Young men with basic classroom experience in mechanics, design, and drafting were better prepared for on-the-job training in their first employment. Progressive educators believed, moreover, that training girls in home management, cooking, and sewing provided them with practical skills essential to their futures as wives and mothers while, at the same time, socializing them to appropriate female norms. As for boys, they were to learn habits of regular and careful work, accuracy and precision, self-discipline, and earnest attention to rules – "fooling around" was not permitted in the school shop. In rural areas farm boys did not have to be taught how to milk cows or make hay, but courses in the fundamentals of "scientific" agronomy and farm management trained them to be more efficient and productive when they took up farming as young adults.

In 1909 the state legislature granted subsidies to schools for the inauguration of applied courses in agriculture, industry, and domestic science. Vocational education was intended "to train the character as well as the intellect," in the words of F. E. Spaulding, superintendent of schools in Minneapolis. St. Paul had established the Mechanic Arts High School in the 1890s. In Minneapolis, the William Hood Dunwoody Industrial Institute was founded in 1914. The Girls Vocational High School, also established that year in Minneapolis, taught home management, dressmaking, millinery, catering, practical nursing, commercial design, sales, and stenography. When the federal government provided matching funds through the Smith-Hughes Act in 1917, Minnesota moved quickly to appropriate state money to expand vocational education.[30]

Industrial arts class at Albert Lea High School, 1940

When the Great Depression arrived, this first initiative in applied education had run its course: young adults, trained or untrained, confronted a job market that had little place for them. Federal programs like the Civilian Conservation Corps (CCC), which included an Indian division, and the National Youth Administration (NYA) took up some of the slack; tens of thousands of young Minnesotans went off to forestry camps or continued their education with part-time jobs subsidized by the NYA on high school or college campuses. The NYA provided opportunities that allowed unemployed youth to stay in school and off the job market. In the process many participants acquired skills on the job as clerks, library and laboratory assistants, and subprofessional workers in galleries and museums.[31]

The military and civilian demands of World War II and the surge of veterans into the job market in 1945 provoked a new wave of interest in applied education. Local school districts demonstrated their eagerness to offer expanded and more sophisticated programs for returning veterans, who brought with them substantial cash subsidies through provisions of the G.I. Bill. The state legislature paved the way for these new programs in 1945 by creating the Area Vocational-Technical schools, which were under the control of local school districts. Mankato Vo-Tech opened first, in 1947, and six more were established within the next five years – in St. Cloud, Winona, Thief River Falls, Duluth, Austin, and St. Paul; by the late 1960s, there were twenty-eight. Earlier programs had stressed acquisition of simple, practical skills and submission to the discipline of the workplace. The new programs, more likely to be called "technical" than "vocational" education, strove for flexibility and adaptability, placing more stress on "theoretical and abstract knowledge" and less on "the manipulative skills."[32]

The vo-techs offered short, intensive courses designed to retrain experienced workers for new technologies, as well as general education programs in mathematics, science, psychology, and management. As the state's economy slowly changed from manufacturing and processing to an emphasis on science and high-technology industries, the vo-tech schools adopted courses in the health sciences, communications, and computer technology.

The Choices in Higher Education

By midcentury, high school graduates wishing to continue their formal education in Minnesota had a rich array of options. Regional vo-tech schools offered practical training with relatively quick and rational entry into the job market. The state colleges still prepared graduates for careers in teaching, but they also offered basic programs in the liberal arts that could lead to professional or graduate work. The University of Minnesota provided the most comprehensive opportunities, with its several undergraduate colleges and many graduate and professional programs. All these options were part of the public education system in Minnesota. In addition, students could choose from among the state's sixteen private liberal arts colleges – seven of them Catholic, five Lutheran, and four rooted in other Protestant traditions.

Community or junior colleges were available as a staging area in which to prepare for a career or for academic work in another institution. Minnesota was in the vanguard in the development of two-year community colleges. As early as 1869 Folwell had articulated the "Minnesota Plan," whereby students would complete the equivalent of college sophomore work within their secondary schools. When public junior colleges were founded at Cloquet, Rochester, and Faribault in 1914–15, there were only fifteen in the entire country. Tax revenues from iron mining supported the opening of five junior colleges on the iron ranges – Hibbing, Eveleth, Virginia, Ely, and Itasca – by 1922. The junior colleges were established to provide economical education close to home for students intending to transfer to four-year institutions, in addition to offering preprofessional courses in a variety of subjects.[33]

Although the junior colleges were intended to make higher education available over a wide geographic area, Minnesota's system experienced the inevitable pressures of declining enrollments on campuses located in rural communities. In 1981 researchers described a "clear dichotomy" within the system between the campuses located in the Twin Cities and Rochester and those in other parts of the state. By 1988 the state included eighteen community colleges with a total enrollment of 37,100 – and two-thirds of those students were attending Twin Cities campuses.[34]

Students in a Greek class at Gustavus Adolphus College, St. Peter, 1907

Private Colleges

Although Minnesota's private colleges reflected the cultural pluralism of the state itself, common themes persisted beneath the diversity. In 1900 the curriculum tended to emphasize classical courses of instruction. The faculty of Hamline University in St. Paul, for example, was qualified in such areas as mental and moral science, chemistry and physics, history, Greek and modern languages, Latin language and literature, English literature, mathematics, pedagogics, and elocution.[35]

Colleges with strong church sponsorship sought to deepen the faith of their students, as at St. Olaf, by building faculties of "Christian character, personality, scholarship, and the gift for teaching." Catholic, Lutheran, and Baptist colleges perceived their mission to be the education of a laity that would remain loyal to denominational truths and the preparation of a saving remnant to enter the priesthood or ministry. Carleton College, which was founded in Northfield in 1867 in the Congregational tradition but without direct sectarian control, was seen by an observer in 1902 as treating "Christian truth as an indispensable part of human knowledge."[36]

Each college followed a path peculiar to its own religious and ethnic constituency, style, and values, but all were gradually transformed in the first three or four decades of the century by the demands of their students (and of the parents who supported them) and by the forces of modernization that operated in the larger society. From their early role of training students for teaching or preparing them for the ministry, the private colleges moved toward strengthening the liberal arts. Modern languages and the new social sciences – economics, political science, sociology, and psychology – and biological sciences were among the first disciplines to be added to the curriculum. The early curriculum at Augsburg College, founded in Minneapolis in 1872, was dominated by the Greek department; by 1921 the school offered majors in English, education, and history, with ancient languages, Norse, social and natural sciences, chemistry, and religion being added the following year. The fine and performing arts were introduced in Minnesota colleges early in the century. F. Melius Christiansen, who became music director at St. Olaf College in Northfield in 1903, brought national and international renown to the college for its choral music. Ernst Krenek, who taught at Hamline in the 1940s, introduced contemporary vocal and instrumental music to resistant – but, in time, appreciative – audiences. In Collegeville, Father Virgil Michel inspired programs in the 1930s that put St. John's University at the center of the movement for liturgical revival.[37]

On campuses both public and private, colleges stood *in loco parentis*, a responsibility of corporate parenting that they took earnestly and even severely through the 1950s. College officials enforced elaborate rules governing student behavior – attendance at chapel services, curfew hours (typically later for men than for women), and appropriate forms of recreation (dancing and competitive sports were forbidden or restricted on some campuses well into the century). But student life was also enriched by intramural sports and intercollegiate athletics, fraternities and sororities, literary and dramatic clubs, competitions in rhetoric and debate, honorary academic societies, and clubs for the discussion of current domestic and world issues. Modestly at first, and at an accelerated pace in the 1920s and 1930s, colleges encouraged students to participate in shaping extracurricular activities and their own social life. These developments involved a good deal of tension on some campuses between student leaders and college administrators, the latter tending to remain sensitive to their obligation to maintain discipline and moral standards.

As student enrollments steadily increased, college presidents had to devote more of their efforts to raising funds for investment in physical facilities (gymnasiums and playing fields, libraries and laboratories, classrooms and dormitories), increased staff, and a more highly qualified faculty. Because student tuition and fee payments typically covered only part of the cost of current expenditures – 62 percent in Minnesota colleges in the 1960s – colleges stayed solvent only if they solicited contributions and grants from alumni, churches, wealthy patrons (whose names still grace hundreds of college buildings), corporations, and public and private philanthropic foundations. Donald J. Cowling, president of Carleton College from 1909 to 1945, perfected a tactic of targeting potential patrons with the kinds of specific projects likely to provoke their interest and generosity, rather than relying on general appeals. His work, which became a model for college fund-raising, was based on the belief that the strength of public education must be balanced by excellence of education in the voluntary sphere (underwritten by private giving). Cowling was among the first to actively cultivate the interest and inspire the participation in this effort of individuals, corporations, and foundations located outside Minnesota and the region.[38]

Economic depression in the 1930s initiated a time of testing for all the colleges. Many wealthy patrons suffered loss of fortune, families that had paid tuition for their sons and daughters had difficulty scraping together cash to support the higher education of younger siblings, corporations operating in the red could hardly afford to continue their underwriting of fellowships and related programs, and churches had missions besides education to fund from declining resources. Endowments provided some colleges with a bit of financial security, but even the more affluent ones faced shrinkage of capital and sharply reduced dividend income. Minnesota colleges survived by postponing upkeep and new construction and by cutting back on library appropriations. But it was the sacrifice of loyal teachers that contributed most to sustaining liberal arts education. Cuts in faculty salary levels were not restored until well after World War II.

Starting in 1946, the colleges experienced a boom in enrollments as men and women discharged from the armed forces entered or returned to school. The highest total enrollment in Minnesota's private colleges before the war had been about nine thousand; in the fall of 1948, the total was more than fifteen thousand. When the boom subsided a few years later, the colleges entered a difficult period of maintaining the quality of their programs in the face of rising costs. Nationally, measures that attempted to ease this situation included federal student loans and the National Merit Scholarship program, which benefited both public and private institutions, as well as increased giving from foundations, business, and alumni.[39]

The University of Minnesota

At the turn of the century the University of Minnesota was not much larger than a number of private colleges would be in the 1980s: about 2,500 regular undergraduate students, fewer than 200 graduate students, and a faculty of some 150. Almost nine decades later it had become one of the largest state universities in the country: 1987 enrollment on all its campuses exceeded 54,000, with more than 4,700 men and women serving as members of the full-time academic staff. In addition to its principal campus in the Twin Cities, the University of Minnesota grew to include a branch at Duluth, originally the state normal school there, and technical colleges at Crookston and Waseca. The branch at Morris had its beginnings in a Catholic boarding school for Indians, which the state acquired in 1909 with the stipulation that the school remain tuition free for Indian students. Morris served as the site for a state agricultural school until it was transformed into a four-year liberal arts college in 1959.[40]

The University of Minnesota derived its mission from its status as a land-grant state university – to provide basic higher education for all qualified citizens of the state who chose to attend; to offer such graduate and professional training as would benefit the community, including applied programs in agriculture, engineering, and business; to sponsor basic and applied research in all fields and academic disciplines; and to serve the people through outreach or extension programs. As university president Lotus D. Coffman put it in 1932, "The State Universities hold that there is no intellectual service too undignified for them to perform."[41]

The undergraduate program involved the largest numbers of students and commanded the most substantial attention of the faculty in the basic disciplines. In 1897, the "academic" department held 57 percent of the students enrolled in postsecondary coursework at the university. In that general education enterprise, the College of Liberal Arts (which carried a variety of official designations over the years) played the central role. It offered a four-year degree of its own as well as providing basic learning in the sciences, social sciences, humanities, and arts for students who earned their baccalaureates in education, engineering, and business, among other fields. In 1932 the university created the General College – initially a two-year junior college for the state – to give "late-blooming" students the opportunity for formal learning beyond high school. Tailoring its courses to the needs of students who entered the program with insufficient academic background, the General College counted its successes both in the numbers of students who earned terminal two-year degrees and in those who transferred to other colleges for upper-division work. In later years it proved to be an effective arena for the higher education of young women and men who were disadvantaged by poverty or other factors.[42]

The university's graduate program took longer to develop. In 1900, work beyond the baccalaureate level was judged by a history professor to be "wholly unorganized," managed essentially "by men who already have their hands full with undergraduate classes." The leadership of Guy Stanton Ford, dean of the Graduate School from 1913 to 1938, created the conditions for the flowering of graduate and professional education. He set out to attract promising young scholars to Minnesota, provided resources for their research, and saw to it that the most productive among them were rewarded by rapid promotion and substantial salary increases. He sought research grants, gathered funds for libraries and laboratories, and played a major role in the founding of the university press. His influence was evident as well in efforts to encourage research across traditional disciplinary lines.[43]

Professional education could show no such coherent and uniform advance, yet solid progress was made in many fields over the years. As in the nation, medicine was just beginning to move toward scientific standards in Minnesota in 1900. The university's Medical Department was established in 1888, and in 1900 admission standards were "raised to those of the freshman class of the academic courses," in the words of one historian, for a seven-year course that conferred a combined bachelor of science and doctor of medicine degree. A School of Nursing was inaugurated in 1909, and 1911 saw the building of the first unit of the University Hospitals, which had been housed since 1909 in a former fraternity house. In 1915 the department entered into a partnership with the Mayo Clinic in Rochester through the Mayo Foundation for Medical Education and Research, and a year later formal internships were established. From such modest beginnings the health sciences at Minnesota emerged to become among the nation's best, achieving early distinction in public health and surgery and later in pioneering organ transplants.[44]

The Law School, which was established in 1888 as the Department of Law, took as its mandate the training of young persons who, upon being certified by passing the bar examination, entered the practice of law or pursued a career in business or government. Gradually the school shifted its focus away from chief reliance on case law; by the 1970s it declared its intention to "take the leadership in encouraging University-wide study of the relationships between the legal order and the social order and the use of law as an instrument for achieving justice among men." It was such an implied commitment, especially as it developed under the deanship of Everett Fraser from 1920 to 1948, that put Minnesota in the advanced guard of schools noted for the civic and public responsibility assumed by its graduates.[45]

The College of Education came into its own under the assertive leadership of Lotus Coffman, dean from 1915 to 1920, who labored effectively to relate research and instruction to the basic academic disciplines and to promote advanced courses in technique and method. In the 1920s and 1930s the college developed specialties in the teaching of children with learning disabilities, remedial reading and arithmetic, occupational therapy, agricultural and commercial education, and graduate programs in administration. By about 1955, 60 percent of public school superintendents and 75 percent of senior high school principals in the state had received master's degrees from the College of Education.[46]

Minnesota won national recognition for research into the wide range of individual differences, at every age, in learning ability and for developing practical strategies to help slow learners and to provide accelerated and enriched programs for the talented. One consequence of these studies, beginning in the early 1920s, was the elaboration of research and training in guidance counseling, including extensive counseling services that were offered to all students on campus through the office of the dean of students. The university's counseling services set a model that public schools throughout the state came to emulate.

A partner of the College of Education was the Institute of Child Welfare (later the Institute of Child Development), which was founded in 1925 and merged with the college in 1957. Its staff concentrated on the physical, psychological, and emotional development of children – their habits and behavior, systems of language, and modes of learning. From the start the institute engaged in basic research, instruction of teachers and counselors, clinical assessment of children and adolescents, and provision of consultation services to educators and parents.

Other professional schools in the university exercised wide influence over policy and practice in their fields in Minnesota. The Institute of Technology – created in 1935 by bringing together existing programs in engineering, mines, chemistry, and architecture – trained engineers and conducted basic research in physics, chemical engineering, electrical engineering, and mining that led to significant developments in nuclear physics, computer technology, and taconite mining. The School of Social Work was formally established in 1942, but the department from which it developed had been strong since the 1920s. The school supplied thousands of human service workers who were certified by a master's degree to work in public welfare departments and in agencies in the voluntary sector. It also provided expert counsel in the shaping of public welfare policies. The School of Public Affairs (renamed in 1977 the Hubert H. Humphrey Institute of Public Affairs) and the School of Business (renamed in 1986 the Curtis L. Carlson School of Management) were other manifestations of the mission of land-grant universities to train practitioners, engage in basic and applied research, and advance the community's economic, social, and political interests.[47]

Education in agriculture provided perhaps the university's most pervasive connection with people throughout the state. A College of Agriculture was established in 1874 but initially had difficulty attracting students to its four-year program. Far more popular among the young people on Minnesota's farms was the School of Agriculture, which in its early years was a secondary school emphasizing practical farm skills. The principal campus opened in St. Paul in 1888, and branches were added at Crookston in 1906, Morris in 1910, Grand Rapids in 1926, and Waseca in 1947. University historian James Gray described the purpose of the schools in 1951 as giving "bright boys and girls who expect to become practical farmers and farmers' wives a thorough look at modern methods." A committee of evaluators had characterized the schools a few years earlier as "something distinctly precious in Minnesota's tradition." By 1960, declining enrollments as more students chose the university's more advanced agricultural programs led to the closing of the schools.[48]

Young men and women received more formal training in the College of Agriculture on the university's St. Paul campus, where they learned advanced techniques in agronomy and farm management. If training was at first simple and folksy, it was also effective. Students advanced quickly from the admonitions of Theophilus L. Haecker, professor of dairy husbandry – "Be gentle with the cow, boys. Remember she's a mother and a lady" – to a curriculum featuring livestock breeding, crop improvement, veterinary science, horticulture, and basic science. A program in home economics that was begun in 1896 offered courses in nutrition, clothing and textiles, housing, home management, and family life (psychology, sociology, and economics). The nation's first plant pathology department was established at the university in the first decade of the century. Norman E. Borlaug, a 1942 graduate of the department's doctoral program, received the Nobel Prize in 1970 for genetic research on wheat that produced the high yields of the "green revolution." The St. Paul campus also became home for programs in forestry, fisheries, and wildlife management and in rural sociology and agricultural economics, the last a department of national distinction.[49]

An essential part of the story of agriculture in Minnesota has been the research conducted at experiment stations using federal funds initially authorized by the Hatch Act of 1887. From the beginning, the stations concentrated on programs having direct and immediate application to the progress of the state's farm economy, such as techniques of tilling and crop rotation, the planting of shelterbelts on treeless plains, and the develop-

Cattle judging at the School of Agriculture of the University of Minnesota, St. Paul, about 1910

ment of rust-resistant wheat. By the 1980s there were six experiment stations in rural Minnesota and one in St. Paul. The agricultural extension service, established in 1909, educated farmers primarily by example and demonstration, engaging in agricultural outreach work and developing linkages to outstate communities through a county agent system and to local farmers through county farm bureaus and 4-H clubs.[50]

Most striking in all these activities was the balance achieved between pure and applied research and between classroom and extension learning. The work of what came in 1973 to be called the Institute of Agriculture, Forestry, and Home Economics, incorporating experiment stations and extension services along with the many programs of its three colleges, generated a loyalty among its diverse constituencies that strengthened the whole university, financially and politically. Over the decades the university's work in agricultural education created a reservoir of good will more powerful in the public imagination, and longer lasting, than even the most victorious of Golden Gopher athletic teams.

The State Universities

Minnesota's state teachers colleges experienced a boom in enrollments that began after World War II and continued to the early 1970s. The five campuses at Bemidji, Mankato, Moorhead, St. Cloud, and Winona grew from a total of 5,300 students in 1940 to 36,000 in 1971. When the legislature approved renaming the institutions simply "state colleges" in 1957, it was a recognition that students attended them because they were "readily accessible, open academically, [and] relatively inexpensive" and because they offered educational opportunities for people "whose career choices had not yet crystalized," wrote G. Theodore Mitau, chancellor of the state college system from 1968 to 1976. Political pressure from residents of western and southern Minnesota led to the establishment of a sixth college, Southwest State College at Marshall, in 1963.[51]

In 1972 the system opened another institution in the Twin Cities – Metropolitan State, an innovative "college without walls" offering upper-division education for adults who wished to earn a bachelor's degree while continuing to work. Metropolitan State aimed "to extend alternative opportunities for higher education at the junior and senior level to citizens throughout the Minneapolis–St. Paul metropolitan area whose needs for such education, for various reasons, have not been met by other institutions of post-secondary education." The university, which was nationally recognized for its nontraditional approach, awarded credit for what it described as "college-level learning gained through experiences outside the classroom" – whether on the job, in community activities, or while pursuing individual study. In the 1980s, Metropolitan State conducted classes throughout the metropolitan area that were instructed by some forty resident faculty members plus more than five hundred teachers recruited from the area's professional community; its 1988 enrollment of about five thousand was comprised primarily of working adults, with a median age of thirty-four.[52]

When the state legislature designated the colleges as "universities" in 1975, the move was not an endorsement of the introduction of new graduate programs or degrees. "Helping these institutions to emerge a little from under the shadows of the University of Minnesota was one thing," wrote Mitau in his 1977 history of the system, but the state continued to regard the University of Minnesota as its principal research and professional center. Despite the name changes, the system retained much of its original mission in preparing teachers for Minnesota schools: in the mid-1980s, half of the elementary and secondary teachers prepared each year within the state were graduates of one of the state universities.[53]

Trends and Changes

It is a truism that all institutions and agencies in society, public and private, respond at different rates to changes in the total environment. Few have proved more sensitive to shifts in economic, political, and cultural realities than the schools. When thousands of migrants from countryside and foreign lands flooded into American towns and cities in the early twentieth century, the nation expected the schools to play the major role in socializing coming generations to American ways and values.

Teachers learning techniques in lesson presentation during summer school at Winona State Teachers College, 1948

To the schools was given the task of preparing workers, technicians, and managers for ever more complex demands of business and government. During wartime, institutions of higher education accelerated courses of learning and established special training programs for various branches of the armed services. When millions of veterans released from military service in 1945 clamored for education under the generous terms of the G.I. Bill, Minnesota's colleges and universities picked up the challenge. When the Soviet Union sent its first satellite tumbling through space in 1957, the citizenry expected the schools to speed up training in mathematics and science so that the nation could catch up and surpass the Russians in the period that became known as the post-Sputnik era. Still later, the transition from an industrial economy to one that emphasized technological and service skills called for new responses from the schools.

The elementary and secondary schools faced their own demographic crisis as the children of the baby boom, those born between 1945 and 1962, passed through the system. Everywhere throughout the state, but with special urgency in the burgeoning suburbs surrounding the Twin Cities, school boards rushed to build new schools and to hire teachers and staff. This dramatic increase in the demand for educators in turn stimulated enrollments in teacher-training programs in all the state's colleges and universities.

Moreover, public elementary and secondary schools confronted the need in this postwar era to consolidate their systems, for by 1945 a multiplicity of small districts could no longer meet the demands of society (and parents) for higher quality and more diversified education. The rising burden of local taxes on real property was another incentive for school boards to cut costs by introducing economies of scale. Although the consolidation of rural and small-town schools had been high on the agenda of the state board of education since the beginning of the century, local resistance held back the movement for decades. Civic pride and the jealousy of local communities for the autonomy of their schools were major factors; practical considerations also played a part – most notably the lack of good, hard-surfaced roads over which to transport pupils from outlying areas. Early efforts to encourage consolidation by providing state aid drew little response in rural Minnesota. A 1947 statute authorized the counties to take the initiative in consolidation, but it was not until 1963 that the state legislature made consolidation mandatory. State law finally made official the measures that economic and educational realities dictated, and there followed a spectacular rush to reduce the number of school districts. By 1972 there were fewer than 450, whereas there had been more than 7,600 as recently as 1945.[54]

Closely related to school consolidation were issues of finance. Diversification of curricular and extracurricular programs, the proliferation of counseling services, the insistence on ever-higher standards of achievement – all combined to raise expenditures per pupil and overall budgetary costs beyond the capacity of local property taxes to support. Moreover, even after consolidation there was a growing disparity in tax bases among school districts: in 1971 wealthy communities invested as much as $1,300 per pupil, while some poorer districts could afford to spend little more than $700.[55]

The passage of a state sales tax law in 1967 led to added revenues available for the expansion of state services at a time when political pressure for property tax relief was mounting. A loose coalition of forces that were often at odds on other issues, composed of organized teachers – the MEA and the Minnesota Federation of Teachers (MFT) – the Minnesota School Boards Association, and the PTA, together with citizen groups seeking tax relief, created a climate favorable to reform. Gov. Wendell R. Anderson seized the opportunity to strengthen education, a goal to which he and his close political associates had long been dedicated. Thanks to brilliant staff work directed by John E. Haynes, at that time a young graduate student in American history, and to the diplomatic skill of state senators Stanley W. Holmquist and Karl F. Grittner, legislators were persuaded to enact a reform soon tagged the Minnesota Miracle.[56]

This reform set in place a complicated new formula for state aid to education. It sharply increased state funds being used to subsidize local schools and at the same time brought a substantial degree of equalization of funding between richer and poorer districts. The relatively affluent suburban schools ringing the Twin Cities, however, benefited the most from new formulas that stressed numbers of pupils enrolled in a system. The reform also regularized categorical aids made available to local districts for transportation, services to children with handicaps, and vo-tech programs. In the years that followed, the state covered from 55 to 65 percent of budgets for education through grade 12, as against the 25 percent or so that it had supplied in the early decades of the century.

As the century progressed, education came to constitute "one of the largest enterprises in Minnesota," in the words of a 1977 observer – involving 25 percent of the state's population and almost 4 percent of its work force. In 1982–83 the total budget for elementary and secondary schooling in Minnesota was more than $2 billion, consuming one-quarter of state tax revenues and one-half of local property taxes. Statistics suggest some of the dramatic forces that have changed education in Minnesota in its later decades: the percentage of citizens over the age of twenty-five who held a high school diploma rose from 44 in 1960 to 70 in 1977; the percentage that earned college degrees rose from 8 to 17. In 1985, an impressive 58 percent of high school graduates continued their education in some postsecondary institution, as opposed to about 15 percent in 1940.[57]

But the structure, quality, and tone of education also changed after 1960. Social movements in those tumultuous years aroused concern for the role and place of minorities in a pluralistic society. Students with physical or learning disabilities had traditionally been neglected or isolated in separate facilities; now the schools sought to integrate or "mainstream" them into regular classroom settings, while also providing them with special services and tutorial assistance. For the gifted, many schools inaugurated enriched sections and opportunities for independent study and field work. Some systems created "open" or "free" schools for students who benefited from being able to shape their own learning experience.[58]

With the accelerated migration of Indian families to urban centers beginning in the 1940s, inner-city schools in Minneapolis, St. Paul, and Duluth faced the challenge of meeting the special needs of young Indians while striving to integrate them into the mainstream. That double task was complicated by persisting differences between Indian and non-Indian cultures and between the cultures of different tribes, by the severe poverty of many urban Indians, and by the back-and-forth flow of the population between home reservations and urban ghettos. Education programs for Indian youths have been frustrated by high "stopout" as well as dropout rates.[59]

Minnesota's educational system has not been uniformly benign or effective, however, and the implementation of educational policy led at every level to a contest of interests and means. The tracking of students through counseling procedures that were often intrusive and misguided rested as often upon considerations of class, race, and gender as upon the presumed "intelligence" of individual students. Youth from working-class and immigrant families were often shunted into terminal high school programs and vocational training, whereas the children of middle-class and professional families were guided into college-preparatory classes. Schools rarely understood or met the special needs of black, Indian, and Hispanic children. As the proportion of minorities increased in urban schools, especially in the decades following World War II, these families joined together to exert community pressure on administrators to desegregate elementary and secondary schools and to initiate compensatory programs and courses in minority culture. Although the percentage of minority youth in the state's school population remained relatively low – less than 7 percent of students in 1983 were Indian, black, Asian, or Hispanic – proponents of integration often had to resort to the courts to win judicial

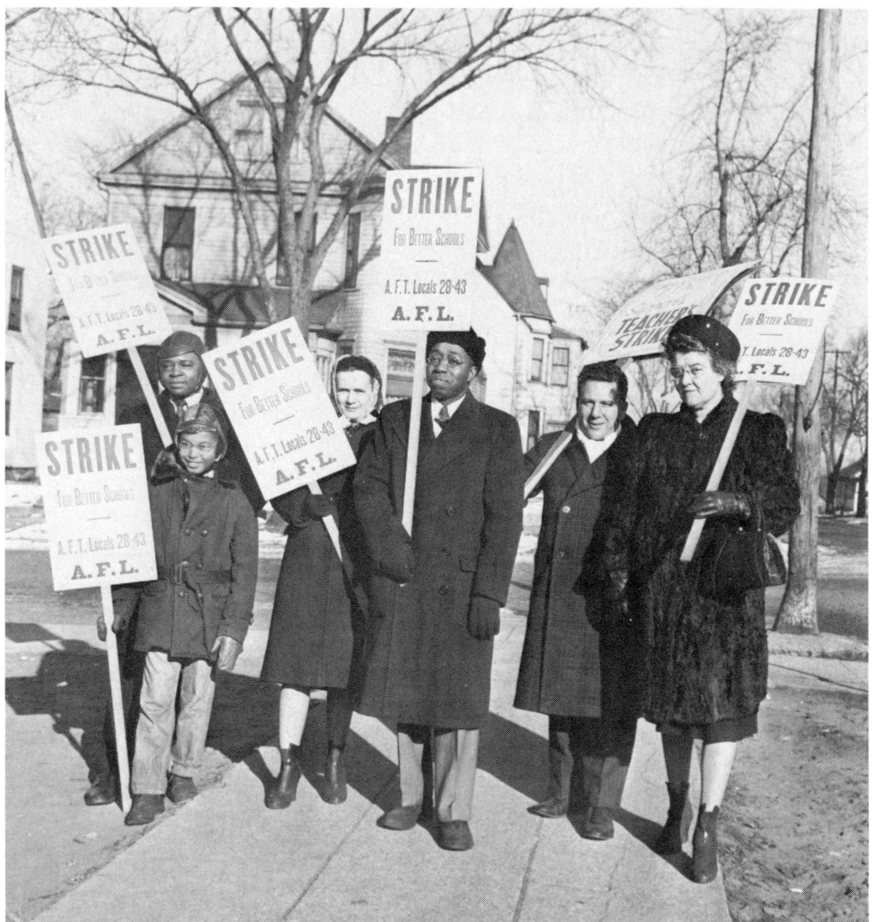

Pickets outside a school during a teachers' strike, St. Paul, 1946

support for institutional changes. Citizen confrontation of school administrators and boards proved to be an effective tactic in achieving modest gains, even if conflict ran against the traditional grain of deference to authority.[60]

Parallel with these developments, teachers accelerated their efforts to organize and bargain collectively through units of either the MEA or the MFT. Bargaining focused not only on salaries but on conditions of labor as well – tenure, retirement, insurance, sick leave, sabbaticals, course load, student load, and grievance procedures. In 1973 the state legislature gave public employees a limited right to strike, leading to a wave of teacher strikes in the late 1970s and early 1980s that were disruptive and divisive in many communities.[61]

In higher education, students during the 1960s and 1970s demanded not only that they be consulted but that they play an active role in shaping the terms of their education and their social lives on campus. Historian Merrill E. Jarchow noted that "no decade in the history of higher learning has been so analyzed, dissected, and described as that of the 1960s," and most of that attention has focused on the actions of students. Mirroring events throughout the country, student protests in Minnesota focused on such issues as the war in Vietnam, the military draft, and civil rights, as well as on securing the right to participate in the governance of the college or university. The inauguration of programs in minority as well as environmental and urban studies came on the insistence of militant students and their allies. The authority of feminist protest was at once subtle and powerful. The Emma Willard Task Force, a grass-roots movement of feminist educators in the Twin Cities, provided strategic leadership and curricular materials for the introduction of women's themes and perceptions into social studies and humanities courses in the schools. Teachers at St. Louis Park High School developed materials on women's issues and experiences to be used in world studies courses. The University of Minnesota was among the first in the nation to develop a program – called Continuing Education for Women – that aimed to prepare mature women to make the break from a life focused principally on family and home into one that included higher education and a career. On many campuses, beginning in the late 1960s, agitation led to the establishment of programs in women's studies. Mirroring the experiences of minorities, women who had suffered generations of discrimination often had to seek judicial rulings to advance affirmative action in the employment of female and minority faculty and staff.[62]

Such efforts to win more effective participation of students and faculty in institutional governance rarely proceeded without prolonged agitation and endless committee work. Competition for resources, arguments about curriculum reform and admissions standards, the award of fellowships, and decisions on hiring, tenure, and merit all aroused hard feelings and sharp debates (sometimes more vehement than the issues reasonably warranted).

During the 1980s, Minnesota and the nation began to take a hard look at the quality of public education. Much of the expressed concern responded to a report produced in 1983 by the National Commission on Excellence in Education that warned of "a rising tide of mediocrity" that threatened to erode the educational foundations of the country. Concerned Minnesotans worked for reforms that would correct the deficiencies that were addressed by the commission's recommendations: strengthen studies in the "new basics" of English, social studies, mathematics, science, and computer studies; raise the expectations for academic performance in high school and the requirements for admission to four-year colleges; make more effective use of instructional time; improve the training, salary, and working conditions of teachers; and increase public fiscal support for education.[63]

Since 1984 Minnesota's national reputation as a leader in public education has suffered little, and several innovative measures have enhanced it – for example, open enrollment between districts and postsecondary courses for high school students at state expense. Still, a critical report by the Office of the Legislative Auditor in 1988 found that "Minnesota's reputation is somewhat overstated and out of date. It results partly from favorable socioeconomic conditions which affect standard education indicators (most notably, college admission test scores)." Among the problems to be solved, the report stated, were a continuing decline in the state's scores on college admission tests; a dissatisfaction among students and the public; the fact that only 27 percent of the state's high schools were officially accredited; and a decline in secondary social-studies test results. These were complex and challenging problems, for which the state and its citizens continued to seek answers.

Throughout the twentieth century, education in Minnesota has been dynamic and evolving. Vida Squier arrived in Ely from the East in 1890 to teach miners' children in a community where most people viewed education as the way in which dreams and personal ambitions could be fulfilled. During the century that followed, Minnesotans attended schools that were shaped by great world events as well as by the major and minor fashions of educational theory. In the process, the schools came to reflect national trends while continuing to respond to the goals and concerns of the people of the state.

NOTES

1. Historical Committee [Ely], Roaring Stoney Days Celebration, *A Souvenir Booklet* ([Ely: The Committee, 1958]), 46–47.

2. William Watts Folwell, "Inaugural Address," in *University Addresses* (Minneapolis: H. W. Wilson, 1909), 75. For more information on nineteenth-century schools, see John N. Greer, ed., *The History of Education in Minnesota,* Contributions to American Educational History no. 31 (Washington, D.C.: U.S. Bureau of Education, 1902).

3. Minnesota Superintendent of Public Instruction, *Fourteenth Biennial Report . . . 1905 and 1906* (Minneapolis: Harrison and Smith Co., 1907), 26, 28.

4. For a broad survey of one-room schools, see Andrew Gulliford, *America's Country Schools* (Washington, D.C.: Preservation Press, 1984).

5. Van D. Mueller, *Paying for the Public Schools: The ABC's of Minnesota School Finance* ([St. Paul]: Public Officials Training Board, 1976), 5; Raymond A. Kent, *A Study of State Aid to Public Schools in Minnesota,* Studies in the Social Sciences no. 11 (Minneapolis: University of Minnesota, 1918), 23–25; William W. Folwell, *A History of Minnesota,* rev. ed., vol. 4 (St. Paul: Minnesota Historical Society, 1969), 186.

6. Minnesota Superintendent, *Fourteenth Biennial Report,* 24; "Report of the Minnesota Educational Association on Teachers' Salaries and Living Expenses," in Minnesota Superintendent, *Fourteenth Biennial Report,* 541–42.

7. For a review of school quality in 1898 see Jennie C. Crays, "The Origin, Growth, and Present Condition of the Public Schools of Minnesota," in *History of Education,* ed. Greer, 147–52.

8. Folwell, *History of Minnesota,* vol. 4, 52.

9. W. E. Peik, "Twenty-five Years of Development in Elementary Education," in *The Changing Educational World, 1905–1930,* ed. Alvin C. Eurich (Minneapolis: University of Minnesota Press, 1931), 238–44 (quotations on 243–44). The comparison was between "common school teachers" in 1904 and "teachers in ungraded elementary schools" in 1926.

10. Information on the development of secondary schools, here and below, is drawn from Fred Engelhardt, *Minnesota Public Schools* (Minneapolis: Educational Test Bureau, Inc., 1934), 83–84; George B. Aiton, "The Beginnings of Secondary Education in Minnesota," in *Changing Educational World,* ed. Eurich, 222–37; Otto E. Domian et al., *Education 1967: A Statewide Study of Elementary, Secondary, and Area Vocational-Technical Education in Minnesota* (College of Education, University of Minnesota, 1967), 53–129, esp. 54; Hugh Graham, "The History of Secondary Education in Minnesota" (Ph.D. diss., University of Minnesota, 1929), 272–96; Minnesota Office of the Legislative Auditor, Program Evaluation Division, *High School Education* (St. Paul: Office of Legislative Auditor, 1988), 170. Data for Minnesota followed national medians rather closely: see, for example, David B. Tyack, *The One Best System: A History of American Urban Education* (Cambridge, Mass.: Harvard University Press, 1974), 183, 269; Edward A. Krug, *The Shaping of the American High School,* vol. 2, *1920–1941* (Madison: University of Wisconsin Press, 1972), 3–17, 42, 218.

11. Engelhardt, *Minnesota Public Schools*, 85-86; Domian et al., *Education 1967*, 104.

12. Engelhardt, *Minnesota Public Schools*, 88; Domian et al., *Education 1967*, 54; Legislative Auditor, *High School Education*, 90.

13. Here and below, see Report of the Superintendent of Schools to the Board of Education, Minneapolis, *The Years of Depression, 1930–1935* (Minneapolis, June 1935), 71–72.

14. Minnesota Department of Education, *The Manual of Standards for All Public Schools* (St. Paul: The Department, 1951), 11, 18, 19. See also Thomas R. Peek, Edward L. Duren, Jr., and Lawrence C. Wells, *Minnesota K-12 Education: The Current Debate, the Present Condition* (Minneapolis: Center for Urban and Regional Affairs, University of Minnesota, 1985); and a special study published by the Minnesota Congress of Parents and Teachers, the Minnesota Education Association, the Minnesota School Board Association, and the Minnesota Citizens Committee for Public Education, *Here Are Your Schools* (1957), pamphlet available at the Minnesota Historical Society (MHS).

15. M. J. Van Wagenen, *Comparative Pupil Achievement in Rural, Town, and City Schools* (Minneapolis: University of Minnesota Press, 1929); G. F. Ekstrom, "Education of Farm Boys and Girls in Minnesota," *The Visitor* 33 (January 1946): 1. See also David L. Nass, "The Rural Experience," *this volume*, 134–36.

16. Here and below, see Jean H. Alexander, "Chronological Outline of the Development of Public Education in Minnesota," in *Changing Educational World*, ed. Eurich, 249–57; O. W. Snarr, "The State Teachers' Colleges in Minnesota's Program of Higher Education," in Minnesota Commission on Higher Education, *Higher Education in Minnesota* (Minneapolis: University of Minnesota Press, 1950), 239–52. For examples, see Donald B. Youel, *Mankato State College: An Interpretive Essay* (Mankato: The College, 1968); Dudley S. Brainerd, *History of St. Cloud State Teachers College* (St. Cloud: The College, 1953); R. A. DuFresne, *Winona State University: A History of One Hundred Twenty-Five Years* (Winona: The State University, 1985). The campus at Duluth was folded into the University of Minnesota system in 1947; the others have been coordinated under the governance of a single state board.

17. Resolution of the MEA, 1901, quoted in Fletcher Harper Swift, "The Increasing Professionalization of Educational Workers," in *Changing Educational World*, ed. Eurich, 205; Alexander, "Chronological Outline," 257–58.

18. Cyril J. Hoyt and Harry C. Johnson, "Studies of Secondary School Teachers in Minnesota," in Commission on Higher Education, *Higher Education in Minnesota*, 301–14.

19. Melvin E. Haggerty, "The University College of Education As Related to Other Divisions of the University," in *Changing Educational World*, ed. Eurich, 93; Minnesota Department of Education, "Information on Minnesota Licensed Public School Staff, 1987–88," District Data/Management Information, December 1988, p. 13.

20. Here and below, George Drayton Strayer, "Progress in City School Administration during the Past Twenty-five Years," in *Changing Educational World*, ed. Eurich, 158–60 (quotation on 160).

21. Graham, "History of Secondary Education," 294–95, 344; Frances Elizabeth Kelley, *A History of Public-School Support in Minnesota, 1858 to 1917*, Current Problems no. 12 (Minneapolis: University of Minnesota, 1920), 12; Engelhardt, *Minnesota Public Schools*, 33; Dean Honetschlager, "Horizons II Presentation: Education," January 1977, p. 1, typescript available at MHS.

22. D. L. Kiehle, "Department of Public Instruction," in *History of Education*, ed. Greer, 9; Alexander, "Chronological Outline," 246, 258, 259. See also Domian et al., "Minnesota State Department of Education," in *Education 1967*, 243–70.

23. *Minnesota Journal of Education* 4 (September 1960), Centennial issue; Theodore C. Blegen, *Minnesota: A History of the State*, 2d ed. (Minneapolis: University of Minnesota Press, 1975), 413; "Organization, Aims and Purpose of the MSBA," *Minnesota School Board Journal* 1 (October 1946): 4; Legislative Auditor, *High School Education*, 56.

24. Here and below, John E. Dobbin, Ruth E. Eckert, and T. J. Berning, "Trends and Problems in Minnesota's Public Schools," in Commission on Higher Education, *Higher Education in Minnesota*, 35. Examples of parish histories are Sister Elizabeth Marie, *Academy for a Century: A History of Saint Joseph's Academy Located in St. Paul, Minnesota* (St. Paul: North Central Publishing, 1951); Mary Karels, "A History of St. Joseph's School, Rosen, Minnesota, 1927-1977" (N.p., 1977), available at MHS. Scholarly surveys include Sister Nora Luetmer, "The History of Catholic Education in the Present Diocese of St. Cloud, Minnesota, 1855–1965" (Ph.D. diss., University of Minnesota, 1970); Donald Arthur Porter, "Factors Influencing Catholic High School Enrollment" (Ph.D. diss., University of Minnesota, 1967).

25. Data for 1987 from telephone conversation with Carol Hokenson, Minnesota Department of Education, District Data/Management Information, Mar. 3, 1989. For histories of these colleges, see Merrill E. Jarchow, *Private Liberal Arts Colleges in Minnesota: Their History and Contributions* (St. Paul, Minnesota Historical Society, 1973).

26. Dan Cohen, *The Spirit of Breck . . . A Journey* (Minneapolis: Breck School, 1986), esp. 13–17; James Dobbin, "The Bishop Seabury Mission and Its Schools," in *History of Education*, ed. Greer, 198–213; Oak Hall, *Oak Hall: A Day and Boarding School for Girls* (St. Paul: [The School], 1927–28), 6–7; St. Paul Academy, *Alumni Report, June 1939: A Short History and Alumni Roster, Covering the Period from 1900–1939* (St. Paul: [Alumni Report Committee, 1939]), 13–21; Benjamin M. Sherman, *The Blake School, 1907–1974: A Chronological History* (Minneapolis: Colwell Press, 1975), 12, 13, 20, 217–19. The elite tenor of some of these schools was reflected in the names of the founding families – at Blake, for example, these names included Bovey, Carpenter, Crosby, Dunwoody, Gale, and Pillsbury, among others. Family names that predominated in the early years of St. Paul Academy included Ames, Driscoll, Lightner, Ordway, Shepard, and Weyerhaeuser.

27. Here and below, Elizabeth Ebbott, League of Women Voters of Minnesota, *Indians in Minnesota*, 4th ed. (Minneapolis: University of Minnesota Press, 1985), 122–25 (quotation on 122). Secondary accounts of Indian education are few and scattered. Useful on the boarding schools is Sister Carol Berg, "Climbing Learners' Hill: Benedictines at White Earth, 1878–1945" (Ph.D. diss., University of Minnesota, 1981), and the pamphlet *Activities of the Red Lake Public Schools* (December 1937, available at MHS) offers some insights. See also "Education in Minnesota," *Roots* 2 (Fall 1973): 19; Roy W. Meyer, "The Prairie Island Community: A Remnant of Minnesota Sioux," *Minnesota History* 37 (September 1961): 281–82; David Beaulieu, "A Place Among Nations: Experiences of Indian People," *this volume*, 403–6, 424.

28. Wesley Lauritsen, *History of the Minnesota School for the Deaf, Faribault, 1863–1963* (Faribault: Privately published, 1963), 68–72 (quotation on 71); David L. Kiehle, *Education in Minnesota*, part 1 (Minneapolis: H. W. Wilson, 1903), 103–7.

29. Minnesota State Board of Control, *History of the State Board of Control . . . 1901–1922* ([St. Paul: The Board, 1922]), 21; Kiehle, *Education in Minnesota*, 107 (quotation).

30. Spaulding is quoted in Paul C. Violas, *The Training of the Urban Working Class: A History of Twentieth-Century American Education* (Chicago: Rand McNally College Publishing, 1978), 210. For a general account of vocational education in Minnesota, see Harold E. PaDelford, "A Historical Study of Vocational Education in Minnesota with Special Reference to the Minnesota Vocational Association" (Master's thesis, Department of Industrial Education, University of Minnesota, 1967), 34, 45–50. See also Will C. Wachtler, "William Hood Dunwoody: A Portrait of Service, Benevolence" (Plan B paper, University of Minnesota, 1963).

31. Frederick K. Johnson, "The Civilian Conservation Corps: A New Deal for Youth," *Minnesota History* 48 (Fall 1983): 295–302; Calvin W. Gower, "The CCC Indian Division: Aid for Depressed Americans, 1933–1942," *Minnesota History* 43 (Spring 1972): 7–12; D. Jerome Tweton, *The New Deal at the Grass Roots: Programs for the People in Otter Tail County, Minnesota* (St. Paul: Minnesota Historical Society Press, 1988), 101–13.

32. Domian et al., *Education 1967*, 131 (quotation), 137. I have drawn extensively from sections dealing with vocational-technical education in this fine study.

33. R. D. Chadwick, "Public Junior Colleges of Minnesota," *Junior College Journal* 4.7 (April 1934): 341–49; Ruth E. Eckert, Robert J. Keller, and W. Donald Olsen, "Development of the Junior College in Minnesota," Commission on Higher Education, *Higher Education in Minnesota*, 119–44; Blegen, *History of Minnesota*, 422.

34. Minnesota Higher Education Coordinating Board, *Report to the Governor and 1981 Minnesota Legislature* (St. Paul: The Board, 1981), 68, and *Basic Data Report: Preliminary Fall 1988 Headcount Enrollment Report* (St. Paul: The Board, 1988).

35. E. F. Maerkle and Henry L. Osborn, "Hamline University, St. Paul," in *History of Education*, ed. Greer, 178–79. On the private colleges, here and below, see Jarchow, *Private Liberal Arts Colleges*.

36. William C. Benson, *High on Manitou: A History of St. Olaf College, 1874–1949* (Northfield: St. Olaf College Press, 1949), 231 (quotation), 241; "Carleton College, Northfield, Minn.," in *History of Education*, ed. Greer, 153. In the 1920s, St. Olaf drew 84 percent of its students from Norwegian families, 95 percent of them members of the Lutheran church; at that time half of the faculty were themselves graduates of St. Olaf.

37. Here and below, Jarchow, *Private Liberal Arts Colleges*, 65, 80, 84, 147, 154.

38. Merrill E. Jarchow, *Donald J. Cowling: Educator, Idealist, Humanitarian* (Northfield: Carleton College, 1974), 225–55.

39. Jarchow, *Private Liberal Arts Colleges*, 143–48.

40. Willis M. West, "The University of Minnesota," in *History of Education*, ed. Greer, 119; data for 1987 from telephone conversation with Pat Kaszuba, News Service, University of Minnesota, Mar. 6, 1989; Ralph E. Miller, *The History of the School of Agriculture, 1851–1960* (St. Paul: University of Minnesota, 1979), 122–23.

41. Lotus D. Coffman, *The State University: Its Work and Its Problems* (Minneapolis: University of Minnesota Press, 1934), 205.

42. West, "University of Minnesota," 125. The indispensable account concerning the development of the University of Minnesota is James Gray, *The University of Minnesota, 1851-1951* (Minneapolis: University of Minnesota Press, 1951); on General College, see p. 308-22.

43. West, "University of Minnesota," 122-23 (quotations).

44. Jay Arthur Myers, *Masters of Medicine: An Historical Sketch of the College of Medical Sciences, University of Minnesota, 1888-1966* (St. Louis, Mo.: Warren H. Green, 1968), 59, 74, 84, 452-54; West, "University of Minnesota," 124 (quotation); James Gray, *Education for Nursing: A History of the University of Minnesota School* (Minneapolis: University of Minnesota Press, 1960); Harold S. Diehl, "Medical Schools and Medical Education over the Past Century," *Minnesota Medicine* 36 (April 1953): 332-36; Gray, *University of Minnesota,* 179.

45. The quotation is from a planning document entitled "Decades Ahead" (1967) in Robert A. Stein, *In Pursuit of Excellence: A History of the University of Minnesota Law School* (St. Paul: Mason Publishing Co., 1980), 286; for an account of the Fraser deanship, see p. 71-120.

46. Here and below I have drawn heavily from Robert H. Beck, *Beyond Pedagogy: A History of the University of Minnesota College of Education* (St. Paul: North Central Publishing, 1980), esp. 57-65, 180-97. See also Swift, "Increasing Professionalization of Educational Workers," 193-211; Ruth E. Eckert, "Preparation of Teachers at the University of Minnesota," Commission on Higher Education, *Higher Education in Minnesota,* 271-75.

47. Gray, *University of Minnesota,* 323-24, 424 27, 436 39; Ruth E. Eckert and T. R. McConnell, "The University of Minnesota: Its Programs, Services, and Problems," in Commission on Higher Education, *Higher Education in Minnesota,* 321.

48. Here and below, see Miller, *History of School of Agriculture,* 7-8, 19, 98; Gray, *University of Minnesota,* 55-59, 94-104, 402-8 (quotations on 407, 408); Sidney M. Owens, "The School of Agriculture," in *History of Education,* ed. Greer, 133-42; Roy V. Scott, "Early Agricultural Education in Minnesota," *Agricultural History* 37 (January 1963): 21-34, and "Pioneering in Agricultural Education," *Minnesota History* 37 (March 1960): 19-26.

49. Gray, *University of Minnesota,* 101; Tony Gray, *Champions of Peace* (N.p.: Paddington Press Ltd., 1976), 290.

50. M. J. Thompson, *The First Twenty-five Years of the Northwest Experiment Station* ([University of Minnesota], April 1938); Andrew Boss, *Minnesota Agricultural Experiment Station: 1885 1935,* Bulletin 319 (May 1935), 5-78, and *Historical Outline of the Minnesota Agricultural Experiment Station,* Bulletin 328 (May 1936); University of Minnesota, *Agricultural Extension Service* (N.p., n.d.), pamphlet available at MHS.

51. G. Theodore Mitau, *Minnesota's Colleges of Opportunity* ([St. Paul]: Alumni Associations of the Minnesota State University System, 1977), 37, 40 (quotation), 72-73.

52. Mitau, *Colleges of Opportunity,* 63-66 (quotation on 64); Minnesota Metropolitan State College, "Accreditation" (Photocopied report, October 1975), 3 (quotation); Metropolitan State University, *Metropolitan State University: The Degree of Choice* (Brochure issued by the university, St. Paul, 1988).

53. Mitau, *Colleges of Opportunity,* 79 (quotation); Minnesota State University System, *Strategic Planning Report* ([St. Paul]: The System, 1986), 3.

54. Peek et al., *Minnesota K-12 Education,* 27-30. On consolidation, also see Janet Kielb, "School District Reorganization: A History" (St. Paul: Minnesota Department of Education, February 1984), typescript available at MHS; Minnesota Department of Education, *Strengthening Education in Minnesota* (St. Paul: The Department, 1951); Domian et al., *Education 1967,* 276-310. By 1984 the distribution of school districts and pupil enrollment, as tabulated in Minnesota Department of Education, *The Condition of Education, 1985* (St. Paul: The Department, 1985), 5, was as follows:

Number of Pupils Enrolled	*Number of Districts*	*Percentage of Districts*	*Percentage of Total Statewide Enrollment*
Fewer than 300	87	20	3
300-999	200	46	16
1,000-2,999	95	22	23
3,000-9,999	42	10	30
10,000 plus	10	2	28

55. A range of $721 to $1,317 is noted in Joyce E. Krupey and Alan Hopeman, "Minnesota School Finance Equity, 1973-1982," *Journal of Education Finance* 8 (Spring 1983): 490-501. Here, as elsewhere, because data on enrollment, costs, and so forth, vary widely from one source to another, I have chosen to round off figures in the belief that exact figures too often give an unwarranted sense of precise accuracy.

56. Here and below, see especially Tim L. Mazzoni, *Deciding State School Policy in Minnesota: An Analysis of Policy Participants, Influence Relationships, and Decision Processes in the 1970s* (Minneapolis: Department of Educational Administration, College of Education, University of Minnesota, December 1980), 119–42, 174–78, 211–23; Peek et al., *Minnesota K-12 Education*, 32–33, 41; Joel Allen Sutter, "Major Trends in Minnesota Public School Spending, 1970 through 1982" (Master's thesis, Program in Public Affairs, University of Minnesota, 1983); Krupey and Hopeman, "Minnesota School Finance Equity," 490–501. In the 1970s, expenditures per pupil in Minnesota's elementary and secondary schools ran well above the national average, ranking eleventh to sixteenth. In 1985–86 the sum was $3,980 per pupil, a figure that placed Minnesota fifteenth among the fifty states (*New York Times*, Nov. 8, 1986, p. 8).

57. Honetschlager, "Horizons II Presentation," 1; Minnesota State Planning Agency, *Educational Attainment in Minnesota, 1977* (St. Paul: The Agency, 1978), 3, 8; Department of Education, *Condition of Education, 1985*, 7, 38; Ruth E. Eckert and John E. Dobbin, "An Overview of Higher Education in Minnesota Today," in Commission on Higher Education, *Higher Education in Minnesota*, 63.

58. Peek et al., *Minnesota K-12 Education*, 62–68; Department of Education, *Condition of Education, 1985*, 24–25, 28–31; "Investigating Openness" and "Public Schools of Choice," both in *CURA Reporter* (University of Minnesota) 2 (October–November 1972): 1–6.

59. For urban Indian education during this period, see studies conducted by Arthur M. Harkins, I. Karon Sherarts, and Richard C. Woods for the Center for Urban and Regional Affairs, University of Minnesota, entitled "Indian Education in Minneapolis: An Interim Report" (December 1969), "The Elementary Education of St. Paul Indian Children: A Study of One Inner-City School" (December 1970), and "Indians and Their Education in Minneapolis and St. Paul" (February 1972). See also Ebbott, *Indians in Minnesota*, 125–30, 141–46.

60. Department of Education, *Condition of Education, 1985*, 25; Peek et al., *Minnesota K-12 Education*, 99–111; "Special Education Efforts for Black Children" and "Indian Education in the Minneapolis Public Schools," both in *CURA Reporter* 1 (February 1971): 2–3. For a commentary on the desegregation struggle in Twin Cities schools, see Ronald D. Clark, "Ideas about School Desegregation Have Traveled Far since '70s," *St. Paul Pioneer Press and Dispatch*, Dec. 3, 1988, p. 15A.

61. Henry Winkels, *The MFT Legacy to the Teaching Profession* ([St. Paul: Minnesota Federation of Teachers], 1986), 25–29. For information on teacher strikes, see *Minneapolis Tribune*, Oct. 4, 1978, p. 7A, Nov. 17, 1981, p. 3B, 9B; *Minneapolis Star*, Oct. 9, 1981, p. 1A, 6A, Oct. 20, 1981, p. 6A.

62. Jarchow, *Private Liberal Arts Colleges*, 148–50, 182–83, 191, 205–7, 236 (quotation on 148); Emma Willard Task Force on Education, *Sexism in Education*, 3d ed. (Minneapolis: The Task Force, 1972), 1–4; Vera M. Schletzer et al., *Continuing Education for Women: A Five-Year Report of the Minnesota Plan* (Minneapolis: University of Minnesota, 1967). The Shyamala Rajender case focused attention on sex discrimination in hiring at the University of Minnesota (*St. Paul Dispatch*, Apr. 21, 1980, p. 7). See also Marjorie Bingham, "Keeping at It: Minnesota Women," *this volume*, 455–56.

63. Here and below, Legislative Auditor, *High School Education*, 3–5, 153. For a survey of public opinion about the state's schools in the 1980s, see William J. Craig and Kumarasiri Samaranayaka, *1985 Minnesota Citizen Opinions on Public Education and Educational Policies* (Minneapolis: Center for Urban and Regional Affairs, University of Minnesota, 1985), 3–9.

RICHARD M. CHAPMAN

Religious Belief and Behavior

The subject of this essay covers a most expansive terrain. Even fenced in by space (Minnesota) and time (the twentieth century), it remains diffuse and unwieldy. Consequently, the problem of choice – how to narrow the field of investigation – intrudes immediately.[1] The history of theology and the narratives of particular denominations, congregations, and institutions remain important areas for research, but the focus here is on the more behavioral aspects of religious experience, on what can perhaps be thought of as simply *belief-in-action.* This focus follows the lead of historian Martin E. Marty, whose discussion of the "religious" stressed the consequences of religious experience for human endeavor. Considered in this light, the historical importance of religion moves beyond what people believe in a narrow sense to who they are and how religion influences their social, cultural, and political behavior.[2]

How has religion, in this behavioral sense, marked the history of the state, its people and its character, during the twentieth century? And how has religion – the interplay of belief and behavior – been altered along the way? These central probes direct the discussion that follows. The historical record seldom satisfies our desire for perfect clarity, especially in a matter as perplexing as religion; but it does reveal that religion has been a vital part of the identity of many Minnesotans, an essential element in what they think and feel.

Religion in the Lives of Newcomers

A glance at Minnesota's religious landscape provides powerful testimony about the central role of religion in the lives of those groups who settled the state. More than half (55 percent) of Minnesotans surveyed in 1980 belonged to a church or synagogue, a figure well ahead of the national average (43 percent). The survey showed that Lutherans were more than one-fourth of the total population in sixty-four of Minnesota's eighty-seven

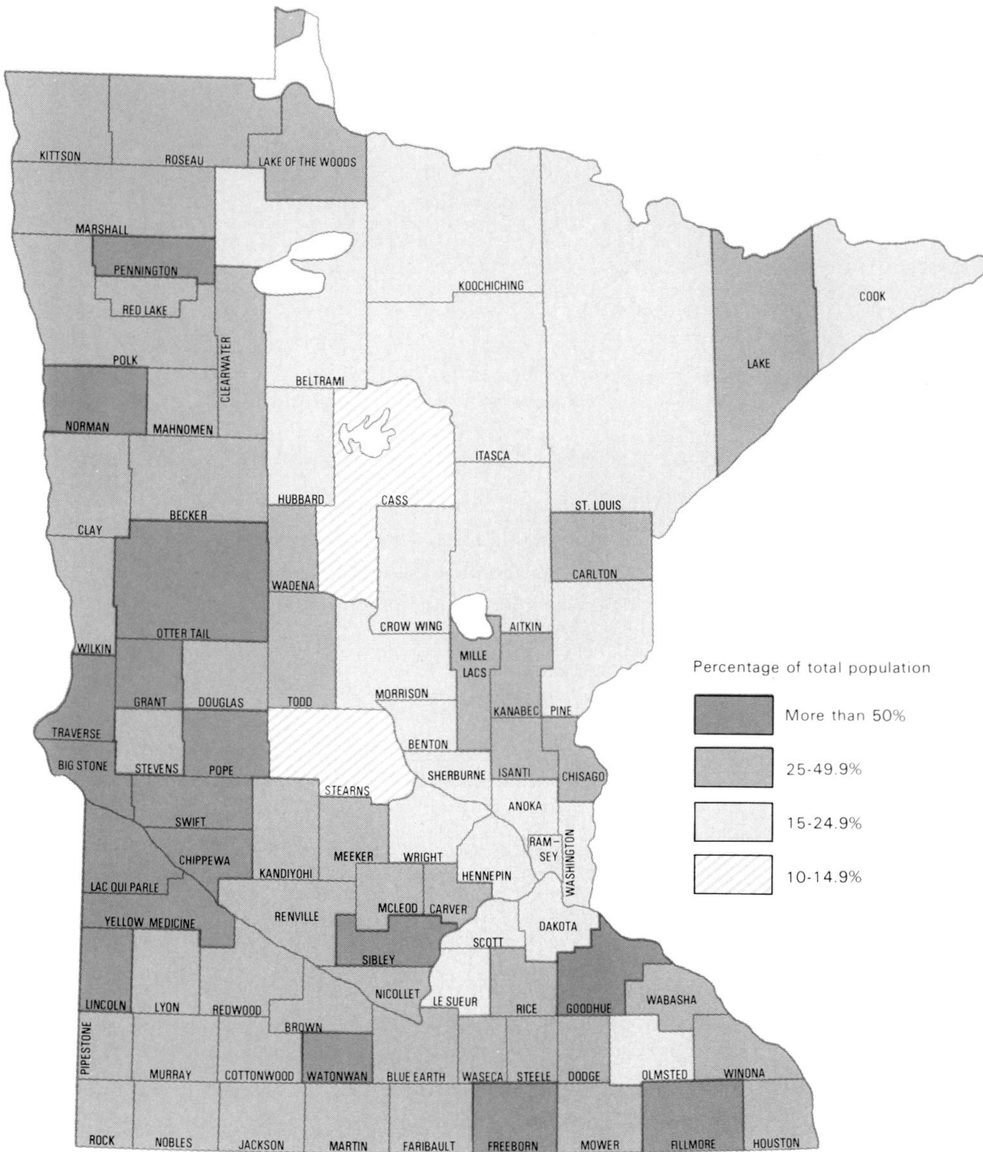

Proportions of Lutherans in Minnesota counties, 1980. Source: *Quinn et al.,* Churches and Church Membership, *150–57.*

counties, whereas Catholics held this position in thirty-five. Lutherans, with roots in the Scandinavian countries and Germany, and Catholics, with antecedents in Ireland, Germany, Italy, eastern Europe, and the Balkans, together constituted a full 82 percent of all Minnesota church members.[3]

This landscape calls attention to the ways in which religion shaped the communities that early settlers and later immigrants established across Minnesota. For many of the state's ethnic groups, the immigrant church

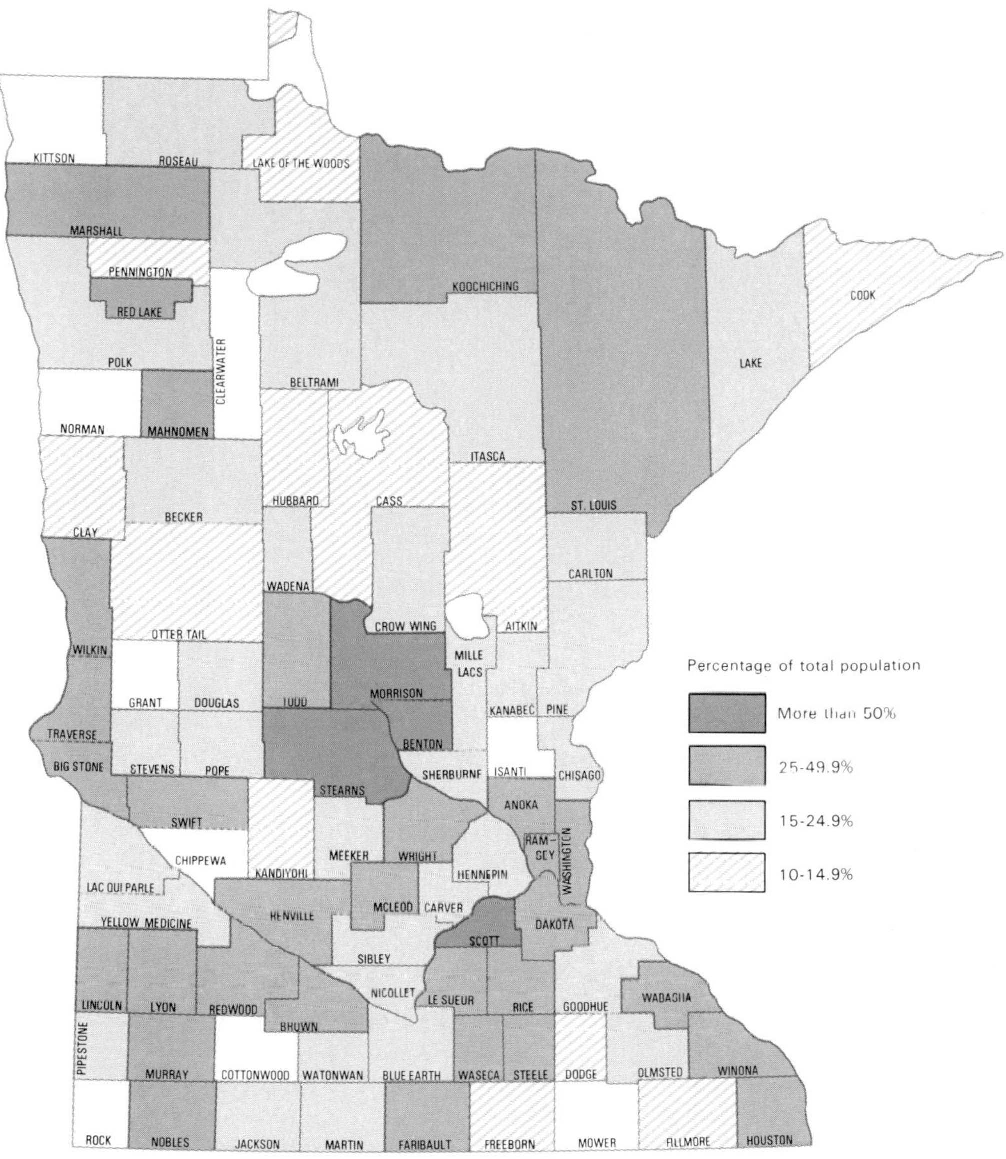

Proportions of Catholics in Minnesota counties, 1980. Source: *Quinn et al.,* Churches and Church Membership, *150–57.*

was the hub around which community life rotated. Frequently the first institutions founded within ethnic enclaves, churches and synagogues provided religious, social, and economic services that softened the shocks of adjusting to life in an alien culture. Over time, the religious festivals and other observances of the immigrant church fostered and sustained ethnic identity as well.

The Old-Stock Americans who came west in the decades after 1840 had

St. Mary's Russian Orthodox Greek Catholic Church in Minneapolis celebrating its twenty-fifth anniversary, 1912

visibly stamped their brands of Protestantism on Minnesota by the turn of the century, not only where they settled but also where their missionizing zeal met success. Especially strong in the Twin Cities and the larger towns of southern Minnesota, Presbyterians, Congregationalists, Episcopalians, and Methodists established a lasting presence, building churches and founding institutions of higher learning – Macalester, Carleton, and Hamline. They produced a flurry of moral reform activities, notably surrounding temperance.[4]

Simultaneously, immigrants to the state settled in large numbers in some communities, at times gaining ethnic-religious dominance not only in individual towns but also in entire counties. German Catholics, from the 1850s, were closely identified with Stearns County in central Minnesota, although many Irish, Slovenian, and Polish Catholics made it their home as well. Swedish (Augustana) Lutherans dominated the history of Chisago County, along the St. Croix River valley, until well into the twentieth century. Isanti County became the home for a substantial cluster of Minnesota's Swedish Baptists. Mountain Lake, in Cottonwood County, was the destination of German Mennonites who fled the Crimea and settled there in the 1870s and 1880s. Similarly, German Lutherans were heavily represented in the state's south-central and southwestern counties, as were Norwegian Lutherans in western Minnesota. These examples are largely rural, but urban ones come quickly to mind – Jews in the Twin Cities and northeastern Minnesota, Finnish Lutherans on the iron ranges, black Baptists and Methodists in St. Paul. Each story is unique, but taken together they underscore "the vitality and force of religion as a factor in defining and preserving ethnic life and character in America," in the words of historians Randall M. Miller and Thomas D. Marzik.[5] In countless ethnic settlements across Minnesota, religion provided social location for its members, fashioned a set of shared values and symbolic expressions linking individuals to the group, and served as a powerful instrument of cultural transmission.

Three years after settling around Chisago Lake, Swedish immigrants in 1854 established Chisago County's first church, the Swedish Evangelical Lutheran. In 1859, members of the young congregation founded a Lutheran school as well. Their reasons were simple: to give their children catechetical instruction and training in the Swedish language.[6] When members of the Scandia Grove Swedish Evangelical Lutheran Church in adjacent Washington County began a school in 1858, they resolved: "We also, in this country, for our own good, want to stay by this church confession and give to our children's children that which we have received." In doing so, they hoped to pass on a way of life – a blend of religion, language, tradition, and custom. By the first two decades of the twentieth century, several of these schools flourished in Chisago County; Emeroy Johnson, longtime resident of Center City and historian of Minnesota's Swedish Lutherans, recalled that "very few children in our community preferred to speak English."[7]

After the first congregation was founded at Chisago Lake, eight more Swedish Lutheran churches sprouted up in the county before 1900. Geographer Robert C. Ostergren calculated that, in the late nineteenth and early twentieth centuries, more than 60 percent of the Swedish-American population in the nine parish communities were members of the Swedish congregations. Although English began to penetrate the county's Lutheran Sunday schools and church services in the 1920s, Swedish was still heard frequently into the 1940s. For many decades, Swedish Lutherans in Chisago County considered "English orthodoxy" logically impossible: to worship rightly meant to do so in Swedish.[8]

A similar pattern emerged among German Catholics in central Minnesota. Passing through Stearns County in 1869, along the road from St. Cloud to Sauk Centre, one traveler remarked on "a very large stone church" that the German Catholics were erecting at St. Joseph, "one that would be an ornament in any of our large cities."[9] A visitor to Stearns County in the 1980s could behold a similar sight: massive Gothic structures rising abruptly before open fields of grain. These impressive parish churches, together with several major Catholic religious and educational institutions – St. John's Abbey and University, the Convent and College of St. Benedict – and numerous parochial schools testify to the strong Catholic presence in the county's history. Throughout the twentieth cen-

Postulants at the Convent and College of St. Benedict, St. Joseph, 1923

tury, Catholics have consistently accounted for about 60 percent of the population of Stearns County.[10]

German Catholics, the largest national grouping to settle the county, demonstrated a persistent inclination to maintain their own religious traditions. In practical terms, this translated into a desire to retain the German language, to follow Catholic practices brought from Germany, and, above all, to secure autonomy at the level of the local parish community. On several occasions – beginning in the 1880s – German Catholics felt these values threatened, most often by the Irish church hierarchy. Archbishop John Ireland, that giant figure in Minnesota and American Catholic history, considered the county's large, traditional German Catholic population a serious challenge to his vision of a truly American Catholic church. He maintained that the children of immigrants should learn English so that they could defend the Catholic faith effectively in the American context. On several occasions, Ireland took issue with Minnesota immigrants whose Catholicism had an ethnic coloration. In 1889, St. Cloud became the diocesan seat for central Minnesota largely at the bidding of Ireland, who hoped to gain leverage over the area's obstreperous German Catholics.[11]

The infamous "school question," more than any other issue, caused turmoil among Stearns County's German Catholics, opening a debate that lingered for decades. Like other religious-minded immigrants, they determined to build schools for their children's education, for religious training and also for instruction in German. In the decades after 1850 they developed district schools that were patterned after the state-supported schools then existing in Germany. They were public, not parochial, schools that the German Catholics controlled because their numerical dominance in many Stearns County townships gave them a virtually unchallenged voice on local school boards. The instructors, known as *kirchen vaeter*, were

Catholic laymen trained at Catholic institutions, many at St. John's and others in Milwaukee. They taught a curriculum that included the basic subjects as well as religion, music, and dramatics. In addition, the visibility of the instructors in the local parish often made them highly esteemed members of the community.[12]

Already a problem by 1880, the school question intensified in the following decade when Rupert Seidenbusch, the first bishop of St. Cloud, and Abbot Alexius Edelbrock of St. John's Abbey began a campaign to establish full-fledged parochial schools, a move spurred by the pronouncements of the Plenary Council of Baltimore in 1884. Entering the debate in New Munich, Edelbrock, in a reference to the lay instructors, reportedly fumed at the parishioners: "A Catholic teacher doesn't make a Catholic school." German Catholics did not accept this argument, however, nor were they pleased when parish priests, under pressure from the church hierarchy, sought to discipline parishioners by installing sisters from St. Benedict's to teach in the district schools.[13]

Disputes arising from the controversy were often protracted and vituperative. For local German Catholics, the parochial schools were clearly unnecessary: they were forced on the people by a distant church bureaucracy, they threatened local autonomy, and they implied financial support of both private and public school systems. But the county's German Catholics were not opposed to parochial schools so long as they retained control. In Melrose Township, for example, when Germans clashed with the majority Irish Catholics they withdrew their children from public school in 1882 and placed them in their own parochial school.[14]

Although pitted against the full weight of the Catholic hierarchy, German Catholic parishes in Stearns County often won at least partial victories. In New Munich, parishioners secured the transfer of their priest to Hastings. The district school remained, with the compromise that sisters be accepted as teachers. In a few instances, priests abruptly left churches when members remained adamant and refused to cooperate. Gradually – and grudgingly – most of the German communities in the 1880s accepted the presence of sisters within the district schools. St. Martin's, however, retained its lay instructors until the school was officially changed to a parochial institution in 1955; conversely, some sisters continued to teach in Stearns County public schools into the 1950s.

As with the Lutheran congregations in Chisago, German Catholic parishes in Stearns County served as strong centers for the preservation of the language and traditions of the old country. Despite the opposition of Archbishop Ireland, German Americans held on to the language into the 1930s. At Meire Grove, one German sermon could be heard each week until the mid-1950s. German Catholics, in the words of historian Sydney E. Ahlstrom, "were convinced that the Christian message could be safely conveyed only in their mother tongue."[15]

Other Americanization efforts were equally unsuccessful. Temperance, a movement rooted in the zeal of Yankee reformers, attracted considerable support among Irish Catholics in the late nineteenth century but did not spread to the German Catholic community. During World War I, when the "100% American" movement reached its height, German Americans came under suspicion nationwide, and their continued use of the German language and beer-drinking habit accelerated the anti-German war hysteria. Joseph Busch, bishop of St. Cloud and disciple of Archbishop Ireland, urged total abstinence from alcohol and the use of English in the Catholic liturgy, positions clearly aimed at German Catholics. Despite intense pressure, including investigations by the Minnesota Commission of Public Safety, German Catholics found temperance an alien movement: beer had always been a part of their lives. Consequently, as one local historian noted, they developed an "inflexible stand against 'temperance' and prohibition." Although the Woman's Christian Temperance Union established fifteen local unions in Stearns County between 1877 and 1939, membership lists suggest that virtually no German-American women participated.[16]

Providing a sense of community identity was a major function of religious institutions, and another was the supplying of essential social services. This function was critical within some ethnic communities, especially when the state's role in meeting social and economic needs was minimal and private agencies were likely to offer help that was tinged with condescension toward the ethnic culture. Among Jewish immigrants, philanthropy – which, along with study and worship, is one of the traditional requirements of the faith – was widely manifest. From the 1870s, historian Hyman Berman observed, Minnesota Jews founded "a bewildering array of fraternal, charitable, cultural, political, and religious groups. Philanthropy became a key ingredient of the voluntary organizations spun off from the pioneer temples, and self-help dominated their philosophies." So prodigious were developments in this area that in 1910 the major Jewish social-service agencies felt the need to integrate their work for greater efficiency, forming in that year the Associated Jewish Charities of Minneapolis and the United Jewish Charities of St. Paul.[17]

For those in the Christian tradition, shared experience, isolation – both geographic and cultural – and social homogeneity made it easy to answer the question that precedes the parable of the Good Samaritan, "And who is my neighbor?" In rural Cottonwood County, Mennonites built an astonishing number of mutual aid organizations, ostensibly to fulfill the injunction to "bear one another's burdens." By the early 1920s, in addition to death and sickness benefits distributed by their churches, Mountain Lake Mennonites had established a preparatory school, hospital, and home for the elderly. One observer in 1939 remarked that the Mennonite sense of obligation "tends to accompany the realization that there is mutual advantage in common association and united efforts."[18]

The churches of black Minnesotans were particularly notable as centers for community well-being. Writing in 1900, W. E. B. Du Bois offered this striking description of one black church: "Various organizations meet here – the church proper, the Sunday-school, two or three insurance societies, women's societies, secret societies, and mass meetings of various kinds. Entertainments, suppers, and lectures are held besides the five or six regular weekly religious services. Considerable sums of money are col-

Congregation of St. James African Methodist Episcopal Church gathering at the construction site at 624 Central Avenue West, St. Paul, 1948

lected and expended here, employment is found for the idle, strangers are introduced, news is disseminated, and charity distributed."[19]

Du Bois's characterization aptly describes the role that the churches played in the black community in St. Paul. Black settlers first arrived in appreciable numbers in the mid-1860s, many as former slaves loosed by the dislocations of war, and they soon established churches that served as community centers. By 1900, four major black congregations existed in St. Paul, of which Pilgrim Baptist, established in 1866, and St. James African Methodist Episcopal, begun in 1878, were the largest and most influential. In the 1890s Pilgrim Baptist supported numerous activities in addition to its regular services, including a women's missionary society, youth group, Sunday school, literary society, and several congregational aid societies.[20]

In the decade after 1910, members of the St. James congregation created an employment clearinghouse. *The Helper*, an official organ of the church, actively solicited employment for members, neighbors, and friends. Initiated in 1915, the publication ran notices that typically read, "DO YOU WANT WORK?"; some issues asserted, "The 'Helper' wants to help you find work," always with information about job leads and contacts. Besides advertising employment openings, St. James's *Helper* gave exposure to black businesses and fostered a spirit of cooperation and generosity among its readers. For years, Hall's Barbershop in downtown St. Paul served to connect the church and community with blacks who were new to the city and looking for work. *Helper* readers were asked in 1925 to phone the Hall brothers if they had information concerning work for men or women. Edward and Orrington Hall developed a range of contacts in the white business community, barbershop patrons who were tapped to provide employment opportunities. Members of St. James church commonly advised friends or relatives to stop in at Hall's as soon as they arrived in the city.[21]

Religion clearly served as a powerful source of communal life, especially for ethnic groups that struggled to maintain their cultural heritage as they built a new life in Minnesota. But it would be remiss to conclude that religion achieved harmonious ends only. Indeed, the element of conflict and, hence, the problem of change are essential in rounding out the picture of many religious communities in Minnesota history. In Chisago County, according to Emeroy Johnson, church discipline and "unchristian conduct" – dancing, drinking, and similar offenses – became problems at the original Swedish Lutheran church by the 1870s. An 1880 pastoral report complained that some members, rather than joining services, remained outside the church talking and visiting. The report also issued a warning against drunkenness. That same year, the completion of a branch line of the Northern Pacific Railroad's St. Paul–Duluth route, which connected Chisago City, Lindstrom, and Center City to the metropolitan area, opened up the county to a wider world of influences. From such transportation and communication developments as this, the use of the English language gained additional impetus. In 1901, several members of the Chisago Lake congregation who lived in nearby Lindstrom organized an English-speaking congregation in their own community. The division stirred a great deal of resentment.[22]

Even with these developments, English was accepted more slowly within the county's Swedish churches than in city congregations, where members were less isolated and faced stronger pressure from the host culture. An 1892 issue of *Svenska Amerikanska Posten* acknowledged that "our youth in the cities are more and more demanding that the services be held in English, and where the circumstances demand, the young people enforce their right in this respect."[23]

The iron ranges, which were sharply different from rural Chisago and Stearns counties in economic and demographic structure, created their own religious patterns. The expansion of the mining industry in northeastern Minnesota that began in the 1880s attracted immigrant laborers from many countries. With so many ethnic and religious backgrounds represented, a kind of ecumenism emerged more by necessity than by design – cooperation was essential in order to build churches and retain the services of clergy. As a rule, this comity (which, in fact, was often strained in mixed congregations) broke off when a group developed the demographic base and financial resources to maintain its own religious institutions.[24]

During the early twentieth century, religion also became a battleground on which factions within single national groups on the ranges fought bitterly. Hostilities occurred between radical Slovenes and their churchgoing compatriots, for example, and churches serving the Italian community faced a potent strain of anticlericalism.[25] But the history of the region's large Finnish population best illustrates the point. Renowned for their "associative spirit," as historian A. William Hoglund described it, the Finns created a vibrant array of ethnic organizations of many types – churches, temperance halls, lodges, as well as Socialist groups and worker unions.[26]

By 1900, church Finns in the United States belonged to three distinct Lutheran bodies: the Suomi Synod, the Apostolic Lutheran church, and the Finnish-American National Evangelical Lutheran church, which differed on theology, points of church polity, and relations with the state church in Finland. Through 1920, however, only about one of every five Finns in northern Minnesota belonged to one of the Finnish Lutheran bodies. A small number joined other Protestant churches, but most Finns were associated with Finnish temperance societies or radical organizations. Temperance halls, begun as secular organizations but quickly attracting the church Finns, were the primary forums where religiously oriented and radical Finns struggled with each other in the 1880s and 1890s to define the meaning of Finnish ethnic identity. The temperance movement split along these lines in 1889, a bifurcation that led to greater trouble ahead.[27]

It was not clear at first that the differences between the factions were unbridgeable. Finnish church leaders tried to remain neutral, at times implying that the contrasting positions were compatible, and some radical Finns emphasized the social thrust of Christ's teachings. But in 1907, following a strident antichurch campaign, Socialist Finns manipulated a stock take-over of the National Evangelical Lutheran church's college and seminary near Duluth, turning the school into the Work People's College and signaling the end of cooperation between the competing groups. After the mining strike of 1907, the division widened still further as the church Finns launched a virulent attack against the Socialists. One study concluded: "Between these two divisions there developed a bitter hostility, so keen that further association of the groups no longer prevailed, and each lived as a separate nationality. Each developed its own set of activities without reference to the others. Even intermarriage between the two bodies was virtually interdicted."[28]

A few exceptional individuals were able to reach out to both parties in ethnic rivalries. Among Finnish Americans, Milma Lappala was a striking example. An immigrant from central Finland, Lappala studied at the Lay College for the Ministry in Revere, Massachusetts, eventually entering the Unitarian ministry along with her husband Risto. In 1911 they accepted a call to create a liberal congregation in Virginia, Minnesota, where Milma Lappala labored until the early 1940s. Because the Virginia congregation took a free-thinking approach to theology, one that allowed integration of Christian tradition with contemporary political and philosophical thought, conservative church Finns considered it anathema; at the same time, radical Finns often viewed the church as a regressive force. Nevertheless, Lappala officiated at burials for both groups, as well as for Finns not connected with any factions. Through her active ministry and

Members of the Ladies Aid Society of Excelsior Lutheran Church, photographed in St. Peter at the home of their pastor, 1931

community involvement, which spanned more than thirty years, Lappala contributed enormously to Finnish-American life on the iron ranges.[29]

As time passed, the ethnic churches took their place alongside the religious institutions that earlier settlers had established in the state. The desire of young people to speak English; assimilationist pressures from the dominant culture, which even in isolated areas were hard to resist indefinitely; government restrictions on further immigration in the 1920s – all came together to transform the immigrant church into an American institution. For example, in 1900 the state's religious landscape included numerous Lutheran groups, each representing an ethnic cluster with its own history of immigration and subsequent settlement in America. The changes that took place across the years were reflected in the 1988 merger of all the major Lutheran churches in the country (with one exception) into a single organization.[30]

The changes were not uniform, however, and cannot be charted with any precision, taking place at different places, different times, and different rates; indeed, the Americanization of ethnic churches continued into the 1980s. The shift to English-language predominance in religious services, which is one way to measure the trend, was well advanced in most locales across the state by the 1930s. In some cases, services in the native language lingered for a longer period, even into the mid-1980s.[31] Choice in religious behavior is another measure. In the 1970s, most Minnesota Jews retained synagogue membership in either the Reform or Conservative branch of American Judaism rather than the Orthodox branch, traditionally the least accommodating of change and diversity. Orthodox Judaism had been pivotal to the faithful continuation of Old World ways for many of the state's Jews whose heritage was eastern European.[32] Among Minnesota's Italian Americans, historian Rudolph J. Vecoli indicated in 1981, "The religious *feste,* once so important, have not been celebrated in the Old Country manner for several decades." Name changes are also telling: at a 1945 church conference in Duluth, Swedish Baptists dropped the modifier "Swedish" from their official designation, taking the name "Baptist General Conference of America."[33]

By the 1980s, ethnicity no longer constituted – in the words of scholar Harry S. Stout – the "vital center of religion" in Minnesota. Nevertheless, as Marty has reminded us, the social eruptions of the 1960s, led by the awakening of black consciousness, spawned a "period of new particularism" that inevitably found expression in American religion, even though the ethnic revival as often expressed a distinctly political as a religious content. Minnesota did not escape the trend. Pilgrim Baptist sponsored a community education program in the 1970s, providing young people with tutorial assistance and an array of class offerings, among them religion and black history. In the late 1970s the church experienced unprecedented growth.[34]

During the same period, other groups in the state brought back a partial schedule of services in the original tongue and resurrected dormant ethnic-religious festivals. Forms of religious expression like the polka Mass, first heard on the iron ranges in the early 1970s, displayed religion's continuing power to convey ethnic identity. But the later brand of ethnic

Italian parishioners during the Feast of the Assumption at St. Ambrose Church on Payne Avenue, St. Paul, 1927

religion differed from that of the immigrants and the first generation in one important respect: it was largely a self-conscious, deliberate practice; in the past, ethnic identity and religion had been imperceptibly joined, blurring the boundaries of each.[35]

New waves of immigrants, however, showed that the phenomenon of ethnic religion, in its original sense, was an ongoing story in Minnesota. The Indochinese peoples – Hmong, Vietnamese, Lao, and Cambodian – who migrated to the state beginning in the mid-1970s represented diverse religious backgrounds, including Buddhism, animism, and both Protestant and Catholic forms of Christianity. Much like the churches, synagogues, and auxiliary bodies created by Minnesotans gone before, the religious organizations established by these immigrants kept alive native languages and traditional rituals, even though altered and reshaped; served as focal points of community activity and identity; and answered basic social-welfare demands of their young, but growing, constituencies. Mutual assistance, in nearly every case, was added to a strictly religious function.[36]

Responses to Twentieth-Century Life

As the twentieth century opened – and as the churches and synagogues of immigrants entered the first stages of Americanization – the religious institutions of earlier settlers confronted other challenges. Churches in rural areas, dwindling in size as members migrated to towns and cities, struggled to remain solvent and alive. Those in urban areas sought to come to terms with a new industrial order of corporate giants and mass production, a universe where their moral authority, dominant in the close-knit world of the old neighborhoods, was much diminished. And everywhere, it seemed, religion had to compete with new entertainments and leisure activities that caught the attention of the people.

On the rural scene, population growth together with improvements in agricultural technology – which meant more productive farms with fewer workers – led inevitably to a rise in out-migration. Church leaders who visualized the deleterious effects on country churches sounded the alarm soon after 1910. The migration of young people, symbols of a congregation's future, caused special dismay. One culprit was education.[37] Big city dreams, it was believed, also enticed the young away but ended in disaster. In the 1930s, the *Catholic Rural Life Bulletin* ran a column entitled "I Am a Country Pastor." One column warned the young, after the biblical passage, that gaining the whole world might mean losing one's soul:

> An event which saddens the country pastor occasionally at this season is the departure of a young boy or girl from the farm home and the rural parish to the cities in quest of a job. . . . The cities entice these youngsters by the promises of big money, the lure of easy living, the supposed gayety and hilarity of life, the bright lights of boulevards and neon signs. They want to get away from the drudgery of farm work; they hope to attain economic security and financial independence. They want to own all

> the nice things displayed in the large stores; they wish to enjoy the lavish life of the cities as they see it in the movies . . . ; they become lost in the maelstrom.[38]

Minnesota's religious leaders were aware of the problems facing rural congregations and turned to various strategies for their solution. The Catholic Rural Life Movement, which aimed to preserve as well as enrich Catholic rural culture, and liturgical renewal, which reached out to all Catholics, were national in scope. Both impulses deepened the spiritual life of rural Catholicism, but because they deplored the worst aspects of individualism and materialism in twentieth-century society they were also rooted in the problems of the day. Minnesota Catholics were at the heart of both movements.[39]

Virgil Michel, a Benedictine theologian and philosopher at St. John's Abbey, became a leading mover and spokesman for liturgical renewal. In 1926, he spearheaded publication of the review *Orate Fratres*, the voice of the liturgical movement, and founded the liturgical press at St. John's Abbey. Pushed forward by Michel's zeal and spiritual commitment – he believed that renewal was indispensable to the religious vitality of Catholicism – and his boundless energy, the liturgical movement encouraged greater lay participation in worship (anticipating the reforms of the Second Vatican Council in the 1960s) and a return to liturgical tradition and ritual. Michel hoped that Catholics might come to a new appreciation of the essentially communal character of the liturgy, to find in its symbolic celebration of Christian unity the basis for human cooperation in all of life's endeavors – economic, social, and spiritual. "To the liturgical awakening of the 1930s," James Hennesey, historian of American Catholicism, maintained, "Virgil Michel brought awareness of the social dimension of Christianity. He was troubled by an 'un-Christian' capitalist system founded on 'greed, selfish egoism, and heartlessness.' Michel's intention in liturgical renewal was to promote human and Christian solidarity."[40]

For Michel, the Catholic Rural Life Movement, which was organized in 1923, originated in much the same source that propelled the liturgical awakening. He argued that in each case the goal was the "spirit of Christian cooperation and mutual aid." In tone, the movement expressed an ideology akin to romantic Jeffersonian agrarianism as it sought to construct what Peter W. Bartholome, coadjutor bishop of St. Cloud, called "a true Catholic philosophy of the land." Proponents articulated the belief that rural life close to nature's cycle was especially virtuous, that agricultural endeavor formed the seat of true spirituality, and that Christ's message became most clear in an agricultural environment. Speaking at the 1946 convention of the National Catholic Rural Life Conference, Bartholome implored his listeners: "Show [the Catholic farmer] that the dignity, independence and freedom of a man can reach its fullest stature on the land and not in the industrial world." To spread its message, the Rural Life movement sponsored a program of reeducation seminars and workshops.[41]

During the 1930s, Catholic Rural Life coincided with a "back-to-the-land" mood and with federal and state programs designed to keep people on the farm. Beyond that, the movement's success is difficult to judge. Martin E. Schirber, dean of St. John's University and director of the university's Institute on Rural Life, gave an ambivalent assessment in 1952. On the one hand, Schirber criticized the movement's rhetorical excess and failure to grasp rural economic realities – "not on vegetables alone doth man live." On the other hand, Schirber believed that the movement "made farm people aware of their life's spiritual values," and he noted that "rural pastors and people have revived old religious customs, and the use of rural blessings from the Roman Ritual has become more common." In this last, the interpenetration of Catholic Rural Life and liturgical renewal was manifest. In Stearns County in the 1980s, the impact of Catholic Rural Life contributed to the pervasive desire among rural Catholics to remain on the land.[42]

By its very nature, the crisis in the rural churches spawned an ecumenical spirit, most often among church planners and administrators, less often within rural congregations themselves. Individual Protestant denominations sponsored programs in the state's rural areas, such as the Country Life movement of the Presbyterian Board of Home Missions, but circumstances – mere survival – often dictated a cooperative response. In the 1920s and 1930s, the Minnesota Federation of Churches, an interdenominational agency that joined with three other groups in 1947 to form the Minnesota Council of Churches (MCC), made the rural church a priority. It established summer schools and conferences for rural ministers and lay people and initiated rural church surveys in cooperation with the agriculture department at the University of Minnesota. Research continued later under the council's Department of Town and Country Church Life through its Town and Country Institutes, again in association with the university.[43]

An emerging synthesis in twentieth-century American historiography has emphasized the spread of bureaucratic forms of organization and control in nearly all avenues of life, including politics, business, government, and even religion.[44] Supporting this line of argument, a 1960 study showed that Minnesota developed a pattern of fewer churches and more members per church during the first half of the twentieth century. Ecumenically minded clergy and church planners certainly worked to promote this pattern, striving to eliminate duplication of effort while articulating a kind of gospel of efficiency. William Jefferson Bell, Presbyterian representative to immigrant miners on the iron ranges, said in 1925 that "the first problem of the rural church is of location, co-operation, elimination, and resident ministry." In "overchurched" – and underpopulated – areas, leaders generally urged church consolidation, criticizing denominationalism as well as the reluctance of the twenty-five-member church to throw in its lot with another congregation.[45]

Withering rural congregations, however, often fought with great determination to preserve their church home. One common strategy was to share clergy with other congregations, a practice that continued into the

1980s, and in other cases members, often women, gave extraordinary efforts to sustain a congregation's life. Raising funds to support the church was especially demanding. For these rural churchgoers, in place of a receding ethnic-religious tie there was evidence of a shared religious experience that helped to cement people and place. At times, the attachment was overlaid with a dimension of ethnic exclusiveness; in 1979, after the Catholic hierarchy ordered the merger of two churches – one Luxembourger-German in origin, the other Irish – in Caledonia, Houston County, some of the Irish protested the disappearance of "their" church.[46]

In addition to changes in the countryside, established Protestant churches faced a shifting social climate in the twentieth century that weakened their stature in the community. In the nineteenth century, towns and cities in the state had often been entirely carried away in the grip of religious revival. As elsewhere in the country, Minnesota saw the proliferation of prayer groups that served as a kind of shock troops of religious ardor. This mood of religious excitement, which was pervasive in its effect, is conveyed in the following newspaper account of a Mankato revival in 1877: "The meetings of the Methodist church continue with unabated interest. The house was crowded on Saturday evening at the gospel temperance meeting, and also on Sunday evening. For ten weeks there has [*sic*] been earnest seekers of salvation, and there were new ones last night. Many say our city has never been so interested in the subjects of religion and temperance as now. Whole families are being saved."[47]

If religious episodes of this scope and intensity recurred, albeit in a different context, in the twentieth century, the religious situation (as Protestant leaders soon discovered) was nonetheless far more complicated. Those in the burgeoning population of immigrants who did not attend an ethnic congregation often had no interest in religion. And, as the pace of life quickened, it became clear that religion was no longer the only game in town. Confronted with these challenges, Protestants disagreed among themselves about the blend of tradition and accommodation that they should apply to the situation. William B. Riley, Baptist pastor in Minneapolis, and Bell, who ministered on the iron ranges, offered very different religious responses to the changing scene. Within the context of a spectrum running from orthodoxy to innovation, Riley and Bell both took older traditions and gave them a new twist.

Riley moved to Minnesota in 1897 to assume the pastorate of First Baptist Church in Minneapolis, a tenure that would last more than forty-five years. Early in his ministry he attacked the status pretensions of the congregation's elite leadership, ending the pew rental system and encouraging people of average means to join. Through a combination of spirited preaching and aggressive leadership, Riley turned First Baptist into a robust congregation numbering 3,500 members in 1937, by far the largest Baptist church in the state. In that year, nearly a third of the Baptists in Minneapolis belonged to Riley's congregation.[48]

Riley became nationally known as an outspoken advocate of fundamentalism, a movement within Protestantism that saw evolutionary science, higher criticism of the Bible, and the social-gospel movement as subvert-

Cowboy evangelist J. C. Kellogg at the Four Square Gospel Church in Minneapolis, 1936

ing the beliefs of the old-time religion. During the 1910s, Riley became a leader in the Minneapolis antisaloon campaign. In the 1920s, he launched an attack on the University of Minnesota for its policy concerning the teaching of evolution, urging his congregation in 1926: "Unite in your demands that the University which belongs to us all shall not become the personal property of a dozen regents or a hundred Darwinized or Germanized, deceived and faithless professors!"[49]

Within the Minnesota Baptist Convention, Riley steered the fight to purge modernist impulses, which by 1910 had attracted many adherents among the state's Baptists. By the mid-1930s, fundamentalists had regained control of the convention and redirected it along conservative lines. To develop a fundamentalist cadre, Riley founded the Northwestern Bible Schools, purposely avoiding the term "seminary," claimed his wife, because of its "association with skepticism." The evangelist Billy Graham became president of the schools in 1947 at the urging of Riley. Graham resigned in 1952 to devote full attention to the work of his evangelistic association, the world-renowned organization that he had established two years before in Minneapolis. As the most visible representative of post-World War II evangelicalism, Graham steered a course away from the separatist posture of fundamentalism and thus also from the style of Protestantism espoused by Riley.[50]

Riley's fundamentalist movement, originating in part as a reaction to the waning of religious uniformity, sometimes blamed immigrants – by association with foreign impulses and ideas – for the increasingly heterogeneous social and religious atmosphere. Riley himself developed a reputation for anti-Semitic pronouncements that tainted the institutions associated with him.[51]

Bell, who was known as Billy Bell in northern Minnesota, worked out a gospel quite different from Riley's. Representing the Presbyterian Home Board, Bell was one of many missionaries sent to work among the mass of unchurched immigrants on the iron ranges. According to the 1906 federal survey of religious groups, fewer than three of every ten persons living in St. Louis County outside of Duluth were affiliated with any religious body. Intending to stay a summer when he arrived in Virginia in 1913, Bell stayed on, his plans to serve a missionary apprenticeship in Europe ultimately thwarted by World War I. He became so committed to the work that he remained until 1931.[52]

Seeing the difficult social and economic conditions in which the immigrants lived and labored, Bell adopted methods that responded to the circumstances. In place of the conventional strategies of evangelism and

Presbyterian missionary William Jefferson Bell (fifth from left) with coworkers at Swan Lake. Bell served his Range Parish from 1913 to 1931.

church planting, Bell pioneered the Range Parish, a nondenominational operation that was not attached to a single location. This informality allowed Bell to be flexible in working with miners and their families, who moved frequently between mine sites. With the help of local recruits, Bell organized a wide range of activities, described by historian Clarke A. Chambers as including "prayer services, Bible study groups, clubs for boys and girls, stereoptican shows, community singing and hymn festivals . . . and, in the summertime, Daily Vacation Bible Schools." Visits to isolated homes, a rigorous and time-consuming task, became a central part of the Range Parish's ministry. Because Bell understood religious education in broad terms, the Range Parish sponsored a children's program for the mind and body – sports, camping, nature study, and creative activities – as well as the soul.[53]

Like the experience of Walter Rauschenbusch in the Hell's Kitchen neighborhood of New York City before him, Bell's exposure to poverty, deprivation, violence, and all manner of human suffering among the immigrants of the iron ranges persuaded him almost immediately that his work must follow a social and economic as much as a spiritual course. Bell did not believe that the church should be foremost a social center, but he considered it expedient that the church conduct studies, provide leadership, and initiate action in situations where social agencies did not exist. If appropriate agencies did exist, the church could perform a referral service, as the Range Parish frequently did. From the premise that the "church group" was the best equipped "to study the entire situation of a community," Bell concluded in 1925 that "the church will always have to pioneer in other areas to get things going in the realm of education, health, recreation." Beyond the myriad small ways in which Bell and his staff contributed to welfare on the iron ranges, he was among several individuals who led in the formation of the Range Conference of Social Workers.[54]

To men like Riley, the social-gospel orientation of Bell made him a Socialist or, worse, a minion of bolshevism. In reality, most proponents of the social gospel were not radicals so much as reformers who believed that the capitalist system ought to be restrained, not destroyed outright, in the interest of workers and of the consumers of the goods they produced. Bell considered the Range Parish part of a "nationwide task of Christianizing America's industrial order," as he informed his supervisory board in 1920. Religious institutions, to Bell, were "co-structures" with schools and communities in the struggle for democracy and the "American way," or, as he put it on another occasion, "the struggle of industrial America at the sources of her wealth."[55]

Bell's work on the iron ranges offers an important lesson about the ethnic religious experience. It is misleading to see only a process of Americanization, of a change that was imposed by the new society upon the traditions of the old. Long-established U.S. religious institutions, as well as ethnic ones, were reshaped as they interacted with each other in a changing environment. The tone of individualism and moral uplift that was characteristic of nineteenth-century evangelism was tempered by the exposure of church social and benevolent agencies to the hardships under which immigrants lived – for example, the conditions that Bell witnessed on the ranges. Thereafter, a new moral economy was espoused by many religious people that was more inclined to equate poverty with social than with individual iniquity.[56] This strand of Protestant thinking, together with the ethnic philanthropic spirit, became especially visible in later years in the form of individual Jewish, Catholic, and Protestant charities and social services. Indeed, one might argue that this religious perspective formed an important ingredient in the state's liberal social consensus.

The divergent outlooks of Riley and Bell illustrate the sharply contrasting ways of being religious that continued to find vital expression in Minnesota. A 1983 survey of religious belief and practice in the state, sponsored by the Institute for Ecumenical and Cultural Research in Collegeville and published in the volume *Faith and Ferment*, pointed to the existence of two distinctive religious styles that cut across denominational lines. The conservative style stressed the centrality of religious experience, often in terms of conversion; took a lofty view of scriptural authority; avoided participation in the secular realm; and had a well-defined notion of the elect church. Social activism was directed to issues of domestic life and personal behavior (for example, sexuality, morality in the media, abortion). The social and political force behind the movement referred to as the "religious right" was clearly derived from this group; further, its social agenda conformed closely with the philosophy of Riley, who believed himself to be a mouthpiece for the "God-believing, God-fearing Minnesota majority." The liberal style, on the other hand, was more open to dialogue with the broader society and less dogmatic about questions of doctrine, authority, and personal behavior. Its affinity with social activism and broad social emphasis (for example, welfare, racial and cultural reconciliation, peace issues) echoed the social philosophy of Bell.[57]

Changing Forms of Religious Cohesion

The composite shape of religion in the state after 1950 has resembled a jumbled picture, with developments as diverse as ecumenism, charismatic renewal, the holiness movement, evangelicalism, the revival of ethnic religious practices, personal religion, and, in the 1980s, the emergence of the religious right in state politics. The trend away from strict denominational identity, whether associated with doctrinal or ethnic exclusivity, emerged as a hallmark of the religious scene in Minnesota during this period.

As patterns of religious cohesion moved away from denominational separatism, new patterns appeared that stressed social and cultural outlooks – ways of being religious – that crossed denominational lines. The resulting religious identities sometimes overlapped in bewildering ways – evangelical, charismatic, liturgical, fundamentalist, liberal, conservative, humanist, and so forth. In this development, Minnesota was part of a larger trend. At the national level, organizations like the National

Service conducted during the anniversary celebration of the Minnesota Council of Churches in Minneapolis, 1959

Council of the Churches of Christ, the National Association of Evangelicals, the Navigators, Campus Crusade for Christ, and the Moral Majority catered to new kinds of religious constituencies that had burst out of denominational wineskins.[58]

In Minnesota, the emergence of nondenominational, or even nonchurch, religious-based networks organized for social and political action represented the culmination of this phenomenon. Examples on the conservative side included the Berean League, various political action groups, and Minnesota Citizens Concerned for Life; on the liberal side were the social action department of the MCC and various peace and justice networks. These groups were part of the conservative-liberal split uncovered in the 1983 survey. In the politics of abortion, remarkable combinations of religious groupings, Protestant, Catholic, and Jew, were lined up on both sides. A Baptist in the 1980s was likely to have more in common with a Lutheran or Catholic than with another Baptist; a Lutheran might share as much, or more, with a Methodist or Episcopalian as with another Lutheran. The sources of this shift were complex and difficult to ascertain with precision, but they can be suggested here.

Ecumenism, the movement toward closer cooperation and fellowship among denominational groupings, had clearly been an important factor in breaking down barriers. The ecumenical spirit, which went back to the turn of the twentieth century among the state's pioneer Protestant churches, came of age in January 1947 when the MCC was formed. During the 1960s, the council significantly broadened its member base when several Lutheran groups and Eastern Orthodox congregations joined the organization. Comity with Minnesota Catholics was also stepped up at that time, and Catholics began to participate in several programs sponsored by the council. Additionally, pronouncements made at the Second Vatican Council (1962–65), particularly the call for broader Christian fellowship

Membership in Mainline Protestant Churches in Minnesota, 1957-80

Church	1957	1980	Change (%)
American Baptist	20,518	13,042	−36
Congregational/United Church of Christ	37,828	45,371	+20
Disciples of Christ	7,572	1,893	−75
Episcopal	34,310	28,481	−17
Presbyterian	61,520	63,765	+4
Methodist/United Methodist	93,389	120,941	+30

Sources: National Council of Churches, *Churches and Church Membership*, tables 50–51; Quinn et al., *Churches and Church Membership*, 18.

and liturgical changes allowing greater lay participation, helped to reduce still further the distance separating Catholics from other religious Minnesotans. Ecumenism, on the whole, emphasized dialogue and a broad social agenda and embraced a spirit that flowed into the formation of the liberal style.[59]

In rural Minnesota, a grass-roots ecumenism emerged in response to the problems of farmers in the 1980s. Catholics and Lutherans in rural areas joined forces to operate a farm-crisis hotline, and the shared hardship eroded what one account called "invisible barriers" between Catholics and Lutherans in rural Minnesota.[60] Church leaders called ecumenical conferences to spell out a new "theology of the land."[61]

The climate of religious consensus that was symbolized by the ecumenical movement allowed sociologist Will Herberg in the 1950s to identify three distinctive strands or "melting pots" – Protestant, Catholic, and Jew – together celebrating a single American way of life.[62] But not everyone was swept up in the call for religious unity. Because it sacrificed distinctive denominational identity in the interest of a broader, but more blurred, religious unity, ecumenism had the effect of spawning a religious reversal, a backlash, in the 1960s and 1970s. People who felt lost in the liberalizing trend or yearned for a more transcendent religious experience sought to recover more distinctive and clearly defined forms of religious self-identity.

As a by-product of the reversal, so-called mainline Protestant churches in Minnesota, those most deeply implicated in the ecumenical impulse, grew very slowly in the decades after 1960, as in the nation as a whole.[63] Membership figures (see table) attest to the pattern. Of these groups, only the Congregational and the United Methodist churches kept up with state population growth, which was 20 percent between 1960 and 1980.[64] In both cases, however, growth reflected church merger more than organic increase. Congregational membership was augmented in 1959 through union with the Evangelical and Reformed church, creating the United Church of Christ. Similarly, Methodists merged in 1968 with Evangelical United Brethren to create the United Methodist church. At least part of the trend toward slow growth reflected a conscious decision by these groups to shift priorities away from church development and toward social action – in the liberal style.[65]

The reverse of this development was the dramatic increase of membership in conservative and evangelical groups over the same period, a trend that is difficult to measure because many of the groups, preferring to stay separate from longer-established denominations, were not represented in membership figures; others were "hidden" within denominational structures. But their growing numbers and increasing confidence were apparent in state politics by the 1980s, most notably as a force within the Independent Republican party. Despite gains registered by conservative churches and associated groups, however, the movement was not as great in Minnesota as in other parts of the country. A survey reported by the Minnesota Poll in 1986 found that 20 percent of Minnesotans identified themselves as "born-again" Christians, a figure half the national rate.[66] Here, as in other religious trends, the presence of Lutherans and Catholics in large numbers in the state was apparently important, since their religious outlooks have generally been shaped more by church teachings than by the intense, often emotional, individual experience associated with being "born again."

But the conservative tide left its mark in Lutheran and Catholic circles as well, demonstrating that a conservative, if not fundamentalist, style was not confined to a segment of Baptist and independent Bible churches. In 1975, a group of parents in Freeport (Stearns County), believing that the parochial as well as the public schools had grown too liberal, established St. Jude's Academy. The headmaster argued that Catholic schools had "watered down" traditional church teachings and introduced such things as sex education and sensitivity training. Sponsors of St. Jude's, which was one of several separatist Catholic schools begun in the county at about the same time, considered the school Catholic but did not seek the sanction of the St. Cloud diocese.[67] Changes emanating from the Second Vatican Council contributed to the conservative rumblings. Two churches in Stearns County – in Rockville and Albany – severed ties with the diocese to form independent churches that would follow the older liturgy.[68]

The increased number of congregations affiliated with the Association of Free Lutheran Congregations, centered in Plymouth, followed the same pattern among Lutherans. These splinter groups left the major Lutheran fellowships because they were dissatisfied with what they perceived as a diminution of biblical authority and moral standards. Some of these breakaway congregations were prompted by the 1988 Lutheran merger, which was viewed as a harbinger of even greater doctrinal compromise, and more congregations were expected to follow.[69]

The Jewish community in the state had seen a conservative reaction earlier in the century. Unhappy with the broad educational and cultural emphasis that had come to characterize the Talmud Torah, which had provided Jewish education since 1894, some Minneapolis Jews began the Torah Academy in 1944 to provide what Berman called "a total Jewish religious education for their children." But most Minnesota Jews moved in secular and liberal directions. They were not plagued by questions of identity to the same extent as other religious groups in the state, for reasons

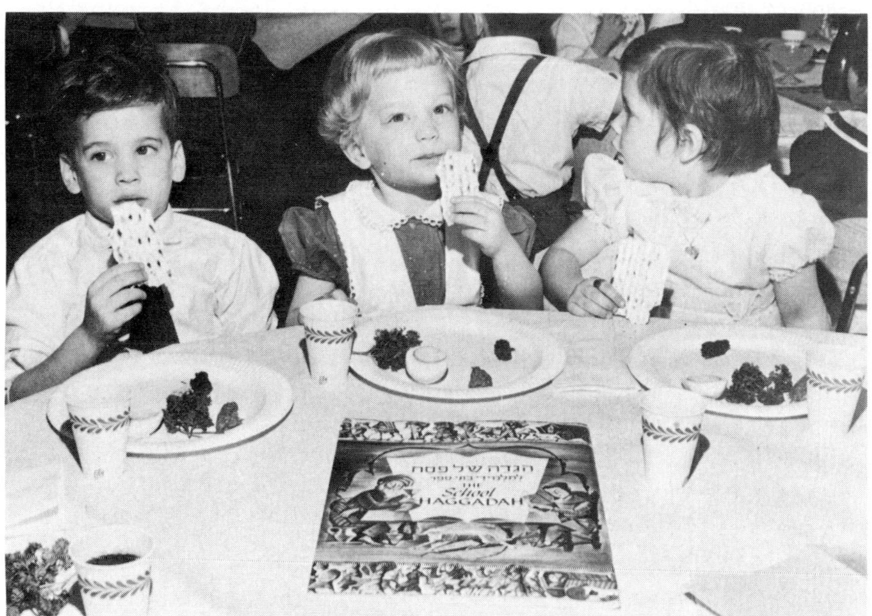

Passover seder at Talmud Torah, Minneapolis, 1960

both internal and external. Many young Jews whose parents had been Orthodox joined Reform congregations in the decades after 1940, and they brought traditional Jewish elements that tempered the Reform spirit. Much farther away, the experience of the Holocaust and political events in the Middle East tended to foster a Jewish identity on secular and political footings. Together with lingering expressions of anti-Semitism, these factors served to mitigate the acuteness of the religious identity crisis that was apparent elsewhere. For the state's Jewish population, Jewishness – in its manifold expressions – was far more than a religious identity.[70]

The charismatic and holiness movements that emerged in the late 1960s and the 1970s were evidence of a deeply felt need for fresh, interior religious experience, the inverse of the broad social emphasis of many church groups. Picking up adherents from diverse traditions – Pentecostalism, Assemblies of God, segments of Catholicism and of Lutheranism and other Protestant churches – the movement was not bounded by denomination. Still other developments fed this mood of seeking personal religious experience. The revival in ethnic religion and in forms of religious experience completely outside the conventions of church – in eastern religions, meditation, and spiritualism – moved the search in many directions. Here, what historian Joseph Blau said of Jews – "Nonaffiliation is by no means the same as nonreligion" – had a much broader application. Indeed, spiritual odysseys that took place outside the church or synagogue pointed to a "measure of indifference to the traditional modes of expressing religious feeling." Even among active Minnesota church members in the 1980s, according to the *Faith and Ferment* survey, half did not believe that a "good relationship with God" demanded church membership, and 48 percent believed it sometimes necessary to follow the dictates of conscience rather than church teachings.[71]

The social movements of the 1960s also left a clear imprint. Eighty-two percent of the respondents in the survey indicated that "the liberation movements of this period have given some new insight into their theology of equality," and 76 percent believed that following Jesus implied "taking the side of the poor and doing what is possible to secure systemic justice."[72] In fact, as calls for social action went forth from the churches, the message penetrated new circles. "Young evangelicalism," as it was called, combined a conservative biblical theology with a new, broadened social consciousness. It appealed to a younger evangelical set who had grown weary of the residual fundamentalism and individualistic moral ethos of the older generation. Park Avenue Methodist Church in Minneapolis, traditional in theology but promoting a progressive social agenda and a message of racial reconciliation, represented an example of the young evangelical spirit. The development moved some congregations that were in the tradition of post-World War II evangelicalism – whether Baptist, Methodist, Evangelical Free, or Lutheran – closer to mainline Protestants and Catholics who had longer social-justice traditions.[73]

But the conservative voice was strong in interviews conducted by the *Faith and Ferment* research team. Researcher Joan D. Chittister remarked that "the 'New Religious Right' has developed within churches of every denomination. . . . It is . . . a movement that transcends denominational boundaries to work for what it believes to be the Christian message: that the activity and authority of God in the world [have] been obscured by the teaching of secular humanism; that pluralism has eroded the absolute value of Christian principles and Americanism; that the family, the unit divinely ordained and above all other human institutions, is under Satanic attack."[74] If the growth in conservative churches in the 1960s and 1970s marked a religious reaction to the ecumenical movement, the religious right became, from the late 1970s, the conservative political reaction to that movement's liberal social agenda. And as religiously conservative Minnesotans gained political confidence, they, too, discovered the usefulness of ecumenical alliances, a practice that they had traditionally avoided.

The women's movement, as it was articulated in the 1960s, also began to alter the old patterns of cohesion that had been based on denomination. Women had always been a fundamental component – indeed the lifeblood – of religious life in the state, and increasingly they sought changes in male-centered theologies and religious practices and demanded religious roles previously reserved for men. By the 1980s, forms of worship and theological perspectives were being debated in many denominations, and some were being refashioned in response to these new demands. Some women had discovered that they shared more with other women, regardless of denomination, than with their coreligionists. Should that awareness continue to grow, the interaction of religiously oriented women in such nondenominational networks as the abortion and peace movements would be likely to play a pivotal role.[75]

Women's group of Central Park Church in St. Paul, about 1910

The religious shifts described above rearranged the structure and profile of many Minnesota churches. Some Protestant groups, in an attempt to reverse membership declines, showed an increased willingness to tolerate diversity, including more conservative theological viewpoints. The role of evangelism – church development – was being reweighed in circles where it had not been a priority for many years. Some church leaders perceived a growing desire among people to combine social action in the spirit of the 1960s and early 1970s with "more family-oriented activities . . . and stricter moral values," according to one newspaper account.[76] Nondenominational fellowships offered other solutions to a fluid and volatile religious climate.

The multiplication of religious styles, behaviors, and experiences in Minnesota after the midcentury mark demonstrated that one could no longer speak, as Herberg did in 1960, of a "common religion" that was identified with the "American Way of Life."[77] During this period, the state witnessed multiple political developments, multiple identities, and multiple visions of what Minnesota, as a social and political unit, should be and become. And the rich diversity of Minnesota's religious history – the interactions among traditions, the interplay of belief and behavior – had promised nothing less.

NOTES

1. The spirituality of Indian peoples, for example, is seen by them as an essential dimension of their whole way of life. Because its particular expressions are considered to be a private matter, Indian spirituality is not included among the religious traditions described in this essay.

2. See Marty's commentary on "religious social behavior" in Martin E. Marty, *A Nation of Behavers* (Chicago: University of Chicago Press, 1976), chap. 2, esp. 33–37.

3. Bernard Quinn et al., *Churches and Church Membership in the United States, 1980* (Atlanta: Glenmary Research Center, 1982), 1, 150–57. The Quinn survey enumerated church members in two separate categories. The first, "communicants/full members," was the most restrictive; the second, "total adherents," added to the first category the children of full members and other "regular participants" who were not considered full members (p. ix). The figure of 55 percent for Minnesota church membership is based on the more restrictive category, except in the case of Catholics and Latter Day Saints, where only the second category was given. Using the less restrictive approach, the survey found that 65 percent of Minnesotans were church members or "near-members" as participants. Either figure was well above the national average. Nevertheless, it would be premature to conclude that Minnesotans were more "religious" than other Americans: church membership is only one way to measure religiousness, and a haphazard one at that. It is safer to conclude that Minnesotans deemed church membership more important than did other Americans. The pattern likely owed a great deal to the proportionately higher number of Catholics and Lutherans in the state than in the nation as a whole, groups that traditionally emphasize the centrality of the church with corresponding strong demands for membership.

4. John G. Rice, "The Old-Stock Americans," in *They Chose Minnesota: A Survey of the State's Ethnic Groups*, ed. June Drenning Holmquist (St. Paul: Minnesota Historical Society Press, 1981), 67–69; C. Hobart, "Religious Movements in Minnesota" (1851; reprinted in *Minnesota Historical Society Collections*, vol. 1 [St. Paul, 1902]), 64–66; Donald B. Marti, "The Puritan Tradition in a 'New England of the West,'" *Minnesota History* 40 (Spring 1966): 1–11; Works Projects Administration (WPA), Minnesota Papers, Minnesota Historical Society (MHS), folder on Social Attitudes – Temperance, 1849–75.

5. Miller and Marzik, eds., *Immigrants and Religion in Urban America* (Philadelphia: Temple University Press, 1977), xxii. See also Timothy L. Smith, "Religion and Ethnicity in America," *American Historical Review* 83 (December 1978): 1155–85; *Ethnicity* 2, no. 2 (1975), entire issue; "Immigrants and Religion: The Persistence of Ethnic Diversity," *Spectrum* (Immigration History Research Center, University of Minnesota) 1 (September 1975): 3.

6. W. H. C. Folsom, *Fifty Years in the Northwest* (St. Paul: Pioneer Press Co., 1888), 311; Emeroy Johnson, "The Swedish Evangelical Lutheran Church at Chisago Lake, Center City, Minnesota" (1940), 30, 70, typescript available at MHS.

7. "Swedish Elementary Schools in Minnesota Lutheran Congregations," *Swedish Pioneer Historical Quarterly* 30 (July 1979): 172–74 (quotations on 173, 174).

8. Robert C. Ostergren, "Cultural Homogeneity and Population Stability among Swedish Immigrants in Chisago County," *Minnesota History* 43 (Fall 1973): 262 (Ostergren's data are calculated for 1885 and 1905); Emeroy Johnson, *God Gave the Growth* (Minneapolis: T. S. Denison and Co., 1958), 73–74, and "Swedish Evangelical Lutheran Church," 107–8; Jim Cordes, *Reflections of Amador* (North Branch: Review Corp., 1976), 22.

9. *St. Paul Daily Press*, July 13, 1869.

10. Proportions of Catholics in the population were 59.8 percent for 1906, 61 percent for 1936, 68.5 percent for 1957, and 59 percent for 1980: U.S. Census Bureau, *Special Reports, Religious Bodies: 1906*, 1:327–29; *1936*, 1:773–74; State of Minnesota, *Census, 1905*, 47; National Council of Churches of Christ in the U.S.A., *Churches and Church Membership in the United States* (New York: The Council, 1957), table 52; Quinn et al., *Churches and Church Membership*, 156. See also Lowry Nelson, *Minnesota Community* (Minneapolis: University of Minnesota Press, 1960), 171.

11. Marvin R. O'Connell, *John Ireland and the American Catholic Church* (St. Paul: Minnesota Historical Society Press, 1988), 217–19, 262–63; Ann Regan, "The Irish," in *They Chose Minnesota*, ed. Holmquist, 144–45; see other references to Ireland's actions on p. 168, 370, 408, 458 of the Holmquist work.

12. The discussion of the school debate is based on several Stearns County local histories: Paulin Blecker, *One Hundred Years in Christ* (St. Cloud: Sentinel Publishing Co., 1957), 38–46, 49–50, and *Deep Roots: One Hundred Years of Catholic Life in Meire Grove* (St. Cloud: Sentinel Publishing Co., 1958), 83; Brice J. Howard, *A History of St. Joseph* (N.p., [1956?]), 47–51; *Stones and Hills: Reflections, St. John the Baptist Parish, 1875–1975* (Collegeville: The Church, 1975), 128; Grace McDonald, *With Lamps Burning* (St. Joseph: St. Benedict's Priory Press, 1957), 110–11, 187–88; Cyril Ortmann, *History of St. Martin's Parish* (N.p., 1958), 45–46.

13. McDonald, *With Lamps Burning,* 110; Sydney E. Ahlstrom, *A Religious History of the American People* (New Haven, Conn.: Yale University Press, 1972), 832; Blecker, *One Hundred Years,* 43 (quotation).

14. Vincent A. Yzermans, *The Mel and the Rose* (St. Cloud: Sentinel Publishing Co., 1972), 302, 305–6.

15. Blecker, *One Hundred Years,* 66, and *Deep Roots,* 85–86; *Stones and Hills,* 114–15; McDonald, *With Lamps Burning,* 201; Ahlstrom, *Religious History,* 830.

16. Stephen John Gross, "German-Americans and the Populist Appeal: The 1918 Elections in Stearns County, Minnesota" (Senior thesis, University of Minnesota, 1984), 24–26; Sister John Christine Wolkerstorfer, "Nativism in Minnesota in World War I: A Comparative Study of Brown, Ramsey, and Stearns Counties, 1914–1918" (Ph.D. diss., University of Minnesota, 1973), 88–89, 96; Blecker, *Deep Roots,* 84 (quotation); Bessie L. Scovell, *A Brief History of the Minnesota Woman's Christian Temperance Union, 1877–1939* (St. Paul: Bruce Publishing Co., 1939), 230–59.

17. Joseph Blau, *Judaism in America: From Curiosity to Third Faith* (Chicago: University of Chicago Press, 1976), 132; Hyman Berman, "The Jews," in *They Chose Minnesota,* ed. Holmquist, 496 (quotation).

18. J. Winfield Fretz, "Mutual Aid Activities in a Single Mennonite Community," *Mennonite Quarterly Review* 13 (July 1939): 191, 194–95, 197–98, 208–9 (quotation); see also Ferdinand Peter Schultz, "The History of the Settlement of German Mennonites from Russia at Mountain Lake, Minnesota" (M.A. thesis, University of Minnesota, 1937).

19. Quoted in *W. E. B. Du Bois: A Reader,* ed. Meyer Weinberg (New York: Harper and Row, 1970), 205.

20. Jon Butler, "Communities and Congregations: The Black Church in St. Paul, 1860–1900," *Journal of Negro History* 56 (April 1971): 118–34; David V. Taylor, "Pilgrim's Progress: Black St. Paul and the Making of an Urban Ghetto, 1870–1930" (Ph.D. diss., University of Minnesota, 1977), 159–79, and "The Blacks," in *They Chose Minnesota,* ed. Holmquist, 73–91; *Pilgrim Baptist Church Centennial, 1863–1963* (St. Paul: The Church, 1963); Butler, "Communities and Congregations," 127; *St. Paul Daily Dispatch,* Feb. 25, 1875.

21. S. Edward Hall, interviews by David Taylor, Dec. 19, 1970, and by Ethel Ray Nance, May 28, 1974, MHS; James Richard Lynn, June 14, 1974, and Ione Brown, July 2, 1974, interviews by David Taylor, MHS. Copies of *The Helper* are available in Eva Neal and Family Papers, MHS.

22. Emeroy Johnson, *A Church Is Planted: The Story of the Lutheran Minnesota Conference* (Minneapolis: The Conference, 1948), 37, 40–41, 356–57, "Swedish Evangelical Lutheran Church," 73, 77, 84, 95, 99, and *God Gave the Growth,* 74, 76. On the topic of religion and communal life, see, for example, French sociologist Emile Durkheim's classic study *The Elementary Forms of the Religious Life,* trans. Joseph Ward Swain (New York: Collier Books, 1961), which offers the compelling insight that religion originates in the celebration of the social life of the group but is not forthcoming in explaining how conflict and change can arise from social unity.

23. *Svenska Amerikanska Posten,* May 17, 1892.

24. M. Mark Stolarik, "The Slovaks," 357, Keith P. Dyrud, "The East Slavs," 410–11, Louis M. deGryse and Anne R. Kaplan, "The Romanians," 447, and Rudolph J. Vecoli, "The Italians," 460, all in *They Chose Minnesota,* ed. Holmquist; William Jefferson Bell, interview by Lila Johnson Goff, Feb. 2, 1968, 7–9, MHS; John Syrjamaki, "Mesabi Communities: A Study of Their Development" (Ph.D. diss., Yale University, 1940), 312. See also Arnold R. Alanen, "Years of Change on the Iron Range," *this volume,* 177–80.

25. Timothy L. Smith, "Religious Denominations as Ethnic Communities: A Regional Case Study," *Church History* 35 (June 1966): 210–17, 223; "Radicals Threaten Priest," *Chisholm Tribune-Herald,* Dec. 10, 1931, p. 15; William J. Bell to W. P. Schriver, Aug. 18, 1913, William J. Bell Papers, MHS.

26. A. William Hoglund, *Finnish Immigrants in America, 1880–1920* (Madison: University of Wisconsin Press, 1960), 38; John I. Kolehmainen, "Finnish Temperance Societies in Minnesota," *Minnesota History* 22 (1941): 391–403.

27. U.S., *Religious Bodies: 1906,* 1:328–29, 2:392; *1916,* 1:278, 2:410–12; Timo Riippa, "The Swedes and Swede-Finns," in *They Chose Minnesota,* ed. Holmquist, 306–8; Arthur E. Puotinen, *Finnish Radicals and Religion in Midwestern Mining Towns, 1865–1914* (New York: Arno Press, 1979), 170, 178; Syrjamaki, "Mesabi Communities," 296–97; Kolehmainen, "Finnish Temperance Societies," 391; Smith, "Religious Denominations," 210.

28. Smith, "Religious Denominations," 214–15; Hoglund, *Finnish Immigrants,* 51; Puotinen, *Finnish Radicals,* 207–25; Syrjamaki, "Mesabi Communities," 302 (quotation).

29. Carol Hepokoski, "Milma Lappala: Unitarian Minister and Humanist," in *Women Who Dared: The History of Finnish American Women,* ed. Carl Ross and K. Marianne Wargelin Brown (St. Paul: Immigration History Research Center, University of Minnesota, 1986), 158–64.

30. Witnessing the difficult decisions that the Lutheran groups were facing as they prepared for the merger, Rabbi Leigh Lerner, Reform rabbi of St. Paul's Mount Zion Temple, made a light-hearted offer to serve as presiding bishop of the new church, claiming that his "utter objectivity" would be useful. See *Minneapolis Star and Tribune*, Apr. 18, 1986, p. 3B.

31. The cases of Stearns and Chisago counties are noted above. See also Hepokoski, "Milma Lappala," 160–61; David Guston and Martin Erikson, eds., *Fifteen Eventful Years: A Survey of the Baptist General Conference, 1945–1960* (Chicago: Harvest Publications, 1961), 17–18; Susan M. Diebold, "The Mexicans," 96, Sarah P. Rubinstein, "The British," 125, Ann Regan, "The Icelanders," 292, Timo Riippa, "The Baltic Peoples," 331, C. Winston Chrislock, "The Czechs," 341, Frank Renkiewicz, "The Poles," 374, June D. Holmquist, Joseph Stipanovich, and Kenneth B. Moss, "The South Slavs," 399, Dyrud, "The East Slavs," 416–17, deGryse and Kaplan, "The Romanians," 447, and Deborah L. Miller, "Middle Easterners," 517, all in *They Chose Minnesota*, ed. Holmquist.

32. Judith B. Erickson and Mitchel J. Lazarus, *The Jewish Community of Greater Minneapolis, 1971–1972* (Minneapolis Federation for Jewish Service, 1973), VII 2–4; Berman, "The Jews," 496–99, 502; Blau, *Judaism in America*, 128, 133–35. In 1973, Minneapolis had two remaining Orthodox synagogues, St. Paul four, and Duluth one.

33. Vecoli, "The Italians," 464; Guston and Erikson, eds., *Fifteen Eventful Years*, 12.

34. Harry S. Stout, "Ethnicity: The Vital Center of Religion in America," *Ethnicity* 2 (1975): 204–24; Marty, *Nation of Behavers*, 177; "Pilgrim Baptist Church 117th Anniversary Commemoration" (1980), booklet available at church office.

35. Carlton C. Qualey and Jon A. Gjerde, "The Norwegians," 242, John G. Rice, "The Swedes," 268, Riippa, "The Finns and Swede-Finns," 313, and Holmquist, Stipanovich, and Moss, "The South Slavs," 399, all in *They Chose Minnesota*, ed. Holmquist.

36. Sarah R. Mason, "The Indochinese," in *They Chose Minnesota*, ed. Holmquist, 582–83, 585, 588–89.

37. G. H. Gerberding, *The Lutheran Church in the Country* (Philadelphia: General Council of the Evangelical Lutheran Church in North America, 1916), 111–12; Carl W. Thompson and Gustav P. Warber, *Social and Economic Survey of a Rural Township in Southern Minnesota* (Minneapolis: University of Minnesota, 1913), 50–51, 68–69; Gustav P. Warber, *Social and Economic Survey of a Community in Northeastern Minnesota* (Minneapolis: University of Minnesota, 1915), 110–12; Karl N. Aho, *Portrait of the Church in an Economic Eclipse* (Minneapolis: Minnesota Council of Churches, 1964), 15–16, 19.

38. *Catholic Rural Life Bulletin* 2 (November 1939): 5.

39. See Aaron I. Abell, *American Catholicism and Social Action* (Notre Dame, Ind.: University of Notre Dame Press, 1963), 217–19; James Hennesey, *American Catholics* (New York: Oxford University Press, 1981), 262–66; Colman J. Barry, *Worship and Work: St. John's Abbey and University, 1856–1980* (Collegeville: Liturgical Press, 1980), 263–66; Edward S. Shapiro, "Catholic Agrarian Thought and the New Deal," *Catholic Historical Review* 65 (1979): 583–99.

40. Paul B. Marx, *Virgil Michel and the Liturgical Movement* (Collegeville: Liturgical Press, 1957), 125–27 (see also chap. 7 for a lengthy discussion of the movement's theological basis and social ramifications as Michel saw them); Hennesey, *American Catholics*, 266.

41. Michel quotation in Paul Folsom, "Rural Ministry: A Response to Change" (D.D. thesis, Aquinas Institute of Theology, Dubuque, Iowa, 1976), 69; Peter W. Bartholome, "The Land and the Spirit," sermon delivered Oct. 13, 1946 (Des Moines, Iowa: National Catholic Rural Life Conference, n.d.), available at MHS.

42. Martin E. Schirber, "Catholic Rural Life," in *The American Apostolate*, ed. Leo R. Ward (Westminster, Md.: Newman Press, 1952), quotations on 137, 145; also Folsom, "Rural Ministry," 70, 316; William L. Cofell, "Rural Stearns County, Minnesota," vertical files under "Stearns County," MHS.

43. L. F. Badger, *A Canvass of Religious Life and Work in Redwood County, Minnesota* (Presbyterian Board of Home Missions, 1914); Hayden L. Stright, *Together: The Story of Church Cooperation in Minnesota* (Minneapolis: T. S. Denison and Co., 1971), 97, 122–23, 259; Glenn I. Nelson, *Social Change and Religious Organizations of Meeker County* (Agricultural Experiment Station, University of Minnesota, 1965), 21–32.

44. Representative works are Robert H. Wiebe, *The Search for Order, 1877–1920* (New York: Hill and Wang, 1967) and Alfred D. Chandler, Jr., *The Visible Hand: The Managerial Revolution in American Business* (Cambridge, Mass.: Harvard University Press, 1977).

45. Nelson, *Minnesota Community*, 120–21; untitled manuscript, 1925, Bell Papers, MHS; Thomas C. Campbell, "Is This Minnesota's Most Overchurched Community?" *Minnesota Messenger* (September 1965): 10, 18; Aho, *Portrait of the Church*, 22; Stright, *Together*, 122.

46. "Workers' Forum," *Home Lands* 5 (February 1924): 16; Regan, "The Icelanders," 294; *Minneapolis Star and Tribune*, June 30, 1986, p. 16A; Louis M. deGryse, "The Low Countries," in *They Chose Minnesota*, ed. Holmquist, 205.

47. *St. Paul Pioneer Press*, Mar. 21, 1877, p. 4. See also *Daily Minnesotian*, Mar. 11, 1858.

48. Marie Acomb Riley, *The Dynamic of a Dream* (Grand Rapids, Mich.: W. B. Eerdmans Publishing Co., 1938), 68–70, chaps. 5, 6; Ernest A. Finstrom, *Baptist Activities: A Description of the Work of the Organized Baptists of Minneapolis and St. Paul* (Twin City Baptist Union, 1937), 3.

49. Riley, *Dynamic of a Dream*, 107.

50. Dell G. Johnson, "The Victory of Fundamentalism in the Minnesota Baptist Convention," *Central Bible Quarterly* 20 (Spring 1977): 36–42; Riley, *Dynamic of a Dream*, 136 (quotation), chap. 10; W. David Lockard, *The Unheard Billy Graham* (Waco, Tex.: Word Books, 1971), 22–23; John Jefferson Davis, *Foundations of Evangelical Theology* (Grand Rapids, Mich.: Baker Book House, 1984), 35.

51. Charles I. Cooper, "The Jews of Minneapolis and Their Christian Neighbors," *Jewish Social Studies* 8 (1946): 36; Berman, "The Jews," 500.

52. Clarke A. Chambers, "Welfare on Minnesota's Iron Range," *Upper Midwest History* 3 (1983): 31–34; Warren Upham, ed., *Congregational Work of Minnesota, 1832–1921* (Minneapolis: Colwell Press, 1921), 217–18; Charles Nelson Pace, ed., *Our Fathers Built: A Century of Minnesota Methodism* (Historical Society of the Minnesota Methodist Conference, 1953), 45–54; U.S., *Religious Bodies: 1906*, 1:327; State of Minnesota, *Census, 1905*, 42–43.

53. Chambers, "Welfare on Minnesota's Iron Range," 31 (quotation), 33.

54. Untitled manuscript, 1925, Bell Papers, MHS; Chambers, "Welfare on Minnesota's Iron Range," 32.

55. "Memo for Eastman – Sept. 15, 1920"; "Two Great Factors, Democracy and Religion," *Home Mission Monthly*, March 1923; untitled manuscript, May 1927 – all in Bell Papers, MHS.

56. See Paul R. Lucas, "The Church and the City: Congregationalism in Minneapolis, 1850–1890," *Minnesota History* 44 (Summer 1974): 69.

57. Joan D. Chittister and Martin E. Marty, *Faith and Ferment: An Interdisciplinary Study of Christian Beliefs and Practices* (Minneapolis and Collegeville: Augsburg/Liturgical Press, 1983), 143–44, 258–63; Riley, *Dynamic of a Dream*, 107 (quotation).

58. Martin E. Marty, *Pilgrims in Their Own Land: 500 Years of Religion in America* (Boston: Little, Brown and Co., 1984), 411–12, 469, 472.

59. Arvel M. Steece, "A Century of Minnesota Congregationalism" (Ph.D. diss., Harvard University, 1957), 314–15, 420–22; Stright, *Together*, 98, 246.

60. Reggie McLeod, "The Rural Church," *Minnesota Monthly*, October 1985, p. 34.

61. *Minneapolis Star and Tribune*, Oct. 18, 1985, p. 4B, May 5, 1986, p. 1A, 6A, Aug. 6, 1986, p. 1B, 4B.

62. Will Herberg, *Protestant – Catholic Jew: An Essay in American Religious Sociology*, rev. ed. (Garden City, N.Y.: Anchor Books, 1960), 26 41.

63. The term *mainline* is often used to denote the Protestant denominations rooted in the American colonial period and those emerging from the revival traditions of the eighteenth and nineteenth centuries. In a more general sense, it also describes denominations closely associated with establishment culture and based in the middle and upper classes. Mainline Protestants in the twentieth century tended to unite around a commitment to social-gospel politics and liberal theology (see Marty, *A Nation of Behavers*, chap. 3). The table excludes Lutherans because, as an ethnic church, Lutheranism was still in the process of becoming a mainline denomination over this period. In Minnesota, the Lutheran church retained a distinct identity that was based on the immigrant history of its Scandinavian and German adherents. On the whole, Lutheran membership in the state remained healthy during this period.

64. State population was 3,413,864 in 1960, 4,075,970 in 1980: U.S., *Census*, 1960, PC(1)-25A, p. 11; 1980, vol. 1, chap. B, part 25, p. 7. In 1957, the Evangelical and Reformed church had 11,705 Minnesota members and the Evangelical United Brethren had 14,432 (National Council of Churches, *Churches and Church Membership*, tables 50–51).

65. See also Steece, "Century of Minnesota," 429–36; Jackson W. Carroll et al., *Religion in America: 1950 to the Present* (New York: Harper and Row, 1979), 41.

66. *Minneapolis Star and Tribune*, Jan. 10, 1986, p. 1A.

67. *Minneapolis Tribune*, Oct. 12, 1975, p. 1B; Folsom, "Rural Ministry," 146–47.

68. *Minneapolis Star and Tribune*, Mar. 16, 1986, p. 1A.

69. *Minneapolis Star and Tribune*, Apr. 8, 1986, p. 1A.

70. Berman, "The Jews," 497 (quotation), 499, 500–503; Marty, *Pilgrims in Their Own Land*, 461–64.

71. Blau, *Judaism in America*, 136; Chittister and Marty, *Faith and Ferment*, 79 (quotation), 95. For the charismatic and holiness movements, see Marty, *Pilgrims in Their Own Land*, 469–70, Richard Quebedeaux, *The New Charismatics II* (New York: Harper and Row, 1983), esp. conclusion, and Erling T. Jorstad, ed., *The Holy Spirit in Today's Church* (Nashville: Abingdon Press, 1973), 7.

72. Chittister and Marty, *Faith and Ferment*, 77, 101.

73. An example of a call for social action is found in Robert Esbjornson, Nancy Eddy, and Barry Stoner, "Social Ministry in the Parish" [1967?], available at MHS. See also Richard Quebedeaux, *The Young Evangelicals* (New York: Harper and Row, 1974); *Minneapolis Star and Tribune*, July 9, 1986, p. 6B.

74. Chittister and Marty, *Faith and Ferment*, 147.

75. *Minneapolis Star and Tribune*, May 10, 1986, p. 17A, Aug. 4, 1986, p. 11A, 12A; *Women's Role in the Archdiocese: A Plan of Action* (Archdiocese of St. Paul and Minneapolis, 1979) and *Woman: Pastoral Reflections* (Roman Catholic Bishops of Minnesota, 1979), both available at MHS.

76. *Minneapolis Star and Tribune*, Jan. 10, 1986, p. 11A, Mar. 30, 1986, p. 1A (quotation).

77. Herberg, *Protestant – Catholic – Jew*, 77.

KARAL ANN MARLING

Culture and Leisure: "The Good Life in Minnesota"

There was a kind of heat wave going on in Cloquet, according to the cynical reporter from the *Los Angeles Times* dispatched to the wilds of Minnesota to soak up local color: in mid-April, that journalist marveled, it was actually thirty degrees above zero![1] In a little house in the woods in nearby Nickerson, the atmosphere was heating up, too. Where in heck was the TV? Wasn't that old black-and-white set down in the basement somewhere? Finally, "Al" found it and hauled it upstairs and perched it on top of the Singer sewing machine in the front room. Then he and "Dorothy" got themselves settled in for the evening to see if their Jessie would win an Oscar out there in Hollywood.[2] Such was life in the heartland – at least as an emissary from the movie capital conceived of it.

Jessica Lange *did* win an Academy Award on that spring night in 1983. Neither of the movies for which she was nominated had made it to the Chief Theater in Cloquet (it was closed most of the winter because of the horrendous heating bills), and *Frances* – her newest picture, a film biography of strong-minded actress Frances Farmer – wouldn't reach Duluth for another month. But most of the regulars in Tillie's Bar had seen her new comedy, *Tootsie*, and were ready to pick the winners on the basis of other factors, anyway. The principal of Cloquet High, from which the actress had graduated as a straight-A student in the late 1960s, thought it was a good thing "anytime a community is recognized for somebody." Though there was no Jessica Lange Day in the planning, no "rah-rah for her," and (in the opinion of the editor of the weekly *Cloquet Pine Knot*) a lot more excitement about the high school hockey team's trip to the state tourney, folks were nevertheless pleased by her success and intrigued by her sporadic local appearances, with Mikhail Baryshnikov – "the famous ballet dancer" – in tow. In recent memory, for instance, the pair had been spotted buying sneakers in Johnson's store.[3]

Ms. Lange, for her part, had an edgy, deeply ambivalent relationship with the series of mill towns in northern Minnesota where she had grown up. On the one hand, she used the proceeds from her first big movie part to buy a 120-acre farm near Holyoke. Her father built her a log cabin on the property, and she always spent Christmases and vacations there. "It's weird," the rising star told a Chicago reporter, "but it's the only place I feel entirely comfortable."[4] At the same time, however, her published recollections of the narrowness and clannishness of small-town life would have done credit to Carol Kennicott, malcontent heroine of *Main Street,* Sinclair Lewis's 1920 satire based on Sauk Centre, Minnesota.[5] Carol rebelled against convention, conformity, conservatism, women's clubs, and a deplorable lack of culture. Frustrated in her desire to transform the grubby mansard storefronts of commercial Gopher Prairie into a neocolonial copy of a New England village, she bullied her neighbors into getting up a drama society instead, only to find that they insisted on performing *The Girl from Kankakee.*[6]

For Carol, and for Sinclair Lewis, nature offered the only real escape from the constraints imposed by the society of Main Street. Throughout the novel, fishing, sledding, and walks in the woods are the symbols of an authenticity wanting in the culture of Gopher Prairie.[7] The young "Jess" Lange of the 1960s had been a rebel, too, against the social hierarchy of Cloquet High School. "I was . . . definitely not a cheerleader," she remembered twenty years later. "They said I was good technically and physically but that my attitude basically sucked. . . . They honestly didn't like me. I think they didn't like my superior attitude. They were very small town and boring and tedious."[8]

But the place still called her home. Jessica Lange had her cabin in the woods, and came back every Christmas to be with the family, and bought sneakers at Johnson's store. And magazine articles about the rising star geared for an audience of fans were apt to be titled "Actress: Minnesota Family 'Pioneer Stock.' "[9] "I am a strong person, honest and frank," she told the press just after a steamy performance in a remake of *The Postman Always Rings Twice* – a movie that, along with the birth of an illegitimate child, brought her a certain measure of unwelcome notoriety. She faced her critics down: "That comes from my upbringing in rural Minnesota."[10]

Although Cloquet, with its one-of-a-kind Frank Lloyd Wright gas station, wasn't exactly the back forty, Lange had, she said, "lived in enough rural communities . . . to be familiar with the problems of farmers and farming" addressed in *Country,* a film she co-produced in 1984.[11] Her own farm gave her special insights into the current crisis as well, Lange felt, even though the usual descriptions of her woodsy, log-cabin retreat did not conjure up pictures of tractors, corn rows, and farmers holding off the auctioneer. "I get back there several times a year," she confided to an emissary from the Minneapolis paper. "I was just back there for a month this summer. I have a little lake and a river and a pond and a big forest. It's my salvation."[12]

It was such glowing testimonials to the recuperative powers of the great Northwest that led *Minneapolis Star and Tribune* columnist Barbara Flanagan to propose casting Jessica Lange in a state-sponsored commercial advertising "Minnesota's glorious fresh air" to tourists. It would show the star with her pale, Finnish-blonde hair ruffled by a gentle breeze, paddling a canoe along a lakeshore, waving at famous native fishermen – singer Bob Dylan, perhaps, or James Arness (television's most durable Western marshal, from "Gunsmoke"), or Franken and Davis, the popular comics. Such an ad might have unleashed a migration unmatched since the coming of the Scandinavians in the 1880s, since (according to *W*, New York's snooty high-fashion magazine) Jessica Lange was very "in" for 1984, along with other wholesome, homey things like mashed potatoes.[13] But Walter Mondale, the unsuccessful Democratic candidate for president that year, was definitely "out," even though, in moments of high triumph and defeat alike, that famous native son was prone to head north and put a boat in the water himself, to do, he declared, "the one thing Minnesotans do best – [go] fishing."[14]

Despite Mondale's much-publicized taste for cold, blue lakes, and despite an annual governor's fishing opener widely held to portend the fate of the incumbent at the polls, politics did not begin to define the ineffable savor of Minnesota that an alluring commercial required.[15] Besides, the recent record of favorite sons competing in the national arena was dismal. Every time the Minnesota Vikings won their pro football conference but lost the Super Bowl, every time the Minnesota Twins (who lost the 1965 World Series) started the season with high hopes and then slid inexorably toward the bottom of the American League (surely the World Series autumn of '87 was some glorious fluke!), local sportswriters seemed instinctively to invoke the name of Harold E. Stassen, Minnesota's perennial – and thus far uninaugurated – presidential hopeful, and took perverse delight in pointing out that Hubert Humphrey was *almost* elected president in 1968. "It's like there's a curse," moaned a soccer fan from Bloomington in 1986, after the Minnesota Strikers lost the championship to San Diego in the final game.[16]

No, given the choice between the glamorous Jessica Lange paddling her canoe and a rejected Walter Mondale trolling for that last elusive lunker, Flanagan and *W* had no trouble deciding who best represented the culture of Minnesota in the 1980s. Lange's self-created rusticity, her farm-cum-log cabin – one part "ma-and-pa" lake resort, one part pure, stereotypical Grandma Moses – and her ambivalent embrace of a small town both romanticized and flawed in memory are all important components of Minnesota's culture. Farm values, hard work, cultivated fields, the beauty of unspoiled nature, play, wilderness: these are what Minnesotans mean when they lay claim to a unique way of life resistant to the homogeneity of mass culture.

And yet Jessica Lange, Hollywood star and proponent of an unconventional family life lived without benefit of clergy, was not exactly your average Minnesota girl from Cloquet any more. She fled to the "U," to "the Cities," like Bob Zimmerman (a.k.a. Bob Dylan) of Hibbing before her, and never, until her spate of celebrity interviews in the early 1980s, looked back.[17] But Minneapolis and St. Paul are Minnesota, too, and they are powerful magnets, luring fresh-faced kids off the farms, out of the dying mining towns and mill towns of the Upper Midwest into colleges, art

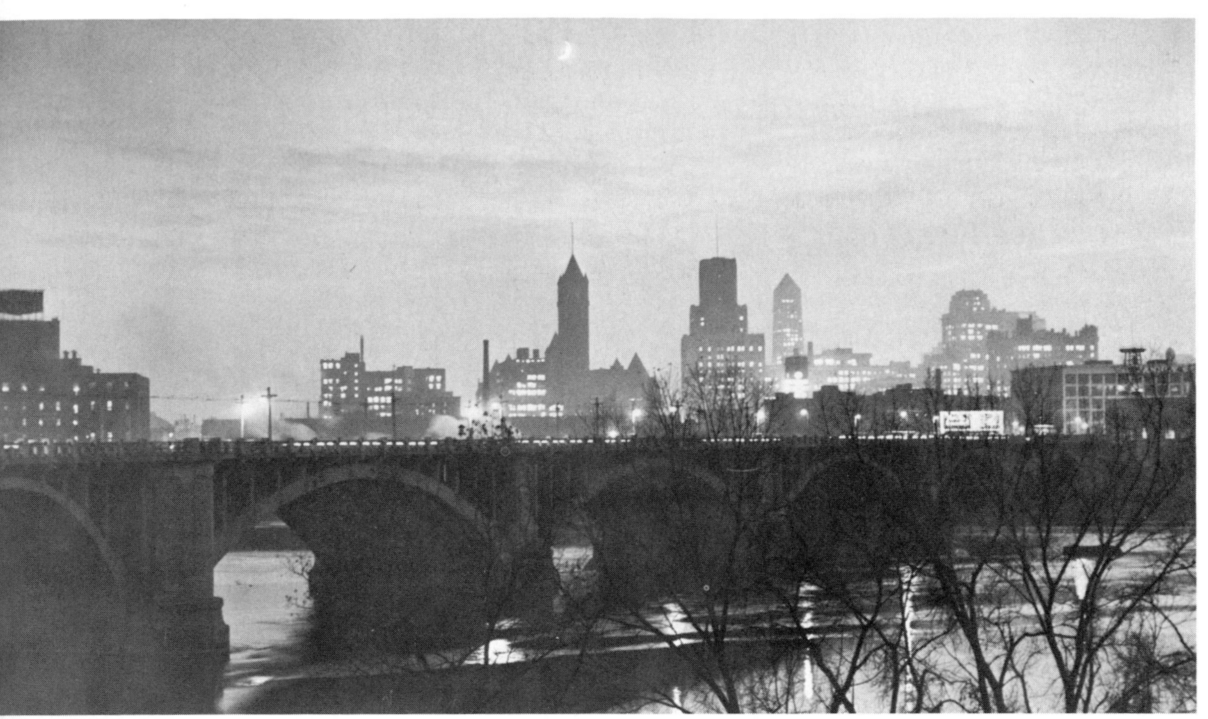

Night skyline of Minneapolis as seen over the Third Avenue Bridge across the Mississippi River, about 1938

galleries, and concert halls, into glittering shopping centers – Southdale, designed by Victor Gruen in 1956, was the nation's first enclosed suburban mall – and, by the 1980s, into movie and recording studios. Beatrice Rutman, Bob Dylan's mother, thought that good stores were one of the state's best features. "We have beautiful dinner parties, lovely entertainment and wonderful shopping," she noted in her encomium to the Iron Range community from which her son repeatedly escaped, lured by the bright lights of Minneapolis.[18]

The young Dylan's response to such litanies of middle-class niceness can readily be imagined. Nonetheless, what the migrant to urban Minnesota found there in the 1960s through 1980s was, in fact, a kind of cultural boutique, stocked with tantalizing samples of the media, the attitudes, the consumer desires, and the ideals that would help make "Jess" Lange and "Bob Zimmerman" national celebrities under other names. In contrast to the Virgilian ethos of farm and forest, the Twin Cities offered a skyscraper or two, night life, a taste of glamour, and the odd glimpse of a Hollywood idol – a Robby Benson or a Mary Tyler Moore, perhaps – before the cameras, with local landmarks prominently displayed behind them.[19]

On Saturday nights in the mid-1970s, the antics of Mary, Murray, Georgette, Ted, and Mr. Grant, the fictional news crew of "The Mary Tyler Moore Show," gave residence in Minneapolis a certain unaccustomed cachet. The sitcom was, admittedly, a Hollywood fantasy of midwesternness. But the situation in which TV's Mary Richards found herself also amounted to a cogent commentary on Minnesotans' changing perceptions of themselves and their lives. The opening credits pictured how the definitive "nice" girl, unlucky in love, arrived in the big city to make a new start. Mary would be a modern career woman of the 1970s. As the series unfolded, she found an apartment in a Victorian house and met her neighbors – Phyllis, the lutefisk-eating native, a reminder of the status quo, and the exotic Rhoda from New York City, tough, streetwise, liberated. The old house, too, was played off against the modern facade of the TV station where Mary worked, and the Crystal Court of the spanking new IDS building in downtown Minneapolis.

As a symbol of fresh beginnings and a sort of militant determination to be up-to-date, Philip Johnson's beautiful skyscraper, looming then above the prairie flatness of the city in almost total isolation, spoke for the TV business, for the high-technology and service industries that would determine the future of small-town girls and farm boys all across Minnesota.[20] But the weekly montage that opened "The Mary Tyler Moore Show" jumped straight from Nicollet Mall in the heart of the business district to a shot of its heroine scampering past one of the city's fabled lakes, trailed by a happy band of kids and ducks. Modern Minnesota was best depicted in a quick cut from towers of glass and steel to lakes and loons, or a pretty girl paddling past the camera, waving to the fishermen.

By December of 1984, when Gov. Rudy Perpich raised eyebrows in churchgoing circles by declaring Christmas week "Prince Days" in honor of the sultry pop music idol from North Minneapolis, motion-picture cameras were no longer a novelty on the local scene.[21] Prince Rogers Nelson, a diminutive black kid with long eyelashes who went to Central High School, invented the salt-and-pepper technofunk-rock blend widely known as the Minneapolis Sound, and often displayed his peculiar omnisexual eroticism in a stage costume consisting of a raincoat worn over a black lace bikini. In 1983–84 he filmed the quasi-autobiographical and wildly successful movie *Purple Rain* in Minneapolis in midwinter.[22] Although script problems were responsible for the late start, it is tempting to believe that Prince was exhibiting something of the same defiant scorn in the teeth of climatic adversity that true Minnesotans had long brought to the building of ice palaces and the conduct of subzero football games.[23] His wintertime feat was, in any case, noted with admiration by the same Hollywood press corps that shuddered over the prospect of visiting Cloquet in April.

The fondness for purple regalia shared by Prince, the star of *Purple Rain,* and the glacial Bud Grant, longtime (1967–84 and 1985–86) coach of the purple-shirted Minnesota Vikings, suggests a kinship, at any rate.[24] And when the editors of the *Minneapolis Star and Tribune* reconsidered the propriety of "Prince Days," they went so far as to suggest that Bud might have a thing or two to learn from the beruffled rocker. "Besides being a local talent who is providing opportunities for other local musicians, Prince has given state politicians and athletes proof that a Minnesotan can reach the top of the charts," the savants decided. "He adds a colorful purple dimension to Minnesota's image."[25] His purple but otherwise unremarkable split-level house on the requisite lake in suburban Chanhassen was as

Prince, the inventor of the Minneapolis Sound, during a performance in the mid-1980s

much a sign of cultural roots in Minnesota as Walter Mondale's fishing reel, or that politician's ritual invocation of a boyhood spent in the fields and farm communities of the Upper Midwest. So were Prince's purple BMWs, his flashy duds, and his lightning visits to the trendy First Avenue nightclub in downtown Minneapolis for a dance in the wee small hours.

Prince is a souped-up version of a Minnesota "yuppie" (a young, upwardly mobile professional, *the* acronym of the 1980s), the sexy Adam of Minnesota's Eden Prairie teendom. When the authoritative rock magazine *Rolling Stone* came to Minnesota in search of what it termed the "Kung Fu Grasshopper" persona Prince adopted for the receipt of Academy Awards, it found instead that the familiar landmarks back home "bring out more Babbitt than Badass in Prince as he leads a leisurely tour down the main streets of his inner-city Gopher Prairie. He cruises slowly, respectfully: stopping completely at red lights, flicking on his turn signal even when no one's at an intersection."[26] Playing Sinclair Lewis's hometown booster to the hilt, Prince turned up unannounced to entertain at the St. Paul Winter Carnival's Fun Fair in St. Paul in February 1986. "Los Angeles ain't got this," he enthused to the freezing crowds, without fear of contradiction. "Minneapolis [*sic*] is the funkiest state on the map."[27]

Lake Wobegon, in Mist County, somewhere in the central reaches of the state, appears on no map at all. Thanks to its imposing statue of the Unknown Norwegian and a rich body of folklore, however, "the little town that time forgot and the decades cannot improve" may have been the best-known place in Minnesota in the 1980s.[28] Its principal historian was Garrison Keillor, who rose to fame in St. Paul – he got there by way of Anoka, the "U," and the *New Yorker* – as host of "A Prairie Home Companion," a weekly radio program that, despite a common thread of mannerly restraint, neatly reversed the urban aspirations of "The Mary Tyler Moore Show."[29]

"Jess" and "Bob Zimmerman" and Mary (and "Gary" Keillor, too, in the early 1960s) came to the Cities in search of the good life. But Keillor beckoned his listeners back to the low-tech countryside, to a fictional realm where macaroni hot dish for Thursday supper perks up the most jaded palates, and boys and girls who never knew the lyrics to Prince's "Dirty Mind" warble "Because God made the stars to shine" while washing up the dirty dishes. "The Mary Tyler Moore Show" embraced the complexities of the urban experience; "A Prairie Home Companion" provided an imaginative alternative, a nostalgic version of small-town Minnesota in the 1950s, before Mary Richards moved to the Cities. The pain of loss is all the sweeter when nothing, in fact, has been lost; and the charm of Anoka-on-Lake-Wobegon glimmered most prettily in the minds of listeners who wouldn't have gone home again if given the chance, or cosmopolitan souls who were already at home in skyscrapers high above the lakes.[30]

Garrison Keillor's quixotic preference for the radio medium favored nostalgia; but it was also a function of pretend backwardness, an established genre of "hick" humor – the same kind of self-deprecating, aw-shucks silliness that led Minnesota's brotherhood of journalists to boast of the state's losing record in national elections and the National Football League. Outstate, the same impulse prompted members of the Rotary

Minnesota Vikings head coach Bud Grant leaving the field after a victory at Met Stadium, 1969

Club and Junior Chambers of Commerce to construct huge parodies of civic monuments in brightly colored fiber glass in order to proclaim their more-often-than-not overlooked towns "The Lutefisk Capital of the U.S.A." or "The Eagle Capital of the World." There were giant walk-through and ride-on fish, and fish simply meant to be gaped at (like the one that got away!). There were colossal ducks, and loons, and ears of corn, and a whole family of mascots drawn from the Paul Bunyan legends, including one statue of Paul that lolled its head about and talked to delighted children. Since the 1930s, the roadsides of Minnesota have been littered with the prototypes of Keillor's Unknown Norwegian, boasting of great hunting and fishing nearby, of Bunyanesque forests, record-breaking corn crops, and vacation-time fun afoot, all the while undercutting the puffery with their own comical hyperbole.[31] The drive to erect tall-tale statuary continued unabated into the 1980s. This form of sly, shy humor was also popular in more evanescent media: in a clever series of TV commercials aired in the 1980s, it was used to sell paramilitary chickens who purportedly guarded the state's dinner tables from invading southern fowl, and New York vanilla ice cream derived from a big, white Minnesota cow covered in graffiti.[32] Jokes about bad weather and the opacity of Scandinavians fall into the same category.[33]

Although the boasting goes back to Babbitt and the frontier boomers before him, and an awareness of the ludicrous aspects of such claims almost that far, humor does not set Minnesota apart from a thousand other provincial places that the media bombard daily with signs of their status as backwaters remote from the real centers of American power and culture. But that does not deter national columnists and commentators from hoping to find out there somewhere a pocket of vibrant regional culture, some sturdy strain of localism resistant to the blandishments of mass culture. In fact, although regionalism has long been believed to percolate upward from the grass roots of Mid-America, it can also filter down from the offices of Time-Life, Inc., and the TV networks.[34] Because *Time* magazine came to Minnesota in August of 1973 in search of its uniqueness, for instance, a TV network could confidently assure viewers a decade later that MacGyver, hero of a weekly action thriller set in any number of espionage hot spots on the back lot, came by his self-reliance naturally: MacGyver, after all, grew up in "The Land of 10,000 Lakes," where even the governor played hockey in the winter and went fishing in a lumberjack shirt every summer.[35]

After an estimated 4.25 million American households had inspected the *Time* cover that featured a Minnesota lake, a plaid shirt, and the boyish Wendell R. Anderson brandishing a trophy northern, the carping started.[36] It had all been a put-up job, ghostwritten by his publicity staff to make Governor Anderson into a vice-presidential contender! The editor was a Brainerd boy! All the so-called average citizens quoted in the story were cronies of Anderson's! Especially indignant over *Time*'s kid-glove treatment of Wendell Anderson's Minnesota was Elmer L. Andersen, who had been governor back in 1961 when the *Saturday Evening Post* (which ceased publication soon after) decided that the state was on its last legs.

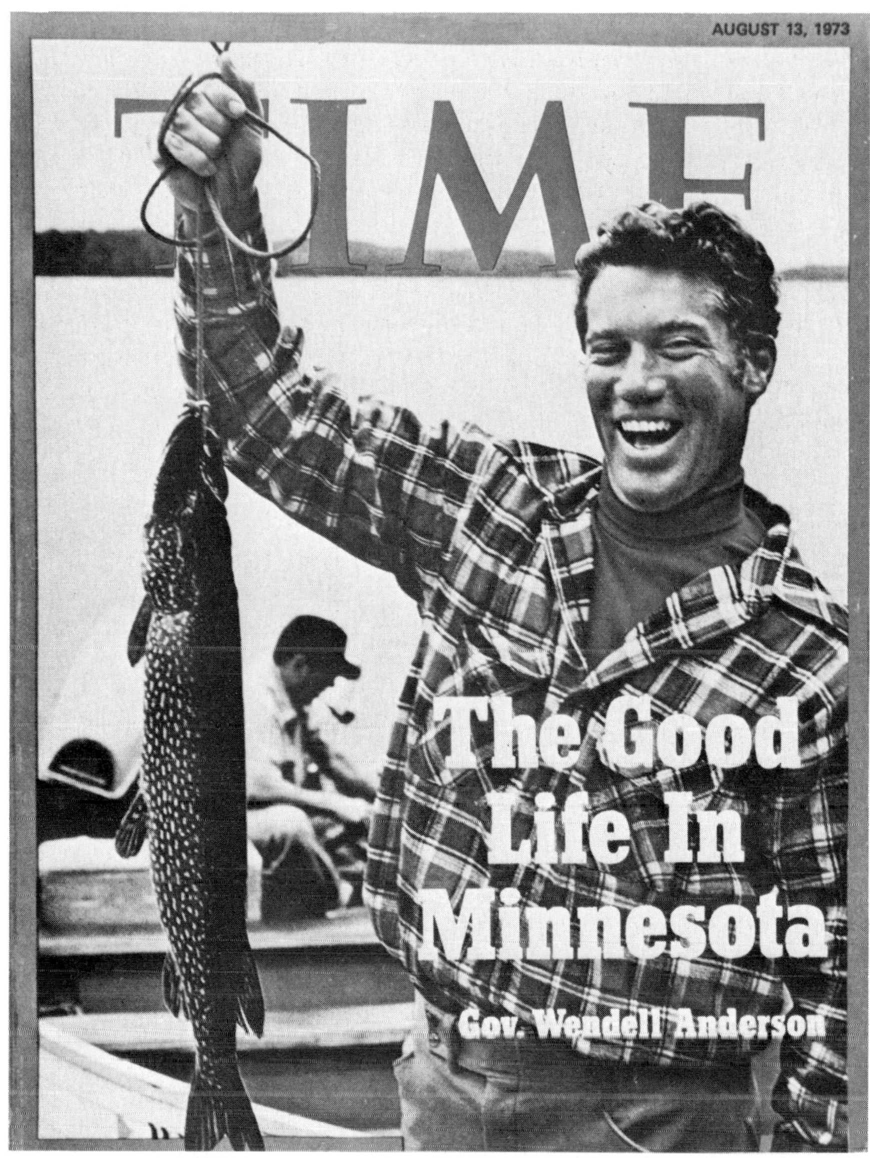

Minnesota and its governor on the cover of Time *magazine*

"In the intervening years, Minnesota seems to have fared much better than the . . . *Post*," he quipped. "Surely things a dozen years ago were not all that bad. And surely things aren't all that glorious now for all our people."[37] The *Post*, and the former governor's critique, were concerned largely with economic facts. According to the offending article, iron and timber resources had been exploited and exported at the expense of a solid industrial base and the tax climate was awful. The prospects for tourism looked equally bleak because the fish population was disappearing and wintertime temperatures were so low that even the natives showed "little enthusiasm for outdoor winter sports."[38]

By contrast, and despite a respectable smattering of statistics on Indian unemployment and sagging taconite production, the *Time* piece focused on the intangibles that comprised an elusive "quality of life"– sunsets over lakes, picnics, and a cultural climate as hot as the winters were said to be cold. Since the *Post* had paid its call, the Guthrie Theater had opened in Minneapolis (in 1963), and the Walker Art Center had moved into contiguous quarters (in 1971), shedding the last vestiges of its old-masters origins together with the earnest amateurism of its adolescence as a WPA community project.[39] The Minnesota Orchestra was flourishing under the baton of Stanislaw Skrowaczewski. The IDS Center was up, along with Minoru Yamasaki's temple for the Northwestern National Life Company and Gunnar Birkert's dramatic catenary arch, from which dangled the Federal Reserve Bank of Minneapolis. *Time* showed them all in tantalizing color, interspersed with shots of grain elevators, farms, Sinclair Lewis's original Main Street, and seven separate lakes that lacked only a sauntering Mary Richards to achieve iconic perfection.[40]

In compensation for Mary's absence, there were two gorgeous shots of "Wendy" Anderson. On the cover, fish in hand, he appeared in the guise of a Nordic hero, patron deity of "The Good Life in Minnesota," the legend set off against the plaid splendor of his outdoor togs. On an inside page (wearing the same shirt), he was posed like a male version of Sleeping Beauty, dozing in the grass in that perfect serenity henceforth characteristic of the pure air and high-mindedness of Minnesota. He dreamt, perhaps, of that stupendous fish of his, talisman of the good life. Or perhaps, as his political enemies surmised, his sleep was soothed by visions of the stupendous vote totals a *Time* cover could produce. After August 13, 1973, Governor Anderson's handsome face was almost as easy to recognize as Bob Dylan's nasal twang, no mean feat considering that barely six months before he had been enlisted to stump the celebrity panels on television's "I've Got a Secret" and "What's My Line?"[41]

That Governor Anderson should have graced the TV game show circuit is not altogether surprising; in his second inaugural address, he quoted pop singer John Denver, whereas (his critics noted) Gov. Patrick Lucey of neighboring Wisconsin alluded to Ralph Waldo Emerson.[42] Anderson's fascination with the mechanisms and messages of mass culture reflected the same frenetic modernity that coaxed Mary Richards, the IDS building, and the thrust stage at the Guthrie Theater into being: in the 1960s and 1970s, Minnesota opted for bright lights, urban glitter, media flash, experimentalism, and hype. That Anderson appeared on programs concerned with the question of identity is particularly telling, since Minnesota's concern with what it is, and why, and how the Land O' Lakes is qualitatively different from other places may be the most distinctive feature of its regional culture. Paradoxically, it was the quest for identity that largely defined Minnesota's identity on the shady side of the twentieth century.

The Iowa jokes and anti-North Dakota billboards of the 1980s express a self-consciousness profound enough to be taken seriously, an almost obsessive interest in the genius loci, in the spirit that makes a "good life in

Minnesota" both unique and very good indeed. New regional and local magazines feed the search for Minnesota rituals and sensibilities. Tourists and homebodies alike are invited to proclaim their belief in a viable communal culture by wearing T-shirts that greet so many square miles of farms and lakes and skyscrapers like a cherished buddy just back from a month up north: "Hello Minnesota!" reads the cheery logo.[43]

Although the late-twentieth-century round of Minnesota-watching owed much of its fervor to *Time* and to energetic marketing by T-shirt makers, the publishers of *Lake Wobegon Days*, and their kin, the booster impulse that preceded it can be traced back to Floral Park, a suburb of the thinly disguised city of "Zenith," Minnesota, described by Sinclair Lewis in 1922. There lived George F. Babbitt, fisher-up-north, rooter for the local baseball team, pillar of the Boosters' Club. And while Babbitt was, throughout most of the book named for him, blissfully unaware of the significance of himself and his affiliations, his creator brought George to bumptious life through a minute examination of the texture of everyday doings in middle-class Minnesota. For satirical purposes, Lewis looked closely at Indian place-names and the vogue for neocolonial houses with hand-tinted Wallace Nutting photos above the mantlepieces; at literary thirsts readily slaked by doggerel in the newspapers; and at dramatic urges satisfied in "The Chateau," a movie theater whose weekly program offered a nice mixture of bathing beauties, cowboys, and fat men eating spaghetti, and whose fabulous entryway was "decorated with crown-embroidered velvet chairs and almost medieval tapestries," where "parrakeets sat on gilded lotos [*sic*] columns."[44] F. Scott Fitzgerald's magazine stories, too, yielded up a devastating portrait of social climbing in St. Paul in the 1920s, and the social insecurities of a raw, monied midwestern elite, as much at home in the Winter Carnival ice palace as Babbitt was in a motion-picture palace just a few fictional miles away.[45]

Hometown friends of both writers had every reason to be distressed at savage lampoons of institutions and situations that seemed to derive unmistakably from Minnesota, and Minnesota alone; however, their novels and short stories aimed at a universality bred of sharp observation of characters in a convincing milieu. Palaces of ice or of plaster and lath were incidental to their larger literary aims. Lewis and Fitzgerald wrote about Minnesota, but they were not Minnesota writers in quite the sense that their near-contemporaries, Margaret Culkin Banning and Grace Flandrau, were. It would be easy to conclude that forgotten novelists are the real regionalists (and that regionalism is a polite term for failure or provincialism), were it not for the sheer intensity with which Flandrau, for example, approached the minutiae of Summit Avenue luncheon menus. There is a ferocity in her scrutiny of a "complicated salad . . . looking like a flower garden and surprisingly compounded of eight different kinds of fruit, and of marshmallows, nuts, dates, French dressing, mayonnaise, and whipped cream" that transcends mere local color.[46] Local ladies of leisure consumed such delicacies: the titanic too-muchness of the dish symbolized material success and material aspirations in a very particular way.[47] The same rec-

Women's club in Winona gathering before a table of refreshments, about 1910

ipe, with slight parochial variations, turned up alongside the macaroni hot dish in all manner of self-published Minnesota church cookbooks of the 1980s, identified as a "Minnesota Heritage" treat and a regional specialty. It is hard to escape the conclusion that the fancy concoction just might be an important cultural marker, a taste of what Minnesotans who elect to ponder the nature of their selfhood, and those who don't, really mean by Minnesota culture.[48]

When, in 1958, the Minnesota Statehood Centennial Commission set about celebrating that important anniversary, a variety of projects was set in motion. One was a centennial cookbook to which, according to surviving records, no major cultural importance was attached: the compilation was something to give the ladies a role in the official observances. But when county chairwomen forwarded the recipes they had garnered to St. Paul, long letters more often than not came with the instructions for making boiled "verenicas," brown bread, old-fashioned cottage cheese, chicken-ginger cookies, and Christmas pudding. To the women who had saved their grandmothers' and great-grandmothers' "receipts," foodways were an important source of pride, fond memories, and historical consciousness.[49]

Brown bread reminded a Sauk Rapids housewife of her husband's grandmother, born in Vermont in 1822, who came west to Minneapolis, she thought, in a covered wagon. Cottage cheese put a Foley woman in mind of good things "my mother used to make" and Grandpa's trek to Minnesota in 1868. Ginger cookies made with chicken fat for shortening recalled frontier privations suffered by a niece of Ralph Waldo Emerson, who was the ancestress of a Crow Wing County contributor. Albeit the stuff of everyday life, cookies and cottage cheese spelled heritage and creativity and the aesthetic pleasures often associated only with the higher reaches of art-as-culture to many Minnesotans for whom the centennial commission's designated cultural artifacts – a statue of Gov. Floyd B. Olson for the Capitol grounds, a short orchestral selection by Antal Dorati (then conductor of the Minneapolis Symphony), and an opera based on a funny story by James Thurber – might have remained somewhat esoteric.[50]

The kinds of activities that did bring beauty and food for thought into the leisure hours of most Minnesotans throughout their first century are difficult to establish with any precision. While few diarists or writers of letters would have used the exalted term "culture" to dignify their own activities, their lists of both routine and extraordinary happenings describe a culture nonetheless – a rich potpourri of books, fashion, lectures, magazines, shows, quilting bees, artistic scrapbooks, movies, popular songs, grand opera, and more besides.

Ilma Cale, a spinster stenographer who worked in Grand Rapids and Minneapolis between 1905 and 1917, wrote long and faintly superior letters to her stay-at-home older sister on the family farm near Worthington, from which she omitted no detail of urban, middle-class taste.[51] A willing slave to fashion as it was represented in shop windows and on the backs of elegant women passing by in the streets, Ilma fussed endlessly over her own hats and shirtwaists, and pitied her poor sister Artie because she was stuck in Worthington, a "town . . . always rather a back number in matters of style."[52] For all her interest in such trivia, however, Ilma could explain the meaning of a French phrase with some precision, chide Artie for missing the chance to hear educator Maria Sanford speak, insist that all young women should know something about painting and music, and take a rather lofty attitude toward the once-popular novel *Trilby* because she considered it badly written.[53]

After a period of refined disdain, Ilma took to motion-picture shows with a passion. She never missed a circus or a Wild West show or the Chautauqua. When she went to see Clara Kimball Young, the greatest silent star of the day, in *The Price She Paid,* Ilma had already read the novel by David Graham Phillips from which the "movie play" was adapted. Although she was a voracious consumer of whatever cultural fare came her way, Ilma Cale was no purist: her most prized book was an illustrated Shakespeare with gilded edges, bound in floppy red leather covers, but she admired the Juliet played by the slinky Theda Bara, siren of the silver screen.[54]

For Miss Cale's contemporaries who stayed on the family farm, the menu of cultural sustenance offered wholesome but limited choices. The diary of Ada Cross, written on a Martin County farmstead in 1917, shows that fixing companionable suppers for passing friends and relatives and talking in the parlor afterward were regular treats. More rarely, she noted the excitement of going into Fairmont for a picture show at the Strand, a parade of doughboys, or an afternoon of sewing in "the Red Cross rooms."[55]

Books and pictures and the like did not bulk large in daily life on the Cross place, but Ada was not insensitive to objects of aesthetic appreciation in the domestic circle: she took pains over the appearance of her needlework and vastly admired the "lovely chair" the family gave her parents for their sixtieth wedding anniversary.[56] For Ada Cross, culture was embedded in the texture of everyday life.

But for James Shields of St. Paul, whose diaries almost totally exclude events that did not take place on a stage or in a concert hall, culture meant something refined, splendid, and altogether out of the ordinary, something to be savored and remembered. One Monday night in the autumn of 1900,

Shields went to the Metropolitan Opera House in St. Paul "to see Joseph Jefferson in his famous impersonation of 'Rip Van Winkle.' " The theater was packed, and the crowd so enthusiastic that Jefferson was forced to make a curtain call after the first act. It had been twenty-five years since he had first played St. Paul, said the old actor with a tear in his eye, "and to play here now in full health of mind and body before the descendants of those ancestors is a privilege." Watching the spectacle, James Shields recalled seeing Jefferson do his Rip twenty-seven years earlier in Faribault, and once again on Thanksgiving afternoon in 1895, and the knowledge that he had done so clearly gave him enormous satisfaction.[57]

Over the course of a long life – he lived to the ripe old age of ninety-six, a sort of modern-day Rip Van Winkle himself – Shields often had occasion to compare the celebrated Madame Nordica singing Meyerbeer in 1900 with Lily Pons doing Donizetti in 1949.[58] To the connoisseur, such opportunities for the exercise of judgment and erudition were among the principal pleasures art had to offer. To Myrtle Fortun, a Lyle, Minnesota, telephone operator who kept a lively scrapbook-cum-diary between 1941 and 1948, a union dispute that barred "all popular music on the radio" so that "we are hearing the Old Masters" was a curiosity and a minor annoyance.[59] Myrtle and her friends dearly loved music of a different sort: they played the latest jazz tunes on the piano, sang hymns for fun sometimes, and kept an ear out for new novelty ditties on the radio.[60]

On her days off, the jolly Miss Fortun found no end of cultural events to fill the idle hour. An admirer of the suave actor Leslie Howard, she went to the movies in Austin and took along her copy of *Gone with the Wind* to check the Technicolor version against the book. She kept up with new regional fiction, too – she especially liked *Song of Years* by Bess Streeter Aldrich, "an Iowa story of Waterloo and Cedar Falls country." She entered a jingle contest in the newspaper (winning a pair of movie tickets for splicing together a group of ads to make a nonsense verse), and felt terrible when one of her favorite comic strips was canceled. Her taste ran to hand-tinted photographs and greeting cards that she bought by the bagful, poring over the racks in the drugstore so the images and verses she picked out would say just what she might have said, had Myrtle been a poet.[61] The instinctive feeling for design that led her to examine cards by the hour was also expressed in the quilt tops she made, and in her massive scrapbook, in which she balanced off the text against an assortment of clippings, comical stickers, and magazine pictures with a practiced eye and enormous care.[62]

Artist Wanda Gág, growing up in New Ulm in the early years of the century, contributed to the support of herself and her numerous siblings by hand-painting greeting cards or "postals."[63] Sold by a sympathetic druggist, her watercolor renderings of chubby children were adapted to suit Halloween, Easter, Thanksgiving, Valentine's Day, and all the other moments on the calendar that called for special commemoration. Hostesses ordered place cards from her for their luncheons and dinners; smart young women commissioned illuminated "birthday books" as reminders of festal days in the lives of their friends and relatives. At the

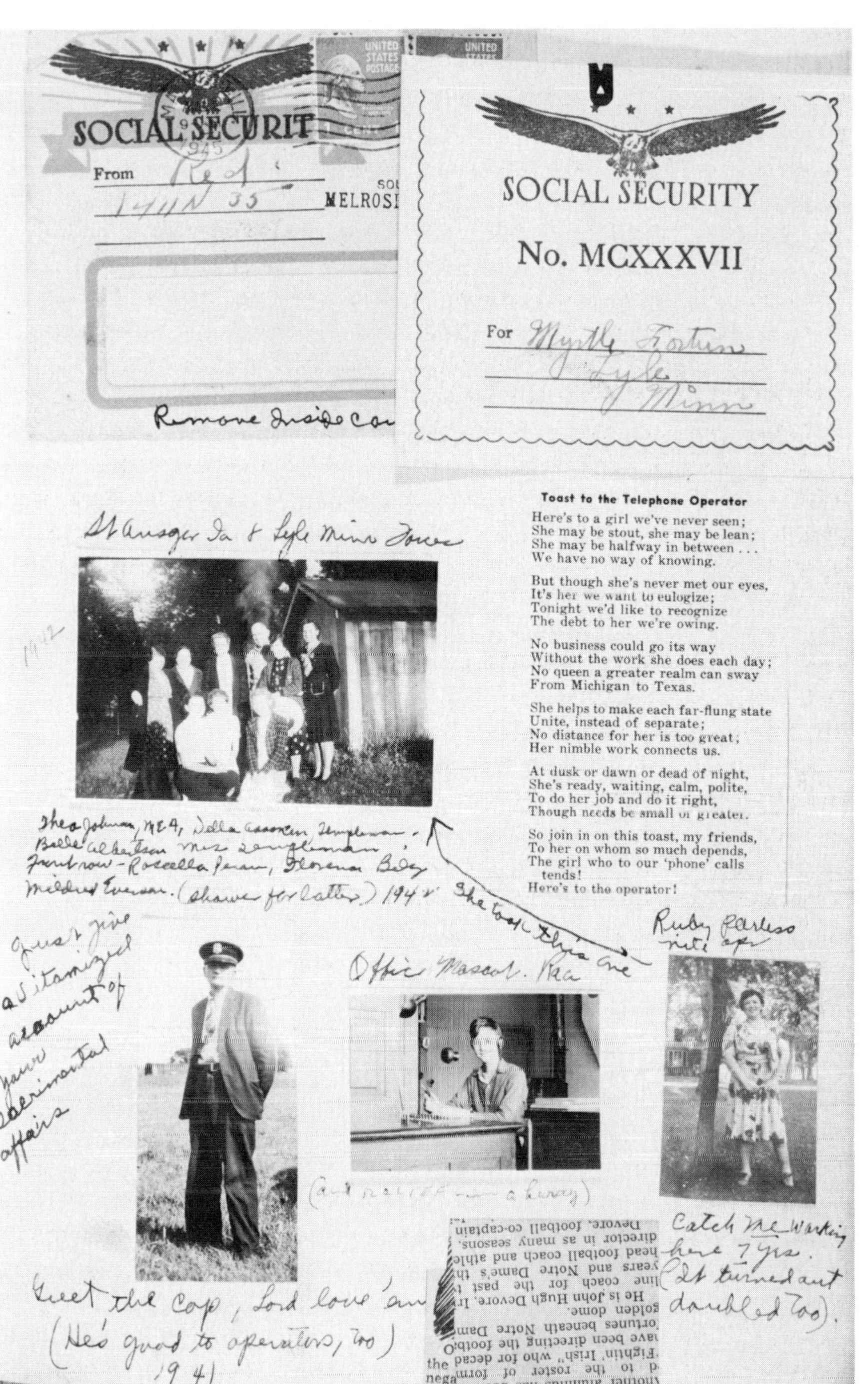

A page from Myrtle Fortun's diary, compiled between 1941 and 1948

age of fifteen, Wanda Gág already had turned an attic room into a studio, much like that of her late Papa, Anton, a painter of church murals, dining-room friezes, and yards-of-roses. She had already hit upon a style derived from the work of popular illustrators of the hour.

In fact, one of the most fascinating aspects of Wanda's New Ulm school days is the ease with which the little "paintress" and her classmates debated the merits of child art by Jessie Wilcox Smith, Mary True Ayer, and Rose O'Neil (who also wrote "snappy" and "fetching" verse), and the dewy beauties celebrated by Howard Chandler Christy, James Montgomery Flagg, and Harrison Fisher. These well-known magazine illustrators were, she told her diary, her "favorite artists," and she pined "to see and talk with" such titans, compared to whose work her own scribblings were "noughts, zeros, nothing."[64] The names of Michelangelo, Raphael, and Rosa Bonheur were also bandied about in her circle, but commanded no greater respect. When her little sister Stella compared her to one of the Harrison Fisher girls, "with their perfect noses, roseleaf skin and lovely wavy hair," Wanda was both embarrassed and thrilled to the quick.[65]

Some of this fervor can be chalked up to normal adolescent enthusiasm, to be sure. But the interest in a certain kind of prettified, sentimental, chocolate-box art – an interest shared by Wanda Gág's New Ulm clients and Myrtle Fortun, spinning the card racks in the Lyle drugstore a generation later – warrants closer attention. It shows the extent to which small-town culture, as early as 1908, had been influenced by the mass-circulation journals for which Fisher, O'Neil, and the others provided illustrations. It suggests that both magazine pictures and those painted by Anton Gág and his daughter filled a need for art in daily life that art galleries, had there been such institutions in southern Minnesota, would not: Michelangelo probably *was*, at bottom, extraneous to a culture geared to bookmarks, paper dolls and cards, holidays, and ritualized moments of leisure from the hard work of making a living.

Wanda's diary also discloses how feminized "artistic" popular culture was in its consumption and, increasingly, in its creation. It shows how important, in this distaff realm, was imagery expressive of the value of feminine pursuits – having babies, dressing and looking well – and of feelings and emotions that seldom found direct expression in the constrained etiquette deemed proper to women. Finally, Wanda Gág's little business should serve as a reminder that aesthetic choices, whether exercised over the purchase of greeting cards or a preference for Raphael in lieu of Michelangelo, are still complex cultural decisions, acts of no little importance.

When Wanda Gág moved to the Cities to attend both the St. Paul and the Minneapolis Schools of Art on scholarship between 1913 and 1917, she learned to question the hometown sureties of her youth. Her new friend Armand Emraad, who went to the University of Minnesota and held strong opinions on matters artistic, did not have much use for New Ulm standards of beauty. "We talked of Harrison Fisher . . . who had sacrificed The Better Art for The Art That the Public Demands," Wanda told her diary. "I said that if I . . . had made a good start, had gone on the wrong path (that of Cleverness and Superficiality) and had then found that I couldn't get back to Good Stuff – " Here, Armand stopped her. "I'd come and choke you," he growled.[66]

In time, Wanda Gág returned to the kind of work with which her precocious career had begun; she is best remembered for the charming *Millions of Cats*, a children's book she wrote and illustrated.[67] But she was exposed to a very different understanding of culture during her sojourn in the Cities. Art and the demands of the public were somehow at odds. "Good Stuff" contained higher truths, wasted on the vulgar horde. The doctrine of art for art's sake had taken root in the soil of Minnesota.

Like nightshade in a field of soybeans, once planted, the notion flourished and held on tenaciously. In 1958, a slender centennial volume, *A History of the Arts in Minnesota*, achieved its attenuated proportions by taking a dim view indeed of illustration, radio music, and movies. It passed over recipes, quilts, and such with nary a word. The section devoted to the visual and plastic arts tells the story of Minnesota artists gradually weaned away from the impulse to paint place cards, or blood-and-thunder panoramas of the wonders of the West (one memorable example took in the territory from Lake Harriet in Minneapolis to Mt. Tacoma, in Washington), or theater curtains (such as the rendering of Ben Hur's famous chariot race that was cheered more loudly than the play during opening night at a Minneapolis opera house in 1910).[68]

As the culture matures, according to this model, the frontier crudity of art-as-entertainment yields by degrees to the genteel tradition of noblesse oblige, uplift, and a higher consciousness. Wealthy patrons of the arts, like St. Paul's James J. Hill or T. B. Walker of Minneapolis, use their fortunes to import true culture to the wilderness. With the support of the best people, institutions slowly arise – mainly urban ones – devoted to the display and elucidation of two kinds of works of art: masterpieces from the mainly European past, and more modern works designated as worthy of attention by taste makers in Paris, New York, and other distant enclaves of refinement. Ordinary people can benefit from seeing such worthy objects, of course, but culture remains something folks must seek out humbly in museums; it is not often made in New Ulm or found along the shores of Lake Harriet at sunset.[69]

Arguments of this sort have never been immune to clever manipulation by the common folk, of course. If art was civilization's highest ornament, a requisite for the good life, then Minnesota had better get some, or risk certain ruin. "Art, music, and literature are the noble princesses of a house of culture," declared a St. Paul newspaper in 1887, in a fit of anxious boosterism. "Is St. Paul to be noted only as a city of real estate booms and business push, wherein [a] man may make his money, but from which, when it is accumulated, he will remove his family to enjoy the advantages in some less short-sighted city?"[70] Eighty-odd years later, *Time*'s paean to the good life in Minnesota dwelt at length on corporate support for cultural institutions as a major reason why businesses kept their headquarters in the Upper Midwest: Shakespeare, Chinese scrolls, Schubert, and the annual Symphony Ball made hard economic sense in 1973, too.[71] John

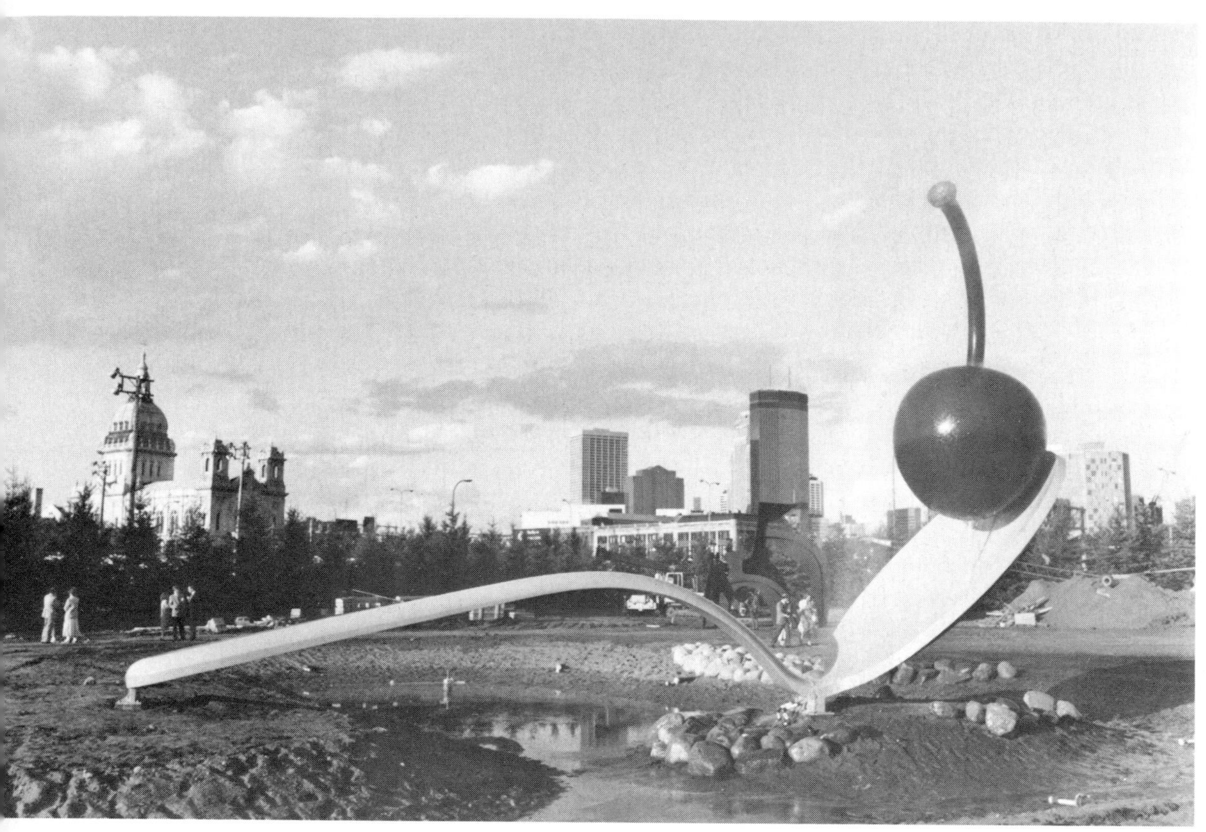

Spoonbridge and Cherry by artists Claes Oldenburg and Coosje van Bruggen being installed in the Minneapolis Sculpture Garden, 1988

Cowles, Jr., of the Minneapolis Star and Tribune Company was cited for contributions to the Guthrie Theater. Bruce Dayton of Dayton's department store was said to be soliciting $26 million for a modern Kenzo Tange addition to the Minneapolis Institute of Arts (finished in 1974), and his brother Kenneth was "deeply involved in fund raising for a new $18.5 million music-center complex [Orchestra Hall, completed in 1974] which he hopes will rival Washington's Kennedy Center."[72]

The yen to impose a culture on Minnesota akin to that of Washington or New York (and the persistent urge on the part of homegrown artists to go "out East" and create culture that counts) comes from a real enough sense of inferiority.[73] Periodic campaigns to make Minneapolis over into an artistic "Minneapple," a Montmartre-on-the-Mississippi, imply that there is nothing much there worth salvaging. Poet Patricia Hampl was intrigued, for that reason, by the case of running back Darrin Nelson, number one draft choice of the Minnesota Vikings in the early 1980s. A Stanford University product, Nelson begged the team not to pick him because, according to published interviews, he thought that being sent to Minnesota would be like being exiled to Siberia. He later changed his mind, but fans from one end of the state to the other were stunned by the slight from "Disco Darrin." "It's the fear lurking in every Minnesotan's heart,"

Hampl argued. "This is a very proud community. It cares about things, and it's nervous, too, about its place in the cultural life. . . . Now this hunk draft choice has said the thing we're afraid they're all thinking."[74]

A free-floating, all-American "rubophobia" (a syndrome defined by columnist and cultural critic Calvin Trillin as "fear of being taken for a rube," not fear of same) is probably responsible for such extraordinary crises of confidence as the Darrin Nelson controversy.[75] Nobody likes to hear that his or her native turf lacks the sophistication of places with taller skyscrapers. But historically Minnesotans seem to have been prone to feelings of cultural inferiority. Patricia Hampl cited F. Scott Fitzgerald's response to the lushly Victorian mansions along "Crest Avenue," the "show street" of St. Paul: "A museum of American architectural failures." Hampl, writing about forty-five years later, said it was the perfection and rigid idealism of modern design that induced disdain and, finally, outright terror. With its brave flourishes of gingerbread and endearing eccentricities, "Summit Avenue avoids, up on its bluff, this abyss." In the end, the avenue acquired a sense of itself as equal to the onslaughts of Fitzgerald, who, by dubbing it a failure, sought to justify his own escape to New York.[76] Hence the appeal of Lake Wobegon, whose resident bard had the good sense to stay home (until he flounced off to parts east in 1987, that is) and the wit to interest bicoastal trend setters in the finer points of hot-dish cuisine. "We're grateful to Garrison for making art out of the materials of Minnesota life," Hampl concluded, taking a relaxed and self-confident approach to the once-prickly issue of what culture in Gopherland might be.[77]

Keillor's *Lake Wobegon Days;* Hampl's reflections on riding the Grand Avenue bus through St. Paul; her poems written at a typical resort on the North Shore; the reminiscences of Macalester College professor Susan Allen Toth on going east to school from a small town in the Midwest; *The Wind Chill Factor,* a thriller by Thomas Gifford that opens by the outdoor pool at the former Minneapolis Sheraton: like the Sleepy Eye and Mankato settings featured on TV's "Little House on the Prairie," the local coloration of these works of the 1970s and 1980s was a source of pride to Minnesota.[78] But beyond considerations of literary chauvinism, the same period also brought a good-natured interest in what one's fellow citizens were up to, and ample time to extend the compass of Main Street's traditional curiosity from the Iowa line to the Rainy River.

In the 1980s, leisure let most Minnesotans so inclined – not just Thorstein Veblen's "leisure class," not just the Kenwood set, or the Summit Avenue crowd, or the lumber barons of Duluth – survey the cultural offerings, and take a hand in fabricating new ones with special relevance to the massive fun-and-sun industry spawned by shorter workweeks. "Back in the 70s when everyone was talking about 'quality of life,' " historian Bruce White noted, the state tourism office produced a booklet devoted to the subject in which was highlighted the remarkable statistic that "nine out of ten Minnesotans are within 20 minutes of a lake." One might well ask, he added in a puckish aside, "What are they doing there when they should be at work?" The answer, of course, is that they, and their lake-bound forebears, were enjoying one of the oldest forms of communal behavior exhibited by Minnesotans.[79]

Even before the Civil War, East Coast disciples of Izaak Walton betook themselves west, quoting snatches of Longfellow on "the great lakes of the Northland," to euphonious Minnesota, "water and smoke country," in search of the perfect crystal lake. Despite the fact that the home of the canny bass was often ringed by mosquitoes as big as largish hummingbirds, visitors were soon almost as thick as the bugs and the Minnesotans themselves.[80] Until well past the turn of the century, booklets designed to promote immigration to Minnesota unfailingly illustrated two alluring sights: one was a heap of monster pumpkins, demonstrating the fertility of the soil to prospective farmers, and the second was a line strung between two trees on the shores of a lake to show off scores of huge fish said to have been "caught in a single day," or sometimes in "a single hour," at such resorts as Geneva Beach near Alexandria or Amber Lake in Martin County.[81]

The names of individual lakes were sublimely unimportant, however. The implication of the whole pictorial convention was that the merest dip of the line into Hiawatha's waters would yield piscatorial riches untold. Fishing pictures are also interesting because they show a social and a sexual democracy at work in Minnesota's resorts. Gentlemen anglers pose alongside farm boys and clerks on holiday. Women in wasp-waisted sports togs made of sturdy twill and broad-brimmed bonnets meant to protect milady's complexion point with pride at their stringers, too. Indeed, the visual evidence suggests that both sport fishing and the milder entertainments of "going to the lake" were family affairs almost from the beginning. And from the beginning the sexes shared an appreciation for the natural beauty of the out-of-doors.

Simple enjoyment of the light on the water still counts as one of the major reasons for praising the state; when Bud Grant retired suddenly in 1984 after seventeen years as head coach of the Vikings, people understood a man who had "some rivers I want to cross, . . . some streams I want to wade."[82] Nor can the sheer bodily pleasures afforded by a hot-weather escape from city and town be discounted. Long before Prince made Lake Minnetonka famous in *Purple Rain*, Willard Dillman wrote a forty-seven-stanza *Rubaiyat of Lake Minnetonka*, in which he waxed lyrical over the loveliness of its wild flowers.[83] But in a line that must have been the last word in naughtiness for 1904 (the year in which Minnesota sent a boxcar load of live game fish for exhibition at the St. Louis World's Fair), he also disclosed a second powerful source of lakeside enjoyment – the fact that "On 'Tonka's shore they wear the fewest clo'es."[84] The "Skipper" (the warm-weather, Minneapolis version of Boreas Rex of St. Paul) of the lake- and river-oriented Minneapolis Aquatennial festival, at which a certain unbuttoned informality has prevailed every summer since 1940, could not have put it better.

In September of 1864, C. Stuart Warren of St. Paul sat down to angle at Lake Minnetonka and in five days caught 554 pounds of fish – mostly bass, he said.[85] The 1956 "muskie craze" at Leech Lake has been com-

A postcard touting the good fishing in Minnesota, 1910

memorated in a mural in Mickey's Cafe in Grand Rapids and a picture postcard to be dispatched to skeptics in the Cities.[86] In a beery rite of spring one observer called "smelt-o-mania," the silvery bounty of spawning fish is harvested by the garbage-can-full along the North Shore.[87] Fishing is a sport celebrating crazy luck and natural abundance. If one of the unique features of Minnesota's culture is a sought-after and oft-discussed balance between the claims of modern urbanism and the pull of nature, then the wintertime Leech Lake Eelpout Festival and the summertime Coon Rapids Carp Festival both merit attention as symbolic representations of that sense of equilibrium.

Begun in 1983 by employees of the Coon Rapids Regional Dam on the Mississippi River, the first Carp Festival commemorated the hundredth anniversary of the importation of that fish by state officials in order to accommodate the dietary preferences of new immigrants drawn to Minnesota by the lure of those "one day's catch" pictures. The carp, a newcomer to the Land of 10,000 Lakes, has become a kind of index of the progress of urbanism. It provides mute testimony, too, to the assimilative powers of the melting pot: carp are so abundant as to be an embarrassment because the Europeans rapidly became Minnesotans, and learned to prefer bass, walleye, and northern pike.[88] Although citizens of "the fishing-est state in America" may well have been "born with a rod and reel in their hands," the carp-fishing contest at the dam mocks the luckless angler who gets stuck with one of them.[89]

Richard Guindon, a nationally syndicated cartoonist who got his start with snow and carp jokes confirming Minnesotans' belief that they are much put-upon survivors, appeared at the first Carp Festival. He later launched a line of "Club Carp" merchandise, gentle put-downs of "Club

Med" resorts in the tropics and other expensive and fashionable hangouts; the T-shirts and book bags were a delight to Minnesotans more often tickled by self-deprecation than by sharper forms of satire, and always pleased to be noticed.[90] Recognition of a similar sort comes when plummeting temperatures in International Falls make the network news, or when regional oddities like "The World's Largest Ball of Twine," saved up by Francis Johnson of Darwin, are exclaimed over on the televised version of "Ripley's Believe It or Not."[91]

The cold and the peculiar have conspired to make the Eelpout Festival at Walker a rousing success. Held every year since 1980 in the dead of winter on the frozen waters of Leech Lake, the festival celebrates a fish said to be so ugly that only strong men, fortified by impressive draughts of peppermint schnapps, can look upon trophy specimens without permanent damage to the eyesight. Ice fishing for eelpout – called "pouting" – requires a minimum of skill because, unlike elusive game fish, they'll bite at anything. But it does take resistance to subzero gales and a keen appreciation for mockery of civilized life and the pretensions of organized and professional sports. Men "pout" in raucous teams that also play ice-basketball or ice-golf in bathing suits when the action is slack inside the fish houses. The shacks themselves, set up in mock towns populated almost entirely by men, dispense with the curtains and niggling points of hygiene favored by wives. Women can and do come to watch the fun, however, and spend money in area motels and restaurants that might otherwise be closed during the off-season. Since 1937, when the elders of Bemidji forgathered to plan the first Paul Bunyan Winter Carnival, resort towns have been trying to convince the public that heading "up North" can be a year-round joy.[92]

Capitalizing on a century of strategic retreats from the coercions of everyday life, tourism has become one of Minnesota's most important growth industries. But increased competition for the tourist dollar has several consequences for the modern-day form of folklife embodied in festivals like those in Coon Rapids and Walker. Only a purist would hold that an authentic manifestation of folk culture in twentieth-century America must be absolutely unique to the group creating it. Nonetheless, for every foot-shaped "De Feet of Jesse James" cookie (these goodies are something to look for at Northfield's annual re-creation of the James gang's legendary 1876 bank raid), Minnesota festivals also continue to spotlight endless squadrons of Shriners on little motorcycles, mobile "mini-donut" and "corn dog" units marking time until the State Fair opens, and craft items assembled from mail-order kits.[93]

But even if Olivia, Minnesota, drew national attention to itself by having singer-celebrity Olivia Newton-John riding at the head of its Corn Capital Days parade in 1978, that incursion of mass cultural glitz did nothing to compromise the pardonable and authentic pride of a corn-growing center whose civic picnic pavilion, set out hospitably along U.S. Highway 212 between Glencoe and Granite Falls, was crowned with a brilliant green and yellow ear of fiber-glass corn about a hundred times life size.[94] And Olivia's celebration proved that tourism no longer required a lake, either

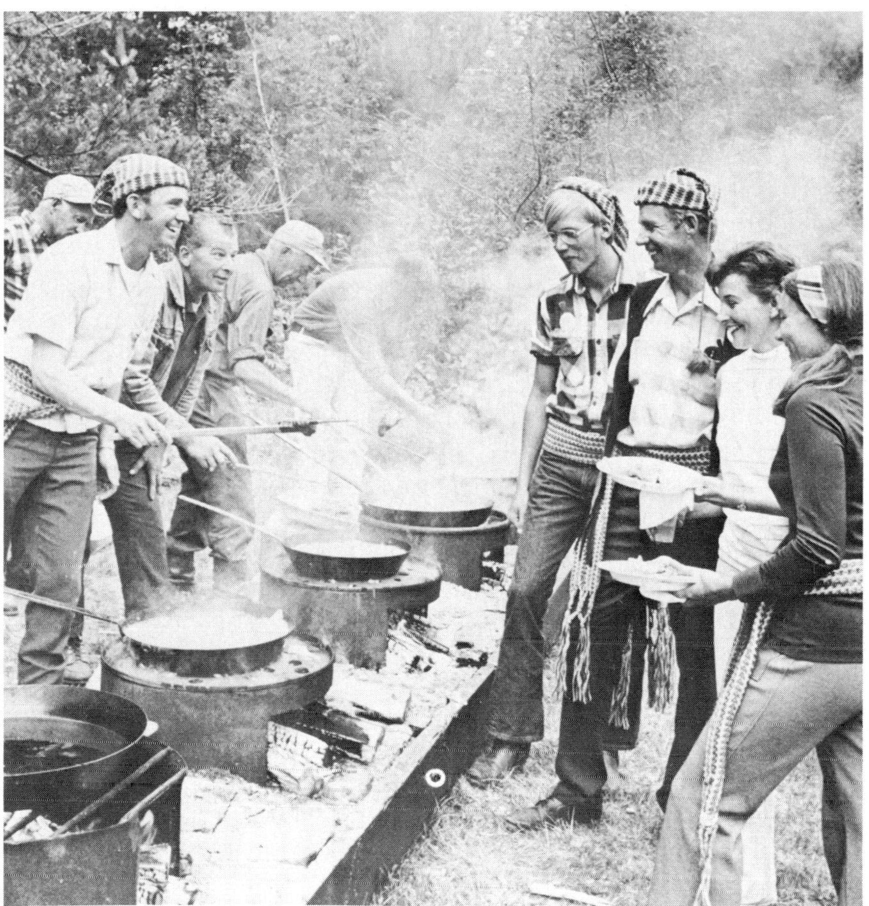

"World's Largest Fish Fry," Crane Lake Voyageur Day, about 1970

in liquid or solid form. Farm country – where most city folks wish they had come from, or really did – had also become a place of spiritual and actual pilgrimage.

A successful festival requires neither a lake nor a surplus of corn, however. Glenwood, for instance, has Lake Minnewaska and an abundance of nearby dairy farms, but Waterama, its thirty-year-old July celebration, has spotlighted instead teams of volunteer fire fighters shooting their hoses at a suspended beer keg in a kind of aerial tug-of-war. There are parades (for "kiddies," for pontoon boats, and for the usual marching units), the coronation of a festival queen, amateur theatricals, comestibles-on-a-stick, informal homecomings, sidewalk sales. In addition to the direct and indirect financial rewards of mounting Waterama, organizers say that "it's a great advertisement for the community," a source of identity, and a way of integrating newcomers into the life of Glenwood. Robert Lavenda, a St. Cloud State University anthropologist with a special interest in the ever-growing number of small-town civic celebrations, agrees. "It looks to me like Minnesota probably has more festivals per capita than any other state," he adds. "I do think putting on a festival is one of the ways we define being a Minnesotan. The whole point of going to the festival is to assert your membership in the community."[95]

"Festival retailing," a concept that mixes crafts, music, finger food, and high fashion in the glass-and-glitter confines of shopping malls like St. Paul's Galtier Plaza, Riverplace in Minneapolis, or the Creamery in downtown Isanti, aims to erase sales resistance by summoning up the comforting illusion of instant community.[96] For those who sell the buttons and drill the bands in places like Glenwood, community means a closed circle of coworkers and interested neighbors. But the combined effect of several hundred such festivals is a broader, statewide definition of community – a happy, pan-Minnesota community in which even the most isolated urbanite can find a temporary place. The dramatized lake-ness, country-ness, hometown-ness, and pioneer-ness that, singly or in suggestive combinations, typify festival life also serve to reintegrate the disparate elements of Minnesota's past with the realities of its present. The chance to be a small-town kid again, or the opportunity to live out a fantasy of being a child of nature, accounts for some of the appeal of these weekend extravaganzas. But the longing to *belong* that unites organizer, booster, local spectator, and curious outsider alike suggests that for many of us, culture is community: a tight-knit, familial community, the way things used to be.

The best families are occasionally racked by sibling rivalry, and the Minnesota family has been no exception. Grudge festivals have been held, for example, and major works of art created out of simple spite. St. Paul's Great Northern Celebration of 1893 was a "wild hurrah" of giant arches crisscrossing Third Street, floats pulled by teams of horses draped in matching blankets, and other gestures of homage to James J. Hill's successful completion of his transcontinental railroad; it was mounted by the city in a conscious effort to outdo the Minneapolis tribute to Hill of nine years before.[97] On that occasion, seventeen prominent Minneapolitans including T. B. Walker, Charles A. Pillsbury, and other flour and lumber magnates with reason to cheer good rail service had commissioned a forty-pound silver tray made by Tiffany, picturing the new Stone Arch Bridge at the Falls of St. Anthony surrounded by scenes from the life of the Empire Builder.[98] St. Paul's civic "hurrah" was one response to upstart Minneapolis; the other was a silver presentation punch bowl adorned with noteworthy St. Paul landmarks in Jim Hill's career.[99]

It was the touchy pride of civic leaders that helped to sustain the great sterling-silver war of the late nineteenth century and the decades of snubs and slights that preceded it. But the animosity trickled down to sports fans in short order, and the rivalry between the fractious Twin Cities was formalized in the 1880s by the annual battles of the Minneapolis Millers and the St. Paul Saints for supremacy in the American Baseball Association. The Millers played in Nicollet Park on East Thirty-First Street. The Saints occupied a succession of Lexington Parks just off University Avenue between Lexington and Dunlap.[100] In the 1920s, split doubleheaders were a big attraction on holidays. There would be a morning game in one city, an afternoon contest in the other. On the morning of July 4, 1929, an intercity riot broke out at a packed Lexington Park when a St. Paul pitcher was spiked by a Millers base runner. With the fans in full cry, "both benches emptied," sportscaster Halsey Hall remembered, "and it took twenty minutes to clear the field. . . . But like so many of those affairs, the afternoon game was peaceful."[101] In 1986, as the Minnesota Twins celebrated twenty-five years of major-league détente between the former rivals with another lackluster season, fans were entitled to wonder whether so much peace was good for local baseball![102]

Long after the teams had been replaced by the Minnesota Twins, the primal loyalties of Saints-vs.-Millers days were still being invoked in the debate over building a sports stadium, the Hubert H. Humphrey Metrodome – "the Dome" – in downtown Minneapolis. That squabble raged throughout the late 1970s. In the end it turned out to be a confusing fight between sober business interests; the "up North" gang, professing to love the camaraderie of shared frostbite during the football season; and the tailgaters (a fraternity that used to launch loud parties from the tail-gates of their station wagons before the game), who feared the loss of pre-game togetherness in the parking lot of old Metropolitan Stadium in Bloomington.[103] Despite the occasional whimpers of some "Dump the Dome" diehards, both factions amicably intermingled within a domed stadium that bears an uncanny resemblance to a cuddly sugar bowl, a soft sculpture expressive of a cultural drive for community sweetness and light strong enough to absorb or deflect most conflict. A place of almost magical amity, it was also the site of the Twins' first World Series triumph, in 1987.[104]

Politeness has become both a social and an artifactual desideratum among Minnesotans. After consultations with the executives at Norwest Corporation, Yale architect Cesar Pelli concluded in 1986 that it would be unwise to make that company's proposed skyscraper taller than the IDS building. "We could have added three feet . . . at almost no cost and claimed to have been the tallest building in town," he told reporters. "[But] we felt that was not the spirit of Minneapolis."[105] By the same token, "it is neither wise nor discreet to discuss matters of great tension at Lutheran church suppers," remarked John Louis Anderson, a local humorist who also detected on the part of non-Scandinavian Minnesotans a "weary urge to blend into the most homogeneous mass since cottage cheese."[106]

The prevailing wholesomeness John Louis Anderson's wry observations serve to endorse and enforce is not a new cultural imperative. From 1902 through the late 1920s, Minnesota called itself "The Bread and Butter State," and touted its simple virtues with sunny pictures of kids eating those talismanic foods with obvious relish.[107] As wheat production fell and dairying caught on, the state gained renown for lavish displays of "pure Minnesota butter" at national fairs and expositions. At great cost in the days before reliable refrigeration, hundreds of sixty-eight-pound butter blocks were brought to far-flung points like Buffalo, New York (for the Pan-American Exposition of 1902), and St. Louis, Missouri (for the Louisiana Purchase Exposition of 1904). There, they were sculpted into towering likenesses of the new State Capitol, the discovery of the Falls of St. Anthony by Father Hennepin and his band (including a life-size voyageur,

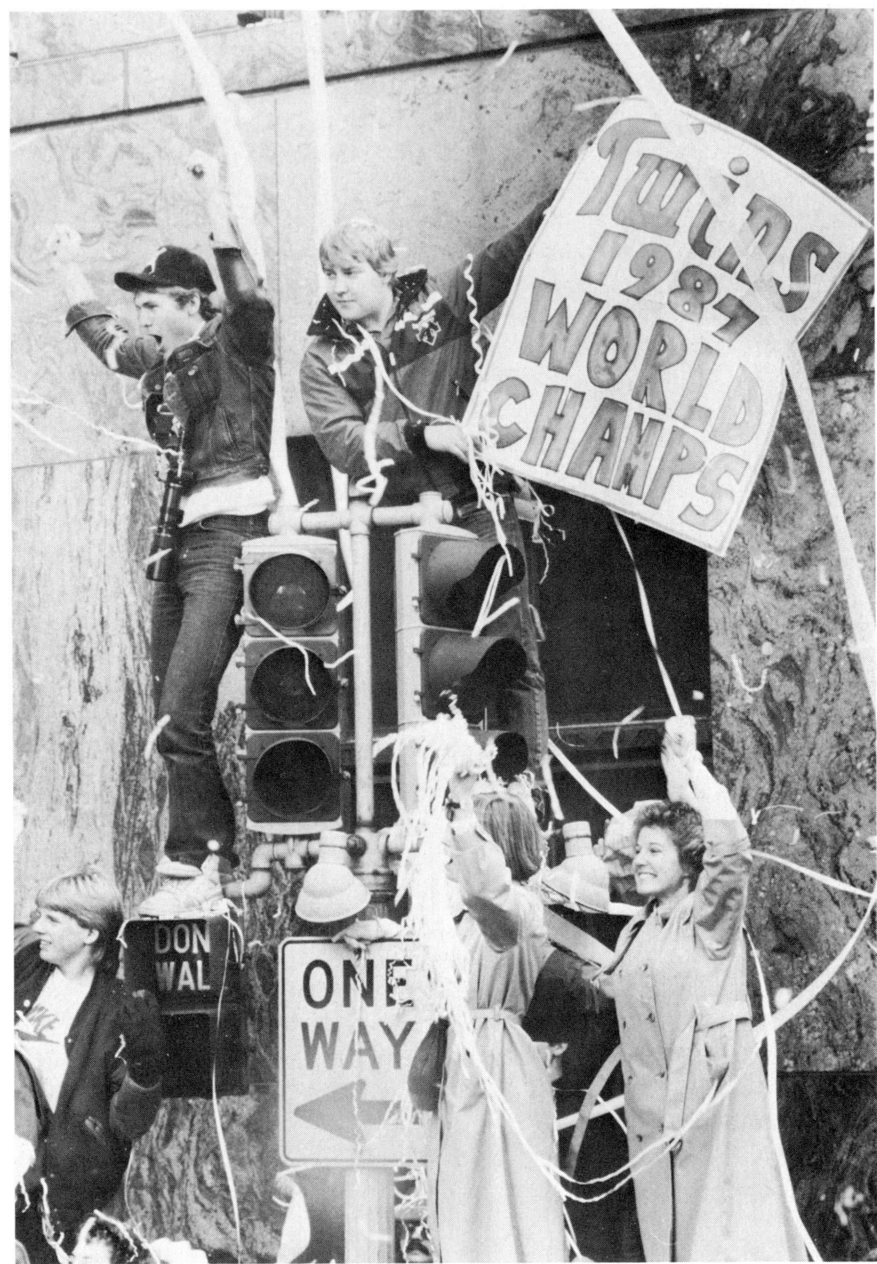

Fans celebrating the World Series victory of the Minnesota Twins over the St. Louis Cardinals, St. Paul, 1987

an Indian wearing a tall butter feather, and a canoe), and other tableaux expressive of a seemly pride in local enterprise, history, and ingenuity.[108] In the 1980s, unhappily, Linda Christensen's annual appearance at the Minnesota State Fair, where she carved small portrait busts of dairy princesses in a revolving glass case in the Dairy Building, hardly began to recapture the scale on which this indigenous art once was practiced.[109]

In its heyday, butter modeling was boosterism in the grand manner, akin to the sometimes backhanded boasting indulged in by sponsors of small-town festivals. As certified, one-of-a-kind, sock-'em-in-the-eye oddities, such statuary conveyed an ever-so-slightly defensive sense of state identity. But golden butter sculptures also suggested a surfeit of purity, a glut of abundance, and the fragility of both those states of grace. They were, in other words, prideful acknowledgments of the dangers of excessive pride, excessive monuments to a fatalistic awareness that small and quiet virtues will probably, in the end, prevail. They were the work of reluctant boosters, uncomfortable with their task. The aesthetic of butter sculpture prefigures the modest claims of those who would later define "the good life in Minnesota" in terms of simple, old-time things like small towns, fish, sunny fields, and lots of lakes, all within twenty minutes or so of up-to-date cities where even the skyscrapers hesitate to get too tall.

Linda Christensen, Wanda Gág, Ilma Cale, and Myrtle Fortun are not household names, even in Minnesota; yet their lives have much to teach us about the shape and meaning of culture in our state. So do the doings of a Bud Grant or a Cesar Pelli. So, in varying degrees, do *Time* magazine, "The Mary Tyler Moore Show," and the other elements of popular culture we share and reject and applaud and adapt to our needs. In their own time, Sinclair Lewis and F. Scott Fitzgerald looked closely at the ordinary facets of Minnesotans' lives and made art of them. History may not rank Jessica Lange among the great theatrical artists of the twentieth century, although her work to date certainly merits the respect her peers have given it. But her story – the chronicle of a small-town girl come to the city, of a famous and accomplished star coming home to find her roots in nature – is worthy of close scrutiny for the sheer attention the media have paid it. It is also, of course, a powerful metaphor for understanding culture and leisure in the Minnesota of the 1980s.

However true or untrue, according to some absolute standard of judgment, that particular story finds resonance in other lives and other tales. It has become an active component of our culture in the twentieth century. As surely as any of Garrison Keillor's lovely monologues or Patricia Hampl's trenchant verses or Prince Rogers Nelson's allusive lyrics, her story helps to determine what others understand us to be and what we, in the end, believe we are about. And so Jessica Lange stands quite nicely for a culture of fish and old-time things, of losers and stars, of lakes and modest skyscrapers. In our hypothetical commercial she *should* be paddling along in a canoe, just as Barbara Flanagan suggested, with a little town peeping over the water in the background and, perhaps, the top of the IDS building just visible in among the pines. And she should be waving in a shy but friendly way at the fishermen along the shoreline – at Garrison Keillor, Bud Grant, Prince, Patricia Hampl, and a couple of guys in snowmobile suits, looking for off-season eelpout. It would make a wonderful movie. Better yet, carve it out of Minnesota butter!

NOTES

The subtitle of this essay was the cover caption on *Time*, Aug. 13, 1973. The accompanying article (p. 24–36) was entitled "Minnesota: A State That Works."

1. Lee Grant, "Will Jessica Lange Score for Cloquet?" syndicated report from *Los Angeles Times*, in *St. Paul Pioneer Press*, Apr. 10, 1983, p. 3E. See also Dave Matheny, "Cloquet Took No Special Notice of Lange or Her Oscar," *Minneapolis Star and Tribune*, Apr. 12, 1983, p. 1C.

2. Nancy Livingston, "Langes Are Proud, but Awards Prove Bore," *St. Paul Dispatch*, Apr. 12, 1983, p. 1A, 4A. See also Nancy Livingston, "Penalties, Rewards of Success Extend to Families of Famous," *St. Paul Pioneer Press*, Nov. 18, 1984, p. 4C.

3. Grant, "Will Jessica Lange Score for Cloquet?" p. 3E.

4. Jan Herman, "Jessica Lange's Come a Long Way from Cloquet," syndicated report from *Chicago Sun-Times*, in *St. Paul Pioneer Press*, Mar. 22, 1981, Lively Arts section, p. 4, 10. Her cabin was about seven miles from her parents' home in Nickerson. In his own way, aviator Charles A. Lindbergh, whose trans-Atlantic flight turned out to be both more and less significant than his contemporaries in the 1920s predicted, is the popular idol most directly comparable to Lange in his love-hate relationship with his roots in rural Little Falls, Minnesota.

5. For his Minnesota settings, see John J. Koblas, *Sinclair Lewis, Home at Last* (Bloomington: Voyageur Press, 1981).

6. Sinclair Lewis, *Main Street* (New York: Harcourt, Brace and Howe, 1920; New York: Signet, New American Library, 1961), 214.

7. For example, see *Main Street*, 257, 431. For a discussion of nature as the alternative to Main Street, see Karal Ann Marling, "My Egypt: The Irony of the American Dream," *Winterthur Portfolio* 15 (Spring 1980): 6–7.

8. Herman, "Jessica Lange's Come a Long Way."

9. This title was used on the second page of Herman, "Jessica Lange's Come a Long Way," p. 10.

10. Vernon Scott, "Lange's New Film May Make Monkeys of Critics," *Minneapolis Tribune*, Feb. 8, 1981, p. 2G. The reference is to *King Kong* (1976), her first feature film. Her father called her farm "King Kong's Retreat." Prof. Robert Silberman, a film historian at the University of Minnesota, said that there is footage of a plump, dark-haired Lange in Twin Cities collections, from an experimental film shot by Paco Grande, her ex-husband, in the late 1960s, when she was a studio arts major at the University of Minnesota. See also Bruce Rubenstein, "Exile on Main Street," *City Pages* (Minneapolis and St. Paul), July 23, 1986, p. 7–12.

11. David Gebhard and Tom Martinson, *A Guide to the Architecture of Minnesota* (Minneapolis: University of Minnesota Press, 1977), 186; Bill Diehl, "Compelling 'Country' Rings True," *St. Paul Pioneer Press*, Oct. 11, 1984, p. 1B. See also Dane Smith, "Movie on Farm Foreclosing Sounds Political Overtones," *St. Paul Dispatch*, Oct. 3, 1984, p. 8A.

12. Bob Lundegaard, "Role as Producer Gives Lange Greater Kinship with 'Country,' " *Minneapolis Star and Tribune*, Oct. 12, 1984, p. 7C.

13. Untitled Barbara Flanagan columns, *Minneapolis Star and Tribune*, Jan. 19, 1983, and Jan. 18, 1984, both on p. 1B. Al Franken and Tom Davis were comedy writers and performers, notably on NBC's Saturday Night Live in the late 1970s.

14. "Mondale Plan for Debate Rejected," *Minneapolis Star and Tribune*, July 21, 1984, p. 1A. He went fishing "up North" after his nomination and again after his defeat. (His excellent recipe for salmon mousse was widely reprinted during the election campaign; my dog-eared version came from the *New York Times*, ca. Feb. 15, 1984.)

15. In the 1950s and 1960s the openers became elaborate affairs and key elements in the state's promotional strategy. Prominent business leaders were often guests of the governor on these jaunts. I am grateful to Colleen Sheehy, assistant director for touring exhibitions at the University Art Museum, University of Minnesota, for sharing her vast knowledge of Minnesota fishing folklore with me.

16. Susan Feyder, "Striker Likers Find Their Affection Defective," *Minneapolis Star and Tribune*, May 27, 1986, p. 1A.

17. Among the best accounts of Zimmerman's self-transformation are Anthony Scaduto, *Bob Dylan, An Intimate Biography* (New York: Grosset and Dunlap, 1971), 9–15; and Wilfred Mellers, *A Darker Shade of Pale: A Backdrop to Bob Dylan* (New York: Oxford University Press, 1985), 111–12. Like Lange, Dylan sometimes claimed to have ridden the rods as a child in an attempt to escape small-town Minnesota; see "Let Us Now Praise Little Men," *Time*, May 31, 1963, p. 40.

18. Lloyd Grove, "Minnesota Chic? It's Loons, Prince and Easy Parking," syndicated report from *Washington Post*, in *Minneapolis Star and Tribune*, Oct. 4, 1984, p. 1C. On South-

dale, see Chester H. Liebs, *Main Street to Miracle Mile: American Roadside Architecture* (Boston: Little, Brown and Co., 1985), 32.

19. The must-see comedy series of the 1970s, "The Mary Tyler Moore Show" was closely associated with the state. See, for example, *Redbook*, December 1976, p. 46. *Ice Castles*, a movie starring teen star Robby Benson, was filmed at several in- and out-state locations in 1978, and premiered in Minneapolis; it marked the beginning of a mature local film industry.

20. For a sound critical appraisal of the IDS Center, designed by Philip Johnson and John Burgee, see Charles Jencks, *Skyscraper-Skyprickers-Skycities* (New York: Rizzoli Books, 1980), 10, 13.

21. "People," *Minneapolis Star and Tribune*, Dec. 14, 1984, p. 11A; untitled Jim Klobuchar column, *Minneapolis Star and Tribune*, Dec. 19, 1984, p. 1B, 4B.

22. Lynn Norment, "Prince: The Story behind His Passion for Purple and Privacy," *Ebony*, November 1984, p. 66–72, 75; Debby Miller, "Prince: The Secret Life of America's Sexiest One-Man Band," *Rolling Stone*, Apr. 28, 1983, p. 18; "His Highness of Haze," *Time*, Aug. 6, 1984, p. 62; Kurt Loder, "Prince Reigns," *Rolling Stone*, Aug. 30, 1984, p. 21.

23. Jean E. Spraker, "The Rollicking Realm of Boreas: A Century of Carnivals in St. Paul," *Minnesota History* 49 (Winter 1985): 322–31; Karal Ann Marling, *The Colossus of Roads: Myth and Symbol along the American Highway* (Minneapolis: University of Minnesota Press, 1984), 75–76.

24. Bill McGrane, *Bud: The Other Side of the Glacier* (New York: Harper and Row, 1986), 162–63.

25. "The Prince and the Perpich," *Minneapolis Star and Tribune*, Dec. 27, 1984, p. 14A.

26. Neal Karlen, "Prince Talks," *Rolling Stone*, Sept. 12, 1985, p. 25. This is the best description of the purple house.

27. Jon Bream, "A Royal Treat," *Minneapolis Star and Tribune*, Feb. 7, 1986, p. 18C.

28. Garrison Keillor, *Lake Wobegon Days* (New York: Viking, 1985), 90–92; "Lonesome Whistle Blowing," *Time*, Nov. 4, 1985, p. 68–73. See also Keillor, *News from Lake Wobegon*, cassette tapes of live broadcasts of "A Prairie Home Companion" (St. Paul: Minnesota Public Radio, 1983).

29. Among the best pieces on Keillor and Lake Wobegon are James Traub, "The Short and Tall Tales of Garrison Keillor," *Esquire*, May 1982, p. 109–17; "Garrison Keillor: The Voice of Lake Wobegon," *Mother Earth News*, May–June 1985, p. 16–22; and Mark Singer, "Welcome to Lake Wobegon, the Town That Time Forgot," *Blair and Ketchum's Country Journal*, January 1982, p. 49–55.

30. The first show of the 1986 season, celebrating the reopening of the renovated World Theater in St. Paul, was televised, and rebroadcasts were made on the Disney Channel. Keillor quit the show at the end of the season but has since held two "farewell" reunion shows and announced plans for a third, a strategy that clarifies his desire to institutionalize nostalgia.

31. Marling, *Colossus of Roads*, 41–63.

32. The Gold'n Plump chicken campaign ran on local television from about 1984 to 1987; the TV and billboard promotion for Kemp's ice cream started in 1986–87. It is not a coincidence that the years that saw the Twin Cities grow into a center of music and film production (1970s and 1980s) also witnessed a dramatic rise in the number and prestige of local advertising agencies.

33. For example, see Al Blair, *Minnesota Shouts, Stomps and Syncopated Hollers: A Jazz Fakebook* (Alexandria: Northcountry Publishing Co., 1985), 5, 9, 10. Blair includes such tunes as "Our Fishhouse of Love Is Freezin' since My Ice-Fishin' Mama Turned Cold," "That's A-Plenty of Lutefisk," and "It's-Snowing-on-Our-Love Blues."

34. "Regionalism" as a term referring to cultural matters is still bound up with the movement in midwestern painting and prose that attracted both attention and controversy in the 1930s. It was named and promoted, if not created, by *Time* magazine. See Karal Ann Marling, *Tom Benton and His Drawings* (Columbia, Mo.: University of Missouri Press, 1985), 18–19.

35. A long prologue on MacGyver's origins as a Minnesota Cub Scout introduced the episode aired on July 16, 1986, by KSTP-TV, St. Paul-Minneapolis.

36. Cover and "Minnesota: A State That Works," *Time*, Aug. 13, 1973, p. 24–35.

37. Steven Dornfeld, "Governor's Aide Worked to Develop 'Time' Article with Anderson on Cover," *Minneapolis Tribune*, Aug. 19, 1973, p. 1A. There was renewed interest in the issue when the governor's reelection campaign proposed to distribute 200,000 reprints of the article; see "Anderson Campaign Uses 'Time' Reprints," *Minneapolis Tribune*, May 16, 1974, p. 6A.

38. Clay Blair, Jr., "Minnesota Grows Older," *Saturday Evening Post*, Mar. 18, 1961, p. 85.

39. For the evolution of the Walker, see "Minneapolis Opens Art Center Built around Walker Gallery," *Newsweek*, Jan. 15, 1940, p. 34; "Reincarnated," *Art Digest*, Jan. 15, 1940, p. 26; "Minneapolis: An Art Center," *Art News*, Jan. 20, 1940, p. 14; *Walker Art Center:*

History-Collections-Activities (Minneapolis: Walker Art Center, 1971), 2–3; and *Walker Art Center: A History* (Minneapolis: Walker Art Center, 1985), 3–6.

40. "Minnesota: A State That Works," 24–27, 31, 34.

41. "Governor to Make TV Appearance," *Minneapolis Tribune*, Mar. 14, 1973, p. 10B; "Kreiger Reacts to TV Dates," *Minneapolis Star*, Mar. 17, 1973, p. 16B.

42. "Two Speeches," *Minneapolis Tribune*, Jan. 23, 1975, p. 8A.

43. Regional magazines include *Minnesota Monthly* and *Sunday Magazine*, the latter published by the *Minneapolis Star and Tribune*. See also Neal St. Anthony, "She's Got World Travelers Shouting 'Hello Minnesota,' " *Minneapolis Star and Tribune*, Nov. 11, 1985, p. 1M.

44. Sinclair Lewis, *Babbitt* (New York: Harcourt, Brace and Co., 1922; Signet, New American Library, 1961), 83, 127–30.

45. Fitzgerald, "Winter Dreams" (1922), in *The Fitzgerald Reader*, ed. Arthur Mizener (New York: Charles Scribner's Sons, 1963), 54–75, and "The Ice Palace" (1920), in *The Stories of F. Scott Fitzgerald* (New York: Charles Scribner's Sons, 1965), 61–82.

46. Grace H. Flandrau, *Being Respectable* (New York: Harcourt, Brace and Co., 1923), 37. This novel owes something to Lewis (and something, perhaps, to a common milieu) in its emphasis on new neocolonial manses and a nervous mockery of nonpopular or noncommercial artists, also marked in *Babbitt*. Lewis is also invoked by one of the characters; see p. 50–51, 177, 274.

47. Margaret Culkin Banning, *Country Club People* (New York: George H. Doran Co., 1923), 57, comments tellingly on the equation between leisure, consumption, and success in a similar view of Minnesota society in a Duluthish sort of town that exhibits many of the physical and social traits of the Twin Cities.

48. *100 Years of Good Cooking* (St. Paul: St. Peter's Lutheran Church, [1986]), 130–34; *Fron Centennial Cook Book* (Starbuck: Fron Lutheran Church Women, 1980), 262–70; *The 125th Anniversary Cookbook* (Dennison: Vang Lutheran Church, [1986]), 175, 179. This last recipe comes closest to the classic formulation. Jell-O, instant pudding, and other "convenience" products were often added by the 1980s. Taste of Minnesota, a food festival held on the grounds of the State Capitol during the Fourth of July holiday starting in 1983, has never offered distinctive Minnesota fare; restaurateurs have served what they hope Minnesotans like. For the most part, like the cookbooks, the festival has confirmed taste rather than creating it.

49. The cookbook was *100 Years of Good Cooking: Minnesota Centennial Cook Book*, ed. Virginia Huck and Ann H. Andersen (St. Paul: Minnesota Historical Society, 1958). The records of the Minnesota Statehood Centennial Commission are in the Minnesota Historical Society (MHS); responses to the call for recipes, arranged by county, occupy a large box. For this and the paragraph below, see, under Becker County, Mrs. Mel Bartelson (Detroit Lakes); under Benton County, Mrs. Alma G. Buckmaster (Sauk Rapids) and Mrs. Robert Tomporowski (Foley); under Crow Wing County, Mrs. Elmer G. Anderson (Crosby) and Ruth Martin Alexander (Brainerd). Many recipes for the famous salad are included, as are directions for making macaroni and rice hot dishes. Chinese-style casserole was another fashionable food of the 1920s (Carol Kennicott might have served it at the ill-fated oriental soiree in *Main Street*) that has slipped down the social ladder from the upper crust to the middle class over the past sixty years. Since none of these dishes is any easier or cheaper to prepare than the kind of light, fresh American cuisine favored by fashionable cookbooks and restaurants later in the twentieth century, the preference for such textures and tastes is worth pondering. The fact that one's mother cooked similar dishes is one reason for their continuing popularity, of course.

50. The Minnesota Statehood Centennial Commission Records at the MHS contain a group of commissioned compositions filed under "Music Scores, 1957–8" and a pamphlet, *The Unveiling and Dedication of the Statue of Floyd B. Olson* ([St. Paul]: Minnesota Statehood Centennial Commission, [1958?]), which describes the unveiling of the statue by A. J. Brioschi, paid for by an appropriation from the legislature that was matched by funds raised by the AFL-CIO.

51. The Cale correspondence is discussed in Joan M. Seidl, "Consumers' Choices: A Study of Household Furnishing, 1880–1920," *Minnesota History* 48 (Spring 1983): 191–93. Ilma also worked across the North Dakota border, in Minot, during this period.

52. Ilma Cale to Artie Cale, Apr. 16, 1912, in Artie M. Cale and Family Papers, MHS.

53. Ilma Cale to Artie, June 21, 1905; June 12, 18, 1912, Cale Papers.

54. Ilma Cale to Artie, July 2, 1912; Feb. 8, 1913; Nov. 8, 14, 1916; Apr. 25, 1917, Cale Papers.

55. Ada Cross, diary, Feb. 17; Sept. 2, 14; Dec. 22, 25, 27, 1917, William Cross and Family Papers, MHS.

56. Cross, diary, Feb. 17, 1917.

57. James A. Shields, diary, Oct. 22, 1900, James A. Shields Papers, MHS. Only the aesthetic aspects of the liturgy of the Catholic church occupy as much space in these remarkable diaries.

58. Shields, diary, Dec. 19, 1900, Jan. 21, 1949, Shields Papers.

59. Myrtle E. Fortun, diary, Jan. 4, 1941, available at MHS. ASCAP (the American Society of Composers, Authors, and Publishers) was protesting radio fees by barring popular songs from the airwaves.

60. Fortun, diary, Feb. 11, 1941.

61. Fortun, diary, Feb. 15, Mar. 31, May 4, June 22, July 13, 1941; Jan. 6, 1942. To follow her reading tastes, see Bess Streeter Aldrich, *Song of Years* (New York: D. Appleton-Century Co., 1939).

62. Fortun, diary, July 3, Sept. 23, 1941.

63. For a brief account of the visual culture of the Gág household, see Rebecca L. Keim, *Three Women Artists: Gág, Greenman and Mairs* (Minneapolis: University [of Minnesota] Gallery, 1980), 5–6.

64. Wanda Gág, *Growing Pains: Diaries and Drawings for the Years 1908–1917* (New York: Coward McCann, 1940; St. Paul: Minnesota Historical Society Press, 1984), 56–59, 67.

65. Gág, *Growing Pains*, 78.

66. Gág, *Growing Pains*, 218.

67. Gág, *Millions of Cats* (New York: Coward, McCann and Geoghegan, 1928).

68. Donald R. Torbert, "A Century of Art and Architecture in Minnesota," in *A History of the Arts in Minnesota*, ed. William Van O'Connor (Minneapolis: University of Minnesota Press, 1958), 18–19. Much of the material in Torbert's essay comes from Roy A. Boe, "The Development of Art Consciousness in Minneapolis and the Problems of the Indigenous Artist" (M.A. thesis, University of Minnesota, 1947), whose treatment of the work of turn-of-the-century crowd-pleasers like Peter Gui Clausen (p. 116–23) is a great deal more sympathetic.

69. Torbert, "A Century of Art," 19–25. Although art history is a highly conservative discipline, a volume on the same topic written on the occasion of the national Bicentennial (with a foreword by Gov. Wendell Anderson) avoids the worst pitfalls of the prevailing elitism; see Rena Neumann Coen, *Painting and Sculpture in Minnesota, 1820–1914* (Minneapolis: University of Minnesota Press, 1976).

70. Quoted in Isaac Oliver Peterson, "Art in St. Paul as Recorded in the Contemporary Newspapers" (M.A. thesis, University of Minnesota, 1942), 187.

71. For a discussion of the wealth on view at Minneapolis concerts of classical music over the years, see Donald Ferguson, interview by Dennis Rooney, Minneapolis, 1972, p. 27, transcript available in the Minneapolis History Collection, Minneapolis Public Library. This tape is no. 13 in a series, "Music in Minnesota: Minnesota Orchestra." Others in the same series contain similar discussions.

72. "Minnesota: A State That Works," 33. At that time, Minoru Yamasaki was expected to design the MIA's addition. See also Gebhard and Martinson, *Architecture of Minnesota*, 66.

73. For a description of how recent recipients of Jerome Foundation fellowships for emerging artists have faced the choice between staying in Minnesota and going East, see Calvin Tomkins, "Out of Town," *New Yorker*, June 23, 1986, p. 89–92.

74. Linda Owen, "Patricia Hampl: Author Gleans Subject Matter from St. Paul Sites, Memories," *St. Paul Dispatch*, May 3, 1982, p. 11A.

75. M. Sue Kendall, *Rethinking Regionalism: John Steuart Curry and the Kansas Mural Controversy* (Washington, D.C.: Smithsonian Institution Press, 1986), 14, discusses the relevance of Trillin's delightful concept to the public reception of Regionalist art in the 1930s. It is perhaps indicative of a new-found self-confidence that cessation of the New York Metropolitan Opera's annual tour of the provinces (1945–86), an endeavor heavily supported by Minnesota contributors and surrounded by the usual displays of social climbing, caused hardly a whimper of protest. A brief history of the tour is included in the souvenir program, *The Metropolitan Opera at Northrop* ([Minneapolis]: Metropolitan Opera in the Upper Midwest, 1986), 13, 62–64.

76. Patricia Hampl, *A Romantic Education* (Boston: Houghton Mifflin Co., 1981), 64–66. The Fitzgerald quote is from "The Crack-Up," published in 1936.

77. Owen, "Patricia Hampl," p. 11A.

78. Hampl, *Resort and Other Poems* (Boston: Houghton Mifflin Co., 1983) was written on the North Shore. For the reception of Toth's *Blooming: A Small-Town Girlhood* (Boston: Little, Brown and Co., 1981) and *Ivy Days: Making My Way Out East* (Boston: Little, Brown and Co., 1984), see Jeff Strikler, "Raves for Second Book Convince Toth She's a Writer," *Minneapolis Star and Tribune*, May 31, 1984, p. 1C, 3C. Gifford's book is a perennial paperback favorite; see *The Wind Chill Factor* (New York: Ballantine Books, 1985). Of interest to the same readership is another Minnesota author's book: Kate Green, *Shattered Moon* (New York: Dell, 1986).

79. Bruce M. White, "Going to the Lake," *Minnesota Monthly*, June 1986, p. 9.

80. [Charles Hallock], "The Red River Trail," *Harper's New Monthly Magazine* 18 (April 1859): 602 (quotations), 610. See also such classics as Oliver Gibbs, Jr., *Lake Pepin Fish-Chowder in Letters to General Spinner* (New York: H. D. McIntyre and Co., 1869).

81. Marling, *Colossus of Roads*, 90–91. Trout and bass were still the fish of choice in 1904, when northerns were still called "snakes" and tossed back.

82. Quoted in Bob Sansevere, "Bud Grant Retires Again as Coach," *Minneapolis Star and Tribune*, Jan. 7, 1986, p. 12A. See also "Bud Bows Out," *Sports Illustrated*, Feb. 6, 1984, p. 16.

83. Untitled Barbara Flanagan column, *Minneapolis Star and Tribune*, July 30, 1986, p. 1B, notes a big demand elsewhere for "Lake Minnetonka" T-shirts and curiosity about the place Prince made famous.

84. Quoted in White, "Going to the Lake," 10.

85. This item from the *St. Paul Pioneer*, Sept. 24, 1864, is in WPA Federal Writers' Project, "Annals of Minnesota," in WPA Records, MHS.

86. The postcard was published by Gallagher's Studio, Duluth.

87. Matti Kaups, "Evolution of Smelt-O-Mania on Lake Superior's North Shore," *Journal of Popular Culture* 11 (Spring 1978): 959–76.

88. KSTP-TV has provided good coverage of the Coon Rapids festival. For her personal recollections of this and the Eelpout Festival, I am grateful to Colleen Sheehy, who spoke on "King for a Day: The Status of Fish in Two Minnesota Festivals" at the Fourteenth Annual History Conference of the MHS, Bloomington, Oct. 11, 1986.

89. *Minnesota: Fishing the No. 1 Spot* (St. Paul: Minnesota Department of Economic Development, [1971?]), unpaginated.

90. For Guindon, see Cristine M. Levenduski, "Schizophrenic City: Souvenirs of Minneapolis," in *Prospects: An Annual of American Cultural Studies*, ed. Jack Salzman, vol. 11 (New York: Cambridge University Press, 1987), 301–10.

91. During the 1982–83 season the Ripley series, carried on the ABC network, dramatized the rivalry between Darwin and Cawker City, Kansas, whose residents claimed, in the teeth of sound evidence to the contrary, that their string ball was larger.

92. Marling, *Colossus of Roads*, 1–3.

93. See *Defeat of Jesse James Days* (Northfield: Defeat of Jesse James Days, Inc., 1986), 5. Although this is one of my favorite festivals, I am grateful to John McGuigan, former managing editor of MHS Press, for his special insights on it. The list of Minnesota festivals has grown yearly. In 1986, the roster of warm-weather events alone ran to more than three hundred entries; "Minnesota Festivals/1986," *Minneapolis Star and Tribune*, June 1, 1986, p. 8E.

94. Marling, *Colossus of Roads*, 58–60.

95. Bruce Benidt, "Festival Forges Community Identity in Glenwood," *Minneapolis Star and Tribune*, July 27, 1986, p. 1B. Works Progress Administration, *The WPA Guide to Minnesota* (New York: Viking Press, 1938; St. Paul: Minnesota Historical Society Press, 1985) lists such festivals as were flourishing in 1938. See, for example, the entry for the Detroit Lakes Summer Carnival sponsored by the Junior Chamber of Commerce, p. 439.

96. A press release, "Galtier Plaza Celebrates Grand Opening with Gala Four-Day Event," Nov. 12, 1985, in Boisclair Corp., publicity office files, notes the "heritage" aspects of the event – a tribute to Father Galtier, who built a church in St. Paul in 1841 – as well as the planned release of ten thousand balloons and entertainment featuring music from "A Prairie Home Companion." I am grateful to Boisclair Corp. for giving me access to publicity materials bearing on their several "festival" ventures and to Marilyn McGriff of Cambridge for introducing me to the recently recycled Creamery mall in Isanti.

97. Susan E. Williams, " 'A Wild Hurrah': The Great Northern Celebration of 1893," *Minnesota History* 48 (Fall 1982): 119.

98. Francis J. Puig, "The Hill Tray," *Minneapolis Institute of Arts Bulletin* 64 (1978–80): 43–44.

99. Williams, " 'A Wild Hurrah,' " 121–22.

100. Tom Sweeney, "The World's Greatest Outfielders," *Minnesota History* 50 (Spring 1986): 18; Patrick Reusse, "Lexington Park: Campy, the Duke, the Babe, and Oh, That Coliseum," in *The Hubert H. Humphrey Metrodome Souvenir Book*, ed. Dave Mona (Minneapolis: MSP Publications, 1982), 26.

101. Quoted in Dave Mona, "Nicollet Park: Home of the Millers," in *Metrodome Souvenir Book*, ed. Mona, 23.

102. See also Dave Mona and Dave Jarzyna, *Twenty-Five Seasons: The First Quarter-Century of the Minnesota Twins* (Minneapolis: Mona Publications, 1986).

103. For a good indication of the diverse ethnic, economic, regional, and religious strata attracted to Minnesota sporting events, see the recipes in Dottie Dekko, *Cooking for Kicks: The Sport of Tailgating – Recipes of Sport Stars and Fans* (Minneapolis: Sprague Publications, 1978).

104. There are still serious intercity sports rivalries at the high school level, although they may prove difficult to sustain when tournaments are held in the vast, absorbent emptiness of the Metrodome. See Joel B. Krenz, *Gopher State Greatness: A Thirty-Year History of Boys High School Basketball 1951–52 – 1980–81* (N.p.: Richtman's Printing, 1984).

105. Quoted in Sharon Schmickle, "Norwest's Design Lets IDS Retain Tallest Title," *Minneapolis Star and Tribune*, July 30, 1986, p. 1A.

106. John Louis Anderson, *Scandinavian Humor and Other Myths* (Minneapolis: Nordbook, 1986), 42, 102.

107. Karal Ann Marling, " 'She Brought Forth Butter in a Lordly Dish': The Origins of Minnesota Butter Sculpture," *Minnesota History* 50 (Summer 1987): 218–28.

108. *The Bread and Butter State: Report of the Minnesota Board of Managers for the Pan-American Exposition at Buffalo, New York* (St. Paul: Pioneer Press Co., 1902), 16–18; David R. Francis, *The Universal Exposition of 1904*, vol. 2 (St. Louis: Louisiana Purchase Exposition Co., 1913), 181.

109. I have personally observed her work with great interest every summer since 1977. See also "Beauty in Butter," *Fairmount Sentinel*, Oct. 18, 1973, clipping in the files of the Publicity Office, Minnesota State Fair. I am grateful to Jerry Hammer for providing access to this collection.

Photo Sources

The photographs used in this book are reproduced through the courtesy of the originators and providers named below. The designation "MHS" refers in most cases to photographs held in the collections of the audio-visual library of the Minnesota Historical Society; when the original object or document is held in a separate MHS collection, the appropriate information is supplied in parentheses. Parentheses also indicate names of photographers, or the organizations or institutions that originally owned the photograph, when known.

Image and Identity
Page 3, MHS (original in Pamphlet Collection); **page 5,** MHS; **pages 7 and 13,** courtesy Minnesota Department of Trade and Economic Development; **page 16,** courtesy National Geographic Society, copyright 1935 (Clifton Adams).

Forces at Work on Landscape
Page 29, MHS (C. L. Merryman); **page 30,** MHS (M. J. Viken); **page 32,** courtesy Thomas J. Baerwald; **page 35,** MHS; **page 36,** MHS (William F. Roleff); **page 37,** MHS (*St. Paul Daily Pioneer Press*); **page 39,** MHS; **page 43,** MHS (*Minneapolis Star*), **page 45,** MHS (Kenneth Wright); **page 47,** MHS (Lee Bros.).

Network of Urban Centers
Page 54, MHS (D. Anderson); **pages 59 and 60,** MHS; **page 63,** MHS (*Minneapolis Star Journal*); **page 66,** MHS (C. P. Gibson); **page 69,** MHS (John Runk); **page 83,** MHS (Basgen Photography); **page 86,** courtesy Richfield Historical Society; **page 87,** MHS (*Minneapolis Star Journal-Tribune*); **page 91,** courtesy Minneapolis Community Development Agency.

Small-Town Minnesota
Page 98, MHS (original in Museum Collections); **page 101,** MHS (Lee Hanley); **pages 106 and 107,** MHS; **page 109,** MHS (C. L. Merryman); **page 111,** MHS; **page 112,** courtesy Northwest Architectural Archives, University of Minnesota; **page 117,** MHS (Gustafson Photo, Olivia); **page 121,** courtesy Thomas Harvey; **page 122,** MHS.

The Rural Experience
Page 128, MHS (William Sharkey); **pages 132, 134, 138 and 140,** MHS; **pages 141 and 145,** MHS (George Luxton Collection); **page 148,** courtesy *St. Paul Pioneer Press Dis-*

patch (Tom Majeski); **page 149,** courtesy *St. Paul Pioneer Press Dispatch* (Joe Rossi); **page 150,** courtesy *St. Paul Pioneer Press Dispatch.*

Change on Iron Range

Page 160, Farm Security Administration (John Vachon); **page 162,** *Hibbing Tribune*; **pages 164 and 167,** MHS; **page 168,** courtesy Northeast Minnesota Historical Center; **page 174,** MHS (courtesy The Bettman Archive); **page 176,** courtesy Bertha Pousi, donor, and Immigration History Research Center, University of Minnesota; **page 183,** courtesy Iron Range Research Center (Oliver Iron Mining Company, USS Collection); **page 184,** courtesy Northeast Minnesota Historical Center; **page 186,** MHS (Basgen Photography).

Labor: Three Key Conflicts

Page 199, courtesy Iron Range Research Center (Arnie Maki Collection); **page 201,** courtesy Immigration History Research Center, University of Minnesota (Edith Kovisto Papers); **page 203,** courtesy Industrial Workers of the World, 3435 N. Sheffield, Chicago, Illinois 60657; **page 205,** MHS (*St. Paul Daily News*); **page 208,** MHS (George Luxton Collection); **page 210,** MHS; **page 211,** MHS (*St. Paul Daily News*); **page 215,** courtesy *St. Paul Pioneer Press Dispatch* (Brian Peterson); **page 216,** courtesy *St. Paul Pioneer Press Dispatch* (John Doman); **page 218,** courtesy *St. Paul Pioneer Press Dispatch* (Richard Marshall).

The Major Manufacturers

Page 227, MHS (Novak Studio Photographers); **page 229,** MHS (C. P. Gibson); **page 230,** MHS; **page 233,** MHS (Minneapolis City Archives); **pages 235 and 240,** MHS (*St. Paul Daily News*); **page 241,** MHS (*Minneapolis Star Journal*); **page 244,** MHS; **page 247,** courtesy Medtronic, Inc.; **page 251,** courtesy General Mills, Inc.

Business of Agriculture

Page 260, MHS (Farm Security Administration, Russell Lee); **page 266,** MHS; **page 268,** MHS (Duluth Chamber of Commerce); **page 273,** MHS (copyright Palmquist Studio, Milaca); **page 274,** MHS; **page 275,** MHS (P. Schawang, St. Paul); **pages 283 and 284,** MHS; **page 286,** MHS (*Minneapolis Tribune*); **page 288,** MHS (Farm Security Administration, Arthur Rothstein).

Print and Broadcast Media

Page 297, MHS (*Minneapolis Journal*); **pages 301 and 303,** MHS; **page 304,** MHS (Norton & Peel and Hibbard Studio); **page 310,** MHS (original in Minnesota State Archives); **page 313,** MHS (*Minneapolis Tribune*); **page 314,** MHS; **page 317,** courtesy *St. Paul Pioneer Press Dispatch*; **page 321,** courtesy *St. Paul Pioneer Press Dispatch* (Don Church).

Model of Moral Government

Page 330, courtesy Steven Linder; **page 337,** MHS (Kenneth J. Berglund); **page 339,** courtesy Iron Range Research Center (IRRRB Mineland Reclamation); **page 342,** MHS (Edward A. Bromley); **page 343,** MHS (*St. Paul Pioneer Press Dispatch,* Ted Strasser); **pages 346 and 347,** MHS; **page 351,** MHS (E. D. Becker); **page 353,** courtesy *St. Paul Pioneer Press Dispatch* (Spence Hollstadt).

Reformers, Radicals, Conservatives

Page 360, MHS (copyright Cole & Wickham, original in Poster Collection); **page 363,** MHS (original in Museum Collections); **pages 376 and 377,** MHS (George Luxton Collection); **page 380,** MHS (original Library and Archives); **page 382,** MHS (George Miles Ryan Studio); **page 386,** courtesy *St. Paul Dispatch* (T. J. Strasser); **page 387,** MHS;

page 388, courtesy *St. Paul Pioneer Press Dispatch* (Spence Hollstadt); **page 393,** courtesy *St. Cloud Times.*

A Place Among Nations

Page 398, MHS (Monroe Killy); **page 401,** MHS; **page 404,** MHS (*St. Paul Dispatch and Pioneer Press,* T. J. Horton); **page 412,** MHS (Randy Croce); **page 416,** MHS; **page 419,** MHS (Hakkerup Studio, Bemidji); **page 422,** MHS (Bill Burnson); **page 423,** courtesy *St. Paul Pioneer Press Dispatch* (Neale Van Ness); **pages 425 and 427,** MHS (Randy Croce); **page 428,** MHS (Monroe Killy).

Keeping at It: Minnesota Women

Page 435, MHS (Monroe Killy); **page 437,** MHS (*St. Paul Pioneer Press Dispatch*); **page 439,** MHS; **page 443,** MHS (C. J. Hibbard); **page 446,** MHS; **page 447,** MHS (Pacific & Atlantic Photos, Inc.); **page 448,** MHS (*Minneapolis Journal*); **page 450,** MHS (WPA); **page 460,** MHS (Tracey Baker); **page 463,** MHS (*Minneapolis Star Journal-Tribune*).

Educating for the Future

Page 472, MHS (*Minneapolis Star Journal*); **page 474,** MHS (Michael Kieger); **pages 475, 481, and 483,** MHS; **page 487,** MHS (*Minneapolis Tribune*); **pages 489 and 495,** MHS; **page 497,** MHS (*St. Paul Pioneer Press*); **page 500,** MHS.

Religious Belief and Behavior

Pages 510, 512, and 515, MHS; **page 518,** MHS (WPA); **page 519,** MHS; **page 524,** MHS (*Minneapolis Star Journal*); **page 525,** MHS; **page 528,** MHS (Bruce Sifford Studio); **page 531,** MHS; **page 533,** MHS (C. P. Gibson).

"Good Life in Minnesota"

Pages 542 and 544, MHS; **page 545,** courtesy AP/Wide World Photos; **page 547,** Copyright 1973 Time Inc. All rights reserved. Reprinted by permission from TIME; **page 550,** MHS; **page 553,** MHS (original in Manuscripts Collection); **page 556,** Collection Walker Center, Minneapolis. Gift of Frederick R. Weisman in honor of his parents, William and Mary Weisman, 1988; **page 559 and 561,** MHS; **page 564,** courtesy *St. Paul Pioneer Press Dispatch* (Spence Hollstadt).

Index

The text of this book is set in Century Expanded; the display faces are Palatino Bold Italic and Gill Sans. The paper is Warren's Patina, which is a coated stock over an acid-free base, and both the paperback and cloth editions are Smyth sewn for durability. Typesetting was performed by Stanton Publication Services, Minneapolis; printing by Viking Press, Eden Prairie; and binding by Midwest Editions, Minneapolis. Lois Stanfield designed the book's cover and interior.